Studien zum Internationalen Investitionsrecht

herausgegeben von
Prof. Dr. Marc Bungenberg, LL.M., Universität des Saarlandes
Prof. Dr. Stephan Hobe, LL.M., Universität zu Köln
Prof. Dr. August Reinisch, LL.M., Universität Wien
Prof. Dr. Andreas R. Ziegler, LL.M., Universität Lausanne

In Kooperation mit dem
International Investment Law Centre Cologne (IILCC)
Prof. Dr. Stephan Hobe, LL.M.
Prof. Dr. Bernhard Kempen
Prof. Dr. Heinz-Peter Mansel
Prof. Dr. Burkhard Schöbener

Band 26
zugleich Band 14 der Schriftenreihe des
International Investment Law Centre Cologne (IILCC)

Nico Basener

Investment Protection in the European Union

Considering EU law in investment arbitrations arising from intra-EU and extra-EU bilateral investment agreements

Nomos

facultas

DIKE

Die Deutsche Nationalbibliothek verzeichnet diese Publikation in der Deutschen Nationalbibliografie; detaillierte bibliografische Daten sind im Internet über http://dnb.d-nb.de abrufbar.

Zugl.: Köln, Univ., Diss., 2017

ISBN 978-3-8487-4347-6 (Nomos Verlag, Baden-Baden, Print)
ISBN 978-3-8452-8571-9 (Nomos Verlag, Baden-Baden, ePDF)

ISBN 978-3-7089-1617-0 (facultas Verlag, Wien)
ISBN 978-3-03751-965-3 (Dike Verlag, Zürich/St.Gallen)

1. Auflage 2017

Für Meike, meine Geschwister und meine Eltern

Vorwort

Die vorliegende Arbeit wurde zum Sommersemester 2017 von der Universität zu Köln als Dissertation angenommen. Bis zur Drucklegung konnte daher Literatur und Rechtsprechung bis Juni 2017 berücksichtigt werden.

Für die vielseitige Unterstützung, die mir bei der Erstellung dieser Arbeit zuteil wurde, möchte ich mich an dieser Stelle ganz herzlich bedanken.

An erster und vorderster Stelle gilt mein herzlicher Dank Herrn Professor Dr. Stephan Hobe für seine stete Unterstützung mit Tat, Rat, Kritik und Anregungen, die er mir als Betreuer und Erstkorrektor dieser Arbeit zuteil wurden ließ. Diese Arbeit hätte ohne seine Förderung und seinen Beitrag in der hier vorliegenden Form niemals erscheinen können.

Ebenfalls gilt mein Dank Herrn Prof. Dr. Bernhard Kempen, der die Arbeit als Zweitkorrektur begutachte, für die äußerst hilfreichen Anmerkungen und Anregungen.

Die Idee zu dieser Arbeit geht zurück auf meinen Studienaufenthalt an der Université de Paris 1 / Panthéon-Sorbonne während des deutsch-französischen Magisterstudiengangs. Während des Verfassens eines Beitrags zu einer dort einzureichenden schriftlichen Seminarbeit, stieß ich erstmals auf die – damals noch sehr junge Fragestellung – der Interaktion von Europarecht und Investitionsschutzrecht. Nachdem die Frage zwei Jahre später immer noch nicht umfassend gelöst schien, wuchs die Idee zu dieser Arbeit.

Mein Dank gilt daher auch Frau Prof. Dr. Dauner-Lieb, die mich während eben dieser Studienzeit als Programmleiterin, aber auch danach, mit Rat und Tat begleitete und förderte. Sie trägt einen erheblichen Anteil daran, dass diese Arbeit heute in dieser Form erscheinen kann.

Bedanken möchte ich mich auch bei meinen Freunden, die mich auf unterschiedlichste Art und Weise bei der Erstellung unterstützten.

Abschließend gilt mein Dank selbstverständlich meinen Eltern, meinen Geschwistern und meiner Lebensgefährtin. Meinen Eltern und meinen Geschwistern, da sie mich auf meinem bisherigen Lebensweg und im Rahmen meiner Ausbildung stets unterstützten und mir diese ermöglichten. Meiner Lebensgefährtin, weil sie es war, die mich stets neu aufbaute, stets Verständnis hatte und durch ihren Rückhalt in wesentlichem Maße dazu beigetragen hat, dass diese Arbeit erfolgreich abgeschlossen wurde.

München, Juli 2017 *Nico Basener*

Inhaltsverzeichnis

Abbreviations:

BIT	Bilateral Investment Treaty
CCP	Common Commercial Policy
cf.	please refer to
Charter	Charter of Fundamental Rights of the European Union
CJEU	Court of Justice of the European Union which shall compromise the reference to the Court of Justice of the European Coal and Steel Communities, the Court of Justice of the European Communities, the Court of First Instance, the General Court and the Court of Justice
ECHR	European Convention on the protection of Human Rights
ECT	Energy Charter Treaty
ECtHR	European Court of Human Rights
et al.	and others
EU	European Union
EU Law	All sources of law deriving from primary or secondary law of the European Union, including the TEU, TFEU, general principles of the law applicable in the European Union as derived by the CJEU, secondary law and those general principles and conventional obligations of international law which are binding within the European Union and its member states
European Treaties	All treaties concluded between the EU member states since the Treaty of Rome, including all amendments (until the Lisbon Treaty) and accession treaties
FCN treaties	Treaties of Friendship Navigation and Commerce
FET	Fair and Equitable Treatment
f / ff	following page / following pages
FPS	Full Protection and Security
ICC	International Chamber of Commerce
IIA	International Investment Agreement (including BITs and multilateral investment treaties as well as trade agreements, which include provisions on investment protection)

ICJ	International Court of Justice
ICSID	International Centre for Settlement of Investment Disputes
ILC	International Law Commission
IMF	International Monetary Fund
LCIA	London Court of International Arbitration
MFN	Most-Favoured Nation
para	paragraph (*Randnummer*)
p.	page / pages
SCC	Stockholm Chamber of Commerce
TEU	Treaty on the European Union
TFEU	Treaty on the Functioning of the European Union
UNCITRAL	United Nations Commission on International Trade Law
VCLT	Vienna Convention on the Law of Treaties

Introduction

Presumably only few aspects of the European Union's common commercial policy currently attract more attention in the public and political sphere than the negotiation of the two trade agreements CETA[1] and TTIP[2] by the European Union (EU) with Canada and the United States of America. Besides fears about the "*blurring*" of consumer protection and environmental standards, the most controversial aspect of these agreements is the inclusion of an investment protection mechanism in both agreements.[3] The most militant oppositions express conclusions such as:

> "The most invidious aspect about TTIP is the investment agreement [...]. It's about stopping parliament[s] from passing regulations that would protect our economy, our people, our health."[4]

The general concept of such investment protection mechanism is as follows: two or more states agree upon a certain number of substantive protection standards for investors abroad in an international agreement. Those standards could e.g. include a prohibition of discriminatory measures towards the investor or a prohibition of expropriation. Whenever a state undertakes a specific measure, *inter alia* as Germany did by adopting the law on the termination of nuclear plants after the accident in Fukushima, foreign investors may not only challenge this measure (the law ordering the termination) under the domestic legal framework but also under the protection standards conferred in the international investment agreement (IIA). Hence, even though the measure may comply with the requirements of national (constitutional) law, it might however breach the protection standards agreed upon on the international level. Additionally, those treaties usually refer the disputes arising from IIAs to international arbitral tri-

1 Comprehensive Economic and Trade Agreement, under negotiation since 2009.

2 Transatlantic Trade and Investment Partnership, under negotiation since 2011.

3 Cf. also: *Lang*, Der EuGH und die Investor-Staat-Streitbeilegung in TTIP und CETA (Beit. zum Transnat. Wirt.-R, Vol. 138, 2015), p. 6.

4 Joseph Stiglitz, Nobel Price winner 2001 (economics) and former head of the IMF and IEA, interview on 10/10/2015 relating to the TTIP regulations with GEDProject, available at https://www.youtube.com/watch?v=sIfO5HRRjQg [last checked on: 28/02/2017].

bunals and hence carve out these investment disputes from the national judicial framework. Most of the current criticism is closely related to this regulation.[5]

Besides all criticism, the EU member states were among the leading countries when concluding and implementing investment protection mechanisms through IIAs. Predominantly the EU member states tried to foster investment protection through the conclusion of bilateral agreements – also referred to as bilateral investment agreements (BITs) – with other states all over the world. The result is an extensive network of IIAs concluded by EU member states either among themselves (intra-EU IIAs) or with non-member states (extra-EU IIAs).

The problem to be addressed in this thesis: Potential conflicts between EU law and intra-EU and extra-EU IIAs

The current debate on TTIP and CETA should not obscure the discussions on a different subject which is closely interlinked but dates back before the first negotiations of those agreements were started in 2009 and 2011. Given that the competence to negotiate such agreements was transferred to the EU in 2009 only, previous IIAs were negotiated by the member states. Approximately in 2006/2007 the question arose how EU law and international investment law interact and how potential conflicts of both systems could be resolved. The questions are of multiple nature. Lets imagine two EU member states that have concluded an IIA including several substantive protection standards. One of these states has granted particular advantages to investors to build up their business in disfavoured regions of the member state, in order to enhance economic development. The European Commission might consider such advantages to constitute state aids in terms of Art. 107 TFEU and thus prohibited under EU law, which leads to their mandatory revocation towards the investor.[6] The investor, besides potentially challenging the revocation of aids before national courts or the

5 Cf. comment by the German Judges Association, available at: http://www.zeit.de/politik/ausland/2016-02/ttip-deutscher-richterbund-schieds gerichte [last checked on: 28/02/2017].

6 The example is provided by reference to the facts in the reknown *Micula Case*, cf.: *Ioan Micula, Viorel Micula & others vs. Romania*, 11.12.2013 – ICSID Case No. ARB/05/20 - Final Award and Decision on Jurisdiction and Admissibility dated 23.09.2008.

CJEU, might also seek judicial protection by an arbitral tribunal, basing its claim on the IIA. Indeed, it can be argued that revoking an advantage previously granted to an investor might violate such investor's legitimate expectations and thus be contrary to the so-called fair and equitable treatment standard guaranteed under an IIA. What should the member state do? Risking infringement proceedings in the European context to avoid being ordered to pay damages by an arbitral tribunal based on the investment treaty? Can arbitral tribunals even be competent to rule upon the legality of a measure which is mandatory under EU law without impeding on the competences of the European Courts? What would be the effect of contradicting decisions by the arbitral tribunal, basing its considerations on the IIA and European Courts, judging the case by reference to national and EU law? The questions become even far more complicated when taking into consideration that both frameworks *ab initio* claim absolute supremacy within their respective framework. Whereas EU law is essentially based on the principle of supremacy as one of the fundamental rules to guarantee its so-called autonomy and its uniform application, international investment law usually refers to the general principle in international law that changes in a state's domestic law cannot excuse violations of international obligations (cf. Art. 27 Vienna Convention on the Law of Treaties (VCLT)).

These questions are more than theoretical. In the last decade, a considerable number of disputes was closely related to the question of the interaction of EU law with international investment law. In 2015, 130 pending investment arbitration cases were based on intra-EU IIAs (19% of all cases).[7] Additionally disputes based on extra-EU IIAs, involving the responsibility of an EU member state, are increasing, a fact which was nearly unconceivable for long times. This increase in procedures raised particular interest for these questions. In several of the arbitral proceedings EU member states tried to demonstrate that IIAs could not set aside the obligations undertaken under EU law. Although taken into consideration by several arbitral tribunals, these objections were mostly dismissed very clearly. The European Commission is actively seeking to face the (alleged) threat to the uniform application of EU law within the member states through such investment proceedings. The last attempt of these interventions were infringement proceedings initiated in 2015 against several member states which accuse them of being in violation of EU law by

---

7 *UNCTAD*, World Investment Report, 2016, p. 105.

keeping IIAs in force, despite the threat to the autonomy of the EU's legal order. Several national courts were also sought with the question in the context of enforcement or setting aside proceedings regarding arbitral awards being rendered based on IIAs involving EU-member states. One of the most prominent proceedings in *Achmea (former Eureko) vs. Slovak Republic* finally led to a preliminary ruling reference of the German Federal Supreme Court on 10.05.2016 to the CJEU regarding the validity of dispute settlement provisions in intra-EU IIAs and their effect on the arbitral tribunal's jurisdiction.[8]

Literature review

Despite the tremendous importance of the subject and the increasing number of arbitral awards rendered in the meantime[9], the current perception of the conflict in literature remains rather fragmented. *Ahner* analysed the possibilities for the EU to conclude future IIAs but expressly carves out the problems arising in the context of intra-EU or extra-EU conflicts.[10] *Schmitt* explored the consequences of the shift of competences for foreign direct investments to the EU through the Lisbon Treaty, without treating the difficulties which derive from the potential conflicts of IIAs and EU law in arbitration proceedings.[11] *Bräuninger* exclusively focuses on the (potential) discrimination of investors in extra-EU IIAs, which will only

8 *Engel*, SchiedsVZ, 2015, 218, 218, cf. also: *Peterson*, IA Reporter Vol. 9, No. 11 (2016), 2, 2 f.

9 Cf. *inter alia* the awards: *Binder vs. Czech Republic*, 06.06.2007 – UNCITRAL - Award on Jurisdiction; *Eastern Sugar vs. Czech Republic*, 27.03.2007 – SCC No. 088/2004 - Partial award; *Euram vs. Slovak Republic*, 22.10.2012 – PCA Case no. 2010-17: First Award on Jurisdiction; *Achmea vs. Slovak Republic*, 26.10.2012 – PCA Case No. 2008-13 - Award on Jurisdiction, Arbitrability and Suspension; *Electrabel vs. Hungary*, 30.11.2012 – ICSID Case No. ARB/07/19: Decision on Jurisdiction, Applicable Law and Liability; *EDF vs. Hungary*, 04.12.2014 – UNCITRAL - Award; cf. also the judgements / orders rendered by national courts, *inter alia*: *Higher Regional Court Frankfurt*, SchiedsVZ (2013), 119, 10.05.2012 – 26 SchH 11/10; *German Federal Supreme Court*, 03.03.2016 – I ZB 2/15; *Swiss Federal Supreme Court, 1èr Cour de droit Civil*, 06.10.2015 – 4A 34/2015.

10 *Ahner*, Investor-Staat-Schiedsverfahren nach Europäischem Unionsrecht, 2015.

11 *Schmidt*, Die Kompetenzen der Europäischen Union für ausländische Investitionen in und aus Drittstaaten, 2013.

be of minor importance for this thesis.[12] General literature and handbooks contain very little on the specific subject matter.[13] Several articles and discussion are centred around the recent decisions of the arbitral tribunals, without however questioning the overall approach of those tribunals.[14] Others try to limit the discussion either on the international law perspective or the EU law perspective, which might lead to, at least partially, ignoring the far-reaching implications of the question in practice for both, investors and states.[15] Additionally, with the upcoming negotiations of the free trade agreements, the focus shifts on particular issues of policy making and potential possibilities how to reconcile investment protection and EU law in future agreements.[16]

Focus of the thesis

However, a comprehensive approach of how the arbitral tribunals should address the question of conflicting provisions in EU law and international investment law, both regarding intra-EU IIAs as well as extra-EU IIAs, is missing so far. From a current perspective, this conflict will subsist for quite a while, given that the negotiations on agreements which should replace pre-existing IIAs are pending and it becomes more and more doubt-

12 *Bräuninger*, Investitionsschiedsgerichtsbarkeit und Diskriminierungsverbote, 2015.

13 The most extensive debates can be found in the different chapters in *Bungenberg/Griebel/Hobe u. a.* (Eds.), International Investment Law, (2015), cf. inter alia: Chapter 4: II. European Bilateral Approaches or Chapter 7: II EU Rules and Obligations related to investment; furthermore the different contributions in *Bungenberg/Griebel/Hindelang* (Eds.), Internationaler Investitionsschutz und Europarecht, (2010) also address the interferences but, however, largely foucs on the future competences of the EU in the context of the Lisbon Treaty.

14 Cf. inter alia: *Reinisch*, LIEI Vol. 39, No. 2 (2012), 157; *Wehland*, ICLQ Vol. 58, Iss. 2 (2009), 297; *Söderlund*, JOIA Vol. 24, Iss. 5 (2007), 455.

15 Among the largest contributions in journals feature: *Burgstaller*, JOIA Vol. 26, No. 2 (2009), 181; *Dimopoulos*, CMLR Vol. 48, No. 1 (2011), 63; *Eilmansberger*, CMLR Vol. 46 (2009), 383; *Hindelang*, LIEI Vol. 39, Iss. 2 (2012), 179; the recent contribution by *Tietje/Wackernagel*, JWIT Vol. 16, Iss. 2 (2015), 205 has a different focus but treats overlapping questions with regard to this thesis.

16 *Hindelang*, AVR Vol. 53 (2015), 68; *Lang*, Der EuGH und die Investor-Staat-Streitbeilegung in TTIP und CETA (Beit. zum Transnat. Wirt.-R, Vol. 138, 2015); *Lenk*, EJLS Vol. 8, No. 2 (2015), 6.

ful, if those agreements will ever (and to which extent) include any particular provisions on investment protection. Hence, a comprehensive analysis of the existing particularities and conflicts in this – existing – situation of overlapping legal frameworks is of predominant importance. As a senior associate of a renowned law firm involved in several of the current disputes puts it:

> „The problem about this subject is that 'Internationalists' do not listen to 'Europeanists' and vice-versa."[17]

This thesis will thus try to overcome these difficulties by furnishing a comprehensive analysis of how arbitral tribunals should consider EU law in arbitration proceedings arising in the context of an international investment protection dispute. The focus will be on disputes based on IIAs concluded by EU member states with other member states as well as non-member states, which engage the responsibility of an EU member state under the respective IIA. Within this analysis, the questions of the interference of EU law with all stages of the arbitration proceedings should be questioned, including the question of whether (or whether not) EU law is part of the applicable law in those disputes, which effects it might have on the arbitral tribunal's jurisdiction or the substantive protection provided under international investment law.

Several questions should however be excluded from this analysis. First, the question of state-contracts will not be further analysed. These contracts, which are usually concluded between investors and states regarding a particular investment, represent several particularities, which could also interact with EU law, but which are subject to a completely different setting than IIAs as international treaties. Second, mixed agreements concluded by the EU and the member states, will not be treated in deeper detail as well. The reason for this omission is basically that the only existing treaty, the Energy-Charter-Treaty, represents particularities linked to its negotiation, which could bias the overall analysis and set a completely different focus. Furthermore, given the recent uncertainties regarding the inclusion of investment protection in further agreements, the situation remains highly uncertain. However, within the analysis, whenever possible, some of the particularities or consequences for mixed agreements will be highlighted. Third, given the considerable amount of contributions regarding the EU's future competences, this subject will only be treated when

---

17 Quote from an off-the-record conversation with a senior associate having been involved in several proceedings based on either intra-EU or extra-EU BITs.

necessary to derive consequences for the existing IIAs. The focus should be exclusively on the conflict between IIAs and EU law.

Structure of the analysis

Addressing this conflict requires a three-step approach.

First, following this introduction, the different mechanisms of investment protection within the EU should be explained (*Part I*). This requires an analysis of the roots of modern investment protection through IIAs as well as its basic features. These features will be contrasted to the most important provisions of EU law which might be advanced by investors in the EU in order to protect their investment against measures from EU member states or the EU. It will be demonstrated that *de facto* both frameworks, EU law as well as investment protection through IIAs, build two overlapping frameworks, which have not been construed in a coordinated approach. The analysis of the different protection standards under both frameworks serves as a basis for the entire understanding in the further thesis and developments. Having compared those two frameworks and having taken into consideration the particular features of each of them, Part I will finish by outlining various potential conflicts of both frameworks regarding investments in the EU.

Second, based on these potential conflicts, the following parts of the thesis will develop solutions how to resolve these conflicts in arbitration proceedings. To be able to develop those solutions, one needs to fundamentally distinguish between intra-EU and extra-EU disputes. Given the different actors in question, the approach to resolve the conflict as well as the considerations to take into account, cannot be identical in the extra-EU and intra-EU context. Hence, the analysis will be separated. The conflict regarding EU law and intra-EU IIAs should be addressed first (*Part II*). It will be demonstrated that the conflict between the provisions of EU law and intra-EU IIAs lead to the arbitration clause and the substantive protection standards contained in IIAs to be set aside by conflicting provisions of EU law. To demonstrate this, it will be first shown that EU law can be considered as international law. Second, it will be developed that under the relevant rules of conflict of law applicable in this context, the provisions of EU law prevail over conflicting provision under any international obligation by the member states and conflicting provisions of international law need to remain unapplied. It will then be outlined that arbitration clauses contained in IIAs actually conflict with EU law and hence need to be set aside and that a substantial guarantee provided in an IIA cannot alter the member states' obligations under EU law.

After having advanced the solution to be applied in the intra-EU context, the question how to consider EU law in the extra-EU context will be deployed (*Part III*). After having a look on the current perception of the conflict, the potential influences and implications of EU law on the arbitration proceedings will be outlined. The major part of this extra-EU analysis will however focus on the development of a new approach how to address questions of EU law in international arbitration proceedings based on extra-EU IIAs which is influenced by similar solutions developed by the ECtHR regarding multi-level legal frameworks in the well-known *Bosphorus-Decision.* These developments should in particular demonstrate that despite of various arbitral tribunals having concluded the contrary, the protection offered by EU law and IIAs can at least be considered equivalent, enabling new procedural approaches to address the conflict between both frameworks. Finally, given the results, a brief outlook should outline several prospects of the solution for the current discussions on trade agreements and the future investment policy of the EU (*Part IV*). The previously found theses will then be summarised in the Conclusion.

Terminological comments

For matters of clarification, several terminological issues should be addressed at this stage as well. For the purpose of this thesis, European Treaties will refer to the integrity of treaties concluded by EU member states since the creation of the European Coal and Steel Community in 1951 and the Treaty of Rome establishing the European Economic Community and European Atomic Energy Community in 1958. Hence, as long as not expressly denominated, this includes all amendments to the Treaty of Rome, such as the Brussels Treaty, Single European Act, etc. until the Lisbon Treaty, as well as the Accession Treaties by new member states.

Similarly, EU law will refer to the integrity of law in relation with the EU, which means: primary law as contained in the European Treaties (TEU, TFEU, Charter), secondary law issued by institutions of the EU (directives, regulations, decisions) as well as all general principles of EU law developed in the jurisprudence.

For further simplification, all decisions by the Court of Justice of the European Coal and Steel Communities, the Court of Justice of the European Communities, the Court of First Instance, the General Court and the

Court of Justice, will be referred to as decisions by the Court of Justice of the European Union (CJEU). Given the inconsistent nomenclature the terms principle of primacy and principle of supremacy should be understood as synonyms and equivalently referring to the fundamental principle in EU law that any conflicting provision should be deemed inapplicable (Vorrang des Europarechts).

Part I: Investment protection in the European Union: the rise of potentially conflicting legal frameworks in the European Union

Addressing the question of investment protection in the EU requires to first admit that the subject involves two distinct evolutions which mostly took place in the 20th century. Based on an immanent necessity of investment protection since the very early existence of foreign investments, the mechanisms for offering this protection shifted dramatically during the last 60-70 years.

From its early roots in the minimum treatment of aliens abroad, investment protection nowadays has become a sub-system of public international law with considerable influence (and efficiency) in the protection of economic operations abroad. However, in the context of investment protection in the EU, one needs to consider the second development which took place since the early 1960s: the raise of the EU as a more and more political and economic union.

The consequence of this union is another sub-system of '*supra-national*'-law which, concerning investors in the EU member states, overlaps with the requirements of international investment law.

As both systems have not been conceived in a cooperative approach but widely independent one from the other, this overlap leads to various potential conflicts in the concrete application of these frameworks (often referred to as the result of a *multi-level system of laws* or the "*fragmentation*" of international law).[18]

Chapter 1: The necessity of investment protection

The necessity of investment protection mechanisms derives from a couple of threats foreign investments face since its appearance in the Middle Ag-

18 *Tietje*, Intra-EU BITs als Herausforderung im Mehrebenensystem des Rechts (Beit. zum Transnat. Wirt.-R, Vol. 104, 2011); *Klabbers*, Treaty conflict and the European Union, 2009, p. 8, cf. also: *International Law Commission*, ILC Report on Fragmentation of International Law, 13/04/2006.

es. As self-evident as it may appear, regardless the kind of investment any investor needs to ensure that its contribution to establish the investment leads to a positive return on investment.

But the question whether a positive return on investment is created, is not only a question of the success or failure of the business model pursued by the investment, but rather a question of a safe, stable and secure (legal and factual) environment the investment is made in. Since its early beginnings foreign investments face a couple of threats which, regardless of any changes in their concrete manifestation, remain similar.

The most obvious threat is the nationalisation of the investment, which may nearly affect each kind of investment. Meaningless if an investor bought shares in a foreign entity, build its own production in the host state or got a concession for offering any kind of (public) service in the host state, if the host state decides to nationalise the business entity, future revenues cannot be realised. [19]

Several other risks can be as detrimental as nationalisations. Discrimination in favour of national competitors or competitors of any other states, changing legal environments which prohibit the activity previously undertaken by the investment or the withdrawal of promises made by the host state may ruin business opportunities and considerably affect any kind of foreign investment.

Even less obvious measures may have considerable impacts. The most important example might be the absence of protection towards unrests or criminality in the host state, even if those activities are not actively undertaken by the host state itself.[20] The recent developments e.g. in Turkey, Syria or Egypt are a prominent example of these threats, which persist until today.[21]

---

19 *Griebel*, (2008), p. 2; *Reinisch* in: *Tietje* (Ed.), Internationales Wirtschaftsrecht, 2015, p. 399; *Herdegen*, 10. Edn. (2014), p. 350; Considering that the major amount of investments is based on a long-term engagement to maximise the return on investments in the later years after amortisation, nationalisation is one of the most important investment risks.

20 *Griebel*, (2008), p. 2; cf. also: *Schöbener/Herbst et al.*, 2010, p. 270 f; *Schreuer* in: *Wolfrum* (Ed.), Max Planck Encyclopedia of Public International Law, 2008, para 4 f.

21 The recent attemped coup in Turkey in July 2016 leaves considerable doubts for investors as to political stability and security, cf.: article in Süddeutsche Zeitung, 20. Juli 2016, accessible at: http://www.sueddeutsche.de/wirtschaft/investitionsklima-der-putsch-in-der-tuerkei-verschreckt-die-unternehmen-1.3085089-2 [last checked on: 28/02/2017].

This set of – non-exhaustive – threats foreign investments may fear is closely linked to three different origins:

First, the investor generally operates under the national law of a foreign state and thus is subject to any changes within this framework.

Second, any investor is submitted to any factual or administrative interference with its investment by the state.

Third, investments are heavily dependent on the factual circumstances in a foreign state, including *inter alia* the general security situation, particular political difficulties or the general enforcement of the rule of law.[22]

The simple fact that the investor generally operates under the national law of the host state and the protection provided to the investor therein, is one of the major challenges. If these laws do not provide a sufficient protection, the investment remains unprotected. If the legal framework changes in detriment of the investor, the investment's business model is affected.[23]

But even if the national framework (theoretically) provides an adequate protection for the investor, a violation of this framework may not have any consequences for the host state. Substantive protection therefore also requires procedural protection. However, national tribunals of the host state may be hostile to foreign entities. They may also – voluntarily or involuntarily – privilege nationals. Being subject to the jurisdiction of the host state therefore is another major threat for foreign investments.[24]

Eliminating or at least diminishing these risks is the principal concern of investment protection measures. These measures have been refined during the last two centuries, which will be shown later, but their key issues remain the same since the early beginning.

---

22 *Herdegen*, 10. Edn. (2014), p. 330; *Schreuer* in: *Wolfrum* (Ed.), Max Planck Encyclopedia of Public International Law, 2008, para 4 f; *Tietje* in: *Ehlers/Schoch* (Eds.), Rechtsschutz im Öffentlichen Recht, 2009, p. 64-67; more generally regarding the development and necessity of protecting aliens abroad: *Hobe* in: *Bungenberg/Griebel/Hobe et al.* (Eds.), International Investment Law, 2015, p. 7-14.

23 *Tietje* in: *Ehlers/Schoch* (Eds.), Rechtsschutz im Öffentlichen Recht, 2009, p. 65 f; *Schöbener/Herbst et al.*, 2010, p. 243 and 248.

24 *Ghouri*, Int. A.L.R. Vol. 14, No. 6, 189, 190; for a detailed analysis of the underlying idea of internationalising the disputes: *Sattorova*, LIEI Vol. 39, No. 2 (2012), 223, 226 ff; *Tietje* in: *Ehlers/Schoch* (Eds.), Rechtsschutz im Öffentlichen Recht, 2009, p. 65 f; cf. for the term internationalising: *Füracker*, SchiedsVZ, 2006, 236, 244.

Contemporary investment protection mechanisms are largely exercised through IIAs, concluded between two or several states.

Generally speaking – nonetheless the differences in details – these treaties establish the terms and conditions of investments for private persons or other entities of one state in another state.[25]

Therefore, these treaties feature a couple of characteristics distinguishing them from other mechanisms used before the raise of IIAs, such as diplomatic protection or individual investment treaties (so-called *state contracts*) concluded by an investor with the government or any other entity of the host state.

About 3000 of these IIAs have been concluded, most of them as bilateral treaties (BITs).[26] They usually contain several standards of conduct (protection standards) that apply to governments or other state entities regarding the treatment of foreign investors in their respective countries.

Besides these standards of conduct, IIAs regularly also contain jurisdiction clauses, which grant jurisdiction to alternative dispute resolutions mechanisms in any case of dispute arising from the investment. Through such clauses, investor may directly claim violation of their rights before international arbitral tribunals, without the necessity to sue the state before domestic courts in the host state.[27]

However, investment protection through IIAs has not been the traditional mode of protecting the interests of foreign nationals abroad. The mechanism has widely changed and developed in the last centuries.

---

25 *Griebel*, (2008), p. 38; *Schöbener/Herbst et al.*, 2010, p. 247 f; *Tietje* in: *Ehlers/Schoch* (Eds.), Rechtsschutz im Öffentlichen Recht, 2009, p. 70-72; *Ipsen*, Völkerrecht, 6. Edn. (2014), p. 757 f.

26 Often referred to as: treaty concerning the encouragement and reciprocal protection of investment, as to the UNCTAD there are currently 2954 IIAs in force, accessible at http://investmentpolicyhub.unctad.org/IIA [last checked on 28/02/2017].

27 *Herdegen*, 10. Edn. (2014), p. 332-334; *Reinisch* in: *Tietje* (Ed.), Internationales Wirtschaftsrecht, 2015, p. 402; *Füracker*, SchiedsVZ, 2006, 236 , 242-245. *Schöbener/Herbst et al.*, 2010, p. 248 and 270 ff (regarding substantive standards).

Chapter 2: The ascent of investment protection through IIA / BITs

Before being able to refer to the currently most effective mechanism of investment protection through IIAs, the historic development of investment protection mechanisms before the prosperity of IIAs should be clarified (A.). These historic roots enable to understand where the actual investment protection derives from, why such mechanisms were necessary as well as its advantages (B.).

A. The historical development of investment protection mechanisms

Seen from a historical perspective, various instruments of investment protection have been developed since the first types of foreign investment appeared. This underlines the need for such mechanisms as soon as cross-border investments and trade developed. More than ever these considerations remain valid in today's largely globalised world, with a total amount of foreign direct investments of USD 1.8 trillion in 2015.[28] Today's protection mechanisms through IIAs are somehow a derivative of their ancestors but also an instrument which was developed as a counter-movement to the failure of further instruments or the impossibility of maintaining several previously used mechanisms.

I. From the Middle Ages until the Colonial Era: the use of force and other individual measures

Generally, the situation for aliens residing abroad in the Middle Ages and even in the Colonial Era was difficult. They were usually considered as outlaws, both by states and sovereigns as well as by other individuals.[29] Thus, security for traders abroad was one of the major concerns. On the one hand, investors faced the fear of physical encroachment, either by pirates, thieves or any other threat. On the other hand, trading in general was usually prohibited in foreign countries. To be able to exercise any business abroad, traders needed to postulate for a trading-right granted by the local

28 *UNCTAD*, World Investment Report, 2016.

29 *Vogel*, Kurze Geschichte der Deutschen Hanse, 1915, p. 14.

sovereign.[30] Hence, traders were heavily dependent on the discretion of the local sovereign. Being disgraced by them, usually led to either the revocation of trade rights or the submission to arbitrary measures by judicial or administrative entities.

In these circumstances, investment protection was mainly exercised through individual measures. Such measures were either the use of force or the negotiation of individual agreements with local sovereigns. Some institutions, such as e.g. the *Hanseatic League*, tried to bundle particular interests to better exercise those mechanisms through collective security measures or bundled negotiations with foreign sovereigns.[31]

With the establishment of the colonial empires the focus shifted. By means of force countries such as the United Kingdom or France invaded several countries especially in America, Africa and Asia. Those occupied territories were safeguarded by military means, which allowed to implement a sort of extraterritorial area within those foreign countries. These areas, which were formally part of the colonial powers' territory, were submitted to the legal system of the colonial powers and governed by delegates, who derived their powers from the colonial power.[32] "*Exporting*" a legal framework abroad thus obviously diminishes the risks for traders and investors from the colonial states, exercising their business in these colonial countries.[33]

Outside the colonial context, with the rise of state territories and more stable sovereigns, "*a blend of diplomacy and force ensured that these states did not interfere with foreign investors too adversely.*"[34] States began to protect the interests of their sovereigns through the building of an espousal system, hence through the mechanism of diplomatic protection.

---

30 Revoking this concession was a significant risk. Without the permission delivered by the sovereigns no access was granted to the local markets and trade was usually prohibited or at least the alien was considered as an outlaw and therefore without rights at all, cf.: *Vogel*, Kurze Geschichte der Deutschen Hanse, 1915, p. 14.

31 *Tietje*, Int. Investitionsschutzrecht im Spannungsverhältnis (Beit. zum Transnat. Wirt.-R, Vol. 93, 2010), 5, 6; *Verosta/Fischer/Köck u. a.* (Eds.), Völkerrecht und Rechtsphilosophie, 1980 p. 348; *Vogel*, Kurze Geschichte der Deutschen Hanse, 1915, p. 47.

32 *Sornarajah*, 3. Edn. (2010), p. 19; *Krajewski*, Wirtschaftsvölkerrecht, 2. Edn. (2009), para 540 ff.

33 *Sornarajah*, 3. Edn. (2010), p. 20: *Hobe* in: *Bungenberg/Griebel/Hobe et al.* (Eds.), International Investment Law, 2015, p. 8.

34 *Sornarajah*, 3. Edn. (2010), p. 20.

In case of interference with its nationals several home states intervened towards the host state to protect their investors.[35] This intervention – although it remained rare in use – was first exercised through diplomatic means and in case of failure often pursued by the use of force (often referred to as "*gunboat diplomacy*").[36]

Thus, at the end of the Colonial Era investment protection shifted from a purely individual approach to a more state-driven concept, which leveraged investment protection to the field of public international law in the 19th and 20th century.

II. The Post-Colonial Era: the gradual rise of public international law as protection mechanism

The post-Colonial Era, especially at the end of the 19th century, was characterised by the raising awareness that the use of force cannot be a final arbitrator. First, military power may be instituted in several places but keeps being an extremely expensive and demanding mean of protection. Second, sustainable economic relations cannot be construed upon the use of force. Third, the acceptance of the use of force declined tremendously after World War I.[37] This initiated a broader discussion about the protection of aliens abroad and foreign investments, especially in the North- and

35 *Hobe* in: *Bungenberg/Griebel/Hobe et al.* (Eds.), International Investment Law, 2015, p. 8; *Ghouri*, Int. A.L.R. Vol. 14, No. 6, 189, 191; cf. also: *Reinisch* in: *Tietje* (Ed.), Internationales Wirtschaftsrecht, 2015, p. 401.

36 *Ghouri*, Int. A.L.R. Vol. 14, No. 6, 189, 191; *Hobe* in: *Bungenberg/Griebel/Hobe et al.* (Eds.), International Investment Law, 2015, p. 8; *Fischer* in: *Verosta/Fischer/Köck et al.* (Eds.), Völkerrecht und Rechtsphilosophie, 1980, p. 347 states that sovereigns and states remain hostile to interfere with other states in favour of particular nationals. However, dependent on who was concerned, this attitude might easily change; *Reinisch* in: *Tietje* (Ed.), Internationales Wirtschaftsrecht, 2015, p. 401; *Engel*, SchiedsVZ, 2015, 218, 219; cf. similar: *Sornarajah*, 3. Edn. (2010), p. 20.

37 *Vandevelde*, U.C. Davis Jour. of Int. Law & Policy Vol. 12, No. 1 (2005), 157, 168 f; cf. also: *Reinisch* in: *Tietje* (Ed.), Internationales Wirtschaftsrecht, 2015, p. 401 with reference to the Drago-Porter Convention signed in 1907 which prohibited the use of force to enforce payment claims towards other states; similar: *Hobe* in: *Bungenberg/Griebel/Hobe et al.* (Eds.), International Investment Law, 2015, p. 8 f.

South-American context.[38] The extension of trade and investments by the end of the 19th century considerably fostered this development. Especially capital exporting nations tried to develop legal mechanisms to protect their interests and nationals abroad. [39]

The underlying idea of this approach was to enable the use of means of diplomatic protection whenever the nationals of a home state were mistreated abroad. Diplomatic protection is generally a mechanism by which one state may take diplomatic or other action against another state whenever its nationals' rights or interests have been injured by the opposite state.[40] Thus, the precondition to exercise this protection is an internationally wrongful act of the host state.[41] In absence of any conventional obligation undertaken by the states, such wrongful acts may only derive from a breach of customary international law (1.). As customary international law did not provide for sufficient clarity, several (mostly) capital exporting states tried to refer to international conventions to regulate further obligations (2.).

1. Customary international law: minimum standard of treatment

Especially the United States of America in its relations to the Latin American countries, started to invoke a minimum standard of treatment of aliens abroad deriving from customary international law. This standard should at least guarantee an alien abroad a treatment in the host state which does not fall short of an internationally recognised minimum of treatment. This should provide for an external, minimal but internationally recognised standard of treatment for aliens abroad, irrespective of how the host state treats its own nationals (which may even be treated way which does not meet the minimum standard).[42]

---

38 *Sornarajah*, 3. Edn. (2010), p. 20 f; *Hobe* in: *Bungenberg/Griebel/Hobe et al.* (Eds.), International Investment Law, 2015, p. 9 f.

39 *Newcombe/Paradell*, Law and Practice of Investment Treaties: Standards of Treatment, 2009, p. 11; *Sornarajah*, 3. Edn. (2010), p. 21-23; *Schöbener/Herbst et al.*, 2010, p. 250.

40 *Schweisfurth*, Völkerrecht, 2006, p. 126; *Ghouri*, Int. A.L.R. Vol. 14, No. 6, 189, 191.

41 *Schweisfurth*, Völkerrecht, 2006, p. 126; *Ipsen*, Völkerrecht, 6. Edn. (2014), p. 574; *Kempen/Hillgruber*, Völkerrecht, 2. Edn. (2012), p. 112 f.

42 *Ghouri*, Int. A.L.R. Vol. 14, No. 6, 189, 191; *Krajewski*, Wirtschaftsvölkerrecht, 2. Edn. (2009), para 541 f; *Hobe* in: *Bungenberg/Griebel/Hobe et al.*

This approach raised considerable resistance especially from the Latin American countries, which denied the existence of the preconditions to establish a rule of customary international law: an *established, constant state practice* carried by an *opinio juris*.[43] Those countries denied that there is any established practice to grant an alien abroad a minimum treatment irrespective of whether nationals are treated differently and any will to recognise such minimum standard as binding (*opinion juris*). Those countries mainly referred to the *Calvo Doctrine* to justify their opposition.[44] The *Calvo Doctrine* is based on the principles of the sovereign equality of states and the principle of equality of nationals and aliens. The only minimum treatment an alien abroad could claim is thus the *national treatment*, which means a treatment equal to the treatment of nationals in the host state.[45] The only remedy left for aliens is to claim that national laws were ignored. Such a claim can, as it deals with the application of the laws of the host state, only be pursued before national courts. Any interference made by foreign powers, e.g. through diplomatic protection or aggression, is an internationally wrongful act, as it challenges the host state's sovereignty.[46]

Hence not only the scope of the international minimum standard remained disputed but even its existence was challenged. Hence, the minimum standard of treatment remained a rather ineffective instrument to protect the interests of investors abroad.[47] Additionally, in any case the standard only grants a *minimum* of protection.

(Eds.), International Investment Law, 2015, p. 9 (regarding the difference with the Calvo-Doctrine (cf. *infra*) and 14 ff regaring the scope).

43 *Shaw*, International law, 6. Edn. (2008); *Kempen/Hillgruber*, Völkerrecht, 2. Edn. (2012) p 81; *Herdegen*, Völkerrecht, 15. Edn. (2016), p. 146; cf. for the difficulties: *Reinisch* in: *Tietje* (Ed.), Internationales Wirtschaftsrecht, 2015, p. 404.

44 *Ghouri*, Int. A.L.R. Vol. 14, No. 6, 189, 191; *Sornarajah*, 3. Edn. (2010), p. 21; *Vandevelde*, U.C. Davis Jour. of Int. Law & Policy Vol. 12, No. 1 (2005), 157, 159.

45 *Ghouri*, Int. A.L.R. Vol. 14, No. 6, 189, 191; *Vandevelde*, U.C. Davis Jour. of Int. Law & Policy Vol. 12, No. 1 (2005), 157, 159; *Hobe* in: *Bungenberg/Griebel/Hobe et al.* (Eds.), International Investment Law, 2015, p. 9.

46 *Notter*, Völkerrechtlicher Investitionsschutz, 1989, p. 26; cf. also: *Hobe* in: *Bungenberg/Griebel/Hobe et al.* (Eds.), International Investment Law, 2015, p. 9.

47 Cf. also: *Herdegen*, 10. Edn. (2014), p. 330; *Füracker*, SchiedsVZ, 2006, 236, 239; *Vandevelde*, U.C. Davis Jour. of Int. Law & Policy Vol. 12, No. 1 (2005), 157, 159; *Hobe* in: *Bungenberg/Griebel/Hobe et al.* (Eds.), International In-

2. Conventional obligations: Treaties of Friendship, Commerce and Navigation

By the end of the 19th century, mostly the United States of America tried to introduce legally binding obligations for host states towards aliens and investors abroad through conventional utilities.[48] As customary international law did not grant a sufficient level of protection, the only way to guarantee a higher standard of protection for aliens abroad, was to negotiate appropriate standards of treatment in international conventions with the respective host states.[49] Whereas in customary international law binding obligations may only result from the general, unanimous and consistent state practice, each state is, under international law, free to agree upon any sort of legal obligation in a bi- or multilateral convention towards another state(s).[50]

The United States of America started to introduce such more demanding protection standards by means of international conventions through Treaties of Friendship, Commerce and Navigation (FCN treaties).[51] FCN treaties did not exclusively deal with investment protection.[52] On the contrary, the typical FCN treaties, at least before World War II, only contained a few provisions concerning investment protections but a lot more

---

vestment Law, 2015, p. 9 and 13 pointing out that these inefficiencies lead to the conclusion of IIAs (cf. *infra*).

48 *Füracker*, SchiedsVZ, 2006, 236, 239; *Ghouri*, Int. A.L.R. Vol. 14, No. 6, 189, 191 f; *Krajewski*, Wirtschaftsvölkerrecht, 2. Edn. (2009), para 547 f; *Reinisch* in: *Tietje* (Ed.), Internationales Wirtschaftsrecht, 2015, p. 401.

49 *Herdegen*, 10. Edn. (2014), p. 332; *Reinisch* in: *Tietje* (Ed.), Internationales Wirtschaftsrecht, 2015, p. 401.

50 *Vitzthum/Bothe*, Völkerrecht, 5. Edn. (2010), para 113 ff.

51 *Coyle*, Columbia Journal of Transnational Law Vol. 51 (2013), 302, 307; *Herdegen*, 10. Edn. (2014), p. 332; *Reinisch* in: *Tietje* (Ed.), Internationales Wirtschaftsrecht, 2015, p. 401; *Füracker*, SchiedsVZ, 2006, 236, 237. At the end of the 18th century, these treaties were originally concluded to obtain political and economic support for the still growing country from the European powers, such as France (treaty concluded in 1778), Netherlands (1782), et al.; cf.: *Coyle*, Columbia Journal of Transnational Law Vol. 51 (2013), 302, 307. In the 19th century this focus shifted, although the name of the instruments remaind mainly unchanged.

52 *Füracker*, SchiedsVZ, 2006, 236, 237; *Krajewski*, Wirtschaftsvölkerrecht, 2. Edn. (2009), para 547.

concerning commerce, navigation and general consular treatments.[53] After World War II a major shift towards more specialised instruments (International Investment agreements: IIAs) took place (cf. *infra* under B.).[54]

The probably most direct provision concerning investments were regulations regarding the *protection and taking of property*. [55] FCN treaties featured among the first to grant compensation in case of expropriations or factual interferences with the right to property.[56] In addition the FCN treaties contained non-discrimination guarantees for foreign traders. [57] The general idea of these guarantees was to assure a more secure environment for aliens. [58]

---

53 *Alschner*, Goettingen Journal of International Law Vol. 5, No. 2 (2013), 455, 458; *Coyle*, Columbia Journal of Transnational Law Vol. 51 (2013), 302, 311 ff; *Krajewski*, Wirtschaftsvölkerrecht, 2. Edn. (2009), para 547.

54 *Alschner*, Goettingen Journal of International Law Vol. 5, No. 2 (2013), 455, 458 f; *Hobe* in: *Bungenberg/Griebel/Hobe et al.* (Eds.), International Investment Law, 2015, p. 13.

55 *Coyle*, Columbia Journal of Transnational Law Vol. 51 (2013), 302, 314; *Vandevelde*, Cornell Int. Law. J. Vol. 21, Iss. 2 (1988), 201, 204 f: e.g. FCN treaties granted "*special protection to the persons and property*" (cf. Venezuelan-American Diplomacy - Treaty of Peace, Friendship, Navigation and Commerce Between the United States and Venezuela; May 31, 1836) or the "*most constant protection and security for property*" often followed by compensation requirements.

56 *Coyle*, Columbia Journal of Transnational Law Vol. 51 (2013), 302, 314.

57 *Coyle*, Columbia Journal of Transnational Law Vol. 51 (2013), 302, 312-315; *Krajewski*, Wirtschaftsvölkerrecht, 2. Edn. (2009), para 547 f; *Vandevelde*, Cornell Int. Law. J. Vol. 21, Iss. 2 (1988), 201, 204 f.

58 The content of the treaties has never been uniform, nevertheless one might compare the basic provisions of such treaties. Generally, FCN treaties contained a number of provisions relating to navigation rights (which granted access to the host state's ports) or establishment rights (which ensured the right to settle down in the host state for commercial or business purposes). The essential backbone of these guarantees was a non-discriminatory treatment for the nationals of the other contracting party (e.g. exemption from discriminatory duties or customs) and a most-favoured-nation treatment concerning economic activities or the import of goods. Traders as well as investors thus needed to be treated at least as favourable as nationals from any other country, cf.: *Reinisch* in: *Tietje* (Ed.), Internationales Wirtschaftsrecht, 2015, p. 401; *Brown* in: *Bungenberg/Griebel/Hobe et al.* (Eds.), International Investment Law, 2015, p. 157. Besides these guarantees, some FCN treaties even contained a "*fair and equitable treatment*" standard, which however had an unclear meaning, cf.: *Vandevelde*, Cornell Int. Law. J. Vol. 21, Iss. 2 (1988), 201, 204; *UNCTAD*, United Nations Conference on the Law of Treaties: Series on issues in international investment: Fair and Equitable Treatment, 2012, p. 5. Besides the

III. Remaining inefficiencies of the protection mechanisms leading to more specific instruments

The aforementioned mechanisms still revealed a couple of inefficiencies regarding the scope of protection as well as the procedural enforcement of investor's rights.

1. Procedural enforcement: dependence on either the home state or the host state

Probably the major insufficiency of FCN treaties was the procedural conception on how to enforce the protection granted to investors.

First, violations of the protection standards regarding the international minimum standard or the FCN treaties did not enable the investors to act by themselves. The violation of the international minimum standard by means of diplomatic protection obviously requires the investor's home state to act in favour of its national.[59] The same applies for the guarantees contained in the FCN treaties, although some of these treaties contained jurisdiction clauses, enabling the case to be brought to the International Court of Justice (ICJ) in case of violation of the treaty. However, this action still needed to be engaged by the home state, as the rights and guarantees contained in the FCN treaties were exclusively granted to the "*High Contracting Parties*" and thus to the ratifying states.[60] This goes along with a classic understanding of the subjects of international law and the place of individuals within this system. Pursuant to the classic understand-

---

aforementioned protections, FCN treaties also contained numerous miscellaneous clauses, which referred to the protection of individuals, basic human rights provisions, and provisions concerning consular relations, cf.: *Coyle*, Columbia Journal of Transnational Law Vol. 51 (2013), 302, 314 f; *Vandevelde*, Cornell Int. Law. J. Vol. 21, Iss. 2 (1988), 201, 204; *Alschner*, Goettingen Journal of International Law Vol. 5, No. 2 (2013), 455, 461.

59 *Herdegen*, 10. Edn. (2014), p. 330; *Engel*, SchiedsVZ, 2015, 218, 219; *Happ*, Int. A.L.R. Iss. 3 (2007), 74, 75.

60 E.g. the French-US-Treaty: „*Any dispute between the High Contracting Parties as to the interpretation or application of the present Convention, not satisfactorily adjusted by diplomacy, shall be submitted to the International Court of Justice, unless the High Contracting Parties agree to settlement by some other pacific means*" cited by Vandevelde, U.C. Davis Jour. of Int. Law & Policy Vol. 12, No. 1 (2005), 157, 165.

ing of public international law, the individual is not considered being a subject of international law. Individuals, independent if they are natural or judicial persons, are objects of public international law.[61] This classic understanding has been questioned by literature and state practice in the last decades, recognising that individuals can be (partial) subjects of public international law[62]. *Ipsen* distinguishes between two different scenarios. On the one hand, individuals may enjoy *benefits* as a reflex of a state's obligation towards another state. This perception still considers the individual as an object of international law, as it may not enforce this right except for the possibility to enforce it through the intervention by another state.[63] On the other hand, individuals may be attributed *enforceable rights*, which leverages the individual as a (partial) subject of international law as it may enforce its rights independently from any state action.[64]

However, the attribution of enforceable rights to an individual is a limitation of the state's sovereignty. Such a limitation, in the absence of customary international law, can only be granted through conventional obligations. The FCN treaties expressly denied to directly attribute enforceable rights to the investor. In case of a violation of any obligation, the investor may only ask its home state to leverage the claim on the interna-

---

61 *Ehlers/Schoch* (Eds.), Rechtsschutz im Öffentlichen Recht, 2009 p.67; *Herdegen*, Völkerrecht, 15. Edn. (2016), p. 111; *Ipsen*, Völkerrecht, 6. Edn. (2014), p. 308 ; *Kempen/Hillgruber*, Völkerrecht, 2. Edn. (2012), p. 38; *Braun*, Ausprägungen der Globalisierung: Der Investor als partielles Subjekt im Internationalen Investitionsrecht, 2012, p. 85.

62 *Hobe*, Einführung in das Völkerrecht, 10. Edn. (2014), p. 169 f; *Herdegen*, Völkerrecht, 15. Edn. (2016), p. 111; *Kempen/Hillgruber*, Völkerrecht, 2. Edn. (2012), p. 38; *Ipsen*, Völkerrecht, 6. Edn. (2014), p. 309; *Braun*, Ausprägungen der Globalisierung: Der Investor als partielles Subjekt im Internationalen Investitionsrecht, 2012, p. 86-90.

63 *Braun*, Ausprägungen der Globalisierung: Der Investor als partielles Subjekt im Internationalen Investitionsrecht, 2012, p. 86 f.

64 *Ipsen*, Völkerrecht, 6. Edn. (2014), p. 309 f, cf. also: *Griebel*, (2008) p.8; *Kempen/Hillgruber*, Völkerrecht, 2. Edn. (2012), p. 39 f; cf. also: *Braun*, Ausprägungen der Globalisierung: Der Investor als partielles Subjekt im Internationalen Investitionsrecht, 2012, p. 77 who distinguishes (i) derivate rights (for which the rights of the individual are mediatised by the states), (ii) direct rights (which grants own substantive rights to the individual) and (iii) contingent rights (which grants the right to claim a substantive right to the individual, provided that the substantive right is still agreed among the states and not directly attributed to the individual).

tional level and engage a process.[65] The home state may take care of the claim but he is deliberately free not to do so, to settle the espousal by any time or to resolve it in any other way.[66] This lack of enforceable rights for the investor constituted a major hurdle for the efficiency of investment protection under these mechanisms.[67]

Second, both diplomatic protection and FCN treaties usually require the investor to exhaust local remedies before any claim could be leveraged on the international level.[68] Thus, investors needed to seek protection before national courts in case their rights were violated, before they could even ask their home state to intervene. Through the requirement of exhausting local remedies, the success of a claim is heavily dependent on the procedural system and guarantees in the host state. In the case the judicial guarantees and the judicial system in general is efficient and unbiased, the action may lead to a fast success for the investor. However, if these requirements are not met, the obligation to exhaust local remedies may considerably delay any compensation for the investor.[69]

2. Unspecific provisions and a general trend to the conclusion of more specific treaties

In addition to the procedural issues, the newly introduced standards in the FCN treaties also lacked efficient substantive protection. Although FCN treaties brought a certain security for investors through the provisions con-

---

65 *Coyle*, Columbia Journal of Transnational Law Vol. 51 (2013), 302, 328; *Braun*, Ausprägungen der Globalisierung: Der Investor als partielles Subjekt im Internationalen Investitionsrecht, 2012, p. 85 ff.

66 *Herdegen*, 10. Edn. (2014), p. 330; *Ghouri*, Int. A.L.R. Vol. 14, No. 6, 189, 191; *Lang*, Der EuGH und die Investor-Staat-Streitbeilegung in TTIP und CETA (Beit. zum Transnat. Wirt.-R, Vol. 138, 2015), p.5; *Vandevelde*, U.C. Davis Jour. of Int. Law & Policy Vol. 12, No. 1 (2005), 157, 160.

67 *Herdegen*, 10. Edn. (2014), p. 330; *Engel*, SchiedsVZ, 2015, 218, 219; cf. also: *Brown* in: *Bungenberg/Griebel/Hobe et al.* (Eds.), International Investment Law, 2015, p. 160.

68 *Engel*, SchiedsVZ, 2015, 218, 219; *Happ*, Int. A.L.R. Iss. 3 (2007), 74, 75; *Vandevelde*, U.C. Davis Jour. of Int. Law & Policy Vol. 12, No. 1 (2005), 157, 165.

69 *Engel*, SchiedsVZ, 2015, 218, 219; *Happ*, Int. A.L.R. Iss. 3 (2007), 74, 75; *Ghouri*, Int. A.L.R. Vol. 14, No. 6, 189, 190; also: *Sattorova*, LIEI Vol. 39, No. 2 (2012), 223, 226 f; *Tietje* in: *Ehlers/Schoch* (Eds.), Rechtsschutz im Öffentlichen Recht, 2009, p. 65 f.

tained in the treaties, these provisions were still too unspecific and unspecialised to guarantee a sufficient protection.[70]

Finally, in the struggles after World War II, the conclusion of general treaties relating to various themes and subjects, became more and more difficult. In this context, especially during the Cold War, the conclusion of very particular and specific treaties raised. Those treaties focused on one subject only, which led to a higher probability to reach a consent at least regarding this topic and reduced interferences with other subjects.[71] Within this context, the current standard of investment protection through specialised IIAs raised.[72]

B. International Investment Agreements: investment protection through bilateral or multilateral international treaties

The need for a reshaped mechanism, which specifically protects foreign investments, has been immanent during the years after World War II. On the one hand mechanisms such as diplomatic protection and the rather unspecific FCN treaties were considered to be ineffective.[73] Simultaneously, especially capital exporting powers feared the risks of substantial losses for their investors abroad, due to a rising trend of nationalisations among developing countries in the post-Colonial Era.[74]

Since the 1950's, there has thus been a change in the perception of investment protection. Especially capital exporting states consequently tried to promote the implementation of a multilateral investment protection mechanism. These negotiations failed. Besides, some states tried to agree on a multilateral investment protection mechanism in the context of the negotiations of the Havana-Charter in 1948, which included further provi-

---

70 *Herdegen*, 10. Edn. (2014), p. 332; *Krajewski*, Wirtschaftsvölkerrecht, 2. Edn. (2009), para 549.

71 *Alschner*, Goettingen Journal of International Law Vol. 5, No. 2 (2013), 455, 466 f.

72 Cf. also: *Alschner*, Goettingen Journal of International Law Vol. 5, No. 2 (2013), 455, 463 f; *Herdegen*, 10. Edn. (2014), p. 332.

73 Summarising the overall insufficiencies: *Griebel*, (2008), p. 24 f; cf. *supra* (A., III.).

74 *Reinisch* in: *Tietje* (Ed.), Internationales Wirtschaftsrecht, 2015, p. 399; *Füracker*, SchiedsVZ, 2006, 236; 238; *Notter*, Völkerrechtlicher Investitionsschutz, 1989 p.74 f; *Sornarajah*, 3. Edn. (2010), p. 22; *Vandevelde*, U.C. Davis Jour. of Int. Law & Policy Vol. 12, No. 1 (2005), 157, 168 ff.

sions on the protection of investments.[75] These multilateral efforts were dismissed in favour of the General Agreement on Tariffs and Trade (GATT) as no consensus had been reached.[76] Similar evolutions took place within the Organisation of Economic Co-operation and Development (OECD) which ended with the adoption of a (non-binding) draft on the "*Treatment of Foreign Property*" (1967) and the "*Draft Negotiating Text for a Multilateral Agreement on Investment*" (1998), which both never entered into force.[77] States thus relied on more specific investment protection standards in bilateral agreements, which are nowadays known as BITs and constitute the core of the actual investment protection mechanism.[78] A certain acknowledgment of the potential of foreign direct investments for the economic development of a country lead to more and more of these BITs being concluded since the 1980s.[79]

The international investment protection mechanism through BITs or IIAs in general represents some core characteristics which guaranteed its success and effectiveness. The mechanism based on international conventions (I.), ensures efficient investment protection through specific substantive protection standards (II.) as well as its enforcement through a specific dispute settlement mechanism (III.). The specific approach in these treaties, also leads to a proliferation of the profiteers of this substantive protection (IV.).

---

75 *Echandi/Sauvé*, Prospects in international investment law and policy, 2013, p. 108 f.

76 *Notter*, Völkerrechtlicher Investitionsschutz, 1989, p. 75, *Echandi/Sauvé*, Prospects in international investment law and policy, 2013, p. 109.

77 *Eilmansberger*, CMLR Vol. 46 (2009), 383, 383 f; *Krajewski*, Wirtschaftsvölkerrecht, 2. Edn. (2009), para 572-574; cf. also: *Sornarajah*, 3. Edn. (2010), p. 25; *Schreuer*, JWIT Vol. 6, No. 3 (2005), 357, 358.

78 The first IIA is said to be concluded by Germany with Pakistan in 1959. The United States first adapted several provisions in their FCN treaties but since 1968 also shifted towards the conclusion of BITs, cf.: *Reinisch* in: *Tietje* (Ed.), Internationales Wirtschaftsrecht, 2015, p. 400 and 402; *Tietje*, Int. Investitionsschutzrecht im Spannungsverhältnis (Beit. zum Transnat. Wirt.-R, Vol. 93, 2010), 5, 7 f.

79 *Reinisch* in: *Tietje* (Ed.), Internationales Wirtschaftsrecht, 2015, p. 400; *Vandevelde*, U.C. Davis Jour. of Int. Law & Policy Vol. 12, No. 1 (2005), 157, 171 f; *Sornarajah*, 3. Edn. (2010), p. 22 ff; *Vandevelde*, Cornell Int. Law. J. Vol. 21, Iss. 2 (1988), 201, 209.

I. Conventional protection of investments through IIAs

Investment protection through IIAs benefits from the knowledge of former instruments. Other than the FCN treaties, IIAs tried to focus especially on investment protection issues and address its peculiar difficulties.[80] IIAs are international conventions, concluded by states as contracting parties, which intend to create legal rights and duties in order to establish a framework of stable terms and conditions for investments by nationals of one state (*home state*) in another state (*host state*).[81] Both contracting parties undertake clearly defined commitments to protect investments according to protection standards they mutually agreed on. Hence, IIAs are "*conventions*" in the sense of Art. 38 (1) of the statute of the International Court of Justice and thus a source of binding obligations for the states under international law.[82]

Since IIAs are international conventions, they are independent of changes and interferences in the host state's domestic law. This has two major implications, taking into account the principle of *pacta sunt servanda* in international law[83]:

First the host state cannot invoke its internal law to justify a breach of the obligations such state undertook in the IIA (cf. Art. 27 VCLT).[84]

Second, once the states agreed to guarantee a certain standard of protection, any of them cannot unilaterally terminate its engagement, unless it achieves the consent of the other party or such possibility to withdraw has been agreed in the agreement.[85]

The independence of IIAs from potential interferences through the instability of the host state's legal framework is thus one of the major differentiators for IIAs compared to other instruments.

---

80 *Sachs*, Berkeley Journal of International Law Vol. 2, Iss. 1 (1984)

81 *Schöbener/Herbst et al.*, 2010, p. 247 f; *Reinisch* in: *Tietje* (Ed.), Internationales Wirtschaftsrecht, 2015, p. 402; *Ipsen*, Völkerrecht, 6. Edn. (2014), p. 759; *Leeks*, U. Toronto Fac. L. Rev. Vol. 65, No. 2 (2007), 1, 5.

82 For the definition *inter alia*: *Kempen/Hillgruber*, Völkerrecht, 2. Edn. (2012), p. 56; *Herdegen*, Völkerrecht, 15. Edn. (2016), p. 120.

83 The principle is unanimously recognised as a general principle of international law and since 1969 established in Art. 26 ff of the Vienna Convention on the Law of Treaties, cf.: *Brownlie*, Principles of public international law, 7. Edn. (2008), p. 620.

84 *Griebel*, (2008), p. 47; also referred to in Art. 27 of the VCLT.

85 *Brownlie*, Principles of public international law, 7. Edn. (2008) p.621; cf. also: Art. 26 and 30 ff VCLT.

II. Higher degree of clarity as to the protection standards

IIAs also lead to a higher degree of security regarding the scope of the protection standards. As far as the parties agreed upon a particular standard, this conventional mechanism also overcomes the necessity to rely on customary international law. Preliminary discussions as to the scope of protection of aliens (and economic entities) abroad in customary international law are no longer necessary as the guarantees undertaken in the IIA supersede customary law in its scope of application.[86]

The major elements of this substantive protection standards, includes eight major guarantees.[87]

The *prohibition of expropriation without due compensation* prohibits state acts which deprive the investor (directly or indirectly through other measures than a formal nationalisation) from its property without paying a fair compensation for the loss suffered from the state measure.[88]

The *principle of non-discrimination and national treatment* mainly guarantees that the host state will not differentiate in its actions on the ground of nationality or other arbitrary criteria, leading to a less favourable treatment for foreign investors than the treatment granted to nationals of the host state.[89]

The *fair and equitable treatment standard* (FET) guarantees a certain stability of the regulatory framework and the absence of arbitrary measures or intentionally caused physical or financial harm by the host state towards the investor.[90]

The standard of *full protection and seccurity* (FPS) obliges the state to ensure that no harm occurs to the investor. The overlap between the FET

---

86 *Herdegen*, 10. Edn. (2014), p. 332 ff; a similar idea was pursued by the FCN treaties concluded in the 18th century, which leads several scholars in literature to state that IIAs are "*renamed*" FCN treaties, cf: *Sachs*, Berkeley Journal of International Law Vol. 2, Iss. 1 (1984), p. 194, cf. also: *Herdegen*, 10. Edn. (2014), p. 332; cf. also: *Ghouri*, ELJ Vol. 16, No. 5 (2010), 806, 807.

87 For their concrete scope, cf. *infra* Chapter 4; cf. also: *Engel*, SchiedsVZ, 2015, 218, 219; for a short overview also: *Leeks*, U. Toronto Fac. L. Rev. Vol. 65, No. 2 (2007), 1, 5-7.

88 *Herdegen*, 10. Edn. (2014), p. 350 ff; *Reinisch* in: *Tietje* (Ed.), Internationales Wirtschaftsrecht, 2015, p. 418 f.

89 *Herdegen*, 10. Edn. (2014), p. 348; *Schöbener/Herbst et al.*, 2010, p. 279.

90 *Herdegen*, 10. Edn. (2014), p. 341 ff; *Desert Line vs. Yemen*, 06.02.2008 – ICSID Case No. ARB/05/17 - Award, para 186; *Reinisch* in: *Tietje* (Ed.), Internationales Wirtschaftsrecht, 2015, p. 414 f.

and the FPS standard and a wider scope of the FPS standard are subject to debate.[91]

Umbrella clauses lead to a particular effect regarding (conventional or other) obligations undertaken by the host state *vis-à-vis* the investor. If specific commitments (under domestic law) were granted to the investor, the breach of these (often contractual) commitments is considered as a breach of the IIA by virtue of the umbrella clause.[92]

IIAs typically also include *most-favoured nation clauses* (MFN) which do not provide an inherent protection standard but guarantee that the investor in the host state will enjoy any (more far reaching) protection the host state granted to any other investor in an international agreement.[93]

Finally, most IIAs also guarantee the *right to establish* an investment in the host state and to freely dispose of all funds generated through the investment (establishment clause and free-transfer of funds clause).[94]

III. Direct enforcement by investors

As already explained regarding FCN treaties and the mechanism of diplomatic protection, public international law was generally not perceived as a legal order granting rights to individuals. Individuals were only indirectly protected through (diplomatic or judicial) action by their home states and the rights attributed to those states.[95]

This renders the enforcement of any obligation far more difficult and subject to the good will of the home state.[96] The attribution of own rights

---

91 *Dolzer/Stevens*, Bilateral Investment Treaties, p. 61 f.; *Schreuer*, Journal of International Dispute Settlement, Vol. 1, No. 2 (2010), 353, 354.

92 *Herdegen*, 10. Edn. (2014), p. 340; *Reinisch* in: *Tietje* (Ed.), Internationales Wirtschaftsrecht, 2015, p. 429 f; *Leeks*, U. Toronto Fac. L. Rev. Vol. 65, No. 2 (2007), 1, 6; *Jensen*, RIW, 2016, 277, 279.

93 *Reinisch* in: *Tietje* (Ed.), Internationales Wirtschaftsrecht, 2015, p. 411 f; *Schöbener/Herbst et al.*, 2010, p. 279.

94 *Leeks*, U. Toronto Fac. L. Rev. Vol. 65, No. 2 (2007), 1, 6.

95 *Herdegen*, 10. Edn. (2014), p. 330; *Ghouri*, Int. A.L.R. Vol. 14, No. 6, 189, 191; *Sattorova*, LIEI Vol. 39, No. 2 (2012), 223, 227; *Lang*, Der EuGH und die Investor-Staat-Streitbeilegung in TTIP und CETA (Beit. zum Transnat. Wirt.-R, Vol. 138, 2015), p. 5; *Vandevelde*, U.C. Davis Jour. of Int. Law & Policy Vol. 12, No. 1 (2005), 157, 159 f.

96 *Vandevelde*, U.C. Davis Jour. of Int. Law & Policy Vol. 12, No. 1 (2005), 157, 160; *Lang*, Der EuGH und die Investor-Staat-Streitbeilegung in TTIP und CETA (Beit. zum Transnat. Wirt.-R, Vol. 138, 2015) p. 5.

to individuals by means of international law is a crucial success factor for effectually enforcing those rights. Consequently, as a countermovement to further shortcomings, IIAs attribute individual rights to investors.[97]

It is generally acknowledged that an attribution of rights by means of international (conventional) law needs to be clear and unambiguous to distinguish the attribution of *own rights* from simple benefits an individual may enjoy through obligations which were undertaken *vis-à-vis* the other state party (so-called: *reflex*).[98]

> IIAs are generally very clear on that subject matter. Wordings such as "Each Contracting State shall in its territory in every case accord investments by investors of the other Contracting State fair and equitable treatment as well as full protection under this Treaty."[99]

or

> "Each Party shall accord to covered investments treatment in accordance with customary international law, including fair and equitable treatment and full protection and security"[100]

refer to the "*covered investments*" or "*investments by investors*" and thus clearly to the foreign investors and not to the contracting parties of the agreement. Consequently, the attribution of individual rights to investors through IIAs is nowadays commonly accepted.[101]

But besides this attribution of own rights, IIAs also grant the investor the possibility to enforce its rights at its own discretion through an independent dispute resolution mechanism. IIAs typically contain dispute resolution clauses which guarantee the investors' access to an arbitral forum in which they may present their claim by their own initiative.[102] These dis-

---

97 Cf. also: *Ghouri*, ELJ Vol. 16, No. 5 (2010), 806, 807.

98 *Kempen/Hillgruber*, Völkerrecht, 2. Edn. (2012), p. 39 f; *Ipsen*, Völkerrecht, 6. Edn. (2014), p. 309 f; cf. also: *Engel*, SchiedsVZ, 2015, 218, 219 f.

99 Article 2 of the German Model BIT (2008).

100 Article 5 of the U.S. Model BIT (2012).

101 *Griebel*, (2008), p. 38; *Sachs*, Berkeley Journal of International Law Vol. 2, Iss. 1 (1984)p. 197; cf. also: *Herdegen*, Völkerrecht, 15. Edn. (2016), p. 113; *Tietje* in: *Ehlers/Schoch* (Eds.), Rechtsschutz im Öffentlichen Recht, 2009, p. 66 f; cf. also: *Braun*, Ausprägungen der Globalisierung: Der Investor als partielles Subjekt im Internationalen Investitionsrecht, 2012, p. 91 ff and 103 ff.

102 *Sachs*, Berkeley Journal of International Law Vol. 2, Iss. 1 (1984), p. 219; *Engel*, SchiedsVZ, 2015, 218, 219; *Tietje* in: *Ehlers/Schoch* (Eds.), Rechtsschutz im Öffentlichen Recht, 2009, p. 66 f; *Braun*, Ausprägungen der Globalisie-

pute settlement clauses (or arbitration clauses) help to overcome difficulties regarding the host state's hostility to refer disputes to an unbiased, international arbitration forum.

Dispute settlement by way of arbitration generally requires the prior consent of the parties to submit the claim to an arbitral tribunal.[103] Without such consent, investors keep being limited to the traditional ways of dispute settlement, such as action brought before national courts, diplomatic protection or a claim by the home state before the ICJ.[104] The disadvantages of these means were already discussed in the previous subsections.

To stabilize this way of private dispute settlement and hence enable the investor to submit a claim whenever a dispute has raised, IIAs generally include arbitration clauses in which the state parties give their (prior) unilateral consent to submit a dispute arising from the alleged breach of the IIA to an arbitral tribunal.[105]

The consent provided by the host state in such arbitration clauses contained in IIAs can be accepted by the investor by any implied conduct, which is generally seen in the submission of the claim to the arbitral tribunal.[106] The main idea behind these considerations is that the parties do not necessarily need to express their consent to arbitration in one single instrument.[107] It is sufficient that there is a consent by both parties: the host state expressed such consent in the IIA whereas the investor expresses its consent through filing the claim.[108] Arbitration clauses contained in IIAs

---

rung: Der Investor als partielles Subjekt im Internationalen Investitionsrecht, 2012, p. 91-93.

103 *Schwab/Walter et al.*, Schiedsgerichtsbarkeit, 6. Edn. (2000), p. 23, *Tietje* in: *Ehlers/Schoch* (Eds.), Rechtsschutz im Öffentlichen Recht, 2009, p. 64.

104 *Engel*, SchiedsVZ, 2015, 218, 219 f; *Vandevelde*, U.C. Davis Jour. of Int. Law & Policy Vol. 12, No. 1 (2005), 157, 159 f.

105 *Sachs*, Berkeley Journal of International Law Vol. 2, Iss. 1 (1984), p. 219, *Tietje* in: *Ehlers/Schoch* (Eds.), Rechtsschutz im Öffentlichen Recht, 2009 p.68, *Dolzer/Stevens*, Bilateral Investment Treaties, 1995, p. 131 f.

106 *Dolzer/Stevens*, Bilateral Investment Treaties, 1995, p. 131; *Engel*, SchiedsVZ, 2015, 218, 219.

107 *Dolzer/Stevens*, Bilateral Investment Treaties, 1995, p. 131 *Griebel*, (2008), p. 92 f; *Füracker*, SchiedsVZ, 2006, 236,244 ; *Schreuer*, The ICSID Convention, 2. Edn. (2009), para 427 f and 448; *Tietje* in: *Ehlers/Schoch* (Eds.), Rechtsschutz im Öffentlichen Recht, 2009, p. 68.

108 This has been a sort of countermovement to prior ideas how to submit investment disputes to arbitration: the consent to arbitration could theoretically be granted to investors in multiple ways. First, the consent to arbitration may be

thus establish a mechanism to ensure an arbitral dispute settlement even if the host state refuses to cooperate.[109]

IV. Enlargement of the scope of rights through the terms investment and investor

Besides the attribution of claimable rights to the investor, IIAs also tend to significantly enlarge the attribution of protection to a larger scope of beneficiaries than others mechanisms before.

Investments may generally imply multi-layer structures of ownership, either due to the operating model of the investment itself (e.g. the subsidiary owned by a parent company) or due to the implication of legal entities running a business, which necessarily requires shareholders owning the legal entity. Efficiently protecting investments hence requires not only protecting the immediate asset (such as a e.g. the factory or the land on which the business operates) but also those which are indirectly affected, such as e.g. the shareholders of a legal entity, which owns the assets.

Under customary law, especially since the *Barcelona Traction Case*, the rights of shareholders were hardly protected at all. The ICJ drew a clear distinction between the rights of the company and the rights of the shareholders, as both are separate legal personalities.[110] The court concluded that an infringement of the company's rights generally does not imply a direct infringement of the shareholders' rights. They may be exposed to "*difficulties or financial losses [...] as a result of the situation of the company*", but this affection of interests cannot involve the host states'

included in a direct individual agreement between the investor and the host state (e.g. included in so-called *state-contracts*, cf. *infra*). However, the negotiation of such individual contracts requires the investor to have a considerable bargaining power, which deprives the mechanism of wider use. Second, the consent to arbitration could theoretically be included in the host state's national legislation. Nevertheless, such unilateral offers included in the national legal framework are rather weak securities. As the consent is given unilaterally in a national law it can as well be unilaterally revoked by the host state at any time. Furthermore, such unilateral consent can include various limitations or ambiguous formulations which may weaken the reference to arbitral tribunals, cf.: *Tietje* in: *Ehlers/Schoch* (Eds.), Rechtsschutz im Öffentlichen Recht, 2009, p. 68, *Dolzer/Stevens*, Bilateral Investment Treaties, 1995, p. 131.

109 *Sachs*, Berkeley Journal of International Law Vol. 2, Iss. 1 (1984), p. 219.

110 *Barcelona Traction Case*, I.C.J. Reports (1970), 3, 35 f; *Griebel*, (2008), p. 63.

responsibility as long as the host state's act does not directly infringe a shareholder's right.[111]

IIAs try to overcome this perception by seeking to include both shareholders and companies, regardless of the nationality of the legal entity conceived in the host state and regardless of whether or not any other shareholder wants to initiate proceedings in the concrete case (proliferation of beneficiaries).

This broadening is a result of a dual determination of the scope of application for IIAs. This scope is determined by the terms "*investment*" and "*investor*". Protection standards in IIAs generally guarantee the "*investor*" that his "*investment*" will not be treated in a detrimental way. The US-Model-BIT (2012) prototypically states "*Each Party shall accord to investors of the other Party treatment no less favorable than that it accords, in like circumstances, to its own investors with respect to the establishment, acquisition, expansion, management, [...] or other disposition of investments (...)*".[112] It can be observed that the "*investor*" is the subject the right is attributed, but the protected object, which should not be accorded a "*treatment no less favourable than that it [is] accord[ed], in like circumstances, to its own investors*"[113] is the "*investment*".[114]

Thus, the scope of beneficiaries of the protection offered in an IIA is determined by analysing the interference of both terms.

First, the term of investment is generally defined in a broad manner in IIAs. Commonly treaties refer to "*every asset that an investor owns or controls, directly or indirectly*"[115] or "*every kind of asset that is indirectly invested by investors of one Contracting State in the territory of the other Contracting State*"[116]. The definition is then followed by a non-exhaustive list of particular assets, which may refer to "*movable and immovable property*"[117], any kind of concession-like contracts, such as "*turnkey, construction, management, production, concession, revenue-sharing, and*

111 *Barcelona Traction Case*, I.C.J. Reports (1970), 3, 35 f.

112 Art. 3 (1) of the U.S. Model BIT (2012).

113 Art. 3 (1) of the U.S. Model BIT (2012).

114 Other investment treaties contain similar provisions, as an example, the German Model BIT (2009) states: "*Each Contracting State shall in its territory promote as far as possible investments by investors of the other contracting State and admit such investments in accordance with its legislation (...)*".

115 Definition of investment in Art. 1 of the U.S. Model BIT (2012).

116 Art. 1 (1) of the German Model BIT (2009).

117 Art. 1 (1) of the German Model BIT (2009).

other similar contracts "[118], "*intellectual property rights*"[119] as well as "*company or business enterprise, or shares, stock, or other forms of equity participation in a company*"[120]. Hence, the term "*investment*", which determines the applicability *ratione materiae* of IIAs, expressly states that shares and other forms of equity participation fall within the scope of protection offered by the treaties.[121] Consequently, if protection is granted to "*investments*" it is granted to "*shares or other interests*" in the same manner as it is granted to "*movable or immovable property*". The difference established in the *Barcelona Traction Case* is evaded and both are equally protected.[122] The term investment hence refers to a broad understanding, including especially structures of indirect control and a wide range of assets.[123]

Some IIAs however contain a certain limit to the protection of shareholders. They require a direct or indirect control of the investment by the shareholder to fall under the scope of protection of the IIA. This is usually understood as the exclusion of portfolio-investments. Portfolio-investments as to *Füracker* are "*mere capital flows intended to raise capital for ventures without the investor putting more interest into the development of the company than the value of his capital.*"[124] An investor protected under the IIA needs to be able to exercise some control on the investment, either by having a sufficient amount of shares, being granted specific rights or other means.[125]

Second, regarding the term "*investors*", the determination of the investor's nationality is crucial to enable an IIA to be invoked. Only investors having the nationality of a certain home state having concluded an IIA with the host state, are protected under the IIA (criteria *ratione perso-*

118 Defintion of investment in Art. 1 lit. e of the U.S. Model BIT (2012).

119 Defintion of investment in Art. 1 lit. f of the U.S. Model BIT (2012).

120 Art. 1 (6) lit. (b) of the Energy Charter Treaty (1994).

121 Cf. also: *Füracker*, SchiedsVZ, 2006, 236, p. 240; *Reinisch* in: *Tietje* (Ed.), Internationales Wirtschaftsrecht, 2015, p. 408.

122 *Griebel*, (2008) p.64; the only limitation is usually conceived by excluding (pure) portfolio-investment by requiring the investor to have direct or indirect control over its investment. Usually the exclusion of those investments does not lead to particular problems.

123 *Bischoff/Happ* in: *Bungenberg/Griebel/Hobe et al.* (Eds.), International Investment Law, 2015, p. 500-502 ; *Schöbener/Herbst et al.*, 2010, p. 257-259.

124 *Füracker*, SchiedsVZ, 2006, 236, 240.

125 *Herdegen*, 10. Edn. (2014) p 335 f; *Schöbener/Herbst et al.*, 2010, p. 263-266.

nae).[126] However, IIAs through particular provisions denominating the conditions to be met – especially for judicial entities – to determine the nationality, lead to a certain security for investors which could now adapt their business structures to enjoy a certain – desired – protection.[127]

C. State-contracts

Another approach, besides IIAs, to guarantee investments abroad were individual contracts concluded between investors and states (so-called state-contracts) to reach a certain level of contractual protection for the investor in the host state. State-contracts can be concluded in various forms, such as Joint-Venture-Treaties, Concessions, etc..[128] State contracts are generally defined as a contract concluded between the host state (or a separate legal entity ruled by the state) and the investor to determine rights and obligations with regard to a specific investment.[129] Such rights and obligations may be substantive guarantees, stabilization clauses with regard to a legal framework, dispute resolution clauses, e.g. to grant jurisdiction to arbitral tribunals or to the host states domestic tribunals, as well as a clause ruling the governing law. The governing law may thus be the host state's domestic law or any other choice of law, including international law. All these instruments could reduce the investor's risk to be (solely) submitted to the national legal and judicial framework of the host state. However, the conclusion of such treaties requires a certain weight in the negotiations, which limits the scope of protection offered through such mechanisms to few economic operators.[130]

126 *Griebel*, (2008), p. 65 f; *Herdegen*, 10. Edn. (2014), p. 334-337.

127 Generally, for natural persons the determination remains subject to the national laws of the host state. To prevent abuse, generally an effective and genuine link is required, cf.: *Griebel*, (2008), p. 65.

128 *Griebel*, (2008), p. 27; *Schöbener/Herbst et al.*, 2010, p. 424 f; *Reinisch* in: *Tietje* (Ed.), Internationales Wirtschaftsrecht, 2015, p. 407.

129 *Schöbener/Herbst et al.*, 2010, p. 242; *Reinisch* in: *Tietje* (Ed.), Internationales Wirtschaftsrecht, 2015, p. 407.

130 *Herdegen*, 10. Edn. (2014), p. 330; *Schöbener/Herbst et al.*, 2010, p. 243.

Chapter 3: The reception of modern investment protection through IIAs / BITs in the EU: doubling the protection?

The emergence of IIAs, especially BITs, is far from being a non-European phenomenon. Most of the current EU member states are capital exporting countries since decades or even centuries and therefore expressed great interest in protecting their investments abroad. Hence, EU member states even significantly pushed the current mechanism of investment protection through IIAs to its current success. They concluded a multitude of IIAs and thus contributed widely to the proliferation of the protection standards and their interpretation. This leads to a multitude of IIAs being concluded between EU member states and non-member states (extra-EU IIAs). Furthermore, mainly driven by the context of the subsequent enlargement of the EU, IIAs were concluded between EU member states and eastern European states, which later acceded the EU. This development leads to the existence of approximately 190 intra-EU IIAs, after the enlargement was successfully conducted.[131] Hence, investors in the EU primarily seem to be submitted to a large framework of IIAs (B.).

However, investors operating in the EU are subject to a second, different legal framework which emerged in coexistence but was never conceived as part of a coordinated approach with the proliferation of IIAs. The ongoing integration process within the EU, and especially the creation of the internal market and the framework of EU law in general, lead to a doubling of legal frameworks for investments in the EU member states. This second framework provides certain guarantees but also particular regulations for economic operators in the EU and thus also for investors (A.).

A. Rise of the EU and the internal market: Investment protection through EU law

The current perception of the EU and the potential implications on matters such as international investment law are the consequence of a long-lasting development since the foundation of the European Coal and Steal Community (ECSC) in 1951. From the perspective of the founders in 1951,

---

131 *Dahlquist/Lenk et al.*, European Policy Analysis, 2016:4, 1, 1 f; *Wehland*, ICLQ Vol. 58, Iss. 2 (2009), 297, 297.

any interference in matters such as cross-border-investment would have been hard to perceive. However, since the Treaty of Rome in 1958, which did not only found the European Economic Community (EEC) and the EURATOM but also created the customs union among the six founding states, the EU, which displaces the former European Community since 1st December 2009, extended not only its member states but also the competences, concepts and objectives.[132]

The creation of the internal market (formerly denominated common market) and the subsequent changes to the European Treaties[133], led to the accomplishment of an economical union and thus a multitude of changes which also affect investment policies.[134]

This formation of the economic union is based on several traces of an ongoing integration in the EU. Within this union, economic operators are subject to a more and more enhanced *'supra-national'*- legal framework.

The first driver for the creation of the economic union is the development and strengthening of the internal market.[135] The internal market, as perceived by the Single European Acts should establish

> "an area without internal frontiers in which the free movement of goods, persons, services and capital is ensured".[136]

The principle is laid down in Art. 26 (2) TFEU.

The overall goal is to achieve a level playing field for economic operators within the territory of the EU member states. Within this entire territory, no national boarders should hinder effective competition between the economic operators and encourage their free economic development.[137]

---

132 *Hobe*, 8. Edn. (2014), para 20 ff; *Oppermann/Classen et al.*, 5. Edn. (2011) § 2, para 12 ff; *Haratsch*, 2016, p. 4; the EEC, EURATOM and ECSC were unified as European Community since the Treaty of Maastricht; with the entry into force of the Lisbon Treaty on 01/12/2009 the former European Community was renamed as European Union.

133 Especially the changes achieved through the adoption of the Single European Act, Official Journal of the European Communities L 169 (1987).

134 *Haratsch*, 2016, p. 7 f; cf. also: *Kleinheisterkamp*, JIEL Vol. 15, No. 1 (2012), 85, 100 referring to the internal market as *„the regulated level playing field that is the backbone of the European intergraton project"*.

135 *Hobe*, 8. Edn. (2014), para 607 ff; *Streinz*, 10. Edn. (2016), p. 304.

136 Art. 26 (2) TFEU, cf. also: *Hobe*, 8. Edn. (2014), para 607 ff.

137 *Streinz*, 10. Edn. (2016), p. 304 f; *Haratsch*, 2016, p. 400; cf. also: *Lenk*, EJLS Vol. 8, No. 2 (2015), 6, 9; *Kilian*, Europäisches Wirtschaftsrecht, 5. Edn. (2016), p. 44.

The creation of the internal market should be achieved by two means:

On the one hand, the adoption of common rules in all member states[138] as perceived by Art. 114 TFEU should significantly equalise (and substitute) the different national environments the economic operators compete within.[139] Common rules applied in all member states considerably facilitate cross-border economic engagements.

On the other hand, the fundamental freedoms (free movement of goods, free movement of workers, freedom of establishment, freedom to provide services, and free movement of capital) operate as major contributors to achieve this level playing field in the internal market.[140] Even in those areas where common rules have not yet been implemented, the fundamental freedoms guarantee the possibility for economic operators and individuals to interact and compete in all member states and across member states in an unhindered, non-discriminatory way.[141] Those freedoms serve as a guarantee against the detrimental interference of national legislators with economic operators and individuals in general.

Derived as part of the prohibition of restrictions deducted from the fundamental freedoms, the principle of mutual trust among member states should further reduce obstacles in *inter se* trades in the EU. *Inter alia*, a product traded in a member state should be deemed to comply with the regulation in this member state if it fulfils all necessary standards and regulations in its country of origin. This fundamental principle enabled to considerably reduce the ability of national legislators to disadvantage foreign *vis-à-vis* national competitors.[142]

The second driver is the ongoing transfer of legislative competencies to the EU through e.g. the Treaties of Rome, Maastricht and Lisbon. Driven by the desire to enable broader regulations in connection with the accomplishment of the internal market but also regarding more complementary fields of action, the EU member states transferred considerable legislative

138 The German expression is „*Rechtsangleichung*".

139 *Hobe*, 8. Edn. (2014), para 614; *Streinz*, 10. Edn. (2016), p. 304, 378 f; *Haratsch*, 2016, p. 667 ff; *Kilian*, Europäisches Wirtschaftsrecht, 5. Edn. (2016), p. 159 f.

140 *Hobe*, 8. Edn. (2014), para 615 f; *Haratsch*, 2016, p. 380; *Dimopoulos*, CMLR Vol. 48, No. 1 (2011), 63, 64 f.

141 *Hobe*, 8. Edn. (2014), para 615 f; *Haratsch*, 2016, p. 380 f; *Dimopoulos*, CMLR Vol. 48, No. 1 (2011), 63, 64 f.

142 *Hobe*, 8. Edn. (2014), para 614; *Streinz*, 10. Edn. (2016), p. 383 f; *Kilian*, Europäisches Wirtschaftsrecht, 5. Edn. (2016), p. 146.

competencies to the EU. This leads to more and more sophisticated regulations in areas of economic relations, trade and competition, which are either directly applicable to the member states (primary law and regulations) or need to be transposed to national law (directives).[143]

The matters governed by EU primary or secondary law now include, *inter alia,* liberalisations in the energy sector, public procurement law, dedicated rules for competition, state monopolies or other obstacles to competition within the markets, etc.

The third driver for the raising importance of the economic union is the enlargement process since the Treaties of Rome. Starting with the entry of the United Kingdom, Ireland and Denmark (1973), followed by Greece (1981), Spain, Portugal (both 1986) and Austria, Sweden and Finland (all 1995) and finally leading to the eastern-enlargement-process in 2004, 2007 and 2013 which makes the internal market to stretch among 28 states in 2016.[144]

All this was predominantly supplemented the CJEU which served as a major contributor to ensure the ongoing processes of integration. Driven by an approach which stresses an interpretation based on the objectives of the European Treaties, the CJEU constantly reduced attempts of the member states which could affect the fundamental freedoms, the unhindered competition in the internal market and the basis of the economic union. The European court system which operates independently from the influence of EU member states, continuously enabled to strengthen the importance of EU law in all member states and for all economic operators.[145]

For investors and investments within the EU, the creation of the internal market and the further integration process has tremendous effects. First, the internal market sets the level playing field for all economic operations within the EU and hence, also for foreign investors operating thereunder.

---

143 *Kilian*, Europäisches Wirtschaftsrecht, 5. Edn. (2016), p. 47.

144 Depending on the outcome of the negotiations following the 'Brexit-Vote' on 23/06/2016 by the United Kingdom, the structure of the member states could be fundamentally changed. Ireland and Scotland expressed their wish to enter the European Union, when the United Kingdom decides to leave it. At the same time the consequences to be drawn by the British Government from the vote are unclear as well, some resistance as to completely leaving the EU formed since the publication of the results. The consequences are not to be determined at the time this thesis was handed in; cf. for an overview of the legal consequences and requirements: *Thiele*, EuR, 2016, 281.

145 *Rengeling/Kotzur* in: *Rengeling/Middeke/Gellermann* (Eds.), Handbuch des Rechtsschutzes in der Europäischen Union, 2014, p. 57 f.

Second, EU law became increasingly important for investors: on the one hand as the legal framework they interact with and hence which (more and more) supersedes the national framework as the predominant legal business environment. On the other hand, EU law became a lever for protection against all sorts of measures issued by the member states, as it has been more and more used by economic operators to prevent particular state measures to affect their businesses.[146]

The last step in this ongoing integration was conceived by the Lisbon Treaty entering into force on 1st December 2009. Besides a large amount of institutional changes and changes relating to the procedures to follow to adopt legislative acts, the Lisbon Treaty also included certain changes with particular relevance for investment protection and investors in the EU.

First, the Lisbon Treaty declared the Charter of Fundamental Rights of the EU (the Charter) to be applicable to all member states, except for Poland, the UK and Ireland (Art. 6 (1) TEU).[147] The Charter includes a wide range of fundamental rights, including economic rights, such as the right to property or freedom to conduct business, which the EU, its institutions and all member states need to respect when implementing EU law, cf. Art. 51 of the Charter.[148] This is a considerable change in the protection standard for individuals and legal entities and thus for investors in the EU.[149]

Second, the Lisbon Treaty unified the EC and the EU and created a distinct, legal personality for the EU.[150] Since 1st December 2009, the EU is entitled, based on the external competences conferred by the Treaties, to conclude legally binding international treaties which would create rights and obligations for all member states.

Third, the Lisbon Treaty introduced several changes in the institutional framework through abolishing the three-pillar structure and especially

146 Cf. similar: *Lenk*, EJLS Vol. 8, No. 2 (2015), 6, 9; *Kleinheisterkamp*, JIEL Vol. 15, No. 1 (2012), 85.

147 *Streinz*, 10. Edn. (2016), p. 23; *Nowak*, Europarecht nach Lissabon, 2011, p. 148 f.

148 The scope of Art. 51 of the Charter will be discussed in further detail in Chapter 4 and 15.

149 *Nowak*, Europarecht nach Lissabon, 2011, p. 148 f.

150 *Streinz*, 10. Edn. (2016), p. 22 f; *Nowak*, Europarecht nach Lissabon, 2011, p. 84 f and, p. 88-90.

modifying the procedures to adopt secondary law.[151] With the extension of the ordinary procedure in Art. 294 TFEU, the EU tremendously simplified the adoption of secondary legislation as unanimous consent by all member states in the European Council is substituted by the requirement of a qualified majority in a large majority of cases.[152]. By abandoning the previous pillar structure, the Lisbon Treaty reinforced the integration procedure within the EU.[153] Besides, the conferral of a distinct legal personality to the EU and the reshaping of the competencies strengthened the internal and external ability to act for the EU.[154] Together with several amendments regarding the access to the CJEU, this can be considered as a milestone to further implement the rule of law in the EU.[155] As a consequence, the Lisbon Treaty may be regarded as the second most important treaty to obtain an integrated legislative framework and the advancement of the internal market after the Single European Acts.

B. Rise of IIAs concluded by EU member states: EU-Investment protection through IIAs

As aforementioned, EU member states concluded various IIAs starting in the 1950s. Nowadays, the amount of IIAs concluded by EU member states in total reaches about 1600 bi- or multilateral treaties.[156]

At first glance, there is nothing special about states concluding international agreements, even though they might be part of a regional organisation of economic integration. *Inter alia*, Mexico, Canada and the United States of America concluded various IIAs besides the conclusion of the NAFTA. Nevertheless, the ongoing process of integration within the EU

---

151 *Hobe*, 8. Edn. (2014), para 68 f, 72 and 74; *Streinz*, 10. Edn. (2016), p. 22 f; *Haratsch*, 2016, p. 144 f; cf. also: *Lenk*, EJLS Vol. 8, No. 2 (2015), 6, 7 f.

152 *Hobe*, 8. Edn. (2014), para 72 ff; *Oppermann/Classen et al.*, 5. Edn. (2011) § 3, para 14; *Haratsch*, 2016, p. 145; cf. also: *Nowak*, Europarecht nach Lissabon, 2011, p. 131-133.

153 *Hobe*, 8. Edn. (2014), para 68 ff; *Oppermann/Classen et al.*, 5. Edn. (2011) § 3, para 14; *Streinz*, 10. Edn. (2016), p. 22 f.

154 *Hobe*, 8. Edn. (2014), para 67, 70; *Oppermann/Classen et al.*, 5. Edn. (2011) § 3, para 14.

155 Cf. also: *Hobe*, 8. Edn. (2014), para 69 and 76.

156 According to UNCTAD the member states had 1385 extra-EU BITs and 195 intra-EU BITs in force in 2016, cf.: http://investmentpolicyhub.unctad.org/IIA [last checked on 28/02/2017].

differentiates this regional system of economic integration from other systems and leads to further difficulties.

The most obvious difference is the particular structure of the EU. On the one hand the EU is not a state in terms of international public law. Consequently, the EU member states keep being subjects of international law and thus exercise their own competences concerning their internal and external matters. Nevertheless, the EU member states decided to confer several competences to the institutions of the EU which are then exercised by the latter. This may concern internal (toward the member states) as well as external (towards non-member states) competencies. The division of competences within the EU and its member states is governed by the principle of conferral, currently expressed in Art. 5 TEU.[157] According to this principle the EU member states keep the full competences to act as long as the subject matter in question has not been voluntarily conferred to the EU.[158] Concerning investment protection and specifically foreign direct investments the conferral of competencies was established through the entry into force of the Lisbon Treaty. The treaty extended the scope of the common commercial policy (CCP) of the EU to foreign direct investments.[159] Art. 207 TFEU now states that the

> "common commercial policy shall be based on uniform principles, particularly with regard to changes in tariff rates, the conclusion of tariff and trade agreements relating to trade in goods and services, and the commercial aspects of intellectual property, [and] foreign direct investment, (…)".

Beforehand it has been mainly unchallenged – and clarified by the Opinion 1/94 of the CJEU – that the CCP does not include regulations of foreign direct investments with regard to third states.[160] Consequently, the competence to adopt measures or conclude international treaties in this

157 *Frenz*, Europarecht, 2011, para 36-40; *Hobe*, 8. Edn. (2014), para 181-198; *Nowak*, Europarecht nach Lissabon, 2011, p. 117-119.

158 Cf. e.g.: *Epping* in: von Heinegg/Vedder EUV/AEUV, Art. 5 TEU, para 2 ff; *Lienbacher* in: Schwarze EU-Kommentar, Art. 5 TEU, para 7 f.

159 *Nowak*, Europarecht nach Lissabon, 2011, p. 264 f.

160 *Burgstaller* in: *Bungenberg/Griebel/Hindelang* (Eds.), International investment law and EU law, 2011, p. 55 f; *Söderlund*, JOIA Vol. 24, Iss. 5 (2007), 455, 461 f; *Johannsen*, Die Kompetenz der EU für ausländische Direktinvestitionen nach Lissabon (Beit. zum Transnat. Wirt.-R, Vol. 90, 2009), p. 6 ff.

subject matter remained with the member states until the shift of powers towards the EU through the Lisbon Treaty.[161]

This distribution of competences and the process of integration leads to a far more divided system of investment protection through IIAs in the EU than in any other regional system.

Before the Lisbon Treaty, the EU member states exercised this competence at various occasions. Germany e.g. concluded about 130 IIAs which entered into force since 1962.[162] Such treaties were originally and mainly concluded with non EU member states (extra- EU IIAs). However, several of those treaties were concluded with states of the former Eastern Bloc after its dissolution in 1991. This leads to a significant amount of IIAs involving two EU member states after the eastern European states accessed the EU in 2004 and 2007 (intra-EU IIAs). The same applies for several other member states.[163]

The conferral of competences for foreign direct investments through the Lisbon Treaty further complicates the landscape.[164] The Treaty also created the consolidated legal personality for the EU.[165] Consequently, the EU has been enabled to negotiate and conclude international agreements itself as long as the subject matter of the agreements fall into the scope of competences conferred to the EU. Future IIAs will thus be concluded either by the EU itself or as conjoint agreements of the EU and its member states.

161 *Burgstaller* in: *Bungenberg/Griebel/Hindelang* (Eds.), International investment law and EU law, 2011, p. 55 f, who points out that previously the EU was competent if the agreement conlcuded by the member states would also include further subjects, which fall into the scope of competence conferred to the EU, cf. p. 58 f; *Eilmansberger*, CMLR Vol. 46 (2009), 383, 397; *Johannsen*, Die Kompetenz der EU für ausländische Direktinvestitionen nach Lissabon (Beit. zum Transnat. Wirt.-R, Vol. 90, 2009), p. 22.

162 *Burgstaller* in: *Bungenberg/Griebel/Hindelang* (Eds.), International investment law and EU law, 2011, p. 55.

163 Before the enlargement to the Eastern European Countries, only two intra-EU BITs existed between Portugal / Germany and Greece / Germany; cf. also: *Wehland*, ICLQ Vol. 58, Iss. 2 (2009), 297, 297 f and *Söderlund*, JOIA Vol. 24, Iss. 5 (2007), 455, 455 f; *Kleinheisterkamp*, JIEL Vol. 15, No. 1 (2012), 85, 95 f.

164 Cf. also: *Kleinheisterkamp*, JIEL Vol. 15, No. 1 (2012), 85, 85 f.

165 Prior to the Lisbon Treaty the EC and the European Atomic Energy Community were granted legal personality, the status of the EU was subject to considerable debate, cf.: *Dörr* in: Grabitz/Hilf/Nettesheim EUV/AEUV, Art. 47 TEU, para 4-7; cf. also: *Nowak*, Europarecht nach Lissabon, 2011, p. 84 f and p. 88-90.

The conclusion of such mixed agreements will be necessary if the treaty includes subject matters for whom the competences are partially conferred to the EU and partially remain with the EU member states. Even before the Lisbon Treaty such mixed agreements were concluded by the EC and the member states, e.g. the Energy Charter.[166] This third category of agreements will probably even gain in impact within the next years, as it was the dedicated intention of the EU to replace the member state IIAs by a coherent community investment and trade policy.[167]

I. Extra-EU IIAs

Currently there are more than 1200 IIAs in force that were concluded by EU member states with non-member states.[168] Considerable doubts as to the continued validity of these agreements were expressed after the transferal of competences for foreign direct investments to the EU in the Lisbon Treaty.[169] Some authors argued that those treaties remain fully in force by an analogous application of Art. 351 TFEU. Article 351 TFEU concerns treaties concluded by member states before their accession to the EU with non-member states and states that the obligations from treaties are not compromised by EU law after the accession. Solely, the member states are obliged to undertake any necessary step to ensure its compliance with EU law by measures of renegotiation or termination. By analogy, the article should also apply if member states concluded treaties with non-member states before a transfer of competences to the EU. [170] Others ad-

166 Energy Charter Treaty (1994); *Burgstaller* in: *Bungenberg/Griebel/Hindelang* (Eds.), International investment law and EU law, 2011, p. 56.

167 *European Commission*, Communication COM(2010)343 final: Communication from the Commission to the Council, the European Parliament, the European Economic and Social Committee and the Committee of the Regions - Towards a comprehensive European international investment policy, 07/07/2010; cf. also: *Dimopoulos*, LIEI Vol. 39, No. 4 (2012), 447, 449. Such new agreements will need to be concluded as mixed agreements, at least if they contain particular dispute settlement clauses, CJEU, 16.05.2017 – Opinion 2/15 = ECLI:EU:C:2017:376 para 285 ff.

168 *Tietje*, Intra-EU BITs als Herausforderung im Mehrebenensystem des Rechts (Beit. zum Transnat. Wirt.-R, Vol. 104, 2011), p. 6.

169 Cf. also: *Kleinheisterkamp*, JIEL Vol. 15, No. 1 (2012), 85, 86.

170 *Johannsen*, Die Kompetenz der EU für ausländische Direktinvestitionen nach Lissabon (Beit. zum Transnat. Wirt.-R, Vol. 90, 2009), 22 and 24 ff; *Tietje*, Die Außenwirtschaftsverfassung der EU nach dem Vertrag von Lissabon (Beit.

vanced the principle of *pacta sunt servanda* and denied any effect of the transferal of competences to the validity of these extra-EU IIAs.[171]

The Commission *de facto* accepted the approach that those IIAs remain in force from a public international law perspective and issued a regulation (Regulation 1219/2012/EU) to redress all doubts.[172] As to Art. 2 of the regulation, the member states should notify the Commission about the extra-EU IIAs in force. Those should be deemed to remain fully in force (Art. 3 of the regulation). However, in a coordinated approach, the compliance with EU law should be ensured.[173] The regulation is often referred to as a grandfathering regulation regarding the existing extra-EU IIAs, as it affirms their continuous validity under EU law.

II. Intra-EU IIAs

The question of intra-EU IIAs, which means that both contracting states are members of the EU, mainly raised through the accession of several states to the EU through the enlargement procedures. In preparation of the accession to the EU the future member states usually enter into an Association Agreement, also called Europe Agreements with the present member states.[174] These agreements tend to prepare the state's accession until the final signature of the accession treaty. Future member states usually need

---

zum Transnat. Wirt.-R, Vol. 83, 2009), p. 17; *Eilmansberger*, CMLR Vol. 46 (2009), 383, 397 f; *Terhechte* in: Schwarze EU-Kommentar, Art. 351 TFEU, para 16; *Schmitt*, 2013, p. 298-300; *Lavranos* in: v. d. Groeben/Schwarze AEUV/EUV, Art. 351 TFEU, para 6, cf. *infra* for a detailed analysis (Chapter 12).

171 *Manzini*, EJIL Vol. 12, No. 4 (2001), 781, 786; *Lavranos*, TDM Vol. 10, Iss. 2 (2013), 1, 3; *Terhechte* in: Schwarze EU-Kommentar, Art. 351 TFEU, para 16, for a detailed analysis cf. *infra* (Chapter 12).

172 Regulation (EU) 1219/2012 on bilateral investment agreements between member states and third countries, Official Journal of the European Union L 351 (12/12/2012), 40; cf. also: *Reinisch* in: *Tietje* (Ed.), Internationales Wirtschaftsrecht, 2015, p. 403; *Engel*, SchiedsVZ, 2015, 218, 222 f.

173 Cf. for further details regarding the procedure: *Engel*, SchiedsVZ, 2015, 218, 222 f.

174 *Dahlquist/Lenk et al.*, European Policy Analysis, 2016:4, 1, 1 f; *Wehland*, ICLQ Vol. 58, Iss. 2 (2009), 297, 297; cf. e.g. the Europe Agreement between the EU member states and the Czech Republic (04/10/1973): the text can be assessed at: https://www.gov.uk/government/uploads/system/uploads/attachment_data/file/272 009 /2437.pdf [last checked: 28/02/2017].

to adopt or change a certain amount of legislations as well as fulfil certain criteria, considered to be essential to align the national legislation with the requirements of the *acquis communautaire* and EU law in general.[175]

The Europe Agreements contained provisions which encouraged the future member states to enter in IIAs with the EU member states. As a result, currently 195 IIAs exist between EU member states in 2016.[176] Those treaties are clearly not covered by the grandfathering regulation (Regulation 1219/2012/EU) for extra-EU IIAs. The Commission and several member states even explicitly challenge the validity and applicability after the states accessed the EU. Those treaties will be referred to as intra-EU BITs or intra-EU IIAs.[177]

III. Mixed agreements including the EU as contracting party

Resulting from the transferal of competences in Art. 207 TFEU and the creation of a distinct, legal personality attributed to the EU, further IIAs will probably be concluded as mixed agreements included in more far-reaching trade-agreements with non-member states.[178]

As previously mentioned mixed agreements that are concluded by both, EU and its member states, will be necessary as long as an the subject covered by the international agreement falls into the competence of both the EU and its member states.[179] The Energy Charter Treaty, which entered into force in 1998, is the most prominent investment related agreement in force, which is binding on the EU and all current member states.[180] The

175 *Dahlquist/Lenk et al.*, European Policy Analysis, 2016:4, 1, 1 f; *Wehland*, ICLQ Vol. 58, Iss. 2 (2009), 297, 297.

176 Number according to http://investmentpolicyhub.unctad.org/IIA [last visited on 20.02.2017]; Italy and Ireland followed the incentive by the European Commission and terminated several of its BITs with EU member states, cf.: *European Commission*, Press Release: Commission asks Member States to terminate their intra-EU bilateral investment treaties, 18/06/2015.

177 Cf. also: *Reinisch* in: *Tietje* (Ed.), Internationales Wirtschaftsrecht, 2015, p. 403; *Kleinheisterkamp*, JIEL Vol. 15, No. 1 (2012), 85, 86 f.

178 Anticipating such evolutions, the EU already issued regulation EU/912/2014 regarding the financial liability and the conduct of procedures in arbitrations arising from mixed agreements, cf. also: *Gramlich/Conen*, SchiedsVZ, 2015, 225, 228 f.

179 Cf. also: *Eilmansberger*, CMLR Vol. 46 (2009), 383, 392.

180 *Kerkemeyer*, EuZW, 2016, 10, 11.

EU-Singapore Free Trade Agreement will be another major treaty, when entered into force.[181]

Several other mixed agreements are currently under negotiation, including the TTIP and CETA- Agreement. However, it remains unclear if and to which degree these agreements will include provisions containing investment protection and dispute settlement mechanisms. Until now there have been no negotiations for exclusive agreements relating to investment protection. After the opinion rendered by the CJEU in 2016, it has now become clear that even specialised IIAs would need to be concluded by the EU as a mixed agreement if they contain particular dispute settlement provisions.[182]

The following table should illustrate the number of IIAs in force including EU member states as contracting parties in 2016[183]:

intra-EU IIAs	extra-EU IIAs	
	pre-accession IIAs	post-accession IIAs
195	332	932

181 Cf. also: *Engel*, SchiedsVZ, 2015, 218, 220; *Gramlich/Conen*, SchiedsVZ, 2015, 225, 228; an overview of the recent negotiations and the current state of free trade agreements negotiated by the EU can be accessed at: http://www.bmwi.de/DE/Themen/aussenwirtschaft,did=666642.html [last checked at: 28/02/2017].

182 *Kerkemeyer*, EuZW, 2016, 10, 11; cf. for the necessity to conlcude those agreements as mixed agreements: *Reinisch* in: *Tietje* (Ed.), Internationales Wirtschaftsrecht, 2015, p. 403; also: *Gramlich/Conen*, SchiedsVZ, 2015, 225, 228; *Tietje*, Die Außenwirtschaftsverfassung der EU nach dem Vertrag von Lissabon (Beit. zum Transnat. Wirt.-R, Vol. 83, 2009), p. 16 f; cf. also *Burgstaller*, LIEI Vol. 39, No. 2 (2012), 207, 208 with further references; *Terhechte* in: *Bungenberg/Griebel/Hindelang* (Eds.), International investment law and EU law, 2011 p.82-84; *Bungenberg* in: *Bungenberg/Griebel/Hindelang* (Eds.), International investment law and EU law, 2011, para 40-42; *Eilmansberger*, CMLR Vol. 46 (2009), 383, 392 and 394-396. The Commission seemed to consider that the EU has the exclusive competence to conclude the agreement and asked for an opinion by the CJEU, cf.: *European Commission*, Press Release: European Commission to request a Court of Justice opinion on the trade deal with Singapore, 04/03/2015; the CJEU rejected this approach: CJEU, 16.05.2017 – Opinion 2/15 = ECLI:EU:C:2017:376 para 285 ff.

183 Based on an own assessment via data available at: http://investmentpolicyhub.unctad.org/IIA; obligations from the ECT are excluded; only treaties (still) in force in 2016 were taken into account.

Chapter 4: The separate legal frameworks of investment protection in the EU

EU law and international investment protection through IIAs in EU member states thus created two distinct but overlapping legal frameworks. The resulting situation is a multilevel system of legal frameworks.[184] In order to determine to what extent those systems could potentially conflict, the substantive and procedural norms providing for investment protection under IIAs (A.) and EU law (B.) will be analysed in order to describe the potential protection offered for investors under both legal frameworks. The following Chapter 5 will then draw the conclusions from the comparison and analysis derived in this Chapter 4.

A. The IIA framework: investment-protection through IIAs

I. Guiding principles of investment protection through IIAs

Investment protection through IIAs follows several principles which will be briefly summarised in the following:

The protection is based on an IIA, which is an international convention between two or more states. The IIA grants several substantive protection guarantees (cf. II.) to investors from the home state in the respective host state.[185] The host state remains *de facto* free to amend its regulations or to undertake whichever measure, but these changes in its domestic legal framework will not alter the obligations under the IIA. On the contrary, the changes might constitute a violation of the IIA.[186]

---

184 Cf. for this term: *Tietje*, Intra-EU BITs als Herausforderung im Mehrebenensystem des Rechts (Beit. zum Transnat. Wirt.-R, Vol. 104, 2011), p. 5.

185 Cf. *inter alia*: *Reinisch* in: *Tietje* (Ed.), Internationales Wirtschaftsrecht, 2015, p. 401 f; *Engel*, SchiedsVZ, 2015, 218, 218-220.

186 *Tietje* in: *Ehlers/Schoch* (Eds.), Rechtsschutz im Öffentlichen Recht, 2009, p. 66; this is a basic feature of public international law: within its territory, the state (and hence its tribunals as well) remain the sole deciding authority, irrespective of any international obligation and its potential violation: cf. *Ipsen*, Völkerrecht, 6. Edn. (2014), p. 110; *Herdegen*, Völkerrecht, 15. Edn. (2016), p. 8-11. The state will however be liable on the international level and hence *de jure* restricted by public international law.

The only way to amend those protection standards is by means of international law, especially, by mutual consent of both, the home state and the host state. However, the investor is not entitled to change the circumstances of the IIA either. Its protection is derived from its home state through the IIA.

If investors from the home state suffer from any state measure in the host state, they can claim the breach of the IIA in (international) arbitration proceedings which are enabled through arbitration clauses in the IIA. This principle of "*internationalisation*" of the dispute was originally conceived to carve out the investment disputes from the domestic legal framework, as an independent court system is needed to enforce rights. Domestic courts may be reluctant as to the attribution of damages to a private entity if the respondent is the "*own*" host state or basic principles of due process may not be observed (cf. III.).[187]

II. Substantive protection: overview and scope of protection standards in IIAs

The substantive guarantees in IIAs should be analysed first to determine the scope of protection generally achieved by IIAs. There are several differences regarding the protection standards in the approximately 3000 IIA currently in force.[188] Even though countries usually conclude IIAs based on model treaties, these treaties are often modified in reciprocal negotiations. The final treaty may thus differ largely from the model treaty. To establish the concrete scope of protection, investors thus need to refer to the particular treaty in force.[189] Nevertheless, there are main structural elements which can be extracted from the treaties, as there is a significant

---

187 Cf. for those hostilities being the underlying idea of internationalising the dispute resolution mechanism: *Sornarajah*, 3. Edn. (2010), p. 217; *Engel*, SchiedsVZ, 2015, 218, 219; *Happ*, Int. A.L.R. Iss. 3 (2007), 74, 75; *Ghouri*, Int. A.L.R. Vol. 14, No. 6, 189, 190; also: *Sattorova*, LIEI Vol. 39, No. 2 (2012), 223, 226 f ; *Herdegen*, 10. Edn. (2014), p. 353; cf. also: *Kleinheisterkamp*, JIEL Vol. 15, No. 1 (2012), 85, 101 f; *Dimopoulos*, CMLR Vol. 48, No. 1 (2011), 63, 92; *Tietje* in: *Ehlers/Schoch* (Eds.), Rechtsschutz im Öffentlichen Recht, 2009, p. 65 f.

188 Cf. *Füracker*, SchiedsVZ, 2006, 236, 240; The current number (2954) can be reviewed on the Investment Policy Hub of the UNCTAD, accessible at http://investmentpolicyhub.unctad.org/IIA [last checked on 28/02/2017].

189 *Füracker*, SchiedsVZ, 2006, 236, 240.

harmonisation in the treaties and the interpretation of the treaties by arbitral tribunals.[190]

As it has already been explained, the current provisions in IIAs are largely influenced by the previously existing rules of customary international law and the shortcomings of these provisions or other investment protection mechanisms. Therefore, some protection standards contained in IIAs are the express stipulation of previously customary rules, others modify or enlarge customary rules to strengthen the protection and some are expressly stipulated to establish a protection standard, which did not exist under customary law.

1. Fair and equitable treatment

The standard of fair and equitable treatment (FET) is currently one of the most common protection standards in IIAs and "*has emerged as perhaps the most important standard of treatment*".[191] The German Model-BIT (2008) e.g. provides in Art. 2 (2):

> "Each Contracting State shall in its territory in every case accord investments by investors of the other Contracting State *fair and equitable treatment* as well as full protection under this Treaty".[192]

Although the standard may be found in nearly every IIA, the scope of rights deriving from this standard is heavily contested.[193] There are gener-

---

190 *Brown* in: *Bungenberg/Griebel/Hobe et al.* (Eds.), International Investment Law, 2015, p. 182.

191 *Newcombe/Paradell*, Law and Practice of Investment Treaties: Standards of Treatment, 2009, p. 255.

192 Art. 2 German Model BIT (2008) [emphasis added].

193 The formulations may vary extensively, cf. Article 10 (1) of the Energy Charter Treaty e.g. provides: "*Each Contracting Party shall [...] encourage and create stable, equitable, favourable and transparent conditions for Investors [...]. Such conditions shall include a commitment to accord at all times to Investments of Investors of other Contracting Parties fair and equitable treatment.*" However arbitral tribunals seem to refer to an underlying standard of FET even though the wording may not even include the words "*fair*" or "*equitable*", cf.: *Jacob/Schill* in: *Bungenberg/Griebel/Hobe et al.* (Eds.), International Investment Law, 2015, p. 705; cf. also: Plama vs. Bulgaria, 27.08.2008 – ICSID Case No. ARB/03/24 - Award, para 164 which clearly admits that to define the scope of protection under the FET standard of the Enery Charter Treaty it will also take into consideration practice under other BITs, which sets aside any argument based on differences or nuances in wording. However, in

ally two difficulties to determine the concrete scope of the standard. The first question is mostly related to several particularities in the NAFTA-context, which should not be deepened at this point of the thesis.[194] The second difficulty relates to the fact that the concrete interpretation of the FET standard remains flux, i.e. which creates uncertainties as to rights be-

---

the NAFTA context, the textual argument gains importance, cf. the considerations below.

194 There is a considerable debate on the FET standard dealing with the question whether the FET standard is different from the minimum standard of protection which is generally considered to form part of customary international law. Some scholars and arbitral tribunals consider the FET standard to be a "*tantamount of the minimum standard of protection required by international law*" (cf. *Dolzer/Stevens*, Bilateral Investment Treaties, 1995 p.59; cf. for an overview: *Reinisch* in: *Tietje* (Ed.), Internationales Wirtschaftsrecht, 2015, p. 414 f and *Jacob/Schill* in: *Bungenberg/Griebel/Hobe et al.* (Eds.), International Investment Law, 2015, p. 708 f). Others support that the FET standard is an independent concept which goes (far) beyond the requirements of treatment under the international minimum standard (cf.: *Dolzer/Stevens*, Bilateral Investment Treaties, 1995, p. 59; especially the tribunal in *Tecmed vs. Mexico*, 29.05.2003 – ICSID Case No. ARB (AF)/00/2 - Award, para 154). The discussion is somehow linked to a specificity of the NAFTA and exudes to the IIAs concluded by the contracting parties of the NAFTA, especially the United States of America, as the in the NAFTA the wording in the FET clause especially refers to customary international law and the NAFTA Free Trade commission adopted an interpretative note stating that the FET standard should reflect what is required under customary international law, cf.: *NAFTA Free Trade Commission*, Notes of Interpretation of Certain Chapter 11 Provisions, issued on 31/07/2001; cf. also: *Schreuer* in: *Hoffmann* (Ed.), Protection of foreign investments through modern treaty arbitration: diversity and harmonisation, 2010, p. 125, 130; cf. also: *Griebel*, (2008) p.69; *Schreuer*, JWIT Vol. 6, No. 3 (2005), 357, 362. Outside the NAFTA-context, arbitral tribunals and various authors in literature generally consider that the FET standard reflects an autonomous and more demanding standard than the (original) international minimum standard, cf. *inter alia*: *Dralle*, Der FET Standard im Investitionsschutzrecht (Beit. zum Transnat. Wirt.-R, Vol. 115, 2011), 5, 12 f; *Dolzer*, Santa Clara Jour. of Int. Law Vol. 12 (2014), 7, 13 f; cf. also: *Schreuer* in: *Hoffmann* (Ed.), Protection of foreign investments through modern treaty arbitration: diversity and harmonisation, 2010, p. 125, 125 ff, especially 129 and *Füracker*, SchiedsVZ, 2006, 236, 242, both with multiple further references. However, treaties such as the Energy Charter Treaty or most European IIAs, on which this thesis focusses, do not include such explicit reference to customary international law. In those treaties, the FET standard should be interpreted as to establish an autonomous standard. This will be discussed in more detail in Chapter 15.

ing attributed to the investors by the FET standard.[195] However, several elements in the judicial practice of arbitral tribunals enable to sharpen the scope of protection.[196] The key elements that are commonly advanced to judge the compliance or breach with the FET standard reveal a dual scope of protection. On the one hand, key elements are protection against *unjust or arbitral* [197] conduct of the state as well as the *lack of due process*[198], which is generally "*unacceptable from the international perspective*"[199]. On the other hand, the standard seems to be – more generally – a protection against objectively unexpected measures and changes committed by the host state, which deter the fundamental legal and factual circumstances, the investment was made in.[200] This second idea relies on the teleological concept behind the guarantee, which is the *"protection of the investor's legitimate expectation through the creation of a transparent and stable legal framework"*[201] complying with the elemental features of the rule of law.[202] In *Tecmed vs. Mexico*[203] the tribunal stated that "*the foreign investor expects the host state to act in a consistent manner, free from ambiguity and totally transparently in its relations with the foreign inves-*

---

195 *Jacob/Schill* in: *Bungenberg/Griebel/Hobe et al.* (Eds.), International Investment Law, 2015, p. 703.

196 Cf. also: *Jacob/Schill* in: *Bungenberg/Griebel/Hobe et al.* (Eds.), International Investment Law, 2015, p. 714.

197 In the *S.D. Myers Case*, the arbitral tribunal defined FET as any treatment in: "*an unjust or arbitrary manner [which] rises to the level that is unacceptable from the international perspective*" (*S. D. Myers vs Canada*, 13.11.2000 – UNCITRAL - Partial Award, para 263).

198 Similar to S.D. Myers but with a slightly broader approach, the arbitral tribunal in Waste Management Case stated that "*fair and equitable treatment is infringed [...] if the conduct is arbitrary, grossly unfair, unjust or idiosyncratic, is discriminatory and exposes the claimant to sectorial or racial prejudice or involves a lack of due process [...] or a complete lack of transparency and candour in an [...] process*" (cf.: para 98).

199 *S. D. Myers vs Canada*, 13.11.2000 – UNCITRAL - Partial Award, para 263.

200 *Inter alia*: *Occidental Exploration vs. Ecuador*, 01.07.2004 – LCIA Case No. UN3467 - Final Award, para 191; cf. also: *Dolzer*, Santa Clara Jour. of Int. Law Vol. 12 (2014), 7, 18-20; *Griebel*, (2008) p.72.

201 *Schreuer* in: *Hoffmann* (Ed.), Protection of foreign investments through modern treaty arbitration: diversity and harmonisation, 2010, p. 125, 126.

202 *Jacob/Schill* in: *Bungenberg/Griebel/Hobe et al.* (Eds.), International Investment Law, 2015, p. 716 ff; *Schreuer* in: *Hoffmann* (Ed.), Protection of foreign investments through modern treaty arbitration: diversity and harmonisation, 2010, p. 125, 126 f.

203 *Tecmed vs. Mexico*, 29.05.2003 – ICSID Case No. ARB (AF)/00/2 - Award.

tors"[204]. Various other tribunals made similar findings.[205] However, the host state is not forced to keep the "*circumstances prevailing at the time the investment is made [...] totally unchanged*"[206], as this cannot be the legitimate expectation of an objective, reasonable and informed third party. But any changes of the host state's legal frameworks need to be foreseeable and offer the investor the possibility to react and plan its investment and to comply with such regulations.[207] The question if the FET standard is violated can only be determined by a consideration of all (legitimate) interests, the purpose of the state measure as well as a balancing of the state's interest, the circumstances the measure was taken in and the way in which the measure was implemented.[208]

For the further understanding of the thesis, the FET standard will be understood as including the following key elements of protection:

- Lack of due process is considered to be a blunt disregard of FET;[209]
- Any obviously arbitrary, discriminatory measure, including financial and physical duress or action intentionally causing (financial or physical) harm is *per se* considered to be a breach of the FET standard;[210]

---

204 *Tecmed vs. Mexico*, 29.05.2003 – ICSID Case No. ARB (AF)/00/2 - Award, para 154.

205 *Saluka vs. Czech Republic*, 17.03.2006 – UNCITRAL - Partial Award, para 307; *El Paso vs. Argentina*, 31.11.2011 – ICSID Case No. ARB/03/15 - Award, para 364; *Metalclad vs. Mexico*, 30.08.2000 – ICSID Case No. ARB(AF)/97/1 - Award cf. also: *Schreuer* in: *Hoffmann* (Ed.), Protection of foreign investments through modern treaty arbitration: diversity and harmonisation, 2010, p. 125, 126 f and *Dolzer*, Santa Clara Jour. of Int. Law Vol. 12 (2014), 7, 20 ff.

206 *Saluka vs. Czech Republic*, 17.03.2006 – UNCITRAL - Partial Award, para 305.

207 *Schreuer* in: *Hoffmann* (Ed.), Protection of foreign investments through modern treaty arbitration: diversity and harmonisation, 2010, p. 125, 126 f; *Jacob/Schill* in: *Bungenberg/Griebel/Hobe et al.* (Eds.), International Investment Law, 2015, p. 730.

208 *Saluka vs. Czech Republic*, 17.03.2006 – UNCITRAL - Partial Award, para 305; *Schreuer* in: *Hoffmann* (Ed.), Protection of foreign investments through modern treaty arbitration: diversity and harmonisation, 2010, p. 125, 126 f; *Dolzer*, Santa Clara Jour. of Int. Law Vol. 12 (2014), 7, 21; *Jacob/Schill* in: *Bungenberg/Griebel/Hobe et al.* (Eds.), International Investment Law, 2015, p. 728-730 and 733 ff.

209 *Rumeli vs. Kazakhstan*, 29.07.2008 – ICSID Case No. ARB/05/16 - Award, para 617; cf. also: *Jacob/Schill* in: *Bungenberg/Griebel/Hobe et al.* (Eds.), International Investment Law, 2015, p. 48 ff.

- Besides those elements, FET requires the host state to act in an impartial and foreseeable manner (*fulfilling legitimate expectations*);[211]
- To determine what is foreseeable the expectations of an objective, reasonable and informed third party will be considered as a benchmark;
- Any measure undertaken by the host state should offer the investor the possibility to react and plan its investment and to comply with such regulations (*obligation of stability, consistency and transparency*);[212]
- Any measure undertaken should be reasonable and proportional compared to the host state's objectives and the public interest in question (*overall proportionality*).[213]

The FET standard thus guarantees a level of legal security and the applicability of the rule of law standard to the investor, which covers several of the most important risks an investor might be exposed to.[214]

---

210 *Waste Management vs. Mexico*, 30.04.2004 – ICSID Case No. ARB(AF)/00/3 - Award, para 98; *Rumeli vs. Kazakhstan*, 29.07.2008 – ICSID Case No. ARB/05/16 - Award, para 609; cf. also: *Jacob/Schill* in: *Bungenberg/Griebel/Hobe et al.* (Eds.), International Investment Law, 2015, p. 731 ff; cf. also: *Schreuer* in: *Hoffmann* (Ed.), Protection of foreign investments through modern treaty arbitration: diversity and harmonisation, 2010, p. 125, 126 f.

211 Cf. also: *Schreuer* in: *Hoffmann* (Ed.), Protection of foreign investments through modern treaty arbitration: diversity and harmonisation, 2010, p. 125, 126 f.

212 *Metalclad vs. Mexico*, 30.08.2000 – ICSID Case No. ARB(AF)/97/1 - Award, para 99; *Maffezini vs. Spain*, 25.01.2000 – ICSID Case No. ARB/97/7 - Decision on Jurisdiction, para 83; *Rumeli vs. Kazakhstan*, 29.07.2008 – ICSID Case No. ARB/05/16 - Award, para 617; *Tecmed vs. Mexico*, 29.05.2003 – ICSID Case No. ARB (AF)/00/2 - Award, para 154; *Jacob/Schill* in: *Bungenberg/Griebel/Hobe et al.* (Eds.), International Investment Law, 2015, p. 728 ff and 733 ff; cf. also: *Schreuer* in: *Hoffmann* (Ed.), Protection of foreign investments through modern treaty arbitration: diversity and harmonisation, 2010, p. 125, 126 f.

213 *Jacob/Schill* in: *Bungenberg/Griebel/Hobe et al.* (Eds.), International Investment Law, 2015; *Jacob/Schill* in: *Bungenberg/Griebel/Hobe et al.* (Eds.), International Investment Law, 2015, p. 735 ff.

214 *Jacob/Schill* in: *Bungenberg/Griebel/Hobe et al.* (Eds.), International Investment Law, 2015, p. 719.

2. Protection against Expropriation

Protection against expropriation is the historically most prominent protection standard. The underlying idea of this standard is not to prevent states from nationalising private property, but to submit it to severe criteria, prevent arbitrary interventions and assuring the payment of a fair compensation.[215] Expropriation clauses can be found in almost every IIA, the U. S. Model BIT e.g. states:

> "Neither Party may expropriate or nationalize a covered investment either directly or indirectly through measures equivalent to expropriation or nationalization ('expropriation'), except:
>
> (a) for a public purpose; (b) in a non-discriminatory manner; (c) on payment of prompt, adequate, and effective compensation; and (d) in accordance with due process of law and [the minimum Standard of Treatment]".[216]

The criteria to constitute a lawful expropriation may slightly differ from treaty to treaty. Despite these differences, the overall statement of almost all clauses is identical: Expropriations or nationalisations are accepted, as long as certain conditions are met. Although there are differences in detail, the following four main conditions have been found in the current investment treaty practice to be met to justify an expropriation[217]:

- the expropriation needs to be for public purpose;
- the expropriation needs to be non-discriminatory;
- compensation needs to be paid for the expropriated good; and

215 *Kniebaum* in: *Bungenberg/Griebel/Hobe et al.* (Eds.), International Investment Law, 2015, p. 962.

216 The above cited clause cannot be generalised. Inter alia the Netherlands-Albania BIT contains a slightly different structure: "*Neither Contracting Party shall take any measures depriving, directly or indirectly, nationals of the other Contracting Party of their investments unless the following conditions are complied with: (a) the measures are taken in the public interest and under due process of law; (b) the measures are not discriminatory [...] (c) the measures are taken against just compensation. Such compensation shall represent the genuine value of the investments affected [and] be paid and made transferable, without undue delay (...)*", cf.: Article 6 of Albania - Netherlands Bilateral Investment Treaty (entry into force: 01.09.1995). One might observe that this BIT does not refer to the criteria "*in accordance with law*" but especially includes the criteria of non-discrimination.

217 *Kniebaum* in: *Bungenberg/Griebel/Hobe et al.* (Eds.), International Investment Law, 2015, p. 1017; *Dolzer/Stevens*, Bilateral Investment Treaties, 1995, p. 97. *Griebel*, (2008) p.76.

- the expropriation procedure needs to comply with the requirements of due process.

Although the above-mentioned conditions impose the host states to respect a certain legal framework before attempting the investor's property, this protection only applies if the measure undertaken by the host state is *qualified as expropriation*. The most crucial point within the protection against expropriation is thus to define whether any act committed by a state is considered to be an expropriation or not.

Historically, expropriations were generally considered as direct legal or administrative acts, which transferred property from an individual to public ownership for public purpose. Various constitutional systems of states even nowadays consider these forms of property taking as the only form of expropriation.[218] Nevertheless, a simple change within the host states legal framework, which does not de jure constitute an act of expropriation, may have identical effects for the investor.[219] States might undertake measures, such as revoking licenses, changing the prerequisites to sell a product or leveraging environmental or security standards, and may thus ruin the investors business. Such measures, having an economic effect which is equivalent to a formal expropriation, are usually called "*indirect*," "*creeping*" or "*de facto*" expropriations.[220] IIAs generally also protect against such indirect expropriations. On the other hand, the state needs to keep the capability to enact legislation, without being obliged to compensate every investor which may be affected by these changes. The determination of the term indirect expropriation thus constitutes a crucial difficulty.[221]. Several elements have been developed in order to distinguish

---

218 *Inter alia* for the German Constitution: *Papier* in: Maunz/Dürig GG, Art. 14 GG, para 531-533.

219 *Dolzer/Stevens*, Bilateral Investment Treaties, 1995, p. 99.

220 *Dolzer/Stevens*, Bilateral Investment Treaties, 1995, p. 99; *Griebel*, (2008), p. 77; *Reinisch* in: *Tietje* (Ed.), Internationales Wirtschaftsrecht, 2015, p. 423 f; *Kniebaum* in: *Bungenberg/Griebel/Hobe et al.* (Eds.), International Investment Law, 2015, p. 971.

221 Cf. for an overview of the various difficulties: *OECD*, "Indirect Expropriation" and the "Right to Regulate" in International Investment Law, 2004; cf. also: *Herdegen*, 10. Edn. (2014), p. 350-352. With regard to this distinction, the clauses within IIAs include several different terms which generally do not provide further clarifications. The German Model BIT (2009) e.g. includes within the scope of protected measures any act which leads to the investor being "*expropriated, nationalized or subjected to any other measure the effects of which would be tantamount to expropriation or nationalization*". The treaty neverthe-

(lawful) exercise of regulatory power from what should be qualified as (indirect) expropriation.[222] The impact of the different approaches will be treated *infra* (cf. Chapter 15). One of the most notable criterion is the *economic impact* of the government action on the investment. It is generally considered to be an indirect expropriation if the investor is de facto deprived of its rights or the benefits of its investment are (quasi-) entirely neutralised. [223]

---

less does not clarify what can be a measure "*tantamount to expropriation or nationalization*". Likewise, the French Model BIT refers "*any measures of expropriation or nationalization or any other measures having the effect of dispossession, direct or indirect, of nationals or companies of the other Contracting Party of their investments*". None of the above cited model BITs, as well as numerous IIAs that entered into force, include further elements to distinguish the (lawful) exercise of regulatory power from what should be qualified as (indirect) expropriation. Nevertheless, some treaties include further explanations in the protocols of the respective treaties, denominating benchmarks such as the economic impact, interference with investment-backed interests and the character of the host state's action, e.g. the US-Model BIT (2012) includes an Annex B which refers to a number of indicators and conditions to sharpen the definition of indirect expropriations, namely to determine whether an *"an action or series of actions by a Party has an effect equivalent to direct expropriation without formal transfer of title or outright seizure" an analysis based on a "case-by case, fact-based inquiry" should be undertaken, "that considers, among other factors: (...) the economic impact of the government action, (...) the extent to which the government action interferes with distinct, reasonable investment-backed expectations; and the character of the government action";* cf. also: *Kniebaum* in: *Bungenberg/Griebel/Hobe et al.* (Eds.), International Investment Law, 2015, p. 969 f.

222 The discussion predominantly concerns the question, whether the impact of the measure should be sufficient to qualify a measure as indirect expropriation. Some tribunals consider the effect of the state measure as the only element which should be taken into account (*sole effect doctrine*), regardless of the state's intention or any public policy necessities to act the way the state did even though they might have considerable economic effects. Such criteria have been used in recent arbitral practice to limit the consequences of the *sole effect doctrine.* Some tribunals exercised an additional test of proportionality, which means that the expropriation will be balanced against the public interest requiring the measure, cf.: *Kniebaum* in: *Bungenberg/Griebel/Hobe et al.* (Eds.), International Investment Law, 2015, p. 982.

223 The tribunal in *S. D. Myers vs Canada*, 13.11.2000 – UNCITRAL - Partial Award, para 282 stated that "*expropriations tend to involve the deprivation of ownership rights; regulations [are] a lesser interference*". The Tribunal in *CME vs. Czech Republic*, 13.09.2001 – UNCITRAL - Partial Award, para 604 held: "*De facto expropriations or indirect expropriations, i.e. measures that do*

3. Full protection and security

The scope of the full protection and security standard (FPS standard) is nearly as disputed as the FET standard. The discussions are based on similar difficulties, i.e. the concrete scope of protection derived therefrom. The wording usually used when referred to the FPS standard reads as follows:

> "Such […] Investments shall also enjoy the most constant protection and security".[224]

The NAFTA as well as the U.S. Model BIT (2012), exemplarily state:

> "Each Party shall accord to investments of investors of another Party treatment in accordance with international law, including fair and equitable treatment and full protection and security".

According to most scholars, the FPS standard is a leftover from the previous FCN treaties and their reference to the protection of aliens abroad through the international minimum standard.[225]

With reference to the international minimum standard, a certain scope of the FPS standard remains unchallenged. As *Schreuer* states,

> "[i]t is beyond doubt that the standard of full protection and security relates to the physical protection of the investor and its assets"[226].

Others state the FPS standard as

> "a general obligation for the host State to exercise due diligence in the [physical] protection of foreign investment"[227].

The standard of FPS hence requires the host state to act in favour of the investor to protect him from any harmful acts. This obligation exists with regard to harmful acts committed by state organs but also by any other

---

not involve an overt taking but that effectively neutralize the benefit of the property of the foreign owner, are subject to expropriation claims (...)".

224 Energy Charter Treaty in Art. 10 (1).

225 *Dolzer/Stevens*, Bilateral Investment Treaties, 1995 p.61; *Griebel*, (2008), p. 75; *Lorz* in: *Bungenberg/Griebel/Hobe et al.* (Eds.), International Investment Law, 2015, para 767; *Noble Ventures vs. Romania*, 12.10.2005 – ICSID Case No. ARB/01/11 - Award, para 164 f.

226 *Schreuer*, Journal of International Dispute Settlement Vol. 1, No. 2 (2010), 353, 354.

227 *Dolzer/Stevens*, Bilateral Investment Treaties, 1995, p. 61; cf. also for this defintion : *Noble Ventures vs. Romania*, 12.10.2005 – ICSID Case No. ARB/01/11 - Award, para 164.

persons.[228] Hence, contrary to the most other standards, FPS not only requires an omission of harmful acts but a positive action, i.e. a state needs to exercise

> "reasonable measures of prevention which a well-administrated government could be expected to exercise under similar circumstances"[229].[230]

Beyond that scope, arbitral tribunals did not reach a consensus on how to interpret the scope of this standard. Some tribunals expressly limited the scope of the standard to physical security.[231] However, other recent decisions also extend the scope of the FPS standard from purely physical protection to a protection of the stability of the legal framework.[232] This extension, which mainly includes the stability of a legal framework and the protection offered through this framework to the investor, has raised considerable debate with a clear opposition by several tribunals but also en-

---

228 *AAP vs. Sri Lanka*, 27.06.1990 – ICSID Case No. ARB/87/3 - Final Award, para 77 ff; *Eastern Sugar vs. Czech Republic*, 27.03.2007 – SCC No. 088/2004 - Partial award, para 203; *Biwater Gauff vs. Tanzania*, 24.07.2008 – ICSID Case No. ARB/05/22 - Award, para 730; *Schreuer*, Journal of International Dispute Settlement Vol. 1, No. 2 (2010), 353, 356 f.

229 *AAP vs. Sri Lanka*, 27.06.1990 – ICSID Case No. ARB/87/3 - Final Award, para 77.

230 *Griebel*, (2008), p. 74 f. It is important to note that through the FPS the state does not undertake a strict liability in terms of an obligation of results, cf.: *Schreuer*, Journal of International Dispute Settlement Vol. 1, No. 2 (2010), 353, 366 f and *Rumeli vs. Kazakhstan*, 29.07.2008 – ICSID Case No. ARB/05/16 - Award, para 668, cf. also : *Lorz* in: *Bungenberg/Griebel/Hobe et al.* (Eds.), International Investment Law, 2015, p. 775.

231 *Rumeli vs. Kazakhstan*, 29.07.2008 – ICSID Case No. ARB/05/16 - Award; *Eastern Sugar vs. Czech Republic*, 27.03.2007 – SCC No. 088/2004 - Partial award, para 302 ; *Suez vs. Argentina*, 30.07.2010 – ICSID Case No. ARB/03/19 - Decision on Liability, para 173, cf. also : *Lorz* in: *Bungenberg/Griebel/Hobe et al.* (Eds.), International Investment Law, 2015, p. 781-785.

232 *CME vs. Czech Republic*, 13.09.2001 – UNCITRAL - Partial Award, para 613: "*The host State is obligated to ensure that neither by amendment of its laws nor by actions of its administrative bodies is the agreed and approved security and protection of the foreign investor's investment withdrawn or devalued.*"; *Occidental Exploration vs. Ecuador*, 01.07.2004 – LCIA Case No. UN3467 - Final Award, para 187; *Biwater Gauff vs. Tanzania*, 24.07.2008 – ICSID Case No. ARB/05/22 - Award, para 729: *"[The FPS-standard] implies a State's guarantee of stability in a secure environment, both physical, commercial and legal."*; cf. also: *Lorz* in: *Bungenberg/Griebel/Hobe et al.* (Eds.), International Investment Law, 2015, p. 783.

dorsement by others.[233] The main issue raised by this extension is the overlap with the FET standard. If FPS essentially guaranteed the stability of a legal framework and the protection offered through this framework, it would rather be a particular sub-category of the FET standard (cf. *supra*).[234] However, it is doubtful if the contracting parties to IIAs really intended to install twice the same standard in a treaty.[235] Hence, one should clearly distinguish both guarantees: whereas the FET standard guarantees the stability of a legal framework and predominantly protects against interferences of the host state with the investor's rights, the FPS standard should be interpreted more restrictively but from another angle. Its predominant focus is to guarantee the absence of physical and financial harm to the investor and the investment.[236] However, the state is obliged to provide such protection and security through actively sharpening a legal and factual environment in which the investor and its investment are protected

---

233 Endorsing an extension: *CME vs. Czech Republic*, 13.09.2001 – UNCITRAL - Partial Award, para 613; *Occidental Exploration vs. Ecuador*, 01.07.2004 – LCIA Case No. UN3467 - Final Award, para 187; *Siemens A.G. vs. Argentina*, 17.01.2007 – ICSID Case No. ARB/02/8 - Award, para 303; for the opposite: *Suez vs. Argentina*, 30.07.2010 – ICSID Case No. ARB/03/19 - Decision on Liability, para 164 ff and 179; *Ronald S. Lauder vs. Czech Republic*, 03.09.2001 – UNCITRAL- Final Award, para 314; cf. for a comprehensive summary: *Lorz* in: *Bungenberg/Griebel/Hobe et al.* (Eds.), International Investment Law, 2015, p. 783 ff.

234 This extension is supported by several arguments: some refer to a systematic interpretation of the investment treaties. If IIAs are directed to protect commercial and financial (tangible or intangible) instruments, it is "*difficult to understand how the physical security of an intangible asset would be achieved*" (cf.: *Siemens A.G. vs. Argentina*, 17.01.2007 – ICSID Case No. ARB/02/8 - Award, para 303). Others refer to the wording of "*full*" to opt in favour of a more demanding standard, cf.: *Azurix Corp. vs. Argentina*, 14.07.2006 – ICSID Case No. ARB/01/12 - Award, para 408: "*The Tribunal is aware that in recent free trade agreements signed by the United States, for instance, with Uruguay, full protection and security is understood to be limited to the level of police protection required under customary international law. However, when the terms "protection and security" are qualified by "full" and no other adjective or explanation, they extend, in their ordinary meaning, the content of this standard beyond physical security.*";cf. also *Biwater Gauff vs. Tanzania*, 24.07.2008 – ICSID Case No. ARB/05/22 - Award, para 729.

235 *Lorz* in: *Bungenberg/Griebel/Hobe et al.* (Eds.), International Investment Law, 2015, p. 788.

236 *Lorz* in: *Bungenberg/Griebel/Hobe et al.* (Eds.), International Investment Law, 2015, p. 789; *Schreuer*, Journal of International Dispute Settlement Vol. 1, No. 2 (2010), 353, 362 and 366.

(as opposed to the simple omission).[237] Hence, the FPS standard puts upon the host state a duty to act (due diligence), which is fundamentally different from the obligation to restrain from harmful acts.[238] This duty to act may very well include legislative changes as well, as a sufficiently developed legal framework which both are necessary prerequisites to be able to protect the investor from fundamental harm to occur.[239]

4. Non-discrimination clauses

Clauses which should protect investors against discrimination can be found in mainly three distinct forms in IIAs: the national-treatment standards, a most-favoured-nations treatment standard as well as general, unspecific non-discrimination clauses.

(1) National treatment

The standard of national treatment "*imposes on the host State [...] to accord the foreign investor the same treatment as that enjoyed by its own nationals*".[240] In other words, national and foreign investors should be treated identically.[241]

The German Model BIT (2009) states in Art. 3.:

> "Each Contracting State shall in its territory subject investments owned or controlled by investors of the other Contracting State to treatment no less favourable than that which it accords to investments of its own investors."

---

237 Cf.: *Biwater Gauff vs. Tanzania*, 24.07.2008 – ICSID Case No. ARB/05/22 - Award, para 729; *Lorz* in: *Bungenberg/Griebel/Hobe et al.* (Eds.), International Investment Law, 2015, p. 789; *Reinisch* in: *Tietje* (Ed.), Internationales Wirtschaftsrecht, 2015, p. 417 f; *Schreuer*, Journal of International Dispute Settlement Vol. 1, No. 2 (2010), 353, 362 and 366.

238 *Lorz* in: *Bungenberg/Griebel/Hobe et al.* (Eds.), International Investment Law, 2015, p. 789; *Reinisch* in: *Tietje* (Ed.), Internationales Wirtschaftsrecht, 2015, p. 417 f; *Schreuer*, Journal of International Dispute Settlement Vol. 1, No. 2 (2010), 353, 366.

239 *Lorz* in: *Bungenberg/Griebel/Hobe et al.* (Eds.), International Investment Law, 2015, p. 789.

240 *Dolzer/Stevens*, Bilateral Investment Treaties, 1995, p. 63.

241 *Reinisch* in: *Tietje* (Ed.), Internationales Wirtschaftsrecht, 2015, p. 411.

The standard is thus a *relative* standard, as it does not impose a specific action or omission.[242] It simply prohibits discrimination in the treatment of nationals and foreign investors.[243] Consequently, the protection offered by the standard is *per se* as strong or as weak as the general legal and factual circumstances in the host state.[244]

Although the definition of the national treatment standard is widely recognised, the actual difficulties in its application are based on how the discrimination of foreign investors compared to nationals is established. This requires three conditions (also referred to as the *three-step-test*) to be fulfilled[245]:

First, the investors need to establish the similarity of situations: [246] most treaties restrain the application of national treatment standards to a treatment in "*similar circumstances*" or "*like circumstances*".[247] How such similarity can be established is subject to considerable debate.[248]

Second, foreign investors need to be discriminated towards national investors. It is nowadays recognised that such less favourable treatment may

242 *Reinisch* in: *Bungenberg/Griebel/Hobe et al.* (Eds.), International Investment Law, 2015, p. 847.

243 *Reinisch* in: *Bungenberg/Griebel/Hobe et al.* (Eds.), International Investment Law, 2015, p. 847.

244 *Reinisch* in: *Tietje* (Ed.), Internationales Wirtschaftsrecht, 2015, p. 412: If the host state generally respects the rule of law towards its nationals, grants compensation for expropriations and guarantees a transparent and stable legal framework, foreign investors may rely on the standard of national treatment to be treated in the same way. But if the rule of law is loosely enforced, no compensation granted, national treatment may not grant sufficient protection, as the treatment is equal, cf. *Dolzer/Stevens*, Bilateral Investment Treaties, 1995 p.64 f; This reveals why the capital exporting powers refused the raise of the Calvo-doctrine in the colonial period, which essentially granted only national treatment as the only treatment aliens may ask for when residing abroad, cf.: *Reinisch* in: *Tietje* (Ed.), Internationales Wirtschaftsrecht, 2015, p. 412.

245 The notion of three-step-test is issued from the Claimants proposal recited by the Methanex – Tribunal in: *Methanex vs. USA*, 03.08.2005 – UNCITRAL- Final Award of the Tribunal on Jurisdiction and Merits, para 13.

246 *Griebel*, (2008), p. 82.

247 Article 1102 (1) of the NAFTA: "*Each Party shall accord to investors of another Party treatment no less favorable than that it accords, in like circumstances, to its own investors (...)*"; Similar Art. 3 of the US-Model BIT (2012), Art. III. 3. of the Wolrd Bank Guidelines on the Treatment of Foreign Investment: "*be as favorable as that accorded by the State to national investors in similar circumstance*".

248 Different tribunals and scholars found diametrically opposed interpretations to determine the similarity: this will be treated *infra* in Chapter 15.

be *de jure* or *de facto.*[249] *De jure* discrimination is often referred to as direct discrimination, as the host states formally (openly) differentiates between nationals and entities with other nationalities.[250] *De facto* (or indirect) discrimination is linked to – at first glance – neutral criteria, which however affect foreign investors differently compared to the host-state's nationals.[251].

Third, the measure by the host state may be exceptionally permitted. The national treatment provision is often granted under several exceptions only. IIAs of EU member states often include exceptions for "*Measures that have to be taken for reasons of public security and order, public health or morality*"[252] which *"shall not be deemed 'treatment less favourable' within the meaning of Article 3*"[253]. But even though IIAs may not provide for such expressly stated exceptions, arbitral tribunals regularly consider the host state's possibility to justify a differential treatment.[254] Such justifications may either be considered separately or introduced in

249 *Reinisch* in: *Tietje* (Ed.), Internationales Wirtschaftsrecht, 2015 p 862; *Griebel*, (2008), p. 82.

250 *Reinisch* in: *Tietje* (Ed.), Internationales Wirtschaftsrecht, 2015, p. 862; cf. also: *ADM and Tate & Lyle vs. Mexico*, 21.11.2007 – ICSID Case No. ARB (AF)/04/5 - Award, para 193.

251 *Reinisch* in: *Tietje* (Ed.), Internationales Wirtschaftsrecht, 2015, p. 862; *ADM and Tate & Lyle vs. Mexico*, 21.11.2007 – ICSID Case No. ARB (AF)/04/5 - Award, para 193. Examples of a *de facto* discrimination might be the enforcement of measures vis-à-vis non-nationals whereas the same applicable laws are not enforced towards nationals or any provision which is linked to facts that foreigners typically fulfil, whereas nationals do not (*or vice versa*, such as diplomas, etc.). To establish this *de facto* or *de jure* discrimination, the current jurisprudence by arbitral tribunals relies on the effect of the measure, irrespective of a discriminatory intent, cf.: *Reinisch* in: *Tietje* (Ed.), Internationales Wirtschaftsrecht, 2015, p. 862; however this remains somehow disputed, as some tribunals still require a subjective element: cf.: *Parkerings vs. Lithuania*, 11.09.2007 – ICSID Case No. ARB/05/8 - Award, para 368.

252 Article 3 of the Protocol to the Agreement between the People's Republic of China and the Federal Republic of Germany on the Encouragement and Reciprocal Protection of Investments (2003).

253 Ad Article 3 of the Protocol to the Agreement between the People's Republic of China and the Federal Republic of Germany on the Encouragement and Reciprocal Protection of Investments (2003); cf. also: *Griebel*, (2008), p. 83.

254 *Reinisch* in: *Tietje* (Ed.), Internationales Wirtschaftsrecht, 2015, p. 863; *Griebel*, (2008), p. 82 f.

the test of "*like circumstances*", denying the similarity of two situations if there are sufficient reasons of "*public policy*" for a differentiation.[255]

(2) Most favoured nation treatment

Most-Favoured-Nation treatment (MFN) is the second relative protection standard included in most IIAs.[256] It essentially aims at creating equal conditions among all foreign investors.[257] *Inter alia*, the NAFTA defines the MFN treatment as follows:

> "Each Party shall accord to investors of another Party treatment no less favorable than that it accords, in like circumstances, to investors of any other Party or of a non-Party (…)"[258].

The standard thus requires states to ensure that

> "[a]ny treatment granted to a national of a third country which is more favourable than national treatment or treatment under the BIT must be accorded to an investor or an investment covered by this BIT"[259].

The host state undertakes to extend any advantage granted to any investor to all other investors, eliminating any less favourable treatment among foreign investors in the host state (level playing field among foreign investors).[260] However, and once again the concrete scope of application for this guarantee remains controversial.[261]

---

255 The approach of introducing justification in the assessment of like circumstances was *inter alia* adopted by: *Pope & Talbot vs. Canada*, 10.04.2001 – UNCITRAL - Awards on the Merits of Phase 2, para 78 and *S. D. Myers vs Canada*, 13.11.2000 – UNCITRAL - Partial Award, para 250; other tribunals admitted the justification as a separate ground for denying a breach of the national treatment standard: *Contact Champion Trading et al vs. Egypt*, 27.08.2006 – ICSID Case No. ARB/02/9 - Award, para 134 and *Parkerings vs. Lithuania*, 11.09.2007 – ICSID Case No. ARB/05/8 - Award, para 368; cf. also: *Reinisch* in: *Tietje* (Ed.), Internationales Wirtschaftsrecht, 2015, p. 863 f and *Ortino* in: *Dupuy/Francioni/Petersmann* (Eds.), Human rights in international investment law and arbitration, 2009, p. 360.

256 *Reinisch* in: *Bungenberg/Griebel/Hobe et al.* (Eds.), International Investment Law, 2015, p. 808.

257 *Griebel*, (2008), p. 79.

258 Article 1103 (1) of the North American Free Trade Agreement (1994).

259 *Füracker*, SchiedsVZ, 2006, 236, p. 242.

260 *Griebel*, (2008), p. 80.

261 *Dolzer/Stevens*, Bilateral Investment Treaties, 1995 p.66; *Griebel*, (2008), p. 80; other than for the national treatment standard, the difficulties are less

The debate is mainly focussed on the question whether jurisdiction clauses may be extended to other investors by virtue of a MFN clause.[262] Whereas some tribunals and scholars consider that a MFN clause may also extend the effects of dispute settlement provisions to other IIAs[263], others firmly reject this approach and limit MFN clauses to substantive provisions only.[264] This will be dealt with in detail *infra* (Chapter 15).

(3) Other non-discrimination clauses

Besides the above-mentioned clauses which constitute specific forms of non-discrimination clauses, IIAs may also include a non-specific prohibition of discriminatory or arbitrary measures. Art. 2 (3) of the German Model BIT (2008) states that

> "[n]either Contracting State shall in its territory impair by arbitrary or discriminatory measures the activity of investors of the other Contracting State with regard

connected to the concrete wording of the MFN clauses (which also widely differs) but to the extend of the principle contained therein, cf.: *Reinisch* in: *Bungenberg/Griebel/Hobe et al.* (Eds.), International Investment Law, 2015, p. 815. Some particular BITs might be cited, where the concept is intentionally limited to particular effects, such as the FET standard, cf. for further examples: *Reinisch* in: *Bungenberg/Griebel/Hobe et al.* (Eds.), International Investment Law, 2015, p. 816; other debates seem to be resolved: it is now rather commonly accepted that other investors may not claim indivudal rights arising from individual contracts to be extended. The same would apply for treaties dealing with completely different subjects, such as a treaty on environmental protection (often referred to as the result of the *ejusdem generis principle*, which limits the MFN clause, cf.:. *Dolzer/Stevens*, Bilateral Investment Treaties, 1995 p.66 ff; *Fietta*, Int. A.L.R. Iss. 4 (2005), 131, 132 f; *Reinisch* in: *Bungenberg/Griebel/Hobe et al.* (Eds.), International Investment Law, 2015, p. 812 f).

262 *Reinisch* in: *Bungenberg/Griebel/Hobe et al.* (Eds.), International Investment Law, 2015, p. 809; *Reinisch* in: *Tietje* (Ed.), Internationales Wirtschaftsrecht, 2015, p. 816 f; *Griebel*, (2008), p. 80 f.

263 *Maffezini vs. Spain*, 25.01.2000 – ICSID Case No. ARB/97/7 - Decision on Jurisdiction, para 35.

264 Cf. *inter alia*: *Wintershall vs. Argentina*, 08.12.2008 – ICSID Case No. ARB/04/14, para 162; *Plama vs. Bulgaria*, 27.08.2008 – ICSID Case No. ARB/03/24 - Award, para 223-225; *Salini vs. Jordan*, 09.11.2004 – ICSID Case No. ARB/02/13 - Award, para 119.

> to investments, such as in particular the management, maintenance, use, enjoyment or disposal of such investments."[265]

Even though, the wordings might differ with references to *"unjustified"* or "*unreasonable*" instead of "*arbitrary*", the majority of tribunals opposes arbitrary/unreasonable/unjustified measures to discriminatory measures.[266] Hence, the standard protects investors not only from discriminatory measures but also from arbitrary measures; each of them is sufficient to demonstrate a violation.[267]

To further sharpen the standard, several objective criteria were developed, which have been summarised by *Schreuer*[268] as the following: to avoid being qualified as *arbitrary*, the measure needs to be undertaken for a public purpose, it needs to have a legal basis and the state needs to respect the principles of due process. Some others include an element of proportionality, meaning that the measure needs to be necessary to achieve the public purpose.[269] Taking into account the evaluation of the FET standard, any arbitrary act as defined above will also violate the FET standard. The importance thus diminishes significantly in practice.

Regarding the protection against *discriminatory* measures, the clauses will mainly serve as a "*backup guarantee*" for measures which are dis-

---

265 Art. 2 (3) of the German Model BIT (2008).

266 *Kniebaum* in: *Bungenberg/Griebel/Hobe et al.* (Eds.), International Investment Law, 2015, p. 792 f with numerous examples of BIT clauses; for the reception by the tribunals: *Siemens A.G. vs. Argentina*, 17.01.2007 – ICSID Case No. ARB/02/8 - Award, para 319.; *Plama vs. Bulgaria*, 27.08.2008 – ICSID Case No. ARB/03/24 - Award, para 184; *AES Summit vs. Hungary*, 23.09.2010 – ICSID Case No. ARB/07/22 - Award, para 10.3.37.

267 *Kniebaum* in: *Bungenberg/Griebel/Hobe et al.* (Eds.), International Investment Law, 2015, p. 793; *Siag and Vecchi vs. Egypt*, 01.06.2009 – ICSID Case No. ARB/05/15 - Award, para 457; *Siemens A.G. vs. Argentina*, 17.01.2007 – ICSID Case No. ARB/02/8 - Award, para 319 and 320; *Azurix Corp. vs. Argentina*, 14.07.2006 – ICSID Case No. ARB/01/12 - Award, para 391; for the opposite: *Ronald S. Lauder vs. Czech Republic*, 03.09.2001 – UNCITRAL- Final Award, para 219.

268 *Schreuer* in: *Rogers/Alford* (Eds.), The future of investment arbitration, 2009, p. 183.

269 *Schreuer* in: *Rogers/Alford* (Eds.), The future of investment arbitration, 2009, p. 183, 188; *EDF vs. Romania*, 08.10.2009 – ICSID Case No. ARB/05/13 - Award, para 303; *SAUR vs. Argentina*, 06.06.2012 – ICSID Case No. ARB/04/4 - Decision on Jurisdiction and Liability, para 488 [only available in French]; cf. also: *Kniebaum* in: *Bungenberg/Griebel/Hobe et al.* (Eds.), International Investment Law, 2015, 719; *AES Summit vs. Hungary*, 23.09.2010 – ICSID Case No. ARB/07/22 - Award, para 10.3.7 ff.

criminatory but not based on the investor's nationality. [270] Hence, the investor is not only protected against measures which discriminate based on its nationality, but more generally, against each differential treatment in a comparable situation, which is unjustified. The questions arising are mainly the same than those under the national treatment standard: what is meant to be a discrimination, which situations are to be compared and how to justify a difference in treatment.[271]

5. Umbrella clauses

Umbrella clauses try to stabilise individual contractual guarantees provided by the host state to the investor.[272] Through this guarantee, the violation of e.g. contractual obligations *vis-à-vis* the investor should not only constitute a violation of this contractual agreement but also of the IIA. The clause leverages a so-called *contract claim* (for fulfilment of a contract, which might also be submitted to the national law of the host state) to a *treaty claim* (for breach of the IIA).[273] The same may apply for other obligations undertaken towards the investor which do not root in contractual commitments.[274]

---

270 Cf. eg.: *Griebel*, (2008) p.73; *Schreuer* in: *Rogers/Alford* (Eds.), The future of investment arbitration, 2009, p. 183, 193

271 *Kniebaum* in: *Bungenberg/Griebel/Hobe et al.* (Eds.), International Investment Law, 2015, p. 802; *Schreuer* in: *Rogers/Alford* (Eds.), The future of investment arbitration, 2009, p. 183, 195. Similar as regarding the national treatment requirement, the main discussion focusses on how to determine the comparable circumstances. The requirements to justify any differential treatment raises questions comparable to those with regard to the national treatment standard (cf. *supra:* (1) National treatment). Second, the question araises how to justify a difference in treement. Overall, as *Kniebaum* points out, the approach to justify the state measure, reveals to be similar to the test of proportionality as know from the European Courts, including the CJEU and the ECtHR, *Kniebaum* in: *Bungenberg/Griebel/Hobe et al.* (Eds.), International Investment Law, 2015, p. 804 f; cf. Chapter 15.

272 *Herdegen*, 10. Edn. (2014), p. 340.

273 *Reinisch* in: *Tietje* (Ed.), Internationales Wirtschaftsrecht, 2015, p. 429; This commonly recognised terminology was also used by the tribunal in: *SGS vs. Pakistan*, 06.08.2003 – ICSID Case No. ARB/01/13 - Decision of the Tribunal on Objections to Jurisdiction, para 146.

274 *Griebel*, (2008), p. 85.

The German Model-BIT (2008) stipulates what is usually understood to be an umbrella clause as follows:

> "Each Contracting State shall fulfil *any other obligations* it may have entered into with regard to investments in its territory by investors of the other Contracting State."[275]

The scope of protection offered by these clauses remains highly controversial, especially due to the meaning of the terms "*any other obligations*".[276] Some consider this term to cover all obligations undertaken by the host state towards the investor, irrespective of their nature.[277] Others restrict the clause to cover contractual obligations only.[278] Irrespective of the correct interpretation of the term obligation, which will be dealt with *infra* (Chapter 15), some confusion should be avoided: an umbrella clause does not create obligations itself, it just renders a breach of an obligation under domestic law claimable on the international level.[279]

6. Free transfer of funds

Nearly every cross-border investment requires the transfer of funds from the investor's home state to the host state and vice-versa.[280] It is pointless to establish a well running investment in a host state and not being able to transfer profits, interests or dividends from bank accounts run in the host state back to the investor's home state. The same idea applies for funds

---

275 Art 7 (2) of the German Model BIT (2008) [emphasis added].

276 *Herdegen*, 10. Edn. (2014), p. 340; *Griebel*, (2008) p.85.

277 *SGS vs. Philippines*, 29.01.2004 – ICSID Case No. ARB/02/6 - Decision of the Tribunal on Objections to Jurisdiction, para 115 f and 127 f, which although dealing with a treaty claim does not seem to limit the scope of the umbrella clause in the BIT to those contractual obligations only; same applies for: *Noble Ventures vs. Romania*, 12.10.2005 – ICSID Case No. ARB/01/11 - Award, para 61; for a wide interpretation also: *Jensen*, RIW, 2016, 277.

278 *Reinisch* in: *Tietje* (Ed.), Internationales Wirtschaftsrecht, 2015, p. 429; *Eureko vs. Poland*, 19.08.2005 – Ad Hoc Arbitration - Partial Award, para 244 and 250 f although it is not expressly stated by the tribunal.

279 *Sinclair* in: *Bungenberg/Griebel/Hobe et al.* (Eds.), International Investment Law, 2015, p. 914 f and p. 919: *"Rather than transforming the provisions of a State contract into an international obligation, the umbrella clause makes the observance of such provisions, so identified accordingly to their proper law, an obligation under the treaty (...)".*

280 *Reinisch* in: *Tietje* (Ed.), Internationales Wirtschaftsrecht, 2015, p. 428; *Griebel*, (2008), p. 91.

which should be transferred from the investor's home state to an affiliate or any other facility in the host state.[281]

However, customary international law generally does not recognise any right to transfer funds to foreign countries or back.[282] The sovereignty of states leaves it to each state's discretion to shape its monetary system at its own conception and prohibit or restrict the transfer of funds to foreign countries. As such restrictions narrow down the investor's ability to invest in the host state, free transfer of funds clauses are included in nearly all IIAs.[283] The first type of transfer of funds which is generally protected by IIAs are outbound transfers.[284] This category usually consists of "*returns*" on investments, such as "*profits, dividends, capital gains [etc.]*" [285]. All these funds are essential elements to enable the investor to successfully enjoy of its investment. The second category consists of the protection of incoming transfers, generally for the purpose to be invested in the investment.[286] The obligations undertaken by the host state concerning funds to which it guarantees "*free transfer*" usually covers four elements: investors should be enabled to transfer funds, in convertible currencies, without delay and at the official exchange rate.[287] All these requirements intend to protect the investor from "*hidden*" ways how to detrimentally affect the investment (e.g. the convertibility of the funds as well as the link to official exchange rates are essential as otherwise host states could heavily circumvent the guarantee by the choice of currencies, e.g. currencies which are subject to substantial alterations).[288]

---

281 *Reinisch* in: *Tietje* (Ed.), Internationales Wirtschaftsrecht, 2015, p. 371; *Griebel*, (2008), p. 91.

282 *Griebel*, (2008), p. 91.

283 *Griebel*, (2008), p. 91 f; *Reinisch* in: *Tietje* (Ed.), Internationales Wirtschaftsrecht, 2015, p. 428.

284 *UNCTAD*, Bilateral Investment Treaties: 1995–2006, 2007UNCTAD, p. 57.

285 Art. 7 of the U.S. Model BIT (2012)US Model BIT 2012 which enumerates further detailed funds to be covered by the provision.

286 *UNCTAD*, Bilateral Investment Treaties: 1995–2006, 2007, p. 57.

287 *Dolzer/Stevens*, Bilateral Investment Treaties, 1995 p.94; *Reinisch* in: *Tietje* (Ed.), Internationales Wirtschaftsrecht, 2015, p. 371.

288 *Reinisch* in: *Tietje* (Ed.), Internationales Wirtschaftsrecht, 2015, p. 428.

7. Admission clauses and right to establish

The admission of foreign investments deals with the treatment of foreign (future) investors in a phase before they established their investment, the so-called *pre-establishment-phase*. There is generally no obligation for any state to admit foreign investments on its territory.[289] Consequently, in absence of treaty obligations, a decision to admit or deny access of foreign investments to its territory is left to the host state's discretion.[290]

The guarantees which might grant such a right to establish in a foreign country are usually subject to a specific regulation in so-called admission clauses or pre-entry obligations.[291] Those clauses cover a completely different aspect of investment protection than the protection standards mentioned before as they guarantee particular rights even before the investment is admitted. Current IIAs in force mainly distinguish between two sort of clauses, which reflect a completely different viewpoint on pre-establishment rights.

Most IIAs and the majority of IIAs signed by EU member states contain so-called "*admission clauses*" only.[292] Through admission clauses the host states guarantee investors from the other contracting party to admit the investments "*as far as possible*"[293], as long as the investment is made "*in accordance with [the host state's] laws and regulations.* "[294] Hence it is left to the host state's national regulatory framework to establish the conditions of admittance of foreign investments. The regulations imposed on the investors may be conditions which are indistinctly applied but may also include regulations that preserve some industries to nationals only or

289 *Mestral* in: *Bungenberg/Griebel/Hobe et al.* (Eds.), International Investment Law, 2015, p. 685 f; *Reinisch* in: *Tietje* (Ed.), Internationales Wirtschaftsrecht, 2015, p. 355; *Füracker*, SchiedsVZ, 2006, 236, 241; however this is disputed among scholars.

290 *Reinisch* in: *Tietje* (Ed.), Internationales Wirtschaftsrecht, 2015, p. 355 f; *Füracker*, SchiedsVZ, 2006, 236, 241.

291 *Mestral* in: *Bungenberg/Griebel/Hobe et al.* (Eds.), International Investment Law, 2015, p. 687 f; *Füracker*, SchiedsVZ, 2006, 236, 241.

292 *Chaisse*, JIEL Vol. 15, No. 1 (2012), 51, 56 and 63 f; *Eilmansberger*, CMLR Vol. 46 (2009), 383, 386.

293 Article 2 (1) of the German Model BIT (2009).

294 Art. 2.I. Russion – Ethopia BIT (2000), Article 2 (1) German Model BIT (2009), Article 2: French Model BIT, BIT between Belgium and China (1984) Article 2, *UNCTAD*, Bilateral Investment Treaties: 1995–2006, 2007, p. 22.

even contain discriminatory regulations.[295] Hence, in this pre-establishment phase the investors are *not* guaranteed a non-discriminatory treatment. Nevertheless, admission clauses restrain the host states discretion to a certain degree as well. First, it may only deny the admittance of an investor "*on ground provided for legislation which is currently in force*"[296]. Secondly the host state at least needs to respect the principles of due process as to the decision if an investment is admitted.[297] Some treaties, mostly concluded by the United States of America and Canada, contain a so-called "*right of establishment*", which establishes far broader rights but should not be developed in detail here.[298]

III. Legal remedies: the dispute settlement mechanism in IIAs

The content of IIAs is not limited to substantive guarantees. As previously demonstrated, IIAs typically contain arbitration clauses which include the host state's consent to submit the dispute to arbitration. This offer can be

---

295 *Reinisch* in: *Tietje* (Ed.), Internationales Wirtschaftsrecht, 2015, p. 355; *UNCTAD*, Bilateral Investment Treaties: 1995–2006, 2007, p. 21 f.

296 *Füracker*, SchiedsVZ, 2006, 236, 241.

297 *Reinisch* in: *Tietje* (Ed.), Internationales Wirtschaftsrecht, 2015, p. 356, *Füracker*, SchiedsVZ, 2006, 236, 241.

298 *Chaisse*, JIEL Vol. 15, No. 1 (2012), 51, 56 and 63 f; *Eilmansberger*, CMLR Vol. 46 (2009), 383, 386; cf. also: *Füracker*, SchiedsVZ, 2006, 236, 241; *Mestral* in: *Bungenberg/Griebel/Hobe et al.* (Eds.), International Investment Law, 2015, p. 687 ff; *Reinisch* in: *Tietje* (Ed.), Internationales Wirtschaftsrecht, 2015, p. 409 f. "*Right of establishment*"-clauses grant foreign investments a right to access the host state if he fulfils the criteria set forth in the IIA. Those criteria may include performance requirements or exceptions as to the right of establishment. These clauses however have a limited impact regarding the EU member states, as those states mostly remain with the more restrictive approach by admission clauses. Nevertheless, the concept of clauses granting a "*right of establishment*" to other countries have become more and more popular also within IIAs concluded by EU member states. The Italian Model BIT (2003) exemplarily provides: "*Investors of either Contracting Parties shall have the right of access to investments activities in the territory of the other Contracting Party, which shall be not less favourable than that under Article III, paragraph 1 [reference to national treatment and most favoured nation treatment]*" (cf. Article II (2) of the Italian Model BIT (2003). Given the limited impact for IIAs in the EU, the focus of this thesis for further comparisons will be mainly on the post-establishment standards.

accepted by the investor at any time, especially by "*simply instituting proceedings pursuant to the proffered 'offer'*"[299].

Generally, there are two different types of clauses addressing different parties: one addressing the investor (and thus leading to mixed arbitrations), others are addressing the investor's home state (thus leading to inter-state arbitrations).[300]

Most of the provisions concerning so-called "*investment disputes*"[301] refer to institutional or pre-existing arbitration rules through a reference in the investment treaty.[302] As an example the German Model BIT (2009) provides that:

> "the dispute being submitted to one of the following dispute settlement mechanisms of the investor's choosing: arbitration under the auspices of the International Centre for Settlement of Investment Disputes (…)[;] an […] arbitral tribunal which is established in accordance with the rules of the United Nations Commission on International Trade Law (UNCITRAL) (…) [or][…] the Dispute Resolution Rules of the International Chamber of Commerce (ICC), the London Court of International Arbitration (LCIA) or the Arbitration Institute of the Stockholm Chamber of Commerce (SCC)."[303]

The references to the above-mentioned institutions (ICSID, UNCITRAL, ICC, SCC or LCIA) are predominantly found in the modern IIAs. Thus, the states consent to arbitration is not given to any kind of *ad-hoc* arbitration but refers to pre-determined mechanisms with an institutional framework and procedural rules concerning the arbitration which grants stability and security for investors.[304]

The most common reference is the reference to the International Centre for Settlement of Investment Disputes (ICSID) which has been established through the Convention of the Settlement of Investment Disputes between

---

299 *Dolzer/Stevens*, Bilateral Investment Treaties, 1995, p. 131 f; *Füracker*, SchiedsVZ, 2006, 236, 244; *Dugan*, Investor-state arbitration, 2008, p. 220 f; *Tietje* in: *Ehlers/Schoch* (Eds.), Rechtsschutz im Öffentlichen Recht, 2009, p. 65 f.

300 *El Paso vs. Argentina*, 27.04.2006 – ICSID Case No. ARB/03/15 - Decision on Jurisdiction, para 35; *Griebel*, (2008), p. 92 f., *Dolzer/Stevens*, Bilateral Investment Treaties, 1995, p. 119; *Füracker*, SchiedsVZ, 2006, 236, 344; *Schreuer*, The ICSID Convention, 2. Edn. (2009), para 427 f and 448.

301 *Dolzer/Stevens*, Bilateral Investment Treaties, 1995, p. 119.

302 *Dolzer/Stevens*, Bilateral Investment Treaties, 1995, p. 119; *Füracker*, SchiedsVZ, 2006, 236, 344.

303 Article 10 of the German Model BIT (2009).

304 *Herdegen*, 10. Edn. (2014), p. 352.

States and Nationals of Other States (ICSID Convention)[305], which will be explained in detail in the following sub-section (1.).

Nevertheless, due to their increasing importance and the differences compared to the ICSID mechanism, the dispute settlement mechanisms governed by the ICC and UNCITRAL rules will be explained as well (2.).

1. Investor-state arbitration governed by the ICSID-Convention

The key characteristic of arbitrations governed by the ICSID Convention is the high degree of institutionalization of the procedures.[306] The ICSID-Framework regulates in detail the procedural rules, the applicable law, the enforcement of decisions as well as numerous other questions related to the disputes.

(1) Jurisdiction of the Centre

The jurisdiction of the Centre is regulated in Art. 25 (1) ICSID-Convention which states that it:

> "shall extend to any legal dispute arising directly out of an *investment*, between a Contracting State (or any constituent subdivision or agency of a Contracting State designated to the Centre by that State) and a national of another Contracting State, which the parties to the dispute consent in writing to submit to the Centre."[307]

Any dispute may thus only be referred to an arbitral tribunal constituted under the rules of the ICSID-Conventions if three prerequisites are met: the parties need to consent to the submittal, the dispute needs to arise from an investment, both parties (or the nationals thereof) need to be contracting states of the convention and the investor must not be a national of the host state.[308]

Concerning the parties' consent to submit the dispute to the centre the key elements have been discussed *supra* (cf. Chapter 2): the consent may be

---

305 *Chaisse*, JIEL Vol. 15, No. 1 (2012), 51, 74; *Schreuer*, JWIT Vol. 5, No. 2 (2004), 231, 231.

306 *Tietje* in: *Ehlers/Schoch* (Eds.), Rechtsschutz im Öffentlichen Recht, 2009, p. 69 and 75.

307 Art. 25 (1) of the ICSID-Convention [emphasis added].

308 *Schöbener/Herbst et al.*, 2010, p. 314 f; *Tietje* in: *Ehlers/Schoch* (Eds.), Rechtsschutz im Öffentlichen Recht, 2009, p. 81 f.

given either by a consensual agreement of the parties or by the host state's unilateral offer, which is generally included in the IIA's arbitration clause.[309]

The dispute referred to the Centre needs to arise directly out of an "*investment*". This element of the jurisdiction *ratione materiae* has been subject to various awards and discussions in literature and jurisprudence. In the context of Art. 25 (1) ICSID Convention, which should not be confused with the term "*investment*" in the IIAs (which the parties may deliberately shape based on their definition in the IIA), the existence of an investment is regularly affirmed by reference to the so-called *Salini-Test*.[310] As to this test, an investment constitutes of the following elements:

> "[a] contribution, a certain duration of performance of the contract and a participation in the risks of the transaction [...] In reading the Convention's preamble, one may add the contribution to the economic development of the host State of the investment as an additional condition."[311]

The criteria enable to implement a certain filter regarding minor transfers of assets and delimit investments from pure trade operations. [312] The justification for each of the criteria remains disputed, however the test constitutes a certain benchmark which keeps being continuously applied.[313]

---

309 *Schreuer*, The ICSID Convention, 2. Edn. (2009), para 427 f and 448; cf. also references *supra* footnotes 107 and 108.

310 The name refers to the decision in *Salini vs. Morocco*, 31.07.2001 – ICSID Case No. ARB/00/4 - Decision on Jurisdiction, para 52. The decision was issed regarding the notion of "*investment*" in the context of Art. 25 of the ICSID-Convention and hence to establish the arbitral tribunal's jurisdiction and not the scope of application of the IIA (which should be separated). However, some suggest to apply the *Salini Test* to determine the term investment regarding the scope of application of IIAs as well, cf.: *Schöbener/Herbst et al.*, 2010, p. 259; The current approach adopted by the EU in the CETA draft also seems to refer to the Salini-Test, cf.: *Lentner*, JOLAS No. 2 (2014), 156, 158; this approach remains contested: cf. *Bischoff/Happ* in: *Bungenberg/Griebel/Hobe et al.* (Eds.), International Investment Law, 2015, p. 515 f.

311 *Salini vs. Jordan*, 09.11.2004 – ICSID Case No. ARB/02/13 - Award, para 52.

312 *Schöbener/Herbst et al.*, 2010, p. 259; *Bischoff/Happ* in: *Bungenberg/Griebel/Hobe et al.* (Eds.), International Investment Law, 2015, p. 510-513.

313 *Schöbener/Herbst et al.*, 2010, p. 259; *Bischoff/Happ* in: *Bungenberg/Griebel/Hobe et al.* (Eds.), International Investment Law, 2015, p. 510-513; cf. also: *Tietje* in: *Ehlers/Schoch* (Eds.), Rechtsschutz im Öffentlichen Recht, 2009, p. 87 f.

As to the last condition, Art. 25 (1) ICSID-Convention requires that the host state and the investor's home state are contracting parties of the ICSID Convention. However, under the ICSID Additional Facility Rules claims may also be submitted if only one of the States ratified the convention.[314] However, in this setting, the Convention will not apply, especially regarding the enforcement proceedings, applicable law, etc..[315] The arbitration under the Additional Facility rules presents the same characteristics as a private forum (cf. *infra* 2.).[316]

(2) Procedural rules and applicable law

The procedural rules are established in the Art. 36 ff. ICSID-Convention. The additional ICSID Rules of Procedure for the Institution of Conciliation and Arbitration Proceedings and the Rules of Procedure for Arbitration Proceedings apply additionally.[317] The ICSID proceedings are highly institutionalised as most of the procedural provisions are binding.[318]

As to the applicable law to the dispute, Art. 42 (1) of the ICSID Convention states:

> The Tribunal shall decide a dispute in accordance with such *rules of law as may be agreed by the parties*. In the absence of such agreement, the Tribunal shall apply the *law of the Contracting State* party to the dispute (including its rules on the conflict of laws) and such *rules of international law* as may be applicable.[319]

In other words: generally, the explicit choice of law of the parties, e.g. contained in the IIA, will need to be respected by the tribunal.[320] In the ab-

314 Art. 2 of the ICSID Additional Facility Rules (April 2006).

315 *Burgstaller*, LIEI Vol. 39, No. 2 (2012), 207, 214 f.

316 *Schöbener/Herbst et al.*, 2010, p. 310.

317 *Tietje* in: *Ehlers/Schoch* (Eds.), Rechtsschutz im Öffentlichen Recht, 2009, p. 75.

318 *Tietje* in: *Ehlers/Schoch* (Eds.), Rechtsschutz im Öffentlichen Recht, 2009, p. 75: The procedural provisions governing the additional facility proceedings are mainly the same.

319 Art. 42 (1) ICSID-Convention [emphasis added]. Besides Art. 42 (1) ICSID-Convention, Art. 42 (3) ICSID-Convention also offers the possibility of a decision ex aequo et bono upon request by the parties. However, this last possibility should not be treated here.

320 Cf. e.g.: *Leeks*, U. Toronto Fac. L. Rev. Vol. 65, No. 2 (2007), 1, 10 ; *Kjos*, Applicable law in investor-state arbitration, 2013, p. 213; *Banifatemi* in:

sence of an *explicit* choice, arbitral tribunals generally tend to apply predominantly international law to the dispute, despite the indistinct reference ("*and*") to domestic and international law in Art. 42 (1) of the Convention.[321] The justifications for this reasoning differ, some try to rely on the IIA, principles of international law as well as other relevant rules of international law to be the *lex causae*.[322] Others tend to refer to an implicit choice of international law as applicable law by basing the claim on the IIA.[323]

In principle, the role of national law is, unless otherwise agreed upon by the parties, reduced to a supplementary function for '*preliminary questions*'. It might as well be considered within the facts relevant to the dispute, especially to determine whether a protection standard under the IIA, was violated.[324] However, in most cases it will not be applied as a legal source which might set away the obligations contained in an IIA.[325] In addition, according to Art. 42 (1) of the ICSID-Convention, the host state's

---

Yannaca-Small (Ed.), Arbitration under international investment agreements, 2010, p. 192.

321 *Spiermann* in: *Muchlinski/Ortino/Schreuer* (Eds.), The Oxford handbook of international investment law, 2008, p. 107 f.; *Schreuer*, McGill Jour of Disp. Res. Vol. 1, No. 1 (2014), 1, 11 ff.

322 *Kjos*, Applicable law in investor-state arbitration, 2013, 223, 224 ff and 229 f; *Annulment Committee in MTD vs. Chile*, 21.03.2007 – ICSID Case No. ARB/01/7 - Decision on Annulment, para 72: *"As noted above, the lex causae in this case based on a breach of the BIT is international law (...)"*.

323 *AAP vs. Sri Lanka*, 27.06.1990 – ICSID Case No. ARB/87/3 - Final Award, para 39; *Wena vs. Egypt*, 08.12.2000 – ICSID Case No. ARB/98/4 - Award, para 78; *MTD vs. Chile*, 25.05.2004 – ICSID Case No. ARB/01/7 - Award, para 87; cf. also: *Spiermann* in: *Muchlinski/Ortino/Schreuer* (Eds.), The Oxford handbook of international investment law, 2008, p. 108; *Tietje*, Intra-EU BITs als Herausforderung im Mehrebenensystem des Rechts (Beit. zum Transnat. Wirt.-R, Vol. 104, 2011), p. 8; *Leeks*, U. Toronto Fac. L. Rev. Vol. 65, No. 2 (2007), 1, 15; the notion of implicit choice is contested, cf. *inter alia*: *Gaillard/Banifatemi*, ICSID Rev. Vol. 18, Iss. 2 (2003), 375, 387.

324 For a comprehensive analysis of the different settings in which domestic law could be respected despite of the general choice in favor of internationa law: *Spiermann* in: *Muchlinski/Ortino/Schreuer* (Eds.), The Oxford handbook of international investment law, 2008 p 110 ff.

325 However, if an arbitral tribunal decides to deny an *implicit* choice of law, the rule set forth in Art. 42 (1) of the ICSID Convention would apply. Then domestic law might indeed be applied by the tribunal, together with international law, cf.: *Kjos*, Applicable law in investor-state arbitration, 2013, p. 207 f; *Leeks*, U. Toronto Fac. L. Rev. Vol. 65, No. 2 (2007), 1, 18; For the hierarchy of both frameworks in this context, cf. *infra* Chapter 13.

domestic law does not constitute the *lex loci arbitri* (the law of the seat of the tribunal, cf. *infra* for private forums) as well. ICSID-arbitration is a delocalised dispute.[326] Hence, although in theory domestic law is applicable to an ICSID-dispute, in most cases its application will be reduced to rather minor settings; this constitutes an important difference to private forums.

(3) Recourse and enforcement

The enforcement of judicial decisions is generally considered to be one of the key elements to guarantee the efficiency of the legal framework. Two elements may deter such efficiency and delay the application of any award rendered by an arbitral tribunal. First the possibilities of appeal or recourse can lead to long lasting appeal-procedures which affect the efficiency of the whole system. Secondly the final awards need to be enforced in the host state.

The ICSID-Convention tries to strengthen the efficiency of its own dispute settlement system by rigorous provision concerning these two elements. The possibilities of appeal are diminished to a strict minimum. Art. 53 of the ICSID Conventions states in principle that

> "[t]he award shall be binding on the parties and shall not be subject to any appeal or to any other remedy except those provided for in this Convention."

Only few exceptions from this principle are considered by the Convention. The convention admits the possibility of annulment proceedings by an ad-hoc annulment committee (Art. 52 ICSID-Convention) and the review of the award if the underlying facts reveal to be erroneous (Art. 51 ICSID-Convention). However, besides these proceedings, no further review should be exercised. No enforcement proceedings should be necessary either.[327]

326 *Spiermann* in: *Muchlinski/Ortino/Schreuer* (Eds.), The Oxford handbook of international investment law, 2008, p. 93; as to *Tietje* this leads to a complete internationalisation of the dispute, cf: *Tietje* in: *Ehlers/Schoch* (Eds.), Rechtsschutz im Öffentlichen Recht, 2009, p. 69.

327 *Tietje* in: *Ehlers/Schoch* (Eds.), Rechtsschutz im Öffentlichen Recht, 2009, p. 74 f.

(a) Annulment proceedings

The ICSID-proceedings are subject to a particular annulment procedure, excluding the challenge of awards under national law.[328] The proceedings enable the control of the award through an ad-hoc-tribunal but is limited to an enumerated number of reasons (Art. 52 ICSID-Convention). Among others, the article states that "*Either party may request annulment of the award [if] the Tribunal has manifestly exceeded its powers*". This reason is the sole reason enumerated in Art. 52 (1) of the ICSID-Convention being of relevance for this thesis.[329] It includes the fact that an arbitral tribunal did not have the competency to rule the case or that it made manifest errors in determining the applicable law to the dispute.[330] If none of the grounds listed in Art. 52 (1) can be proven, the ICSID-Convention provides for no further possibility to review the award. It has thus to be accepted as binding by both parties.

(b) Enforcement of ICSID-Awards

The award, once it is binding, needs to be enforced. The ICSID-Convention does not provide a separate system of enforcement but relies on enforcement through the national tribunals.

However, ICSID-Awards represent a particularity as to enforcement measures. Usually, foreign arbitral awards need to be submitted to specific national enforcement procedures by national tribunals to be finally granted the necessary status to be enforced in this country.[331] As to Art. 53, 54 ICSID-Convention an award rendered under the ICSID-Framework should be granted the same status as a national judgment in all signatory states of the convention. In other words, there is no need for an enforce-

---

328 *Engel*, SchiedsVZ, 2015, 218, 220; *Tietje* in: *Ehlers/Schoch* (Eds.), Rechtsschutz im Öffentlichen Recht, 2009, p. 74 f.

329 The other reasons enumerated by Art. 52 (1) of the ICSID-Convention are: "*the Tribunal was not properly constituted*"; "*there was corruption on the part of a member of the Tribunal*", "*there has been a serious departure from a fundamental rule of procedure*" or the "*award has failed to state the reasons on which it is based*", cf.: Art. 52 (1) of the ICSID-Convention.

330 Cf. *infra* (Chapter 5 and 13) for a deeper analysis.

331 *Tietje* in: *Ehlers/Schoch* (Eds.), Rechtsschutz im Öffentlichen Recht, 2009, p. 74 f; *Engel*, SchiedsVZ, 2015, 218, 220; *Kniebaum*, ELTE Law Journal, 27, 34; *Kleinheisterkamp*, JIEL Vol. 15, No. 1 (2012), 85, 102.

ment procedure and there are – in principle – no grounds to refuse enforcement.[332]

2. Investor-state arbitration in private forums: ICC / SCC, etc.

For the scope of this thesis it should be sufficient to briefly address the differences of private arbitration frameworks compared to the rules that apply for investment disputes under the ICSID-Convention.

(1) Jurisdiction of the arbitral tribunal

Other than the ICSID-Proceedings, private forums do not contain a specific regulation as to the tribunal's scope of jurisdiction in their institutional frameworks. This is mainly due to the fact that those forums were initially conceived for commercial arbitrations dealing with diverse subjects. Hence, the tribunal's jurisdiction depends entirely on the existence of a valid arbitration agreement between the two parties covering the subject of the dispute.[333] In the case of investment proceedings the tribunals will *inter alia* need to verify:

- the validity of the consent given by the host state in the IIA and the investor through filing its claim;
- the applicability of the IIA to the parties of the dispute, which might contain questions linked to the investor's nationality or the qualification of the economic activity as "*investment*" in terms of the IIA the dispute is based on;[334]

---

332 *Tietje* in: *Ehlers/Schoch* (Eds.), Rechtsschutz im Öffentlichen Recht, 2009, p. 74; cf. however: *Tietje/Wackernagel*, JWIT Vol. 16, Iss. 2 (2015), 205, 210 and 235 ff., who argue that with respect to EU law there might be a risk of non-enforcement for awards being contrary to substantial provisions of EU law; cf. also: *Wehland*, ICLQ Vol. 58, Iss. 2 (2009), 297, 308 f; the European Commission also considers that an award contrary to EU law may not be enforced: *European Commission*, Amicus Curia Brief filed in Electrabel vs. Hungary (ICSID Case n° ARB/07/19) - arbitration proceedings, 12/06/2009, para 136-138.

333 *Tietje* in: *Ehlers/Schoch* (Eds.), Rechtsschutz im Öffentlichen Recht, 2009, p. 68 and 82.

334 Cf. also: *Böckstiegel*, Arbitration International Vol. 28, Iss. 4 (2012), 577, 583; this was e.g. the second major objection raised by the Slovak Republic in

- the determination, whether the concrete dispute is covered by the particular arbitration clause, as several clauses might contain restrictions such as limitations to violations of particular protection standards only, etc.[335]

Once this is established, the tribunal has *prima facie* jurisdiction to rule the case. However, this does not exclude further objections to the tribunal's jurisdiction, such as e.g. non-compliance with waiting-periods, objection of *res judicata*, etc.

(2) Applicable law and procedural rules

The procedural rules offered by the private forums are much more flexible than the proceedings under the ICSID-Convention. Most of these rules can be derogated by the parties. Also, the density of regulation is far less developed.[336] The only exception are the procedural rules of the ICC, which contain a considerable amount of regulations with regard to the proceedings.[337]

Regarding the applicable law private forums however present a major difference to the ICSID-Proceedings. One needs to differentiate between the law applicable to the procedural framework and the tribunal's jurisdiction and the law applicable to the merits

(a) The law applicable to the proceedings and to determine jurisdiction

Although the parties are deliberately free to choose a law applicable on the merits, the procedural rules of the proceedings are generally limited by the

---

Binder vs. Czech Republic, 06.06.2007 – UNCITRAL - Award on Jurisdiction, para 21 ff.

335 Cf. Art. 24 of the U.S. Model BIT (2012) which limits the potenital disputes to breaches of *"(...) (A) an obligation under Articles 3 through 10, (B) an investment authorization, or (C) an investment agreement (...)"*; cf. also: *Schreuer*, McGill Jour of Disp. Res. Vol. 1, No. 1 (2014), 1, 6 ff; the investor's claim in *Austrian Airlinces vs. Slovak Republic*, 09.10.2009 – UNCITRAL - Final Award was entirely dismissed based on such considerations, cf. para 85 ff.

336 *Tietje* in: *Ehlers/Schoch* (Eds.), Rechtsschutz im Öffentlichen Recht, 2009, p. 76 f.

337 *Tietje* in: *Ehlers/Schoch* (Eds.), Rechtsschutz im Öffentlichen Recht, 2009, p. 76.

mandatory provisions of the *lex loci arbitri*, the national law at the place of arbitration.[338] The parties still enjoy considerable freedom as to design the procedural framework upon mutual agreement. The outer limits of this freedom are however provided by the mandatory provisions of the *lex loci arbitri*.[339]

Besides setting the boundaries to potential modifications of the procedural framework, the *lex loci arbitri* also determines the validity of the arbitration clause.[340] Hence, and for the purpose of this thesis, if the seat of the tribunal is designated within the EU, the *lex loci arbitri* may also include EU law.

(b) Law applicable to the merits

Regarding the law applicable to the merits, the procedural rules of private forums either contain no statement at all or they leave it to the parties' discretion to choose the law applicable to the dispute. If the parties do not denominate the applicable law, the tribunals under ICC, SCC or UNCITRAL proceedings are entitled to judge the case in accordance with the law they consider appropriate to rule the case.[341]

---

338 *Trittmann*, SchiedsVZ, 2016, 7, 10; *Böckstiegel*, Arbitration International Vol. 28, Iss. 4 (2012), 577, 580; *Tietje* in: *Ehlers/Schoch* (Eds.), Rechtsschutz im Öffentlichen Recht, 2009, p. 69; *Poudret/Basson*, Comparative law of international arbitration, 2. Edn. (2007), para 112 ff.

339 *Trittmann*, SchiedsVZ, 2016, 7, 10; *Böckstiegel*, Arbitration International Vol. 28, Iss. 4 (2012), 577, 579 f; *Horn*, SchiedsVZ, 2008, 209, 211 who refers to the challenges for the concept of *lex loci arbitri* by the acceptance of delocalised arbitration proceddings (such as under the ICSID Convention), cf. also: *Fouchard/Gaillard et al.*, Fouchard, Gaillard, Goldman on international commercial arbitration, 1999, p. 213 ff; However *Park*, The International and Comparative Law Quarterly Vol. 32, No. 1 (1983), 21, 22 f; and *Tietje* in: *Ehlers/Schoch* (Eds.), Rechtsschutz im Öffentlichen Recht, 2009, p. 69 both correctly point out that *in fine* it is up to the national arbitration law to decide to which degree it desists from imposing boundaries by virtue of the *lex loci arbitri*; this is also advanced by *Poudret/Basson*, Comparative law of international arbitration, 2. Edn. (2007), para 120 ff.

340 Cf. references above; cf. also: *Higher Regional Court Frankfurt*, SchiedsVZ (2013), 119, 10.05.2012 – 26 SchH 11/10, 122.

341 Art. 22 of the SCC Arbitration Rules (2010); Art. 21 (1) of the ICC Arbitration Rules (2012); Arrt. 35 of the UNCITRAL Arbitration Rules (2013); cf. also: *Schreuer*, McGill Jour of Disp. Res. Vol. 1, No. 1 (2014), 1, 11 ff.

Hence, as to the applicable law to the merits, the differences to ICSID-Proceedings are less obvious. If the IIA contains a choice of law, this needs to be respected.[342] The same applies for any subsequent choice of law by the parties.[343] In case of missing consent as to the applicable law, the tribunal will exercise its discretion. Similarly as in the ICSID-Context, due to the international nature of IIAs, this will predominantly lead to the application of international law. Domestic law might apply e.g. for the determination of contract-breaches under national law.[344]

Generally, the reference to domestic law is one of the only differences one might conceive between the applicable law provisions in ICSID-proceedings and private forums.[345] Whereas Art. 42 (1) ICSID Convention expressly refers to domestic law as applicable law whenever the parties did not chose the applicable law, this reference is missing in private forums.[346] This should however not limit the arbitrator's discretion to apply domestic law to parts or even the integrity of the dispute, depending on the particular facts. Overall the differences in the proceedings are minimal.[347]

(3) Recourse and enforcement of arbitral awards issued in private forums

Other than for the ICSID-Proceedings, private forums do not contain particular regulations regarding a recourse or the enforcement in the procedural regulations itself. Those questions are regulated by other instruments. An award rendered under the procedural rules of a private forum may potentially be challenged in setting aside proceedings, which are sim-

---

342 The underlying idea is that through accepting the arbitration by virtue of the arbitration clause, host state and investor also accepted the choice of law contained in the IIA, *Siemens A.G. vs. Argentina*, 17.01.2007 – ICSID Case No. ARB/02/8 - Award, para 76; cf. also: *Schreuer*, McGill Jour of Disp. Res. Vol. 1, No. 1 (2014), 1, 11 f; *Trittmann*, SchiedsVZ, 2016, 7, 8 f.

343 *Trittmann*, SchiedsVZ, 2016, 7, 8 f.

344 *Böckstiegel*, Arbitration International Vol. 28, Iss. 4 (2012), 577, 580; *Kjos*, Applicable law in investor-state arbitration, 2013, p. 207 f; *Leeks*, U. Toronto Fac. L. Rev. Vol. 65, No. 2 (2007), 1, 18 f.

345 Similar: *Schreuer*, McGill Jour of Disp. Res. Vol. 1, No. 1 (2014), 1, 13; *Böckstiegel*, Arbitration International Vol. 28, Iss. 4 (2012), 577, 580 even considers that the difference becomes less important, as most new BITs contain a reference to domestic law in their provisions regarding the applicable law.

346 *Schreuer*, McGill Jour of Disp. Res. Vol. 1, No. 1 (2014), 1, 11 ff.

347 *Schreuer*, McGill Jour of Disp. Res. Vol. 1, No. 1 (2014), 1, 11 f.

ilar to the ICSID Annulment proceedings. To enforce the award in any other state than the award's origin, enforcement proceedings need to be initiated in the specific country.

(a) Setting aside proceedings

Arbitral proceedings under other forums (such as ICC, SCC, etc.) usually – except for the particular case in which the parties agreed on an appeal mechanism – will be a one-stage only procedure. However, regarding those forums, 'setting-aside'- proceedings might be initiated by recourse to national courts.[348] Those courts will not exercise a full control of the award, but ensure that certain minimum standards were followed during the arbitration proceedings by evaluation of specific 'annulment grounds'. Both mechanisms, ICSID Annulment proceedings and 'setting-aside'-proceedings are similar in effect.

Whether or not an arbitral award may be challenged in 'setting-aside' proceedings is a question of national law in the respective country the award derives from (its origin).[349] There is – other than for the enforcement of the award – no international convention regulating these proceedings.[350] Each national (procedural) law dealing with arbitration might include its own stipulations as to 'setting-aside' proceedings. Therefore, the grounds and procedures to follow can heavily diverge. However, the in-

---

348 *Engel*, SchiedsVZ, 2015, 218,220; this possibility (and its risks for the annulment of the award) is also clearly recognised by the Tribunal in *Electrabel vs. Hungary*, 30.11.2012 – ICSID Case No. ARB/07/19: Decision on Jurisdiction, Applicable Law and Liability, para 4.112

349 *Pavic* in: *Knahr* (Ed.), Investment and commercial arbitration, 2010, p. 131, 133; *Engel*, SchiedsVZ, 2015, 218, 220; There are two prevailing ways to determine the "*origin*" of an award, either by referring to the procedural framework or to the place of the arbitral tribunals legal seat, cf. *Pavic* in: *Knahr* (Ed.), Investment and commercial arbitration, 2010, p. 131, 133. For the purpose of the analysis the choice of criteria to determine the awards origin does not impact, as the analysis is based on the grounds for annulment only, which may anyways diverge from one country to the other, displaying however a certain uniformity on key elements; cf. also: *Engel*, SchiedsVZ, 2015, 218, 220; *Abedian*, JOIA Vol. 28, Iss. 6 (2011), 553, 554 f, for a comparative analysis p. 555 ff.

350 Cf. *infra* (b) for the New York Convention governing the enforcement proceedings.

troduction of the revised UNCITRAL Model law[351] in 2006 in multiple national legislations has created a certain uniformity among countries.[352] Art. 34 of the Model law includes several grounds to challenge an arbitral award, which should – in the Model law's conception – be the only recourse to challenge the validity of a rendered award.[353] For the purpose of this thesis the relevant parts of Art 34 of the Model law reads as follows:

> "An arbitral award may be set aside (…) if:
>
> (a) the party making the application furnishes proof that:
>
> (i) a party to the arbitration agreement […] was under some incapacity; or the said agreement is not valid under the law to which the parties have subjected it or, failing any indication thereon, under the law of this State; *or* […]
>
> (b) the court finds that:[…]
>
> (ii) the award is in conflict with the public policy of this State"

The UNCITRAL Model law is in no way mandatory for the states. They may – and indeed a couple of states did – introduce other grounds of annulment or modify the grounds provided in Art. 34 Model Law.[354] Nevertheless, a certain consensus, especially regarding the grounds for annulment being relevant for this thesis (public policy and missing validity of the arbitration agreement), has subsisted.[355]

(b) Enforcement proceedings

Private forums do not contain separate enforcement provisions in the procedural framework. Arbitral awards rendered under any forum except IC-

---

351 UNCITRAL Model Law (as amended in 2006).

352 *Pavic* in: *Knahr* (Ed.), Investment and commercial arbitration, 2010, p. 131, 133; *Engel*, SchiedsVZ, 2015, 218, 220.

353 Cf. Art. 34 (1) of the Model law text: "*Recourse to a court against an arbitral award may be made only by an application for setting aside in accordance with paragraphs (2) and (3) of this article*".

354 *Pavic* in: *Knahr* (Ed.), Investment and commercial arbitration, 2010, p. 131, 135.

355 Compare e.g. the German § 1059 Code of Civil Procedure (ZPO), Art. 41 and 42 of the Spanish Arbitration Act (Ley 60/2003 de arbitraje); Art. 190 (2) of the Swiss Federal Statute on Private International Law; for a further, comparative analysis: *Pavic* in: *Knahr* (Ed.), Investment and commercial arbitration, 2010, p. 131; for the Spanish Arbitration Act: *Cairns*, Arbitration International Vol. 22, No. 4 (2006), 573.

SID, fall under the scope of the New York Convention.[356] Thus, awards need to be recognised in the country where enforcement of the award is desired. The Convention recognises several (conclusive) grounds, which might be invoked to deny enforcement to the award and thus may constitute gateways to challenge the award based, e.g. on (potential) conflicts with EU law.[357] The convention has largely been transposed to national laws, allowing similar if not identical grounds to refuse the enforcement of an arbitral award as those under the UNCITRAL Model Law. Art. V of the New York Convention stipulates that enforcement may be refused if:

> "(1) (a) the said [arbitration] agreement is not valid under the law to which the parties have subjected it or, failing any indication thereon, under the law of the country where the award was made; or [...]
>
> (2) (b) The recognition or enforcement of the award would be contrary to the public policy of that country."

Hence, the two potential reasons to set aside an award in annulment proceedings, reappear in the context of enforcement proceedings as potential grounds to refuse enforcement in the respective country.

3. Other remedies such as inter-state and local remedies

Despite the predominant use of mixed arbitrations mechanisms, the further possibilities of dispute settlement mechanisms should not be unmentioned. First, most IIAs also include inter-state dispute resolution clauses which enable the home state to engage action against the host state in case of a breach of the IIA.

Second, investors do not necessarily need to rely on the mixed arbitration mechanism. They might also engage proceedings before national courts. These proceedings offer a particular advantage compared to the arbitration proceedings. Whereas arbitral tribunals might in general only engage the state responsibility and order compensation for a breach of the IIA, they are – in the predominant understanding, which is challenged – unable to order the invalidity of a state measure or to impose the duty to

356 New York Convention on the Recognition and Enforcement of Foreign Arbitral Awards (1958).

357 Cf. for mandatory provisions regarding consumer-protection, cf.: *Wilske/Fox* in: Wolff New York Convention, Art. V, para 110.

take or omit from a certain measure.[358] Such measures, – usually referred to as *restitution in kind* – can only be order by the national courts (primary relief). Judicial protection by arbitral tribunals will be limited to secondary protection by compensation.[359]

B. The EU-Law framework: „investment"-protection in EU law

The legal framework nowadays called EU law recognises different sources of law: EU primary law, which includes the EC Treaty and protocols as well as its amendments, EU secondary legislation, which includes regulations, directives, decisions and opinions, general principles of EU law as developed in the jurisprudence of the CJEU, as well as customary law and the rights and obligations deriving from international agreements undertaken by the EU.[360]

After addressing several guiding principles of EU law first, the most essential provisions in EU law with particular significance for investment protection within EU member states will be described in the following. This should demonstrate the second angle of protection offered to investors in EU member states.

358 For a recent example of a tribunal which seems to be willing to order restitution of a legal framework instead of compensation: *Ioan Micula, Viorel Micula & others vs. Romania*, 23.09.2008 – ICSID Case No. ARB/05/20 - Decision on Jurisdiction and Admissibility, para 166-168; some consider restitution to be in practice impossible (e.g. *CME vs. Czech Republic*, 13.09.2001 – UNCITRAL - Partial Award, para 618; cf. also for the general challenge of restitution in kind to be the appropriate measure to be ordered by an arbitral tribunal: *inter alia*: *Hindelang*, AVR Vol. 53 (2015), 68, 78; others point out the fact that BITs generally (with several exceptions) are not limited to secondary relief but given e.g. Art. 53, 54, which only relate to the enforcement of awards attributing compensation, restitution may not be the best choice for the investors, cf.: *Dugan*, Investor-state arbitration, 2008, p. 569 f; under public international law however restitution should be the first option to be addressed: cf.: *ICJ*, Case concerning the factory at Chrozow, p. 47.

359 Similar: *Ghouri*, ELJ Vol. 16, No. 5 (2010), 806, 807; *Hindelang*, AVR Vol. 53 (2015), 68, 78; cf. also references above.

360 *Hobe*, 8. Edn. (2014), para 363; *Haratsch*, 2016, p. 196-198; *Schwarze* in: Schwarze EU-Kommentar, Art. 19 TEU, para 22, 27 f.

I. Guiding principles of EU law

EU law is essentially based on two sort of provisions: on the one hand the European Treaties as well as the implementing secondary law guarantee a certain level playing field for economic operators within the internal market. The essential idea behind these regulations is to remove the interference of state measures with economic operators for national purposes. Business or economic activity should be freely enjoyed, irrespective of the actor's nationality within the internal market.[361]

On the other hand, EU law also includes a certain common understanding of competition, market (de)regulation and consumer protection. The absence of competition within a market, due to the predominant position of one of its actors, is judged to be inadmissible as it would have considerable detrimental effects on consumers and the economy in general.[362] Therefore, EU law contains various provisions which set up boundaries for economic activities within the market affecting effective competition.

Furthermore, with the Lisbon Treaty, EU law admitted a more elaborated submission to a further control regarding individual fundamental rights which – given the economic nature of the Union – include far reaching economic rights in the Charter of Fundamental Rights.[363]

The entire legislative framework of the EU is characterised by its autonomy as one of the most fundamental principles. The member states, when signing the European Treaties and thus creating the EU, agreed to limit their sovereignty with regard to the competences transferred to the EU. The legal framework based upon this transferal of competences is a sell-sufficient body of law, which is binding on all member states.[364] The autonomy of the EU's legal order is the guarantee of its functioning. It ensures that no national legislation or unilateral act of the member states will waive the uniform and constant application of EU law within all member

361 *Hobe*, 8. Edn. (2014), para 996; *Haratsch*, 2016, p. 671; *Hatje* in: Schwarze EU-Kommentar, Art. 119 TFEU, para 9-10; *van Voet Vormizeele* in: v. d. Groeben/Schwarze AEUV/EUV, Art. 26 TFEU, para 25-27.

362 *Hobe*, 8. Edn. (2014), para 996; *Haratsch*, 2016, p. 671; *Hatje* in: Schwarze EU-Kommentar, Art. 119 TFEU, para 9-11; cf. also: *Oppermann/Classen et al.*, 5. Edn. (2011) § 18, para 8 f; *van Voet Vormizeele* in: v. d. Groeben/Schwarze AEUV/EUV, Art. 26 TFEU, para 28.

363 *Hobe*, 8. Edn. (2014), para 652 and 654.

364 *CJEU*, 15.07.1964 – C-6/64 - Flaminio Costa vs. E.N.E.L. = ECLI:EU:C:1964:66, 1269; *Nettesheim* in: Grabitz/Hilf/Nettesheim EUV/AEUV, Art. 1 TFEU, para 60.

states.[365] Any changes to this framework may only be agreed upon in a conjoint, mutual action by all member states (except if one state exits the EU by virtue of Art. 50 TEU).

Two further principles are a consequence and at the same time part of this autonomy.[366] First, the principle of supremacy of EU law guarantees the recognition of EU law as supreme legal order. Every conflicting national provision, which might affect the effective and full application of EU law, is inapplicable.[367] Second, the direct effect of EU law enables all individuals to directly invoke certain provisions of EU law before national courts or the CJEU. This guarantees that EU member states may not circumvent the principle of supremacy and the autonomy of the legal order by non-application or non-transposal of EU law.[368]

II. Substantive protection and its limits under EU law

Based on these sources, one could determine several particular frameworks of EU law, designed to protect the investor's operations in an EU member state. This includes guarantees derived from the fundamental freedoms (1.) as well as through the Charter of Fundamental Rights of the EU (2.).

1. Investment protection through the fundamental freedoms

The five fundamental freedoms shape the internal market in the EU. Their underlying idea is to abolish any restrictions to the free movement of goods and capital, the freedom of establishment of individuals and legal entities within all member states and the free movement of workers and

365 *Nettesheim* in: Grabitz/Hilf/Nettesheim EUV/AEUV, Art. 1 TFEU, para 61; *Streinz*, 10. Edn. (2016), p. 63; *Oppermann/Classen et al.*, 5. Edn. (2011) § 9, para 12.

366 *Streinz*, 10. Edn. (2016), p. 71; cf. also: *Hindelang*, AVR Vol. 53 (2015), 68, 72.

367 *Nettesheim* in: Grabitz/Hilf/Nettesheim EUV/AEUV, Art. 1 TFEU, para 73 f; *Streinz*, 10. Edn. (2016), p. 73 and 75; *Haratsch*, 2016, p. 68-89.

368 *Nettesheim* in: Grabitz/Hilf/Nettesheim EUV/AEUV, Art. 1 TFEU, para 73 f; *Haratsch*, 2016, p. 68-89; *Oppermann/Classen et al.*, 5. Edn. (2011) § 9, para 14 f.

services in this same territory. Hence, they support the general idea of investment protection which is to protect the investors from interventionist measures by the host state. With respect to the protection of investments against harmful state measures the most predominant protection will be offered through the freedom of establishment (1) and the free movement of capital (2). However, it should not be neglected that additional protection is offered through the free transfer of payments (3) as well as the free movement of goods and the freedom to provide services (4).

(1) Freedom of establishment

The freedom of establishment in Art. 49 ff TFEU guarantees the (free) right to establish a business or to perform an economic activity in all member states by individuals or legal entities, including companies or partnerships in a cross-border context.[369] This guarantee is a prerequisite to the functioning of an unhindered economic development and interaction within the internal market, as it guarantees the very first step to develop an economic activity: the access to the member state's market.[370] Given the interpretation and application of the provisions by the CJEU, notwithstanding the wording, the freedom of establishment is a protection against all kind of hindrances by member states to the free establishment of individuals and legal entities in the entire area of the internal market for economic purposes and the subsequent exercise of this activity. Any measure potentially reducing the freedom is subject to justification. Consequently, it provides substantial protection to investors operating in the EU.

---

369 *Hobe*, 8. Edn. (2014), para 779 ff; *Tietje* in: Becker/Ehlers Europäische Grundfreiheiten (2014), § 10, para 24; *Korte* in: Calliess/Ruffert EUV/AEUV, Art. 49 TFEU, para 1; *Schlag* in: Schwarze EU-Kommentar, Art. 49 TFEU, para 2. The German expression is "*grenzüberschreitender Bezug*"

370 *Hobe*, 8. Edn. (2014), para 779; *Schlag* in: Schwarze EU-Kommentar, Art. 49 TFEU, para 4; *Tietje* in: Becker/Ehlers Europäische Grundfreiheiten (2014), § 10, para 2.

(a) The type of action protected under the freedom of establishment

As to the CJEU, an "*establishment*" could be any form of "actual pursuit of an economic activity through a fixed establishment in another Member State for an indefinite period".[371] There is no necessity to form a distinct legal entity. A location which serves as a hub to manufacture goods or provide services is perfectly sufficient.[372] Given the broad terms, a large variety of investments are covered by the term establishment.

The freedom of establishment mainly guarantees three types of actions: the set up for an entirely new main establishment (creation of a new primary business)[373], the movement of an existing establishment (relocation

371 *CJEU*, 25.07.1991 – C-221/89 - Factortame = ECLI:EU:C:1991:320, para 20.

372 *Tiedje* in: v. d. Groeben/Schwarze AEUV/EUV, Art. 49 TFEU, para 1 ff; *Hobe*, 8. Edn. (2014), para 783; *Tietje* in: Becker/Ehlers Europäische Grundfreiheiten (2014), § 10, para 26 f; *Korte* in: Calliess/Ruffert EUV/AEUV, Art. 49 TFEU, para 26 and 34. To differentiate the freedom of establishment from the freedom to provide services, the durability of the activity, its actual use and the weight of the economic activity are major criteria. An establishment is met, whenever the activity is a surplus to "*only*" providing cross-border services, cf.: *Tiedje* in: v. d. Groeben/Schwarze AEUV/EUV, Art. 49 TFEU, para 11; *Korte* in: Calliess/Ruffert EUV/AEUV, Art. 49 TFEU, para 25 f.

373 *Tiedje* in: v. d. Groeben/Schwarze AEUV/EUV, Art. 49 TFEU, para 38 ff; *Schlag* in: Schwarze EU-Kommentar, Art. 49 TFEU, para 19; *Hobe*, 8. Edn. (2014), para 782 ff; *Oppermann/Classen et al.*, 5. Edn. (2011) § 28, para 21. The criterion of a cross-border-context (grenzüberschreitender Bezug) is interpreted widely by the CJEU, which diminishes more and more its impact on the delimiation of the fundamental freedoms. As to the CJEU any element establishing that the measure *"concerns"* (even potential) interests of economic operators in other member states is sufficient. This is settled case law, cf. e.g.: *CJEU*, 19.07.2012 – C-470/11 - SIA Garkalns = ECLI:EU:C:2012:505, para 21:" *[Art.49] applies to situations connected with trade between the Member States, it is far from inconceivable that operators established in Member States other than the Republic of Latvia have been or are interested in opening amusement arcades in Latvia"* [footnotes omitted]; cf. also: *Ehlers* in: Becker/Ehlers Europäische Grundfreiheiten (2014), § 7, para 25.

of the main or secondary business)[374] or the creation of an entirely new secondary establishment (creation of a subsidiary)[375].

Generally, the above mentioned three actions are protected against any hindering measure in a cross-border-context. Although the wording of Art. 49 TFEU seems to prohibit only discriminatory measures, the CJEU – same as for the other freedoms – extended the prohibition contained in Art. 49 TFEU to all measures which are either discriminatory or "*liable to hinder or make less attractive the exercise of fundamental freedoms guaranteed by the Treaty*".[376] Thus, the CJEU developed a general prohibition of restrictions.[377] This prohibition applies both to measures which are either directly discriminatory (because they are applied to foreigners only), indirectly discriminatory (although the criteria of application is neutral, non-nationals are typically affected by this measure)[378] or even those measures which are indistinctly applied to nationals and non-nationals but which are liable of hindering the fundamental freedom or making it less attractive.[379] Such measures might be inter alia the prohibition to establish a subsidiary[380], minimum tariffs to register companies for particular services[381], the requirement to prove further diploma or documents[382], or dif-

374 *Tiedje* in: v. d. Groeben/Schwarze AEUV/EUV, Art. 49 TFEU, para 38 ff, *Schlag* in: Schwarze EU-Kommentar, Art. 49 TFEU, para 19 and 20 *Hobe*, 8. Edn. (2014), para 782 ff; *Oppermann/Classen et al.*, 5. Edn. (2011) § 28, para 22.

375 *Tiedje* in: v. d. Groeben/Schwarze AEUV/EUV, Art. 49 TFEU, para 41 ff; *Schlag* in: Schwarze EU-Kommentar, Art. 49 TFEU, para 20; *Oppermann/Classen et al.*, 5. Edn. (2011) § 28, para 21.

376 *CJEU*, 30.11.1995 – C-55/94 - Gebhard = ECLI:EU:C:1995:411, para 37 – settled case law since then, cf. *inter alia*: *CJEU*, 01.02.2001 – C-108/98 - Mac Quen = ECLI:EU:C:2001:67, para 26, *Tiedje* in: v. d. Groeben/Schwarze AEUV/EUV, Art. 49 TFEU, para 98 ff, *Schlag* in: Schwarze EU-Kommentar, Art. 49 TFEU, para 45 ff; *Oppermann/Classen et al.*, 5. Edn. (2011) § 28, para 33.

377 The German expression is "*Beschränkungsverbot*".

378 *Schlag* in: Schwarze EU-Kommentar, Art. 49 TFEU, para 36 ff; *Tiedje* in: v. d. Groeben/Schwarze AEUV/EUV, Art. 49 TFEU, para 75; *Tietje* in: Becker/Ehlers Europäische Grundfreiheiten (2014), § 10, para 52.

379 *Schlag* in: Schwarze EU-Kommentar, Art. 49 TFEU, para 45; *Tiedje* in: v. d. Groeben/Schwarze AEUV/EUV, Art. 49 TFEU, para 98.

380 *CJEU*, 12.07.1984 – C-107/83 - Klopp = ECLI:EU:C:1984:270.

381 *CJEU*, 12.12.2013 – C-327/12 - SOA Nazionale Costruttori = ECLI:EU:C:2013:827.

ferent tax rules applying based on the nationality of the company or its shareholders.[383]

Thus, restrictions through the regulatory environment to be applied on investments are clearly part of the measures which need to be justified as they impede on the freedom of establishment, regardless of whether this measure is indistinctly applied to nationals and non-nationals.[384] This sets a considerable protection framework for investors in the EU, if the freedom of establishment can be applied to them.

(b) Personal scope of application: individuals and entities being able to invoke the freedom of establishment

The freedom of establishment is guaranteed to each national of any member state, irrespective of its domicile.[385] Regarding investment protections, shareholders or other individuals being nationals of an EU member state and wanting to establish a new legal entity in the EU could invoke Art. 49 ff TFEU.[386] Investors having exclusively the nationality of a non-member state would need to rely on the free movement of capital (cf. *infra*). Art. 54 TFEU also guarantees the freedom of establishment to legal entities ("*companies or firms*"), which are formed according to the law of a member state and which have their *"registered office, central administration or principal place of business within the [European] Union"* [387]. Hence it also protects the legal entity itself which wants to extend its busi-

382 *CJEU*, 12.05.2005 – C-278/03 - Commission vs. Italy = ECLI:EU:C:2005:281; *CJEU*, 30.03.2006 – C-451/03 - Servizi Ausillari Dottori = ECLI:EU:C:2006:208.

383 *CJEU*, 21.11.2002 – C-436/00 - X and Y = ECLI:EU:C:2002:704, para 36; *Schlag* in: Schwarze EU-Kommentar, Art. 49 TFEU, para 49.

384 This seems to be misunderstood by the arbitral tribunal in *Achmea vs. Slovak Republic*, 26.10.2012 – PCA Case No. 2008-13 - Award on Jurisdiction, Arbitrability and Suspension, para 251 which still seems to focus on the element of discrimination instead of a general prohibition of unjustified restrictions.

385 *Hobe*, 8. Edn. (2014), para 780: whether the individual is also national of a third country, is irrelevant.

386 This somehow presents similarities to the overcoming of the limits in the *Barcelona Traction-Case* as to the rights of a legal entity and the possibility to invoke such rights for the shareholders. The TFEU – same as the IIA – personally attributes the rights to individuals wanting to perform an economic activity through a distinct legal entity.

387 Art. 54 (2) TFEU.

ness by either accessing another EU member state market itself or forming a subsidiary in another market.

The terms "*companies or firms*" are interpreted autonomously from the law of the EU member states.[388] The CJEU generally refers to all kind of legal entities, distinct from individuals, which perform an economic activity (other than those attributed to the public sphere).[389] The criteria of registered office, central administration or principal place of business are interpreted rather extensively.[390] Irrespective of certain limits which will be

---

388 *Jung* in: Schwarze EU-Kommentar, Art. 54 TFEU, para 2; *Forsthoff* in: Grabitz/Hilf/Nettesheim EUV/AEUV, Art. 49 TFEU, para 3; *Müller-Graff* in: Streinz EUV/AEUV, Art. 54 TFEU, para 2; *Oppermann/Classen et al.*, 5. Edn. (2011) § 28, para 13.

389 *Jung* in: Schwarze EU-Kommentar, Art. 54 TFEU, para 2; *Müller-Graff* in: Streinz EUV/AEUV, Art. 54 TFEU, para 2; *Forsthoff* in: Grabitz/Hilf/Nettesheim EUV/AEUV, Art. 49 TFEU, para 4 f; *Oppermann/Classen et al.*, 5. Edn. (2011) § 28, para 13. Entities which need to be attributed to the public sphere, as they are exercising sovereign rights, will be excluded (cf. Art. 51 TFEU), cf: also: *Tietje* in: Becker/Ehlers Europäische Grundfreiheiten (2014), § 10, para 43.

390 The requirement of performing an economic activity only relates to the aim to generate revenues, the entity does not necessarily need to be profit oriented, cf.: *Jung* in: Schwarze EU-Kommentar, Art. 54 TFEU, para 7 which refers to the exclusion of *inter alia* purely cultural, educational or philanthropic entities which are only engaged in the promotion of their respective aims without wanting to interfere by any means with the market; *Müller-Graff* in: Streinz EUV/AEUV, Art. 54 TFEU, para 2; *Oppermann/Classen et al.*, 5. Edn. (2011) § 28, para 13. The first criterion of registered offic) only refers to the seat of the entity as designated upon establishment. Other than the two criteria of central administration or principal place of business it refers to a formal link. This would also extend the application of Art. 49, 54 TFEU to offshore companies ("*Briefkastenfirmen*"), which do not exercise any real business in the EU member state, cf. for the further debate: *Jung* in: Schwarze EU-Kommentar, Art. 54 TFEU, para 16; *Forsthoff* in: Grabitz/Hilf/Nettesheim EUV/AEUV, Art. 49 TFEU, para 17; There remains considerable uncertainty with regard to the question if a purely offshore company would enjoy the freedom of establishment, cf. *Tietje* in: Becker/Ehlers Europäische Grundfreiheiten (2014), § 10, para 36a; also: *Jung*, NZG, 2008, 681, 682. The term central administration refers to the place where administration and / or supervisory board generally meet. The general principal place of business is conceived as the location of the major utilities and operating sources, cf.: *Jung* in: Schwarze EU-Kommentar, Art. 54 TFEU, para 15 f; *Tiedje* in: v. d. Groeben/Schwarze AEUV/EUV, Art. 54 TFEU, para 27 f. If one of these conditions is fulfilled, the registered office of the entity could even be designated to a non-member state.

addressed *infra* (Chapter 15), it can thus be concluded that from the perspective of investment protection, all legal entities having a business or at least the general administration within an EU member state will be able to invoke by the freedom of establishment upon further action (cf. *infra*). Even entities from non-member states may enjoy protection if they either create a subsidiary within an EU member state as a host state or if the registered office is in an EU member state.[391]

(c) Limitations to the freedom of establishment

The freedom of establishment is not an unlimited right. It may be restricted by either the EU or the member states, provided that several criteria are fulfilled. The European Treaties and the CJEU established an elaborated set of criteria differentiating between different types of measures limiting the fundamental freedoms:

First a fundamental freedom may be restricted by any measure which is based on an explicit exception which is foreseen in the European Treaties. For the freedom of establishment, limitations or restrictions may be based on Art. 52 TFEU. The article allows exceptions from the freedom of establishment for measures taken on grounds of public policy, public security or public health, if those measures are overall proportional to the goal they seek to implement. [392]

Second, the CJEU developed a further, unwritten, possibility to limit a fundamental freedom: Indistinctly applied restrictions to the freedom of establishment – hence excluding limitations which are discriminatory – may be admissible if they are justified

> "by imperative requirements in the general interest; […] suitable for securing the attainment of the objective which they pursue; and […] not go beyond what is necessary in order to attain it."[393] The test is somehow referred to as the "Cassis-

391 *Forsthoff* in: Grabitz/Hilf/Nettesheim EUV/AEUV, Art. 49 TFEU, para 17; *Tietje* in: Becker/Ehlers Europäische Grundfreiheiten (2014), § 10, para 36a.

392 *Schlag* in: Schwarze EU-Kommentar, Art. 52 TFEU, para 6; *Tiedje* in: v. d. Groeben/Schwarze AEUV/EUV, Art. 52 TFEU, para 14 ff: Being construed as exceptions, Art. 52 TFEU should *per se* be applied in a restrictive way; in addition, several further limitations apply: cf. *infra* (Chapter 15) for a deeper analysis thereof.

393 *CJEU*, 30.11.1995 – C-55/94 - Gebhard = ECLI:EU:C:1995:411, para 37; cf. also: *Oppermann/Classen et al.*, 5. Edn. (2011) § 28, para 36 ff.

de-Dijon-Formula"[394], as the test has primarily been conceived regarding the free movement of goods, or also as the *"rule of reason"*.[395]

The test implies a strict evaluation if the measure is necessary to fulfil an imperative requirement, if the measure is actually suitable to attaint this objective, if it is necessary to do so (which implies the absence of less hindering means) and if it is overall proportionate by balancing the importance of the requirement against the importance of the freedom of establishment in the concrete circumstances.[396]

Restrictions which do not fulfil either all criteria under Art. 52 TFEU or the rule of reason, are considered to be in breach of the freedom of establishment under Art. 49, 54 TFEU.[397] Like for all fundamental freedoms, the freedom of establishment might be limited or specifically regulated through secondary law (especially directives and regulations). Once issued, any member state measure then needs to comply with secondary law.[398] Within its scope of application, the secondary law blocks the possibility to immediately rely on Art. 49 TFEU. However, when issuing the directive or regulation, the EU itself is bound by respecting the fundamental freedom and limiting it only under the conditions explained *supra*.[399]

---

394 *CJEU*, 20.02.1979 – C-120/78 - Cassis de Dijon = ECLI:EU:C:1979:42, para 8 which introduces the possibility to justify an indistinctly applicable restriction by *"provisions [which] may be recognized as being necessary in order to satisfy mandatory requirements"*.

395 Cf. also: *Steiner/Woods et al.*, EU law, 9. Edn. (2006), p. 378 ff.

396 *Schlag* in: Schwarze EU-Kommentar, Art. 49 TFEU, para 48 f.

397 The current discussion on the question whether (indistinctly applied) particular policy measures of an EU member state, which only generally set the legal framework for exercising business in a member state also fall under the prohibition of restrictions will be treated *infra* (Chapter 15): with reference to the CJEU's decision in the *Keck-Case* (*CJEU*, 24.11.1993 – Joined Cases C-267/91 and C-268/91 - Keck = ECLI:EU:C:1993:905) related to the free movement of goods, several scholars argue that measures restricting the access to the internal market through restrictions of the freedom of establishment should be separated from measures only framing the exercise of economic operations within the market (*Marktzugangsbeschränkungen vs. reine Verkaufsmodalitäten / Ausübungsbeschränkungen*).

398 *Korte* in: Calliess/Ruffert EUV/AEUV, Art. 49 TFEU, para 59; *Oppermann/Classen et al.*, 5. Edn. (2011) § 22, para 6

399 *Ehlers* in: Becker/Ehlers Europäische Grundfreiheiten (2014), § 7, para 53; *Oppermann/Classen et al.*, 5. Edn. (2011) § 22, para 6; given the hierarchy of norms, this result is obvious, cf.: *Bieber/Epiney et al.*, Die Europäische Union, 11. Edn. (2015), p. 199 f.

(2) Free movement of capital

The free movement of capital in Art. 63 TFEU is one of the most relevant provisions in the European Treaties when it comes to protecting investments, either in the intra-EU or in the extra-EU context.[400] There are two reasons for this conclusion: Frist, the free movement of capital is the only one among the fundamental freedoms which also applies to individuals or entities from non-member states (b).[401] Second, the CJEU applies a very broad definition of the terms in Art. 63 TFEU which leads to an extensive protection range arising from this provision (a).[402]

(a) The type of action protected under Art. 63 TFEU

The term movement of capital is neither entirely defined by the European Treaties, nor by secondary legislation or the CJEU. The CJEU refers to the *"transfer of assets"*, which implies a very broad understanding.[403] The "*Capital directive*" 88/361/EEC[404] on the movement of capital provides a non-exhaustive nomenclature of what should be understood by movement of capital, which the CJEU usually refers to when defining the terms.[405] The terms mentioned in directive 88/361/EEC lead to the conclusion that the movement of capital includes all sorts of creation, establishment, transmission and somehow even use of pecuniary rights.[406] The directive e.g. refers to direct investments such as the *"[e]stablishment and extension of branches or new undertakings belonging solely to the person providing the capital, and the acquisition in full of existing undertakings*",

400 Cf. *inter alia*: *Hindelang/Maydell* in: *Bungenberg/Griebel/Hindelang* (Eds.), International investment law and EU law, 2011.

401 *Oppermann/Classen et al.*, 5. Edn. (2011) § 30, para 1; *Glaesner* in: Schwarze EU-Kommentar, Art. 63 TFEU, para 1.

402 *Oppermann/Classen et al.*, 5. Edn. (2011) § 30, para 7.

403 *Wilmowsky* in: Becker/Ehlers Europäische Grundfreiheiten (2014), § 12, para 2 f; *CJEU*, 23.02.1995 – Joined Cases C-358/93 and C-416/93 - Bordessa and others = ECLI:EU:C:1995:54, para 13.

404 Council Directive 88/361/EEC - Capital Directive, Official Journal of the European Communities L 178 (24.06.1988), 5

405 *Hobe*, 8. Edn. (2014), para 855; *Steiner/Woods et al.*, EU law, 9. Edn. (2006), p. 346; *Bröhmer* in: Calliess/Ruffert EUV/AEUV, Art. 63 TFEU, para 14 f.

406 *Wilmowsky* in: Becker/Ehlers Europäische Grundfreiheiten (2014), § 12, para 2; *Hobe*, 8. Edn. (2014), para 856.

participations within "*new or existing undertaking with a view to establishing or maintaining lasting economic links*", reinvestment of profits, long term loans, investments in real estate, dealing with or holding of shares, bonds or other financial instruments, insurances or even guarantees or securities provided.[407]

As soon as these assets by any means "*cross*" the border between EU member states or between third-states and EU member states, the protection under the "*free movement of capital*" applies.[408] It can easily be observed that typical foreign investment situations as conceived by IIAs, such as establishing a joint-venture, acquiring shares in a subsidiary, etc. are comprehensively covered by this definition of capital movement.

As for the freedom of establishment, the CJEU considers every discriminatory or indistinctly applied measure which hinders the free movement of capital or makes it less effective as an impediment on Art. 63 TFEU which needs to be justified.[409] Thus, Art. 63 TFEU generally prohibits any restriction on capital movement, even though it might be non-discriminatory.[410]

Prohibited restrictions may be *inter alia* the necessity for a prior approval or preconditions to acquire or sell private property, shares or any other kind of asset considered to be capital in terms of Art. 63 TFEU. Generally, the prohibition of restrictions also covers various regulatory

---

407 Annex I of the Council Directive 88/361/EEC - Capital Directive, Official Journal of the European Communities L 178 (24.06.1988), 5.

408 *Wilmowsky* in: Becker/Ehlers Europäische Grundfreiheiten (2014), § 12, para 3; *Glaesner* in: Schwarze EU-Kommentar, Art. 63 TFEU, para 17 f.

409 *Hobe*, 8. Edn. (2014), para 862; *Oppermann/Classen et al.*, 5. Edn. (2011) § 30, para 14; *Wilmowsky* in: Becker/Ehlers Europäische Grundfreiheiten (2014), § 12, para 6; *Bröhmer* in: Calliess/Ruffert EUV/AEUV, Art. 63 TFEU, para 48.

410 *Bröhmer* in: Calliess/Ruffert EUV/AEUV, Art. 63 TFEU, para 48; *Glaesner* in: Schwarze EU-Kommentar, Art. 63 TFEU, para 16 f; *Wojcik* in: v. d. Groeben/Schwarze AEUV/EUV, Art. 63 TFEU, para 14 f, who backs up the transferal of the *Dassonville-Doctrine* to Art. 63 TFEU by the similar wording in Art. 63 and Art. 34, 35 TFEU and regarding the exceptions to both fundamental freedoms. Furthermore, which is correct, the CJEU continuously applies considers that Art. 63 TFEU can be limited by reference to imperative requirements of general interest and applies the rule of reason (cf. for this: *CJEU*, 05.03.2002 – Joined Cases C-515/99 to C-524/99 - Reisch et al = ECLI:EU:C:2002:135). However, this test was designed to relieve the consequences of the general prohibition of restrictions, cf.: *Wojcik* in: v. d. Groeben/Schwarze AEUV/EUV, Art. 63 TFEU, para 15.

provisions by member states.[411] As an example, the prohibition to sell parts of a state-owned company to private investors or restraints in connection with such privatisations were judged to be restrictions under Art. 63 TFEU.[412] Tax law provisions which are in any way (indirectly discriminatory) or could even only hinder investments or make them less attractive have – on various occasions – been considered to be a restriction in terms of Art. 63 TFEU which needs further justification.[413] Whether this general protection is weakened through the overlap with other fundamental freedoms, especially the freedom of establishment, will be analysed *infra* (Chapter 15).[414]

(b) Personal scope of application

Art. 63 ff TFEU apply both to nationals from EU member states and to nationals from non-member states, irrespective of whether an individual or a legal entity wants to invoke the provisions.[415] Consequently, the scope of protection fully applies to all sort of investors from abroad wanting to invest in the EU and to all legal entities, irrespective of their concrete status,

---

411 *CJEU*, 21.10.2010 – C-81/09 - Idryma Typou = ECLI:EU:C:2010:622; cf. also: *Wojcik* in: v. d. Groeben/Schwarze AEUV/EUV, Art. 63 TFEU, para 19; In *CJEU*, 09.10.2014 – C-326/12 - van Caster = ECLI:EU:C:2014:2269, para 25 the CJEU held that, restrictions on the free movement of capital "*include those that are such as to discourage non-residents from making investments in a Member State or to discourage that Member State's residents from doing so in other States*" and consideres this to be settled case law; cf. also: *Oppermann/Classen et al.*, 5. Edn. (2011) § 30, para 14.

412 *CJEU*, 22.10.2013 – Joined cases C-105/12 to C-107/12- Essent = ECLI:EU:C:2013:677; cf. also: *Wojcik* in: v. d. Groeben/Schwarze AEUV/EUV, Art. 63 TFEU, para 29.

413 *Wojcik* in: v. d. Groeben/Schwarze AEUV/EUV, Art. 63 TFEU, para 37 ff. *CJEU*, 06.06.2000 – C-35/98 - Verkooijen = ECLI:EU:C:2000:294; *CJEU*, 18.12.2007 – C-436/06 - Groenfeldt = ECLI:EU:C:2007:820.

414 The question will be treated regaring extra-EU IIAs and the equivalence of protection under EU law. For an overview cf.: *Glaesner* in: Schwarze EU-Kommentar, Art. 63 TFEU, para 11; *Wojcik* in: v. d. Groeben/Schwarze AEUV/EUV, Art. 63 TFEU, para 62; *Khan/Eisenhut* in: von Heinegg/Vedder EUV/AEUV, Art. 63 TFEU, para 15.

415 *Hobe*, 8. Edn. (2014), para 861; *Wojcik* in: v. d. Groeben/Schwarze AEUV/EUV, Art. 63 TFEU, para 10; *Steiner/Woods et al.*, EU law, 9. Edn. (2006), p. 345; *Wilmowsky* in: Becker/Ehlers Europäische Grundfreiheiten (2014), § 12, para 4.

which are exercising their business in the EU.[416] *Wojcik* provides the pertinent example of a

> "(...) Brazilian investor, being domiciled in Mexico, investing in a property in the Netherlands and selling it to company in Singapore (...)[417]"

as being perfectly covered by the free movement of capital, although the only link to the EU is the *situs* of the property.[418]

(c) Limitations to the free movement of capital

Limitations to the free movement of capital may either be justified based on the provisions of Art. 63-65 and 75 TFEU, or, for indistinctly applied measures, based on the "*rule of reason/Cassis-de-Dijon-Doctrine*".[419]

Art. 64 and Art. 65 TFEU contain particular provisions to enable restrictions on the free movement of capital. Whereas Art. 64 (1) TFEU mainly contains a grandfathering rule for existing limitations, Art. 64 (2) and (3) TFEU enable restrictions on the free movement of capital with third countries if those are adopted following the ordinary legislative procedure (para 2) or in a specific procedure (para 3). Such restrictions are only enabled regarding particular types of capital movements.[420] Additionally, the general limits to such restrictions apply, *inter alia* the principle of non-discrimination and the test of proportionality regarding the restricting measure.[421] Art. 65 TFEU enables national measures in the domain of tax law or for the reasons of protecting public policy or public security. Additionally, Art. 66 TFEU generally admits restrictions to counter

---

416 *Wojcik* in: v. d. Groeben/Schwarze AEUV/EUV, Art. 63 TFEU, para 10; *Wilmowsky* in: Becker/Ehlers Europäische Grundfreiheiten (2014), § 12, para 1, 4.

417 *Wojcik* in: v. d. Groeben/Schwarze AEUV/EUV, Art. 63 TFEU, para 10.

418 *Wojcik* in: v. d. Groeben/Schwarze AEUV/EUV, Art. 63 TFEU, para 10.

419 *CJEU*, 03.02.1993 – C-148/91 - Veronica = ECLI:EU:C:1993:45, para 10-12; *Hobe*, 8. Edn. (2014), para 864; *Oppermann/Classen et al.*, 5. Edn. (2011) § 30, para 22 f; *Glaesner* in: Schwarze EU-Kommentar, Art. 63 TFEU, para 22 f.

420 The scope of application is limited to direct investments, establishments, the provision of financial services or the admission of securities to capital markets.

421 *Wojcik* in: v. d. Groeben/Schwarze AEUV/EUV, Art. 64 TFEU, para 21; *CJEU*, 13.05.2003 – C-463/00 - Commission vs. Spain = ECLI:EU:C:2003:272, para 72 and 73, „*However, the Court has also held that the requirements of public security, as a derogation from the fundamental principle of free movement of capital, must be interpreted strictly [...] and [that the restrictions] do not go beyond what is necessary for that purpose.*"

serious difficulties for the EU or the Eurozone. Neither Art. 66, nor Art. 64 (2), (3) TFEU have ever been used so far.[422] Lastly, Art. 75 TFEU enables the European Parliament and the European Council to restrict the free movement of capital if such a restriction is necessary to prevent or fight terrorism. The provision is mostly used to execute sanctions issued by the UN Security Council.[423]

(3) Free transfer of funds

Art. 63 (2) TFEU also guarantees the free transfer of funds to all EU member states and to all third countries. Free transfer of funds essentially relates to the payment of debts and the transfer of any currency (including electronic currencies) from one state to another.[424] Just as for the free movement of capital, the CJEU considers every measure hindering the free transfer of funds to be an impediment on Art. 63 (2) TFEU.[425]

The exceptions to the free transfer of funds are mainly identical with those to the free movement of capital. However, Art. 64 TFEU does not apply to the free transfer of funds. On thc other hand, Art. 143 f TFEU enable limitations to the free transfer of funds which do not apply to Art. 63 TFEU.[426]

(4) Free movement of goods and freedom to provide services

In matters not being covered by either the freedom of establishment or the free movement of capital, investors could potentially invoke the free movement of goods (Art. 34, 35 TFEU) and the freedom to provide services as well (Art. 56 TFEU). The free movement of goods generally refers to the unhindered circulation of those "*products which can be valued*

422 *Bröhmer* in: Calliess/Ruffert EUV/AEUV, Art. 66 TFEU, para 1.

423 *Bröhmer* in: Calliess/Ruffert EUV/AEUV, Art. 75 TFEU, para 1; cf. also: *CJEU*, 03.03.2009 – C-249/06 - Commission vs Sweden = E-CLI:EU:C:2009:119, para 32.

424 *Oppermann/Classen et al.*, 5. Edn. (2011) § 31, para 27; *Wilmowsky* in: Becker/Ehlers Europäische Grundfreiheiten (2014), § 12, para 5.

425 *Oppermann/Classen et al.*, 5. Edn. (2011) § 30, para 26 ff; *Wilmowsky* in: Becker/Ehlers Europäische Grundfreiheiten (2014), § 12, para 6.

426 *Wojcik* in: v. d. Groeben/Schwarze AEUV/EUV, Art. 63 TFEU, para 6.

in money and which are capable, as such, of forming the subject of commercial transactions".[427] The term goods also includes electricity and gas.[428] The freedom to provide services refers to activities which are immaterial, performed independently, provided for remuneration and which are not covered predominantly by any other of the fundamental freedoms.[429]

The scope of prohibitions as well as the requirements to limit the freedoms are basically identical to what has already been explained for the freedom of establishment and the free movement of capital (cf. *supra*).

The freedom to provide services could especially cover those situations in which the requirements for an establishment under Art. 49 TFEU are not fulfilled due to a relatively short-term investment or the scope of business not being of sufficient weight.[430] However, as both freedoms only apply to nationals or judicial persons of an EU-member state, they essentially might be invoked in either intra-EU investments or regarding state measures which try to interfere with an subsidiary established in an EU member state but owned by foreign investors.[431]

2. Charter of Fundamental Rights of the EU

Further protection for investments in the EU is guaranteed by the Charter of Fundamental Rights of the EU.

The Charter essentially establishes protections against sovereign measures either by the EU member states or by the EU itself. The business-related protection standards are integrated in Art. 15-17 of the Charter. Those articles guarantee the freedom to choose an occupation and right to engage in work (Art. 15 of the Charter), the freedom to conduct business (Art. 16 of the Charter) and the right to property (Art. 17 of the

427 *CJEU*, 21.10.1999 – C-97/98 - Jägerskiöld = ECLI:EU:C:1999:515.

428 *CJEU*, 27.04.1994 – C-393/92 - Almelo = ECLI:EU:C:1994:171, para 28.

429 *Holoubek* in: Schwarze EU-Kommentar, Art. 56, 57 TFEU, para 17 ff.

430 Cf. for the delimitation: *Tiedje* in: v. d. Groeben/Schwarze AEUV/EUV, Art. 49 TFEU, para 11 and *supra* (1).

431 This will only apply if the state measure potentially might affect intra-EU trade relations ("*grenzüberschreitender Bezug*"), which cannot be excluded at least for larger-scale investments which are not exclusively limited to the territory of one member state.

Charter). The guarantees provided therein can be considered as the fundamental pillars for economic protection within the EU.[432]

(1) Scope of application of the Charter (Art. 51 of the Charter)

The Charter, and hence the rights contained therein, are not unconditionally applied to all acts by all member states. The scope of application of the Charter is laid down in Art. 51 (1) of the Charter. It reads as follows:

> "The provisions of this Charter are addressed to the institutions and bodies of the Union with due regard for the principle of subsidiarity and to the Member States only when they are implementing Union law."

It clearly results from the provision that there is a difference with regard to the addressees under the Charter. The organs and institutions or other bodies of the EU need to comply with the provisions of the Charter by all means and whenever they act.[433] Hence, all acts directly issued by those institutions, bodies, offices and agencies, including *inter alia* secondary regulations and directives but also decisions on state aids by e.g. the European Commission, need to respect the fundamental freedoms and rights guaranteed by the Charter.[434]

Member states are not bound to the same extent by the provisions of the Charter. However, they need to respect the Charter, whenever they are "*implementing European Union law*". The interpretation given to the two terms "*implementing*" and *"European Union law"* considerably influences the degree to which the member states are deemed to respect the rights and guarantees of the Charter.[435] Both terms were recently interpreted in a very extensive way by the CJEU, which extends the application of the Charter to a nearly exhaustive set of potential actions which somehow refer to EU law. As to the CJEU, the term "*European Union law*" is not

---

432 *Wollenschläger* in: v. d. Groeben/Schwarze AEUV/EUV, Preface to Art. 15-16 of the Charter, para 1.

433 *Terhechte* in: v. d. Groeben/Schwarze AEUV/EUV, Art. 51 of the Charter, para 5 ff; *Borowsky* in: Meyer (Ed.) Charta der Grundrechte der EU, Art. 51 of the Charter, para 19.

434 Cf. also: *Terhechte* in: v. d. Groeben/Schwarze AEUV/EUV, Art. 51 of the Charter, para 5 f; *Jarass*, EU-Grundrechte, 2005, p. 35.

435 *Oppermann/Classen et al.*, 5. Edn. (2011) § 17, para 13; *Jarass*, EU-Grundrechte, 2005, p. 38; *Franzius*, ZaöVR, 2015, 383, 385 - 387.

meant to limit the scope of application of the Charter. [436] It refers to all kinds of primary and secondary law.[437] This might include the European Treaties and the Charter itself (as primary law), as well as regulations and directives but also all additional forms of interaction which are conceived in Art. 289 TFEU or might be conceived in future provisions.

With regard to the term "*implementing*", the CJEU dismissed attempts in literature and among other courts to interpret this term in a more restrictive way.[438] In the *Fransson-Case*[439] and the subsequent judgements, the

436 *Terhechte* in: v. d. Groeben/Schwarze AEUV/EUV, Art. 51 of the Charter, para 8; *Borowsky* in: Meyer (Ed.) Charta der Grundrechte der EU, Art. 51 of the Charter, para 26.

437 *Terhechte* in: v. d. Groeben/Schwarze AEUV/EUV, Art. 51 of the Charter, para 8; *Borowsky* in: Meyer (Ed.) Charta der Grundrechte der EU, Art. 51 of the Charter, para 26.

438 It has been argued that the term "*implementing*" in Art. 51 (1) of the Charter should contradict this jurisprudence and considerably limit the scope of application of the Charter to those situations in which EU member states execute EU law as a public authority for the EU, cf.: *Borowsky* in: Meyer (Ed.) Charta der Grundrechte der EU, Art. 51 of the Charter, para 24 ff; *Kingreen* in: Calliess/Ruffert EUV/AEUV, Art. 51 of the Charter, para 17; *Streinz/Michl* in: Streinz EUV/AEUV, Art. 51 of the Charter, para 7 ff, especially, para 9 pleading that the transposition of directives should not be considered as "*implementing*" EU law; *Cremer*, NVwZ, 2003, 1452, 1455; for an exhaustive overview of the different positions: *Heuer*, Art. 51 Abs. 1 Satz 1 GRC: Die Bindung der Mitgliedstaaten an die Unionsgrundrechte, 2014, p. 156 ff. Others, stated that the term needs to be interpreted in the light of the ERTA-Jurisprudence and is not meant to limit the scope of appication, cf.: *CJEU*, 12.11.1969 – C-29/69 - Stauder = ECLI:EU:C:1969:57; *CJEU*, 17.12.1970 – C-11/70 - Internationale Handelsgesellschaft = ECLI:EU:C:1970:114; cf. also: *Hobe*, 8. Edn. (2014), para 650; *Oppermann/Classen et al.*, 5. Edn. (2011) § 17, para 13.

439 *CJEU*, 26.12.2013 – C-617/10 - Hans Åkerberg Fransson = ECLI:EU:C:2013:105. The preliminary ruling in the case was related to a Swedish citizen having incorrectly declared its revenues in the tax declarations regarding the Swedish VAT. The citizen was first 'punished' by being order to pay a tax surcharge as administrative penalty. Later, the same conduct was at the origin of criminal proceedings initiated against the citizen based on tax fraud (potentially) leading to a sentence of imprisonment. The Swedish Court doubted if the tax fraud provision in Swedish national law is contrary to the principle of *ne bis in idem* (Art. 50 of the Charter), expressing considerable doubts as to the applicability of the Charter to the case as the provisions dealt with are in no way the consequence of binding provisions in EU primary or secondary law. The CJEU however stated: "*Since the fundamental rights guaranteed by the Charter must therefore be complied with where national legislation falls within the scope of EU law, situations cannot exist which are covered*

CJEU sharpened the term interpretation of the term "*implementing*" as follows[440]:

> "(…) the concept of 'implementing Union law', as referred to in Article 51 of the Charter, requires a certain degree of connection above and beyond the matters covered being closely related or one of those matters having an indirect impact on the other.
>
> In order to determine whether national legislation involves the implementation of EU law for the purposes of Article 51 of the Charter, some of the points to be determined are whether that legislation is intended to implement a provision of EU law; the nature of that legislation and whether it pursues objectives other than those covered by EU law, even if it is capable of indirectly affecting EU law; and also whether there are specific rules of EU law on the matter or capable of affecting it (…)"[441]

A provision should not be considered to implement EU law if the later does not "*impose any obligation on Member States with regard to the situation at issue*".[442] Hence, although the CJEU defines limits as to the scope of the term "*implementing*" in Art. 51 (1) of the Charter, the overall scope of actions remains considerably large.[443] According to the CJEU, the Charter is binding on the EU member states whenever:

- the state measure is mandatory under EU law[444] *or*
- the state measure limits fundamental freedoms, as such limitations can only be justified if they also comply with the rights and guarantees of the Charter[445] *or*

---

in that way by EU law without those fundamental rights being applicable. The applicability of EU law entails applicability of the fundamental rights guaranteed by the Charter", cf.: *CJEU*, 26.12.2013 – C-617/10 - Hans Åkerberg Fransson = ECLI:EU:C:2013:105, para 21. For a further analysis of the doubts the decision raised before the following judgements *CJEU*, 06.03.2014 – C-206/13 - Siragusa = ECLI:EU:C:2014:126 and *CJEU*, 10.07.2014 – C-198/13 - Hernández = ECLI:EU:C:2014:2055: *Wegner*, HRRS, 2013, 126.

440 *CJEU*, 06.03.2014 – C-206/13 - Siragusa = ECLI:EU:C:2014:126, para 24 ff.

441 *CJEU*, 06.03.2014 – C-206/13 - Siragusa = ECLI:EU:C:2014:126, para 24 and 25.

442 *CJEU*, 06.03.2014 – C-206/13 - Siragusa = ECLI:EU:C:2014:126, para 26 repeated in *CJEU*, 10.07.2014 – C-198/13 - Hernández = ECLI:EU:C:2014:2055, para 35.

443 *Jarass*, EU-Grundrechte, 2005, p. 38-41.

444 *Terhechte* in: v. d. Groeben/Schwarze AEUV/EUV, Art. 51 of the Charter, para 10; *Ehlers* in: Becker/Ehlers Europäische Grundfreiheiten (2014), § 14, para 74-76.

- in all other cases where the state measure is somehow related to EU law by its objective, by the intention to implement EU law or even if it only indirectly affects provisions of EU law as long as the specific characteristics of EU law such as the principle of supremacy, the direct effect or the autonomy are questioned.[446]

Consequently, not all state measures ordered by EU member states fall under the scope of the Charter. A considerable amount of actions will only be controlled *vis-à-vis* the national constitutions and potential fundament rights guaranteed therein. However, this thesis focusses on potential interferences and/or conflicts of IIAs and EU law when a state measure undertaken towards the investor is challenged before an arbitral tribunal. If EU law is not in question at all in those proceedings, the conflict will not rise. However, in those questions where a potential conflict is in question (those situations will be demonstrated in Chapter 5), at least the CJEU's third criteria is fulfilled and the state measure also needs to comply with the rights and guarantees contained in the Charter.

(2) Freedom to conduct business (Art. 16 of the Charter)

Through its large scale of application, Art. 16 of the Charter features essential guarantees for investors and investments and their businesses in the EU member state as a host state. The freedom to conduct business in Art. 16 of the Charter guarantees all business and enterprises, irrespective of whether they are natural persons or legal entities, the right to freely conduct their business. It protects all kinds of economic businesses or enterprises, which should include, all entities regardless of their legal status or their mode of financing, as long as the economical or commercial activity is pursued for a certain timeframe and provided against any sort of remuneration.[447]

---

445 *Terhechte* in: v. d. Groeben/Schwarze AEUV/EUV, Art. 51 of the Charter, para 10; *Ehlers* in: Becker/Ehlers Europäische Grundfreiheiten (2014), § 14, para 75.

446 *CJEU*, 10.07.2014 – C-198/13 - Hernández = ECLI:EU:C:2014:2055, para 37; *Terhechte* in: v. d. Groeben/Schwarze AEUV/EUV, Art. 51 of the Charter, para 11; *Ehlers* in: Becker/Ehlers Europäische Grundfreiheiten (2014), § 14, para 77; *Jarass/Beljin*, NVwZ, 2004, 1, 6-10.

447 Cf.: *Jarass*, 2. Edn. (2013) Art. 16, para 7; the definition is based on the interpretation of the term undertaking in Art. 101 TFEU. Discussions remain as to

The material scope of protection under Art. 16 of the Charter extends to the freedom to engage in business, the contractual autonomy and the freedom of competition.[448]

The freedom to engage in business encompasses the right to start or end a business (*if* to conduct business) as well as the right to conduct it unhindered (*how* to conduct business).[449] The latter also includes the protection of an established position within the market and a certain degree of conformity, transparency and stability for the undertakings in their economic and strategic planning.[450] This may even extend to the protection against enforcing undue or unfair costs for conducting the business or altering the substance of a business[451], a protection which seems to be very similar to what is guaranteed under the FET or indirect expropriation standard under an IIA (cf. *infra* Chapter 15). For certain circumstances, the freedom to

---

the demarcation of Art. 16 and Art. 15 of the Charter (freedom to choose an occupation). Several scholars consider both to form a uniform right, with Art. 16 of the Charter being *lex specialis* to Art. 15 if the conditions of Art. 16 are fulfilled, cf.: *Wollenschläger* in: v. d. Groeben/Schwarze AEUV/EUV, Preface to Art. 15-16 of the Charter, para 6; *Jarass*, 2. Edn. (2013), para 4a; *Ruffert* in: Becker/Ehlers Europäische Grundfreiheiten (2014), § 19, para 11; others suggest that Art. 15 refers to interferences with personal implications on the beneficiary, whereas Art. 16 should remain for all other types of interferences. The jurisprudence of the CJEU does not clearly differentiate between both articles so far.

448 *CJEU*, 22.01.2013 – C-283/11 - Sky Österreich = ECLI:EU:C:2013:28, para 42; *Jarass*, 2. Edn. (2013) Art. 16, para 8; further discussion as to the wording of Art. 16 of the Charter and the question whether the scope of guarantees is subject to the protection guaranteed by the national legislation should be considered obsolete after the recent decisions issued by the CJEU which clearly demonstrate that any limitation to Art. 16 of the Charter needs to be justified by a public interest and the principle of proportionality, e.g. *CJEU*, 22.01.2013 – C-283/11 - Sky Österreich = ECLI:EU:C:2013:28, para 45 ff; cf. also: *Wollenschläger* in: v. d. Groeben/Schwarze AEUV/EUV, Preface to Art. 15-16 of the Charter, para 6.

449 *Jarass*, 2. Edn. (2013) Art. 16, para 9; *Everson/Goncalves* in: Peers, Hervey et al. - European Union Charter of Fundamental Rights, Art. 16 of the Charter, para 16.34.

450 *CJEU*, 05.10.1994 – C-280/93 - Germany vs. Council = ECLI:EU:C:1994:367, para 80 f; *Everson/Goncalves* in: Peers, Hervey et al. - European Union Charter of Fundamental Rights, Art. 16 of the Charter, para 16.36.

451 *Opinion of Advocate General Bot in C-283/11 - Sky Austria*, C-283/11 - Sky Austria, para 37; affirmed by the CJEU in: *CJEU*, 22.01.2013 – C-283/11 - Sky Österreich = ECLI:EU:C:2013:28, para 45 ff.; *CJEU*, 22.01.2013 – C-283/11 - Sky Österreich = ECLI:EU:C:2013:28, para 43.

conduct business also extends to the freedom of competition by protecting an entity having obtained a settled market position[452] or against influences to the (economic and) competitive landscape for a business.[453]

However, Art. 16 of the Charter does not guarantee unlimited rights. Limitations can be justified if they are in line with Art. 52 (1) of the Charter. This requires any limitation to be based on law (either primary or secondary legislation or any provision of the law of the member states) and a legitimate interest to be pursued to limit the freedom. Furthermore, Art. 52 (1) 2 of the Charter requires the limitation to respect the principle of proportionality. Thus, the limitation needs to be suitable to pursue the legitimate interest, necessary to obtain it and appropriate "*in order to attain the objectives legitimately pursued by the legislation in question*".[454] As a consequence, state measures affecting various domains of how to conduct the business (and i.e. an investment in any EU member state) are subject to the guarantees provided in Art. 16 of the Charter and are thus subject to a strict control based on the principles laid down in Art. 52 (1) 2 of the Charter.

(3) Right to property (Art. 17 of the Charter)

Art. 17 of the Charter, the right to property, is considered to be one of the most essential provisions to protect individuals and hence investors against interventionist measures by either the EU or the member states, e.g. when it comes to balance the public interest, such as the fostering of competition, and private interests of economic operators.[455] Examples might *inter alia* be the regulations relating to unbundling provisions in the

---

452 *CJEU*, 05.10.1994 – C-280/93 - Germany vs. Council = ECLI:EU:C:1994:367, para 81.

453 This would e.g. apply to measures implementing Art. 101 ff. TFEU as they might heavily alter the competitive landscape of a business, cf.: *Wollenschläger* in: v. d. Groeben/Schwarze AEUV/EUV, Art. 16 of the Charter, para 8; *Bernsdorff* in: Meyer (Ed.) Charta der Grundrechte der EU, Art. 16 of the Charter, para 14; *Jarass*, 2. Edn. (2013) Art. 16, para 9.

454 *CJEU*, 22.01.2013 – C-283/11 - Sky Österreich = ECLI:EU:C:2013:28, para 50; *Jarass*, 2. Edn. (2013), Art. 16, para 21 ff; *Blanke* in: Stern/Sachs EU GrCH, Art. 16 of the Charter, para 16; *Bernsdorff* in: Meyer (Ed.) Charta der Grundrechte der EU, Art. 16 of the Charter, para 15.

455 *Wollenschläger* in: v. d. Groeben/Schwarze AEUV/EUV, Art. 16 of the Charter, para 1.

energy sector (cf. *infra Chapter 5, B.*), limitations of the free transfer of payments / funds or free movement of capital and general competition law (Art. 101 ff TFEU).[456]

(a) The scope of protection ratione personae: protected individuals and entities

The right may be invoked by any individual or legal persons, regardless of the place of residence, the registered office or the nationality. Only public law bodies or public undertakings are excluded from the personal scope of protection guaranteed under Art. 17 of the Charter.[457] Hence, *ab initio*, each and every investor in an EU member state may rely on the right to property.[458]

(b) The scope of protection ratione materiae: right to property

The right to property in Art. 17 of the Charter provides similar protection as the provisions in IIAs protecting against unlawful expropriation. However, Art. 17 of the Charter generally protects the right to property, against all kinds of measures (not only against the complete deprivation of the right to property, i.e. an expropriation). On the other hand the definition of property might be different in an IIA compared to the Charter. This will be assessed in detail *infra* (Chapter 15).

The term property in terms of Art. 17 (1) of the Charter needs to refer to an autonomous definition of property by EU law.[459] Consequently, even rights which are not recognised as "*property*" by the law or constitution of the member states, may constitute property in terms of Art. 17 of the Char-

---

456 Cf. also: *Wollenschläger* in: v. d. Groeben/Schwarze AEUV/EUV, Art. 16 of the Charter, para 1.

457 *Wollenschläger* in: Peers, Hervey et al. - European Union Charter of Fundamental Rights, Art. 17 (1) of the Charter, para 17(1).14

458 There is a substantial debate regarding the interference of Art. 345 TFEU with Art. 17 of the Charter, this will be dealt with *infra* (Chapter 15).

459 *Wollenschläger* in: Peers, Hervey et al. - European Union Charter of Fundamental Rights, Art. 17 (1) of the Charter, para 17(1). 15; *Wollenschläger* in: v. d. Groeben/Schwarze AEUV/EUV, Art. 17 of the Charter, para 8.

ter.[460] The term is generally defined as all pecuniary rights exclusively assigned to the individual for its private use and interest.[461] It appears from the recent case-law, especially the *Sky Austria Case*[462], that the CJEU would strengthen the requirement of (final) personal attribution to qualify a right as property in terms of Art. 17 of the Charter.[463]

The property needs to be lawfully acquired to be protected by Art. 17 of the Charter. [464] The protection refers to the possession of property, its use and the right to dispose of it at any time.[465]

The most critical question regarding the scope of Art. 17 of the Charter for the protection of economic activities is the question whether the enterprise, economic activity, market position and the good-will are protected as such by Art. 17 of the Charter. The question is matter of intense debates and of particular importance for the scope of protection offered to investors in an EU member state.[466] The general guideline can be described as follows:

The general interference with a certain market position, with general and unspecified business opportunities as well as the altering of chances or

460 *Bernsdorff* in: Meyer (Ed.) Charta der Grundrechte der EU, Art. 17 of the Charter, para 15.

461 *Wollenschläger* in: Peers, Hervey et al. - European Union Charter of Fundamental Rights, Art. 17 (1) of the Charter, para 17(1).16; *Jarass*, 2. Edn. (2013), Art. 17, para 6.

462 *CJEU*, 22.01.2013 – C-283/11 - Sky Österreich = ECLI:EU:C:2013:28.

463 *CJEU*, 22.01.2013 – C-283/11 - Sky Österreich = ECLI:EU:C:2013:28, para 34: "*rights with an asset value creating an established legal position under the legal system, enabling the holder to exercise those rights autonomously and for his benefit.*"; cf. also: *Jarass*, 2. Edn. (2013) Art. 17, para 6.

464 As to the prevailing opinion this only requires the possession to be legally valid under the law of the member states. It however does not relate to any further illegality, even if the legally valid acquisition results from any illegality, cf.: *Wollenschläger* in: Peers, Hervey et al. - European Union Charter of Fundamental Rights, Art. 17 (1) of the Charter, para 17(1).18; *Bernsdorff* in: Meyer (Ed.) Charta der Grundrechte der EU, Art. 17 of the Charter, para 16; *Jarass*, 2. Edn. (2013), Art. 17, para 7.

465 *Bernsdorff* in: Meyer (Ed.) Charta der Grundrechte der EU, Art. 17 of the Charter, para 17; *Wollenschläger* in: Peers, Hervey et al. - European Union Charter of Fundamental Rights, Art. 17 (1) of the Charter, para 17(1).24; *Jarass*, 2. Edn. (2013) Art. 17, para 15.

466 *Bernsdorff* in: Meyer (Ed.) Charta der Grundrechte der EU, Art. 17 of the Charter, para 14 ff; *Wollenschläger* in: Peers, Hervey et al. - European Union Charter of Fundamental Rights, Art. 17 (1) of the Charter, para 17(1).20 ff; *Jarass*, 2. Edn. (2013) Art. 17, para 10 ff.

economic interests does not constitute property in the sense of Art. 17 of the Charter.[467] This also excludes market shares.[468] However, those general interferences with the market activity and the business activity are protected under Art. 16 of the Charter (cf. *supra "(2) Freedom to conduct business (Art. 16 of the Charter)"*). Hence, the economic enterprise or the estate as such are not protected under Art. 17 of the Charter. The protection is only granted under two conditions: either an impediment with the substance of the enterprise (its facilities, assets or the place of production)[469] or the degree of interference sums up to such a considerable de-

---

467 *Wollenschläger* in: Peers, Hervey et al. - European Union Charter of Fundamental Rights, Art. 17 (1) of the Charter, para 17(1).20: *Jarass*, 2. Edn. (2013) Art. 17, para 11 and 14; *Wollenschläger* in: v. d. Groeben/Schwarze AEUV/EUV, Art. 17 of the Charter, para 14 ff; cf. *inter alia*: *CJEU*, 18.03.1980 – Joined cases 154/78, 205/78 et al - SpA Ferriera Valsabbia = ECLI:EU:C:1980:81, para 89: *"the guarantee afforder to the ownership of property cannot be extended to protect commercial interests, the uncertainties of which are part of the very essence of economic activity (...)"*. Such uncertain rights need to be opposed to rights granted under public law schemes, such as benefits from social securities or concessions, authorizations or back-payments of taxes, which are qualified as property in the sense of Art. 17 of the Charter. This requires however that either those rights were granted in return for any (monetary or non-monetary) contribution or, alternatively, protected by legitimate expectations of the owner (protection of *acquired rights*), cf.: *Bernsdorff* in: Meyer (Ed.) Charta der Grundrechte der EU, Art. 17 of the Charter, para 15; *Jarass*, 2. Edn. (2013) Art. 17, para 10 f; and 14 *CJEU*, 23.02.1995 – Joined Cases C-358/93 and C-416/93 - Bordessa and others = ECLI:EU:C:1995:54, para 50: *"transfer for consideration would confer on undertakings purchasing quotas ownership over them"; European Court of Human Rights*, 29.11.1991 – Application no. 12742/87 - Pine Valley *"When Pine Valley purchased the site, it did so in reliance on the permission which had been duly recorded in a public register kept for the purpose and which it was perfectly entitled to assume was valid. That permission amounted to a favourable decision as to the principle of the proposed development, which could not be reopened by the planning authority (see paragraph 29 above). In these circumstances it would be unduly formalistic to hold that the Supreme Court's decision did not constitute an interference [with the right to property]. Until it was rendered, the applicants had at least a legitimate expectation of being able to carry out their proposed development and this has to be regarded, for the purposes of Article 1 of Protocol No. 1 (P1-1), as a component part of the property in question (...)." [footnotes omitted].*

468 *Wollenschläger* in: v. d. Groeben/Schwarze AEUV/EUV, Art. 17 of the Charter, para 14.

469 *Wollenschläger* in: Peers, Hervey et al. - European Union Charter of Fundamental Rights, Art. 17 (1) of the Charter, para 17(1).20: *Jarass*, 2. Edn. (2013)

gree that the exercise of any (reasonable) economic activity becomes impossible.[470] All other measures will be evaluated with regard to Art. 16 of the Charter.[471]

Despite these restrictions, the right of property under Art. 17 of the Charter, conjointly read with the protection offered under Art. 16 of the Charter, covers wide fields of essential interactions of the member states and the EU with investors. Especially the guarantees provided with regard to detrimental interferences with the undertaking or the revocation of public rights, cover situations which constitute basic features of foreign investments (such as e.g. granted concessions, etc.).

(c) Limitations, restrictions and justifications

According to Art. 17 of the Charter, the right to property can be limited in three different ways: either by deprivation of its possession (expropriation) or by regulating the use of property or by other (factual) impediments on the right to property.

(i) Direct and indirect expropriations and its requirements for lawfulness

The possibility for public authorities to expropriate the owner is recognised by Art. 17 (1) 2 of the Charter. However, expropriation is subject to strict prerequisites to be considered lawful. The systematic approach is similar to the protection accorded by an IIA. The major criteria are the following:

Art. 17, para 12; *Wollenschläger* in: v. d. Groeben/Schwarze AEUV/EUV, Art. 17 of the Charter, para 16.

470 *Jarass*, 2. Edn. (2013) Art. 17, para 12; *Vosgerau* in: Stern/Sachs EU GrCH, Art. 17 of the Charter, para 35; *Wollenschläger* in: Peers, Hervey et al. - European Union Charter of Fundamental Rights, Art. 17 (1) of the Charter, para 17(1).20; *Wollenschläger* in: v. d. Groeben/Schwarze AEUV/EUV, Art. 17 of the Charter, para 16; *a contrario* from *CJEU*, 18.03.1980 – Joined cases 154/78, 205/78 et al - SpA Ferriera Valsabbia = ECLI:EU:C:1980:81, para 89: "*(...) Morover, it should be noted that no close of an undertaking as a result of the application of [the regulation] has been recorded (...)*".

471 Cf. *inter alia*: *Jarass*, 2. Edn. (2013), para 4 and 12; *Vosgerau* in: Stern/Sachs EU GrCH, Art. 17 of the Charter, para 32-35.

- Any expropriation needs to be based on a precise legal basis which sets forth the major modalities of the expropriation.[472]
- The expropriation needs to be justified by a public interest and comply with the test of proportionality laid down in Art. 52 (1) of the Charter: thus the deprivation needs to be suitable to pursue the public interest, necessary to obtain it and appropriate compared to the interest pursued.[473]
- A due compensation needs to be paid in return to the expropriation: the compensation needs to be "*fair*", which refers to the amount, and such amount needs to be paid in good time (cf. Art. 17 (1) 2 of the Charter).[474]

As in the context of an IIA, expropriations can be formal or *de facto*. A formal expropriation consists of a transfer of ownership by a "*measure completely and errantly depriving the owner of her/his ownership*"[475].[476] *De facto* expropriation are measures which, similar to the IIA context, leave the formal right of property to the owner but the effects of the measure are equivalent to a formal expropriation by the severity of the re-

472 *Wollenschläger* in: Peers, Hervey et al. - European Union Charter of Fundamental Rights, Art. 17 (1) of the Charter, para 17(1).39.

473 *Jarass*, 2. Edn. (2013) Art. 17, para 28; cf. also: *Wollenschläger* in: Peers, Hervey et al. - European Union Charter of Fundamental Rights, Art. 17 (1) of the Charter, para 17(1).40; *Wollenschläger* in: v. d. Groeben/Schwarze AEUV/EUV, Art. 17 of the Charter, para 33. When balancing the interests in order to determine whether the expropriation can be considered as lawful, one needs to bear in mind that the complete deprivation of property is the hardest possible interference with the right to property and thus requires a considerable public interest to be justified, cf.: *Jarass*, 2. Edn. (2013) Art. 17, para 28.

474 This is generally understood to be a reference to the *Hull-Formula*: *Bernsdorff* in: Meyer (Ed.) Charta der Grundrechte der EU, Art. 17 of the Charter, para 20; *Jarass*, 2. Edn. (2013) Art. 17, para 29; The fair amount should – in principal – be conceived by reference to the market value of the expropriated property. Exceptions to the payment of the full market value may be accepted if justified by fundamental public interest. Such derogations will only be admitted referring to particular circumstances and the extent to which the market value is undershot needs to be reasonable, cf.: *Jarass*, 2. Edn. (2013) Art. 17, para 29; *Wollenschläger* in: v. d. Groeben/Schwarze AEUV/EUV, Art. 17 of the Charter, para 34.

475 *Wollenschläger* in: Peers, Hervey et al. - European Union Charter of Fundamental Rights, Art. 17 (1) of the Charter, para 17(1).32.

476 *Jarass*, 2. Edn. (2013) Art. 17, para 18; *Calliess* in: Becker/Ehlers Europäische Grundfreiheiten (2014), § 20, para 29 f; *Vosgerau* in: Stern/Sachs EU GrCH, Art. 17 of the Charter, para 60-62.

strictions and the implications a measure has on the use, possession or disposal of the property.[477]

(ii) Other limitations to the right of property and its justifications

Besides formal or *de facto* expropriations, the right to property can be limited either by regulations of the use of property (Art. 17 (1) 3 of the Charter) or by factual impediments on the right to property by either the EU or the member state.

Regulatory measures as conceived by Art. 17 (1) 3 of the Charter refer to normative regulations which prohibit or require to use property in a particular way, without being qualified as expropriation. Such regulations could be, *inter alia*, the prohibition to use a property in a particular way[478], prohibitions to rent a property or the freezing of money on bank accounts[479].[480]

Regulations of the use of property or factual impediments can generally only be justified when based on law and passing the test of proportionality. [481] In addition, the legal / administrative proceedings in the context of regulating the right to property need to satisfy the requirements of a due process.[482] Regulations having major consequences on particular property

477 *Jarass*, 2. Edn. (2013) Art. 17, para 18 f and references above, cf. para 19: "*the owner needs to be deprived of any useful exploitation of its property rights*".

478 *CJEU*, 13.12.1978 – C-44/79 - Hauer = ECLI:EU:C:1979:290, para 19 for the prohibition of new plantings on an imovable property.

479 *CJEU*, 21.09.2005 – T-306/01 - Yusuf = ECLI:EU:T:2005:331, para 299 for the freezing of funds as a precautionary measure constituting a regulation of the use of property but not an expropriation.

480 Cf. also: *Jarass*, 2. Edn. (2013) Art. 17, para 20; *Calliess* in: Becker/Ehlers Europäische Grundfreiheiten (2014), § 20, para 27 f.

481 *Jarass*, 2. Edn. (2013) Art. 17, para 42 f; cf. also but in the context of Art. 17 (1) 2 of the Charter: *Bernsdorff* in: Meyer (Ed.) Charta der Grundrechte der EU, Art. 17 of the Charter, para 21. The impediment needs to be proportional. If the consequences are close to a *de facto* expropriation, the test of proportionality may require either transitory measures or even the payment of compensation, cf. *Jarass*, 2. Edn. (2013) Art. 17, para 42 f.

482 *Jarass*, 2. Edn. (2013) Art. 17, para 38; *Wollenschläger* in: Peers, Hervey et al. - European Union Charter of Fundamental Rights, Art. 17 (1) of the Charter, para 17(1).57.

rights may not be enacted without prior hearing the addressee of the measure.[483]

3. Other principles, including the general principles of EU law and principles of access to justice and due process / relief

The substantive guarantees (i.e. the fundamental freedoms and the rights issued from the Charter) are flanked by procedural guarantees, also conceived as subjective rights attributed to the individual or legal entity, to ensure the proper and fair application of EU law during legal remedies (for the legal remedies cf. "*IV. Legal remedies: judicial review as conceived under* EU law")). Among these provisions, Art. 47 of the Charter and Art. 19 TEU can be conceived as the cornerstones of procedural guarantees.

As to Art. 19 TEU, Art. 47 (1) of the Charter, the EU member states are obliged to establish sufficient (national) legal remedies to ensure proper application of EU law in all member states and to guarantee that the individual might challenge any act potentially harmful to any individual rights conferred on him ("*arguable claim*"). Art. 47 (1) of the Charter grants a subjective, claimable right to the individual or legal entity in case of non-respect of the obligation from Art. 19 TEU.[484]

---

483 *Jarass*, 2. Edn. (2013) Art. 17, para 38; *CJEU*, 03.09.2008 – Joined Cases C-402/05 P and C-415/05 P - Kadi = ECLI:EU:C:2008:461, para 368 ff: *"It is to be borne in mind in this respect that the applicable procedures must also afford the person concerned a reasonable opportunity of putting his case to the competent authorities. In order to ascertain whether this condition, which constitutes a procedural requirement inherent in Article 1 of Protocol No 1 to the ECHR, has been satisfied, a comprehensive view must be taken of the applicable procedures." (...) The contested regulation, in so far as it concerns Mr Kadi, was adopted without furnishing any guarantee enabling him to put his case to the competent authorities, in a situation in which the restriction of his property rights must be regarded as significant (...) It must therefore be held that [the regulation] constitutes an unjustified restriction of his right to property*" ; cf. also: *CJEU*, 30.09.2010 – T-85/09 - Kadi = ECLI:EU:T:2010:418, para 192 ff.

484 *Jarass*, 2. Edn. (2013) Art. 47, para 3; *Streinz* in: Streinz EUV/AEUV, Art. 47 of the Charter, para 1.

The legal remedies provided need to be effective. This includes, access to justice and a fair process.[485]

In this regard, the CJEU developed two principles which are now reinforced in Art. 47 of the Charter: the *principle of effectiveness*[486] and *equivalence*[487]. The principle of effectiveness ensures that no rule of national law – irrespective whether it is applied in a legislative, judicial or administrative procedure – should, even temporarily, prevent EU law from "*having full force and effect*".[488] The principle of equivalence however, ensures that the administrative procedures and judicial remedies to implement and properly apply EU law should be at least as favourable as those regarding provisions of national law.[489]

Both principles are supposed to guarantee that the formal possibility to challenge any act is duly respected and EU law is fully applied within the member states. Administrative or judicial proceedings should not be able to circumvent the uniform application of EU law.[490]

Art. 47 (2) of the Charter guarantees the right to a fair trial, addressing the member states' obligations *vis-à-vis* any individual seeking judicial or administrative review. This includes the right to be heard, the independence of the courts as well as the impartiality of the courts and the publicity of any proceedings except in particular circumstances. The right to a fair

485 *Jarass*, 2. Edn. (2013) Art. 47, para 3; *Alber* in: Stern/Sachs EU GrCH, Art. 47 of the Charter, para 2.

486 The German expression is "*Effektivitätsgrundsatz*".

487 The German expression is "*Äquivalenzgrundsatz*".

488 *CJEU*, 19.06.1990 – C-213/89 - Queen vs. Secretary of State for Transport = ECLI:EU:C:1990:257, para 20; *CJEU*, 13.03.2007 – C-432/05 - Unibet = ECLI:EU:C:2007:163, para 43; *CJEU*, 19.09.2006 – Joined Cases C-392/04 and C-422/04 - i24 Germany et al = ECLI:EU:C:2006:586, para 57 with further references; *Gundel* in: Becker/Ehlers Europäische Grundfreiheiten (2014), § 27, para 49 f.

489 *CJEU*, 13.03.2007 – C-432/05 - Unibet = ECLI:EU:C:2007:163, para 43; *CJEU*, 19.09.2006 – Joined Cases C-392/04 and C-422/04 - i24 Germany et al = ECLI:EU:C:2006:586, para 57; *Gundel* in: Becker/Ehlers Europäische Grundfreiheiten (2014), § 27, para 49 f. *Bogdandy/Schill* in: Grabitz/Hilf/Nettesheim EUV/AEUV, Art. 4 TEU, para 84-90.

490 Cf. inter alia: *CJEU*, 19.09.2006 – Joined Cases C-392/04 and C-422/04 - i24 Germany et al = ECLI:EU:C:2006:586, para 57 f; *Gundel* in: Becker/Ehlers Europäische Grundfreiheiten (2014), § 27, para 49 f; *Bogdandy/Schill* in: Grabitz/Hilf/Nettesheim EUV/AEUV, Art. 4 TEU, para 90 f.

trial also includes obligations as to the delays to respect upon issuing a decision.[491]

Furthermore, the general principles of EU law provide several guarantees of substantive protection against interventionist measures of either the EU or the member states. As general principles, these guarantees apply to the entire scope of actions of either the EU or the member states when implementing any measure related to EU law.[492] Three basic principles should be particularly mentioned.

The first general principle is the *principle of legal certainty* which refers to the general prohibition of retroactivity.[493] As to the CJEU,

> "[t]he principle of legal certainty precludes a [...] measure from taking effect from a point in time before its publication. It may exceptionally be otherwise where the purpose to be achieved so demands and where the legitimate expectations of those concerned are duly respected."[494]

Hence, the legitimate expectations of the addressees of the provisions becomes a crucial point to determine the validity or invalidity of a regulation creating retroactive effects. If those expectations are worth being protected and effectively jeopardised by an (objectively or subjectively) unpredictable measure, the retroactive measure will be considered unlawful. However, if such expectations do not exist or are not worth being protected, the state measure may even – exceptionally – take retroactive effects. This precautious balancing of interests, contains a considerable safeguard for measures which might affect business related activities as well, especially with regard to the changes of the current legal framework.[495]

---

491 *Jarass*, 2. Edn. (2013) Art. 47, para 42 ff; *Neumann* in: *Rengeling/Middeke/Gellermann* (Eds.), Handbuch des Rechtsschutzes in der Europäischen Union, 2014 § 21, para 21-25.

492 *Kilian*, Europäisches Wirtschaftsrecht, 5. Edn. (2016), p. 146, 151.

493 *Lasok/Millett et al.*, 2004, p. 346-349; *Streinz* in: Streinz EUV/AEUV, Art. 6 TEU, para 33; *CJEU*, 25.01.1979 – C-98/78 - Racke = ECLI:EU:C:1979:14; *CJEU*, 25.01.1979 – C-99/78 - Decker = ECLI:EU:C:1979:15.

494 *CJEU*, 25.01.1979 – C-98/78 - Racke = ECLI:EU:C:1979:14, para 20, settled case law since then.

495 *Lasok/Millett et al.*, 2004, p. 346 f; *Streinz* in: Streinz EUV/AEUV, Art. 6 TEU, para 33; *Bungenberg* in: *Heselhaus/Nowak* (Eds.), Handbuch der Europäischen Grundrechte, 2006, para 42-47; also the CJEU distinguishes between those situations in which the regulation affects events which already took place before the entry into force ("*echte Rückwir*kung"), which is generally prohibited, and regulations which alter a situation which is ongoing at the time of entry into force, but not yet terminated ("*unechte Rückwirkung*"). In the later situation, the principle or retroactivity does per se not apply, however

This understanding of the principle of legal certainty also reveals two further general principles of EU law, which are not limited to this particular setting: the *protection of legitimate expectations* in general and the *principle of proportionality*.

The first generally obliges to take into account legitimate expectations of the addressee of a measure, especially regarding administrative decisions and their revocation.[496] These expectations need to be balanced against the interest of the EU or the member states to undertake the measure. The second principle requires all acts which limit any (legal or natural) person's freedom to be submitted to the test of reason as one of the most basic features of the rule of law.[497] All three principles implement the rule of law within EU law and considerably limit the discretion of a host state to interfere with individuals and legal entities outside a reasonable, justified degree.[498]

III. Dual provisions offering protection but also enabling interventionist measures

Besides the predominantly protection oriented provisions (such as the fundamental freedoms and the Charter of Fundamental Rights), EU law contains provisions and regulations which are more interventionist and thus have a dual scope.[499] On the one hand, they are designated to guarantee an unhindered competition in the internal market but on the other hand they might limit certain freedoms previously enjoyed by economic operators relating to certain business models. Without being exhaustive, three sets of

---

in situations having particularly detrimental effects and affecting legitimate expectations, transition periods to moderate these effects are necessary. cf.: *Bungenberg* in: *Heselhaus/Nowak* (Eds.), Handbuch der Europäischen Grundrechte, 2006, para 42 and 45 and *Lasok/Millett et al.*, 2004, p. 346 f.

496 *Ruffert* in: Becker/Ehlers Europäische Grundfreiheiten (2014), § 19, para 18; *Calliess* in: Calliess/Ruffert EUV/AEUV, Art. 2 TEU, para 26; *Lasok/Millett et al.*, 2004, p. 353 f.

497 *Calliess* in: Calliess/Ruffert EUV/AEUV, Art. 2 TEU, para 26; *Oppermann/Classen et al.*, 5. Edn. (2011) § 17, para 23; cf. also: *Lasok/Millett et al.*, 2004, p. 335-338.

498 *Calliess* in: Calliess/Ruffert EUV/AEUV, Art. 2 TEU, para 25 f; *Lasok/Millett et al.*, 2004, p. 317.

499 Cf. also: *Eilmansberger*, CMLR Vol. 46 (2009), 383, 407.

provisions will be briefly explained to provide examples of those provisions with particular interest for this thesis.

1. Competition law: Art. 101, 102 TFEU

Art. 101 and 102 TFEU are crucial elements of the antitrust-policy of the EU. Whereas Art. 101 TFEU prohibits competition-restricting agreements between two undertakings, Art. 102 TFEU generally prohibits the abuse of a dominant market position to enable substantial competition among economic operators.[500] Both provisions seek to limit abusive behaviour which detriments competition in general and in particular leads to negative effects on competitors and consumers and thus disturbs the overall allocation of public welfare.[501] Hence, those provisions present a dual nature: on the one hand they protect consumers as well as competitors from abusive behaviour of economic undertakings. Perceived from this side, they also offer a considerable protection, as they guarantee the freedom of competition, as also protected under Art. 16 of the Charter (cf. *supra*). However, from the perspective of the targeted undertaking, which seeks to foster its own market share through agreements falling under Art. 101 TFEU or which holds a monopoly, potentially enabling him to make use of its dominant market position, Art. 101 and 102 TFEU do not offer protection but rather restrict the freedom of this particular undertaking. Hence, the provisions represent an interventionist ratio as well.

2. State aid provisions: Art. 107 ff TFEU

EU law generally prohibits state aids, leaving room for few exceptions for policy objectives (Art. 107 ff TFEU). The state aid system is characterised

500 *Hobe*, 8. Edn. (2014), para 997; *Haratsch*, 2016, p. 558 and 582; *Oppermann/Classen et al.*, 5. Edn. (2011) § 20, para 14 and 27.

501 *Oppermann/Classen et al.*, 5. Edn. (2011) § 20, para 4; *Haratsch*, 2016, p. 553-557; *Brinker* in: Schwarze EU-Kommentar, Art. 101 TFEU, para 8 f; generally regarding the ongoing changes towards a "*more economic approach*" also with regard to the state aid provisions: *Rusche* in: Immenga/Mestmäcker AEUV, D. Art. 107 (3) TFEU, para 43-53.

by preliminary investigation and the necessity of prior approval[502]. Hence, without prior approval, even a state measure being in line with the exceptions in Art. 107 (2), (3), 106 (2), 108, 109 TFEU (or the secondary law issued based on these provisions) is considered illegal, if the Treaties do not provide for further exceptions (e.g. Art. 42 or 93 TFEU).[503] Except for particular cases (e.g. block exemptions), any state aid needs to be notified to the Commission before being granted, default of which the state aid is considered at least formally illegal, notwithstanding if it complies with the material criteria in Art. 107 ff TFEU.[504] Subsidies or other forms of state aids issued by a member state, which do not comply with these requirements, will need to be revoked.

Even without a deeper analysis of the provisions one can – once again – perceive the dual nature of the provision: whereas on the one hand these provisions protect the unhindered competition and prevent the member states from interfering with the market by favouring particular undertakings, the provisions also have an interventionist character. Hence, similar as for Art. 101, 102 TFEU, the provisions enable to protect certain undertakings through an impediment with the economic interests of another undertaking.

3. Secondary legislation

Similar as for the Art. 101, 102 TFEU and the state aid-rules in Art. 107 TFEU, various provisions in the secondary legislation represent a dual nature as well. Whereas several of these rules might seek to protect particular interests or economic activities, they put restrictions on others at the same time. Such measures are often implemented in order to protect

---

502 The German expression is "*Präventives Verbot mit Erlaubnisvorbehalt*", cf.: *Hobe*, 8. Edn. (2014), para 1067; *Oppermann/Classen et al.*, 5. Edn. (2011) § 21, para 30; *Beljin/Schulze et al.*, Europarecht, 2. Edn. (2010) §28, para 82; *Haratsch*, 2016, p. 611.

503 *Hobe*, 8. Edn. (2014), para 1067 ff; *Oppermann/Classen et al.*, 5. Edn. (2011) § 21, para 4, 13 ff; *Mestmäcker/Schweitzer* in: Immenga/Mestmäcker AEUV, A. Die Beihilfenregeln im System des EU-Vertrags, para 14-18.

504 *Hobe*, 8. Edn. (2014), para 1067 ff; *Haratsch*, 2016, p. 611; *Oppermann/Classen et al.*, 5. Edn. (2011) § 21, para 30.

particular consumer, health or general security interests.[505] Several examples of these measures will be demonstrated *infra* (Chapter 5).

IV. Legal remedies: judicial review as conceived under EU law

EU law provides in principle a full set of legal remedies to enforce compliance of the member states and its authorities with EU law. The system perceived by Art. 19 TEU is a mixed system. It relies on the national courts of the member states, being in principle competent to rule any case, notwithstanding if the case implies the application of EU law.[506] The jurisdiction of the CJEU is limited to the procedures enumerated in the European Treaties (Art. 274 TFEU).[507] These provisions (Art. 256 ff TFEU) exclude any interpretation or application of provisions of national law, which exclusively remain with the member state courts.[508]

In cases which could be related to investment protection, the following procedures might be initiated by the investor.

1. Proceedings before national courts and preliminary ruling procedure (Art. 267 TFEU)

Proceedings before national courts are conceived as the norm in the system of legal remedies in the EU (cf. Art. 19 TEU and Art. 274 TFEU).[509] Any state measure issued by the host state, either directly or indirectly implementing EU law, should in principle be challenged before national courts. Within these national proceedings, EU law requires the principle of effectiveness[510] and equivalence[511] to be respected.[512] National courts have

505 For the changes relating to the aims of the EU in matters of environment protection and energy politics after the Lisbon Treaty: cf. *Nowak*, Europarecht nach Lissabon, 2011, p. 246-255.

506 *Oppermann/Classen et al.*, 5. Edn. (2011) § 13, para 2 and 3 ff; cf. also: *Hobe*, 8. Edn. (2014), para 480 ff.

507 *Hobe*, 8. Edn. (2014), para 482; *Oppermann/Classen et al.*, 5. Edn. (2011) § 13, para 3.

508 *Hobe*, 8. Edn. (2014), para 482; *Schwarze* in: Schwarze EU-Kommentar, Art. 19 TEU, para 44.

509 *Oppermann/Classen et al.*, 5. Edn. (2011) § 13, para 3; *Pache* in: von Heinegg/Vedder EUV/AEUV, Art. 19 TEU, para 1 and 5.

510 The German expression is *„Effektivitätsgrundsatz"*.

the duty to guarantee the full effectiveness of EU law and respect the principle of primacy in any national proceedings relating to either national law or EU law.[513].

Within these national proceedings, various questions of EU law may arise. First, a measure, law or regulation issued by the host state is considered to be (potentially) incompatible with EU law. Second, a court may be sought with implementing measures based on (directly applicable or transposed) provisions of EU law which it considers contrary to EU law (e.g. the Treaties or the Charter or paramount secondary law).[514] Third, a national court might have doubts about the correct interpretation of EU law.

In such cases, where the interpretation or validity of EU law is relevant for the judgement in the proceedings, the system of the preliminary ruling procedure in Art. 267 TFEU allows the interaction of national courts with the CJEU.[515] The procedure enables to refer a question of interpretation or

---

511 The German expression is "*Äquivalenzgrundsatz*".

512 *Oppermann/Classen et al.*, 5. Edn. (2011) § 13, para 3; *Gundel* in: Becker/Ehlers Europäische Grundfreiheiten (2014), § 27, para 49 f; *Bogdandy/Schill* in: Grabitz/Hilf/Nettesheim EUV/AEUV, Art. 4 TEU, para 90 f.

513 This may lead to the necessity for the member state to recognise or grant a – formerly – unknown or inadmissible relief against state measures, if otherwise the full effectiveness or the principle of supremacy of EU law may be questioned, cf.: *Oppermann/Classen et al.*, 5. Edn. (2011) § 13, para 3 f; *CJEU*, 25.07.1991 – C-221/89 - Factortame = ECLI:EU:C:1991:320, para 20 ff, particularly para 23: "*Consequently,[...] Community law must be interpreted as meaning that a national court which, in a case before it concerning Community law, considers that the sole obstacle which precludes it from granting interim relief is a rule of national law must set aside that rule (...)*".

514 *Gaitanides* in: v. d. Groeben/Schwarze AEUV/EUV, Art. 267 TFEU, para 17 f and 26; *Hobe*, 8. Edn. (2014), para 536-538; cf. also: *Oppermann/Classen et al.*, 5. Edn. (2011) § 13, para 5 and 70.

515 Art. 267 (2) TFEU enables the possibility to refer to the preliminary ruling procedure for all courts of the member states. The CJEU refers to several criteria to determine whether a dispute settlement body can be considered as a court in the terms of Art. 267 TFEU, "*such as whether the body is established by law, whether it is permanent, whether its jurisdiction is compulsory, whether its procedure is inter partes, whether it applies rules of law and whether it is independent*", cf.: *CJEU*, 06.07.2000 – C-407/98 - Abrahamsson = ECLI:EU:C:2000:367, para 29; cf. also: *Gaitanides* in: v. d. Groeben/Schwarze AEUV/EUV, Art. 267 TFEU, para 41. Private arbitral tribunals are not considered to be courts in the meaning of Art. 267 TFEU, cf.: *CJEU*, 23.03.1982 – C-102/81 - Nordsee = ECLI:EU:C:1982:107, para 12; *CJEU*, 01.06.1999 – C-126/97 - Eco Swiss = ECLI:EU:C:1999:269, para 34; *Gaitanides* in: v. d. Gro-

validity of EU law to the CJEU.[516] The CJEU will render the decision on the interpretation or validity and re-refer the case to the national court, which – given the CJEU's judgement and its binding force – will finally decide the case it was sought with.[517] In case the CJEU declares a provision of EU secondary law invalid, the provisions is considered void *erga omnes*.[518]

Art. 267 TFEU distinguishes the possibility to engage the preliminary ruling procedure and the duty to do so for national courts. Whenever the *validity* of a provision of EU law is questioned, all courts, irrespective of their status as courts of last resort, have the duty to refer the question of validity to the CJEU.[519] If the *correct interpretation* of EU law is in question, courts of last resort must in principle refer the question, whereas other courts are granted discretion to do so (cf. Art. 267 (3) TFEU).[520] In any case, the CJEU accepts two exceptions to the duty to refer the question: either the CJEU already decided the question (*acte éclairé*) or the correct interpretation is unambiguous (*acte clair*).[521]

---

eben/Schwarze AEUV/EUV, Art. 267 TFEU, para 45; *Hobe*, 8. Edn. (2014), para 535 based on the argument that arbitral tribunals exercise their jurisdiction based on the parties' consents and the "*public authorities are not involved in the decision to opt for arbitration*", cf. *CJEU*, C-102/81 – Nordsee, cited above.

516 *Gaitanides* in: v. d. Groeben/Schwarze AEUV/EUV, Art. 267 TFEU, para 4 f and references above.

517 *Hobe*, 8. Edn. (2014), para 543; *Oppermann/Classen et al.*, 5. Edn. (2011) § 13, para 83; *Gaitanides* in: v. d. Groeben/Schwarze AEUV/EUV, Art. 267 TFEU, para 86 ff.

518 *Oppermann/Classen et al.*, 5. Edn. (2011) § 13, para 83; *Gaitanides* in: v. d. Groeben/Schwarze AEUV/EUV, Art. 267 TFEU, para 90.

519 *CJEU*, 21.02.1981 – Joined Cases C-143/88 and C-92/89 - Zuckerfabrik Süderdithmarschen = ECLI:EU:C:1991:65, para 14 f; *Oppermann/Classen et al.*, 5. Edn. (2011) § 13, para 79; *Gaitanides* in: v. d. Groeben/Schwarze AEUV/EUV, Art. 267 TFEU, para 65.

520 *Oppermann/Classen et al.*, 5. Edn. (2011) §13, para 76 f; *Gaitanides* in: v. d. Groeben/Schwarze AEUV/EUV, Art. 267 TFEU, para 62.

521 *CJEU*, 06.10.1982 – C-283/83 - CILFIT = ECLI:EU:C:1982:335, para 14 and 16; *Gaitanides* in: v. d. Groeben/Schwarze AEUV/EUV, Art. 267 TFEU, para 66; If doubts about the correct interpretation arise in interim proceedings, the court may also restraint from referring, based on the fact that the decision is not the final decision in the main proceedings, cf. para 65.

2. Immediate proceedings before the CJEU: legal actions enumerated in the European Treaties

Opposed to the general competency of the national courts of the member states, EU law provides for certain exceptions which directly attribute the competency for a legal remedy to the CJEU without referring to the national courts before. In the context of this thesis, the relevant actions are the action for annulment (Art. 263, 264 TFEU) and the infringement proceedings (Art. 258, 259 TFEU).

(1) Action for annulment (Art. 263, 264 TFEU)

The action for annulment in Art. 263, 264 TFEU enables to directly challenge acts of the European institutions producing legal effects *vis-à-vis* third parties. It is a complement which takes into account that acts of the European institutions which produce direct effects and are not subject to further implementation measures by the member state, cannot be challenged before national courts. Art. 263, 264 TFEU compensate this gap in the legal protection.[522]

As to Art. 263 (1) TFEU two sorts of acts of the institutions can be challenged:

First, all legislative acts (cf. Art 289 (3) TFEU) of the Council, the Commission or the European Central Bank, except for recommendations and opinions (which lack a legally binding effect (Art. 288 (5) TFEU)). This includes directives and regulations.

Second, all acts of the European Parliament or the European Council or other bodies, offices or agencies of the EU which are intended to produce legal effects towards third parties. There is no limitation as to the act in question. Hence, all types of acts can be challenged under Art. 263 (1) TFEU as long as they are intended to produce legal effects towards third parties.[523]

With regard to investment protection and investors the action for annulment constitutes a particularly interesting legal remedy as it enables –

522 *Oppermann/Classen et al.*, 5. Edn. (2011) § 13, para 5; *Wegener* in: Calliess/Ruffert EUV/AEUV, Art. 19 TEU, para 44 f.

523 *Pache* in: von Heinegg/Vedder EUV/AEUV, Art. 263 TFEU, para 16; *Hobe*, 8. Edn. (2014), para 506; *Oppermann/Classen et al.*, 5. Edn. (2011) § 13, para 44.

in principle – to directly challenge actions by European institutions in proceedings before the CJEU.

However, the general possibility to challenge acts in the action for annulment is limited by two set of provisions. First, the plaintiffs need to demonstrate that any the challenged act is invalid for any of the reasons laid down in Art. 263 (2) TFEU (*"cas d'ouverture"*). This includes a lack of competence, the infringement of an essential procedural requirement, the violation of the (European) treaties or any provision relating to its application (i.e. a violation of primary law contained in the European Treaties, any general rule of law derived therefrom, obligations deriving from public international law which are binding on the EU as well as senior provisions of secondary law) or the misuse of powers which is mainly a control of the correct use of discretionary powers by the institutions.[524]

Second, Art. 263 (4) TFEU retracts some of this attraction by limiting the *locus standi* for the action for annulment as long as individuals and legal entities are concerned (i.e. for investors).[525] Individuals and legal entities (other than the entities enumerated in Art. 263 (2) TFEU, such as the Commission, which are considered to be privileged plaintiffs) can only bring an action for annulment if they fulfil the criteria set forth in Art. 263 (4) TFEU.[526] The interpretation given to these criteria remains rather restrictive, despite of an enlargement pursued in the Lisbon Treaty.[527] Currently Art. 263 (4) TFEU reads as follows:

> "Any natural or legal person may (…) institute proceedings against an act addressed to that person or which is of direct and individual concern to them, and against a regulatory act which is of direct concern to them and does not entail implementing measures."

---

524 *Pache* in: von Heinegg/Vedder EUV/AEUV, Art. 263 TFEU, para 49 ff; *Hobe*, 8. Edn. (2014), para 511; *Oppermann/Classen et al.*, 5. Edn. (2011) § 11, para 45 ff. The *"infringement of the Treaties or of any rule of law relating to their application";* cf. also:. *Gaitanides* in: v. d. Groeben/Schwarze AEUV/EUV, Art. 263 TFEU, para 139.

525 *Schwarze* in: Schwarze EU-Kommentar, Art. 263 TFEU, para 38; *Gaitanides* in: v. d. Groeben/Schwarze AEUV/EUV, Art. 263 TFEU, para 49; cf. also: *Hobe*, 8. Edn. (2014), para 512; *Oppermann/Classen et al.*, 5. Edn. (2011) § 13, para 42 and 56 ff.

526 *Schwarze* in: Schwarze EU-Kommentar, Art. 263 TFEU, para 38; *Gaitanides* in: v. d. Groeben/Schwarze AEUV/EUV, Art. 263 TFEU, para 49; cf. also: *Hobe*, 8. Edn. (2014), para 512; *Oppermann/Classen et al.*, 5. Edn. (2011) § 13, para 42 and 56 ff.

527 *Hobe*, 8. Edn. (2014), para 513.

The consequences of this provision as well as its concrete scope of application will be assessed *infra* (Chapter 15). However, for instance it can be observed that to pursue a direct action before the CJEU, an investor will need to have a particular burden of proof with regard to the measure affecting its business. Otherwise, the regular remedy available to investors will be proceedings before national courts, with however the possibility to refer the any question of EU law to the CJEU by means of the preliminary ruling procedure (Art. 267 TFEU).

(2) Infringement proceedings as inter-state remedies for violation of EU law (Art. 258 ff TFEU)

The CJEU might also be directly sought for either the EU itself or any member state (allegedly) violating its obligations under EU law in case of the infringement proceedings laid down in Art. 258, 259 TFEU. However, these proceedings are inter-state-remedies.[528]

The CJEU will evaluate if any act by a member state, its authorities or subsidiaries, its organs or any private entity (at least considerably) controlled by the member state, violated EU law through any of its acts. The court held that acts by the member states could be either legislative acts (laws, regulations, etc.), executive acts (decisions, etc.) or even acts issued by judicial bodies (the member state courts) if those fail to comply with EU law.[529] This control exercised on the courts and authorities, organs or subsidiaries of the member states is exercised notwithstanding the fact that those institutions may be independent from any control of either the executive or legislative authorities in the member states.[530] The most prominent failure to apply EU law committed by national courts is the non-respect of the preliminary ruling procedure in Art. 267 TFEU.[531]

528 *Hobe*, 8. Edn. (2014), para 499 ff; *Oppermann/Classen et al.*, 5. Edn. (2011) § 13, para 32 f; *Haratsch*, 2016, p. 212.

529 *Oppermann/Classen et al.*, 5. Edn. (2011) § 13, para 32 f; *Wunderlich* in: v. d. Groeben/Schwarze AEUV/EUV, Art. 258 TFEU, para 7 ff; *Pache* in: von Heinegg/Vedder EUV/AEUV, Art. 258 TFEU, para 4 f. *Schwarze* in: Schwarze EU-Kommentar, Art. 258 TFEU, para 8.

530 *CJEU*, 09.12.2003 – C-129/00 - Commission vs. Italy = ECLI:EU:C:2003:656, para 28 f; *Wunderlich* in: v. d. Groeben/Schwarze AEUV/EUV, Art. 258 TFEU, para 7 ff; *Schwarze* in: Schwarze EU-Kommentar, Art. 258 TFEU, para 8; cf. also: *Oppermann/Classen et al.*, 5. Edn. (2011) § 13, para 33.

531 *Wunderlich* in: v. d. Groeben/Schwarze AEUV/EUV, Art. 258 TFEU, para 8.

The act of the member state accused of having violated EU law is controlled by reference to its compliance with primary and secondary law as well as the general principles of EU law.[532] The violation of EU law can also be an omission, especially in the case of non-transposing or delayed transposal of directives to national law.[533]

However, individuals do not have a *locus standi* in those proceedings.[534] The infringement proceedings are conceived as objective proceedings to enforce compliance of the member state with its obligations under EU law.[535] An investor would therefor need to rely on its home state to engage the proceedings. The mechanism conceived in Art. 258, 259 TFEU can be compared to the inter-state dispute settlements in an IIA. However, given the possibility attributed to the Commission to initiate the proceedings, and its role to observe the member states' compliance with EU law, the infringement proceedings remain a powerful instrument for the European institutions to ensure this compliance.[536]

3. Action for damages

Especially regarding investment protection another particular remedy available to individuals and / or legal entities needs to be addressed. EU law contains a full set of action for damages either for actions of the EU (and its institutions) itself or for actions by the EU member states which violate EU law.

---

532 *Oppermann/Classen et al.*, 5. Edn. (2011) § 13, para 33; *Haratsch*, 2016, p. 217; *Pache* in: von Heinegg/Vedder EUV/AEUV, Art. 258 TFEU, para 21.

533 *Hobe*, 8. Edn. (2014), para 501; *Schwarze* in: Schwarze EU-Kommentar, Art. 258 TFEU, para 5; *Wunderlich* in: v. d. Groeben/Schwarze AEUV/EUV, Art. 258 TFEU, para 6.

534 Cf. Art. 258 and 259 TFEU; cf. also: *Hobe*, 8. Edn. (2014), para 499 and *Haratsch*, 2016, p. 212.

535 *Hobe*, 8. Edn. (2014), para 499 and 501; *Pache* in: von Heinegg/Vedder EUV/AEUV, Art. 258 TFEU, para 3.

536 Cf. for the role of the Commission: *Oppermann/Classen et al.*, 5. Edn. (2011) § 5, para 119 and 130; *Epping* in: von Heinegg/Vedder EUV/AEUV, Art. 5 TEU, para 5; In the proceedings of Achmea (former Eurkeo B.V.) against Slovak Republic the investors actually seek to engage this instrument and filed a complaint against the Slovak Republic with the European Commission for breach of EU law, cf.: *European Commission*, Amicus Curia Brief filed in Achmea (former Eureko BV) vs. Slovak Republic (PCA Case n°2008-13) - arbitration proceedings, 07/07/2010, para 6.

(1) Extra-contractual action for damages against the EU

The liability of the EU for damages occurred to individuals is laid down in Art. 340 (2) TFEU and Art. 41 (3) of the Charter, whereas the latter refers to the liability in accordance with the general principles of EU law.[537] If a violation of any provision attributing individual rights to the individual by any organ or institution of the EU results in a – directly linked – damage for legally protected interests (including the wealth of a person), this damage needs to be compensated.[538]

The type of institution or act does not influence the liability. Other than in several national legal frameworks, the liability of the EU extends to legislative, judicial or executive acts of any organ, body or agency acting within its duties. This includes the liability for illegal directives or regulations.[539]

The act subject to engage the liability needs to violate a provision of EU law conferring rights on individuals (subjective rights).[540] However, the CJEU applies a broad approach to determine subjective rights. Even provisions which are overwhelmingly conceived in a general interest, are not excluded from also serving particular interest and hence – in case of a breach – potentially enabling the liability.[541] Potential provisions include the rights contained in the Charter, the fundamental freedoms, the principle of non-discrimination, the rules on competition and state aid even the provisions in Art. 108 (2) TFEU which essentially deal with procedural issues, but also the general principles of EU law, including the principle of

537 *Oppermann/Classen et al.*, 5. Edn. (2011) § 14, para 3 ff; *Jarass*, 2. Edn. (2013) Art. 41, para 32 f.

538 *CJEU*, 02.07.1974 – C-153/73 - Holtz & Willemsen = ECLI:EU:C:1974:70, para 7 and *CJEU*, 04.03.1980 – C-49/79 - Pool = ECLI:EU:C:1980:64, para 7; cf. also: *Pache* in: von Heinegg/Vedder EUV/AEUV, Art. 340 TFEU, para 6.

539 *Hobe*, 8. Edn. (2014), para 592; *Oppermann/Classen et al.*, 5. Edn. (2011) § 14, para 5; *Gellermann* in: Streinz EUV/AEUV, Art. 340 TFEU, para 14-16.

540 *Augsberg* in: v. d. Groeben/Schwarze AEUV/EUV, Art. 340 TFEU, para 41; *Hobe*, 8. Edn. (2014), para 593; *Gellermann* in: Streinz EUV/AEUV, Art. 340 TFEU, para 20 f.

541 *Augsberg* in: v. d. Groeben/Schwarze AEUV/EUV, Art. 340 TFEU, para 42; cf. also: *CJEU*, 04.10.2006 – T-193/04 Tillack vs. Commission = ECLI:EU:T:2006:292, para 110.

proportionality, the protection of legitimate expectations or the principle of legality.[542]

Depending on the degree of discretion attributed to the acting institution, the simple violation of any provision of EU law is not sufficient to engage the liability of the EU.[543] If relating to the act in question the respective institution enjoys considerable discretion, the breach of EU law needs to be sufficiently serious, which can be demonstrated in the case of a manifest and grave disregard of the limits of its discretion. However, where an institution only has reduced discretion or no discretion at all, the infringement itself is sufficient without any need to demonstrate a particular severity.[544] To demonstrate the sufficiently serious breach of EU law, the CJEU usually relies on several (non-exhaustive) criteria, including the importance of the violated provision and the obviousness of the violation, the addressed audience as well as the importance of the damage suffered.[545]

(2) Extra-contractual action for damages against the member states

The action for damages against the member states for impediments on EU law is subject to the same conditions than the action for damages against the EU itself (parallelism of liability).[546] Since the *Francovich-Case* the liability of the member states for violation of EU law is well established.[547]

---

542 *Jacob/Kottmann* in: Grabitz/Hilf/Nettesheim EUV/AEUV, Art. 340 TFEU, para 78 ff with further cases from the jurisprudence of the CJEU and an extensive overview of potential provisions.

543 *Pache* in: von Heinegg/Vedder EUV/AEUV, Art. 340 TFEU, para 9.

544 *CJEU*, 10.07.2003 – C-472/00 P - Fresh Marine Company A/S = ECLI:EU:C:2003:399, para 27; considered by the court to be settled case law since: *CJEU*, 04.07.2000 – C-352/98 - Bergaderm and Goupil = ECLI:EU:C:2000:361, para 43 and 44; the former distinction relating to the legislative or administrative nature of the act is abandoned (at least) since then; cf. also: *Augsberg* in: v. d. Groeben/Schwarze AEUV/EUV, Art. 340 TFEU, para 51 ff.

545 *Pache* in: von Heinegg/Vedder EUV/AEUV, Art. 340 TFEU, para 9; *Augsberg* in: v. d. Groeben/Schwarze AEUV/EUV, Art. 340 TFEU, para 51 ff; *Berg* in: Schwarze EU-Kommentar, Art. 340 TFEU, para 84 f.

546 *Pache* in: von Heinegg/Vedder EUV/AEUV, Art. 340 TFEU, para 16.

547 *CJEU*, 19.11.1991 – Joined cases C-6/90 and C-9/90 - Francovich = ECLI:EU:C:1991:428; cf. *inter alia*: *Hobe*, 8. Edn. (2014), para 586-588.

Although the action for liability against the member states is – other than the action against the EU – subject to the legal remedies in the national judicial frameworks, the principle of effectiveness and equivalence require the national courts to fully implement the action in the national legal framework.[548] Consequently, no further condition – other than those required by the CJEU for the action against the Union – shall be required by national courts to engage the liability and the proceedings need to effectively enforce the rights regarding the member state's liability.[549]

A particular case is the action for liability relating to the non-compliance with the duty to engage the preliminary ruling procedure by a court of the member states. The non-compliance may in itself be a breach of EU law. However, additionally, when assessing whether a breach of other provisions of EU law is sufficiently serious, the omission of a court to refer a question by virtue of the preliminary ruling to the CJEU is considered to be a decisive factor.[550] The possibility to trigger the liability claim can be a considerable incentive to engage the procedure of Art. 267 TFEU.

Chapter 5: Potential conflicts of EU law and international investment law

As a consequence of the previously described developments, the current investment protection system in the EU is a multi-level legal framework that integrates different subjects and sources of law. The two legal frameworks, EU law as well as IIAs, will both (at least *a priori*) apply to investors operating in EU member states. Although one might think that conceptually both regimes are largely conceived to offer further protection for individuals or legal entities against the member states' interferences with their rights, the frameworks are not identical and can thus create conflicts in their application on the same factual circumstances.

---

548 *Gellermann* in: Streinz EUV/AEUV, Art. 340 TFEU, para 53; *Haratsch*, 2016, p. 276 f; *Berg* in: Schwarze EU-Kommentar, Art. 340 TFEU, para 77 f.

549 *Pache* in: von Heinegg/Vedder EUV/AEUV, Art. 340 TFEU, para 20 ff; *Gellermann* in: Streinz EUV/AEUV, Art. 340 TFEU, para 53; *Haratsch*, 2016, p. 276 f.

550 *Augsberg* in: v. d. Groeben/Schwarze AEUV/EUV, Art. 340 TFEU, para 100; cf. also: *Wegener*, EuR, 2002, 785, 789.

Several arbitral tribunals and scholars denied the possibility for both legal frameworks to enter into conflict. The *Achmea-Tribunal* e.g. stated that:

> "Nor can it be said that the provisions of the BIT are incompatible with EU law. The rights to fair and equitable treatment, to full protection and security, and to protection against expropriation at least, extend beyond the protections afforded by EU law; and there is no reason why those rights should not be fulfilled and upheld in addition to the rights protected by EU law."[551]

Similar arguments have been advanced in other proceedings. [552] Most of these decisions and discussions lack a clear distinction and definition of the notion of (a potential) conflict between two legal frameworks and the potential consequences thereto. This leads to a certain confusion when addressing the question how to resolve any conflict.

Consequently, this Chapter 5 aims to first clarify how the notion of conflicting legal frameworks should be assessed. It will be demonstrated that even frameworks aiming to contribute to the same overarching goal might conflict regarding particular questions. This might e.g. be the case if the scope of admissible actions under one legal framework is outside the scope of admissible actions for the other legal framework. In such situations, an action required by framework A will necessarily lead to the violation of the rules under framework B (cf. "*A. Preliminary remarks as to the notion of conflict regarding different legal frameworks*").

Second, it will be demonstrated that, based on this notion of conflict, international investment law and EU law may conflict in various situations. In particular such conflicts may occur regarding state aid provisions under EU law but also regarding public procurement law, limitations to the fundamental freedoms as well as the principle of non-discrimination. EU law and IIAs could conflict in various (typical) fields of investment protection (cf.: "*B. Potential conflicts between EU law and IIAs*").

Having assessed these situation, this chapter will provide a summary of the detrimental consequences for investors, arbitral tribunals and host

---

551 *Achmea vs. Slovak Republic*, 26.10.2012 – PCA Case No. 2008-13 - Award on Jurisdiction, Arbitrability and Suspension, para 263.

552 Cf. e.g.: *Achmea vs. Slovak Republic*, 26.10.2012 – PCA Case No. 2008-13 - Award on Jurisdiction, Arbitrability and Suspension, para 254 f and *Achmea vs. Slovak Republic*, 07.12.2012 – PCA Case No. 2008-13 - Award, para 275 f; *Euram vs. Slovak Republic*, 22.10.2012 – PCA Case no. 2010-17: First Award on Jurisdiction, para 228; *Eastern Sugar vs. Czech Republic*, 27.03.2007 – SCC No. 088/2004 - Partial award, para 169.

states if such conflicts are ignored. Addressing and resolving the potential conflicts between IIAs and EU law contributes to legal security for both, host states and investors, as the questions of how to address these conflict reoccurs on multiple stages of arbitral proceedings dealing with an investment dispute (cf.: "*C. Potential implications of the conflict*").

Finally, after having developed that there is a fundamental need to carefully address and resolve the potential conflicts between EU law and IIAs, Subsection D. of this Chapter 5 will distinguish three different settings in which such conflicts may occur (intra-EU conflicts, extra-EU conflicts and mixed-agreement conflicts). This distinction shall establish the base for the following considerations in Part II and Part III.

A. Preliminary remarks as to the notion of conflict regarding different legal frameworks

As demonstrated supra (*"Chapter 3: The reception of modern investment protection through IIAs / BITs in the EU: doubling the protection?"*), EU law and IIAs have not been construed in complete cooperation. Both mechanisms, i.e. the integration within the EU and investment protection through IIAs, grew in parallel. However, the missing, at least explicit, harmonization, could potentially trigger conflicts between both legal frameworks.

Several arbitral awards and scholars denied such a potential conflict, stating that both frameworks would rather complement each other but not contradict.[553] However, this analysis is too short-sighted. It should therefore be clarified, before developing the concrete examples of such potential incompatibilities, to what extent incompatibilities in two legal frameworks could occur. To determine such conflicts, the host state's remaining margin of action under the different frameworks needs to be analysed first.

The guarantees attributed in an IIA generally limit the host states' margin of action compared to the situation in which no IIA would exist. EU law will also provide certain guarantees to an investor, which might be similar to what is guaranteed under the IIA. They might also be more ex-

553 Cf. inter alia: *Söderlund*, JOIA Vol. 24, Iss. 5 (2007), 455, 462 stating that both legal frameworks regarding substantive protection are in perfect harmony as they provide similar guarantees; similar: *Reinisch*, LIEI Vol. 39, No. 2 (2012), 157, 174 and 176.

tensive than the guarantees under the IIA or less extensive than the guarantees provided by the IIA.

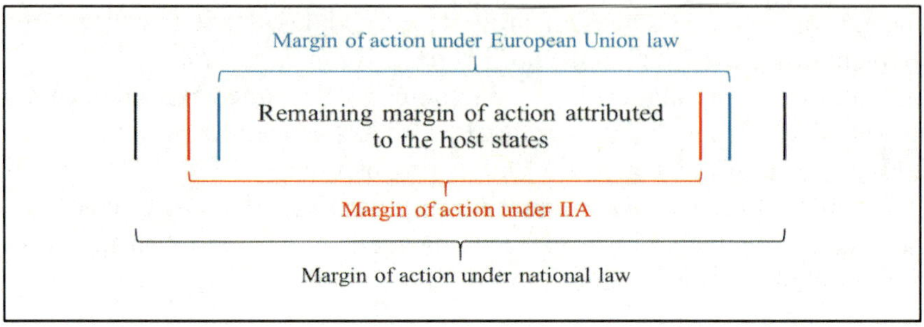

Illustration 1

The graphic above illustrates the setting in which several guarantees from EU law will be more extensive, whereas others are less extensive than the guarantees provided in the IIA. Consequently, the host state's general margin of action is limited by both, EU law and the IIA. In this (hypothetic) general setting, it can be perfectly argued, as the *Achmea-Tribunal* did, that no conflict will occur.[554] The only consequence is that the host state would be forced to obey to both, EU law and the IIA, further reducing its margin of action. This setting, or similar settings, seem to be predominantly taken into account by the arbitral tribunals having dealt with questions of conflicts between EU law and an IIA.[555]

However, there might be different settings which will lead to a conflict of both frameworks. These conflicts will occur, when one of the legal frameworks reduces the host state's margin of action to such a degree that

554 *Dimopoulos*, CMLR Vol. 48, No. 1 (2011), 63, 70 provides the example of an unilateral extension to all foreigners of certain rights granted to nationals, which would potentially be in perfect compliance with both frameworks; cf. similar . *Dahlquist/Lenk et al.*, European Policy Analysis, 2016:4, 1, 6 who however argue that under EU law the difference in scope may already constitute a conflict.

555 Cf. e.g.: *Achmea vs. Slovak Republic*, 26.10.2012 – PCA Case No. 2008-13 - Award on Jurisdiction, Arbitrability and Suspension, para 254 f and *Achmea vs. Slovak Republic*, 07.12.2012 – PCA Case No. 2008-13 - Award, para 275 f; *Euram vs. Slovak Republic*, 22.10.2012 – PCA Case no. 2010-17: First Award on Jurisdiction, para 228; *Eastern Sugar vs. Czech Republic*, 27.03.2007 – SCC No. 088/2004 - Partial award, para 169.

the remaining possible action(s) are outside the remaining margin of action under the other legal framework.[556]

The situation is illustrated in the following graphic:

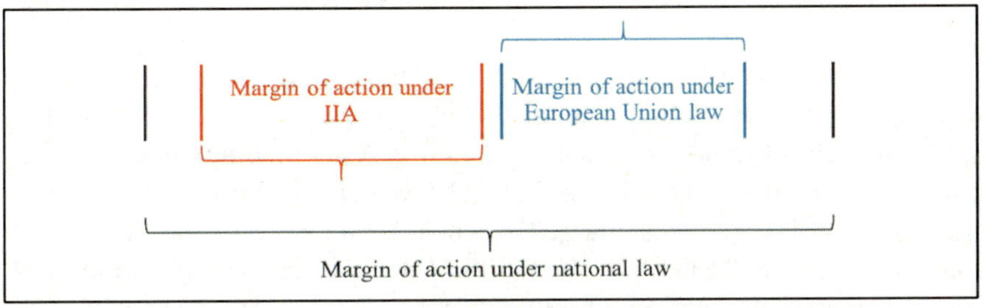

Illustration 2

The example becomes even clearer when one legal framework (e.g. EU law) mandates the state to take a certain action (leaving no margin of action at all) and this action will necessarily cause a breach of the IIA.[557] In other words, a conflict between the two legal frameworks occurs if the remaining potential margins of action for the host state under framework A is prohibited under framework B.

However, the notion of conflict cannot be reduced to analysing the host state's margin of action. A conflict may also be derived from the general concept of two legal frameworks including its guarantees, prohibitions or mechanisms.

As an example, legal framework A may collide with framework B if framework A prohibits to grant a certain guarantee or right which is however expressly granted under framework B.

In this situation the conflict of the competing legal frameworks does not occur on the stage of a host state's margin of action at a stage when both

556 *Eilmansberger*, CMLR Vol. 46 (2009), 383, 407; cf. also: *Tietje/Wackernagel*, JWIT Vol. 16, Iss. 2 (2015), 205, 207 for conflicts between EU law and the ICSID-Convention, cf. *infra*: "*C. Potential implications of the conflict*"; *Klabbers*, Treaty conflict and the European Union, 2009, p. 34 with further examples of general conflicts under international law; *Dahlquist/Lenk et al.*, European Policy Analysis, 2016:4, 1, 6.

557 This is a situation which the Tribunal in *Achmea vs. Slovak Republic*, 26.10.2012 – PCA Case No. 2008-13 - Award on Jurisdiction, Arbitrability and Suspension, para 254 raised as well. However, it concluded that such situations could not occur under the BIT, which will be disproved in the following; approving such conflicts: *Kniebaum*, ELTE Law Journal, 27, 33.

frameworks *have been concluded.* The conflict rather relates to the question if it was legally permissible for the host state under one framework (A) to *also conclude (or engage itself in) the other framework* (B), i.e. it relates to the act of establishing a (potentially) conflicting alternative legal framework.

This sort of conflict will be of particular interest for the question whether the dispute settlement mechanism of resolving investment disputes through arbitral tribunals as agreed in IIAs is incompatible with EU law (cf. *infra*). If one concludes that EU law generally prohibits the conclusion of a diverging dispute settlement mechanism outside the general concept of Art. 19 TEU, Art. 257 ff TFEU, the two legal frameworks (EU law and IIAs) would also enter into conflict.

B. Potential conflicts between EU law and IIAs

Both types of conflicts demonstrated under (A.) might occur with regard to EU law and international investment law. Whereas the more general, conceptual conflicts will rather occur regarding the legal remedies available under an IIA (cf. "*II. Conflicting provisions between EU law* and *IIAs* regarding jurisdiction"), the particular conflicts regarding the host state's margin of action will often be a question of the substantive guarantees under an IIA (cf. "*I. Conflicting provisions between EU law and IIAs regarding substantive guarantees*").[558]

I. Conflicting provisions between EU law and IIAs regarding substantive guarantees

There are numerous provisions in the European Treaties which address situations or measures undertaken by a host state regarding foreign investors and their investments and which are at least potentially triggering a conflict as previously described. The most apparent provisions are the state aid regulations in Art. 107 ff TFEU (1.). However, potential conflicts between substantive provisions of an IIA and EU law may also emerge

558 The conflicts may be reduced or even eliminated by way of interpreation of the obligations, which was e.g. suggested in the *Bosphorus*-Decision by the ECtHR and will be treated *infra* (Chapter 14).

from European public procurement or competition law (2.). Furthermore, it could be considered that state measures in favour of one investor are contrary to the fundamental freedoms in general (3.). Substantive guarantees contained in an IIA could also reveal to be discriminatory under Art. 18 TFEU (4.). Guarantees of the free transfer of funds in IIAs might e.g. conflict with (mandatory) limitations in EU law on the free transfer of capital (5.).

Obviously, whether any of the aforementioned provisions will be applicable to the host state's acts primarily depends on the particular facts of the case. Furthermore, some or even numerous measures might even be permissible under EU law as they might be covered by exemptions in the European Treaties or under secondary EU law. However, the purpose of the following demonstration is to show that numerous incentives and measures undertaken by host states, at least potentially conflict with EU law.[559] It should be noted that some authors tend to limit particular conflicts to intra-EU or extra-EU situations.[560] However, nearly all of the situations apply both to intra-EU as well as extra-EU contexts. *Inter alia*, state aid rules, competition law as well as public procurement law applies to both, EU nationals and non-EU nationals as well as legal entities.[561] Identical considerations are conceivable for secondary legislation limiting the fundamental freedoms as well as the general restrictions on fundamental freedoms in the treaties.[562]

559 Cf. also: *Eilmansberger*, CMLR Vol. 46 (2009), 383, 388; the author wishes to acknowledge that not all of the possible cases, particular conditions and exemptions of the above mentioned substantive provisions can be treated in detail. There are numerous specific cases which, for one reason or another, might not fall under the scope of either European primary or secondary law. The purpose of the demonstration is to show the numerous potential cases in which EU law may apply to "*classic*" situations of foreign investments in the EU member states.

560 A pertinent example is the nomenclature of *Eilmansberger*, CMLR Vol. 46 (2009), 383, 407 ff. (extra-EU) vs 413 ff (intra-EU), ignoring that even in the extra-EU context investors could be affected by e.g. the state-aid rules.

561 *Lenk*, EJLS Vol. 8, No. 2 (2015), 6, 17; *Jung* in: Grabitz/Hilf/Nettesheim EUV/AEUV, Art. 102 TFEU prar 32; cf. also generally: *Kleinheisterkamp*, JIEL Vol. 15, No. 1 (2012), 85, 89-95.

562 *Johannsen*, Die Kompetenz der EU für ausländische Direktinvestitionen nach Lissabon (Beit. zum Transnat. Wirt.-R, Vol. 90, 2009), 22.

1. State aid rules (Art. 107 ff TFEU)

As previously explained, EU law generally prohibits state aids, if it is not exceptionally admissible, either *de jure* (Art. 107 (2), 106 (2), 108, 109 TFEU) or by decision of the Commission (Art. 107 (3) TFEU). Given the wide interpretation of "*state aid*" in terms of Art. 107 (1) TFEU, a range of potential agreements between host states and investors is (at least potentially) subject to prior approval by the Commission and needs to comply with the provided procedures as well as with the substantive provisions in Art. 107 ff TFEU.[563]

State aid is defined by Art. 107 (1) TFEU as any measure, no matter its concrete implementation, by the state directly or through state resources, which displays a sort of selectivity by favouring certain undertakings or the production of goods and distorts or may distort competition, as long as it affects the internal market.[564]

The measures potentially being qualified as state aids are numerous. The CJEU points out that:

> "[t]he concept of aid [under Art. 107 TFEU] is more general than that of a subsidy. It embraces not only positive benefits, but also measures which, in various forms, mitigate the charges which are normally included in the budget of an undertaking and which, without therefore being subsidies in the strict meaning of the word, are similar in character and have the same effect."[565]

Various incentives offered to investors could constitute measures which *"mitigate the charges [...] normally included in the budget of an undertaking"*, including *inter alia*, tax exemptions, refunds for certain costs occurred or even subsidies paid to incentivise the investment.[566] Further-

563 *Eilmansberger*, CMLR Vol. 46 (2009), 383, 413 ff.

564 *Hobe*, 8. Edn. (2014), para 1071; *Bär-Bouyssière* in: Schwarze EU-Kommentar, Art. 107 TFEU, para 23; generally *inter alia*: *CJEU*, 08.11.2001 – C-143/99 - Adria Wien Pipeline vs. Finanzlandesdirektion für Kärnten = ECLI:EU:C:2001:598, para 34, 38.

565 *CJEU*, 23.02.1961 – C-30/59 - De Gezamenlijke Steenkolenmijnen = ECLI:EU:C:1961:2, 19; *CJEU*, 15.03.1994 – C-387/92 Banco Exterior de España = ECLI:EU:C:1994:100, para 13; *CJEU*, 08.11.2001 – C-143/99 - Adria Wien Pipeline vs. Finanzlandesdirektion für Kärnten = ECLI:EU:C:2001: 598, para 38.

566 *Calliess/Ruffert*, in: *Calliess/Ruffert EUV/AEUV*. Art. 107, para 38; *Hobe*, 8. Edn. (2014), para 1078; *Oppermann/Classen et al.*, 5. Edn. (2011) § 21, para 6, The case of *Ioan Micula, Viorel Micula & others vs. Romania*, 11.12.2013 – ICSID Case No. ARB/05/20 - Final Award is a perfect example for a range of

more, support measures such as credits at reduced interests or preferential prices to purchase goods, services or general supply from state-owned suppliers or manufacturers would possibly fall under the scope of measures target by Art. 107 (1) TFEU.[567]

Similarly, agreements such as inter alia long term purchase agreements by the government for fixed prices after the privatisation of certain sectors (e.g. the energy sector) are likely to be qualified as state aids. Except for particular circumstances, such agreements will probably mitigate the charges to bear in a competitive market in favour of the investor.[568]

Privatizations, one of the most traditional forms of foreign investments, could be qualified as state aids as well, if the price paid for the entity is not "*equivalent to the market price*" or, in other words, does not *"correspond to the price which could have been obtained by the purchaser under normal market conditions"* (so-called: *"private operator in a market economy test"*).[569]

Eilmansberger also (correctly) advances the possible "*sale of land under market prices or the promise to establish and maintain a certain infrastructure*".[570] Indeed, the CJEU qualified such measures to fall under the state aid prohibition if they also meet the further criteria of Art. 107 (1) TFEU.[571]

---

measures undertaken by Romania to incentivise investments in the declared "*disfavored regions*" which fall under the scope of Art. 107 (1) TFEU; for a short summary of the case: *Peterson*, IA Reporter Vol. 9, No. 6 (2016), 7, 7 ff.

567 *Calliess/Ruffert*, in: *Calliess/Ruffert EUV/AEUV.* Art. 107, para 38; *Oppermann/Classen et al.*, 5. Edn. (2011) § 21, para 6.

568 Such an long term power purchase agreement is at the origin of a claim brought by *Electrabel vs. Hungary*, 30.11.2012 – ICSID Case No. ARB/07/19: Decision on Jurisdiction, Applicable Law and Liability cf. also: *Peterson*, IA Reporter Vol. 5, No. 23 (2012), 3; *Eilmansberger*, CMLR Vol. 46 (2009), 383, 414 (also) attributes this category to the field of competition law, cf. *infra* (2.).

569 Settled case law, cf. e.g.: *CJEU*, 16.09.2004 – T-274/01 - Valmont vs. Commission = ECLI:EU:T:2004:266, para 45; *CJEU*, 02.09.2010 – C 290/07 P - Commission vs. Scott = ECLI:EU:C:2010:480, para 68; *CJEU*, 16.12.2010 – C-239/09 Seydaland Vereinigte Agrarbetriebe = ECLI:EU:C:2010:778, para 34; *CJEU*, 28.02.2012 – Joined Cases T-268/08 and T-281/08 - Burgenland = ECLI:EU:T:2012:90, para 48, cf. also: *Eilmansberger*, CMLR Vol. 46 (2009), 383, 414.

570 *Eilmansberger*, CMLR Vol. 46 (2009), 383, 414.

571 *Kliemann/Catalán* in: v. d. Groeben/Schwarze AEUV/EUV, Art. 107 TFEU, para 124 ff; *Bartosch*, EU-Beihilfenrecht, 2. Edn. (2016) Art. 107, para 135 f; cf. also: Commission Communication on State aid elements in sales of land and buildings by public authorities (97/C209/03), Official Journal of the Euro-

Most of these measures, as they will be attributed to specific investors or specific industries only, will also fulfil the criteria of selectivity. In terms of Art. 107 (1) TFEU, a measure is selective as soon as it favours certain undertakings or industry sectors and is not applied in a general manner.[572] Hence, they are likely to be considered as state aid according to Art. 107 (1) TFEU.

Some of the measures enumerated *supra* might not be illegal in terms of Art. 107 ff TFEU as they will be covered by exceptions.[573] However, the overwhelming amount is at least potentially subject to prior approval by the Commission or will include difficult questions of lawful or unlawful state aid regulations to be determined by the Commission. Failure to comply with these procedurals rules or if the benefit is not justified by an exception, the Commission will – except particular circumstances – order the recovery of the aid through the host state (Art. 10 ff of the 2013 State aid procedural regulation[574]).[575] This decision will be mandatory for the host state (cf. Art 288 TFEU).[576]

However, recovering the aid, or recovering the advantage taken of the aid by the investor may – at first glance – seem contradictory to the guar-

---

pean Communities C 209 - Vol. 40 (1997), 3; cf.also: *Cremer* in: Calliess/Ruffert EUV/AEUV, Art. 107 TFEU, para 11-13.

572 *Hobe*, 8. Edn. (2014), para 1081; *Oppermann/Classen et al.*, 5. Edn. (2011) § 21, para 10; *Bartosch*, EU-Beihilfenrecht, 2. Edn. (2016), para 105 f.

573 Besides the possibility for the Commission to admit state aids by virtue of Art. 107 (3) TFEU, the most far reaching exceptions regarding the prohibition of state result from the block excemptions isseud based on the Art. 109 (especially the Regulation (EU) No 1407/2013 - De Minimis State Aid, Official Journal of the European Union L 352/1 (24/12/2013), 1 and Regulation (EU) No 651/2014 - General Block Exemption Regulation, Official Journal of the European Union L 187/1 (17/06/2014), 1). With further relevance for this thesis also: *European Commission*, Commission letter SG (2001) D/290869 of 06/08/2001: Commission Communication relating to the methodology for analysing State aid linked to stranded costs, adopted by the Commission on 26/07/2001; cf. also: *Hobe*, 8. Edn. (2014), para 1084 ff and generally *Bartosch*, EU-Beihilfenrecht, 2. Edn. (2016), p. 155 ff.

574 Council Regulation (EU) No 734/2013 of 22 July 2013 amending Regulation (EC) No 659/1999.

575 *Hobe*, 8. Edn. (2014), para 1099 ff; *Oppermann/Classen et al.*, 5. Edn. (2011) § 21, para 34 ff.

576 Cf. e.g.: *Cremer* in: Calliess/Ruffert EUV/AEUV, Art. 108 TFEU, para 27; *Oppermann/Classen et al.*, 5. Edn. (2011) § 21, para 34; *Streinz*, 10. Edn. (2016), para 1106; *Beljin/Schulze et al.*, Europarecht, 2. Edn. (2010) § 28, para 189.

antees provided under the IIA, *inter alia* the guarantee of FET.[577] Thus, in case of a mandatory order by the Commission to revoke the incentive, the host state's margin of action is reduced to a measure which will necessarily compromise the incentive towards the investor. At the same time, this remaining margin of action might be outside the scope of eligible actions under the IIA, raising an above mentioned conflict.[578]

2. European public procurement and competition law

European public procurement law may also limit the host states ability to confer particular rights to investors or to enter into specific agreements. Three different types of situations may be distinguished, which refer to typical situations of foreign investments:

The first would target agreements through which investors are granted exclusive rights to run a certain (often formerly state owned) business, creating a monopoly within this particular market. Such agreements could be illegal under Art. 106 (1), (2), 102 TFEU. Granting exclusive rights, even if this leads to a monopoly in a certain market segment, is not by itself illegal under Art. 106 (1), (2) TFEU.[579] However, it is prohibited under Art. 106 (1), (2), 101, 102 TFEU if the situation resulting from the transfer of those exclusive rights results in the risk of an abuse of a dominant position by the profiteer of the transfer.[580] The relevance of these provisions for foreign investments appears clearly in the *DEI-Case's* (brought to the CJEU in 2014) although its factual basis did not imply foreign investors.[581]

DEI, a former state owned company, in which the Republic of Greece still held a majority of shares, was conferred the right to exploit nearly the entire public deposits of lignite, leaving only a minuscule share of deposits

577 Cf. also *Kleinheisterkamp*, JIEL Vol. 15, No. 1 (2012), 85, 91 ff; more generally: *Kniebaum*, ELTE Law Journal, 27, 33.

578 Cf. *supra* (A.) and *Eilmansberger*, CMLR Vol. 46 (2009), 383, 414.

579 *Grabitz/Nettesheim/Bandilla/Hilf*, in: *Grabitz/Hilf/Nettesheim EUV/AEUV.* Art. 106, para 55; *Calliess/Ruffert*, in: *Calliess/Ruffert EUV/AEUV.* Art. 106, para 27.

580 *CJEU*, 17.07.2014 – C-553/12 P - Commission vs. Dimosia Epicheirisi Ilektrismou AE (DEI) = ECLI:EU:C:2014:2083, para 42.

581 *CJEU*, 17.07.2014 – C-553/12 P - Commission vs. Dimosia Epicheirisi Ilektrismou AE (DEI) = ECLI:EU:C:2014:2083; cf. also for further potential conflicts: *Eilmansberger*, CMLR Vol. 46 (2009), 383, 414.

to other competitors. By this transferal, and the exclusion of competitors to access further deposits, the Greek Republic was held liable of having potentially created the risk of abuse of a dominant position by DEI in the lignite market as well as in the downstream wholesale electricity market.[582] The DEI case becomes an international investment law case, if *inter alia* DEI was a foreign investor which entered into an agreement with the Greek Republic to exploit the lignite deposits.

In such cases, according to Art. 106 (3) TFEU the Commission is entitled to address mandatory decisions to the member states, obliging them to omit from illegal measures or even to revoke them.[583] Upon revocation the same situation as regarding state aid may occur, i.e. the host state would be required to implement a decision which necessarily compromises the investor's rights. Although under the IIA, the same rights might be protected by the FET standard, an indirect expropriation clause or an umbrella clause.

The second type of situation which might create conflicts between IIAs and EU public procurement and competition law, would be the application of Art. 101, 102 TFEU to private economic operators (i.e. investors). Especially Art. 102 TFEU and its specifications through the application of the *essential facilities* doctrine and the interpretation given to the material scope of application of Art. 102 TFEU in general could largely interfere with investments by foreign investors in the EU.[584] Art. 102 TFEU prohibits any abuse of a dominant position of one or more undertakings as long as the undertakings behaviour may affect trade between member states. An abuse of a dominant position is generally defined by obtaining a position of economic strength which puts the undertaking into the position to "*hinder the maintenance of effective competition on the relevant market*"[585]. Such a position could also be achieved through a particular position in a market segment which enables the undertaking not only to keep its dominant position in one market but also to deny access to a separate, e.g. downstream, market. The undertaking being in the possession of either a particular knowledge, structural facilities or any other kind of influ-

582 *CJEU*, 17.07.2014 – C-553/12 P - Commission vs. Dimosia Epicheirisi Ilektrismou AE (DEI) = ECLI:EU:C:2014:2083, para 11-16, 36, 42 ff.

583 *Wernicke* in: Grabitz/Hilf/Nettesheim EUV/AEUV, Art. 106 TFEU, para 82 ff.

584 Cf. also: *Eilmansberger*, CMLR Vol. 46 (2009), 383, 415.

585 *CJEU*, 09.11.1983 – C-322/81 - Michelin = ECLI:EU:C:1983:313, para 10.

ence to efficiently control the entry to the market, may be forced to grant access to competitors or to change substantial parts of its business.[586]

To obtain such changes, the Commission is entitled to impose specific obligations to the undertaking, including fines up to 10% of the annual revenue.[587] Such specific obligations could range from the obligation to include an application enabling to choose between different internet browsers in an "*Operating PC-System*",[588] compulsory licenses or the access to scripting codes or other know-how.[589]

Given the typically interventionist type of measure rendered by the European Commission to enforce compliance with Art. 101, 102 TFEU, the investor may suffer from considerable losses of potential revenues with regard to its business model. Such actions are *per se* suspect to potential claims under an IIA, including either the FET standard, an indirect expropriation or the failure of particular agreements by the host state under an umbrella clause.[590]

The third situation where conflicts could occur relates to all kind of public procurement processes or the attribution of concession which fall under the scope of the (new) public procurement regulations, especially

---

586 *Brinker* in: Schwarze EU-Kommentar, Art. 102 TFEU, para 38-41 and 48; *Schröter/Bartl* in: v. d. Groeben/Schwarze AEUV/EUV, Art. 102 TFEU, para 283-286; Among the most prominent cases were the decisions by the Commission against Microsoft regarding access to scripting codes, which lead to the CJEU's decision *CJEU*, 17.09.2007 – T-201/04 - Microsoft = ECLI:EU:T:2007:289 and the fines imposed on Microsoft regarding their non-compliance with the previously accepted offering of choices for web browsers, cf.: *European Commission*, Press Release: Commission fines Microsoft for non-compliance with browser choice commitments, 06/03/2013. Other cases may concern gas-transmission networks, as the example of the German energy supplier RWE shows: *European Commission*, Press Release: Commission opens German gas market to competition by accepting commitments from RWE to divest transmission network, 18/03/2009.

587 Cf. Art. 23 (2) of the Council Regulation (EC) No 1/2003 - Implementation of Antitrust Regulations, Official Journal of the European Communities L 1/1 (16/12/2002), 1; cf. also: *Brinker* in: Schwarze EU-Kommentar, Art. 102 TFEU, para 49, 50; *Jung* in: Grabitz/Hilf/Nettesheim EUV/AEUV, Art. 102 TFEU, para 382.

588 *European Commission*, Press Release: Commission fines Microsoft for non-compliance with browser choice commitments, 06/03/2013.

589 *Weiß* in: Calliess/Ruffert EUV/AEUV, Art. 102 TFEU, para 75; cf. for the access to scripting codes: *CJEU*, 17.09.2007 – T-201/04 - Microsoft = ECLI:EU:T:2007:289.

590 Cf. also: *Eilmansberger*, CMLR Vol. 46 (2009), 383, 415.

the regulations 2014/24/EU, 2014/25/EU (last amended by regulation 2015/2171[591]) and 2014/23/EU[592]. Through the extension of secondary regulations to procurements in the segments of energy, transportation and concessions for services these provisions gain particular importance for investment proceedings as well.[593]

Generally, procurement or concession processes need to be conducted in a public call for tenders, by using non-discriminatory, objective criteria which are published in advance, within a procedural framework which guarantees equal treatment of all participants.[594]

If a host state does not follow the procedural requirements, e.g. by omitting to perform a call for tenders or by not following the above set criteria in the tender procedure, the contract can – under certain conditions – be declared void (cf. Art. 2d of the directive 2007/66/EC which the member states need to transpose in their national law)[595]. Otherwise the Commission may initiate infringement proceedings against the host state. In case

---

591 Regulation 2015/2171 of 24 November 2015 amending Directive 2014/25/EU of the European Parliament and of the Council in respect of the application thresholds for the procedures for the award of contracts.

592 For an overview of the new regulations: *Neun/Otting*, EuZW, 2014, 446.

593 Even before regulation 2014/25 and the extension to procurements for energy, water and transportation, the mandatory application of general principles of European primary law, including transparency and non-discrimination could have had an impact on e.g. concessions attributed to foreign investments if the general principles were not observed, cf. *Eilmansberger*, CMLR Vol. 46 (2009), 383, 414 f.

594 Assuming that the different thresholds in the regulations are exceeded; *Oppermann/Classen et al.*, 5. Edn. (2011) § 21, para 67 ff; *Hobe*, 8. Edn. (2014), para 914 regarding public procurement and in, para 912 an interesting example which could serve as a blueprint for an investment dispute: The City of Cologne in Germany entered into a 30 year lend for an edifice to be used as exhibition hall. The private contractor was granted a remuneration of EUR 600 million, for which it also agreed to build the entire edifice based on the City's specifications. The CJEU declared that the contract violated EU procurement law as the lending and construction could not be separated and hence the centre of gravity regarding the contract was on the construction, which would have required the City to call for public tenders, cf.: *CJEU*, 29.10.2009 – C-536/07 - Koelnmesse = ECLI:EU:C:2009:664.

595 Germany transposed the directive 2007/66/EC, especially the legal consequences, in the §§ 101 b ff. Act against Restraints of Competition (GWB); for the appeal procedures cf. §§ 102 ff GWB.

the CJEU recognises the non-compliance with European procurement regulations, the judgment obliges the member state to revoke the contract.[596]

Again, for each of these situations, the revocation or non-performance of agreements *vis-à-vis* the investor could potentially rise a claim under the IIA.[597] The host states margin of action is limited by the mandatory provisions of EU law. However, under the IIA, the revocation itself might be outside the remaining margin of action considering the guarantees provided to investors under the IIA, especially the FET standard or even the prohibition of expropriation without prompt and adequate compensation.

3. Fundamental freedoms and their limitations in general

Outside the scope of application of the previous, specific, provisions there are numerous ways how member states could be forced to imply or apply a certain behaviour by EU law, limiting the fundamental freedoms and potentially infringing substantive guarantees in an IIA.

At first glance it is difficult to perceive a conflict of substantive provision in the IIAs and the fundamental freedoms in the European Treaties, as both seem to have a protective nature. However, conflicts may occur wherever the fundamental freedoms are subject to limitations (such as *inter alia* Art. 48, 51, etc. TFEU), as those limitations are generally broader than the limits to substantive protections in IIAs. Not all of these situations will result in a conflict properly speaking. If the member state (only) has the discretion to limit a fundamental freedom, it may decide not to limit it to comply with its obligations under the IIA. On the other hand, there are various cases in which secondary legislation mandates the EU member state to limit the scope of fundamental freedoms.[598] In those cases, if secondary legislation requires the host state to act within a certain margin of action which is outside the remaining margin under the IIA, the

596 *Oppermann/Classen et al.*, 5. Edn. (2011) § 21, para 71.

597 *Eilmansberger*, CMLR Vol. 46 (2009), 383, 414 f.

598 *Dimopoulos*, LIEI Vol. 39, No. 4 (2012), 447, 458 with reference to the potential conflicts with the EU competence in external relations in Art. 206, 207 TFEU as to set up exceptions to the freedoms and, p. 461 with explicit reference to sector specific new regulations; cf. for a more undifferentiated approach: *Kleinheisterkamp*, JIEL Vol. 15, No. 1 (2012), 85, 90 f who seems to consider the possibility of a conflict even thouth the member state is not entitled to act.

obligations issued from both frameworks collide.[599] Two examples, one from the banking sector and one from the energy sector, should illustrate these ideas:

The operational setting for banks operating in the EU is usually covered either by the free movement of services, the freedom of establishment or the free movement of capital.[600] Art. 58 (2) TFEU provides that the liberalization of those services should be pushed according to the liberalization of the free movement of capital. Based on several directives[601] the banking sector is now widely liberalised. However, since the Euro-Crises more interventionist secondary legislation has been adopted.[602] Especially the powers granted to the authorities under the Single Supervisory Mechanism (*inter alia* Art. 16 of the SSM-Directive[603]) could potentially lead to conflicts with investors in the banking sector. The provisions in the SSM-Directive are either binding on the member states or the authorities of the SSM are granted individual powers to directly act towards banks which fall within the scope of application of the directive.[604] Any of these measures, which include the mandatory use of profits to back up equity capital (Art. 16 (2) lit h. of the Directive) or financial penalties (Art. 19 of the Directive) could potentially be outside the margin of action allowed under an IIA (especially the guarantee of free transfer of funds or the FET). Hence, once again EU law and the IIA do not necessarily need to be complementary, but the member state could be forced to undertake an action to comply with EU law which is a potential breach of the IIA.

Similarly, the unbundling in the energy sector is a perfect example of the host states having a reduced margin of action which might potentially

599 *Eilmansberger*, CMLR Vol. 46 (2009), 383, 414 f with the reference to sector-specific rules and functional or structural separation as well as general changes in secondary legislation.

600 *Hobe*, 8. Edn. (2014), para 846 ff ; *Oppermann/Classen et al.*, 5. Edn. (2011) § 31, para 5 ff.

601 Directive 2006/48/EC - Capital Markets Directive, Official Journal of the European Communities L 177 (14.06.2006), 1 which replaced Directive 2000/12/EC - Capital Markets, Official Journal of the European Communities L 126 (20.03.2000 (repealed)), 1.

602 *Hobe*, 8. Edn. (2014), para 981.

603 Council Regulation (EU) No 1024/2013 - SSM Regulation, Official Journal of the European Union L 287 (15.10.2013).

604 Cf. also: *Hobe*, 8. Edn. (2014), para 982 f; *Kleinheisterkamp*, JIEL Vol. 15, No. 1 (2012), 85, 93 uses the example in another context but it perfectly reveals the conflict as well.

violate guarantees under the IIA (such as e.g. protection against expropriation or FET). Based on secondary legislation, especially since two directives in 2003[605] and the directives 2009/72/EC[606] and 2009/73/EC[607] the EU member states needed to adopt far reaching national legislations, aiming *inter alia* to separate electricity suppliers from the transitions networks (Art. 9 of the directives) and exercising a strict control on non-member state operators (Art. 11 of the directives), which seek to enter the European electricity market.[608] The obligation for a member state to adopt an unbundling regime which e.g. leads to a – forced – separation of previously joint legal entities and their obligation to offer an unhindered, non-discriminatory access to competitors could constitute a violation of an IIA under the (partial) expropriation standard.[609] Similarly, the investors could

---

605 Directive 2003/55/EC - Common rules for the internal market in natural gas, Official Journal of the European Communities L 176 (26.06.2003 (repealed)), 57 and Directive 2003/54/EC - Common rules for the internal market in electricity, Official Journal of the European Communities L 176 (26.06.2003 (repealed)), 37; for an overview of the evolution cf: *Roggenkamp/Redgwell/Rønne u. a.* (Eds.), Energy law in Europe, 3. Edn. (2016), para 4.197 ff.

606 2009/72/EC - Common Rules for the Internal Market in Electricity Directive, Official Journal of the European Communities L 211 (13/07/2009), 55.

607 2009/73/EC - Common Rules for the Internal Market in Natural Gas Directive, Official Journal of the European Communities L 211 (13/07/2009), 94.

608 *Roggenkamp/Redgwell/Rønne u. a.* (Eds.), Energy law in Europe, 3. Edn. (2016), para 3.45 and 3. 47; For further explanations for the (alleged) impact of the measures and their overall goal as well as an interpretative note of the directives: *European Commission*, Commission Staff Working Document SWD(2013) 177 final: Ownership Unbundling, 08.05.2013; *European Commission - Commission Staff Working Document*, Interpretative note on Directive 2009/72/EC concerning common rules for the internal market in electricity and Directive 2009/73/EC concerning common rules for the internal market in natural gas, 22/10/2010.

609 *Roggenkamp/Redgwell/Rønne u. a.* (Eds.), Energy law in Europe, 3. Edn. (2016), para 3.45; this conflict was e.g. raised in the arbitration proceedings of *Gazprom vs. Lithuania*, PCA Case No. 2011-16 (ongoing), which have been discontinued in 2015 due to the investor withdrawing from the claim: cf. : http://investmentpolicyhub.unctad.org/ISDS/Details/466 and http://www.naturalgaseurope.com/gazprom-lithuania-arbitration-case-23046 [last checked: 28/02/2017]. It should be noted that although the member states may choose between several models how to obtain the result set forth in the directives, each of these models requires substantial interference with the investor's business model and structure. A conflict could thus not only occur if there is only one

also claim that their guarantee of FET was violated.[610] Also mandatory joint procedures to assign capacities (Art. 7 of the directives) could potentially infringe with long-term agreements given to investors in the energy sector. The recent decision by the CJEU in infringement proceedings against the Slovak Republic demonstrates this conflict. According to the CJEU, the transposition of the 2003 directives would have violated the substantive guarantees under the IIA (cf. Chapter 12 for a further analysis).[611]

4. Non-discrimination (Art. 18 TFEU or the fundamental freedoms)

It should be referred to a further potential conflict, which will however be treated in detail *infra* (cf. Chapter 9). EU law generally prohibits discrimination between nationals of EU member states through Art. 18 TFEU or more generally by virtue of the fundamental freedoms (if applicable).[612] As the substantive protection offered by IIAs, especially in the intra-EU context, offers additional guarantees to some EU nationals but excludes others, the IIAs may constitute a violation of this principle of non-discrimination.[613] Hence, a conflict may occur between the IIA and EU law, if member states, through the IIA, would need to offer an investor a certain treatment, which is denied to other nationals of EU member states, which may not rely on the IIA.[614]

---

action remaining for the member state, but even if several actions are possible but all are outside the remaining margin of action allowed under the BIT.

610 For possible interferences with investment standards, cf. : *Roggenkamp/Redgwell/Rønne u. a.* (Eds.), Energy law in Europe, 3. Edn. (2016), para 3.43 ff.

611 *CJEU*, 15.09.2011 – C-264/09 = ECLI:EU:C:2011:580, para 47-51.

612 The principle of non-discrimination is considered as the cornerstone of all fundamental freedoms, which are *lex specialis* to Art. 18 TFEU if they are applicable, cf.: *Streinz* in: Streinz EUV/AEUV, Art. 18 TFEU, para 13 f; *Holoubek* in: Schwarze EU-Kommentar, Art. 18 TFEU, para 50.

613 *Akçay/Gaffney* in: *Bungenberg/Griebel/Hobe et al.* (Eds.), International Investment Law, 2015, p. 33; the argument will be dealt with *infra* (Chapter 9).

614 *European Commission*, Amicus Curia Brief filed in U.S. Steel Golbal Holdings I B.V. vs. Slovak Republic (PCA Case n°2013-6) - arbitration proceedings, 15/05/2014, para 31 f; *European Commission*, Amicus Curia Brief filed in Achmea (former Eureko BV) vs. Slovak Republic (PCA Case n°2008-13) - arbitration proceedings, 07/07/2010, para 33 ff; several tribunals did not analyse this conflict in detail by reference to the argument that even if the guarantees

5. Free movement of capital

The guarantee of free movement capital in Art. 63 TFEU has a large overlap, if not a nearly identical scope, with provision contained in IIAs, guaranteeing the free transfer of funds.[615] As already demonstrated, the TFEU also includes several possibilities for the EU to restrain the free movement of capital to third countries and within the EU in the Art. 64-66 and 75 TFEU. Whereas the former Art. 60 EC-Treaty was limited to third countries, Art. 75 TFEU does no longer contain such a restriction. Hence, restrictions are possible towards member and non-member states.[616]

If measures are adopted based on any of these provisions, they are mandatory for the member states. Thus, the member states are obliged to implement the restrictions on the free transfer of capital to states concerned by these measures. Such provisions raise a conflict with the free transfer of funds clauses contained in various IIAs, as they specifically guarantee the absence of any obstacle to transfer funds from or to the host state from any third country.[617] One might argue that also IIAs contain, either explicit or implicit reservations (through the scope of comparison or by means of the general possibility to justify restrictions based on public policy). However, this does not necessarily eliminate any conflict as the

---

under an IIA would constitute a discrimination, the advantages need to be extended to other investors but could not deprive any investor from relying on an IIA, cf. among others: *Euram vs. Slovak Republic*, 22.10.2012 – PCA Case no. 2010-17: First Award on Jurisdiction, para 268 ff; the German Supreme Court seems to consider that there is such discrimination, cf.: *German Federal Supreme Court*, 03.03.2016 – I ZB 2/15, para 62 ff. For the detailed analysis of this objection and especially the alleged possibility to eliminate a discrimination by extending its benefits to all potential addressis, cf. *infra* (Chapter 9).

615 *CJEU*, 03.03.2009 – C-249/06 - Commission vs Sweden = ECLI:EU:C:2009:119, para 25 ff; *CJEU*, 03.03.2009 – C-205/06 - Commission vs. Austria = ECLI:EU:C:2009:118, para 24 ff; *CJEU*, 19.11.2009 – C-118/07 - Commission vs. Finland = ECLI:EU:C:2009:715, para 18 ff.

616 Cf. also: *Johannsen*, Die Kompetenz der EU für ausländische Direktinvestitionen nach Lissabon (Beit. zum Transnat. Wirt.-R, Vol. 90, 2009), p. 29.

617 *CJEU*, 03.03.2009 – C-249/06 - Commission vs Sweden = ECLI:EU:C:2009:119, para 33 *Eilmansberger*, CMLR Vol. 46 (2009), 383, 408; *Kleinheisterkamp*, JIEL Vol. 15, No. 1 (2012), 85, 90; *Dimopoulos*, LIEI Vol. 39, No. 4 (2012), 447, 456; *Johannsen*, Die Kompetenz der EU für ausländische Direktinvestitionen nach Lissabon (Beit. zum Transnat. Wirt.-R, Vol. 90, 2009), 22.

degree of reservations may be different.[618] Implementing restrictions on the free movement of capital may thus be considerably challenged by the guarantees of the IIA and *vice versa*.[619]

6. Changing legal framework

Besides the already mentioned cases, there might be – especially secondary – EU law which changes the conditions upon which the investor relied when making the investment.[620] The recent discussions in 2016 regarding the prolongation of the admittance of glyphosate in the EU demonstrates a perfect example of how an investment might be affected by EU law. The member state will not have the discretion to admit the production of a good if this is prohibited under EU law. Such changes might occur regarding various determining circumstances, including *inter alia* the raise of costs due to new or aggravated regulations, changes in the general market structure or other business related regulations.[621] However such detrimental changes might be contrary to e.g. the FET-standard.

II. Conflicting provisions between EU law and IIAs regarding jurisdiction

It should now be demonstrated that conflicts are also conceivable regarding the dispute settlement mechanism set forth in IIAs. As already outlined in the preliminary remarks under (A.), the type of (potential) conflicts between EU law and IIAs regarding jurisdictional provisions contained in IIAs is different from the type of conflict demonstrated with regard to substantive protection (cf. *supra* B. I.). Looking at jurisdictional provisions, potential conflicts do not relate to an action which is imple-

618 Cf. also: *Dimopoulos*, CMLR Vol. 48, No. 1 (2011), 63, 79 f; *Tietje*, Intra-EU BITs als Herausforderung im Mehrebenensystem des Rechts (Beit. zum Transnat. Wirt.-R, Vol. 104, 2011), p. 13.

619 *CJEU*, 03.03.2009 – C-249/06 - Commission vs Sweden = ECLI:EU:C:2009:119, para 39 ff; *CJEU*, 03.03.2009 – C-205/06 - Commission vs. Austria = ECLI:EU:C:2009:118, para 38 ff; *CJEU*, 19.11.2009 – C-118/07 - Commission vs. Finland = ECLI:EU:C:2009:715, para 31 ff; cf. also: *Dimopoulos*, CMLR Vol. 48, No. 1 (2011), 63, 79 f.

620 *Eilmansberger*, CMLR Vol. 46 (2009), 383, 415.

621 *Eilmansberger*, CMLR Vol. 46 (2009), 383, 415.

mented by the host state or the EU. The conflict is rather related to the question whether the European Treaties permit investment arbitration proceedings as foreseen under an IIA.

1. Conflict between arbitration clauses and Art. 344 TFEU

It could be argued that arbitration clauses in IIAs which enable investor-state arbitration and inter-state arbitration might be a breach of Art. 344 TFEU. The European Commission expressly supports this argument.[622] As to the Commission, the EU member states, through Art. 344 TFEU, granted a jurisdictional monopoly to the CJEU to render binding decision on the interpretation of EU law and to ensure its uniform interpretation. Accordingly, the European Treaties would include the obligation to submit any dispute regarding an EU member state's responsibilities under EU law to the CJEU. As a consequence, any arbitration clause contained in an IIA, which refers an investment dispute dealing with such responsibility to any dispute settlement mechanism other than the CJEU would be prohibited by the European Treaties. From this perspective, arbitration clauses contained in IIAs would, as to the Commission, generally conflict with EU law.

Hence, through conclusion of the IIA, the member states enabled themselves to recourse to an arbitration mechanism and thus created the prerequisites for a possible circumvention of EU law and paved the way for its non-uniform application. As to the Commission, creating this prerequisite is prohibited under Art. 344 TFEU.[623]

---

622 *European Commission*, Amicus Curia Brief filed in Achmea (former Eureko BV) vs. Slovak Republic (PCA Case n°2008-13) - arbitration proceedings, 07/07/2010, para 27 f, 79 and 90; *European Commission*, Amicus Curia Brief filed in EURAM vs. Slovak Republic (PCA Case n°2010-17) - arbitration proceedings, 13/10/2011, p. 4 f.

623 *European Commission*, Amicus Curia Brief filed in U.S. Steel Golbal Holdings I B.V. vs. Slovak Republic (PCA Case n°2013-6) - arbitration proceedings, 15/05/2014, para 44 f.

2. Conflict between arbitration clauses and the dispatch of competencies in the EU

More generally it could be (and was) argued that Art. 344 TFEU expresses a series of more general principles, including the exclusive interpretation of EU law by the CJEU, the pre-eminence of the judicial system in the EU and the prohibition to enable member states by any means to "*circumvent the application of relevant rules of [European] Union law*"[624].[625] All nationals from EU member states should in general (and to the extent that intra-EU relationships are concerned) exclusively recourse to the judicial system provided by EU law. This system consists of national courts and their ability to refer questions to the CJEU within the framework of the preliminary ruling procedure (Art. 267 TFEU) and the possibility for the Commission to initiate infringement proceedings (Art. 258 ff TFEU) against member states.[626] Both mechanisms (the preliminary ruling procedure as well as the infringement proceedings) would guarantee the exclusive competence for the CJEU to interpret – as last resort – EU law and guarantee its uniform application in all member states. However, granting access to a – separate and private – arbitral tribunal, which, as it is not considered to be a "*court*" in the sense of Art. 267 TFEU[627], is unable to

---

624 *European Commission*, Amicus Curia Brief filed in U.S. Steel Golbal Holdings I B.V. vs. Slovak Republic (PCA Case n°2013-6) - arbitration proceedings, 15/05/2014, para 45.

625 *European Commission*, Amicus Curia Brief filed in U.S. Steel Golbal Holdings I B.V. vs. Slovak Republic (PCA Case n°2013-6) - arbitration proceedings, 15/05/2014, para 37, 44; *European Commission*, Amicus Curia Brief filed in Achmea (former Eureko BV) vs. Slovak Republic (PCA Case n°2008-13) - arbitration proceedings, 07/07/2010, para 26; *European Commission*, Amicus Curia Brief filed in EURAM vs. Slovak Republic (PCA Case n°2010-17) - arbitration proceedings, 13/10/2011, p. 3 and 5.

626 *European Commission*, Amicus Curia Brief filed in U.S. Steel Golbal Holdings I B.V. vs. Slovak Republic (PCA Case n°2013-6) - arbitration proceedings, 15/05/2014, para 44 ff; *European Commission*, Amicus Curia Brief filed in Achmea (former Eureko BV) vs. Slovak Republic (PCA Case n°2008-13) - arbitration proceedings, 07/07/2010, para 24; to some extent also: *European Commission*, Amicus Curia Brief filed in Micula vs. Romania to the U.S. Court of Appeals, 04/02/2016, p. 27.

627 *CJEU*, 23.03.1982 – C-102/81 - Nordsee = ECLI:EU:C:1982:107, para 13 and *CJEU*, 01.06.1999 – C-126/97 - Eco Swiss = ECLI:EU:C:1999:269, para 34; cf. also: *Dimopoulos*, CMLR Vol. 48, No. 1 (2011), 63, 87; *Burgstaller*, LIEI Vol. 39, No. 2 (2012), 207, 219 f.

recourse to the preliminary ruling procedure would hence violate this principle of exclusive interpretation. *De facto* arbitral tribunals would possibly apply and interpret EU law even contrary to the interpretation given by the CJEU, which might cause distortions to the effective application of EU law in the member states.[628] Consequently, the arbitration clauses contained in IIAs would conflict with such general principle of exclusive jurisdiction of the CJEU. As a consequence of this conflict, the arbitral tribunals would lack jurisdiction to judge an investment dispute involving EU law.[629]

3. Conflict between arbitration clauses and the principle of non-discrimination (Art. 18 TFEU)

Furthermore, the European Commission considers arbitration clauses in IIAs to breach the principle of non-discrimination in Art. 18 TFEU, as some investors from several EU member states are treated differently than investors from other member states.[630] In fact, investors from some EU

---

628 *European Commission*, Amicus Curia Brief filed in Achmea (former Eureko BV) vs. Slovak Republic (PCA Case n°2008-13) - arbitration proceedings, 07/07/2010, para 24 and 79; Letter of the European Commission to the Czech Department of Finance from 13.01.2006, handed over to the arbitral tribunal in *Eastern Sugar vs Czech Republic* and published in *Eastern Sugar vs. Czech Republic*, 27.03.2007 – SCC No. 088/2004 - Partial award, para 119.

629 *European Commission*, Amicus Curia Brief filed in Achmea (former Eureko BV) vs. Slovak Republic (PCA Case n°2008-13) - arbitration proceedings, 07/07/2010, para 26 with reference to: *CJEU*, 30.05.2006 – C-459/03 - Mox Plant = ECLI:EU:C:2006:345, para 123; cf. also: *Binder vs. Czech Republic*, 06.06.2007 – UNCITRAL - Award on Jurisdiction; *Eastern Sugar vs. Czech Republic*, 27.03.2007 – SCC No. 088/2004 - Partial award; *Electrabel vs. Hungary*, 30.11.2012 – ICSID Case No. ARB/07/19: Decision on Jurisdiction, Applicable Law and Liability; *Euram vs. Slovak Republic*, 22.10.2012 – PCA Case no. 2010-17: First Award on Jurisdiction; *Achmea vs. Slovak Republic*, 26.10.2012 – PCA Case No. 2008-13 - Award on Jurisdiction, Arbitrability and Suspension; *Oostergetel & Laurentius vs. Slovak Republic*, 30.04.2010 – UNICTRAL - Award on Jurisdiction.

630 *European Commission*, Amicus Curia Brief filed in Achmea (former Eureko BV) vs. Slovak Republic (PCA Case n°2008-13) - arbitration proceedings, 07/07/2010, para 33 ff; Letter of the European Commission to the Czech Department of Finance from 13.01.2006, handed over to the arbitral tribunal in *Eastern Sugar vs Czech Republic* and published in *Eastern Sugar vs Czech Republic*, para 119.

member states can rely on an IIA which grants access to international arbitration, whereas investors from member states which have not concluded such an agreement are prevented from recourse to such a dispute resolution mechanism.[631]

The consequence of the three aforementioned conflicts between EU law and the jurisdictional provisions (i.e. the arbitration clauses) in IIAs would be that EU member states are generally prohibited to refer investment disputes to arbitral tribunals through arbitration clauses contained in IIAs. Consequently, this conflict would lead to the arbitral tribunal lacking jurisdiction to rule the investment dispute.[632]

---

631 The question will be treated *infra* (Chapter 9). It has been raised in numerous arbitration proceedings, cf. the Respondents' and Commission's arguments in the following proceedings: *Binder vs. Czech Republic*, 06.06.2007 – UNCITRAL - Award on Jurisdiction; *Eastern Sugar vs. Czech Republic*, 27.03.2007 – SCC No. 088/2004 - Partial award; *Electrabel vs. Hungary*, 30.11.2012 – ICSID Case No. ARB/07/19: Decision on Jurisdiction, Applicable Law and Liability; *Euram vs. Slovak Republic*, 22.10.2012 – PCA Case no. 2010-17: First Award on Jurisdiction; *Achmea vs. Slovak Republic*, 26.10.2012 – PCA Case No. 2008-13 - Award on Jurisdiction, Arbitrability and Suspension; *Oostergetel & Laurentius vs. Slovak Republic*, 30.04.2010 – UNICTRAL - Award on Jurisdiction cf. also for a discussion of the issue: *Eilmansberger*, CMLR Vol. 46 (2009), 383, 402 f, 407; *Wehland*, ICLQ Vol. 58, Iss. 2 (2009), 297, 311 ff; *Reinisch*, LIEI Vol. 39, No. 2 (2012), 157, 176; *Dimopoulos*, CMLR Vol. 48, No. 1 (2011), 63, 84; the position of *Dahlquist/Lenk et al.*, European Policy Analysis, 2016:4, 1, 5 is not entirely clear: rights should be extended but if this was not possible, the (extra-EU) BITs would need to be terminated; cf. also: *Söderlund*, JOIA Vol. 24, Iss. 5 (2007), 455, 462. Mainly due to this objection the German Federal Supreme Court made use of the preliminary ruling procedure to the CJEU in *German Federal Supreme Court*, 03.03.2016 – I ZB 2/15.

632 *European Commission*, Amicus Curia Brief filed in U.S. Steel Golbal Holdings I B.V. vs. Slovak Republic (PCA Case n°2013-6) - arbitration proceedings, 15/05/2014, para 31 f; and 38; *European Commission*, Amicus Curia Brief filed in Achmea (former Eureko BV) vs. Slovak Republic (PCA Case n°2008-13) - arbitration proceedings, 07/07/2010, para 30-32; *European Commission*, Amicus Curia Brief filed in EURAM vs. Slovak Republic (PCA Case n°2010-17) - arbitration proceedings, 13/10/2011, p. 5; cf. also the Respondent's argument in: *Achmea vs. Slovak Republic*, 26.10.2012 – PCA Case No. 2008-13 - Award on Jurisdiction, Arbitrability and Suspension, para 114-116 and *Euram vs. Slovak Republic*, 22.10.2012 – PCA Case no. 2010-17: First Award on Jurisdiction, para 98 ff.

C. Potential implications of the conflict

The previous section demonstrated various potential conflicts which could occur between IIAs and EU law regarding both, substantive guarantees provided for in IIAs and the dispute settlement mechanism as conceived by an IIA. In the following, the potential implications of such conflicts for arbitration proceedings will be analysed. It will be demonstrated that ignoring such conflict is not an option (for both, host states as well as investors) as such potential conflicts of EU law with IIAs could impact the claim and enforcement of the investors (alleged) rights on various occasions. Analysing such conflict and developing a solution how to deal with this conflict is a fundamental requirement in order to establish legal security in investment proceedings involving subject matters of EU law.

The first stage where such interference might occur is the stage of the arbitral proceedings (I.). If objections are raised by the host state during the arbitration proceedings dealing with an "EU"-investment dispute, the arbitral tribunal will need to address such objections and determine how to deal with a potential conflict of EU law and IIAs.

However, the conflict is not limited to this occasion. Once, the award is rendered, and even assuming a tribunal would completely ignore any conflict (as it has been done by various tribunals) the conflict between EU law and IIAs could (re-)occur at the stage of setting-aside proceedings or annulment proceedings (II.). During those proceedings the tribunal rendering its decision whether the arbitral award has to be set aside or annulled may need to deal with a conflict between EU law and the provisions contained in IIAs if objections relating thereto are raised by the host states.

Supposing the award is not set-aside, the investor will probably seek enforcement of its award, which may – once again – rise the conflict with EU law (III.). Besides the framework of proceedings initiated by the investor, the conflict could also occur on the level of infringement proceedings initiated by the European Commission (IV.).[633]

---

633 The case of infringement proceedings will not be dealt with in this thesis as the perspective and focus should be on the arbitration proceedings initiated by the investor. It is however obvious that some of the results and findings, especially those regarding the compatibility or incompatibility of IIAs with EU law may also be transposed to any infringement proceedings initiated against member states, as it happened in 2015 regarding several intra-EU IIAs, cf. *European Commission*, Press Release: Commission asks Member States to terminate their intra-EU bilateral investment treaties, 18/06/2015.

I. Arbitration proceedings

Predominantly the interference of EU law with IIAs or its guarantees might be raised in the arbitration proceedings where measures influenced by EU law are challenged by an investor. The host states might – and did – argue that the tribunal lacks jurisdiction, as the arbitration clause is rendered void or at least inapplicable by virtue of conflicting EU law. Furthermore, if the tribunal dismisses these jurisdictional objections, the EU member states might still argue that damages could not be attributed for an alleged violation of the IIA, if this would be contrary to substantive provisions of EU law.[634]

Such objections have effectively been raised in several arbitration proceedings in the past years which reveals the importance of this subject matter for both, investors and host states.

II. 'Setting-aside' or 'vacatur' proceedings and annulment proceedings

Once an arbitral award has been rendered in an investment dispute, the conflict may "*reappear*" at various occasions. However, in this context, one needs to distinguish between the different procedural rules the arbitration was based on. If the tribunal was set up based on the ICSID-Convention, the award is suspect to an annulment proceeding following Art. 52 of the ICSID-Convention.[635] In these annulment proceedings, the question of conflict with EU law may – once again – be raised (2.).[636] However, regarding other forums (such as ICC, SCC, etc.), 'setting-aside'- proceedings might be initiated by recourse to national courts.[637] Although, those courts will only evaluate specific 'grounds' to challenge

634 For the analysis cf. *infra* (Chapter 9).

635 *Engel*, SchiedsVZ, 2015, 218, 220.

636 *Engel*, SchiedsVZ, 2015, 218, 220; In *Ioan Micula, Viorel Micula & others vs. Romania*, 11.12.2013 – ICSID Case No. ARB/05/20 - Final Award Romania – after not having succeeded with its objections in the arbitration proceedings – to seek annulment of the award based on the "*intra-EU-defense*", cf. for a summary of the arguments in the annulment proceedings: *Peterson*, IA Reporter Vol. 9, No. 6 (2016), 7, 9 ff.

637 *Engel*, SchiedsVZ, 2015, 218,220; This possibility (and its risks for the annulment of the award) is also clearly recognised by the Tribunal in *Electrabel vs. Hungary*, 30.11.2012 – ICSID Case No. ARB/07/19: Decision on Jurisdiction, Applicable Law and Liability, para 4.112.

the awards, some of these grounds enable to reintroduce the aforementioned objections and conflicts with EU law (1.).

1. Setting-aside an award rendered in private forums (ICC, SCC, etc.)

As previously described, whether or not an arbitral award may be challenged in '*setting-aside*' proceedings, is a question of the national law, in the country of the award's origin.[638] However, the transposition of the UNCITRAL Model law in 2006 in various states lead to a certain consensus on the grounds which allow to challenge an arbitral award. Especially two grounds (an award being contrary to the country's public policy and the invalidity of the arbitration agreement) are of further relevance for this thesis as they enable to challenge the award based on its non-compliance with EU law.[639]

(1) Invalidity of the arbitration clause (Art. 34 (2) lit. a UNCITRAL Model Law (Lack of jurisdiction))

According to the UNCITRAL Model Law, an arbitral award should be set aside if the arbitration clause was invalid, leading to a lack of jurisdiction

638 *Pavic* in: *Knahr* (Ed.), Investment and commercial arbitration, 2010, p. 131, 133; *Engel*, SchiedsVZ, 2015, 218, 220; There are two prevailing ways to determine the "*origin*" of an award, either by referring to the procedural framework or to the place of the arbitral tribunals legal seat, cf. *Pavic* in: *Knahr* (Ed.), Investment and commercial arbitration, 2010, p. 131, 133. For the purpose of the analysis the choice of criteria to determine the awards origin does not impact, as the analysis is based on the grounds for annulment only, which may anyways diverge from one country to the other, displaying however a certain uniformity on key elements.

639 Compare e.g. the German § 1059 Code of Civil Procedure (ZPO), Art. 41 and 42 of the Spanish Arbitration Act (Ley 60/2003 de arbitraje); Art. 190 (2) of the Swiss Federal Statute on Private International Law; for a further, comparative analysis: *Pavic* in: *Knahr* (Ed.), Investment and commercial arbitration, 2010, p. 131; for the Spanish Arbitration Act: *Cairns*, Arbitration International Vol. 22, No. 4 (2006), 573 and the references *supra* regarding the general system of setting-aside in arbitration proceedings.

for the tribunal.[640] An invalid arbitration clause will lead to the missing consent of the parties (or at least the host state's consent) to submit their dispute to arbitration.

Thus, this ground for annulment enables any host state to reintroduce its objections with regard to conflicting provisions in EU law which would prevent the tribunal from having jurisdiction to rule the case: if the arbitration clause is itself invalid or inapplicable by virtue of EU law, the arbitral tribunal would lack jurisdiction.[641] Such argument, based on a conflict of IIAs with Art. 344, 257 or Art. 18 TFEU have been demonstrated *supra*. If the national courts follow these arguments, any award could be set aside based on these considerations.

A prominent example of the risk of an award getting challenged on such grounds are the setting aside proceedings in *Achmea (former Eureko) vs. Slovak Republic*[642] which lead to a couple of decisions by German Courts and *in fine* to a preliminary ruling reference by the German Supreme Court to the CJEU in Mai 2016 to examine the validity of the IIA's arbitration clause with regard to EU law.[643] In these proceedings the Slovak Republic expressly argued that the award needs to be set aside as the arbitral tribunal did not have jurisdiction to rule the case as the arbitration clause contained in the IIA would conflict with EU law. The German Supreme Court referred the question to the CJEU through the preliminary ruling procedure. From the investor's perspective, the challenge to the award based on a conflict with EU law already considerably delayed the enforcement.

640 *Pavic* in: *Knahr* (Ed.), Investment and commercial arbitration, 2010, p. 131, 136; *Lachmann*, Handbuch für die Schiedsgerichtspraxis, 3. Edn. (2008), p. 524 f.

641 For a complete discussion of this topic, cf. *infra* (Chapter 9).

642 *Achmea vs. Slovak Republic*, 26.10.2012 – PCA Case No. 2008-13 - Award on Jurisdiction, Arbitrability and Suspension and *Achmea vs. Slovak Republic*, 07.12.2012 – PCA Case No. 2008-13 - Award.

643 *German Federal Supreme Court*, 03.03.2016 – I ZB 2/15. This is the second time the Federal Supreme Court had been sought with the Achmea/Eureko proceedings. The first appeal was rejected as inadmissible, cf. : *German Federal Supreme Court*, 19.09.2013 – III ZB 37/12. During the appeal the arbitral tribunal rendered the final award, leading to the loss of interest in legal protection for the host state as the same objections could be advanced in the setting aside proceedings against the final award.

(2) Award contrary to public policy

Furthermore, objections as to a contradiction of the award with substantive provisions of EU law may also be invoked in the setting-aside proceedings. The UNCIRTAL Model Law enables the annulment of the award if the award is contrary to public policy. The definition of rules forming part of the term "*public policy*" by national courts varies widely. However, public policy is often defined as those norms being the fundamental and inalienable norms and legal principles of a state.[644] Hence, an arbitral award rendered in disregard of EU law could only be set-aside, if the (potentially) conflicting provision of substantive EU law constituted such fundamentals and inalienable norms for the state in which the host state applied for annulment.[645]

It might be doubtful if the substantive provisions of EU law are of such character. However, the CJEU clearly stated that the misapplication of EU competition rules (in the concrete case: Art. 101 TFEU) by an arbitral tribunal would constitute a violation of the member states' public policy.[646] From the reasoning provided in the judgment, one might conclude that the scope of the decision is not limited to EU competition law or Art. 101 TFEU. The CJEU stated:

> "(…) [Art. 101 TFEU] constitutes a fundamental provision which is *essential* for the accomplishment of the tasks entrusted to the Community and, in particular, *for the functioning of the internal market.* […]
>
> For [this] reasons […], the provisions of [Art. 101 TFEU] may be regarded as a matter of public policy (…)."[647]

There are numerous substantive provisions in the European Treaties and even in EU secondary law, which are of a similar importance for the functioning of the internal market within the EU and which could be circumvented by enforcing an award. The CJEU in another decision also included provisions concerning the protection of consumers in the term of public

---

644 *Lachmann*, Handbuch für die Schiedsgerichtspraxis, 3. Edn. (2008), p. 549.

645 *Wehland*, ICLQ Vol. 58, Iss. 2 (2009), 297, 308.

646 *CJEU*, 01.06.1999 – C-126/97 - Eco Swiss = ECLI:EU:C:1999:269, para 36 and 39, the dispute concerned the enforcement of an agreement between Benneton and Eco Swiss regarding market distribution, which presumably was void under EU competition law, cf. for an extensive analysis of the judgement: *Komninos*, CMLR Iss. 37 (2000), 459.

647 *CJEU*, 01.06.1999 – C-126/97 - Eco Swiss = ECLI:EU:C:1999:269, para 36 and 38 [emphasis added].

policy which should lead to an annulment of an arbitral award.[648] Indeed, from the EU law perspective, the protection of the internal market is the EU's most fundamental task. The scope of substantive provisions which might therefore (at least potentially) fall under the term "*public policy*" could be extended to most of the cases in which potential conflicts of investment law with EU law could occur: including the state aid provisions, the provisions on public procurement law and the fundamental freedoms (cf. *supra*).[649]

Furthermore, the CJEU backed up its reasoning by the conclusion that the legal effects of Art. 101 TFEU (the invalidity of the agreement contrary to competition law) would be circumvented if an award is allowed to enforce the obligations contained therein.[650] This would also apply to state aid provisions, public procurement law or most of the EU secondary law. Enforcing an award contrary to these provisions, would lead to a legal situation completely contrary to what is mandated by EU law. Thus, the ground of annulment for a violation of public policy offers a gateway for the host state to claim its objections as to contradicting substantive provision of EU law, at least if these setting aside proceedings take place in an EU member state.

Recently in 2015, a host state (Hungary regarding the award rendered in *EDF vs. Hungary*[651] which is unfortunately unpublished) tried to challenge an (unfavourable) award in such setting-aside proceedings based on the argument that the award was contrary to "*public policy*". As the arbitral tribunal was based in Switzerland, Hungary initiated setting-aside proceedings in Switzerland before the Swiss Federal Court.[652] Being a claim in Switzerland, EU law will not necessarily apply as *lex loci arbitri*, which lead to a particular shape of the reasoning by Hungary. It tried to demonstrate that by rendering an award which condemns Hungary to pay compensation to EDF, the arbitral tribunal forces Hungary to violate its obliga-

---

648 *CJEU*, 26.10.2006 – C-168/05 - Elisa Maria Mostaza Claro = ECLI:EU:C:2006:675, para 35 ff.

649 Cf. also: *Engel*, SchiedsVZ, 2015, 218, 221; similar but in the context of enforcement proceedings: *Tietje/Wackernagel*, JWIT Vol. 16, Iss. 2 (2015), 205, 224.

650 *CJEU*, 23.03.1982 – C-102/81 - Nordsee = ECLI:EU:C:1982:107, para 14 f; cf. also: *Komninos*, CMLR Iss. 37 (2000), 459, 465.

651 *EDF vs. Hungary*, 04.12.2014 – UNCITRAL - Award.

652 *Swiss Federal Supreme Court, 1èr Cour de droit Civil*, 06.10.2015 – 4A 34/2015.

tions under the European Treaties and hence the principle of *pacta sunt servanda*. This principle should be part of the Swiss public policy which is recognised as setting-aside-ground by the Swiss national arbitration law in Art. 190 (2) lit. e LDIP.[653] This is rejected by the Swiss Federal Court. However, it seems as if the reasoning is more based on procedural issues than on a clear dismissal of Hungary's arguments.[654] However, the proceedings demonstrate the imminent danger for an investor that the award is challenged based on a conflict between IIAs and EU law even after the award has been rendered by the arbitral tribunal.

2. ICSID-Annulment proceedings

With regard to ICSID-Proceedings the situation is different. Other than arbitral awards rendered in a private forum, an ICSID-Award can only be subject to annulment procedures for grounds stated in Art. 52 (1) of the ICSID-Convention. The only ground for annulment being relevant for potential objections by the host state (in the context of this thesis) is the *man-*

---

653 *Swiss Federal Supreme Court, 1èr Cour de droit Civil*, 06.10.2015 – 4A 34/2015, para 5.2.

654 After addressing the arbitral tribunal's reasoning and expressly referring to the fact that the tribunal did not find any incompatibility between EU law and the IIA in question, the Swiss Federal Court does not accept the violation of the *pacta sunt servanda* principle as part of the Swiss public policy (cf. *Swiss Federal Supreme Court, 1èr Cour de droit Civil*, 06.10.2015 – 4A 34/2015, para 5.3.2; cf. also: *Hepburn*, IA Reporter Vol. 8, No. 25 (2015), 16, 18 f.). Regarding further arguments by Hungary, especially the ignorance of the tribunal to refer to material and procedural requirements under the Art. 107 ff TFEU, the tribunal seems to dismiss them primarily for formal considerations, without necessarily addressing the substance. The tribunal states that the alleged errors by the arbitral tribunal would need to be addressed under the violation of the right to be heard, which has not been invoked by Hungary. Hence, the tribunal cannot properly address the question (cf. *Swiss Federal Supreme Court, 1èr Cour de droit Civil*, 06.10.2015 – 4A 34/2015, para 5.3.2; cf. also: *Hepburn*, IA Reporter Vol. 8, No. 25 (2015), 16, 18 f). However given these limits, the decision does not contribute a clear answer to the pending questions of how EU law would influence the potential setting-aside grounds regarding an arbitral award allegedly violation EU law, *Swiss Federal Supreme Court, 1èr Cour de droit Civil*, 06.10.2015 – 4A 34/2015, para 5.3.2.2; *Hepburn*, IA Reporter Vol. 8, No. 25 (2015), 16, 19.

ifest excess of powers by the arbitral tribunal.[655] However, manifest excess of powers has a dual nature in the case-law of the annulment committees under the ICSID-Convention. An excess of powers can either occur if the arbitral tribunal (incorrectly) admitted its jurisdiction or if the arbitral tribunal "*fails to apply the applicable law*"[656].[657]

Similar as for private arbitration forums, the manifest excess of powers constitutes a perfect gateway for the host state to invoke conflicts with EU law in the annulment proceedings, if those have been disrespected in the arbitral award and *vice versa*. It could e.g. be argued that the arbitral tribunal erroneously admitted its jurisdiction despite of contradicting provisions of EU law or that the tribunal omitted to apply (or fundamentally misapplied) fundamental norms of the European Treaties, which conflict with substantive guarantees under the IIA.[658]

The annulment-proceedings in the *Micula vs. Romania-Case*[659] illustrate the risk for the investor of having its award being challenged in annulment proceedings based on objections relating to EU law. Romania introduced annulment proceedings after having been condemned by the arbitral tribunal to pay damages to the investor. The challenges were mainly based on a conflict of the IIA with state-aid rules under EU law and the

655 In the case *Ioan Micula, Viorel Micula & others vs. Romania*, 11.12.2013 – ICSID Case No. ARB/05/20 - Final Award, Romania tried to seek annulment on several other grounds, including the departure from fundamental rules of procedure and the failure to state reasons. Whereas the procedural objection was based on particular facts of the case, Romania tried to introduce a control on the quality of the reasoning and its correctness through the "*failure to state reasons*", cf. : *Annulment Committee in Micula vs. Romania*, 26.02.2016 – ICSID Case No. ARB/05/20 - Decision on Annulment, para 159 ff. The tentative is clearly dismissed by the annulment committee, stating at para 135: "[…] *as long as reasons have been stated, even if incorrect, unconvincing or non-exhaustive, the award cannot be annulled on this ground*".

656 *Annulment Committee in Micula vs. Romania*, 26.02.2016 – ICSID Case No. ARB/05/20 - Decision on Annulment, para 127 with reference to *inter alia*: *Annulment Committee in MTD vs. Chile*, 21.03.2007 – ICSID Case No. ARB/01/7 - Decision on Annulment, para 44.

657 *Annulment Committee in Micula vs. Romania*, 26.02.2016 – ICSID Case No. ARB/05/20 - Decision on Annulment, para 125 and 127.

658 Cf. also for the similarity of the grounds of annulment and the grounds to set aside an award regarding the lack of the tribunal's jurisdiction and the applicable law: *Steindl*, Yearbook on International Arbitration Vol. 4 (2015), 181, 186-188.

659 *Annulment Committee in Micula vs. Romania*, 26.02.2016 – ICSID Case No. ARB/05/20 - Decision on Annulment.

objections to the arbitral tribunal's jurisdiction which have been demonstrated *supra*.[660] Although the annulment-committee dismissed Romania's objections, the proceedings demonstrate the inherent risk that the questions of a potential conflict of EU law with IIAs reappears at various occasions during and subsequent to arbitral proceedings in an investment dispute.

III. Enforcement proceedings

Even if neither the arbitral tribunal in the main proceedings, nor the ad-hoc committee in the annulment proceedings or a national court in setting-aside proceedings followed a host state's objection regarding a conflict of the IIA in question and EU Law, such objections may reappear if the investor seeks to enforce the arbitral award. Again, one needs to distinguish between arbitration proceedings under the ICSID-Convention and other forums (ICC; SCC, etc.), as the ICSID-Convention imposes a major difference compared to a private forum.

1. Enforcement in private forums (ICC, SCC, etc.)

Regarding enforcement proceedings, arbitral awards rendered under any forum except ICSID, fall under the scope of the New York Convention.[661] The convention states that if an investor seeks enforcement of the award, the award needs to be recognised in each jurisdiction where such enforcement is desired. The Convention enumerates several (conclusive) grounds, which can be invoked to deny enforcement to the award and which might be gateways to challenge the award based on the above mentioned (poten-

---

660 *Annulment Committee in Micula vs. Romania*, 26.02.2016 – ICSID Case No. ARB/05/20 - Decision on Annulment, para 144 ff where Romania as applicant tries to demonstrate the arbitral tribunals failure to apply the applicable law by ignoring the interaction between the BIT in question and EU law; the additional argument advanced which tries do advance the same argument on the "*failure to state reasons*" fails, cf. footnote 655. Romanias reasoning and the reasons by the arbitral tribunal are summarized by*Peterson*, IA Reporter Vol. 9, No. 6 (2016), 7, 9 ff.

661 New York Convention on the Recognition and Enforcement of Foreign Arbitral Awards (1958), *Ehle* in: Wolff New York Convention, Art. I, para 20-22 and 151 ff.

tial) conflicts with EU law. The convention has largely been transposed to national laws, allowing similar if not identical grounds to refuse the enforcement of an arbitral award as those under the UNCITRAL Model Law. Art. V of the New York Convention stipulates that enforcement may be refused:

> "(1) (a) the said [arbitration] agreement is not valid under the law to which the parties have subjected it or, failing any indication thereon, under the law of the country where the award was made; or […]
>
> (2) (b) The recognition or enforcement of the award would be contrary to the public policy of that country."

Hence, upon request to enforce an arbitral award, the host state may once again invoke jurisdictional as well as substantive challenges to the award, if the awards conflicts with EU law. The basis for those challenges are (nearly) identical with those already discussed with reference to possible setting-aside proceedings (i.e. a lack of jurisdiction and an award being contrary to public policy).[662] The predominant difference to the setting-aside proceedings is that a foreign arbitral award – to be enforced – needs to be recognised in every foreign jurisdiction where enforcement measures should take place.[663] Hencc, whenever the investor seeks enforcement in *any* EU member state, the objects may be raised in *any of such enforcement proceedings*.

2. Enforcement of ICSID-Awards

As already demonstrated, by virtue of Art. 53, 54 ICSID-Convention an award rendered under the ICSID-Framework should be granted the same status as a national judgment. In principle there should be no grounds to refuse enforcement.[664]

However, although there is no settled case-law regarding the denial of an enforcement of an ICSID award, some scholars argue that *exequatur* will be refused to the award in the EU member states, if such award re-

---

662 *Engel*, SchiedsVZ, 2015, 218, 220; *Wehland*, ICLQ Vol. 58, Iss. 2 (2009), 297, 308; *Tietje/Wackernagel*, JWIT Vol. 16, Iss. 2 (2015), 205, 224.

663 *Herdegen*, 10. Edn. (2014), p. 359; regarding the determination of the awards "*nationality*" cf.: *Pavic* in: *Knahr* (Ed.), Investment and commercial arbitration, 2010, p. 131, 133 f.

664 *Engel*, SchiedsVZ, 2015, 218, 220.

veals to be contrary to fundamental provisions of EU law, despite Art. 53, 54 of the ICSID-Convention.[665]

The argument is based on a treaty conflict between the European Treaties and the ICSID-Convention and the reception of international conventions concluded by the member states within the EU.[666] In the European Treaties the member states agreed to grant EU law absolute primacy in their *inter se* relations. Hence, no international convention could set away this principle. An award being contrary to EU law could therefore potentially not be enforced in the EU. Art. 53, 54 ICSID-Convention would be inapplicable as they conflict with EU law.[667] The argument is similar to considerations regarding intra-EU IIAs and the relevant rule of conflict for these treaties (cf. *infra "Chapter 8: The relevant rule of conflict of laws*").[668] Without wanting to develop the argument further at this stage, there is a considerable risk that even for arbitral awards rendered under the ICSID-Convention, a disrespect of EU law could lead to the non-enforceability of such award in the EU.[669]

---

665 *Tietje/Wackernagel*, JWIT Vol. 16, Iss. 2 (2015), 205, 210 and 235 ff., who argue that in their point of view Art. 27 VCLT should apply by analogy due to the '*sui generis*' character of EU law but who however admit that courts within the EU member states being sought for enforcement, would potentially not apply the same perspective and thus deny the enforcement. The Commission also supports this view, cf.: *European Commission*, Amicus Curia Brief filed in Electrabel vs. Hungary (ICSID Case n° ARB/07/19) - arbitration proceedings, 12/06/2009, para 136-138; *Wehland*, ICLQ Vol. 58, Iss. 2 (2009), 297, 308 f; against such a possibility: *Engel*, SchiedsVZ, 2015, 218, 220; *Kniebaum*, ELTE Law Journal, 27, 34; *Kleinheisterkamp*, JIEL Vol. 15, No. 1 (2012), 85, 102.

666 *Tietje/Wackernagel*, JWIT Vol. 16, Iss. 2 (2015), 205, 210 ff, cf. also discussion *infra* (Chapter 13).

667 *Tietje/Wackernagel*, JWIT Vol. 16, Iss. 2 (2015), 205, 277 ff, 235 ff, cf. also discussion *infra* (Chapter 13).

668 *Tietje/Wackernagel*, JWIT Vol. 16, Iss. 2 (2015), 205, 217 ff with a focus on Art. 30 VCLT, admitting that one could also base the argument on an inherent conflict rule in the principle of supremacy, cf. p. 218; *Wehland*, ICLQ Vol. 58, Iss. 2 (2009), 297,308 f with reference to the principle or primacy as a conflict rule or Art. 31 (3) (c)VCLT which might force EU member states to interprete the ICSID-Convention restrictively.

669 *Tietje/Wackernagel*, JWIT Vol. 16, Iss. 2 (2015), 205, 235; the Commission seems to actively promote this standpoint as well, cf. the reference to the amicus curia brief filed in Micula vs. Romania, *Ioan Micula, Viorel Micula & others vs. Romania*, 11.12.2013 – ICSID Case No. ARB/05/20 - Final Award, para 336.

IV. The impact of further potential EU proceedings on the enforcement of an award

The recent action by the European Commission in the Micula-Case and in other cases reveals a further risk for the investor which cannot be assessed in its entirety as the CJEU did not yet have the opportunity yet to pronounce any decision with regard to those actions. The European Commission is actively seeking two additional paths of action which might considerably hinder investors to rely on IIAs in the European context and which are the immediate consequence of the several arbitral tribunals admitting damages to investors which the Commission considers to be a contravention of EU law.

As a first path of action the Commission rendered a decision prohibiting Romania to obey to an award rendered by the arbitral tribunal, considering that the payment of the attributed damages to the investor, would constitute state aid prohibited by the provisions of Art. 107 ff. TFEU.[670] Hence, the Commission is trying to force the host state not to comply with the unfavourable award and hence tries to impede on the investor's rights. As long as this decision by the Commission exists (and has not yet been declared void by the CJEU), Romania and all other member states will need to comply with this decision.

A second path of action consists in initiating infringement proceedings. The Commission actively tries to force EU member states to terminate existing intra-EU IIAs by all possible means, including infringement proceedings, the latest initiated in 2015 against five member states (Sweden, Austria, Romania, Netherlands and Slovakia).[671] If such proceedings succeed, the member states will be forced to terminate the IIAs, which might have detrimental consequences for the investor.

---

670 *European Commission*, Commission Decision (EU) 2015/1470 - notified under C(2015) 2112: Decision on State aid SA.38517 (2014/C) (ex 2014/NN) implemented by Romania-Arbitral award Micula v Romania of 11 December 2013 (30/03/2015).

671 *European Commission*, Press Release: Commission asks Member States to terminate their intra-EU bilateral investment treaties, 18/06/2015.

V. Conclusion on potential conflicts in the arbitration proceedings

It has been demonstrated that potential conflicts of IIAs with EU law are not limited to the stage of the arbitration proceedings. Even having obtained an award in its favour, an investor cannot rely on the award. On the contrary, numerous challenges might occur until the award could finally be enforced and the investor obtains satisfaction. The insecurity arising from this scenario and the various (different) tribunals which may need to deal with the same questions, lead to the need for a solid evaluation of the potential conflicts of EU law and IIAs involving EU member states and an approach on how to resolve these conflicts. It is indeed inconceivable to ignore either the EU law angle or the public international law principles. For EU law, especially in setting aside proceedings in EU member states, courts might be very attentive to EU law principles and provisions. On the contrary, as IIAs are primarily subject to public international law, this angle cannot be ignored either without rendering the investor's rights and investment security useless. The following section will distinguish different settings or scenarios which need to be analysed to address the aforementioned conflicts in more detail.

D. Handling EU law in international investment arbitration proceedings: different scenarios but similar interests

To address the question how and whether the conflict described *supra* (cf. B. and C.) should be addressed by arbitral tribunals in an international investment dispute, it is necessary to distinguish different types of scenarios in which such conflicts might occur. These scenarios should be outlined first, before developing the solution on how to address the conflict in such scenarios in Part II and Part III of this thesis.

I. Distinguishing different types of situations raising the conflict: intra-EU vs. extra-EU IIAs

To address the question whether and how the conflict between EU law and international investment law can be resolved, one needs to distinguish three different types of situations, depending on the acting agents:

- The contracting parties of the international investment agreement are EU member states only (intra-EU IIA conflict); or

- The contracting parties of the international investment agreement are (at least) one EU member state and (at least) one non-member state (extra-EU IIA conflict); or
- The EU itself is (together with the EU member states) contracting party of an international investment agreement with a non-member state (mixed agreement conflict).

Depending on whether one needs to deal with an intra-EU dispute or an extra-EU dispute the solutions might differ as the contracting parties to an IIA and the European Treaties will differ. It should be assumed for both situations that the host state in such dispute is a member state of the EU and thus – in one way or another – will be bound by EU law. Depending on the status of the investor's home state, the European Treaties will either apply to both contracting parties to an IIA (intra) or to the host state only (extra). Hence, the intra-context is characterised by an overlap of two treaty frameworks: EU law and the IIA, whereas in the extra context, the overlap is only unilateral.

The differences in both situations should be illustrated by the illustrations below.

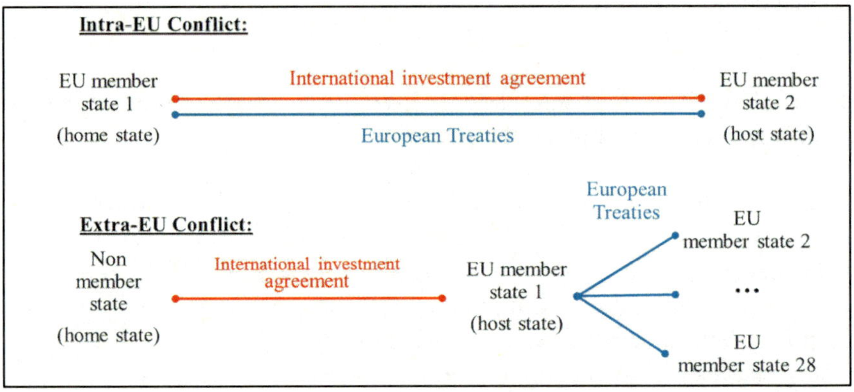

Illustration 3

The thirds scenario, including the EU as a contracting party to an IIA, will not be analysed separately. The consequences and questions arising in this context are mainly the same than for the intra-EU and extra-EU context, depending on the parties involved in a concrete dispute arising from the mixed agreement. *De facto*, the agreement is a regrouping of bilateral treaties between member states, non-member states and the EU.[672] The solutions which will be developed for each of these scenarios can be transposed to the mixed agreements as well. However, whenever adequate, a reference to particularities which might arise in the context of a mixed agreement or the consequences thereon, will be highlighted.

II. „Enjeux en question" – Guiding principles which should be respected by any solution to this conflict of laws

Independently of the particular scenario, the conflict between EU law and international investment law involves diverging interests by investors, states and the EU as well as several fundamental principles. Those need to be respected when developing solutions on how to address conflicts between EU law and IIAs in the intra-EU and extra-EU scenario. The solutions developed in Part II and Part III will be benchmarked against these principles. As the International Law Commission puts it, success or failure of solutions in a fragmented and multilevel system of legal frameworks *"is measured by how the legal world will view the outcome"*.[673]

Therefore, three angles should be analysed to adopt a coherent view on the issue:

The first angle is the nature and the principles of the legal frameworks involved. The respective underlying ideas of both frameworks should be respected to the most possible extend by any solution to a conflict.

Regarding EU law this refers to its specific characteristics, such as the principle of supremacy, the direct effect and the aims of the internal market to create an economic union based on identical ideas, rules and values as provided for in primary and secondary law.

The specific nature of IIAs as international agreements between two states from which the investor derives its particular rights should also be respected. To the extent that the states mutually agreed to grant and maintain such agreements, the aim of IIAs is to guarantee the investor a minimum level of protection for its investment. This idea also includes the safeguard against the host state's interference with the investors' rights

672 This is the perception conducted under Art. 30 VCLT, cf.: *Tietje/Wackernagel*, JWIT Vol. 16, Iss. 2 (2015), 205, 227 who however questions this approach.

673 *International Law Commission*, ILC Report on Fragmentation of International Law, 13/04/2006, para 419.

through influences on national courts, which could deprive the investor from the integrity of its rights.

The second angle should focus on the parties involved.

A solution needs to respect, to the most possible extent, the mandatory character of EU law for the EU member states. Their choice to enter into an organisation with a unique degree of integration at the international level should be respected whenever possible.

At the same time, the investor should not be deprived of its reasonable protection. Investors should be able to rely on a minimum of protection guaranteed but which also takes into account that such rights could only be protected to a reasonable degree. The investors' rights are dependent on the home state's and host state's will to maintain the IIA. Cherry-picking or forum-shopping which seek to extend the protection to a degree which was not conceived by the states, cannot be a legitimate interest deserving to be protected.

The third angle is a question of practical issues and consequences of any solution. It should be kept in mind that the protection of the investors' rights is a multilevel approach which does not only include the level of the main arbitral proceedings, potentially granting the investor damages, but also the later stages, including the risk that an award is set-aside or annulled and the necessity to enforce an award. Only if the investor is ensured of actually being able to enforce a decision rendered in its favour, even though the conflict might deal with questions that arise within the context of EU law, the solution can be reliable in the long term.

Any solution, whether it concerns intra-EU or extra-EU disputes should be challenged against these principles. Only compliance with the aforementioned principles can guarantee the lasting acceptance of the solution by the different parties involved.

Part II: Conflicts between EU Law and IIAs in the intra-EU setting

The specific nature of this constellation is due to the fact that all contracting parties of the IIA are EU member states, which also (either) signed the Treaty of Rome and its amendments until the Lisbon Treaty or an accession treaty, granting them the status of an EU member state.

The situation deriving from this fact can be considered as the most classic constellation of a conflict of laws: the acting agents (i.e. the home state and the host state) are (both) bound by two legal instruments, which the acting agents both considered to be binding on them and which might – as demonstrated *supra* – require non-compatible acts.[674]

As aforementioned, both legal frameworks, IIAs as well as EU law, can create inconsistencies in specific situations. One might argue that these inconsistencies do not need to be taken into consideration as long as EU law is considered to be treated as internal law of the host state.[675] The general principle laid down in Art. 27 VCLT seems to provide a particularly clear answer, which should be that internal law (i.e. EU law) cannot justify the breach of an international obligation (i.e. the IIA).[676] However, if both frameworks originate in the international order, Art. 27 VCLT is inapplicable and numerous potential conflicts occur. The latter alternative will be the approach of this thesis, as it will be demonstrated that EU law, despite its particularities, still remains international law (cf. *infra: "Chapter 7: EU law as international law applicable* to the dispute"). But irrespective of this qualification, Art. 27 VCLT would not provide the allegedly clear answer. This is due to a particularity in international investment law, regarding the potential applicable laws and the influence of domestic laws on the protection standards, which will be treated at a later stage in the context of extra-EU IIAs (cf. *infra* Part III, Chapter 13).

674 *Mus*, Netherlands International Law Review, 1998, 208, 210.

675 With reference to EU law being supranational but not international and should thus be treated as internal law only: *Tietje*, Intra-EU BITs als Herausforderung im Mehrebenensystem des Rechts (Beit. zum Transnat. Wirt.-R, Vol. 104, 2011); *Tietje/Wackernagel*, JWIT Vol. 16, Iss. 2 (2015), 205.

676 This is actually argued by *Tietje* and *Wackernagel* in *Tietje/Wackernagel*, JWIT Vol. 16, Iss. 2 (2015), 205.

The question of a conflict between the IIA and EU law in the intra-EU context will thus address three touchpoints:

- The question of applicable law to an international investment arbitration dispute rising from an IIA;
- The potential challenges for the tribunal's jurisdiction as the arbitration clause contained in an IIA might collide with EU law;
- The influence of EU law on the substantive guarantees and protection standards in the IIA on the merits, if the tribunal does not deny its jurisdiction.

In order to be able to determine a solution how to handle the conflict on intra-EU IIAs with EU law, this Part II will be subdivided into six chapters. Chapter 6 will serve as a dogmatic basis for the further developments and hence explain the structure which will be followed. It will be demonstrated that in order to address the conflicts of EU law and IIAs in intra-EU relationships, the first question to resolve is the nature of EU law and its qualification as international law (Chapter 7). Only being qualified as such, there is a conflict of laws properly speaking between IIAs (as international conventions and hence international law) and EU law (as international law). Chapter 8 will then deduct the applicable rule of conflict which determines the question which of both legal frameworks shall prevail upon which conditions. Having found that the applicable rule of conflict is the principle of primacy, issued from EU law, Chapter 9 will then address the question on whether arbitration clauses contained in IIAs are incompatible with EU law and will hence need to remain unapplied in application of the principle of primacy. Having demonstrated that the arbitral tribunal indeed lacks jurisdiction as arbitration clauses contained in IIAs conflict with EU law, Chapter 10 provides some ancillary thoughts on the question how to resolve conflicts on the merits (i.e. between EU law and substantive guarantees contained in IIAs) if an arbitral tribunal comes to a different conclusion with regard to its jurisdiction. Chapter 11 will challenge the aforementioned results regarding the particular nature of rights attributed to investors in IIAs and the general principles to be respected by each solution to a conflict which has been presented *supra* (cf.: *supra* Chapter 5).

Chapter 6: Intra-EU IIAs in arbitration proceedings: how to address the interaction of EU law and intra-EU IIAs

The question of potential interactions (and/or conflicts) between EU law and IIAs has been raised in a couple of arbitral proceedings by several EU member states (being sued in such proceedings as host states having allegedly violated substantive provisions of existing IIAs). These proceedings were mostly initiated after the EU enlargement process which lead to the "*appearance*" of a considerable number of intra-EU IIAs.[677] Among the most prominent decisions involving intra-EU IIAs feature *Eastern Sugar vs. Czech Republic*[678], *Achmea B.V. (former Eureko B.V.) vs. Slovak Republic*[679] and *Electrabel vs. Hungary*[680]. A multitude of other cases is reported to address the question; however, those proceedings were either terminated without an award or the proceedings are not published.[681]

Furthermore, the European Commission is – after a certain period of omission[682] – actively seeking to influence arbitral proceedings involving

677 Cf. *Dahlquist/Lenk et al.*, European Policy Analysis, 2016:4, 1; *Kniebaum*, ELTE Law Journal, 27, 27; *Dimopoulos*, CMLR Vol. 48, No. 1 (2011), 63, 63; *Kleinheisterkamp*, JIEL Vol. 15, No. 1 (2012), 85, 86.

678 *Eastern Sugar vs. Czech Republic*, 27.03.2007 – SCC No. 088/2004 - Partial award.

679 *Achmea vs. Slovak Republic*, 26.10.2012 – PCA Case No. 2008-13 - Award on Jurisdiction, Arbitrability and Suspension.

680 *Electrabel vs. Hungary*, 30.11.2012 – ICSID Case No. ARB/07/19: Decision on Jurisdiction, Applicable Law and Liability.

681 *EDF vs. Hungary*, 04.12.2014 – UNCITRAL - Award award not yet published but annulment proceedings were initiated in Switzerland, cf.: *Swiss Federal Supreme Court, 1èr Cour de droit Civil*, 06.10.2015 – 4A 34/2015; *U.S. Steel vs. Slovak Republic*, PCA Case No. 2013-6 (ongoing) which was discontinued by notice of the parties; *Cargill vs. Poland*, 01.03.2008 – UNCITRAL - Award *Nepolsky vs. Czech Republic*, 01.10.2010 – UNCITRAL - Award which was also discontinued, cf.: *Peterson*, IA Reporter Vol. 3, No. 9 (2010), 10; *Vattenfall vs. Germany I*, 11.03.2011 – ICSID Case No. ARB/09/6 - Award (discontinued upon agreement by the parties). Most recently an ICSID-Tribunal rendered an award in favour of the investor in *Edenred S.A. vs. Hungary*, 13.12.2016 – ICSID Case No. ARB/13/21 - Award (unpublished award). The proceedings are reported having dealt with the legality of Hungary's decisions to nationalise a particular sector related to social 'vouchers'; the measure has been declared illegal by the CJEU under EU law, cf.: *Peterson*, IA Reporter 2016 (Vol.9, No. 29), 8, 8 f. Recently further claims based on intra-EU IIAs are notified, cf. *inter alia*: *Peterson/Dahlquist* Vol. 9, No. 16 (2016), 2.

682 The existence of intra-EU BITs and the possible difficulties arising from those treaties have been known by the European Institutions since the enlargement in

intra-EU IIAs. Mostly this intervention is taking place through the filing of several *amicus curia* briefs to arbitral tribunals or state courts in the case of appeal proceedings.[683]

All these proceedings (and the European Commission's intervention) share in common that the host states relied on EU Law as an objection to demonstrate that either the arbitral tribunal lacks jurisdiction to judge the case based on the alleged breach of the IIA or it was claimed that any of the host state's action being in conformity with EU Law could not be a breach of any provision of an IIA. The underlying idea is that in an intra-EU context, the home state and the host state, both being EU member states, could not agree on any mechanism which would contravene any applicable EU law. This should be called the "*intra-EU objection*".[684]

In a nutshell, the line of argumentation advanced by either the host states or the European Commission reads as follows and refers to several of the conflicts which have been previously demonstrated in Chapter 5:

Some argue that the IIA as a whole has been terminated through accession of the host state to the EU.[685] The rights and obligations arising from

---

2004. The issue has even been expressly treated by the Economic and Financial Committee in 2006 in a report adressed to the Commission: *European Financial Committee*, Report ECFIN/CEFCPE(2006)REP/56882 final: Annual EFC Report to the Commission and the Council on the Movement of Capital and the Freedom of Payments, 15/11/2006, p. 7; However, until 2015, the Commission has limited itself to negotiate with the member states and submit *amicus curia* briefs to pending arbitral proceedings (cf. *infra*). Cf. also: *Dahlquist/Lenk et al.*, European Policy Analysis, 2016:4, 1, 1 f.

683 Most of these filings, especially regarding the pending proceedings, are not publicly available and cannot be acceded via the Commission's access to documents service either. However, the filings in several (closed) proceedings can be accessed, including *Achmea (former Eureko) vs. Slovak Republic, EURAM vs. Slovak Republic, U.S. Steel vs. Slovak Republic, Elecrabel vs. Hungary and EDF vs. Hungary*.

684 The denomination is following the nomenclature of the tribunal in *Achmea vs. Slovak Republic*, 26.10.2012 – PCA Case No. 2008-13 - Award on Jurisdiction, Arbitrability and Suspension, para 57.

685 This has been mainly advanced by the host states being sued in investment arbitration proceedings, cf. *Binder vs. Czech Republic*, 06.06.2007 – UNCITRAL - Award on Jurisdiction, para 13 ff; *Eastern Sugar vs. Czech Republic*, 27.03.2007 – SCC No. 088/2004 - Partial award, para 99; the European Commission *so far did not* argue that intra-EU BITs became invalid through the accession of the host state to the European Union, cf. e.g.: *European Commission*, Amicus Curia Brief filed in Achmea (former Eureko BV) vs. Slovak

an IIA would be incompatible with the rights and obligations arising from EU law. Hence the states could not maintain both legal frameworks.[686]

In any case the arbitral tribunal would lack jurisdiction as the arbitration clause contained in an IIA would be incompatible with EU law. Either by virtue of the principle of primacy or by application of the Articles 59 and 30 VCLT, the arbitration clause needs to remain unapplied. The incompatibility would result from two arguments: First EU law should attribute a monopoly of interpretation to the CJEU which should be the only court ultimately deciding on the correct interpretation of EU law.[687] Second, in the *MOX-Plant Case*[688], the CJEU is meant having said that according to Art. 344 TFEU, the member states could not submit any dispute to any

---

Republic (PCA Case n°2008-13) - arbitration proceedings, 07/07/2010, para 31 and 41.

686 *European Commission*, Amicus Curia Brief filed in Achmea (former Eureko BV) vs. Slovak Republic (PCA Case n°2008-13) - arbitration proceedings, 07/07/2010, para 30 and 47 ff; *European Commission*, Amicus Curia Brief filed in EURAM vs. Slovak Republic (PCA Case n°2010-17) - arbitration proceedings, 13/10/2011, p. 3 f; *European Commission*, Amicus Curia Brief filed in Electrabel vs. Hungary (ICSID Case n° ARB/07/19) - arbitration proceedings, 12/06/2009, para 135. For the European Commission this follows from either Art. 30 VCLT or the principle of primacy.

687 As to the European Commission there is an exclusive competence for the CJEU to interpret – as last resort – EU law and guarantee its uniform application in all member states. Granting access to a – separate – arbitrate tribunal, which, as it is not considered to be a "*court*" in the sense of Art. 267 TFEU, is unable to recourse to the preliminary ruling procedure would therefore violate this principle of exclusive interpretation, cf.: *European Commission*, Amicus Curia Brief filed in Achmea (former Eureko BV) vs. Slovak Republic (PCA Case n°2008-13) - arbitration proceedings, 07/07/2010, para 24 and 79; Letter of the European Commission to the Czech Department of Finance from 13.01.2006, handed over to the arbitral tribunal in *Eastern Sugar vs Czech Republic* and published in *Eastern Sugar vs Czech Republic*, para 119. Through conclusion of the IIA, the member states enabled themselves to recourse to an arbitration mechanism and thus created the prerequisites for a possible circumvention of EU law and paved the way for its non-uniform application, cf.: *European Commission*, Amicus Curia Brief filed in U.S. Steel Golbal Holdings I B.V. vs. Slovak Republic (PCA Case n°2013-6) - arbitration proceedings, 15/05/2014, para 44 ff, *European Commission*, Amicus Curia Brief filed in Achmea (former Eureko BV) vs. Slovak Republic (PCA Case n°2008-13) - arbitration proceedings, 07/07/2010, para 24; to some extent also: *European Commission*, Amicus Curia Brief filed in Micula vs. Romania to the U.S. Court of Appeals, 04/02/2016, p. 27.

688 *CJEU*, 30.05.2006 – C-459/03 - Mox Plant = ECLI:EU:C:2006:345.

other dispute settlement mechanism than those provided for in the European Treaties as soon as substantial matters of EU law are concerned.[689]

Furthermore, the access to arbitration and the attribution of particular substantive guarantees under the IIA for some investors only would constitute a discrimination which would generally be prohibited under EU law (Art. 18 TFEU).[690]

---

689 This is predominantly advanced by the European Commission. Regarding inter-state arbitrations, the Commission refers to the clear wording of Art. 344 TFEU and its interpretation by the CJEU in the *MOX Plant-Case*. As to Art. 344 TFEU, the CJEU would have ruled in the *MOX Plant-Case* that any reference to any other method of dispute resolution is prohibited between EU member states, as soon as matters of EU law are – at least to some extent – concerned, cf.: *European Commission*, Amicus Curia Brief filed in Achmea (former Eureko BV) vs. Slovak Republic (PCA Case n°2008-13) - arbitration proceedings, 07/07/2010, para 25 ff. This should follow from the principle that the member states cannot set aside the rights and obligations agreed upon in the European Treaties by virtue of a separate agreement (such as international treaties). The European Treaties would include the obligation to submit any dispute regarding responsibilities under EU law to the CJEU, as well as the recognition of the autonomy of the EU's legal framework and the obligation by the member states to guarantee the uniform and effective application of EU law in all member states, cf.: *European Commission*, Amicus Curia Brief filed in Achmea (former Eureko BV) vs. Slovak Republic (PCA Case n°2008-13) - arbitration proceedings, 07/07/2010, para 27 f, 79 and 90; *European Commission*, Amicus Curia Brief filed in EURAM vs. Slovak Republic (PCA Case n°2010-17) - arbitration proceedings, 13/10/2011, p. 4 f. For the Commission, the principle of Art. 344 TFEU also applies to investor-state arbitration, at least if only member states and parties which were conferred their rights by member states are concerned. Even though the wording of Art. 344 TFEU does not directly include private parties, the Commission argues that Art. 344 TFEU expresses a series of more general principles, including the exclusive interpretation of EU law by the CJEU, the pre-eminence of the judicial system in the EU and the prohibition to enable member states by any means to "*circumvent the application of relevant rules of [European] Union law"*, cf.: *European Commission, Amicus Curia Brief filed in U.S. Steel Golbal Holdings I B.V. vs. Slovak Republic (PCA Case n°2013-6) - arbitration proceedings, 15/05/2014, para* 45.

690 The European Commission and several host states consider arbitration clauses in IIAs to breach the principle of non-discrimination in Art. 18 TFEU, as some investors from several EU member states are treated differently than investors from other member states. The investors from some EU member states could rely on an IIA which grants access to international arbitration, whereas investors from member states which have not concluded such an agreement are prevented from recourse to such a dispute resolution mechanism, cf.: *European Commission*, Amicus Curia Brief filed in Achmea (former Eureko BV) vs.

In any case, the implementation of EU law could not violate any provision of an IIA. Any result to the contrary would be a violation of the principle of primacy of EU law.[691]

Without entering into details of these decisions or arguments (which will be analysed in the course of the following sub-paragraphs) the current perception of the conflict by tribunals and the European Commission demonstrates fundamentally contrasting positions. The Commission stolidly reiterates the EU's perspective on the disputes, based on EU principles,[692] whereas the arbitral tribunals tend (or at least try) to completely

---

Slovak Republic (PCA Case n°2008-13) - arbitration proceedings, 07/07/2010, para 33 ff; Letter of the European Commission to the Czech Department of Finance from 13.01.2006, handed over to the arbitral tribunal in *Eastern Sugar vs Czech Republic* and published in *Eastern Sugar vs Czech Republic*, para 119. Generally, discrimination could be eliminated in two separate ways: either the party not being granted the benefit, is being granted the benefit as well (extending the benefit) or the benefit is entirely denied for everybody (removing the benefit). In the European Commission's view, the discrimination could only be resolved by denying effect to the arbitration clause. Extending the benefit of an arbitration clause to those investors from EU member states not having signed an IIA would breach with the judicial system within the EU and thus aggravate the incompatibility, cf.: *European Commission*, Amicus Curia Brief filed in Micula vs. Romania to the U.S. Court of Appeals, 04/02/2016, p. 11; *European Commission*, Amicus Curia Brief filed in Achmea (former Eureko BV) vs. Slovak Republic (PCA Case n°2008-13) - arbitration proceedings, 07/07/2010, para 32-34.

691 The Commission concludes that there could be no material provision of the IIA preventing the state from executing its obligations under EU law. Whenever an act of the host state would be contrary to provisions of the IIA but in line with its obligations under EU law, the IIA provision must be considered as incompatible. According to the Commission, at least no breach of the IIA could occur by adopting a measure by which the host state complies with its obligations under EU law, cf.: *European Commission*, Amicus Curia Brief filed in U.S. Steel Golbal Holdings I B.V. vs. Slovak Republic (PCA Case n°2013-6) - arbitration proceedings, 15/05/2014, *para* 66 f; *European Commission*, Amicus Curia Brief filed in Achmea (former Eureko BV) vs. Slovak Republic (PCA Case n°2008-13) - arbitration proceedings, 07/07/2010, para 31 and 47; *European Commission*, Amicus Curia Brief filed in Electrabel vs. Hungary (ICSID Case n° ARB/07/19) - arbitration proceedings, 12/06/2009, para 135.

692 Cf. as an example: *European Commission*, Amicus Curia Brief filed in Achmea (former Eureko BV) vs. Slovak Republic (PCA Case n°2008-13) - arbitration proceedings, 07/07/2010, para 41; *European Commission*, Amicus Curia Brief filed in U.S. Steel Golbal Holdings I B.V. vs. Slovak Republic (PCA Case n°2013-6) - arbitration proceedings, 15/05/2014, para 23-26 (although the Commission uses the terms "*superseded*" the facts invoked relate to the "*in-*

ignore the effects which EU law might have on the arbitral proceedings. So far none of the tribunals or courts having dealt with intra-EU IIAs admitted to deny its jurisdiction. Some, however, admitted a (certain) primacy of EU law when dealing with the merits of the claims.[693]

This Part II hence aims to resolve such conflicts and carefully analyse how to address potential compatibilities or incompatibilities of EU law and IIAs and answer the question if those incompatibilities exist. Before addressing the main questions, some preliminary remarks should highlight the perspective of an arbitral tribunal on the conflict and set the scene on how to address the questions raised by the (alleged) conflict.

A. Structure of the analysis

It was previously demonstrated that the procedural and substantial provisions under EU law and IIA may contradict and hence host states may be subject to (at least at first glance) contradicting provisions and/or obligations under EU law and the provisions of an IIA. The diversity of questions raised by the arbitral tribunals so far in the most prominent decisions lead to a certain dogmatic confusion how to correctly address the question of – possible – conflicts of EU law and intra-EU IIAs. This confusion is caused by mixing – or at least not sufficiently distinguishing – the question of applicable law, jurisdiction and the merits of the arbitration proceedings.[694]

The fact that two legal systems provide for different regulations and are applied to the same facts, even though they might be contradictory, does not as such imply any further consequences.

---

compatibility" of the FET-Clause in the BIT and Europen Union law, cf.: para 19 ff).

693 *Achmea vs. Slovak Republic*, 07.12.2012 – PCA Case No. 2008-13 - Award *Electrabel vs. Hungary*, 25.11.2015 – ICSID Case No. ARB/07/19 - Award, para 4.197.

694 One can observe this on multiple occasions in the referred arbitral awards: e.g. in *Electrabel vs Hungary* the Tribunal addressed the question of the "*nature*" of EU law together, the relevant conflict rules and a possible incompatibility of the arbitration clause with EU law under the subtitle of "*applicable law*" to the dispute, whereas the considerations in the "*Jurisdiction*" section merely contain no considerations at all about a possible incompatibility of the arbitration clause with EU law, leading to a lack of jurisdiction of the arbitral tribunal.

Any subject of laws may be confronted with different regulations which set forth different rules the respective subject needs to comply with. The question which then needs to be answered is whether there is a rule of conflict of laws which resolves this conflict. This rule of conflict may be different within each legal system and highly depends on the nature of the rules involved. As an example, the rules of conflict for a national legal system are generally set forth in the constitution, which provides for a particular hierarchy (generally setting the constitutional document at the top of the hierarchy of norms).

An analysis of which rule of conflict of laws to apply and which consequences to derive thereof, should hence, at a first step, take into consideration the nature of the legal provisions involved.

Hence, to resolve a conflict of laws four steps need to be undertaken:

- the nature of the legal provisions involved needs to be determined in order to be able to identify the correct rule of conflict of law (cf. *infra* Chapter 7);
- among the rules of conflict of law for the respective nature of the legal provisions, the rule of conflict applicable to the case needs to be identified (cf. *infra* Chapter 8);
- the consequences of the rule of conflict so identified needs to be addressed (cf. *infra* Chapter 8) and
- it needs to be determined whether the provisions actually are incompatible and hence conflict (cf. *infra* Chapter 9).

Since IIAs are rules of public international law, the conflict needs to be addressed by referring to rules of conflict of international law. A conflict of laws between international law and national law is generally resolved by Art. 27 of the VCLT, which declares that provisions of national law may not justify a breach of the state's obligations under international law. Hence, if EU law would be considered as internal law only, a conflict between any provision contained in an IIA and EU law would not have any immediate impact on the *validity* of the IIA (cf. Art. 27 VCLT). Other impacts, i.e. on the interpretation of an obligation will be shown in Chapter 10, 12 and Chapter 13.

However, this section should demonstrate that the conflict between the provisions of EU law and IIAs lead to the arbitration clause and the substantive protection standards contained in IIAs to be set aside by conflicting provisions of EU law.

To demonstrate this, it will be first demonstrated that EU law can be considered as international law. Second, it will be developed that under the relevant rules of conflict of laws applicable in this context, the provisions of EU law prevail over conflicting provision under any international obligation by the member states and conflicting provisions of international law need to remain unapplied. Third, it will be argued that arbitration clauses contained in IIAs actually conflict with EU law and hence need to be set aside. Finally, it will be demonstrated that a substantial guarantee provided in an IIA cannot alter the member states' obligations under EU law. The aforementioned steps correspond to the logical steps an arbitral tribunal should undertake when being confronted with an investment dispute based on an intra-EU IIA. To demonstrate this parallelism, the following sub-section will briefly address the perspective of the arbitral tribunal when being confronted with an intra-EU investment dispute.

B. The perspective of an arbitral tribunal in an intra-EU investment dispute

Analysing the question of how arbitral tribunals should consider EU law, should start from the arbitral tribunals view on the dispute.[695] The tribunal is confronted with a dispute on the basis of an IIA under a certain procedural framework (e.g. ICSID, ICC, etc.).

As correctly pointed out by the *Eureko-Tribunal*, as long as – and this should be presumed for the purpose of this thesis – the conditions set forth in the IIA, such as an "*investment*" under the IIA, the nationality of the investor and possible further conditions of the arbitration clause are fulfilled,

> "the tribunal established in accordance with the BIT has at least prima facie jurisdiction over the dispute". [696]

However, this can only be considered as the starting point of the analysis: the tribunal then is under the duty to first verify and affirm its jurisdiction[697] and – in case of a positive response – proceed to the merits by ana-

695 Cf. for this approach: *Hindelang*, LIEI Vol. 39, Iss. 2 (2012), 179, 181; *Tietje*, Intra-EU BITs als Herausforderung im Mehrebenensystem des Rechts (Beit. zum Transnat. Wirt.-R, Vol. 104, 2011), p. 7.

696 *Achmea vs. Slovak Republic*, 26.10.2012 – PCA Case No. 2008-13 - Award on Jurisdiction, Arbitrability and Suspension, para 223.

697 *Tietje* in: *Ehlers/Schoch* (Eds.), Rechtsschutz im Öffentlichen Recht, 2009, p. 81.

lysing the applicable substantive standards to the dispute and whether or not they were violated by the host state.[698]

As to the tribunal's jurisdiction, the tribunal derives its own capacity to adjudicate from the parties' consent, expressed for the host state in the IIA's arbitration clause, combined with the acceptance of the investor through filing its claim.[699] Consequently, the validity of the arbitration clause is a crucial prerequisite to the tribunals jurisdiction. This validity could be set aside if either:

- the IIA as a whole was terminated as there would be no valid arbitration clause, *or*
- the IIA as a whole was still in force, but the arbitration clause itself became invalid or inapplicable.[700]

The tribunal needs to address the validity of the arbitration clause by applying the applicable law to determine its jurisdiction. This is not necessarily the law applicable to the merits of the dispute.[701] Arbitral tribunals constantly held that the applicable law to determine the tribunal's jurisdiction is linked to the instrument which contains the parties' consent to arbitration, hence the IIA.[702] As this instrument is an instrument of international law, the applicable law to determine if the tribunal has jurisdiction should be primarily the IIA and other rules of international law which could either influence the IIA or set aside the consent expressed in the

698 *Achmea vs. Slovak Republic*, 26.10.2012 – PCA Case No. 2008-13 - Award on Jurisdiction, Arbitrability and Suspension, para 220-223, *Tietje*, Intra-EU BITs als Herausforderung im Mehrebenensystem des Rechts (Beit. zum Transnat. Wirt.-R, Vol. 104, 2011), p. 7, *Wehland*, ICLQ Vol. 58, Iss. 2 (2009), 297, 302 f; *Hindelang*, LIEI Vol. 39, Iss. 2 (2012), 179, 181.

699 *Tietje* in: *Ehlers/Schoch* (Eds.), Rechtsschutz im Öffentlichen Recht, 2009, p. 68, 82.

700 *Schreuer*, The ICSID Convention, 2. Edn. (2009) Art. 25, para 429; cf. also: *Wehland*, ICLQ Vol. 58, Iss. 2 (2009), 297, 303; to some extend also: *Hindelang*, LIEI Vol. 39, Iss. 2 (2012), 179, 181 f.

701 *Inter alia*: *Daimler Financial Services AG vs. Argentina*, 22.08.2012 – ICSID Case No. ARB/05/1 - Award, para 50; *Tietje*, Applicability of the ECT in ICSID Arbitration (Beit. zum Transnat. Wirt.-R, Vol. 78, 2008), 5, 5 f; *Schreuer*, McGill Jour of Disp. Res. Vol. 1, No. 1 (2014), 1, 2 ff for a multitude of further references.

702 Cf. *Schreuer*, McGill Jour of Disp. Res. Vol. 1, No. 1 (2014), 1, 2 ff; *Banifatemi* in: *Yannaca-Small* (Ed.), Arbitration under international investment agreements, 2010, p. 191 f; *Tietje*, Applicability of the ECT in ICSID Arbitration (Beit. zum Transnat. Wirt.-R, Vol. 78, 2008), 5, 6.

IIA's arbitration clause.[703] Any source of international law which would set aside the IIA, would also eliminate the consent to arbitration. Hence, the tribunal will have to apply the relevant rules of international law as to determine its jurisdiction.[704]

Therefore, EU law could *a priori* only affect the validity of the IIA, if is qualified as international law in terms of the applicable law to the dispute.[705] If it is qualified as international law, and thus can be applied to the investment dispute, there would be a conflict of two competing frameworks of international law.

Obviously, the arbitration clause itself would be set aside if the IIA as *a whole* has been terminated by virtue of EU law. If the IIA has not been *terminated as a whole*, one needs to examine whether EU law could render invalid or inapplicable the arbitration clause (as a particular provision contained in the IIA). In case of an affirmative response, the tribunal is forced to deny its jurisdiction. Which legal effect shall prevail can only be determined by reference to a rule of conflict of laws.

As to the merits, the tribunal will need to evaluate whether the host state violated any substantive guarantee under the IIA. Similar as for the question of jurisdiction, to determine the scope of protection guaranteed in the IIA, the tribunal will need to take into account the IIA itself as well as all other rules of international law applicable to the parties.[706]

---

703 Cf. also: *Schreuer*, McGill Jour of Disp. Res. Vol. 1, No. 1 (2014), 1, 3 ff; this is in line with the tribunals having dealt with the intra-EU objection in the arbitration proceedings before: cf. *inter alia: Achmea vs. Slovak Republic, 26.10.2012 – PCA Case No. 2008-13 - Award on Jurisdiction, Arbitrability and Suspension, para* 220 ff.

704 Cf. e.g.: *Tietje*, Intra-EU BITs als Herausforderung im Mehrebenensystem des Rechts (Beit. zum Transnat. Wirt.-R, Vol. 104, 2011), p. 7; *Hindelang*, LIEI Vol. 39, Iss. 2 (2012), 179, 182.

705 *Wehland*, ICLQ Vol. 58, Iss. 2 (2009), 297, 301; *Burgstaller*, JOIA Vol. 26, No. 2 (2009), 181, 192; *Eilmansberger*, CMLR Vol. 46 (2009), 383, 420 ff; *Hindelang*, LIEI Vol. 39, Iss. 2 (2012), 179, 181; *a contrario,* denying that EU law should be qualified as international law: *Tietje*, Intra-EU BITs als Herausforderung im Mehrebenensystem des Rechts (Beit. zum Transnat. Wirt.-R, Vol. 104, 2011), p. 7, 11; *Tietje*, Applicability of the ECT in ICSID Arbitration (Beit. zum Transnat. Wirt.-R, Vol. 78, 2008), 5, 6 cf. also however more implicitly: *Kniebaum*, ELTE Law Journal, 27, 28 f.

706 Cf. also: *Hindelang*, LIEI Vol. 39, Iss. 2 (2012), 179, 181.

A violation of the substantive standards under the IIA would, *a priori*, be impossible if either:

- the IIA as a whole has been terminated as there would be no substantive guarantees anymore the investor could rely on, *or*
- the IIA as a whole would still be in force, but certain substantive standards (or their legal effects) could not be applied as these standards themselves became invalid or inapplicable.[707]

One can observe certain similarities regarding the questions of interference of EU law with arbitration proceedings: the first question is to qualify the nature of EU law: if EU law can be considered as international law in terms of the applicable law to the investment dispute, there are two competing legal frameworks on the international level (both regarding the question of the tribunal's jurisdiction and the merits). If, on the contrary, one would consider that EU law cannot be applied as a *legal* source to the dispute, it would – at best – be seen as a fact which the tribunal may take into account when analysing the host states behaviour and potential violations of the guarantees in the IIA.[708]

It will therefore first be demonstrated that EU law needs to be considered as international law in terms of the law applicable to investment disputes (Chapter 7).

Second, the relevant conflict rule to settle any potential conflict (regarding both jurisdiction or the substantive guarantees in the IIA) of EU law and the IIA will be determined (Chapter 8).

However, any rule of conflict requires that there is an incompatibility / conflict between the IIA and EU law.[709] Hence, the question will be addressed next:

To that regard it will first be analysed whether the arbitration clause contained in the IIAs conflicts with EU law (Chapter 9). It will be demonstrated that given the incompatibilities with EU law, the arbitral tribunals lack jurisdiction.

In a second step, the consequences for any conflict on the merits will be demonstrated (Chapter 10). EU law takes primacy on the merits and com-

707 Cf. also: *Wehland*, ICLQ Vol. 58, Iss. 2 (2009), 297, 303; *Hindelang*, LIEI Vol. 39, Iss. 2 (2012), 179, 181.

708 Similar: *Hindelang*, LIEI Vol. 39, Iss. 2 (2012), 179, 191; for the opposite: *Tietje*, Applicability of the ECT in ICSID Arbitration (Beit. zum Transnat. Wirt.-R, Vol. 78, 2008), 5, 6.

709 Cf. also for the relationship between EU Law and the ICSID-Convention: *Tietje/Wackernagel*, JWIT Vol. 16, Iss. 2 (2015), 205, 218 f.

pliance with the obligations under EU law cannot infringe the IIA's substantive guarantees.

Finally, it will be examined if the results conform with the set of interests, which has been previously outlined as cornerstones of any solution to the conflict (cf. Chapter 11).

Chapter 7: EU law as international law applicable to the dispute

It will first be demonstrated that EU law can be considered as applicable law to the dispute concurrently with the IIA in question (on which the investor might base its claim). Consequently, two frameworks of international law (EU law and IIAs) will collide immediately and on the same level. The demonstration shall be as follows: The applicable law in an international investment proceeding usually refers to the IIA and the *relevant* rules of international law applicable to the parties of the IIA (A.). EU law can and should be qualified as such rule of international law (B.).

A. The relevance of any other rule of law than the IIA in the proceedings

Each arbitral tribunal will need to decide the dispute based on the applicable law to the dispute.[710] As aforementioned, the applicable law to the jurisdictional and merits stage need to be separated. Regarding the tribunal's jurisdiction, as the IIA is an instrument of international law, the latter should also be the applicable law to determine whether or not the arbitral tribunal has jurisdiction. This includes the provisions of the IIA but also all other relevant rules of international law, especially the general principles applicable to international conventions. Those principles generally govern the rights and obligations issued from international treaties. Hence, they are also applicable to determine whether the host state's consent contained in an IIA is still valid.

As to the merits, the applicable law in an investment dispute can either derive from the parties' explicit choice of law or – in absence of such an

710 *Tietje*, Intra-EU BITs als Herausforderung im Mehrebenensystem des Rechts (Beit. zum Transnat. Wirt.-R, Vol. 104, 2011), p. 7; *Wehland*, ICLQ Vol. 58, Iss. 2 (2009), 297, 301; *Burgstaller*, JOIA Vol. 26, No. 2 (2009), 181, 192; *Eilmansberger*, CMLR Vol. 46 (2009), 383, 420 ff.

explicit choice – the applicable law is determined by referring to the arbitration rules the dispute is based on.[711]

An explicit choice of law between the parties is rare, notwithstanding if such an agreement exists, it is binding on the tribunal. However, although IIAs mostly do not expressly include a provision regarding the choice of law, some explicitly do so and usually render applicable the provisions of the IIA as well as any *relevant* rule of international law.[712]

Even in case an explicit choice of law is missing, arbitral tribunals, especially if an international investment disputes based on IIAs are concerned, generally tend to admit that the applicable law is essentially determined by the (nature of the) body of law the arbitration claim is based on and can be supplemented by other relevant rules of law.[713] As the IIA (being the instrument the claim is based on) by itself is an international agreement, arbitral tribunals usually consider the IIA and any other *relevant* rule of international law as to be the applicable law to the dispute.[714]

Consequently, any other rule besides the IIA (and thus e.g. EU law) will generally only be applied if it is considered to be a "*relevant rule of international law applicable to the parties*".[715]

If one would assume for the moment – which will be demonstrated *infra* (B.) – that EU law can be qualified as international law, it still needs to be a "*relevant*" rule of international law for the dispute. At first glance this seems questionable, as the IIA itself contains a comprehensive set of rules and usually "*relevant*" rules have been only those rules of interna-

711 *Banifatemi* in: *Yannaca-Small* (Ed.), Arbitration under international investment agreements, 2010, p. 199.

712 *Tietje*, Intra-EU BITs als Herausforderung im Mehrebenensystem des Rechts (Beit. zum Transnat. Wirt.-R, Vol. 104, 2011), p. 7.

713 *Tietje*, Intra-EU BITs als Herausforderung im Mehrebenensystem des Rechts (Beit. zum Transnat. Wirt.-R, Vol. 104, 2011), p. 7.

714 *Tietje*, Intra-EU BITs als Herausforderung im Mehrebenensystem des Rechts (Beit. zum Transnat. Wirt.-R, Vol. 104, 2011), p. 7; *Wehland*, ICLQ Vol. 58, Iss. 2 (2009), 297, 301; *Burgstaller*, JOIA Vol. 26, No. 2 (2009), 181, 192; *Eilmansberger*, CMLR Vol. 46 (2009), 383, 420 ff; *inter alia* in *Annulment Committee in Vivendi vs. Argentina*, 03.07.2002 – ICSID Case No. ARB/97/3 - Decision on Annulment, para 102 the Committee expressly stated that the BIT and rules of international law should be applied to the dispute.

715 This shall be the rule in the vast majority of the cases. However, it excludes the cases in which the parties agree, or the tribunal finds to, apply national law (on the merits) as well which would then render irrelevant the question how to qualify EU law as it would be applied to the dispute anyway (even if one concluded that it needs to be considered as internal law of the host state).

tional law which were applied by the tribunal in case of a lacuna of the IIA. EU law is in particular invoked to set aside the IIA or specific provisions therein, thus neither the host states nor the respondent alleges that there is any lacuna at all.

However, a treaty which would set aside another treaty (i.e. the IIA) is *per se* relevant for the application of the IIA. Such a treaty would even be of the most predominant relevance for the dispute. This is supported by Art. 31 (3) of the VCLT.[716] Although it deals with the interpretation of a treaty, the article clearly demonstrates a fundamental rule of international law: any interpretation of an international treaty – and *a forteriori* the application of a treaty – should take into account the other agreements and rules of international law applicable between the parties in question.[717]

Hence, if EU law can be qualified as international law, EU law is considered to be part of the law applicable to the (investment) dispute and might cause a conflict of laws with the (provisions of the) IIA.

B. The qualification of EU law as international law

The qualification of EU law is thus crucial to determine whether there is even the possibility of the two legal systems, i.e. EU law and international investment law, to conflict on the same level. Only if EU law is not qualified as domestic law only but qualified as international law, it might ultimately challenge the validity of an IIA or provisions contained in an IIA.

The characterization of EU law has not been uniform among investment tribunals and among scholars. Three different concepts can be distinguished, leading to different outcomes.[718]

---

716 *Eilmansberger*, CMLR Vol. 46 (2009), 383, 421.

717 Cf. *Sorel/Evenó* in: Corten/Klein VCLT - I, Art. 31 VCLT, p. 826 which states: "*According to doctrine and practice, this subsequent practice reflects what the parties intended (...)*"; cf. also: *Eilmansberger*, CMLR Vol. 46 (2009), 383, 420 f which clearly states that there is "*no justification for granting BITs an automatic status of supremcay with regard to other international obligations*" and refers to the rules of interpretation and application of international law; similar: *Leeks*, U. Toronto Fac. L. Rev. Vol. 65, No. 2 (2007), 1, 31; cf. also: *CMS vs. Argentina*, 12.05.2005 – ICSID Case No. ARB/01/8 - Award, para 324 regarding Argentina's reliance on the state of necessity.

718 Whereas several scholars oppose two sort of classifications (international law and suprantational law / *sui generis*, cf. *inter alia*: *Streinz*, 10. Edn. (2016), p. 46 f; *Hindelang*, LIEI Vol. 39, Iss. 2 (2012), 179, 184 and 191 f)), given the

First and foremost, EU law can be classified as *internal law of the host state*. This is the approach of the tribunal in *AES Summit vs. Hungary*[719] and the most predominant line of argumentation of several claimants when dealing with the question of EU law in arbitration proceedings.[720] Indeed, given this perception, one must deny any relevant conflict between EU law and the IIA. It is common ground in public international law that the state's internal law may not justify a breach of the state's international obligations (Art. 27 VCLT).[721] Consequently, the effect of EU law would be adverse. It would not influence the protection standard under the IIA or the tribunal's jurisdiction, but could only be evaluated as one fact besides several others to evaluate if those standards have been violated.[722]

The tribunal in *AES Summit vs. Hungary*adopted such an approach and hence concludes:

> "The question whether Hungary was, may have been or may have felt obliged under [EU] law to act as it did, is only an element to be considered by the tribunal when determining the rationality, reasonableness, arbitrariness and transparency of [Hungary's behaviour]."[723]

---

scope of this thesis and the focus on arbitration, the different conclusions from the arbitral tribunals should be taken into account as well, leading to a distinction between three different types of qualification, which additionally takes into account to refer to EU law as internal law of the host state only, without refering to its supranational character (cf. footnote 720 for further references to the investor's reasonings to that regard).

719 *AES Summit vs. Hungary*, 23.09.2010 – ICSID Case No. ARB/07/22 - Award.

720 Cf. the investor's statements in *Electrabel vs. Hungary*, 30.11.2012 – ICSID Case No. ARB/07/19: Decision on Jurisdiction, Applicable Law and Liability, para 4.24-4.26 and 4.29 stating that provisions of EU law would depart *"significantly from 'rules and principles of international law'"*; the investor's argued similarly in *AES Summit vs. Hungary*, 23.09.2010 – ICSID Case No. ARB/07/22 - Award, para 7.3.4; cf. also: *Ioan Micula, Viorel Micula & others vs. Romania*, 11.12.2013 – ICSID Case No. ARB/05/20 - Final Award, para 302.

721 Art. 27 VLCT is generally observed to be a highly recognised rule of customary international law, cf. *inter alia*: *Schaus* in: Corten/Klein VCLT - I, Art. 27 VCLT, p. 691.

722 Cf. also: *Eilmansberger*, CMLR Vol. 46 (2009), 383, 420; *Hindelang*, LIEI Vol. 39, Iss. 2 (2012), 179, 191 and the considerations of the tribunals in: *AES Summit vs. Hungary*, 23.09.2010 – ICSID Case No. ARB/07/22 - Award, para 7.5.2 f; *Ioan Micula, Viorel Micula & others vs. Romania*, 11.12.2013 – ICSID Case No. ARB/05/20 - Final Award, para 319-329.

723 *AES Summit vs. Hungary*, 23.09.2010 – ICSID Case No. ARB/07/22 - Award, para 7.6.9. However, it should be noted that the conclusion also derives from

Others state that EU law is limited to be taken into account as a fact in the arbitration proceedings but derive this conclusion from a slightly different qualification of EU law. For those authors, the founding treaties of the EU may have been instruments of international law, but the development since then made EU law to "*transpose*" its nature into a *legal order sui generis,* which can no longer be qualified as international law.[724] Some authors even characterise EU law as a novel form of body of laws, which cannot be characterised within the common classifications.[725] The most striking consequence of this classification is to *deny* EU law the status of international public law or at least not to apply rules of conflict between international treaties but to rely on an analogous application of Art. 27 VCLT which means that EU law could not alter any obligation undertaken on the international level.[726]

There are several arguments to support this denial.

First, as a consequence of the ongoing process of integration within the EU, the legal framework created by the EU member states should have

---

the particularities of the facts: both the investor and the host state mutually agreed that the tribunal should apply EU law as a fact only. They hence made an explicit choice of law. It is doubtful if the tribunal would – in absence of such choice – have come to the same conclusion as it refers to the "*dual nature*" of EU law, cf.: *AES Summit vs. Hungary*, 23.09.2010 – ICSID Case No. ARB/07/22 - Award, para 7.6.6 as to which EU law is both, international law but also part of the internal law of the host state. This will be analysed in Part III. The tribunal in *Micula vs. Romania* also adopted a similar approach but by stating that at the time when the (alleged) breach of the IIA occurred only the IIA and the Europe Agreements have been in place. As to the *Micula-Tribunal* the IIA could hence not conflict with the European Treaties as Romania has not yet acceded to the EU, cf.: *Ioan Micula, Viorel Micula & others vs. Romania*, 11.12.2013 – ICSID Case No. ARB/05/20 - Final Award, para 319.

724 *Happ*, Int. A.L.R. Iss. 3 (2007), 74, 76 f; *Ličková*, EJIL Vol. 19, No. 3 (2008), 463, 470; *Tietje*, Intra-EU BITs als Herausforderung im Mehrebenensystem des Rechts (Beit. zum Transnat. Wirt.-R, Vol. 104, 2011), p. 8, *Tietje/Wackernagel*, JWIT Vol. 16, Iss. 2 (2015), 205, 214 ff; cf. also: *Nettesheim* in: Grabitz/Hilf/Nettesheim EUV/AEUV, Art. 1 TFEU, para 61-64 and *Streinz*, 10. Edn. (2016), p. 46 f for the general arguments.

725 C.f. e.g.: *Oppermann/Classen et al.*, 5. Edn. (2011) § 9 Rn. 5 ff; *Nettesheim* in: Grabitz/Hilf/Nettesheim EUV/AEUV, Art. 1 TFEU, p. 63.

726 *Ličková*, EJIL Vol. 19, No. 3 (2008), 463; *Happ*, Int. A.L.R. Iss. 3 (2007), 74, 76 f; *Tietje*, Intra-EU BITs als Herausforderung im Mehrebenensystem des Rechts (Beit. zum Transnat. Wirt.-R, Vol. 104, 2011), p. 8, *Tietje/Wackernagel*, JWIT Vol. 16, Iss. 2 (2015), 205, 214 ff and 228 ff; this also seems to be supported by *Kottmann*, EuZW, 2016, 512, 519.

reached a degree of regulation that forms an autonomous body of law, incomparable to any obligations states could have undertaken based on international law.[727] This finding is usually supported by the judgement of the CJEU in the *Costa/E.N.E.L-Case*[728] which stated that

> "by contrast with ordinary international treaties, the EEC treaty has created its own legal system which, on the entry into force of the treaty, became an integral part of the legal systems of the member states and which their courts are bound to apply. By creating a community of unlimited duration, having its own institutions, its own personality, its own legal capacity and capacity of representation on the international place and, more particularly, real powers stemming from a limitation of sovereignty or a transfer of powers from the states to the community, the member states have limited their sovereign rights, albeit within limited fields, and have thus created a body of law which binds both their nationals and themselves."[729]

In other words: the high degree of integration within the EU which leads to a transferal of numerous competences to the EU, the specificity of application of EU law within the EU member states (direct effect and primacy) and the autonomy of the EU law in the perception of the EU, its institutions and the member states, disqualify EU law from being international law.[730]

---

727 *Ličková*, EJIL Vol. 19, No. 3 (2008), 463, 470; *Tietje*, Intra-EU BITs als Herausforderung im Mehrebenensystem des Rechts (Beit. zum Transnat. Wirt.-R, Vol. 104, 2011), p.8, *Blanke/Mangiameli*, The Treaty on European Union (TEU), 2013, Art. 1, para 15; *Oppermann/Classen et al.*, 5. Edn. (2011) § 9, para 5 f, *Tietje/Wackernagel*, JWIT Vol. 16, Iss. 2 (2015), 205, 214 ff; *Happ*, Int. A.L.R. Iss. 3 (2007), 74, 76.

728 *CJEU*, 15.07.1964 – C-6/64 - Flaminio Costa vs. E.N.E.L. = ECLI:EU:C:1964:66, 1269.

729 *CJEU*, 05.02.1963 – C-26/62 - Van Gend & Loos = ECLI:EU:C:1963:1, p. 25; *CJEU*, 15.07.1964 – C-6/64 - Flaminio Costa vs. E.N.E.L. = ECLI:EU:C:1964:66, 1269; established case law of the CJEU; constantly reiterated by the CJEU, e.g. with further relevance for this thesis in *CJEU*, 08.03.2011 – Opinion 1/09 - Patents Court = ECLI:EU:C:2011:123, para 65 and *CJEU*, 18.12.2014 – Opinion 2/13 - ECHR = ECLI:EU:C:2014:2454, para 166 f.

730 *Ličková*, EJIL Vol. 19, No. 3 (2008), 463, 470; *Tietje*, Intra-EU BITs als Herausforderung im Mehrebenensystem des Rechts (Beit. zum Transnat. Wirt.-R, Vol. 104, 2011), p. 8, *Blanke/Mangiameli*, The Treaty on European Union (TEU), 2013, Art. 1, para 15; *Oppermann/Classen et al.*, 5. Edn. (2011), § 9, para 5 f, who seems to accept that EU law may rely on mechanisms of public international law whenever "*adequate*"; *Tietje/Wackernagel*, JWIT Vol. 16, Iss. 2 (2015), 205, 217; *Wackernagel*, EU Judicial Proceedings, Consenual Termination of Intra-EU BITs (Beit. zum Transnat. Wirt.-R, Vol. 140, 2016), 5, 11.

Second, it is argued that under EU law the member states remain autonomous subjects of international law and can conclude (international) agreements among them, as long as the subject matter of the agreement does not fall within the scope of a community competency.[731] As to the scholars, this underlines that EU law considers itself as a distinct order, which *cannot* compete with other sources of international law.[732] Thus, EU law stands outside public international law and disqualifies itself – from its very own point of view – as international law.[733] Some further support this argument by referring to so-called *disconnection clauses* in international treaties concluded by the member states within their remaining competences.[734] Such clauses usually remind that the present treaty may not derogate from any obligation under EU law and that, if any changes occur in the split of competences between the EU and the member states which leads to any incompatibility with EU law in the future, the later should prevail.[735] According to those authors, such disconnection clauses would not be necessary under international law, as they only repeat customary rules of conflict regarding two subsequent treaties. As the

731 *Tietje*, Intra-EU BITs als Herausforderung im Mehrebenensystem des Rechts (Beit. zum Transnat. Wirt.-R, Vol. 104, 2011), p. 10.

732 *Tietje*, Intra-EU BITs als Herausforderung im Mehrebenensystem des Rechts (Beit. zum Transnat. Wirt.-R, Vol. 104, 2011), p. 10, 11.

733 *Tietje*, Intra-EU BITs als Herausforderung im Mehrebenensystem des Rechts (Beit. zum Transnat. Wirt.-R, Vol. 104, 2011), p. 10, *Tietje/Wackernagel*, JWIT Vol. 16, Iss. 2 (2015), 205, 216 who describe EU law as alien to international law.

734 *Tietje*, Intra-EU BITs als Herausforderung im Mehrebenensystem des Rechts (Beit. zum Transnat. Wirt.-R, Vol. 104, 2011), p. 12; similar: *Ličková*, EJIL Vol. 19, No. 3 (2008), 463, 470.

735 *Tietje*, Intra-EU BITs als Herausforderung im Mehrebenensystem des Rechts (Beit. zum Transnat. Wirt.-R, Vol. 104, 2011), p. 12 referring to Art. 47 (1) of the Prüm-Convention (or Schengen III-Agreement) concluded between 11 European Union member states and Norway which reads: "*The provisions of this Convention shall apply only in so far as they are compatible with EU law. Should the European Union in future introduce arrangements affecting the scope of this Convention, EU law shall take precedence in applying the relevant provisions of this Convention. The Contracting Parties may amend or replace the provisions of this Convention in view of those new arrangements resulting from EU law.*" Text of the Convention available at: http://register.consilium.europa.eu/doc/srv?l=EN&f=ST%2010900%202005%20INIT [last checked on: 28/02/2017].

member states consider such a clause to be necessary, EU law could not be international law.[736]

Third, the international character of EU law is rejected by reference to its criteria of application within the member states.[737] International law would apply among states by an act of the state, expressing its will to apply international law.[738] EU law should be disconnected from this willingness of the member states and apply by its own justifications, the autonomy of EU law and its supremacy on the law of the member states.[739]

Nevertheless, these characterizations are erroneous. In terms of the applicable law in investment arbitration proceedings, EU law should be qualified as international law.[740]

Qualifying EU law as a *legal framework sui generis* or a *supra-national* legal order does not provide a sufficient answer outside the context of the EU.[741] The disqualification due to its high degree of integration follows the idea that public international law is a body of laws that stagnates without evaluating. However, as every body of laws, international law needs to take into account new forms and characteristics as the result of a constant

---

736 *Tietje*, Intra-EU BITs als Herausforderung im Mehrebenensystem des Rechts (Beit. zum Transnat. Wirt.-R, Vol. 104, 2011), p. 12.

737 *Ličková*, EJIL Vol. 19, No. 3 (2008), 463, 470; *Tietje/Wackernagel*, JWIT Vol. 16, Iss. 2 (2015), 205, 215 f.

738 *Tietje/Wackernagel*, JWIT Vol. 16, Iss. 2 (2015), 205, 215 f. It should not be entered into the discussion or the choice whether states opt for a monist or dualist reception of international law in their legal framework, as both rely on the state's will to apply public international law, cf. for the monist and dualist approach in general e.g.: *Kempen/Hillgruber*, Völkerrecht, 2. Edn. (2012), p. 11-13; *Hwang*, EuR, 2016, 355, 372 f clearly opting for a monist approach in the EU context.

739 *Tietje/Wackernagel*, JWIT Vol. 16, Iss. 2 (2015), 205, 215 f; similar: *Haratsch*, ZaöVR 66 (2006), 927, p. 27 f; *Frenz* qualifies this as the distinctive character, more than any other particularity of EU law: cf.: *Frenz*, Europarecht, 2011, para 3.

740 *Kokott* in: Streinz EUV/AEUV, Art. 47 TEU, para. 10, *Hindelang*, LIEI Vol. 39, Iss. 2 (2012), 179, 186, *Wehland*, ICLQ Vol. 58, Iss. 2 (2009), 297, 301 f. and who (cf. footnote 6) by referring to Van Gend & Loos, even puts it drastically by saying that: "*there is no doubt that the European Treaties are instruments of public international law*"; *Hindelang*, LIEI Vol. 39, Iss. 2 (2012), 179, 184 but in 191 f argues why in any case even adopting the supranationalists intra-EU BITs could not escape to the principle of primacy.

741 *Wehland*, ICLQ Vol. 58, Iss. 2 (2009), 297, 302; cf. also: *Streinz*, 10. Edn. (2016), p. 49.

evolution and reciprocal influences by national and international law. As *Shaw* perfectly describes:

> "The range of topics covered by international law has expanded hand in hand with the upsurge in difficulties faced and the proliferation in the number of participants within the system. It is no longer exclusively concerned with issues relating to the territory or jurisdiction of states narrowly understood, but is beginning to take into account the specialised problems of contemporary society. "[742]

Given this approach EU law still needs to be considered as a part of international public law, at least in the context of IIAs, although some of its characteristics are novel compared to "*classic*" manifestations of international law.[743] It may be characterised as a "*regional-international law sub system*"[744], but it remains – as to its main characteristics – international law.[745]

This should be demonstrated in the following sub-sections.

The starting point of any characterization needs to be the definition of international law, which is generally defined as binding rules governing the relations between subjects of international law, without however being considered as part of the internal law of one of these subjects.[746]

Consequently, there are three key elements a body of law needs to meet to be qualified as international law.

It first needs to determine a *set of rules applicable to subjects of international law* (cf. *infra*: *"III. EU law regulates rights between subjects of* international law*"*).

Second, the body of laws needs to determine a *set of rules binding in the relations of subjects of international law* (cf. *infra*: "*II. EU law primarily creates rights and obligations towards member states and as an auxiliary* individual rights").

---

742 *Shaw*, International law, 6. Edn. (2008), p. 47.

743 *Burgstaller*, JOIA Vol. 26, No. 2 (2009), 181, 192; *Hindelang*, LIEI Vol. 39, Iss. 2 (2012), 179, 186; *Wehland*, ICLQ Vol. 58, Iss. 2 (2009), 297, 301 f; *Streinz*, 10. Edn. (2016), p. 48.

744 *Shaw*, International law, 6. Edn. (2008), p. 46.

745 *Hindelang*, LIEI Vol. 39, Iss. 2 (2012), 179, 186, *Wehland*, ICLQ Vol. 58, Iss. 2 (2009), 297, 301 f; cf. also: *Streinz*, 10. Edn. (2016), p. 47 f.

746 *Kempen/Hillgruber*, Völkerrecht, 2. Edn. (2012), p. 2, *Stein/Buttlar*, Völkerrecht, 13. Edn. (2012), para 6; *Vitzthum/Bothe*, Völkerrecht, 5. Edn. (2010), p. 17.

Third, the body of law needs to be *based* on generally recognised *sources of international law* (cf. *infra* : "*I. EU law is sourced in* international law").

EU law fulfils all of these criteria, and has not yet transgressed the boarder to the final building of a federal state.[747]

I. EU law is sourced in international law

First, EU law is based on (international) conventions and thus on generally recognised sources of international law (cf. Art. 38 of the statute of the ICJ). These international conventions are the TEU and the TFEU, which determine the entire functioning of the EU, both regarding legislative acts or the European institutions, and thus the entire legal framework which is nowadays called EU law.[748]

The TEU as well as the TFEU continue to be international conventions.[749] Both, the TEU and the TFEU are the result of several amendments of the Treaty of Rome, entered into force in 1958. The Treaty of Rome has never been challenged to be an international convention in terms of Art. 38 of the statue of the ICJ. It created the tariffs union and the common markets of goods, services and capital within the territory of the six contracting parties. By this agreement six states, i.e. (West-) Germany, Luxemburg, Belgium, France, Netherlands and Italy established a binding set of rules for a certain field of their reciprocal relationship. Consequently, the Treaty of Rome meets all criteria to be qualified as an international convention.

---

747 Indeed, an evolution to a federal state would entirely requalify EU law. However, several mechanisms of EU law, such as the recognition of the member states as subjects of international law and the principle of conferal differ so widely from a federal state that this evolution cannot yet be recognised, cf. also: *Ghouri*, ELJ Vol. 16, No. 5 (2010), 806, 811; *Hobe*, 8. Edn. (2014), para 119 and 121; *Oppermann/Classen et al.*, 5. Edn. (2011) § 4, para 29.

748 *Hobe*, 8. Edn. (2014), para 416, *Wehland*, ICLQ Vol. 58, Iss. 2 (2009), 297, 302; *Hindelang*, LIEI Vol. 39, Iss. 2 (2012), 179, 185; this is even admitted by *Tietje/Wackernagel*, JWIT Vol. 16, Iss. 2 (2015), 205, 214; in so far: *Ličková*, EJIL Vol. 19, No. 3 (2008), 463, 467.

749 *Hobe*, 8. Edn. (2014), para 416, *Kokott* in: Streinz EUV/AEUV, Art. 47 TEU, para 10, *Wehland*, ICLQ Vol. 58, Iss. 2 (2009), 297, 302; similar: *Ličková*, EJIL Vol. 19, No. 3 (2008), 463, 467.

Since 1958 the Treaty of Rome has been amended several times, last in 2009 with the Lisbon Treaty, creating the EU and the TFUE and TUE, but without losing its character of being an international convention. The treaties are still amended by a unanimous decision of all member states, followed by a ratification procedure within each member state.[750] They still establish reciprocal rights and obligations within the EU member states. The EU member states still remain to be subjects of international law. Hence, EU law still remains to be international law. Neither the transferal of competencies, nor the particular principles established by EU law, alter this qualification.

1. Transferal of competencies and rights to legislate

The density of integration within the EU, the conferral of competences, the establishment of the European institutions and their power to independently create legally binding acts for the EU member states and their nationals does not alter the qualification of EU law as international law.[751] All of these functions, are based on the European Treaties which are instruments of international law.

Art. 13 (1) TEU enumerates the European institutions which "*shall aim to promote its values, advance its objectives, serve its interests (...)*"[752]. None of the institutions exists outside the framework of the European Treaties. The creation of the High Representative of the Union for Foreign Affairs and Security (Art. 18 TEU) through the Lisbon Treaty perfectly demonstrates that the member states keep the power to create, change or abandon these institutions or parts of them.[753] In any case, the creation of

---

750 *Hobe*, 8. Edn. (2014), p. 416; *Burgstaller*, JOIA Vol. 26, No. 2 (2009), 181, 192; *Hindelang*, LIEI Vol. 39, Iss. 2 (2012), 179, 185.

751 *Kokott* in: Streinz EUV/AEUV, Art. 47 TEU, para 10, *Wehland*, ICLQ Vol. 58, Iss. 2 (2009), 297, 302, *Shaw*, International law, 6. Edn. (2008), p. 46: "*International organizations have now been accepted as possessing right and duties of their own and a distinctive legal personality*"; *Streinz*, 10. Edn. (2016), p. 47-49; *Ipsen*, Völkerrecht, 6. Edn. (2014), p. 218; for the opposite: *Tietje/Wackernagel*, JWIT Vol. 16, Iss. 2 (2015), 205, 214 ff who consider this conferral of powers as sort of a '*game-changer*' for EU laws characteristics; *Ličková*, EJIL Vol. 19, No. 3 (2008), 463, 470.

752 Art. 13 (1) TEU.

753 Clearly supporting this idea: *Dörr* in: Grabitz/Hilf/Nettesheim EUV/AEUV, Art. 47 TEU, para 77.

institutions in international organisations is nothing particular to the EU.[754] It is even a necessary element of qualification for international organisations and numerous international institutions created (executive) organs with particular rights without anybody questioning the qualification of the body of law surrounding these institutions as international law.[755]

The second atypical element of EU law, and particularly secondary law, is the fact that the EU's institutions were enabled – through the primary law – to create legally binding acts for the member states. But similarly, the conferral of powers to these institutions and their right to engage legally binding acts (and thus the entire secondary law of the EU) remain the consequence of its establishment through the European Treaties.[756] As the principles in Art. 5 ff TEU clearly acknowledge, the EU may only exercise its legislative powers upon referral of a competence to the EU through the European Treaties. The source of these legislative powers and its application in each and every member state remains the European Treaties.[757] Whereas it is true that some of the procedures, especially the references to the qualified majority in Art. 238 ff TFEU derogate from requiring the unanimous consent by all member states (which is somehow deemed to be principal process of decision making in international organisations), this cannot be a determining factor.[758] First, the Security Council

754 *Streinz*, 10. Edn. (2016), p. 48; similar: *Hindelang*, LIEI Vol. 39, Iss. 2 (2012), 179, 185 f.

755 Cf. for the existence of organs as being a necessary criteria: *Stein/Buttlar*, Völkerrecht, 13. Edn. (2012), p. 121; *Ipsen*, Völkerrecht, 6. Edn. (2014), p. 214; examples of such executive organs are the security council of the United Nations, which according to Art. 25 UN-Charter issues binding decisions for all member states; the board of directors at the World Bank or as a dispute settlement body which issues external control on its member states; one might also refer to the European Court of Human Rights within the European Council or the Dispute Settlement Body at the WTO, cf. for several further examples: *Ipsen*, Völkerrecht, 6. Edn. (2014), p. 137 ff.

756 *Wehland*, ICLQ Vol. 58, Iss. 2 (2009), 297, 302; *Hindelang*, LIEI Vol. 39, Iss. 2 (2012), 179, 185 f who consider that those effects are the result of a pure application of *pacta sunt servanda*; also admitted to be the internationalist view by *Tietje/Wackernagel*, JWIT Vol. 16, Iss. 2 (2015), 205, 215; *Ghouri*, ELJ Vol. 16, No. 5 (2010), 806, 811; cf. also in so far: *Haratsch*, 2016, p. 28.

757 *Streinz*, 10. Edn. (2016), p. 47 f; for the German perspective cf. *German Constitutional Court*, BVerfGE 123, 267, 30.06.2009 – 2 BvE 2/08, 397 f (para 332, 333 and 334).

758 Cf. also: *Streinz*, 10. Edn. (2016), p. 48; In fact, the new procedural rules to enact legislation since Lisbon Treaty widely disconnected the creation of new legislative acts from a prior (unanimous) consent of the member states and en-

of the United Nations as one of the most prominent institutions of an international organisation, does not require the unanimous consent of all member states to the UN to adopt a resolution either.[759] Second, one needs to consider that the basis of these authorization is a prior consent of all member states to this procedure in the treaties building the EU primary law.[760] Each act engaged by the EU's institutions must remain within the scope of action that has been conferred by the EU member states. The act must respect the procedures laid down in the treaties for this kind of acts and the member states themselves accepted the binding nature of any act that has been created through the respect of the TFEU and TEU. The process of prior consent perfectly respects the sovereignty of the member states. The only reason why the EU can oblige these states to conform themselves with any act of secondary law, is because the states through their own exercise of sovereignty by signing the amendments of the European Treaties, consented to this primacy.[761] The mechanism is well known from other international organisations without questioning the character of international law. Art. 27, 38 ff of the Charter of the United Nations e.g. provide that the measures taken by the security council are binding on, and need to be executed by, all member states of the United Nations. Nevertheless, the simple fact that the scope of action within the EU is much broader than known from any other international organisation does not af-

---

able a qualified majority as described in Art. 238 TFEU to adopt decisions in the European Council. Several particularly sensible legislative domains still prerequisite an unanimous decision by the Council; cf. for an overwiev after Lisbon: *Bieber/Epiney et al.*, Die Europäische Union, 11. Edn. (2015), p. 208-220.

759 *Stein/Buttlar*, Völkerrecht, 13. Edn. (2012), p. 131 f; *Ipsen*, Völkerrecht, 6. Edn. (2014), p. 203 with reference to the arrest warrant issued by the International Criminal Court which is deemed to have immediate effect as well.

760 The Tribunal in *Electrabel vs. Hungary*, 30.11.2012 – ICSID Case No. ARB/07/19: Decision on Jurisdiction, Applicable Law and Liability, para 4.123 correctly holds: "*(...) it would be artificial to categorise, as an international legal rule, Article 87 EC (precluding 'any aid granted by a Member State or through State resources ... incompatible with the internal market') and refuse the same status to the necessary implementation of that international rule by the non-national organ created by the same EU treaty (...)";* cf. also: *Streinz*, 10. Edn. (2016), p. 48.

761 Cf. also: *Ghouri*, ELJ Vol. 16, No. 5 (2010), 806, 811.

fect the nature of the acts engaged by this entity.[762] The fact that the EU got conferred substantial fields of action in the last decades is the result of a general consensus on the economic and political system to be established in Western Europe.[763] As international law requires a consensus of all acting parties to develop, such a consensus is much easier to find – and therefore easier to imply – in a relatively equivalent surrounding of political and economic ideas.[764]

Tietje/Wackernagel and *Frenz* argue that the application of EU law by the member states does no longer rely on the state's will through the signing of the European Treaties, but on the autonomy of this legal order.[765] This argumentation seems to confound the basis of the application of the order and its perception within the legal order that has been created from the European Treaties. Any application of EU law and the decisions by its institutions is still the result of the ongoing will of the member states to comply with this legal order and the (particular) conflict rules and statues of the institutions foreseen in the Treaties (cf. *infra*). The current debate and activation of Art. 50 TEU by the United Kingdom delivers the best proof of the underlying idea. The EU remains an institution to which states may adhere or quit. If they decide to quit, which is the most straightforward expression of their will, the application of EU law ends after elapse of the timeframe as stated in Art. 50 (3) TEU.[766] Similarly, the reception of EU law by the EU member states demonstrates the member states' perception that it still depends on their will to integrate EU law in their respective frameworks.[767] Also, if a member state decides not to comply

---

762 *Hindelang*, LIEI Vol. 39, Iss. 2 (2012), 179, 185 f; *Streinz*, 10. Edn. (2016), p. 48 considers the EU to be a new form of international organisation which however keeps being such an institution.

763 Cf. the recitals 1, 3,4 of the TEU; *Terhechte* in: Grabitz/Hilf/Nettesheim EUV/AEUV, Preamble of the TEU, para 15 f, 20; similar: *Streinz*, 10. Edn. (2016), p. 8 f; cf. also: *Kempen/Hillgruber*, Völkerrecht, 2. Edn. (2012) p 147 f.

764 *Streinz*, 10. Edn. (2016), p. 8 f; cf. also: *Kempen/Hillgruber*, Völkerrecht, 2. Edn. (2012) p 147 f.

765 *Tietje/Wackernagel*, JWIT Vol. 16, Iss. 2 (2015), 205, 215; *Frenz*, Europarecht, 2011, para 3.

766 *Dörr* in: Grabitz/Hilf/Nettesheim EUV/AEUV, Art. 50 TEU, para 7.

767 Cf. *German Constitutional Court*, BVerfGE 123, 267, 30.06.2009 – 2 BvE 2/08, 397 f (para 332, 333 and 334), *French Constitutional Court*, Journal Officiel du 29 décembre 2007, p. 21813, text n° 96, 20.12.2007 – Décision n° 2007-560 DC - Traité de Lisbonne, para 7 and 8; cf. also: *Streinz*, 10. Edn. (2016), p. 48.

with EU law, it may be exposed to the consequences laid down in the European Treaties (*inter alia* the mechanisms provided for in Art. 258-260 TFEU).[768] However, under no circumstances, EU law applies without the states willingness to apply it. There is no ultimate enforcement of EU law by itself.[769] Once again the recent developments in the refugee crisis and the non-compliance of certain member states with the agreed 'resettlement-quotas' provides best proof of this approach.[770] The autonomy of the EU legal order[771], same as the principle of supremacy and direct effect, are principles in EU law designed to safeguard to the most possible extent the uniform application of legal framework in all member states. However, none of these principles disable the character of EU law as international law.[772]

2. Irrelevance of principles set forth in the European Treaties for its qualification

EU law's specific principles such as the autonomy and primacy do not disqualify the body of laws of being international law either.

Regarding the principle of primacy, it will be demonstrated *infra* that this principle can be considered as a rule of conflict of laws the European

768 *Karpenstein* in: Grabitz/Hilf/Nettesheim EUV/AEUV, Art. 258 TFEU, para 63 ff also referring to preventive measures under Art. 3 TEU and informal warnings by the Commission.

769 *Hindelang*, LIEI Vol. 39, Iss. 2 (2012), 179, 185 f; It should be pointed out that even the judgment by the CJEU in infringement proceedings declaring the incompatibility of an act by the member state with EU law does not have effect the validity of the state-measure, cf.: *Karpenstein* in: Grabitz/Hilf/Nettesheim EUV/AEUV, Art. 258 TFEU, para 11 ff.

770 The resettlement quotas agreed upon in 2015 for refugees being located in Greece to other EU member states, 937 have been relocated until March 2016 due to the resistence of the member states to implement the binding decision issued in 2015; cf: http://europa.eu/rapid/press-release_IP-16-829_en.htm [last accessed on 20.02.2017].

771 Cf. *CJEU*, 15.07.1964 – C-6/64 - Flaminio Costa vs. E.N.E.L. = ECLI:EU:C:1964:66.

772 Cf. also: *Burgstaller*, JOIA Vol. 26, No. 2 (2009), 181, 191; *Hindelang*, LIEI Vol. 39, Iss. 2 (2012), 179, 185 f; *Ghouri*, ELJ Vol. 16, No. 5 (2010), 806, 812; for the opposite: *Ličková*, EJIL Vol. 19, No. 3 (2008), 463, 470; *Tietje/Wackernagel*, JWIT Vol. 16, Iss. 2 (2015), 205, 217.

member states agreed upon.[773] Indeed, no one would challenge the member states capacity to determine a conflict rule for any regulation applied in a legal relationship between them.[774] Thus, it is doubtful how the establishment of a conflict rule, as predominant as the rule might be, would alter the qualification of the entire legal framework.[775] *A contrario* this would mean that states would be limited in their discretion to choose any rule of conflict of laws, if they do not want to change the nature of the acts concerned. However, under the general principle of sovereignty and autonomy of each state such a limitation would be hard to perceive.[776]

Also the principle of autonomy of EU law should not affect the classification of EU law. Authors regularly refer to the statement of the CJEU in the *Costa/E.N.E.L.-Case*:

> "By contrast with ordinary international law, the [European Treaties] created its own legal system"[777]

---

773 Cf. for the qualification of the principle of primacy as a conflict rule: *Eilmansberger*, CMLR Vol. 46 (2009), 383, 425; cf. also: *Burgstaller*, JOIA Vol. 26, No. 2 (2009), 181; for the opposite: *Kleinheisterkamp*, JIEL Vol. 15, No. 1 (2012), 85, 96; *Tietje/Wackernagel*, JWIT Vol. 16, Iss. 2 (2015), 205, 236.

774 This capacity is expressly granted by Art. 30 (2), (3) and (4) VCLT and *in fine* safeguards the states will to submit themselves to a certain legal framework and to enforce – to the most possible extent – the states will in their bilateral or multilateral relations, cf. Art. 31 VCLT. To be able to submit itself to a certain framework, even though it might result in the loss of its quality as a state vis à vis international law, is the most elemental expression of sovereignty exercised by states, cf. also: *Repasi*, EuR, 2013, 45, 62.

775 *Shaw*, International law, 6. Edn. (2008), p. 834; *Klabbers*, Treaty conflict and the European Union, 2009, p. 16 f who points out the freedom of the parties to agree upon any mechanism they want; cf. also: *Repasi*, EuR, 2013, 45, 62.

776 *Streinz*, 10. Edn. (2016), p. 48; *Tietje/Wackernagel*, JWIT Vol. 16, Iss. 2 (2015), 205 describe this point of view as the "*European perspective*". Although it might be that this principle is an inherent rule of EU law, the search for further perspectives and classifications does not help to address the itnra-EU conflict. If states agree to confer primacy to certain rules in their respective relations, this should be recognised as a conflict rule in accordance with Art. 30 VCLT. The European Union member states simply agreed upon a certain hierarchy of norms in their respective relations; cf. also: *Klabbers*, Treaty conflict and the European Union, 2009, p. 16 f and *Repasi*, EuR, 2013, 45, 62.

777 *CJEU*, 15.07.1964 – C-6/64 - Flaminio Costa vs. E.N.E.L. = ECLI:EU:C:1964:66, 1269; cf. for the reference to this quote: *Tietje/Wackernagel*, JWIT Vol. 16, Iss. 2 (2015), 205, 215; also *Tietje*, Intra-EU BITs als Herausforderung im Mehrebenensystem des Rechts (Beit. zum Transnat. Wirt.-R, Vol. 104, 2011), p. 8 f refering to an inconsistent behaviour of the EU.

Nothing in this judgement requalifies EU law and it cannot be assumed that the CJEU through this judgement or the following reiterations in other judgements wanted to influence the qualification of EU law from an external perspective (i.e. a lens other than by the member states as contracting parties to the European Treaties).[778] Certainly EU law heavily differs from 'ordinary' international law, simply due to the fact that the degree of cooperation and the density of the legal framework cannot be compared to 'ordinary' international law.[779] What the CJEU intended to strengthen in these cases, is the particular interest of EU law when it comes to preserve the legal framework deriving from the European Treaties and the secondary legislation.[780] The court intends to contrast these principles to classic international law. Compared to this "*classic*" international law, EU law is a specialised, unique, form of international law as no other regional organisation found itself in the situation and the premises to agree upon a similar cooperation.[781]

Additionally, as *Wehland* correctly points out:

> "(…) the self-proclamation of EC law as an autonomous legal order cannot be relevant from a public international law viewpoint."[782]

Indeed, if the self-proclamation of a legal order would enable to alter the character of the legal order, it could easily jeopardise the entire structure of public international law. For all other actors outside the EU, keeping in mind a minimum of legal certainty, the only relevant classification can be

---

778 *Burgstaller*, JOIA Vol. 26, No. 2 (2009), 181, 192; *Hindelang*, LIEI Vol. 39, Iss. 2 (2012), 179, 186, *Wehland*, ICLQ Vol. 58, Iss. 2 (2009), 297, 301 f.

779 *Burgstaller*, JOIA Vol. 26, No. 2 (2009), 181, 191; *Hindelang*, LIEI Vol. 39, Iss. 2 (2012), 179, 185; *Streinz*, 10. Edn. (2016), p. 48.

780 This has recently been clarified by the CJEU in *CJEU*, 18.12.2014 – Opinion 2/13 - ECHR = ECLI:EU:C:2014:2454, para 157 f.: *"The fact that the EU has a new kind of legal order, the nature of which is peculiar to the EU, its own constitutional framework and founding principles, a particularly sophisticated institutional structure and a full set of legal rules to ensure its operation, has consequences as regards the procedure for and conditions of accession to the ECHR."*.

781 *CJEU*, 18.12.2014 – Opinion 2/13 - ECHR = ECLI:EU:C:2014:2454, para 168: *"This legal structure is based on the fundamental premiss that each Member State shares with all the other Member States, and recognises that they share with it, a set of common values on which the EU is founded, as stated in Article 2 TEU."*; *Burgstaller*, JOIA Vol. 26, No. 2 (2009), 181, 191; cf. similar: *Streinz*, 10. Edn. (2016), p. 47 ff.

782 *Wehland*, ICLQ Vol. 58, Iss. 2 (2009), 297, 302.

a distinction between internal or international law based on objective criteria.[783]

Similarly, the reception of public international law within the legal hierarchy in the EU does not affect its qualification either.[784] Each state, and this needs to be admitted for international organisations as well, is deliberately free to choose its mechanism of integrating public international law.[785] The character of international law of a legal instrument has never been challenged due to a state adopting a monist or dualist or even any other mean of reception of public international law in such state's legal framework. If the CJEU states that:

> "the provisions of the Agreement, from the coming into force thereof, form an integral part of Community law"[786]

this is nothing else than the acknowledgment that as to the European Treaties, all agreements concluded by the EU also have binding effects for the member states. Neither does it alter the nature of the agreement, nor does it make prove of a distinction between the European Treaties and public international law.[787]

---

783 *Burgstaller*, JOIA Vol. 26, No. 2 (2009), 181, 191; Similarly: *Eilmansberger*, CMLR Vol. 46 (2009), 383, 424 who tends to ignore the statement for the classification as it cannot alter the character by itself, similar: *Wehland*, ICLQ Vol. 58, Iss. 2 (2009), 297, 302; *Klabbers*, Treaty conflict and the European Union, 2009, p. 16 f.

784 *Streinz*, 10. Edn. (2016), p. 49; similar *Hobe*, 8. Edn. (2014), p. 438-439 who distinguishes between internal and external effects and principles to be applied; also denying any effect of the way EU law is recepted within EU member states: *Dörr* in: Grabitz/Hilf/Nettesheim EUV/AEUV, Art. 47 TEU, para 79.

785 *Hindelang*, LIEI Vol. 39, Iss. 2 (2012), 179, 188 considers that the direct effect is a mean to ensure the uniform application by disabling the member states to breach the European Treaties, hence it is a mechanism conceived to follow the principle of *pacta sunt servanda.*

786 *CJEU*, 30.04.1974 – C-181/73 - Haegeman = ECLI:EU:C:1974:41, para 5, which has been advanced by *Tietje*, Intra-EU BITs als Herausforderung im Mehrebenensystem des Rechts (Beit. zum Transnat. Wirt.-R, Vol. 104, 2011), p. 8 f. to disqualify EU law from being international law.

787 *Bungenberg* in: v. d. Groeben/Schwarze AEUV/EUV, Art. 218 TFEU, para 120 ff. This also applies for the alleed differentiation due to the existence of disconnection clauses. It is difficult to perceive that these clauses are anything different than a statement which is made for the avoidance of doubt and to reiterate the principle of primacy as governing rule of conflict, cf. *infra* (Chapter 8).

II. EU law primarily creates rights and obligations towards member states and as an auxiliary individual rights

The second criterion to qualify international law is that the legal framework needs to be applicable to subjects of international law. EU law, despite its evolution, remains a body of law applicable to the EU member states and thus to subjects of international law. This applies to primary as well as secondary law.[788]

For EU primary law, the contracting parties of the European Treaties are primarily the EU member states. The fact that particularly the provisions for the fundamental freedoms, the principle of non-discrimination and the Art. 101 ff TFEU *also* have direct effect among individuals, does not change this relation.[789]

The same applies for secondary law. The main addresses of these legislative acts remain the EU member states. Besides, all three types of binding legislative acts (regulations, directives and decisions) may also create rights and obligations for individuals. But the fact that these legislative acts do *also* create rights and duties for individuals, does not justify a divergent classification of EU law.

This is based on two considerations:

First because the fact that individuals are subject matters which are affected by an inter-state regulation does not alter the character of the regulation, such rights derive from. Moreover, because through the last century the classic understanding of individuals being only the subject matter of international law has substantially decreased.[790] Since 1950 several treaties such as the European Convention on Human Rights, the Inter-American Convention on Human Rights and nearly all IIAs since the 1960's have attributed individual rights to their nationals and granted direct access to international courts or tribunals.[791] All these agreements

---

788 Obviously distinguishing: *Ličková*, EJIL Vol. 19, No. 3 (2008), 463, 467 and the investors submissions in *Electrabel vs. Hungary*, 30.11.2012 – ICSID Case No. ARB/07/19: Decision on Jurisdiction, Applicable Law and Liability, para 4.40.

789 Similar: *Hindelang*, LIEI Vol. 39, Iss. 2 (2012), 179, 185 f; *Streinz*, 10. Edn. (2016), p. 48.

790 *Shaw*, International law, 6. Edn. (2008), p. 232 f; *Kempen/Hillgruber*, Völkerrecht, 2. Edn. (2012), p. 37.

791 *Shaw*, International law, 6. Edn. (2008), p. 233; relating to this mediatised attribution of rights: *Ipsen*, Völkerrecht, 6. Edn. (2014), p. 311-314; cf. also

have been concluded by states and thus subjects of international law, which by exercising their sovereignty granted claimable rights and obligations to an individual. Despite this effect, nobody questions that these conventions are part of the legal system called "*public international law*". Hence the fact that through the exercise of sovereignty a state (*also*) creates (directly claimable) rights and obligations to an individual, does not affect the qualification of the act constituting these rights and obligations itself.[792] On the contrary the last century demonstrated that individuals got attributed an essential role within the framework of international law.[793] *A contrario*, if the fact that an international convention contains directly claimable rights for individual was sufficient to disqualify such convention of being international law, an IIA would also need to be disqualified from being international law.

One might further question this analysis by referring to the principle of direct effect which leads to the possibility for the individual to invoke certain rights contained in i.e. secondary legislation directly before national courts (even though they might not be transposed yet). It can be argued that this principle is somehow unusual for any international convention. However, the principle does not alter the nature of EU law as well. The principle of direct effect is conceived to strengthen the uniform application of EU law and engage its observance to the most possible extent. The way (member) states try to guarantee the enforcement of an international convention and the legal framework construed therein, cannot alter the nature of the agreement itself.[794] Therefore, EU law also fulfils the second criterion to qualify a legal framework as international law.

III. EU law regulates rights between subjects of international law

Given these considerations, the EU law also fulfils the third criteria, which one could describe as the criterion *ratione materiae*. A legal framework

---

Herdegen, Völkerrecht, 15. Edn. (2016), p. 111 f; *Vitzthum/Bothe*, Völkerrecht, 5. Edn. (2010), p. 158 ff.

792 Cf. also: *Evans*, International law, (2006), p. 32-313 and especially p. 319-321 regarding investment arbitration.

793 *Ipsen*, Völkerrecht, 6. Edn. (2014), p. 311-314; cf. also *Herdegen*, Völkerrecht, 15. Edn. (2016), p. 111 f, who also refers to the mechanisms of investment protection as examples of such individuals being protected.

794 Cf. also: *Repasi*, EuR, 2013, 45, 49.

needs to regulate the relations of subjects of international states. EU creates such binding set of rules in the relations of subjects of international law, which are the member states. *Shaw* puts it as follows:

> "Such regional organizations have added to the developing sophistication of international law by the insertion of 'regional-international law sub-systems' within the universal framework and the consequent evolution of rules that bind only member states."[795]

What has happened through the creation of the EU is the creation of a set of rules which applies to the EU member states. The member states – jointly – agreed to be – jointly – bound by different rules which can either derive from changing the primary law or from derivate secondary law. *De facto* the member states created a sub-system of law, but this sub-system remains international law as it regulates the rights and obligations *vis-à-vis* to subjects of international law.[796] As it has just been demonstrated the simple fact that the EU law also creates rights and obligations that are directly enforceable by individuals does not alter the character of the source of these laws. Regulations, directives as well as decisions under EU law are all based on the TFEU and the TEU, which remain sources of international law. The entire legal framework of the EU is based on the TEU and the TFEU, which both remain international conventions. Neither the institutions of the EU, nor any legislative act, nor any right or obligation within the EU operates outside the set of rules, which has been set by EU primary law.[797] *Streinz* therefore stresses out that the EU law has never been

---

795 *Shaw*, International law, 6. Edn. (2008), p. 46.

796 Cf. *Shaw*, International law, 6. Edn. (2008), p. 46, similar: *Wehland*, ICLQ Vol. 58, Iss. 2 (2009), 297, 302; *Hindelang*, LIEI Vol. 39, Iss. 2 (2012), 179, 185 f points out: "*While it is true that the TEU and TFEU contain elements [...] that go, in terms of integration, far beyond what has been seen in respect of any other international organization, this does not render these treaties an aliud but 'merely a 'treaty plus'' compared to other public international law treaties establishing an international organization.*" [emphasis in original]; The European Court of Human Rights did not even hesitate to consider the European Treaties as well as regulations deriving from secondary law as international law in terms of the VCLT, cf. : *European Court of Human Rights*, 30.06.2005 – Application n° 45036/98 - Bosphorus, para 150 ff.

797 This delimitation is settled case law and was again stressed by the CJEU in the Opinion regarding the EU's accession to the ECHR, *CJEU*, 18.12.2014 – Opinion 2/13 - ECHR = ECLI:EU:C:2014:2454, para 38: "*[The accession to the ECHR under the EC treaty] would therefore have been such as to go beyond the scope of Article 235 of the EC Treaty (which became Article 308 EC),*

separated from its sources which are laid down in international law and that a separation from international law can only be executed through the foundation of a distinct (European) federal state.[798] But since this creation of a (new) federal state did not take place yet, neither the density of regulations within the EU, nor the legal principles governing this legal entity alter the qualification of EU law as international law.

Chapter 8: The relevant rule of conflict of laws regarding EU law and IIAs

As both, EU law as well as the IIA, should be considered as international law, the conflict between the frameworks needs to be determined by means of international law as well.[799] There are several instruments that can be, and have been invoked to resolve this conflict. However, the reception by the arbitral tribunals and scholars so far has been (by far) dominated by the question of whether Art. 59 and Art. 30 (3) of the VCLT are applicable to intra-EU IIA disputes and whether their conditions are met.[800]

Instead of fixing the debate on these articles, the full set of potential rules governing the conflict should be kept in mind, when addressing the question (A.). Given the diverging legal effects of several of these rules (complete invalidity vs. invalidity of particular provisions) the potential invalidity of the entire IIA in accordance with Art. 59 VCLT should be examined first (B.). It will be argued that the criteria set forth in this article are not met. Hence, the next logical step consists in analysing conflict rules in the TFEU, especially Art. 351 TFEU and the principle of primacy in EU law (C.).

---

a provision now contained in Article 352(1) TFEU, which could have been brought about only by way of amendment of that Treaty" [emphasis added].

798 *Kokott* in: Streinz EUV/AEUV, Art. 47 TEU, para 10.

799 Similar: *Hindelang*, LIEI Vol. 39, Iss. 2 (2012), 179, 183 and 186 f; *Ghouri*, ELJ Vol. 16, No. 5 (2010), 806, 811.

800 Cf. decisions in: *Eastern Sugar vs. Czech Republic*, 27.03.2007 – SCC No. 088/2004 - Partial award *Oostergetel & Laurentius vs. Slovak Republic*, 30.04.2010 – UNICTRAL - Award on Jurisdiction *Achmea vs. Slovak Republic*, 26.10.2012 – PCA Case No. 2008-13 - Award on Jurisdiction, Arbitrability and Suspension; *Euram vs. Slovak Republic*, 22.10.2012 – PCA Case no. 2010-17: First Award on Jurisdiction.

It shall be demonstrated that the principle of primacy is the conflict rule which applies in intra-EU relationships even if such relationships result from international conventions and that this principle renders incompatible or conflicting provisions inapplicable. The same result would be obtained by 'application' of settled rules in public international law, which should be demonstrated by reference to the principles in the VCLT (D.).

A. Preliminary remarks how to resolve conflicts between several rules of laws

Public international law contains a multitude of principles how to settle conflicts between different rules of laws or legal frameworks in general. Art. 59 and Art. 30 (3) VCLT are only two examples of codified rules of customary international law.[801] However, before returning to customary international law, one should focus on conventional agreements undertaken by the parties, e.g. in conflict clauses.[802] Such clauses contain the parties' intention how a conflict of different rules of law should be resolved.[803] Those clauses might have numerous effects, such as granting priority to a later treaty, priority to an older treaty, partial priority in specific circumstances or any other type of solution one might imagine.[804] Provided that there is such an expression of the parties' will, such will should be respected. The reason is that the parties to an international agreement keep the power to modify its application by mutual agreement whenever they wish to do so.[805] Hence, if they wish to amend or terminate a treaty, they are entirely free to do so. This fundamental principle is

801 *Mus*, Netherlands International Law Review, 1998, 208, 213; *Dubuisson* in: Corten/Klein VCLT - II, Art. 59 VCLT, para 2.

802 *Mus*, Netherlands International Law Review, 1998, 208, 214; *Leeks*, U. Toronto Fac. L. Rev. Vol. 65, No. 2 (2007), 1, 37; cf. also *Repasi*, EuR, 2013, 45, 62.

803 *Mus*, Netherlands International Law Review, 1998, 208, 214 ff; e.g. the Europe Agreements in Art. 118 contain a conflict rule; similar Art. 350 TFEU or the "*disconnection clauses*" by EU member states in several agreements constitute such clauses.

804 *Mus*, Netherlands International Law Review, 1998, 208, 214.

805 *Mus*, Netherlands International Law Review, 1998, 208, 214 f.; for the same idea underlying Art. 59 VCLT: *Dubuisson* in: Corten/Klein VCLT - II, Art. 59 VCLT, para 1; similar: *Giegerich* in: Dörr/Schmalenbach VCLT, Art. 59 VCLT, para 1 and 3; obviously denying such a possibility: *Söderlund*, JOIA Vol. 24, Iss. 5 (2007), 455, 460 without further arguments.

(fragmentarily) codified in Art. 30 (2) VCLT and cannot be derogated by any other rule of customary international law, such as the principle of *lex specialis* or even the principle of *pacta sunt servanda*.[806] It is important to note that such conflict clauses do not necessarily need to be explicit. Conflict rules may as well result from treaty interpretation in accordance with the principles laid down in Art. 31 ff VCLT.[807] Only if and to the extent such a conflict clause is missing and cannot be deducted from one or the other treaty by means of interpretation, the general rules of customary international law laid down in Art. 59 and 30 (3), (4) VCLT should apply. Hence, public international law recognises a certain hierarchy which should be observed when dealing with a conflict of legal frameworks. Generally, any rule of conflict (irrespective whether such rule is explicit or implicit) takes primacy over Art. 59 and/or Art. 30 VCLT, as the latter only reflect rules of customary international law. Art. 59 and Art. 30 VCLT also reveal to follow a certain hierarchy. Regarding the scope of application and its legal consequences, Art. 59 VCLT has priority over Art. 30 (3) and (4) VCLT.[808] First, the legal consequences of Art. 59 VCLT (termination or suspension in application of the *entire* (dismissed) treaty) are more far reaching than those under Art. 30 (3), (4) VCLT (which will only lead to the non-application of a particular provision).[809]

Second, Art. 30 (3) VCLT expressly refers to Art. 59 VCLT when stating:

> "When all the parties to the earlier treaty are parties also to the later treaty *but the earlier treaty is not terminated or suspended in operation under article 59*, the earlier treaty applies only to the extent (…)"

806 *Mus*, Netherlands International Law Review, 1998, 208, 214 f.

807 Art. 30 (2) VCLT stating: "*whenever a treay specifies*", *Mus*, Netherlands International Law Review, 1998, 208, 217; cf. also: *Hindelang*, LIEI Vol. 39, Iss. 2 (2012), 179, 187; for the opposite: *Leeks*, U. Toronto Fac. L. Rev. Vol. 65, No. 2 (2007), 1, 37; similar and clearly admitting this point: *Wackernagel*, EU Judicial Proceedings, Consenual Termination of Intra-EU BITs (Beit. zum Transnat. Wirt.-R, Vol. 140, 2016), 5, 14; *Burgstaller*, JOIA Vol. 26, No. 2 (2009), 181, 208 f.

808 *Giegerich* in: Dörr/Schmalenbach VCLT, Art. 59 VCLT, para 4; cf. also: *Burgstaller* in: *Bungenberg/Griebel/Hindelang* (Eds.), International investment law and EU law, 2011, p. 75.

809 Cf. dilligently distinguishing between the legal effects of both provisions: *Achmea vs. Slovak Republic*, 26.10.2012 – PCA Case No. 2008-13 - Award on Jurisdiction, Arbitrability and Suspension, para 240.

This reference clearly shows the hierarchy between Art. 59 VCLT and Art. 30 (3), (4) VCLT. Only to the extent that Art. 59 VCLT does not lead to a termination or suspension, Art. 30 (3), (4) VCLT may be applied.[810]

Given the aforementioned considerations, one should assume that potential inherent conflict rules in either the IIA, the Europe Agreements or the European Treaties should be analysed first.

I. Absence of explicit provisions dealing with the conflict in IIAs and the European Treaties

The question of potential conflicts between IIAs and EU law could be easily resolved if either the IIA or the European Treaties contained a conflict clause, explicitly addressing the question. Neither the IIA, nor the Europe Agreements, nor the European Treaties contain a provision which *expressly* targets the 'sake' of IIAs in an inter-member state relationship.[811]

So far, as to the authors' knowledge, none of the IIAs explicitly addresses the question. IIAs omit addressing any particular interference with other international treaties. The only reference which can be found is Art. 16 of the Energy Charter Treaty which addresses the relation to other agreements.[812] Besides the fact that mixed agreements should not be part of the main analysis, it will be demonstrated that within intra-EU conflicts this clause remains irrelevant (cf. *infra* Chapter 8).

The Europe Agreements concluded prior to the accession of the new (Eastern European) member states to the EU, do not contain an explicit rule either. From the regulations contained therein, one cannot deduct any (explicit or implicit) conflict rule.

The Europe Agreements signed prior to the accession of the Eastern-European member states contain only two provisions which might be rele-

810 *Giegerich* in: Dörr/Schmalenbach VCLT, Art. 59 VCLT, para 4.

811 This has also been the conclusion of the arbitral tribunal in *Eastern Sugar vs. Czech Republic*, 27.03.2007 – SCC No. 088/2004 - Partial award, para 156.

812 *Wackernagel*, EU Judicial Proceedings, Consenual Termination of Intra-EU BITs (Beit. zum Transnat. Wirt.-R, Vol. 140, 2016), 5, 14 raises the question whether the sunset clauses contained in several IIAs do not constitute a conflict clause. However, given the wording and their intent to regulate the effects of a termination (which is different from preventing a treaty to be terminated, as it is considered to remain in force), this seems doubtful, cf. Chapter 11 for a further analysis.

vant in this context.[813] The first is Article 74 of the Europe Agreements which reads:

> "1. Co-operation shall aim to establish a favourable climate for private investment, both domestic and foreign, which is essential to economic and industrial reconstruction in the Slovak Republic.
>
> 2. The particular aims of co-operation shall be:
>
> - to improve the institutional framework for investments in the Slovak Republic;
>
> - the extension by the Member States and the Slovak Republic of agreements for the promotion and protection of investment;"

The second one is Art. 118 of the Europe Agreements which stipulates:

> "This Agreement shall not, until equivalent rights for individuals and economic operators have been achieved under this Agreement, affect rights assured to them through existing agreements binding one or more Member States, on the one hand, and the Slovak Republic, on the other."

Although Art. 118 of the Europe Agreements might be read as a conflict rule and has indeed be cited by claimants in investment proceedings[814], the article does not relate to the conflict of European Treaties and an IIA. The provision clarifies that any provision in the *Europe Agreement* should not affect obligations undertaken in prior treaties. However, first, IIAs between EU member states and the accession-candidates have mostly been concluded by the acceding member states after the conclusion of the Europe Agreements (some following the incentive in Art. 74 (2) of the Europe Agreements) and will therefore not be affected by Art. 118 of the Europe Agreements.[815] Second, even if an IIA was concluded before,

---

813 Those provisions have indeed been adressed by various arbitral tribunals: *Eastern Sugar vs. Czech Republic*, 27.03.2007 – SCC No. 088/2004 - Partial award, para 143 ff; *Euram vs. Slovak Republic*, 22.10.2012 – PCA Case no. 2010-17: First Award on Jurisdiction, para 193 ff; *Achmea vs. Slovak Republic*, 26.10.2012 – PCA Case No. 2008-13 - Award on Jurisdiction, Arbitrability and Suspension, para 244.

814 Cf. *inter alia*: *Achmea vs. Slovak Republic*, 26.10.2012 – PCA Case No. 2008-13 - Award on Jurisdiction, Arbitrability and Suspension, para 87: *"the BIT was merely an accessory to the Association Agreements and since those were terminated by the accession of the new Member States, so was the applicability of the BIT."*

815 The Czech Republic concluded the latest BIT with a European Union member state on 09/04/2002 with the Republic of Malta, most of the other Agreements being concluded between 1989 – 1993, cf. for an exhaustive display of the existing BITs by country: http://investmentpolicyhub.unctad.org/IIA/IiasByCountryGrouping#iiaInnerMenu [last checked on 28/02/2017].

Art. 118 does not set any rule of conflict with regard to the European Treaties, which were exclusively concluded *after* the signature and entry into force of any intra-EU IIA.[816]

Similarly, Art. 74 of the Europe Agreements, which encourages the conclusion of IIAs to prepare the accession to the EU, does not contain a conflict rule for the conflict between EU law and existing IIAs. The provision is mostly unclear and does not state a sufficiently clear statement beyond the fact that it encourages the states to deepened their economic relationship during the accession process. Hence, the ambiguity of the Europe Agreements as to IIAs reveals no clear intention of the contracting parties which would allow to deduce an implicit conflict rule from these agreements.[817]

II. Absence of conflict rule leading to the termination of an entire treaty

In the absence of any explicit rule in the European Treaties, the Europe Agreements or the IIAs, one should – in a second step – primarily address *implicit* conflict rules which could be derived from either the IIA or EU

816 Cf. *Dimopoulos*, CMLR Vol. 48, No. 1 (2011), 63, 75.

817 The Slovak Republic tried to demonstrate that it follows from Art. 74 (2) of the Europe Agreements that the BIT was conceived as a transition treaty only, cf.: *Achmea vs. Slovak Republic*, 26.10.2012 – PCA Case No. 2008-13 - Award on Jurisdiction, Arbitrability and Suspension, para 86 f; The *Euram-Tribunal* concluded the opposite and stated that "*Moreover, although the Europe Agreement does not deal expressly with the termination of the BITs, it appears, in the view of the Tribunal, that [Art. 74 of the Europe Agreement] implies that unless rights equivalent to those from which they benefitted under BITs before accession to the EU were conferred upon investors by the EU law, such rights should be maintained. This leans rather in the direction of maintaining the BIT since it is quite difficult to deny that, under the EU framework, the foreign investors do not have, for example, the direct right to bring international arbitration proceedings against the State in which they have invested, a right which is a central feature of the BIT*". This line of argumentation rather opts for the opposite of the demonstration the Slovac Republic supported. As to the author, Article 74 (2) of the Europe Agreement is inconclusive. Given the rather vague terms and the missing reference to any legal effects one could hardly deduct any general principle from both articles in the Europe Agreements. The *Eastern-Sugar-Tribunal* also stated that "*[...] One cannot say that the Europe Agreements or Accession Treaty by their terms epxressly superseded the BIT*", cf.: *Eastern Sugar vs. Czech Republic*, 27.03.2007 – SCC No. 088/2004 - Partial award, para 147 and following paragraphs.

law. It will be demonstrated that EU law contains such an implicit conflict rule which is the principle of primacy (cf. *infra* C.). However, this conflict rule only leads to the non-application of a particular provision (cf. *infra*). EU law does not contain any provision which would lead to the *termination* of an entire international agreement. On the contrary, even in the relationship between EU law and national law, the principle of supremacy of EU law does not render the contrary provision void but simply inapplicable.[818] It is arguable that this disqualifies any application of Art. 59 VCLT *per se* (which would result in the termination of the entire conflicting treaty) as the parties intended to expressly set forth a legal consequence other than the termination of a treaty. However, given the more far reaching consequences of Art. 59 VCLT and the considerable attention paid to this provision by the arbitral tribunals in the arbitral proceedings dealing with intra-EU investment disputes, it should be demonstrated first, why this Art. 59 VCLT could not lead to a termination of the IIA (cf. *infra* B.) Furthermore, if one of the legal frameworks (i.e. the IIA) is rendered void, no conflict exists as there is only one set of legal frameworks left to be applied to the facts. This justifies to treat the question of whether by virtue of Art. 59 VCLT the IIAs are terminated after the accession of the former host-states to the EU first. After finding that still both legal frameworks (EU Law / European Treaties and IIAs) remain in force, the question of the inherent conflict rule in the European Treaties as to the application or non-application of particular provisions to be applied in the intra-EU conflict can be addressed (cf. *infra* C.).[819]

B. Art. 59 of the Vienna Convention on the Law of Treaties

As previously explained the question of termination of the *entire* IIA by virtue of Art. 59 VCTL (as opposed to the inapplicability of particular provisions of an IIA by virtue of the principle of primacy) has to be addressed first. Art. 59 VCLT has been regularly invoked by host states in arbitration proceedings involving intra-EU IIAs. As to the host states,

818 *Hobe*, 8. Edn. (2014), para 463; *CJEU*, 09.03.1978 – C-106/77 - Simmenthal = ECLI:EU:C:1978:49, para 17; *CJEU*, 22.10.1998 – Joined cases C-10/97 to C-22/97 - Ministero delle Finanze vs. IN.CO.GE.'90 Srl and others = ECLI:EU: C:1998:498, para 21; *Haratsch*, 2016, para 179; *Oppermann/Classen et al.*, 5. Edn. (2011) §10, para 9 f.

819 *Dubuisson* in: Corten/Klein VCLT - II, Art. 59 VCLT, para 2 f.

since both, EU law and IIAs, address the question of promoting economic freedom in the internal market, but both legal frameworks are (allegedly) incompatible to a certain extent, Art. 59 VCLT would necessarily lead to a termination of the IIA.[820] This argumentation is erroneous.

It is generally admitted that Art. 59 VCLT prerequisites two strands of conditions to be met[821]: the conflicting treaties need to cover the *same subject matter* (prerequisite) and *additionally* either:

> "(a) it appears from the later treaty or is otherwise established that the parties intended that the matter should be governed by that treaty;"

or – alternatively –

> "(b) the provisions of the later treaty are so far incompatible with those of the earlier one that the two treaties are not capable of being applied at the same time." [822]

Whereas it can be argued that IIAs and the European Treaties share the same subject matter, the additional requirements of Art. 59 (1) lit. a or lit. b are not fulfilled.

I. Same subject matter in terms of Art. 59 VCLT

The condition of "*sameness*" under Art. 59 VCLT has been intensively discussed with regard to the intra-EU objection in international investment arbitration.

---

820 Several host states tried to argue in the respective arbitral proceedings that by virtue of Art. 59 VCLT the IIAs on which the claims were based have been terminated, cf.: *Binder vs. Czech Republic*, 06.06.2007 – UNCITRAL - Award on Jurisdiction, para 19; *Eastern Sugar vs. Czech Republic*, 27.03.2007 – SCC No. 088/2004 - Partial award, para 100-103; *Euram vs. Slovak Republic*, 22.10.2012 – PCA Case no. 2010-17: First Award on Jurisdiction, para 83 ff; *Achmea vs. Slovak Republic*, 26.10.2012 – PCA Case No. 2008-13 - Award on Jurisdiction, Arbitrability and Suspension, para 63.

821 Art. 59 of the VCLT is deemed to reflect customary international law, cf. : *Dubuisson* in: Corten/Klein VCLT - II, Art. 59 VCLT Art. 59, para 6 and 14 ff.

822 Cf. also: *Kniebaum*, ELTE Law Journal, 27, 29; *Eilmansberger*, CMLR Vol. 46 (2009), 383, 400; the tribunal in *Euram vs. Slovak Republic*, 22.10.2012 – PCA Case no. 2010-17: First Award on Jurisdiction referred to lit. a being the "*subjective condition*" and lit. b being the objective condition of Art. 59 VCLT: this denomination will be followed if suitable.

1. The notion of sameness in Art. 59 VLCT as interpreted by the arbitral tribunals dealing with intra-EU disputes

The notion of "*same subject matter*" adopted so far by the arbitral tribunals is predominantly driven by a very strict interpretation. The *Eastern Sugar-Tribunal*[823] concluded that both treaties need to address the same "*precise subject matter*".[824] Two treaties could only address the same "*precise*" subject matter, if their guarantees and the rules and regulations they provide for overlap to an extend which renders the provisions in the respective treaties nearly identical. Given that EU law would miss an access to mixed arbitration (usually contained in IIAs) and would only provide for less extensive guarantees than the guarantees set forth in an IIA, both legal frameworks could, as the tribunal, not address the same "*precise subject matter*".[825] Similarly, the tribunal in *Oostergetel & Laurentius vs. Slovak Republic*[826] adopts a very restrictive approach when determining whether two treaties share the same subject matter in terms of Art. 59 VCLT: it even seems to consider that to cover the same subject matter the

823 *Eastern Sugar vs. Czech Republic*, 27.03.2007 – SCC No. 088/2004 - Partial award.

824 *Eastern Sugar vs. Czech Republic*, 27.03.2007 – SCC No. 088/2004 - Partial award, para 160; apparently supporting such a restrictive approach: *Kleinheisterkamp*, JIEL Vol. 15, No. 1 (2012), 85, 95 but without further arguments.

825 *Eastern Sugar vs. Czech Republic*, 27.03.2007 – SCC No. 088/2004 - Partial award, para 160; the tribunal argues that the guarantees in the European Treaties and the IIA are only partially overlapping with IIAs offering for a wider range of protection especially regarding the investment phase itself (e.g. through FET and FPS clauses), cf. paras 161 ff.; Secondly, EU law would not provide a dispute resolution mechanism similar to the mixed (international) arbitration offered by the IIA. Given the – in the arbitral tribunal's view – tremendous importance of such a mechanism for the effectiveness of the investment protection, both regulations cannot be considered to cover the same "*precise*" subject matter, cf. *Eastern Sugar vs. Czech Republic*, 27.03.2007 – SCC No. 088/2004 - Partial award, para 165 stating that the arbitration clause can be considered as the „*most essential provision*" of the BIT and para 180 considering it to be for itself sufficient to reject an equivalency. Through this reasoning the Tribunal takes the counterpart of the reasoning in *Binder vs. Czech Republic*, 06.06.2007 – UNCITRAL - Award on Jurisdiction, para 65, considering legal action in front of a national court a sufficient equivalent to prevent an investor from a member state protected by a BIT (and thus having access to a mixed arbitration mechanism).

826 *Oostergetel & Laurentius vs. Slovak Republic*, 30.04.2010 – UNICTRAL - Award on Jurisdiction.

treaties nearly have to be identical.[827] According to the tribunal, the IIA focuses on long-term investments and the European Treaties on all kinds of cross-border activity, the substantive safeguards are not "*identical*"[828] and the European Treaties are missing the possibility for an investor to rely on arbitration proceedings. Hence both treaties would not cover the same subject matter.[829] Some – allegedly – broader definitions were applied by the following tribunals, *inter alia* by the *EURAM Tribunal*[830], which concludes that sameness needs to be addressed by identifying the issues "*with which the provisions deal, i.e. its topics or its substance*".[831] Although the definition seems broader, the arguments advanced by the tribunal reveal a very restrictive approach as well. The tribunal advances two arguments why IIAs and the European Treaties by its topic or its substance do not relate to the same subject matter, which reflect this restrictive approach. First, whereas the European Treaties focused on the creation of an (unified, common) internal market, IIAs apply to foster investments through creating a stable legal framework for investors. Given this difference in its focus, as to the *EURAM Tribunal*, both treaties could not be of the same subject matter.[832] Second, referring to Art. 207 TFEU, the tribunal concludes that, as the competence for foreign direct investments had been attributed to the EU only since the Lisbon Treaty, IIAs and the European Treaties could not have the same subject matter before this referral of competence.[833]

Hence, for the arbitral tribunals having dealt with the question so far, the notion of „*same subject matter*" is a criterion which limits the ability

---

827 *Oostergetel & Laurentius vs. Slovak Republic*, 30.04.2010 – UNICTRAL - Award on Jurisdiction, para 75 ff.

828 *Oostergetel & Laurentius vs. Slovak Republic*, 30.04.2010 – UNICTRAL - Award on Jurisdiction, para 76.

829 *Oostergetel & Laurentius vs. Slovak Republic*, 30.04.2010 – UNICTRAL - Award on Jurisdiction, para 104.

830 *Euram vs. Slovak Republic*, 22.10.2012 – PCA Case no. 2010-17: First Award on Jurisdiction.

831 *Euram vs. Slovak Republic*, 22.10.2012 – PCA Case no. 2010-17: First Award on Jurisdiction, para 172.

832 *Euram vs. Slovak Republic*, 22.10.2012 – PCA Case no. 2010-17: First Award on Jurisdiction, para 178 ff, also stressing that aceeding a regional organization is simply not the same than setting up a specific investment protection regime (para 184), which is doubtful given the particular nature of the internal market within the regional organization called European Union.

833 *Euram vs. Slovak Republic*, 22.10.2012 – PCA Case no. 2010-17: First Award on Jurisdiction, para 183.

of two separate legal frameworks to enter into a conflict in the sense of Art. 59 VCLT. As the further criteria in Art. 59 (1) lit. a and lit. b will only apply if the conflicting treaties share the same subject matter, a restrictive interpretation given to the notion of sameness, considerably narrows down the scope of application for Art. 59 VCLT in general. Hence, any deeper assessment of the conflict between the legal frameworks is eliminated *ab initio*. It is highly doubtful if this is the underlying idea of the notion of "*same subject matter*" in Art. 59 VCTL.

2. The misuse of the notion of "same subject matter" to eliminate conflicts ab initio

The approaches adopted by the majority of the tribunals so far are too narrow and (at least probably) driven by the desire to eliminate any potential conflict on a very preliminary stage.

To address the scope of "*sameness*" in Art. 59 VCLT it should first be pointed out that the terms are used both in Art. 59 VCLT and Art. 30 VCLT. Denying the attribute of sameness to two treaties under Art. 59 VCLT necessarily leads to the non-application of Art. 30 VLCT as well.[834]

From a literal interpretation the notion "*same*" indicates that there needs to be a certain form of identity or a lack of difference between two comparatives.[835] However, the notion of sameness in Art. 59 VCLT relates to the term "*subject matter*". Subject matter is defined as the topic to be dealt with in the respective context.[836] Hence, "*same subject matter*" should be a lack of difference of the topic to be dealt with in the respective context. However, the topic could either be the topic of the treaty or the topic of

834 Given the explicit reference in Art. 30 (3) VCLT to Art. 59 VCLT there is no indication that both terms of sameness could be of different scope in the respective articles, cf. also: *Dubuisson* in: Corten/Klein VCLT - II, Art. 59 VCLT, para 24; similar also: *Eilmansberger*, CMLR Vol. 46 (2009), 383, 425; this was also correctly pointed out by the tribunal in *Oostergetel & Laurentius vs. Slovak Republic*, 30.04.2010 – UNICTRAL - Award on Jurisdiction, para 104; for the opposite: *Reinisch*, LIEI Vol. 39, No. 2 (2012), 157, 165 f who considers that the notion of sameness differs in both articles; somehow confuse on this matter: *Giegerich* in: Dörr/Schmalenbach VCLT, Art. 59 VCLT, para 11 which seems to completely ignore the fact that Art. 30 also contains the term "*same subject matter*".

835 *Stevenson*, Oxford dictionary of English, 3. Edn. (2010), p. 1573.

836 *Stevenson*, Oxford dictionary of English, 3. Edn. (2010), p. 1773.

the circumstances to which the treaty is allied. Consequently, a literal interpretation given to the terms used in Art. 59 VCLT would either justify a narrow as well as a broad understanding of "*same subject matter*" in Art. 59 VCLT, depending on what should be understood by the "*topic*" to be dealt with in a treaty.

From the preparatory works, little can be drawn as well. As to the expert in the meetings, the provision should not "*cover cases where a general treaty impinged indirectly on the content of a particular provision of an earlier treaty*".[837] However, the particular discussion seemed to be focused on the principles of how to resolve the conflicts, as the reports state that Art. 59 VCLT should not lead to a circumvention of the principle of *generalia specialibus non derogant* by admitting a conflict with every far-reaching general treaty.[838] However, this could also be achieved by a reasonable interpretation of the further conditions.

Hence, one should address the question from a teleological lens. Art. 59 and Art. 30 VCLT are supposed to serve as conflict rules for two treaties. The notion of same subject matter therefore provides a certain filter for those conflict rules to apply. The shorter the scope of application of those articles is drawn, the less space is left for applying the different concepts of conflict-resolution laid down in Art. 59 (1) lit. a (tacit or implicit abrogation) and lit. b (incompatibility) or Art. 30 VCLT (explicit conflict rule designated by the parties, particular incompatibility, etc.). These considerations would opt for a wide interpretation of the notion of "*same subject matter*" in Art. 30 and 59 VCLT.[839]

In line with these considerations, the ILC adopts the opinion that the precondition of same subject matter should be met as soon as both treaties

---

837 *United Nations Conference on the Law of Treaties*, Summary records of the plenary meetings and of the meetings of the Committee of the Whole Second session, 09/04.1969 to 22/05/1969, p. 222.

838 *United Nations Conference on the Law of Treaties*, Summary records of the plenary meetings and of the meetings of the Committee of the Whole Second session, 09/04.1969 to 22/05/1969, p. 222; similar: *Giegerich* in: Dörr/Schmalenbach VCLT, Art. 59 VCLT, para 12.

839 *Dubuisson* in: Corten/Klein VCLT - II, Art. 59 VCLT, para 25; cf. also: *Wehland*, ICLQ Vol. 58, Iss. 2 (2009), 297,304 f who looks at the purpose of both treaties (promotion and protection of investments) without requiring an identity for the level of protection; However, for the opposite: *Kniebaum*, ELTE Law Journal, 27, 29 f; cf. also: *European Commission*, Amicus Curia Brief filed in EDF vs. Hungary (PCA Case n°2009-13) - arbitration proceedings, 14/05/2013, para 54.

apply to the same facts.[840] As correctly pointed out by the ILC report on the fragmentation of international law[841], one cannot limit the scope of the application of Art. 30 and 59 VLCT by referring to the classification of the treaty (environmental law vs. investment law vs. trade law), its substantive content (the scope of rights and obligations) or even its subjects (internal market vs. investment protection).[842] First, such classifications are highly doubtful and of little clarity. Second, this would considerable limit the parties' possibility to derogate from existing obligations without modifying the original treaty. To the extreme, two parties to a multilateral treaty e.g. relating to trade issues would find themselves impossible to modify a specific obligation in a bilateral treaty dealing e.g. with human rights[843], just because – as the treaties do not relate to the same subject matter – Art. 30 (2), (3) and (4) VCLT could not apply.[844] Third, one cannot reasonably argue that two treaties need to provide for equivalent pro-

840 *International Law Commission*, ILC Report on Fragmentation of International Law, 13/04/2006, para 21 ff. and regarding Art. 30 VCLT with reference to: *Vierdag*, British Yearbook of International Law Vol. 58, Iss. 1 (1988), 75, 100; cf. also: *Hindelang*, LIEI Vol. 39, Iss. 2 (2012), 179, 193 f; this was also supported by the Slovak Republic in *Euram vs. Slovak Republic*, 22.10.2012 – PCA Case no. 2010-17: First Award on Jurisdiction, para 85.

841 *International Law Commission*, ILC Report on Fragmentation of International Law, 13/04/2006.

842 This approach is however adopted by several host states when supporting their argumentation in the arbitration proceedings: cf. *Binder vs. Czech Republic*, 06.06.2007 – UNCITRAL - Award on Jurisdiction, para 13 ff; *Eastern Sugar vs. Czech Republic*, 27.03.2007 – SCC No. 088/2004 - Partial award, para 101 f; Implicitly referred to in *Oostergetel & Laurentius vs. Slovak Republic*, 30.04.2010 – UNICTRAL - Award on Jurisdiction, para 75 as well. It is also promoted by *Reinisch*, LIEI Vol. 39, No. 2 (2012), 157, 167 ff who considers EU law to only partially reflect the guatantees under an IIA and *vice-versa*, which would lead to different subject-matters; similar also: *Eilmansberger*, CMLR Vol. 46 (2009), 383, 400 f; *Hindelang*, LIEI Vol. 39, Iss. 2 (2012), 179, 193 f; *Dimopoulos*, CMLR Vol. 48, No. 1 (2011), 63, 73 f seems to consider that a potential conflict would be sufficient but also demonstrates that the overlap is by far sufficient to fulfill the condition of sameness.

843 For a similar example cf.: *International Law Commission*, ILC Report on Fragmentation of International Law, 13/04/2006, para 23-25 and 253-255; cf. similar: *Euram vs. Slovak Republic*, 22.10.2012 – PCA Case no. 2010-17: First Award on Jurisdiction, para 169, however the tribunal derives the opposite conclusion.

844 Cf. also: *International Law Commission*, ILC Report on Fragmentation of International Law, 13/04/2006, para 21 ff, *Dubuisson* in: Corten/Klein VCLT - II, Art. 59 VCLT, para 25 f.

tection in order to trigger the application of Art. 59 or Art. 30 VCLT. A conflict rule is by definition made to provide a solution to a conflict of potentially applicable set of norms. Such conflict will – at least predominantly – occur if two sets of rights are not necessarily the same or equivalent.[845] Limiting a conflict rule to a situation where applying the same rule would lead to fairly the same result, *de facto* renders the conflict rule useless. Hence, this cannot be the outcome of a teleological interpretation of the notion of sameness in Art. 59 VCLT. What the *Euram-Tribunal* and *Eastern Sugar-Tribunal* did when adopting the restrictive approach how to define the notion of "*same subject matter*", is to read the potential conditions to argue for an implicit abrogation under Art. 59 (1) lit. a VCLT into the notion of sameness.[846] It can indeed be argued that it is hard to demonstrate that the contracting parties had the tacit or implicit intention to replace a more far reaching treaty by concluding another treaty which does not provide for equivalent rights.[847] However, this should not be a question of sameness but of demonstrating the parties' intention as a separate condition in Art. 59 VCLT.

It should therefore be sufficient for the notion of sameness, if both treaties apply to the same facts.[848] Treaties will apply to the same facts, whenever the factual circumstances fall into the scope of application of both treaties. Applied to the potential conflict between the European Treaties and an IIA, these treaties should be considered to have the same subject

845 Several host states tried to demonstrate such equivalence, however it should be assumed that this demonstration was driven by the precendent awards which required such equivalence between the protection offered to the investory by IIAs and EU law in order to apply Art. 59 VCLT. As an example, for the arguments by the host states, cf.: *Binder vs. Czech Republic*, 06.06.2007 – UNCITRAL - Award on Jurisdiction, para 15; *Achmea vs. Slovak Republic*, 26.10.2012 – PCA Case No. 2008-13 - Award on Jurisdiction, Arbitrability and Suspension, para 69 ff.

846 This seems to be implicitly admitted by *Reinisch*, LIEI Vol. 39, No. 2 (2012), 157,172 f; somehow apparently favouring this approach: *Giegerich* in: Dörr/Schmalenbach VCLT, Art. 59 VCLT, para 13.

847 *Eilmansberger*, CMLR Vol. 46 (2009), 383, 401.

848 For the opposite: *Euram vs. Slovak Republic*, 22.10.2012 – PCA Case no. 2010-17: First Award on Jurisdiction, para 168 ff: the tribunal considers that such wide interpretation would not be in ligne with a "*good faith interpretation*" in accordance with the Vienna Convention of the Law on the Treaties. However, it is doubful why a broad interpretation, supported by a teleological interpretation of the Articles 30 and 59 VCLT should not be considered as a good faith interpretation of the latter.

matter, as they are applied to the same facts, an intra-EU investment.[849] The question whether this leads to setting aside the entire IIA or even provisions contained therein, is irrelevant for the determination of the same subject matter.

This is why the considerations by the arbitral tribunals in this regard should be rejected as well. In any case, it cannot be decisive if the guarantees provided for investors are equivalent under both treaty frameworks.[850] Even – for the sake of the argument – admitted that this is not the case, this equivalence is not a precondition for the application for the conflict rules in Art. 30 or 59 VCLT. First, Art. 59 VCLT would hardly make any sense because it would be limited to treaties which provide for equivalent guarantees but are still incompatible.[851] When applied to investment protection, it is hard to image a treaty being incompatible but keeping the same guarantees and same remedies. Second, both conflict rules would be *de facto* reduced to a marginal importance

Also the broader definition in *Euram vs. Slovak Republic* cannot be followed.[852] As previously pointed out, the classification of a treaty is subject

849 Similar: *Clodfelter*, Santa Clara Jour. of Int. Law Vol. 12, Iss. 1 (2013), 159, 178.

850 Cf. also: *Wehland*, ICLQ Vol. 58, Iss. 2 (2009), 297, 304 f; *Dimopoulos*, CMLR Vol. 48, No. 1 (2011), 63, 74; for the opposite: *Reinisch*, LIEI Vol. 39, No. 2 (2012), 157, 167 ff; *Eilmansberger*, CMLR Vol. 46 (2009), 383, 401; *Tietje*, Intra-EU BITs als Herausforderung im Mehrebenensystem des Rechts (Beit. zum Transnat. Wirt.-R, Vol. 104, 2011), p. 14 who however, regarding the ICSID-Convention and EU law (which certainly do not have equivalent protection, because the provisions aim at completely different topics), seems to admit the same subject matter, cf.: *Tietje/Wackernagel*, JWIT Vol. 16, Iss. 2 (2015), 205, 214.

851 *Dimopoulos*, CMLR Vol. 48, No. 1 (2011), 63, 74. However, this seems to be the position of *Reinisch*, LIEI Vol. 39, No. 2 (2012), 157, 167 ff who compares several substantial and procedural guarantees to conclude that their lacking *full* overalap, dismisses the notion of sameness.

852 The Tribunal stated: "*Even if two different rules deal with issues arising from the same facts, it does not necessarily mean that they have the same subject matter. This can be seen from a simple example: a treaty on environmental protection and a treaty on trade may both apply to the same factual situation but the subject matter with which they deal is quite different*" (para 169). However, if the Treaty related on environment protection contained a clause stipulating: "*Article X of this treaty should take supremacy on the obligations flowing from any other treaty between the parties, including the treaties regarding trade issues*", the Tribunal would still not be able to apply Art. 30 (2) VCLT.

to considerable doubts.[853] Furthermore, it would disable the parties to provide express stipulations regarding obligations from a previous treaty in the later treaty which addresses the sake of this previous obligation, if this treaty cannot be classified in the same "*subject matter*". Such limitations would be a major violation of the contracting parties' intention when concluding the treaty and is certainly not in line with the principles of interpretation in Art. 31 ff VCLT.

Given these considerations, both treaty frameworks indeed share the same subject matter as required by Art. 30 and Art. 59 VCLT.

II. Tacit intention to terminate the IIA subsequent to a member state's accession to the European Union (Art. 59 (1) lit. a VCLT)

Art. 59 (1) lit. a VCLT orders the termination of the treaty if it appears from the text of a subsequent treaty or is "*otherwise established*" that the parties intended to terminate one treaty upon conclusion of another treaty. As already mentioned it does not appear expressly from the European Treaties that they intended to abrogate the validity of any IIA concluded prior to the accession (cf. above: "*A. II. Absence of conflict rule leading to the termination of an entire treaty*").[854]

However, one could argue that this intention has been shown otherwise, tacitly, by the EU member states. Under Art. 59 VCLT such tacit intention can be derived from any other evidence supporting the parties' intention to terminate the IIA through the accession.[855] Effectively, several host states

---

This seems to be clearly contrary to the underlying idea in Art. 30 and Art. 59 VCLT.

853 A simple example might be the two opposites regarding the classification of EU law: *Wehland*, ICLQ Vol. 58, Iss. 2 (2009), 297, 304 f who considers that the "*purpose and effect of promoting and protecting investments can hardly be disputed*" against the ruling by the *EURAM-Tribunal.*

854 *Eilmansberger*, CMLR Vol. 46 (2009), 383, 401 correctly points out that the intention to abrogate a more demanding treaty tacitly is questionable.

855 Although details as to some shreds of evidence are disputed, it is generally admitted that under Art. 59 VCLT the tacit intention by the parties can lead to the termination of a treaty if there is sufficient evidence to prove such the states' will to do so, cf. : *Dubuisson* in: Corten/Klein VCLT - II, Art. 59 VCLT, Art. 59, para 35 ff and *Giegerich* in: Dörr/Schmalenbach VCLT, Art. 59 VCLT, para 21 ff; this was e.g. also admited by the *Achmea Tribunal*, cf.: *Achmea vs. Slovak Republic*, 26.10.2012 – PCA Case No. 2008-13 - Award on Jurisdiction, Arbitrability and Suspension, para 244 ff.

tried to demonstrate by various means that through the accession the parties' intended to end the IIAs in force.[856] Basically there were two lines of argumentation, which are both not convincing. First, the host states tried to argue that any state, by acceding to the EU, shows its intention that any intra-EU commercial relations should be exclusively governed by the rules and provisions contained in the European Treaties. The member states, by acceding to the EU, should have shown the (implicit) common intention to terminate and/or supersede all existing, potentially conflicting treaties at the moment of accession to the EU.[857] The second line of argumentation relates to the nature of the IIAs in intra-EU relationships. [858] The intra-EU IIAs should have been *ab initio* conceived as "*transition-treat[ies]*", which would automatically terminate upon the accession of the respective host state to the EU.[859]

However, both arguments are not convincing and contradict with the essence of EU law: the very nature of EU law is the best proof that such an intention cannot be established with sufficient clarity. As already men-

---

856 Cf. *inter alia* the demonstration of the Slovak Republic in *Achmea vs. Slovak Republic*, 26.10.2012 – PCA Case No. 2008-13 - Award on Jurisdiction, Arbitrability and Suspension, para 87 ff in which the Slovak Repulic cites several e-mails exchanged and other documents in order to support the idea that the Slovak Republic as host state and the Netherlands as home state intended to terminate the BIT. Similar in *Eastern Sugar vs. Czech Republic*, 27.03.2007 – SCC No. 088/2004 - Partial award, p. 23 ff where the Czech Republic refers to several notes and exchanges with the home state and the European Commission. None of this can be interpreted in an absolutly conclusive way.

857 *Euram vs. Slovak Republic*, 22.10.2012 – PCA Case no. 2010-17: First Award on Jurisdiction, para 96; *Achmea vs. Slovak Republic*, 26.10.2012 – PCA Case No. 2008-13 - Award on Jurisdiction, Arbitrability and Suspension, para 87.

858 *Eastern Sugar vs. Czech Republic*, 27.03.2007 – SCC No. 088/2004 - Partial award, para 103 ff; *Euram vs. Slovak Republic*, 22.10.2012 – PCA Case no. 2010-17: First Award on Jurisdiction, para 92.

859 *Achmea vs. Slovak Republic*, 26.10.2012 – PCA Case No. 2008-13 - Award on Jurisdiction, Arbitrability and Suspension, para 86: the Slovac Republic in this award referred to a provision in the Europe Agreements which states that any rights and obligations of the Slovac Republic assumed prior to enter into the Europe Agreement should not be affected, unless and until equivalent protection was achieved under EU law. This should reveal the parties' intention to maintain the IIA only until this equivalent protection has been reached. As this has been achieved upon accession to the EU, the IIA would have become void automatically, cf. for this argumentation: *Eastern Sugar vs. Czech Republic*, 27.03.2007 – SCC No. 088/2004 - Partial award, para 103 ff. ; *Achmea vs. Slovak Republic*, 26.10.2012 – PCA Case No. 2008-13 - Award on Jurisdiction, Arbitrability and Suspension, para 86.

tioned, EU law, even though it takes supremacy over contradicting legal frameworks in the member states, including international obligations, never orders the invalidity of any act. As *Hobe* points out:

> "In case the collision of two regulations ceases to exist, the national [or international] regulation revives."[860]

A contrario, the very nature of EU law never intended to render any contradictory set of rules to be void. Hence, from the simple accession to the EU and the acceptance of the principle of primacy, it cannot be deduced that through this accession the parties intended to *terminate* the IIAs because this would never have been the effect established through the principle of primacy.[861] Furthermore, as correctly pointed out by the arbitral tribunals, the exchange of notes subsequent to the first disputes arising from intra-EU IIAs demonstrates that the states were well aware of the continuing validity of the IIA.[862] Consequently, although nobody might have thought about the consequences of the continued existence of the IIAs after the accession, this does not yet establish the parties' intention to terminate the IIA.[863]

---

860 *Hobe*, 8. Edn. (2014), para 463.

861 Similar: *Eilmansberger*, CMLR Vol. 46 (2009), 383, 401.

862 *Inter alia*: *Euram vs. Slovak Republic*, 22.10.2012 – PCA Case no. 2010-17: First Award on Jurisdiction, para 205; cf. also: Note of Czech Republic's minster of finance to the government, recited in *Eastern Sugar vs. Czech Republic*, 27.03.2007 – SCC No. 088/2004 - Partial award, para 127; similar: *Dimopoulos*, CMLR Vol. 48, No. 1 (2011), 63, 73. However, other arguments advanced by e.g. the *Eastern Sugar Tribunal* do not strike: the tribunal *inter alia* stated that the fact that no infringement proceedings were initiated so far and that none of the parties claimed the invalidity before the proceedings should demonstrate that there was no tacit intention to end the IIA. It should be kept in mind that even for the European Commission there is no obligation to initiate infringement proceedings, neither does the fact that anyone claims an invalidity actually affect the validity of a treaty, cf. also: *Burgstaller*, JOIA Vol. 26, No. 2 (2009), 181, 187; cf. also: *Burgstaller* in: *Bungenberg/Griebel/Hindelang* (Eds.), International investment law and EU law, 2011, p. 73.

863 *Wehland*, ICLQ Vol. 58, Iss. 2 (2009), 297, 305 further points out that the tacit intention to terminate a treaty which could be qualified as lex specialis to the overriding treaty seems difficult; this line of argumentation is also followed by the *Achmea-Tribunal* which states: "*Thus, EU law does not provide substantive rights for investors that extend as far as those provided by the BIT. There are rights that may be asserted under the BIT that are not secured by EU law. Consequently, it cannot be said that it is implicit in the text of the EC Treaties that Respondent and the Netherlands intended that it should supplant the*

III. Incompatibility of EU law and IIAs (Art. 59 (1) lit. b VCLT)

The second, alternative, condition under Art. 59 VCLT to terminate the IIAs upon accession of the host states to the EU would be that IIAs and the European Treaties are incompatible to such extend that the IIA needs to be terminated. Hence, by virtue of Art. 59 (1) lit b VCLT the IIA would be terminated, if EU law and IIAs were in so far incompatible that both legal frameworks could not co-exist. Such incompatibilities have been subject to extensive debates between arbitral tribunals, the respective host states and the European Commission. Whereas several host states focused on potential conflicts of provisions in EU law and the IIA (which lead to contradicting results when applying EU law and IIAs to the same facts)[864], others submit that it is sufficient that the goal of one treaty will be frustrated by application of the other treaty, which is a less demanding test for Art. 59 VCLT.[865] The European Commission supported the host states in their line of argumentation that the provisions of IIAs and EU law are incompatible. However, the Commission expressly did not agree that this incompatibility necessarily leads to the termination of the IIA by application of Art. 59 VCLT.[866]

BIT.", cf. *Achmea vs. Slovak Republic*, 26.10.2012 – PCA Case No. 2008-13 - Award on Jurisdiction, Arbitrability and Suspension, para 262. It is however highly doubtful if the tacit intention to terminate a treaty could only be proven in the case where such treaties provide for at least equivalent guarantees. Such an interpretation would render the scope of application of Art. 59 VCLT *de facto* worthless (cf. *infra* and *supra*). The *Eastern Sugar Tribunal* limits its considerations to the simple sentence that *"(...) the Czech Republic has not established that the common intention of the Czech Republic and the Kingdom of the Netherlands was that the EU Treaty should supersede the BIT"*, cf.: *Eastern Sugar vs. Czech Republic*, 27.03.2007 – SCC No. 088/2004 - Partial award, para 167.

864 Focusing on concrete incompatibilities: *Eastern Sugar vs. Czech Republic*, 27.03.2007 – SCC No. 088/2004 - Partial award, para 95-110; *Achmea vs. Slovak Republic*, 26.10.2012 – PCA Case No. 2008-13 - Award on Jurisdiction, Arbitrability and Suspension, para 113-118; for the approach that frustrating the overall goal of a treaty being sufficient: *Euram vs. Slovak Republic*, 22.10.2012 – PCA Case no. 2010-17: First Award on Jurisdiction, para 99 f but also establishing concrete incompatibilites in para 101 ff.

865 *Euram vs. Slovak Republic*, 22.10.2012 – PCA Case no. 2010-17: First Award on Jurisdiction, para 99.

866 Other than several host stastes, the European Cmmission so far did not argue that the intra-EU BITs became invalid through the accession of the host state to the EU, cf. e.g.: *European Commission*, Amicus Curia Brief filed in Achmea

However, without entering into the question whether such incompatibilities actually exist (which should be the subject of *"Chapter 9: Jurisdiction of the arbitral tribunal: Incompatibility of the intra-EU IIA's arbitration clause"* and *"Chapter 10: Primacy of EU law on the merits"*), it should be demonstrated that it cannot be argued that the framework of the European Treaties (or EU law in general) renders an IIA incompatible *to such degree* that the latter needs to be *terminated*. This conclusion is not even based on a comparison of any provisions contained in the treaties but can be drawn by the legal consequences provided by EU law for any conflict.[867] EU law only leads to an inapplicability of any provision being be contrary to EU law. The conflicting provision is expressly not considered to be void. If a legal framework, which should lead to the termination according to Art. 59 VCLT, does not consider any conflicting provision to be void but simply inapplicable, this legal framework cannot be considered to be "*so far incompatible*" with the IIA in terms of Art. 59 VCLT that the IIA needs to be terminated.[868]

(former Eureko BV) vs. Slovak Republic (PCA Case n°2008-13) - arbitration proceedings, 07/07/2010, para 31 and 41.

867 For the same result but being based on the overlap of guarantees which would only adds protection for investors: *Reinisch*, LIEI Vol. 39, No. 2 (2012), 157, 173 f.; however arguing for the opposite: *Clodfelter*, Santa Clara Jour. of Int. Law Vol. 12, Iss. 1 (2013), 159, 178 f; the Euram Tribunal supports the same result however based on the too generic statement that an incompatibility in terms of Art. 59 VCLT could only appear where "*(...) one treaty requires what the other treaty prohibits; in other words, conflict occurs when compliance with one treaty necessarily causes a breach of the other treaty. The Tribunal does not consider that incompatibility extends to a situation where something that is forbidden under the BIT is merely permitted by EU law, or vice versa*", and that EU law and IIAs would not contradict but provide for additional ("*double*") guarantees, cf.: *Euram vs. Slovak Republic*, 22.10.2012 – PCA Case no. 2010-17: First Award on Jurisdiction, para 218, 220 ff, 228, 230; such general statement seems to be too broad, as incompatibilties may occur on various levels which are not necessarily linked to a "*breach*" of one or the other treaty: the essential question for Art. 59 VCLT should be whether the termination of one treaty is the necessary consequence of such incompatibilties.

868 This reveals to be the preeminence of the parties' intention, which is supproted to be the underlying idea of Art. 59 VCLT by *Giegerich* in: Dörr/Schmalenbach VCLT, Art. 59 VCLT para 30 f. It should be noted that several arbitral tribunals dismissed the legal consequence of terminating the IIAs by virtue of Art. 59 VCLT based on another argument: as to e.g. the *Eastern Sugar Tribunal* any inequality and/or potential discrimination by appying IIAs to some investors only could never lead to a termination of the IIA, as this would disfavour the investor. The only legal consequence, as to the tribunal,

IV. Conclusions on the effect of Art. 59 VCLT on intra-EU IIAs

It follows from the foregoing that even though IIAs and the European Treaties cover the same subject matter, the further conditions required by Art. 59 VCLT to order the *termination* of the IIAs upon accession of the host states to the EU are not met. Thus, the IIA was not terminated by the member state's accession to the EU and the conclusion of the European Treaties. This leads to a pure conflict of laws, as two – valid – international treaty frameworks (EU law and the applicable IIA) compete whenever the behaviour ordered under one of the frameworks is prohibited by the other framework.[869]

C. Conflict rules of the TFEU (Art. 350, 351 TFEU and the principle of primacy)

As Art. 59 VCLT does not lead to a termination of the IIA, one needs to determine conflict rules under the European Treaties which deal with the *applicability or inapplicability of particular provisions* of either the IIA or the European Treaties. Such conflict rules contained in the European Treaties would have priority over the (default) conflict rules contained in Art. 30 (3) and (4) VCLT (reflecting rules of customary international law).

In the absence of a more explicit provision in the IIAs[870] and as none of the *inter se* IIAs was concluded after a member states accession to the EU, the European Treaties constitute the latest treaties concluded between the parties. Hence, if the European treaties, namely the TEU and the TFEU, include a conflict rule dealing with the question of so-called *inter se* agreements, this rule of conflict should be observed, as the TEU and the TFEU contain the latest expression of the EU member states' will.[871]

---

could be that all investors are entitled to claim the rights under the IIA, cf.: *Eastern Sugar vs. Czech Republic*, 27.03.2007 – SCC No. 088/2004 - Partial award, para 169 f. This reasoning should be analysed further in Chapter 9.

869 *Mus*, Netherlands International Law Review, 1998, 208, 209 ff.; *Klabbers*, Treaty conflict and the European Union, 2009, p. 22; cf. also *supra* Chapter 5 and 7.

870 It has already been stated *supra* that such provision cannot be found in the BITs concluded by the member states, cf. *supra* (A.).

871 Cf. also: *Hindelang*, LIEI Vol. 39, Iss. 2 (2012), 179, 187.

Regarding the European Treaties, namely the TEU and the TFEU two articles (Art. 350 and Art. 351 TFEU) can be identified, which deal with the conflict of laws between the European Treaties and other international agreements by the member states.

I. Ordinary meaning and scope of Art. 351 TFEU

Art. 351 (1) TFEU reads as follows:

> "The rights and obligations arising from [post – accession] agreements (...) between one or more member states on the one hand, and one or more third countries on the other, shall not be affected by the provisions of the treaties."

The wording "*between one or more member states (...) and one or more third countries*" indicates that the article constitutes *prima facie* a rule concerning the conflict of laws between international agreements of an EU member state and a non-member state.[872] Any other EU member state is obviously not meant by the terms "*third countries*", which has been pointed out by the CJEU in various cases dealing with obligations deriving from international agreements between member states.[873]

It is – nearly – universally accepted that through Art. 351 (1) TFEU the principle of *pacta sunt servanda* in international treaties applies to treaties of EU member states with non-member states concluded before the foundation or accession to the EU.[874]

---

872 *Hummer* in: von Heinegg/Vedder EUV/AEUV, Art. 351 TFEU, para. 5; *Kokott* in: Streinz EUV/AEUV, Art. 351 TFEU, para. 2; cf. also: *Ghouri*, ELJ Vol. 16, No. 5 (2010), 806, 819.

873 *CJEU*, 11.03.1986 – C-121/85 - Conegate = ECLI:EU:C:1986:114: "*Article [351 TFEU] mus be interpretetd as meaning that an agreement concluded prior to the entry into force of the [European Treaties] may not be relied upon in order to justify restrictions on trade between member states. That provision (...) concerns only the rights and obligations established beween the member states and non-member countries.*"; *CJEU*, 20.05.2003 – C-469/00 - Ravil = ECLI:EU:C:2003:295, para 37; cf. also: *Klabbers*, Treaty conflict and the European Union, 2009 p122; this is ignored by *Söderlund*, JOIA Vol. 24, Iss. 5 (2007), 455, 463.

874 *Kokott* in: Streinz EUV/AEUV, Art. 351 TFEU, para 1, *Hobe*, 8. Edn. (2014), para 445 f, *Oppermann/Classen et al.*, 5. Edn. (2011) § 9, para 160 ff; *Ghouri*, ELJ Vol. 16, No. 5 (2010), 806, 820; however, with reference to the CJEU-ruling in *CJEU*, 28.03.1995 – C-342/93 - Evans = ECLI:EU:C:1995:84, para 32, underlines that the CJEU requires a member state to omit from taking

However, the question of treaties among member states is not expressly dealt with in Art. 351 TFEU.[875]

II. Ordinary meaning and scope of Art. 350 TFEU

Art. 350 TFEU reads as follows:

> "The provisions of the Treaties shall not preclude the existence or completion of regional unions between Belgium and Luxembourg, or between Belgium, Luxembourg and the Netherlands, to the extent that the objectives of these regional unions are not attained by application of the Treaties."

This article contains a conflict rule with regard to the treaties regarding the Benelux-Union and the European Treaties.[876] The article states that until the objectives of these "*Benelux*"- Treaties have not been reached, the European Treaties do not put an obstacle to the existence and the execution of the Benelux-Treaties. Thus, the provision regulates a very particular case of conflict between an international agreement among member states and the European Treaties, which is linked to the progress of integration already achieved within these three member states upon conclusion of the European Treaties. Hence, this particular rule cannot as such be extended to further regional integrations or any other situation.[877]

III. Art. 350, 351 TFEU as opposition to the (inherent) general principle of primacy

Thus the European Treaties do not positively contain a rule of conflict dealing with a conflict between the European Treaties and any other treaty concluded by EU member states *inter se*, except for the particular case of the treaty regarding the Benelux-Union. Nevertheless, the CJEU interpreted Art. 351 TFEU as an exception to a more general principle. In fact, there is no need for an express statement of an exception, if there is no general rule the exception should apply to. Both Art. 350 and

any actions under the pre-accession treaty which is not mandatory but conflicting with EU law.

875 *Kokott* in: Streinz EUV/AEUV, Art. 351 TFEU, para 2.

876 *Kokott* in: Streinz EUV/AEUV, Art. 350 TFEU, para 1 f.

877 *Kokott* in: Streinz EUV/AEUV, Art. 350 TFEU, para 5.

Art. 351 TFEU confirm an exception to the general principle of supremacy which is the inherent rule of conflict in intra-EU relations, including *inter se*-agreements of the member states.[878]

When Art. 351 TFEU expressly states that the rights and obligations from post accession treaties should not be affected by EU law, this is meant to be an exception to the (opposite) principle that in any other situation, these rights and obligations should not remain unaffected by EU law.[879]

---

878 *Burgstaller*, JOIA Vol. 26, No. 2 (2009), 181, 195; *Eilmansberger*, CMLR Vol. 46 (2009), 383, 421 f; *CJEU*, 27.02.1962 – C-10/61 - Commission vs. Italy = ECLI:EU:C:1962:2. For the opposite: *Kleinheisterkamp*, JIEL Vol. 15, No. 1 (2012), 85, 96; *Tietje/Wackernagel*, JWIT Vol. 16, Iss. 2 (2015), 205, 236; *Dahlquist/Lenk et al.*, European Policy Analysis, 2016:4, 1, 6; this position is also supported by the Slovak Republic in *Achmea vs. Slovak Republic*, 26.10.2012 – PCA Case No. 2008-13 - Award on Jurisdiction, Arbitrability and Suspension, para 132 ff; the tribunal in *Binder vs. Czech Republic* even seems to consider the principle of primacy to be the applicable conflict rule, when stating: "*The Arbitral Tribunal further cannot find that the invoked substantive provisions of the Czech-German BIT (...) are in any way in conflict with EC law. Consequently, there is no substantive conflict with EC law, and the question of the primacy of EC law does not arise in respect of these provisions*" cf.: *Binder vs. Czech Republic*, 06.06.2007 – UNCITRAL - Award on Jurisdiction, para 63 [emphasis added]. The tribunal seems to consider the principle of primacy of EU law as the applicable conflict rule, although – as there would be no conflict between the substantive provisions of EU law and the IIA– its conditions are not met in the present case. The endorsement of this line of argumentation is by far more obvious in *Electrabel vs. Hungary*, 30.11.2012 – ICSID Case No. ARB/07/19: Decision on Jurisdiction, Applicable Law and Liability, para 4.182 f and 4.191; cf. also: *Repasi*, EuR, 2013, 45, 48 f stating that the member states agreed to set a mechanism through which each change outside the mechanism forseen by the European Treaties is considered void.

879 Cf. also: *Lavranos* in: v. d. Groeben/Schwarze AEUV/EUV, Art. 351 TFEU, para 7; in the same direction but referring to Art. 30 (3) VCLT: *Hummer* in: von Heinegg/Vedder EUV/AEUV, Art. 351 TFEU, para 6; similar. *Johannsen*, Die Kompetenz der EU für ausländische Direktinvestitionen nach Lissabon (Beit. zum Transnat. Wirt.-R, Vol. 90, 2009), p. 28 who however denies "*external*" effect to the principle or primacy; clearly stated also by the CJEU that conflicting *inter-se* agreements do not survive the conclusion of the European Treaties: *CJEU*, 27.02.1962 – C-10/61 - Commission vs. Italy = ECLI:EU:C:1962:2; *CJEU*, 10.11.1992 – C-3/91 - Exportur vs Confiserie du Tech SA = ECLI:EU:C:1992:420 recital 1. This is also clearly stated by the *Electrabel Tribunal*, which refers to this as the "*negative interpreation*" of Art. 351 TFEU, cf.: *Electrabel vs. Hungary*, 30.11.2012 – ICSID Case No.

In the *Conegate-Case*[880] the CJEU concluded:

> "[…] [I]t must therefore be stated, that article 234 of the treaty must be interpreted as meaning that an agreement concluded prior to the entry into force of the [EC] treaty may not be relied upon in order to justify restrictions on trade between member states."

Similarly, this was confirmed in *Commission vs. Austria*:

> "[…] whilst Article 307 ECT allows Member States to honour obligations owed to non-member States under international agreements preceding the Treaty, it does not authorise them to exercise rights under such agreements in intra-Community relations."[881]

In fact, the CJEU considers Art. 351 TFEU to be a (modified) (re)codification of the general provisions in the VCTL in Art. 30 (4),[882] which states that between the same parties (EU member states) the later treaty (the European Treaties) should apply (Art. 30 (4) lit. a, (3) VCLT: *lex posterior derogate legi priori*) but between parties which are not all parties to the same treaties (EU member states and non-member states) the prior treaty should apply (Art. 30 (4) lit. b VCLT).[883]

This interpretation of the CJEU is convincing and should be applied to the conflict between EU law and intra-EU IIA's as well.

First, the interpretation aligns with general principles of interpretation of international treaties. For these general principles of interpretation, it should be referred to the VCTL.

ARB/07/19: Decision on Jurisdiction, Applicable Law and Liability, para 4.183 and 4.191.

880 *CJEU*, 11.03.1986 – C-121/85 - Conegate = ECLI:EU:C:1986:114, para 24.

881 *CJEU*, 07.07.2005 – C-147/03 - Commission vs. Austria = ECLI:EU:C:2005:427, para 73, referring to this principle as settled case law with reference to: *CJEU*, 01.02.2005 – C-203/03 - Commission vs. Austria = ECLI:EU:C:2005:76, para 57 ff and to 59 and *CJEU*, 02.07.1996 – C-473/93 - Commission vs. Luxembourg = ECLI:EU:C:1996:263, para 40; clearly stated also in: *CJEU*, 10.11.1992 – C-3/91 - Exportur vs Confiserie du Tech SA = ECLI:EU:C:1992:420 recital 1.

882 Vgl. *Hummer* in: von Heinegg/Vedder EUV/AEUV, Art. 351 TFEU, para 3; *Schmalenbach* in: Calliess/Ruffert EUV/AEUV, Art. 351 TFEU, para 1.

883 Art. 30 (4) of the VCLT reads as follows: "When the parties to the later treaty do not include all the parties to the earlier one: (a) as between States parties to *both treaties* the same rule applies as in paragraph 3; (b) as between a *State party to both treaties and a State party to only one of the treaties*, the treaty to which both States are parties governs their mutual rights and obligations."

Art. 32 VCTL describes the general guideline for the interpretation of an international treaty:

> "A treaty shall be interpreted in good faith in accordance with the ordinary meaning to be given to the terms of the treaty in their context and in the light of its object and purpose."

Besides the wording of a treaty, it is thus the context, objective and purpose of the treaty, which are designated as crucial elements of interpretation. This includes, as Art. 31 (3) VCLT points out, the subsequent practice by the parties and the parties' intentions when concluding the agreement (Art. 31 (1), (2) VCLT).

In the context of the European Treaties, Art. 351 TFEU seems to be an exception to the general purpose and objective of EU law. The EU member states agreed to create a reciprocally binding legal framework through the TEU, the TFEU, as well as the European institutions that have been created since the Treaty of Rome. Part of this legal framework is the acceptance of the primacy of EU law for the member states as well as the consideration that none of them is permitted to unilaterally revoke its obligation, neither by the conclusion of new treaties with non-member states, neither by simple disrespect, nor by the conclusion of treaties with other member states.[884] The only possible way to set aside EU law obligations, is by following the proper procedure to amend the European Treaties.[885] Thus the objective behind the principle of primacy requires the non-survival of inconsistent international obligations concluded by the member states *inter se*. Consequently, even without any provision in the treaties, the European Treaties contain an *immanent conflict rule* which is the principle of non-survival of conventional obligations of the member states which are inconsistent with EU law.[886]

---

884 Clearly supporting this view: *Hindelang*, LIEI Vol. 39, Iss. 2 (2012), 179, 186 ff; cf. also for the conflict of *inter-se* agreements with the fundamental freedoms: *CJEU*, 10.11.1992 – C-3/91 - Exportur vs Confiserie du Tech SA = ECLI:EU:C:1992:420, para 16 ff.

885 *Lavranos* in: v. d. Groeben/Schwarze AEUV/EUV, Art. 351 TFEU, para 7; *Hindelang*, LIEI Vol. 39, Iss. 2 (2012), 179, 186 ff; cf. also with regard to the jurisprudence of the CJEU: *Ghouri*, ELJ Vol. 16, No. 5 (2010), 806, 822; cf. also: *Repasi*, EuR, 2013, 45, 48 f.

886 Cf. also: *Eilmansberger*, CMLR Vol. 46 (2009), 383, 425 f; *Hindelang*, LIEI Vol. 39, Iss. 2 (2012), 179, 187; this has also been supported by several host states, e.g. Romania in: *Ioan Micula, Viorel Micula & others vs. Romania*, 11.12.2013 – ICSID Case No. ARB/05/20 - Final Award, para 309 ff. It is rejected by *Söderlund*, JOIA Vol. 24, Iss. 5 (2007), 455, 464 who denies any ap-

As this primacy derives from the European treaties, the only way to dismiss this principle is a provision included in the treaties (such as Art. 351 TFEU). But consequently, as long as the requirements of this article are not met, the exception does not apply.[887]

Second a conjoint lecture of Art. 350 TFEU and Art. 351 TFEU underlines this argument. Art. 350 TFEU sets another rule of conflict for treaty establishing the Benelux Union between the Benelux countries (Netherlands, Belgium and Luxemburg) and the European Treaties.[888]

Consequently, the article states a rule of conflict for a specific kind of intra-EU conflicts. Generally speaking, it grants primacy to an international convention (Treaty establishing the Benelux-Union) concluded by specific EU member states (Belgium, the Netherlands and Luxemburg) existing before the entry into force of the European Treaties under the condition that the obligations undertaken cannot be reached through application of the EU law. Hence, if there is the necessity for such a rule of conflict, there must be a general principle which would prohibit such obligations to prevail *posterior* to the member states' accessions to the EU.[889] Any other interpretation would render Art. 350 TFEU meaningless.[890]

Hence Art. 351 TFEU contains two principles for the conflict of international conventions with EU law. First, it (expressly) states that the Eu-

---

plicability to the principle of supremacy because the CCP would not include investment treaties. However, first, intra-EU BITs are not a question of the CCP, second the principle of primacy is of general applicability whenever a (valid) provision of EU law is put into question; *Kleinheisterkamp*, JIEL Vol. 15, No. 1 (2012), 85, 96 also rejects this arguments, stating that the principle of supremacy is a purley internal rule for the EU member states; *Ghouri*, ELJ Vol. 16, No. 5 (2010), 806, 829 f only seems to admit this conclusion for those provisions, where EU law and IIAs govern the same subject matter, which would not be the case for arbitration clauses. This again ignores that there can be conflicts with provisions which do not precisely govern the same subject, but which reveal to be incompatible again for other reasons (cf. *infra* Chapter 5 and 9).

887 *Hummer* in: von Heinegg/Vedder EUV/AEUV, Art. 351 TFEU, para 6; *CJEU*, 10.11.1992 – C-3/91 - Exportur vs Confiserie du Tech SA = ECLI:EU:C:1992:420 recital 1 and *CJEU*, 27.02.1962 – C-10/61 - Commission vs. Italy = ECLI:EU:C:1962:2, p. 7.

888 *Kokott* in: Streinz EUV/AEUV, Art. 350 TFEU, para 1.

889 Cf. also: *Hummer* in: von Heinegg/Vedder EUV/AEUV, Art. 351 TFEU, para 6, *Khan* in: GKK EUV/AEUV, Art. 351 TFEU, para 1; *Eilmansberger*, CMLR Vol. 46 (2009), 383, 425 f.

890 *Hindelang*, LIEI Vol. 39, Iss. 2 (2012), 179, 187 ff.

ropean Treaties do not impede on any right or obligation arising from a post-accession agreement in an extra-EU conflict. Second, in an intra-EU conflict, EU law prevails, regardless if the derogating treaty has been concluded before or after the accession to the EU.[891]

This would also apply to a conflict rule contained in IIAs, as long as this conflict rule would not expressly modify the European Treaties (which could only be obtained by following the procedures and the mutual agreement of all member states). A specific conflict clause contained in an IIA between two member states would not be able to set away the principle of primacy contained in the European Treaties as well. This again would be a circumvention of several states of the predominant principle of supremacy in EU law, which all member states agreed upon.[892]

D. Applicable conflict rule under the principles of the Vienna Convention on the Law of Treaties

It should *in fine* (for the sake of completeness) be demonstrated that regarding the existing IIAs, which were exclusively concluded prior to the member states having acceded the EU, the same results would have been achieved by application of the principles contained in Art. 30 (3) and (4) of the VCLT. The principle of *pacta sunt servanda* in public international law is diminished by the provisions in Part III of the VCLT, especially the

891 *Hindelang*, LIEI Vol. 39, Iss. 2 (2012), 179, 187 f; *Hindelang*, LIEI Vol. 39, Iss. 2 (2012), 179, 187 ff; This result is also supported by the ILC in its 2006 Report: *International Law Commission*, ILC Report on Fragmentation of International Law, 13/04/2006, para 283; cf. also but without expressly naming the principle of primacy as a conflict clause: *Wehland*, ICLQ Vol. 58, Iss. 2 (2009), 297, 306; similar: *Eilmansberger*, CMLR Vol. 46 (2009), 383, 401 and 425 f.

892 Smilar: *Hindelang*, LIEI Vol. 39, Iss. 2 (2012), 179, 188 ff; the *Electrabel-Tribunal* derives this same conclusion by application of the *lex posterior* principle, concluding that as the European Treaties are the “*latest*” treaties concluded between the parties, the conflict rules contained therein shall prevail, cf.: *Electrabel vs. Hungary*, 30.11.2012 – ICSID Case No. ARB/07/19: Decision on Jurisdiction, Applicable Law and Liability, para 4.177. This is at least doubtful for the case that the conflict rule in the IIA would clearly anticipate the conclusion of a later treaty. However, one could still argue that during the negotiation of the latest treaty, the parties also revoked the previous conflict rule in the IIA.

Art. 30 VCLT. Art. 30 (3) states that for successive treaties concerning the same subject matter,

> "[w]hen all the parties to the early are parties also to the later treaty [...] the earlier treaty applies only to the extent that its provisions are compatible with those of the later treaty."

Dealing with a treaty between the same parties, concerning the same subject matter, the VCLT thus denominates the *principle of lex posterior* as the prevailing rule of conflict for successive treaties. This principle sets aside the principle of *pacta sunt servanda.*[893]

This principle of lex *posterior* in Art. 30 (3) VCLT also applies to multilateral treaties, as long as all parties to the earlier treaty are also parties to the multilateral treaty, cf. Art. 30 (4) VCLT. Thus the VCLT clearly accepts the parties' possibility to set aside obligations from previously concluded treaties by later treaties if they are incompatible.[894]

As to the application of Art. 30 (3), (4) VCLT, it has already been demonstrated that both treaties apply to the same subject matter. Thus, in application of Art. 30 (3) VCLT the same result as by application of the principle of primacy can be deducted by the simple finding that the European Treaties (at least the Lisbon Treaty) were concluded after the IIAs. In application of the *lex posterior* principle laid down in Art. 30 (3) VCLT the European Treaties, and thus EU law, prevails in case of conflict.[895]

---

893 Cf. *supra* (A.) and *Mus*, Netherlands International Law Review, 1998, 208, 214 f.; for the same idea underlying Art. 59 VCLT: *Dubuisson* in: Corten/Klein VCLT - II, Art. 59 VCLT, para 1; cf. also: *Reinisch*, LIEI Vol. 39, No. 2 (2012), 157,158; *Dimopoulos*, CMLR Vol. 48, No. 1 (2011), 63, 73 ff.

894 Cf. also for the relationship of EU law and the ICSID-Convention: *Tietje/Wackernagel*, JWIT Vol. 16, Iss. 2 (2015), 205, p. 218 f.

895 *Dimopoulos*, CMLR Vol. 48, No. 1 (2011), 63, 75; This seems to be the view supported by *Ahner*, Investor-Staat-Schiedsverfahren nach Europäischem Unionsrecht, 2015, p. 205; cf. also for the relationsship of EU law and the ICSID-Convention: *Tietje/Wackernagel*, JWIT Vol. 16, Iss. 2 (2015), 205, p. 218 f; this has been the main line of argumentation set forth by the *Electrabel Tribunal*, cf.: *Electrabel vs. Hungary*, 30.11.2012 – ICSID Case No. ARB/07/19: Decision on Jurisdiction, Applicable Law and Liability, para 4.177.

E. Conclusion and summary concerning the rule of conflict in the intra-EU hypothesis

The findings so far can be summarized as follows:

Chapter 7 demonstrated that EU law can be qualified as international law. Hence, IIAs and EU law are two sets of rules of international law which are both applicable to an intra-EU investment and which compete on the same level in case of an investment dispute.

This Chapter 8 further developed the rule of conflict which should be applied in order to determine which of the two orders shall prevail in case there is an inconsistency. It was demonstrated that public international law acknowledges the primacy of conflict rules as agreed upon by the parties (cf. Art. 30 (2) VCLT). In the intra-EU hypothesis, this rule of conflict needs to be derived from the principle of primacy contained in the European Treaties which clearly denominates EU law as the paramount legal framework in *inter se* relations. EU law cannot be unilaterally set aside, neither by international conventions, nor by the adoption of national laws, except for an amendment of the European Treaties itself.

Given these considerations – irrespective of an IIA being concluded between EU member states before (1st sub-hypothesis) or after their accession (2nd sub-hypothesis) to the EU – EU law needs to prevail in case of a conflict.

I. First sub-hypothesis: IIA concluded before accession

The first sub-hypothesis should be the IIA being concluded before the accession to the EU. This is the current case for all of the IIAs concluded between EU member states. In this hypothesis, the negative interpretation of Art. 351 TFEU and the general principle of primacy clearly state that in any case where EU law and intra-EU IIAs conflict, EU law prevails over any obligation undertaken by the member states before their accession. As Art. 351 TFEU only grants an exception to obligations undertaken *vis-à-vis* to non-member states, *inter se* obligations cannot sustain. The same result can be derived from the application of Art. 30 (3) VCLT, even if one would deny that the European Treaties contain any conflict rule.

II. Second sub-hypothesis: IIA concluded after accession

Upon accession to the EU, all member states agreed that the obligations undertaken under the European Treaties, including the principle of supremacy, cannot unilaterally be set aside by any of their members or parts of the member states, except by an amendment of the European Treaties itself. This has been reiterated on various occasions by the CJEU as well.[896] This limitation of sovereignty constitutes a conflict rule which denies (full) effect even to later agreements, as accepted by Art. 30 (2) VCLT.[897] Hence, even in this sub-hypothesis, which did not occur yet, EU law needs to prevail. Given the newly attributed competence to the EU in Art. 207 TFEU, one could even argue that the situation will very likely never exist as the EU member states will most likely no longer conclude isolated IIAs.

III. Necessity of a conflict and the legal consequences

However, the principle of supremacy only applies whenever there is an incompatibility or conflict between the provisions in the IIA and the EU law.[898] Whether such a conflict exists, will be treated in the following two chapters. Only if the arbitration clause contained in the IIA conflicts with EU law, this particular provision remains unapplied. This leads to a lack of jurisdiction for the tribunal (cf. Chapter 9).[899] If a provision regarding the substantive guarantees contained in IIAs conflicts with EU law, the

---

896 Among others: *CJEU*, 08.04.1976 – C-43/75 - Defrenne vs. Sabena = ECLI:EU:C:1976:56, para 58; *Cremer* in: Calliess/Ruffert EUV/AEUV, Art. 48 TEU, para 19-21; *Ohler* in: Grabitz/Hilf/Nettesheim EUV/AEUV, Art. 48 TFEU, para 51, 56.

897 Admitting the possibility of such clauses: *Dimopoulos*, CMLR Vol. 48, No. 1 (2011), 63 and 77; *Burgstaller*, JOIA Vol. 26, No. 2 (2009), 181, 208 f; also *Wackernagel*, EU Judicial Proceedings, Consenual Termination of Intra-EU BITs (Beit. zum Transnat. Wirt.-R, Vol. 140, 2016), 5, 14 who correctly points out that Art. 103 of the UN-Charter is the best example of the existence (and acceptance) of such clauses.

898 Cf. *inter alia*: *Geismann* in: v. d. Groeben/Schwarze AEUV/EUV, Art. 288 TFEU, para 8; *Nettesheim* in: Grabitz/Hilf/Nettesheim EUV/AEUV, Art. 288 TFEU, para 52.

899 *Eilmansberger*, CMLR Vol. 46 (2009), 383, 425 f ; cf. in so far similar: *Dimopoulos*, CMLR Vol. 48, No. 1 (2011), 63, 69-71 and 78.

particular substantive provision needs to be unapplied to the extent the conflict arises. Compliance with on obligation under EU law cannot constitute a breach of the IIA (cf. Chapter 10).

Chapter 9: Jurisdiction of the arbitral tribunal: Incompatibility of the intra-EU IIA's arbitration clause

After having deducted the relevant conflict rule to resolve potential incompatibilities of EU law and IIAs, the following chapter should address the question whether or not there is a conflict in terms of an incompatibility of arbitration clauses contained IIAs and EU law. A potential conflict on the merits (i.e. substantive guarantees in an IIA) will be treated in the following Chapter 10.[900]

The compatibility of the arbitration clause contained in an IIA with EU law gave rise to a couple of debates in literature and deep analysis by arbitral tribunals in their awards.[901] However, the debate has been pushed in a specific direction, which focuses on the compatibility of the clause with Art. 344 TFEU and neglects the findings of the CJEU with regard to the creation of dispute settlement mechanisms outside the judicial framework of the European Treaties. The question therefore needs to be addressed from a different angle. Three potential incompatibilities should be analysed. First, it will be analysed whether the investment dispute mechanism settlement usually contained in IIAs is compatible with the specific characteristics of the EU's legal order and judicial framework (A.). Second, it is doubtful whether the EU member states had or have the competences to agree upon a diverging dispute settlement mechanism in their intra-EU relations: this question will be evaluated next (B.). Third, taking those results into consideration, the question of a potential discrimination through the arbitration clause should be addressed (C.).

---

900 Cf. also supporting a clear distinction: *Söderlund*, JOIA Vol. 24, Iss. 5 (2007), 455, 458.

901 Cf. *inter alia*: *Reinisch*, LIEI Vol. 39, No. 2 (2012), 157, *Söderlund*, JOIA Vol. 24, Iss. 5 (2007), 455; *Tietje*, Intra-EU BITs als Herausforderung im Mehrebenensystem des Rechts (Beit. zum Transnat. Wirt.-R, Vol. 104, 2011) but also: *Hindelang*, LIEI Vol. 39, Iss. 2 (2012), 179 and *Eilmansberger*, CMLR Vol. 46 (2009), 383.

A. Incompatibility of arbitration clauses with the specific characteristics and the autonomy of EU law (the exclusive jurisdiction of the CJEU)

The incompatibility of arbitration clauses contained in the IIAs with EU law could first result from an incompatibility of such clauses with specific characteristics and the autonomy of EU law, such as they are deducted by the CJEU.

However, when analysing such potential incompatibilities of arbitration clauses contained in intra-EU IIAs with EU law, one needs to first address the question why arbitral tribunals should respect the jurisprudence of the CJEU on this subject matter.[902] Having found that arbitral tribunals should consider the CJEU's judgments, this jurisprudence needs to be analysed and reveals that the current debate in the arbitral awards had an erroneous focus on the question of compatibility and/or incompatibility.[903] Correctly analysing the CJEU's previous judgements leads to the necessity to address the arbitration clause's conflict with EU law from a different perspective. Adopting this perspective reveals that arbitration clauses offering access to mixed arbitration in intra-EU IIAs are incompatible with the autonomy of EU law and its specific characteristics.[904] This Chapter will terminate by an interim conclusion on the validity of arbitration clauses containes in intra-EU IIAs.[905]

I. Why the arbitral tribunal should consider the interpretation of the CJEU in its arbitration proceedings

The arbitral tribunals so far, expressed a certain restraint as to take into account specific principles and interpretations of EU law in settled EU case law. The *Electrabel-Tribunal*[906] even expressly rejected the approach

902 This will be treated *infra*: "*I. Why the arbitral tribunal should consider the interpretation of the CJEU in its arbitration proceedings*".

903 This will be treated *infra*: "*II. The erroneous view on the criteria to be observed by a dispute settlement mechanism within the European Union*".

904 This will be treated *infra*: "*III. Violation of the principles deducted by the CJEU by arbitral tribunals in investment proceedings*".

905 This should be addressed in subsection (D.).

906 *Electrabel vs. Hungary*, 30.11.2012 – ICSID Case No. ARB/07/19: Decision on Jurisdiction, Applicable Law and Liability; for a short summary of the underlying facts, cf.: *Stier*, Arbitration International Vol. 31 (2015), 163, 167.

to adopt a EU law perspective as to the hierarchy of norms and legal principles.[907] The same could be argued relating to any interpretation given to the principles derived from the European Treaties and especially any possible incompatibility with Art. 344 TFEU, Art. 18 TFEU or any general principle of EU law. However, even though arbitral tribunals are tribunals constituted under international law, having the task to apply the IIA and the provisions contained therein between two EU member states, the specific interpretation of the European Treaties and their provisions, especially through the CJEU, should be respected by the arbitral tribunal(s). By doing so, the tribunals do not exercise any "*judicial restraint*" doctrine[908] or adopt a purely internal EU law perspective. On the contrary, the tribunals would follow the relevant rules of treaty interpretation with regard to the European Treaties and EU law.[909]

It is widely recognised in literature that the principles of interpretation developed and used by the CJEU with regard to EU law differ to a certain degree from those applied in traditional public international law.[910] The CJEU's approach is much more driven by the principles of *effet utile* and a teleological interpretation, favouring the overall process of integration in the EU.[911] Public international law, on the other hand, is more reluctant to those principles, somehow driven by the mere fact that a common ground and sense of a treaty, such as the process of integration within the EU, has hardly been perceived in any other international judicial framework.[912]

However, the different approaches in interpreting EU law compared to traditional public international law should not lead to the conclusion that the means of interpretation used by the CJEU, and especially the results of this interpretation, should be ignored by any other international (judicial) institution, dropping back on the traditional, internationalist, means of interpretation.

---

907 *Electrabel vs. Hungary*, 30.11.2012 – ICSID Case No. ARB/07/19: Decision on Jurisdiction, Applicable Law and Liability, para 4.112.

908 *Posner*, California Law Review Vol. 100, No. 3 (2012), 519, 520 f.; cf. for the term "*judicial restraint*" doctrine also: *Nettesheim*, EuR, 2006, 737, 770 ff.

909 Cf. also: *Wehland*, ICLQ Vol. 58, Iss. 2 (2009), 297, 305 f.

910 Cf.: *Hobe*, 8. Edn. (2014), para 407 ff, *Oppermann/Classen et al.*, 5. Edn. (2011) § 9, para 5, *Herdegen*, Europarecht, 17. Edn. (2015) § 8, para 79 ff.

911 *Hobe*, 8. Edn. (2014), para 411 ff, *Oppermann/Classen et al.*, 5. Edn. (2011) § 9, para 5, *Herdegen*, Europarecht, 17. Edn. (2015) § 8, para 79 ff.

912 *Sorel/Evenó* in: Corten/Klein VCLT - I, Art. 31 VCLT *Corten/Klein*, in: *Corten/Klein VCLT - I*.p 830; *Wehland*, ICLQ Vol. 58, Iss. 2 (2009), 297, 306.

This is mainly based on two considerations:

First, international law should seek to empower, to its best, the parties' (true) intention expressly when dealing with a bi- or multilateral treaty, which is the overall goal of the Art. 31 and 32 VCLT.[913]

Second, the principles of treaty interpretation laid down in Art. 31 (3) and (4) VCLT accept and expressly denominate the parties' intention and their practice in applying an international treaty as a major mean to interpret a treaty.[914] Since the creation of the CJEU and the application of those principles of interpretation, all EU member states have constantly observed the jurisprudence of the CJEU and applied it in their respective relations.[915] The method of interpretation, as well as the principles deduced by the CJEU, have thus been approved by the member states through their constant practice. Furthermore, the member states are proving their will to support this process of integration by various amendments to the European Treaties conferring further competences to the EU since its creation. [916]

In other words: provisions of intra-EU treaties, no matter if those of the IIA or those of the European Treaties, should be perceived from an intra-EU perspective.

II. The erroneous view on the criteria to be observed by a dispute settlement mechanism within the European Union

Arbitral tribunals so far rejected the argument advanced by several host states and the European Commission that the arbitration clause contained

---

913 *Sorel/Evenó* in: Corten/Klein VCLT - I, Art. 31 VCLT, p. 807 f; cf. also: *Wackernagel*, EU Judicial Proceedings, Consenual Termination of Intra-EU BITs (Beit. zum Transnat. Wirt.-R, Vol. 140, 2016), 5, 9.

914 *Sorel/Evenó* in: Corten/Klein VCLT - I, Art. 31 VCLT, p. 827 ff; *Wehland*, ICLQ Vol. 58, Iss. 2 (2009), 297, 306; similar but in another context: *Hindelang*, LIEI Vol. 39, Iss. 2 (2012), 179, 187.

915 *Wehland*, ICLQ Vol. 58, Iss. 2 (2009), 297, 306.

916 *Sorel/Evenó* in: Corten/Klein VCLT - I, Art. 31 VCLT, p. 830 referring to the „*Community meaning*“ as a valid mean of interpretation for international treaties in the European Context, deduced from the common parties' intention; cf. also to the travaux preparatoires: *Wetzel/Rauschning*, The Vienna Convention on the Law of Treaties, 1978, p. 246 f indicating the overlap in the draft as to the parties' intention and their subsequent practice; cf. also: *Wehland*, ICLQ Vol. 58, Iss. 2 (2009), 297, 306; *Wackernagel*, EU Judicial Proceedings, Consenual Termination of Intra-EU BITs (Beit. zum Transnat. Wirt.-R, Vol. 140, 2016), 5, 9.

within the IIAs could be incompatible with EU law.[917] The debate in the respective arbitration proceedings was mainly focussed on the question whether Art. 344 TFEU is applicable to mixed arbitration proceedings and whether investment arbitration would be contrary to this provision.

The arbitral tribunals so far mainly rejected any incompatibility of the investment arbitration mechanism with Art. 344 TFEU. As to the arbitral tribunals, the scope of application of Art. 344 TFEU should be limited to inter-state litigations only. Investor-State arbitration, being a mixed arbitration mechanism, should not be covered by the provision.[918]

Some of the arbitral awards further discussed the question whether investor-state arbitration would conflict with a judicial monopoly of the CJEU in matters of interpreting EU Law.[919] This objection has also been rejected.

---

917 *Euram vs. Slovak Republic*, 22.10.2012 – PCA Case no. 2010-17: First Award on Jurisdiction, para 249, *Achmea vs. Slovak Republic*, 26.10.2012 – PCA Case No. 2008-13 - Award on Jurisdiction, Arbitrability and Suspension, para 278 ff, *Electrabel vs. Hungary*, 30.11.2012 – ICSID Case No. ARB/07/19: Decision on Jurisdiction, Applicable Law and Liability, para 4.153, 4.166. The European Commission expressly supported this argument in its amicus curia briefs to the respective tribunals, cf.: *European Commission*, Amicus Curia Brief filed in Micula vs. Romania to the U.S. Court of Appeals, 04/02/2016, p. 27; *European Commission*, Amicus Curia Brief filed in EURAM vs. Slovak Republic (PCA Case n°2010-17) - arbitration proceedings, 13/10/2011, p. 5 ff; *European Commission*, Amicus Curia Brief filed in U.S. Steel Golbal Holdings I B.V. vs. Slovak Republic (PCA Case n°2013-6) - arbitration proceedings, 15/05/2014, para 34, 37 and 44; *European Commission*, Amicus Curia Brief filed in Electrabel vs. Hungary (ICSID Case n° ARB/07/19) - arbitration proceedings, 12/06/2009, para 65 ff.

918 Cf. *Achmea vs. Slovak Republic*, 26.10.2012 – PCA Case No. 2008-13 - Award on Jurisdiction, Arbitrability and Suspension, para 276; cf. also: *Euram vs. Slovak Republic*, 22.10.2012 – PCA Case no. 2010-17: First Award on Jurisdiction, para 263.

919 This question has been discussed e.g. in *Euram vs. Slovak Republic*, 22.10.2012 – PCA Case no. 2010-17: First Award on Jurisdiction, para 248, *Achmea vs. Slovak Republic*, 26.10.2012 – PCA Case No. 2008-13 - Award on Jurisdiction, Arbitrability and Suspension, para 273 f, 278 f, *Electrabel vs. Hungary*, 30.11.2012 – ICSID Case No. ARB/07/19: Decision on Jurisdiction, Applicable Law and Liability, para 4.153, 4.166; cf. also: *Wehland*, ICLQ Vol. 58, Iss. 2 (2009), 297, 318 f; *Söderlund*, JOIA Vol. 24, Iss. 5 (2007), 455, 458 f; cf. also: *Clodfelter*, Santa Clara Jour. of Int. Law Vol. 12, Iss. 1 (2013), 159, 179.

As to the arbitral tribunals having dealt with this question, there are mainly three reasons why such judicial monopoly should not exist:

- First, national courts (others than the respective court of last resort in such member state) would regularly apply EU law without being obliged to refer the question of how to interpret a provision of EU law to the CJEU; hence an arbitral tribunal could not be forced to do either;[920]
- Second, even national courts being the court of last resort are not necessarily obliged to refer a question of interpretation of EU law to the CJEU, they could also make use of the doctrine of *acte claire* or *acte eclairé* and hence resolve the question of how to interpret a particular question of EU law by their own; arbitral tribunals should be enabled to proceed in the same way.[921]
- Third, arbitral tribunals regularly referred to several judgements of the CJEU, including i.e. the opinion rendered on the creation of the European and Community Patents Court ("*PC-Opinion*")[922], in order to demonstrate that private arbitration is a common place in the EU and hence investor state arbitration needs to be admitted as well.[923]

The *Achmea Tribunal*[924] as well as the Higher Regional Court in Frankfurt[925], where the Slovak Republic applied for annulment of the award

920 *Euram vs. Slovak Republic*, 22.10.2012 – PCA Case no. 2010-17: First Award on Jurisdiction, para 252; *Electrabel vs. Hungary*, 30.11.2012 – ICSID Case No. ARB/07/19: Decision on Jurisdiction, Applicable Law and Liability, para 4.148 f;

921 *Euram vs. Slovak Republic*, 22.10.2012 – PCA Case no. 2010-17: First Award on Jurisdiction, para 252.

922 *CJEU*, 08.03.2011 – Opinion 1/09 - Patents Court = ECLI:EU:C:2011:123.

923 *Euram vs. Slovak Republic*, 22.10.2012 – PCA Case no. 2010-17: First Award on Jurisdiction, para 263; *Electrabel vs. Hungary*, 30.11.2012 – ICSID Case No. ARB/07/19: Decision on Jurisdiction, Applicable Law and Liability, para 4.153 and 4.155; some additional arguments advanced are e.g. the fact that the CJEU would only have a jurisdictional monopoly regarding the validity or invalidity of acts rendered by the EU itself but not for acts committed by the EU member states, cf. *Euram vs. Slovak Republic*, 22.10.2012 – PCA Case no. 2010-17: First Award on Jurisdiction, para 263. It is also regularily argued that subsequent proceedings, such as enforcement proceedings, would be sufficient to ensure compliance with EU law, cf.: *Euram vs. Slovak Republic*, 22.10.2012 – PCA Case no. 2010-17: First Award on Jurisdiction, para 256.

924 *Achmea vs. Slovak Republic*, 26.10.2012 – PCA Case No. 2008-13 - Award on Jurisdiction, Arbitrability and Suspension.

925 The arbitration proceedings in *Achmea vs. Slovak Republic* led to two orders by the Higher Regional Court of Frankfort. The first order concerns proceed-

rendered by the *Achmea Tribunal*, further analysed the question whether there would be a more general principle under EU law prohibiting mixed arbitration mechanisms such as investor-state arbitrations. Some other tribunals touchbased more or less clearly on this question. This objection has been mainly rejected by stating that the CJEU only has a particular duty under EU law to interpret particular questions of EU law or particular disputes referred to the CJEU, whereas the ordinary courts under EU law are the national courts. Hence, attributing a task, which is usually referred to the national courts, to an arbitral tribunal, could *per se* not compete with any task referred to the CJEU. Furthermore, subsequent proceedings, such as setting-aside proceedings, would enable a sufficient control to guarantee the correct application and interpretation of EU law.[926]

However, the current focus of the debates ignore that the question cannot be limited to the applicability or non-applicability of Art. 344 TFEU to investor-state arbitration. The debate should rather focus on the more general principle that can be deducted from Art. 344 TFEU and the provisions regarding the judicial framework in the European Treaties in general. This general principle must be the guideline to evaluate the compatibility or incompatibility of the IIA's arbitration clause with EU Law. Hence, the validity of such clauses needs to be addressed under a different angle which should be developed in the following (cf. *infra*: 3 and 4). Given this standard of review, the arbitration clause in IIAs reveals to be incompatible with EU law (cf. *infra* subsection III).

---

ings which were initiated based on Section 1040 (3) of the German Code of Civil Procedure, claiming that the arbitral tribunal erred in admitting its jurisdiction to render the awards, cf.: *Higher Regional Court Frankfurt*, SchiedsVZ (2013), 119, 10.05.2012 – 26 SchH 11/10, 120. The second ruling was rendered in the setting aside proceedings based on Section 1059 German Code of Civil Procedure after the final award had been issued by the arbitral tribunals, cf. *Higher Regional Court Frankfurt*, BeckRS (2015, 06323), 18.12.2014 – 26 Sch 3/13.

926 Cf. *Achmea vs. Slovak Republic*, 26.10.2012 – PCA Case No. 2008-13 - Award on Jurisdiction, Arbitrability and Suspension, para 281 and 283; this is analysed in more detail by the Higher Regional Court, cf.: *Higher Regional Court Frankfurt*, SchiedsVZ (2013), 119, 10.05.2012 – 26 SchH 11/10, 123 f and 124, with reference to *CJEU*, 01.06.1999 – C-126/97 - Eco Swiss = ECLI:EU:C:1999:269.

1. The irrelevance of the EU's competencies to regulate arbitration for the question of compatibility

Before entering in this analysis, one principal confusion should be avoided. It was argued that the provisions regarding the CJEU in the European Treaties (especially Art. 344 TFEU) could not have an impact on the validity of the arbitration clause, as IIAs were concluded based on an exclusive member state competence before the Lisbon Treaty. Given that only the Lisbon Treaty (by changing Art. 207 TFEU) granted competencies in the fields of IIAs to the EU, there could be no conflict for agreements which have been concluded earlier.[927] However, this argument is not striking. First, *intra-EU IIAs* from a systematical point of view, do not fall under the CCP, which is a competence to be exercised *vis-à-vis* non-member states. Intra-EU IIAs would fall under the competencies for constructing the internal market.[928] Second, the fact that there might not be a direct competency for the conclusion of IIAs does in no way, even with regard to Art. 344 TFEU, exclude that IIAs enter into conflict with other provisions of the European Treaties.[929]

---

927 *Söderlund*, JOIA Vol. 24, Iss. 5 (2007), 455, 465; *Eilmansberger*, CMLR Vol. 46 (2009), 383, 404.

928 *Burgstaller*, JOIA Vol. 26, No. 2 (2009), 181, 190 f; *Lenk*, EJLS Vol. 8, No. 2 (2015), 6, 9; Art. 344 TFEU generally requires that a dispute "*concerning the interpretation or application of the treaties*" is not submitted to another dispute settlement mechanism. Following the rather extensive application of these terms in the *MOX-Plant* judgement, one needs to admit that the possibility of interference with the provisions of the internal market, e.g. the competition law rules, state aid rules or the fundamental freemdoms are sufficient to generally render Art. 344 TFEU applicable, cf. also for the wider interpretation: *Gáspár-Szilágyi*, LIEI Vol. 40, No. 2 (2013), 163, 166 and 168; *Athen/Dörr* in: Grabitz/Hilf/Nettesheim EUV/AEUV, Art. 344 TFEU, para 27 ff.

929 Expressly referring to the integrity of EU law: *Athen/Dörr* in: Grabitz/Hilf/Nettesheim EUV/AEUV, Art. 344 TFEU, para 27 ff; similar, but without a clear conclusion: *Ahner*, Investor-Staat-Schiedsverfahren nach Europäischem Unionsrecht, 2015, p. 214. Simliar also: *Dimopoulos*, CMLR Vol. 48, No. 1 (2011), 63, 86 who however tends to demonstrate that the matters of IIAs are largely covered by EU law and hence the condition is fulfilled; *Tietje*, Intra-EU BITs als Herausforderung im Mehrebenensystem des Rechts (Beit. zum Transnat. Wirt.-R, Vol. 104, 2011), p. 17 argues that EU law does not contain any mixed arbitration mechanism, which ignores that this omission might be the very essence of the conflict.

2. The scope of application of Art. 344 TFEU

The first and most obvious argument regarding the scope of application of Art. 344 TFEU starts from a strict and literal interpretation of Art. 344 TFEU which reads as follows:

> "Member States undertake not to submit a dispute concerning the interpretation or application of the Treaties to any method of settlement other than those provided for therein."

Given the wording, one could conclude – as the tribunal in *Euram vs Slovak Republic* did:

> "As far as arbitration is concerned, it appears that Article 344 TFEU (...) precludes arbitration *between Member States* regarding their obligations under EU law. This has indeed been decided by the ECJ in the Mox Plant case (...), where the ECJ stated that EU Member States are prevented from submitting their disputes to 'any other method of dispute settlement' than the ones provided for by EU law, and that the ECJ has exclusive jurisdiction in resolving a dispute between two EU Member States that is at least partially covered by EU law.
>
> However, the Tribunal does *not consider that this solution can be transposed* to a case like the present one. There is no provision in the ECT, equivalent to Article 344 TFEU, dealing with arbitration between two or more private parties, nationals of Member States, or with the so-called *mixed disputes settlement mechanisms* like investment arbitration between individuals who are nationals of Member States and Member States."[930]

In other words: the tribunal argues that Art. 344 TFEU would refer to disputes directly involving two EU member states and dealing with their respective obligations under EU law. Disputes between private parties or disputes between a private party and a member state (mixed disputes) are not covered by Art. 344 TFEU.[931] This analysis is equivalent to the rejection of a more general principle underlying Art. 344 TFEU, which is advanced by the European Commission.[932]

---

930 *Euram vs. Slovak Republic*, 22.10.2012 – PCA Case no. 2010-17: First Award on Jurisdiction, para 254 f [emphasis added].

931 Supporting this analysis: *Dittert* in: v. d. Groeben/Schwarze AEUV/EUV, Art. 344 TFEU, para 4; also: *Achmea vs. Slovak Republic*, 26.10.2012 – PCA Case No. 2008-13 - Award on Jurisdiction, Arbitrability and Suspension, para 276 f; *Wehland*, ICLQ Vol. 58, Iss. 2 (2009), 297, 318 f; *Söderlund*, JOIA Vol. 24, Iss. 5 (2007), 455, 459.

932 Clearly adressed in: *European Commission*, Amicus Curia Brief filed in Achmea (former Eureko BV) vs. Slovak Republic (PCA Case n°2008-13) - arbitration proceedings, 07/07/2010, para 24-28 or *European Commission*, Amicus

However, it is doubtful whether the wording of Art. 344 TFEU requires such a restrictive interpretation.[933]

Though, at first glance the argument of the narrow wording of Art. 344 TFEU seems convincing, it does not stand to a deeper analysis.

Starting with the wording of Art. 344 TFEU, it clearly refers to the *member states*. The *MOX Plant-Case*[934] features among the most prominent cases in which reference was made to Art. 344 TFEU. This case, to which several arbitral tribunals as well as the European Commission in its *amicus curia* filings refer, deals with a dispute between member states, as it opposed the United Kingdom to the Republic of Ireland. Some tribunals concluded that *a contrario*, and given the wording, Art. 344 TFEU shall be limited to such disputes between member states only.[935] However, the CJEU states in the *MOX Plant-Case*:

> "Furthermore, as it is between two Member States in regard to an alleged failure to comply with Community-law obligations resulting from those provisions of the Convention, this dispute is *clearly* covered by one of the methods of dispute settlement established by the EC Treaty within the terms of Article 292 EC, namely the procedure set out in Article 227 EC."[936]

Curia Brief filed in U.S. Steel Golbal Holdings I B.V. vs. Slovak Republic (PCA Case n°2013-6) - arbitration proceedings, 15/05/2014, para 37 f and 44; rejected by the tribunals in: *Euram vs. Slovak Republic*, 22.10.2012 – PCA Case no. 2010-17: First Award on Jurisdiction, para 249, *Achmea vs. Slovak Republic*, 26.10.2012 – PCA Case No. 2008-13 - Award on Jurisdiction, Arbitrability and Suspension, para 278 ff, *Electrabel vs. Hungary*, 30.11.2012 – ICSID Case No. ARB/07/19: Decision on Jurisdiction, Applicable Law and Liability, para 4.153, 4.166; cf. also: *Tietje*, Intra-EU BITs als Herausforderung im Mehrebenensystem des Rechts (Beit. zum Transnat. Wirt.-R, Vol. 104, 2011), p. 17; cf. also for a limited analysis of the jurisprudence of the CJEU: *Stier*, Arbitration International Vol. 31 (2015), 163, 168 ff.

933 *Dahlquist/Lenk et al.*, European Policy Analysis, 2016:4, 1, 4 also seem to support a more extensive interpretation; in the same direction *Clodfelter*, Santa Clara Jour. of Int. Law Vol. 12, Iss. 1 (2013), 159, 179; *Burgstaller*, JOIA Vol. 26, No. 2 (2009), 181, 191; for the opposite clearly: *Ahner*, Investor-Staat-Schiedsverfahren nach Europäischem Unionsrecht, 2015, p. 215.

934 *CJEU*, 30.05.2006 – C-459/03 - Mox Plant = ECLI:EU:C:2006:345.

935 *Achmea vs. Slovak Republic*, 26.10.2012 – PCA Case No. 2008-13 - Award on Jurisdiction, Arbitrability and Suspension, para 276; *Euram vs. Slovak Republic*, 22.10.2012 – PCA Case no. 2010-17: First Award on Jurisdiction, para 254.

936 *CJEU*, 30.05.2006 – C-459/03 - Mox Plant = ECLI:EU:C:2006:345, para 128 [emphasis added].

One could argue that there would be no need for the CJEU to expressly state that the dispute in question in the proceedings is *"clearly"*[937] covered by Art. 344 TFEU, if it was the only dispute the provision covers. It could therefore be perceived from the *MOX Plant-Case* that Art. 344 TFEU indeed does not limit itself to disputes between member states only. However, in further cases, the CJEU expressly limited the scope of application of Art. 344 TFEU either to disputes among member states or disputes between member states and the EU itself.[938] Thus, Art. 344 TFEU has only been extended from disputes among member states to disputes between member states and the EU.

In the opinion regarding the EU's accession to the ECHR[939] the CJEU stated:

> "Consequently, where EU law is at issue, the Court of Justice has exclusive jurisdiction in any dispute between the Member States and between those Member States and the EU regarding compliance with the ECHR [as it would form an integral part of EU law after the EU's accession to the ECHR] (…)
>
> Consequently, the fact that Member States or the EU are able to submit an application to the ECtHR is liable in itself to undermine the objective of Article 344 TFEU (…)
>
> In the light of the foregoing, it must be held that the agreement envisaged is liable to affect Article 344 TFEU […]"[940]

This is in line with the previous findings in e.g. the PC-Opinion[941], where the CJEU held:

> „Nor can the creation of the PC be in conflict with Article 344 TFEU, given that that article merely prohibits Member States from submitting a dispute concerning the interpretation or application of the Treaties to any method of settlement other than those provided for in the Treaties. The jurisdiction which the draft agreement intends to grant to the PC *relates only to disputes between individuals* in the field of patents."[942]

---

937 The German translation refers to "*offenkundig*" (i.e. "*obvious*"), underlining the argument.

938 Cf. also: *Bücheler/Vasiljevic*, SchiedsVZ, 2016, 328, 337.

939 *CJEU*, 18.12.2014 – Opinion 2/13 - ECHR = ECLI:EU:C:2014:2454.

940 *CJEU*, 18.12.2014 – Opinion 2/13 - ECHR = ECLI:EU:C:2014:2454, para 204, 212, 214.

941 *CJEU*, 08.03.2011 – Opinion 1/09 - Patents Court = ECLI:EU:C:2011:123.

942 *CJEU*, 08.03.2011 – Opinion 1/09 - Patents Court = ECLI:EU:C:2011:123, para 63 [emphasis added].

Thus, so far the CJEU disregarded the application of Art. 344 TFEU to disputes involving (only) private parties[943] but applies the prohibition to disputes between member states[944] or member states and the European Institutions[945]. Mixed arbitration is precisely in between both situations.[946] However, as to the authors view and in line with the predominant opinion, Art. 344 TFEU itself does indeed not cover mixed arbitration proceedings involving a member state on the one hand and a private investor on the other hand.[947]

Both types of disputes for which the CJEU applied Art. 344 TFEU so far, are characterised by the fact that the European Treaties themselves include specific provisions which cover these disputes (*inter alia*: infringement proceedings for actions of the European Commission against the

---

943 *CJEU*, 08.03.2011 – Opinion 1/09 - Patents Court = ECLI:EU:C:2011:123; *CJEU*, 01.06.1999 – C-126/97 - Eco Swiss = ECLI:EU:C:1999:269.

944 *CJEU*, 30.05.2006 – C-459/03 - Mox Plant = ECLI:EU:C:2006:345; *CJEU*, 08.03.2011 – Opinion 1/09 - Patents Court = ECLI:EU:C:2011:123.

945 *CJEU*, 08.03.2011 – Opinion 1/09 - Patents Court = ECLI:EU:C:2011:123; *CJEU*, 18.12.2014 – Opinion 2/13 - ECHR = ECLI:EU:C:2014:2454.

946 Cf. also: *German Federal Supreme Court*, 03.03.2016 – I ZB 2/15, para 28 raising considerable doubt for the German Supreme Court whether to apply or not to apply Art. 344 TFEU to mixed arbitrations and leading to a preliminary ruling reference to the CJEU.

947 Cf. *inter alia*: *Schill*, JWIT Vol. 16, No. 3 (2015), 379, 384 *Tietje*, Applicability of the ECT in ICSID Arbitration (Beit. zum Transnat. Wirt.-R, Vol. 78, 2008), 5, 14 f; cf. also: *Lang*, Der EuGH und die Investor-Staat-Streitbeilegung in TTIP und CETA (Beit. zum Transnat. Wirt.-R, Vol. 138, 2015), p. 11 f; this interpretation is in line with the tribunals' decisions in: *Achmea vs. Slovak Republic*, 26.10.2012 – PCA Case No. 2008-13 - Award on Jurisdiction, Arbitrability and Suspension, para 273, 274 (denying an incompatibility of arbitration in general with EU law) and para 278, 279 (denying the jurisdictional monopoly for the CJEU), *Euram vs. Slovak Republic*, 22.10.2012 – PCA Case no. 2010-17: First Award on Jurisdiction, para 261 ff. (which somehow – although the tribunal denies to admit a more general principle of jurisdictional monopoly – contains an analysis to what extent the judicial order is *de facto* not affected: an argument which should have been used to determine whether – after admitting that there is a more general principle – these principles have been violated: cf. *infra* (C., I.) for this analysis; *Electrabel vs. Hungary*, 30.11.2012 – ICSID Case No. ARB/07/19: Decision on Jurisdiction, Applicable Law and Liability, para 4.155; *German Federal Supreme Court*, 03.03.2016 – I ZB 2/15; *Higher Regional Court Frankfurt*, SchiedsVZ (2013), 119, 10.05.2012 – 26 SchH 11/10, *Higher Regional Court Frankfurt*, BeckRS (2015, 06323), 18.12.2014 – 26 Sch 3/13 for the opposite however: *Clodfelter*, Santa Clara Jour. of Int. Law Vol. 12, Iss. 1 (2013), 159, 179.

member states, claims for annulment against the European institutions, etc.). In contrast, disputes between private parties are by itself not covered by a specific recourse in the European Treaties but attributed – at first hand – to the courts of the member states.[948] This seems to be the determining factor for the (non-)application of Art. 344 TFEU. As the European Treaties do not include a specific recourse for investor state arbitration but, in the absence of an arbitration clause contained in an IIA, would attribute the dispute to the national courts, Art. 344 TFEU does not apply to mixed arbitrations.[949]

3. The existence of a duty to respect the fundamental elements of the European Union's legal order and judicial system

However, the arbitral tribunals so far, as well as most of literature commenting on these principles, ignored the fact that the CJEU's jurisprudence reveals an underlying principle that is not derived from Art. 344 TFEU itself, but from Art. 19 TEU, the principle of autonomy of the EU's legal order and the principles of judicial review laid down in Art. 258, 267 TFEU and 251 ff TFEU in general.[950] Hence, and this is the erroneous focus of the debate, the analysis of a potential incompatibility of an arbitration clause contained in an IIA with EU law cannot be simply answered by deducting whether Art. 344 TFEU would prohibit such arbi-

948 Cf. also: *Reinisch*, LIEI Vol. 39, No. 2 (2012), 157,176.

949 Similar: *Tietje*, Applicability of the ECT in ICSID Arbitration (Beit. zum Transnat. Wirt.-R, Vol. 78, 2008), 5,16.

950 Cf. also: *Lang*, Der EuGH und die Investor-Staat-Streitbeilegung in TTIP und CETA (Beit. zum Transnat. Wirt.-R, Vol. 138, 2015), p. 7 ff, *Schill*, JWIT Vol. 16, No. 3 (2015), 379, 384 ff; *Dimopoulos*, LIEI Vol. 39, No. 4 (2012), 447, 468; *Dimopoulos*, CMLR Vol. 48, No. 1 (2011), 63, 87; similar also: *Clodfelter*, Santa Clara Jour. of Int. Law Vol. 12, Iss. 1 (2013), 159, 179 f; and *Ahner*, Investor-Staat-Schiedsverfahren nach Europäischem Unionsrecht, 2015, p. 207; *Reinisch*, LIEI Vol. 39, No. 2 (2012), 157, 176 argues that EU law does not provide for a mixed arbitration mechanism and hence there cannot be any incompatibility. However, this ignores that conflicts may appear from other provisions, which do not necessarily set up an equivalent setting but (deliberatly) a completely different court system. *Kottmann*, EuZW, 2016, 512, 519 seems to limit the discussion beside the compliance with Art. 344 TFEU to the compatibility of the arbitration mechanism with Art. 267 TFEU, which also ignores the existence of a more general principle of the EU's legal and judicial order under EU law.

tration clauses. On the contrary, Art. 344 TFEU cannot be considered as a stand-alone provision.[951] It should – and must – be read in the context of the system of judicial remedies provided by the European Treaties and the underlying idea behind Art. 344 TFEU which is the guarantee of the autonomy of the judicial order within the EU and the uniform application of EU law within member states.[952] The European Treaties express a more general principle of the EU's judicial system and the respect of the fundamental elements of the European Union's legal order *each* judicial mechanism within the EU needs to comply with.

The admittance of a more general principle of respect of the "*fundamental elements of the legal order and judicial system of the European Union*"[953] can be perfectly observed when analysing the opinion delivered in the *Patents Court-Case*:

After having stated that the Patents Court would only be granted jurisdiction for disputes among private parties and hence the creation of the Patents Court by virtue of the agreement does not violate Art. 344 TFEU[954], the CJEU states:

> "Since the draft agreement establishes, in essence, a new court structure, it is appropriate to bear in mind, first, the *fundamental elements of the legal order and judicial system of the European Union, as designed by the founding Treaties* and developed by the case-law of the Court, in order to assess *whether the creation of the PC is compatible with those elements*."[955]

The CJEU, makes this statement immediately after having determined that the creation of the Patents Court does not interfere with Art. 344 TFEU. Hence it reveals that the compatibility with the "*fundamental elements of*

951 *Dittert* in: v. d. Groeben/Schwarze AEUV/EUV, Art. 344 TFEU, para 3.

952 *Dittert* in: v. d. Groeben/Schwarze AEUV/EUV, Art. 344 TFEU, para 1; cf. also: *Hindelang*, LIEI Vol. 39, Iss. 2 (2012), 179, 199 in footnote 82; cf. also *Bücheler/Vasiljevic*, SchiedsVZ, 2016, 328, 338.

953 *CJEU*, 08.03.2011 – Opinion 1/09 - Patents Court = ECLI:EU:C:2011:123, para 64, in *CJEU*, 18.12.2014 – Opinion 2/13 - ECHR = ECLI:EU:C:2014:2454, para 164 and 200 the court refers to "*the specific characteristics of the EU and EU law*" or the "*specifics of EU law and its autonomy*", in fine referring to identical idea of protecting the inherent basics of EU law by guaranteeing certain characteristics also through the judicial framework established by the European treaties and the member states.

954 *CJEU*, 08.03.2011 – Opinion 1/09 - Patents Court = ECLI:EU:C:2011:123, para 63.

955 *CJEU*, 08.03.2011 – Opinion 1/09 - Patents Court = ECLI:EU:C:2011:123, para 64 [emphasis added].

the legal order and judicial system of the European Union" is a more general principle, which is *not* limited to the scope addressed in Art. 344 TFEU. The CJEU expressly reiterated this approach in the opinion delivered on the EU's accession to the ECHR, when it carefully distinguishes a violation of the principle of autonomy and judicial system in the EU and a violation of Art. 344 TFEU.[956]

Both fundamental elements (of the EU's legal order and its judicial system) somehow interact and reciprocally influence the respective other principle.[957]

When the CJEU refers to the fundamental element of the *EU's legal order,* it mainly refers to the autonomy of EU law.[958] The autonomy is essentially characterised by the principle of primacy, the direct effect and the (binding) conferral of competences to the EU's institutions.[959] Some consider the (divergent) principles of interpretation developed by the CJEU to be part of the EU law's autonomy as well.[960]

On the other side, the fundamental elements of the *EU's judicial system* are characterised by four main elements: the role of the CJEU as interpretative authority of EU law which may (solely) render finally binding deci-

---

956 *CJEU*, 18.12.2014 – Opinion 2/13 - ECHR = ECLI:EU:C:2014:2454, para 179 ff and 201 ff, although regarding the EU's accession to the ECHR the CJEU considers both principles to be potentially violated by the draft agreement; *Ahner*, Investor-Staat-Schiedsverfahren nach Europäischem Unionsrecht, 2015, p. 209 who refers to *CJEU*, 14.12.1991 – Opinion 1/91 - EEC-Treaty = ECLI:EU:C:1991:490, para 46 ff, which indeed also reveals the dualism.

957 Cf. *CJEU*, 08.03.2011 – Opinion 1/09 - Patents Court = ECLI:EU:C:2011:123, para 67: "*Moreover, it is for the Court to ensure respect for the autonomy of the European Union legal order thus created by the Treaties*", *CJEU*, 18.12.2014 – Opinion 2/13 - ECHR = ECLI:EU:C:2014:2454 par 174, *Lang*, Der EuGH und die Investor-Staat-Streitbeilegung in TTIP und CETA (Beit. zum Transnat. Wirt.-R, Vol. 138, 2015), p. 8 f considers the judicial provisions to be part of the autonomy.

958 *CJEU*, 08.03.2011 – Opinion 1/09 - Patents Court = ECLI:EU:C:2011:123, para 65 and 67.

959 *CJEU*, 14.12.1991 – Opinion 1/91 - EEC-Treaty = ECLI:EU:C:1991:490, para 21; *CJEU*, 08.03.2011 – Opinion 1/09 - Patents Court = ECLI:EU:C:2011:123, para 65; *Herdegen*, Europarecht, 17. Edn. (2015), § 5, para 9 ff; *Hindelang*, LIEI Vol. 39, Iss. 2 (2012), 179, 188; *Ahner*, Investor-Staat-Schiedsverfahren nach Europäischem Unionsrecht, 2015, p. 205 and 208 f.

960 *Oppermann/Classen et al.*, 5. Edn. (2011) § 9, para 7. For a comparison of the traditional principles of interpretation with those applied by the CJEU: *Hobe*, 8. Edn. (2014), para. 407 ff; *Hindelang*, AVR Vol. 53 (2015), 68, 72.

sions on how to interpret EU law, the (exhaustive set of) legal remedies laid down in the European Treaties, the role of the national courts of the member states and their possibility to interact with the CJEU and the principle of mutual trust among EU member states.[961]

Regarding the CJEU as sole authority to interpret EU law, the CJEU stated, as settled case law that it is inadmissible if any other dispute settlement mechanism is granted the right to render binding decisions upon EU member states, on how to interpret EU law.[962] Only this exclusivity would guarantee the uniform application of EU law in the member states.[963]

As to the role of the member states' national courts, the CJEU stressed out, on various occasions that the possibility (and for courts of last resort, their duty) of interaction with the CJEU, especially by virtue of the preliminary ruling procedure laid down in Art. 267 TFEU, is one of the most important elements of the EU's judicial system.[964] It enables, through the ability to refer a question of interpretation of EU law to the CJEU, to ensure that inherent questions of interpreting EU law can be referred to the CJEU and consequently be uniformly applied in all member states.[965] *De facto* this ensures the principle of effectiveness[966] under EU law.

As to the CJEU the European Treaties provide a complete system of legal remedies and an institutional framework, as set forth in Art. 19 TEU. The national courts of the member states are supposed to act as 'ordinary'

---

961 Cf. *CJEU*, 08.03.2011 – Opinion 1/09 - Patents Court = ECLI:EU:C:2011:123, para 65 ff., *Lang*, Der EuGH und die Investor-Staat-Streitbeilegung in TTIP und CETA (Beit. zum Transnat. Wirt.-R, Vol. 138, 2015), p.7 who does include the principle of "*mutual trust*".

962 *CJEU*, 14.12.1991 – Opinion 1/91 - EEC-Treaty = ECLI:EU:C:1991:490, para 54 ff, especially para 58.

963 *CJEU*, 18.12.2014 – Opinion 2/13 - ECHR = ECLI:EU:C:2014:2454, para 184.

964 *CJEU*, 18.12.2014 – Opinion 2/13 - ECHR = ECLI:EU:C:2014:2454, para 175 ff, *CJEU*, 08.03.2011 – Opinion 1/09 - Patents Court = ECLI:EU:C:2011:123, para 69, 77, *CJEU*, 14.12.1991 – Opinion 1/91 - EEC-Treaty = ECLI:EU:C:1991:490, para 58; cf. also: *Lang*, Der EuGH und die Investor-Staat-Streitbeilegung in TTIP und CETA (Beit. zum Transnat. Wirt.-R, Vol. 138, 2015), p. 15; *Hindelang*, LIEI Vol. 39, Iss. 2 (2012), 179, 188 and 195 ff.

965 *Hobe*, 8. Edn. (2014), para 533 f; *Oppermann/Classen et al.*, 5. Edn. (2011), para 68; *Haratsch*, 2016, p. 244 f; *Parish*, EJIL Vol. 23, No. 1, 141, *Hindelang*, LIEI Vol. 39, Iss. 2 (2012), 179, 195.

966 The German expression is "*Effektivitätsgrundsatz*".

courts of the EU and 'guardians' of its legal order.[967] In this position the national courts are entitled to observe the legality of any act and its compliance with EU law and should secure the uniform implementation and application of EU law. Thus, the judicial framework of the EU and the observance of its specific criteria is not only preserved through the CJEU, but also through national remedies in the member states.[968]

Lately, the CJEU also focussed on the principle of mutual trust between EU member states, which is an essential prerequisite to the functioning of the EU.[969] By requiring each member state to presume the observance of EU law by any other member state, the principle guarantees the overall uniform application of EU law.[970] Indeed, mistrust as to the observance of EU law in other member states would potentially encourage the non-observance in the mistrusting member state as well.

4. The criteria to determine the incompatibility with the general principles of the European Union's legal and judicial order

However, the CJEU does not consider every dispute settlement mechanism besides the national courts and the CJEU itself to be an impediment on the above-mentioned principles.[971] Indeed, and as the tribunal in *Eureko vs. Slovak Republic* puts it:

---

967 *CJEU*, 08.03.2011 – Opinion 1/09 - Patents Court = ECLI:EU:C:2011:123, para 66; *CJEU*, 18.12.2014 – Opinion 2/13 - ECHR = ECLI:EU:C:2014:2454, para 174 ff; cf. also: *Parish*, EJIL Vol. 23, No. 1, 141, 144 f.

968 *CJEU*, 18.12.2014 – Opinion 2/13 - ECHR = ECLI:EU:C:2014:2454, para 175.

969 *CJEU*, 18.12.2014 – Opinion 2/13 - ECHR = ECLI:EU:C:2014:2454, para 168 and 191.

970 *CJEU*, 18.12.2014 – Opinion 2/13 - ECHR = ECLI:EU:C:2014:2454, para 191-194.

971 Clearly stated in *CJEU*, 18.12.2014 – Opinion 2/13 - ECHR = ECLI:EU:C:2014:2454, para 183 with reference to *CJEU*, 08.03.2011 – Opinion 1/09 - Patents Court = ECLI:EU:C:2011:123, para 74 and *CJEU*, 14.12.1991 – Opinion 1/91 - EEC-Treaty = ECLI:EU:C:1991:490, para 40 and 70.

> "(…) transnational arbitration is a commonplace throughout the EU (…). It cannot be asserted that all arbitrations that involve any question of EU law are conducted in violation of EU law."[972]

(Private) arbitration is admitted in the EU and does not necessarily constitute a violation of the above mentioned general principle. The CJEU admitted that there are numerous ways of creating new dispute settlement mechanisms, even by virtue of international conventions and outside the framework described by Art. 19 TEU, which are "*not, in principle, incompatible with EU law*".[973] Notably as to arbitration proceedings between private parties, this has been admitted by the CJEU in the *Nordsee*[974] and *Eco Swiss*[975] cases:

> "In that context attention must be drawn to the fact that if questions of Community law are raised in an arbitration (…) the ordinary courts may be called upon to examine them either in the context of their collaboration with arbitration tribunals (…) or in the course of a review or an arbitration award (…)"[976]

and

> "It is to be noted, first of all, that, where questions of Community law are raised in an arbitration resorted to by agreement, the ordinary courts may have to examine those questions, in particular during review of the arbitration award"[977]

Arbitral tribunals generally advance these decisions to conclude from the CJEU's statement that there is no general principle in EU law which prohibits arbitration. This analysis however neglects two facts: on the one hand the CJEU ruled that EU law has to be – if applicable – mandatorily observed by arbitral tribunals, whether or not they are considered to be outside the framework of Art. 19 TEU.[978] On the other hand the court reserves itself (and/or the national courts) the last resort on EU law's interpretation by assigning the duty on the member state's national courts to

---

972 *Achmea vs. Slovak Republic*, 26.10.2012 – PCA Case No. 2008-13 - Award on Jurisdiction, Arbitrability and Suspension, para 274.

973 *CJEU*, 08.03.2011 – Opinion 1/09 - Patents Court = ECLI:EU:C:2011:123, para 74, *CJEU*, 18.12.2014 – Opinion 2/13 - ECHR = ECLI:EU:C:2014:2454, para 182; also stressed out by: *Parish*, EJIL Vol. 23, No. 1, 141, 146; cf. also *Hindelang*, AVR Vol. 53 (2015), 68, 73; *Lang*, Der EuGH und die Investor-Staat-Streitbeilegung in TTIP und CETA (Beit. zum Transnat. Wirt.-R, Vol. 138, 2015), p. 8 f.

974 *CJEU*, 23.03.1982 – C-102/81 - Nordsee = ECLI:EU:C:1982:107.

975 *CJEU*, 01.06.1999 – C-126/97 - Eco Swiss = ECLI:EU:C:1999:269.

976 *CJEU*, 23.03.1982 – C-102/81 - Nordsee = ECLI:EU:C:1982:107, para 14.

977 *CJEU*, 01.06.1999 – C-126/97 - Eco Swiss = ECLI:EU:C:1999:269, para 32.

978 *CJEU*, 01.06.1999 – C-126/97 - Eco Swiss = ECLI:EU:C:1999:269, para 36 ff.

ensure the respect and (correct) application of EU law, either within the enforcement or annulment proceedings or any other kind of interaction with the arbitral tribunal.[979] Within those proceedings, remaining questions regarding the interpretation of EU law, should be resolved by virtue of the preliminary ruling procedure.[980] The CJEU even considers this to be a duty for the member state courts, as otherwise the autonomy of the legal order is endangered.[981]

Hence, as to the CJEU, regarding arbitration between private individuals, the mechanism of judicial review on the later stage, subsequent to the arbitration proceedings, guarantees – to a sufficient degree – the respect of the autonomy of the EU's legal order and its uniform application within the member states, as well as the respect of the fundamental judicial system in the Union, designed to safeguard the legal order.[982] This is mainly based on the consideration that such judicial review on the later stage (i.e. setting-aside proceedings or enforcement proceedings), include the possibility of referring questions to the CJEU through the national courts and the preliminary ruling procedure.[983] Thus, neither the *Ecoswiss*- nor the

---

979 *CJEU*, 01.06.1999 – C-126/97 - Eco Swiss = ECLI:EU:C:1999:269, para 32, *CJEU*, 23.03.1982 – C-102/81 - Nordsee = ECLI:EU:C:1982:107, para 14 f.

980 *CJEU*, 01.06.1999 – C-126/97 - Eco Swiss = ECLI:EU:C:1999:269, para 33, *CJEU*, 23.03.1982 – C-102/81 - Nordsee = ECLI:EU:C:1982:107, para 15; this seems to be an idea which was observed by the tribunal in *Electrabel vs. Hungary*, 30.11.2012 – ICSID Case No. ARB/07/19: Decision on Jurisdiction, Applicable Law and Liability, para 4.153 as well.

981 *Komninos*, CMLR Iss. 37 (2000), 459, 467 f; cf. also: *Hindelang*, AVR Vol. 53 (2015), 68, 76 f.

982 *CJEU*, 01.06.1999 – C-126/97 - Eco Swiss = ECLI:EU:C:1999:269, para 36-37 which underlines the importance of the subsequent proceedings.

983 This interaction seems to be the predominant purpose of the CJEU, reiterated at various occasions:, *CJEU*, 08.03.2011 – Opinion 1/09 - Patents Court = ECLI:EU:C:2011:123, para 89; *CJEU*, 18.12.2014 – Opinion 2/13 - ECHR = ECLI:EU:C:2014:2454, para 176: "*In particular, the judicial system as thus conceived has as its keystone the preliminary ruling procedure provided for in Article 267 TFEU (...)*"; cf. also: *Lang*, Der EuGH und die Investor-Staat-Streitbeilegung in TTIP und CETA (Beit. zum Transnat. Wirt.-R, Vol. 138, 2015), p. 7-9 and 15 ff; *Hindelang*, AVR Vol. 53 (2015), 68, 72 ff; *Dimopoulos*, CMLR Vol. 48, No. 1 (2011), 63, 87 f; *Burgstaller*, LIEI Vol. 39, No. 2 (2012), 207, 219 f seems to consider that the circumvention of Art. 267 TFEU would be sufficient to render the mechanism incompatible; The incompatibility is challenged by *Parish*, EJIL Vol. 23, No. 1, 141, 147 who stresses that a violation of the public policy cannot easily be admitted in any case of missapplication of EU law.

Nordsee-Case give a *carte blanche* to any dispute settlement mechanisms which grants any individual the possibility to refer a dispute to arbitration. Instead, the CJEU found that this particular mechanism of arbitration between private individuals – although being outside the framework of Art. 19 TEU – does not (gravely) endanger the fundamental principles of EU law, as the subsequent proceedings in front of the national member state courts contain sufficient safeguards. This is clearly stated in the *PC-Opinion*:

> "[A]n international agreement may affect [the CJEU's] powers provided that the indispensable conditions for safeguarding the essential character of those powers are satisfied and, consequently there is no adverse effect on the autonomy of the European Union legal order […]."[984]

Hence, every dispute settlement mechanism, i.e. also the mixed investment arbitration mechanism as conceived by IIAs, needs to respect these safeguards. This is clearly demonstrated in the *PC-Opinion*, where such safeguards were missing. This lead to the CJEU's hostility as to the draft agreement.

> "However, the [permissible] judicial systems [analysed beforehand] were designed, in essence, to resolve disputes on the interpretation or application of the actual provisions of the international agreements concerned. Further, while providing particular powers to the courts of third countries to refer cases to the Court for a preliminary ruling, those systems did not affect the powers of the courts and tribunals of Member States in relation to the interpretation and application of EU law, nor the power, or indeed the obligation, of those courts and tribunals to request a preliminary ruling from the Court of Justice *and the power of the Court to reply*.
>
> By contrast, the [PC] is to be called upon to interpret and apply not only the provisions of that agreement but also the future regulation on the Community patent and other instruments of EU law, in particular regulations and directives in conjunction with which that regulation would, when necessary, have to be read, namely provisions relating to other bodies of rules on intellectual property, and rules of the FEU Treaty concerning the internal market and competition law. Likewise, the PC may be called upon to determine a dispute pending before it in the light of the fundamental rights and general principles of EU law, or even to examine the validity of an act of the European Union."[985]

---

984 *CJEU*, 08.03.2011 – Opinion 1/09 - Patents Court = ECLI:EU:C:2011:123, para 76.

985 *CJEU*, 08.03.2011 – Opinion 1/09 - Patents Court = ECLI:EU:C:2011:123, para 77 and 78 [emphasis added].

In other words: Not only the Patents Court would have circumvented the member states possibility to refer questions of interpreting EU law to the CJEU by virtue of the preliminary ruling procedure (and thus the CJEUs ability to render a binding decision on issues of EU law) but also the Patents Court would regularly apply – substantive and important – provisions of EU law without the above mentioned procedural safeguard. Last, the Patents Court would have even be able to judge on the validity of acts of the EU, a power expressly and exclusively conferred to the CJEU in the European Treaties.[986]

In the opinion regarding the draft agreement on the EU's accession to the ECHR the CJEU reiterates several of these ideas and puts it straightforward[987]:

> "Nevertheless, the Court of Justice has also declared that an international agreement may affect [the Court's] own powers only if the indispensable conditions for safeguarding the essential character of those powers are satisfied and, *consequently, there is no adverse effect on the autonomy of the EU legal order* (…)
>
> [However] the mechanism established by that protocol could (…) affect the autonomy and effectiveness of the preliminary ruling procedure provided for in Article 267 TFEU […]
>
> [and furthermore it cannot be ruled out that this mechanism may create] a risk that the preliminary *ruling procedure provided for in Article 267 TFEU might be cir-*

986 Cf. also: *Lang*, Der EuGH und die Investor-Staat-Streitbeilegung in TTIP und CETA (Beit. zum Transnat. Wirt.-R, Vol. 138, 2015) p. 15 f; The tribunal in *Electrabel vs. Hungary*, 30.11.2012 – ICSID Case No. ARB/07/19: Decision on Jurisdiction, Applicable Law and Liability, para 4.156 seems to consider the conferral of powers to examine the validity of acts of the European Union (cf.: para 4.156 and 4.157) as the most decisive fact for the CJEU to consider the Patents Court draft agreement to be incompatible with EU law. However, the CJEU's analysis in para 77 f reveals the inverse. The Court stresses the constant interference of the Court with analyzing EU law while the words "*or even*" indicate that the control of validity of acts of the European Union is only another, complementary factor; cf. also *Ahner*, Investor-Staat-Schiedsverfahren nach Europäischem Unionsrecht, 2015, p. 215, 230.

987 As *Schill*, JWIT Vol. 16, No. 3 (2015), 379, 383 underlines correctly: "*Certainly, the rhetoric of Opinion 2/13 is harsher than that of earlier decisions. In substance, however, Opinion 2/13 adds few, if any (...). Instead, it reiterates concerns already expressed in Opinion 1/91 (Economic Area Agreement I), Opinion 1/00 (European Common Aviation Area), and Opinion 1/09 (European and Community Patents Court), and sharpens them.*".

> *cumvented,* a procedure which, as has been noted in paragraph 176 of this Opinion, is the keystone of the judicial system established by the Treaties."[988]

These impediments on the EU's judicial order and its consequences, especially the risk for the autonomy of the EU's legal order, leads the CJEU to the conclusion that

> "it must be held that the accession of the EU to the ECHR as envisaged by the draft agreement is liable adversely to affect the specific characteristics of EU law and its autonomy (…)"[989]

A conjoint reading of the several decisions rendered by the CJEU in this regard, thus demonstrates the standard of review for an incompatibility with the specific characters of EU law: whether or not a provision or an agreement providing for a dispute settlement mechanism is considered to be incompatible with the above mentioned principles has to be determined by a comprehensive evaluation of the degree of impediment on the autonomy of EU law and its specific characters.[990] A provision, like the IIA's arbitration clause will be considered incompatible with EU law if it is "*liable adversely to affect the specific characteristics*"[991] of the EU's legal and judicial framework, especially its autonomy.[992]

The same conjoint reading also provides the set of criteria used by the CJEU to determine the severity of the impediments and hence allows to deduct the compatibility or incompatibility of a dispute settlement mecha-

988 *CJEU*, 18.12.2014 – Opinion 2/13 - ECHR = ECLI:EU:C:2014:2454, para 183, 197 and 198 [emphasis added].

989 *CJEU*, 18.12.2014 – Opinion 2/13 - ECHR = ECLI:EU:C:2014:2454, para 200.

990 *Lang*, Der EuGH und die Investor-Staat-Streitbeilegung in TTIP und CETA (Beit. zum Transnat. Wirt.-R, Vol. 138, 2015), p. 8; *Burgstaller*, LIEI Vol. 39, No. 2 (2012), 207, 216 f and 219 f.

991 *CJEU*, 18.12.2014 – Opinion 2/13 - ECHR = ECLI:EU:C:2014:2454, para 200.

992 *CJEU*, 18.12.2014 – Opinion 2/13 - ECHR = ECLI:EU:C:2014:2454, para 200; cf. also: *Burgstaller*, LIEI Vol. 39, No. 2 (2012), 207, 216 f; *Lang*, Der EuGH und die Investor-Staat-Streitbeilegung in TTIP und CETA (Beit. zum Transnat. Wirt.-R, Vol. 138, 2015), p. 8; *Hindelang*, AVR Vol. 53 (2015), 68, 73 f; this seems to be what *Parish*, EJIL Vol. 23, No. 1, 141, 145 refers to the risk for the *"'homogenity' of [EU] law*"; *Ahner*, Investor-Staat-Schiedsverfahren nach Europäischem Unionsrecht, 2015, p. 209 refers to three (aparently) distinct categories; However, as it was demonstrated, the overall criteria is the impediment on the autonomy of EU law, which can only be evaluated in an overall approach; for additional thoughts on the implications especially for TTIP and CETA: *Schill*, JWIT Vol. 16, No. 3 (2015), 379, 379 f.

nism with the general principles of the EU legal order and its judicial system:

- The fact that a dispute settlement system operates outside the judicial framework of the European Treaties and substitutes the national courts in their function as ordinary courts of the EU's legal order, especially the number of cases in which this function is eliminated;[993]
- The questions addressed by the dispute settlement mechanism, especially its interpretation and application of EU law and the importance of provisions to be dealt with;[994]
- The question whether the interpretation of EU law by the dispute settlement body would be (if only *de facto*) binding on the member states or any institution of the EU;[995]
- The degree to which the preliminary ruling procedure in Art. 267 TFEU is circumvented or could be substituted by a control *a posteriori* e.g. during the enforcement, setting-aside proceedings or any other review of the award or judgement;[996]

---

993 *CJEU*, 08.03.2011 – Opinion 1/09 - Patents Court = ECLI:EU:C:2011:123, para 80: "*the Member States cannot confer the jurisdiction to resolve such disputes on a court created by an international agreement which would deprive those courts of their tasks as 'ordinary courts within the European legal order*" as well as para 72 which also refers to the number of cases the Patent-Court would have dealt with and the fact that its jurisdiction would be exclusive; *Hindelang*, AVR Vol. 53 (2015), 68, 76 ff who seems to bundle this criteria with criteria n°3 and n°4 which all together relate to interrupting the "*judicial dialogue*".

994 *CJEU*, 08.03.2011 – Opinion 1/09 - Patents Court = ECLI:EU:C:2011:123, para 78; *CJEU*, 14.12.1991 – Opinion 1/91 - EEC-Treaty = ECLI:EU:C:1991:490, para 41 ff.

995 *CJEU*, 18.12.2014 – Opinion 2/13 - ECHR = ECLI:EU:C:2014:2454, para 184; cf. also: *Lang*, Der EuGH und die Investor-Staat-Streitbeilegung in TTIP und CETA (Beit. zum Transnat. Wirt.-R, Vol. 138, 2015), p. 9 who denominates the *de facto* effects as a "*spillover-effect*" of decision rendered in arbitration proceedings on EU law which might, depending on their severity, breach with the principles laid down by the CJEU *Hindelang*, AVR Vol. 53 (2015), 68, 74 ff also referring to this as the "*spillover*" on the CJEU interpretation of EU law; *Ahner*, Investor-Staat-Schiedsverfahren nach Europäischem Unionsrecht, 2015, p. 216 f.

996 *CJEU*, 08.03.2011 – Opinion 1/09 - Patents Court = ECLI:EU:C:2011:123, para 80 ff but also *CJEU*, 01.06.1999 – C-126/97 - Eco Swiss = E-CLI:EU:C:1999:269 *Hindelang*, AVR Vol. 53 (2015), 68, 76 ff cf. also comment on his perception in footnote 1000.

- The potential to ensure the uniform application of EU law by other means in case of misapplication or failure to bring EU law to full effect in the member states through the dispute settlement mechanism;[997]
- The infringement through the dispute settlement mechanism on basic principles, such as the principle of mutual trust.[998]

All these criteria serve to determine the degree of interference of the mechanism and the potential risk to alter the autonomy of the legal order in the EU, including the institutional framework, the principle of supremacy and the effective and uniform application of EU law in the member states.[999] It should be noted that none of these criteria is in itself sufficient to render a dispute settlement mechanism incompatible with the specific characteristics of the EU's legal order and judicial framework.[1000] The criteria should be used as benchmarks of different importance which need to be weighted in an overall approach.[1001]

---

997 *CJEU*, 08.03.2011 – Opinion 1/09 - Patents Court = ECLI:EU:C:2011:123, para 86 f; *Hindelang*, AVR Vol. 53 (2015), 68, 78, cf. also comment on his perception in footnote 1000; *Hindelang*, LIEI Vol. 39, Iss. 2 (2012), 179, 195; *Lang*, Der EuGH und die Investor-Staat-Streitbeilegung in TTIP und CETA (Beit. zum Transnat. Wirt.-R, Vol. 138, 2015), p. 15.

998 *CJEU*, 18.12.2014 – Opinion 2/13 - ECHR = ECLI:EU:C:2014:2454, para 168, 173 and 191 ff.

999 *CJEU*, 08.03.2011 – Opinion 1/09 - Patents Court = ECLI:EU:C:2011:123, para 85, 89; cf. also: *Hindelang*, AVR Vol. 53 (2015), 68, 72 ff; *Lang*, Der EuGH und die Investor-Staat-Streitbeilegung in TTIP und CETA (Beit. zum Transnat. Wirt.-R, Vol. 138, 2015), p. 8 f.

1000 *Lang*, Der EuGH und die Investor-Staat-Streitbeilegung in TTIP und CETA (Beit. zum Transnat. Wirt.-R, Vol. 138, 2015) p.8 f puts only three criteria (the binding interpretation of EU law, the influence on the allocation of competencies and the circumvention of Art. 267 TFEU) but however evaluates a couple of the above-mentioned criteria within those three. In the authors view this reduction of the criteria leads to an unsuitable prioritization of one or the other and is questionable as the CJEU takes a holistic approach by weighting all criteria to determine the degree of impediment an risk for the specific criteria of EU law, cf. for the approach: *CJEU*, 08.03.2011 – Opinion 1/09 - Patents Court = ECLI:EU:C:2011:123, para 89.

1001 *Lang*, Der EuGH und die Investor-Staat-Streitbeilegung in TTIP und CETA (Beit. zum Transnat. Wirt.-R, Vol. 138, 2015), p. 9, who, as to the potential conflict with the CJEU's exclusive competence to render binding decisions on how to interpret EU law, refers to a "*spillover-effect*". It seems that the term is appropriate, however it is suggested not to examine one criteria separate from the other, as the overall approach of the CJEU is to evaluate the potential influ-

III. Violation of the principles deducted by the CJEU by arbitral tribunals in investment proceedings

Thus, the question of compatibility between the IIA's arbitration clause and the CJEU's jurisdictional monopoly cannot be addressed as it has been previously done by the arbitral tribunals. The question is not whether or not a more general principle behind the European Treaties' jurisdictional provisions (including Art. 344 TFEU, but also Art. 267, 258 TFEU and Art. 19 TEU, Art. 251 ff TFEU) exists, but whether the IIA's arbitration clause leads to a sufficiently serious impediment on this – existing – principle leading to an incompatibility of the arbitration clause with EU law (cf. *supra*: "*II. The erroneous view on the criteria to be observed by a dispute settlement mechanism within the* European Union").

The current – erroneous – focus of the arbitral tribunals somehow distorts the analysis if an impediment of sufficient gravity exists. Hence, these criteria should be analysed in the following.

1. Quantity of cases and quality of provisions concerned (criteria n° 1 and n° 2)

The first criteria to evaluate is the quality of the provisions to be dealt with by the dispute settlement mechanism and the quantity of cases to be conferred upon the tribunal / court. As to the quality of provisions concerned, the risk to the autonomy of the EU's legal order will in principle only be affected if the dispute settlement mechanism would be entitled to interpret or apply provisions of EU law. One could argue that arbitral tribunals do apply the IIA but not EU law.[1002] The *Eureko-Tribunal* indeed points out that "*(...) the tribunal does not have jurisdiction to rule on alleged*

ence and impediment of the effectiveness and stability of the specific legal order in the EU.

1002 This argument is also advanced by: *Wehland*, ICLQ Vol. 58, Iss. 2 (2009), 297, 318 who however recognises that it does not completely exclude a threat to an uniform interpretation exists; *Ahner*, Investor-Staat-Schiedsverfahren nach Europäischem Unionsrecht, 2015, p. 216 f who however recognises a *de facto* interpretation of substantive provisions of EU law; *Hindelang*, AVR Vol. 53 (2015), 68, 73 f.

breaches of EU law as such."[1003] However, such a limited viewpoint, which has been expressed by several arbitral tribunals, would ignore the setting of intra-EU disputes.[1004] As already demonstrated the tribunals might need to (also) deal with a multitude of questions regarding EU law which might – through one way or another – interfere with provisions of the IIA. This could e.g. lead to the question if a certain state measure is covered by a particular provision of EU law. If this is the case, the arbitral tribunal will need to consider the legal effects of this provisions and its interaction with the protection standard contained in the IIA.[1005] Even if one denies any (immediate legal) impact of EU law on the substantive guarantees of an IIA, the question whether a state acted in conformity with the IIA, while being obliged to act in a certain way by EU law, remains an important question of the case's factual matrix.[1006] Thus, the arbitral tribunal will need to apply and interpret EU law even though its major task is interpreting the IIA.[1007] Having in mind the potential conflicts of IIAs and EU law which might occur regarding substantive protection standards, the arbitral tribunals will need to deal with provisions which belong to the most fundamental provisions of the EU's legal framework, including *inter alia*: state aid provisions (Art. 107 ff TFEU), competition law (Art. 101

1003 *Achmea vs. Slovak Republic*, 26.10.2012 – PCA Case No. 2008-13 - Award on Jurisdiction, Arbitrability and Suspension, para 290.

1004 Similar: *Hindelang*, AVR Vol. 53 (2015), 68, 74.

1005 *Hindelang*, LIEI Vol. 39, Iss. 2 (2012), 179, 197; *Lang*, Der EuGH und die Investor-Staat-Streitbeilegung in TTIP und CETA (Beit. zum Transnat. Wirt.-R, Vol. 138, 2015), p. 10 f.

1006 Cf. especially: *Hindelang*, LIEI Vol. 39, Iss. 2 (2012), 179, 196 f; *Hindelang*, AVR Vol. 53 (2015), 68, 79 f; in the same direction: *Ahner*, Investor-Staat-Schiedsverfahren nach Europäischem Unionsrecht, 2015, p. 218 ff; cf. also *Ioan Micula, Viorel Micula & others vs. Romania*, 11.12.2013 – ICSID Case No. ARB/05/20 - Final Award, para 328 and *AES Summit vs. Hungary*, 23.09.2010 – ICSID Case No. ARB/07/22 - Award, para 7.6.9.

1007 Cf. also: *Parish*, EJIL Vol. 23, No. 1, 141, 142 f. In the opinion regard the EEA, the CJEU even admitted that not only the application of provisions of EU law but even of those provisions of the EEA which have the same content might *de facto* influence the autonomy of the legal order. The underlying idea is that the *de-facto* effect on the autonomy of the EU's legal order is sufficient which does not require the application of EU law but might also result from the application of other norms if this impacs; cf. also: *Lang*, Der EuGH und die Investor-Staat-Streitbeilegung in TTIP und CETA (Beit. zum Transnat. Wirt.-R, Vol. 138, 2015), p. 10 f however argues that in the EEA agreement, the provisions to be interpreted were mainly identical, which is not the case in investor-state arbitrations.

ff TFEU), public procurement law, etc. (cf. the potential fields of conflicts which have been explained in Chapter 5).[1008] Consequently, in intra-EU disputes arbitral tribunals will regularly need to interpret multiple provisions of EU law.

Also the number of cases for which arbitral tribunals might deprive the member state courts from their role as ordinary courts as conceived in Art. 19 (1) TEU is considerable. Other than in the *PC-Opinion* arbitral tribunals do not have exclusive jurisdiction regarding investment claims. Investors might, and probably will, seek protection of their rights before national courts.[1009] However, the type of protection investors seek before national courts and arbitral tribunals heavily differs. This will have comparable effects to an exclusive jurisdiction attributed to arbitral tribunals for compensation claims brought in an investment disputes. IIAs only contain legal remedies as to the allocation of compensation for damages occurred.[1010] It does not enable to recourse against the initial act causing the damage, e.g. the law, any type of regulation or an administrative decision. This primary relief or primary legal protection[1011] will be exclusively handled by the national courts. However, under IIAs investors are generally not obliged to seek this primary relief first. Investors might as well decide to solely rely on the arbitral tribunal. For this type of dispute, arbitral tribunals have sort of an exclusive jurisdiction. The arbitration mechanism thus presents the inherent risk that a state act is only and exclusively challenged under the arbitration forum, depriving the national courts of their attributed role as ordinary courts.[1012]

By its very nature and the broad definition of investments under the IIAs, the potential number of disputes arising under the IIAs is considerable. Other than particular inter-state disputes, as they have been conceived in e.g. the *EEA-Opinion*[1013], a dispute settlement mechanism offering pri-

---

1008 Similar: *Hindelang*, AVR Vol. 53 (2015), 68, 74 f.

1009 *Hindelang*, AVR Vol. 53 (2015), 68, 78.

1010 *Hindelang*, AVR Vol. 53 (2015), 68, 78.

1011 *Hindelang*, AVR Vol. 53 (2015), 68, 78.

1012 Cf. also: *Hindelang*, AVR Vol. 53 (2015), 68, 78; similar: *Hindelang*, LIEI Vol. 39, Iss. 2 (2012), 179, 197.

1013 *CJEU*, 14.12.1991 – Opinion 1/91 - EEC-Treaty = ECLI:EU:C:1991:490: the opinion was rendered on the agreement by which the former member states of the EU wanted to establish the European Economic Area by conclusion of an agreement with the members of the European Free Trade Association. As to Art. 96 of the draft agreement, a court should have been established which was

vate parties access to claim their rights is always suspect to a larger number of cases. The current "*trend*" of more than 130 pending intra-EU investment proceedings demonstrates the impact of mixed arbitration.[1014] Thus given the first criteria, the basis for an impediment on the EU's specific characteristics, especially its autonomy are well set.

2. Interpretative monopoly – (*de facto*) binding interpretation (criterion n° 3)

Also from the perspective of a possible interference with the uniform application and interpretation of EU law, investment arbitration presents a major risk.[1015] One of the predominant concerns of the CJEU is to safe its role as ultimate instance of interpretation for EU law.[1016] It is one of the cornerstones of the EU's legal order. A multitude of interpreting authorities would considerably hinder the uniform application of EU law in the member states.[1017] As just developed, arbitral tribunal are regularly applying and thus interpreting EU law in investment arbitration proceedings. Although the interpretation given by the tribunals to a particular question of EU law is neither binding on the CJEU nor the member state courts, there is a risk of a *de facto* binding force or '*spillover*'.[1018] This effect might raise through two diverging interpretations given to the same questions by the CJEU and the arbitral tribunals. As an example, one might easily conceive a question of unbundling operators in the energy sector,

---

intended to serve as a dispute settlement body for mainly inter-state claims based on the agreement only without access for any private individuals.

1014 *UNCTAD*, World Investment Report, 2016, p. 105.

1015 Cf. also: *Hindelang*, AVR Vol. 53 (2015), 68, 74 ff; for the opposite, considering that there can be no risk as the CJEU expressly admitted this type of proceedings in private arbitration, which should be transposed to mixed arbitrations: *Engel*, SchiedsVZ, 2015, 218, 221; *Kerkemeyer*, EuZW, 2016, 10, 13 f.

1016 *Hindelang*, AVR Vol. 53 (2015), 68, 72; *Kerkemeyer*, EuZW, 2016, 10, 14; *Clodfelter*, Santa Clara Jour. of Int. Law Vol. 12, Iss. 1 (2013), 159, 180 f.

1017 *Hindelang*, AVR Vol. 53 (2015), 68, 72; *Kerkemeyer*, EuZW, 2016, 10, 14; *Clodfelter*, Santa Clara Jour. of Int. Law Vol. 12, Iss. 1 (2013), 159, 180 f.

1018 Cf. for the use of the term '*spillover*' to describe the *de facto* effects of diverging interpretations by the CJEU and arbitral tribunals: *Hindelang*, AVR Vol. 53 (2015), 68, 72 ff and *Lang*, Der EuGH und die Investor-Staat-Streitbeilegung in TTIP und CETA (Beit. zum Transnat. Wirt.-R, Vol. 138, 2015), p. 9; *Kerkemeyer*, EuZW, 2016, 10, 14 f; rejecting this argument: *Stier*, Arbitration International Vol. 31 (2015), 163, 168 f.

based on the regulation (2009/72/EC or 2009/73/EC) being brought before an arbitral tribunal. Although the CJEU might have decided that those regulations are in perfect compliance with EU law, the arbitral tribunal may still consider the act based on the regulation to be a breach of the IIA. The same would apply for the *Micula-Case*.[1019] The Commission decided to oblige Romania to revoke certain benefits granted to the investors (i.e. certain incentives promised to the investors to develop a disfavoured region in Romania). The arbitral tribunal however declared the revocation to be a breach of the FET standard. Through the attribution of damages in the award, *de facto* the investor obtains its benefits.[1020] The CJEU's ruling on the Commission's decision qualifying the benefits as state aid would be worthless, undermining any *effet utile* to these provisions.[1021] Still this is not a legally binding impact on the interpretation of EU law. However, the *de facto* implication is tremendous as for investors not being protected by an IIA, the same measure would be illegal under EU law, whereas others will – at the final stage – obtain state aid notwithstanding the prohibition in Art. 107 TFEU.[1022] But even for cases with smaller implications, the

---

1019 *Ioan Micula, Viorel Micula & others vs. Romania*, 11.12.2013 – ICSID Case No. ARB/05/20 - Final Award; cf. also: *Hindelang*, AVR Vol. 53 (2015), 68, 74 f and *Lang*, Der EuGH und die Investor-Staat-Streitbeilegung in TTIP und CETA (Beit. zum Transnat. Wirt.-R, Vol. 138, 2015), p. 9 f, both with a reference to the award in *Micula* as well; for a summary of the facts: *Peterson*, IA Reporter Vol. 9, No. 6 (2016), 7, 8 ff.

1020 *Kleinheisterkamp*, JIEL Vol. 15, No. 1 (2012), 85, 92; *Kerkemeyer*, EuZW, 2016, 10, 16; *Hindelang*, AVR Vol. 53 (2015), 68, 74 f; *Tietje/Wackernagel*, JWIT Vol. 16, Iss. 2 (2015), 205, 222; *Lang*, Der EuGH und die Investor-Staat-Streitbeilegung in TTIP und CETA (Beit. zum Transnat. Wirt.-R, Vol. 138, 2015), p. 10; Although generally reluctant, this seems to be admitted by *Dimopoulos*, LIEI Vol. 39, No. 4 (2012), 447, 470 as well.

1021 *Hindelang/Reuling et al.*, Investor State Dispute Settlement Provisions in the EU's International Investment Agreements, 04/09/2014, p. 147 f; *Kerkemeyer*, EuZW, 2016, 10, 15; in so far also: *Eilmansberger*, CMLR Vol. 46 (2009), 383, 406; *Hindelang*, LIEI Vol. 39, Iss. 2 (2012), 179, 197; *Tietje/Wackernagel*, JWIT Vol. 16, Iss. 2 (2015), 205, 222; this is ignored by *Ahner*, Investor-Staat-Schiedsverfahren nach Europäischem Unionsrecht, 2015, p. 224 who considers the potential pressure on the CJEU to change its jurisprudence following contradicting awards by arbitral tribunal as the purpose of a neutral dispute settlement mechanism in IIAs. This is highly doubtful regarding (a) the supranational role of the CJEU and (b) keeping in mind that the question is whether existing IIAs are compatible with the autonomy of EU law.

1022 *Hindelang*, AVR Vol. 53 (2015), 68, 74 f; *Tietje/Wackernagel*, JWIT Vol. 16, Iss. 2 (2015), 205, 222.

risk of diverging *de facto* interpretation is well set. Even arbitral decisions which are limited to deny the scope of application of EU law to a certain behaviour of an investor might create similar distortions. *Inter alia*, as to the interpretation given by the CJEU, certain rules of EU law might apply to the investor, whereas arbitral tribunals may set a completely different legal environment for the investment with all potential consequences.[1023] This is even aggravated considering the fact that arbitral tribunals tend to rely on previous decisions (*de facto precedents / stare decisis*).[1024] A measure or provision of EU law having been considered unlawful by one tribunal is very likely to be considered unlawful by several following tribunals as well. Hence, the diverging interpretation reoccurs at various occasions. *Hindelang* even raises doubts whether such decisions by arbitral tribunals might influence further rulings by the CJEU or member state courts in their interpretation of EU law seeking to adopt a converging view in order to prevent further disruptions.[1025] But even without such an adoption, given the considerable importance attributed by the CJEU to an uniform application to preserve the autonomy of the legal system in the EU, the impediment by an unequal interpretation and handling of the same factual case is a major distraction.[1026] Furthermore, the CJEU expressly stated that even the *risk* of some member states considering an interpretation of EU law by any other institution than the CJEU as binding, is a non-tolerable risk for the autonomy of the EU's legal order.[1027] This risk how-

---

1023 Cf. also: *Kerkemeyer*, EuZW, 2016, 10, 15.

1024 Cf. for this evolution in international investment law: *Commission*, JOIA Vol. 24, Iss. 2 (2007), 129; *Reinisch*, Austrian Arbitration Yearbook, 2008, 495. *Potestà*, ICSID Rev., 2013, 88, 90: *"subsequent tribunals feel they have a 'duty to adopt solutions established in a series of consistent cases'(...)"*; *Lang*, Der EuGH und die Investor-Staat-Streitbeilegung in TTIP und CETA (Beit. zum Transnat. Wirt.-R, Vol. 138, 2015), p. 12 questions this influence by arguing that *ad hoc* tribunals could never have the same authority, which is doubtful given the *stare decisis doctrine*.

1025 *Hindelang*, AVR Vol. 53 (2015), 68, 75; for the contrary opinion and denying any *de facto* impediment (but for the case of potential future EU agreements with third countries): *Dimopoulos*, LIEI Vol. 39, No. 4 (2012), 447, 469.

1026 Cf. also: *Kerkemeyer*, EuZW, 2016, 10, 15; *Hindelang*, LIEI Vol. 39, Iss. 2 (2012), 179; 197; However, *Eilmansberger*, CMLR Vol. 46 (2009), 383, 405 f agrees that there is a risk of opposite decisions, but considers e.g. infringement porceedings to be a sufficient safeguard.

1027 *CJEU*, 14.12.1991 – Opinion 1/91 - EEC-Treaty = ECLI:EU:C:1991:490, para 63; also admitting that a risk is sufficient: *Hindelang*, AVR Vol. 53 (2015), 68, 76.

ever, is clearly conceivable by arbitral tribunals in international investment proceedings.[1028]

3. Circumvention of preliminary ruling procedure – disrupting the interaction of the courts (criterion n° 4)

When assessing the effects of a separate dispute settlement mechanism on the specific nature of the EU's legal order, the CJEU paid particular importance to the preliminary ruling procedure in Art. 267 TFEU, which enables the interaction of the member state courts with the CJEU on matters of EU law. Arbitral tribunals are deprived of such interaction possibilities by ordinary means, as the CJEU does not consider them to be "*courts of the member states*" in terms of Art. 267 TFEU.[1029] Hence, the arbitral tribunals will not be entitled to interact with the CJEU regarding questions of interpretation of EU law. Thus, it follows from the application of the arbitration clause that national courts of the member states will be deprived of their function to interact with the CJEU at least for the main stage of the proceedings.[1030]

A couple of tribunals argued that the preliminary ruling procedure is not mandatory for all member state courts.[1031] As they would also have a discretion whether to engage the procedure, EU law would accept that the procedure is not mandatory. Hence, if through arbitral tribunals the procedure could not be engaged either, this could not be a reason to consider the arbitration clauses incompatible.[1032] However, the CJEU clearly stated that

1028 Cf. generally also supporting this view: *Parish*, EJIL Vol. 23, No. 1, 141, 148 f, with reference to the subjects, implications and frequency in which (important) matters of EU law are subject to investment proceedings; cf. also: *Clodfelter*, Santa Clara Jour. of Int. Law Vol. 12, Iss. 1 (2013), 159, 180 f; for the opposite: *Lang*, Der EuGH und die Investor-Staat-Streitbeilegung in TTIP und CETA (Beit. zum Transnat. Wirt.-R, Vol. 138, 2015), p. 12.

1029 *CJEU*, 23.03.1982 – C-102/81 - Nordsee = ECLI:EU:C:1982:107, para 13 and *CJEU*, 01.06.1999 – C-126/97 - Eco Swiss = ECLI:EU:C:1999:269, para 34; cf. also: *Dimopoulos*, CMLR Vol. 48, No. 1 (2011), 63, 87; *Burgstaller*, LIEI Vol. 39, No. 2 (2012), 207, 219 f.

1030 *Hindelang*, AVR Vol. 53 (2015), 68, 86; *Lang*, Der EuGH und die Investor-Staat-Streitbeilegung in TTIP und CETA (Beit. zum Transnat. Wirt.-R, Vol. 138, 2015), p. 16; *Burgstaller*, LIEI Vol. 39, No. 2 (2012), 207, 219 f.

1031 This is also pointed out by *Parish*, EJIL Vol. 23, No. 1, 141, 142.

1032 *Euram vs. Slovak Republic*, 22.10.2012 – PCA Case no. 2010-17: First Award on Jurisdiction, para 250 and 252. As to the tribunal, even national courts of

the possibility to make use of the preliminary ruling procedure is a substantial safeguard for the autonomy of the legal order in the EU.[1033] Second, the member state courts are under a certain pressure to make use of the procedure. The non-observance of Art. 267 TFEU could lead to infringement proceedings or the possibility of claims for extra-contractual liability. Third, as already pointed out, the criteria are not of an absolute character. They serve as a determinant for the degree to which the specific characteristics of EU law are endangered, which might lead to an incompatibility with autonomy of its legal order.

Other tribunals stated that private arbitration is a commonplace in the EU, expressly admitted by the CJEU in the *Eco Swiss-Case,* and thus could not lead to an incompatibility with EU law.[1034]

Indeed, as previously pointed out, arbitration between private parties has been admitted by the CJEU in *Eco Swiss*. However, the tribunals seem to prejudge the case.

First, the *Eco Swiss* decision contained a considerable constraint. The CJEU expressly referred to the possibility of setting-aside proceedings or enforcement proceedings which enable national courts of the EU member states to activate the preliminary ruling procedure on a later stage of the proceedings and to ensure compliance of the award with the interpretation of EU law given by the CJEU. Through this safeguard the respect of fundamental provisions of EU law, such as e.g. the rules on competition law contained in Art. 101 ff TFEU which were in question at this case, could

---

last resort do not necessarily refer the question to the CJEU. By applying the *acte clair* doctrine, they might apply and interpret EU law if they consider that there is no reasonable doubt about the interpretation and application. Whether courts admit to have reasonable doubts or not, would be subject to a wide range of discretionary power; the same has been argued by the tribunal in *Achmea vs. Slovak Republic*, 26.10.2012 – PCA Case No. 2008-13 - Award on Jurisdiction, Arbitrability and Suspension, para 278 ff and *Electrabel vs. Hungary*, 30.11.2012 – ICSID Case No. ARB/07/19: Decision on Jurisdiction, Applicable Law and Liability, para 4.148.

1033 Cf. also: *Hindelang*, LIEI Vol. 39, Iss. 2 (2012), 179, 197; *Hindelang*, AVR Vol. 53 (2015), 68, 76; *Burgstaller*, LIEI Vol. 39, No. 2 (2012), 207, 217 and 219 f.

1034 *Achmea vs. Slovak Republic*, 26.10.2012 – PCA Case No. 2008-13 - Award on Jurisdiction, Arbitrability and Suspension, para 274; *Euram vs. Slovak Republic*, 22.10.2012 – PCA Case no. 2010-17: First Award on Jurisdiction, para 256 ff ; *Electrabel vs. Hungary*, 30.11.2012 – ICSID Case No. ARB/07/19: Decision on Jurisdiction, Applicable Law and Liability, para 4.153 and 4.155; cf. also: *Engel*, SchiedsVZ, 2015, 218, 221.

be ensured.[1035] For investment arbitration proceedings, these considerations are not necessarily true. Regarding proceedings under the ICSID-Convention, the annulment proceedings will not enable any interaction with the CJEU, as the annulment committee cannot be considered to be a "*court*" under Art. 267 TFEU as well. When it comes to enforce an ICSID-Award, such respect is not guaranteed either. If enforcement is sought outside the EU, which is highly probably given the (probably sufficient) assets each state holds even in non-member states, no control will be exercised at all.[1036] But even if enforcement is sought within an EU member state, the consequences are highly doubtful. Art. 53, 54 ICSID-Convention in principle provides for an unhindered enforcement of the award without any further preconditions.[1037] Even if some scholars (cf. *supra*) doubt that an award contrary to EU law could be enforced, this uncertainty presents a major risk to the autonomy of the legal order as even awards heavily disrespecting EU law could potentially be enforced in or outside the EU member states.[1038]

Second, it is rather doubtful if the setting of private arbitration in the *Eco Swiss-Case* can that easily be transposed to mixed arbitrations in in-

---

1035 *Wehland*, ICLQ Vol. 58, Iss. 2 (2009), 297, 319; *Engel*, SchiedsVZ, 2015, 218, 221; *Komninos*, CMLR Iss. 37 (2000), 459, 468 f.

1036 Cf. also: *Kleinheisterkamp*, JIEL Vol. 15, No. 1 (2012), 85, 101 in footnote 76; *Hindelang*, LIEI Vol. 39, Iss. 2 (2012), 179, 198; *Hindelang*, AVR Vol. 53 (2015), 68, 75; *Ahner*, Investor-Staat-Schiedsverfahren nach Europäischem Unionsrecht, 2015, p. 211 f; *Dimopoulos*, CMLR Vol. 48, No. 1 (2011), 63, 87 f.

1037 Cf. also: *Hindelang*, LIEI Vol. 39, Iss. 2 (2012), 179, 198; *Kleinheisterkamp*, JIEL Vol. 15, No. 1 (2012), 85, 101 in footnote 76; for a summary of the diverging views: *Eilmansberger*, CMLR Vol. 46 (2009), 383, 427 f; cf. also: *Ahner*, Investor-Staat-Schiedsverfahren nach Europäischem Unionsrecht, 2015, p. 211 f; *Dimopoulos*, CMLR Vol. 48, No. 1 (2011), 63, 87 f.

1038 In this sense also: *Komninos*, CMLR Iss. 37 (2000), 459, 467 ff, particularily p. 469: who considers the limits in *Eco Swiss* to be necessary to prevent forum shopping which heavily endangers the autonomy of the EU's legal order; *Eilmansberger*, CMLR Vol. 46 (2009), 383, 427 f agrees that it is doubtful if an ICSID-award can be challenged, but considers that EU courts would probably exercise such control in line with the principle or primacy; this was also advanced by the Slovak Republic in *Achmea vs. Slovak Republic*, 26.10.2012 – PCA Case No. 2008-13 - Award on Jurisdiction, Arbitrability and Suspension, para 116. Against this approach and denying an incompatibility: *Wehland*, ICLQ Vol. 58, Iss. 2 (2009), 297, 319; *Bücheler/Vasiljevic*, SchiedsVZ, 2016, 328, 338 and *Kottmann*, EuZW, 2016, 512, 519.

vestment disputes.[1039] Private arbitration is a dispute between private parties. It is a crucial element of their private autonomy to submit themselves to any potential legal framework worldwide with all its consequences.[1040] In principle the parties are deliberately free to shape their relations, which might also include the decision to refer their dispute to a completely different legal framework. The substantial interest of a state, to ensure certain fundamental values, is ensured through the recognition and enforcement procedures, whenever the parties' agreement takes contact with the respective state (i.e. if the parties seek to enforce the award in the respective state).[1041] If the parties decide to submit their dispute to a foreign legal order and enforce it in this foreign order, a different legal order does not have any necessity to intervene as its own legal framework remains unaffected.[1042] Under this lens indeed submitting a dispute to an arbitral tribunal does not even necessarily challenge the function of a member state court as 'ordinary' court in the judicial system.[1043]

However, mixed arbitration proceedings necessarily challenge state measures undertaken on the territory of the host state. Thus, there is *per se* a point of contact of the dispute with the host state. Those disputes, regarding state measures in the host state, would in principle always be submitted to the national courts of the member states as any other state would miss the competence to interfere with this measures. Hence, in investment arbitration disputes the subject matter of the dispute and the parties involved form a completely different setting than in purely private arbitrations.[1044] The result of an enforcement outside the EU would indeed

---

1039 This argument of comparing private arbitration to mixed arbitraiton is advanced by: *Wehland*, ICLQ Vol. 58, Iss. 2 (2009), 297, 319; *Engel*, SchiedsVZ, 2015, 218, 221.

1040 Cf. *inter alia*: *Ferrari* in: Ferrari/Kieninger/Mankoswki Internat. Vertragsrecht, Art. 3 Regulation (EC) 593/2008 - Rome I, para 1 f; *Kropholler/Neuhaus*, Internationales Privatrecht, 6. Edn. (2006), p. 290 – 301; also admitted by *Parish*, EJIL Vol. 23, No. 1, 141, 147 who however questions why states should not be entitled to follow this example.

1041 *Sänger* in: Sänger/ZPO, Art. 1061 German Code of Civil Procedure, para 15; *Pavic* in: *Knahr* (Ed.), Investment and commercial arbitration, 2010, p. 131, 141 f.

1042 Slightly different however: *Parish*, EJIL Vol. 23, No. 1, 141, 151.

1043 Cf. also: *Parish*, EJIL Vol. 23, No. 1, 141, 147 f.

1044 This is questioned by *Parish*, EJIL Vol. 23, No. 1, 141, 147 f who considers that states may as well choose to submit their dispute to any other forum; however *Komninos*, CMLR Iss. 37 (2000), 459, 469 seems to support this view, when stating that mandatory provisions of EU law involving in particular pub-

be that exclusively alien courts would have to evaluate a state measure of a member state, which is necessarily linked to the host state and at least potentially to EU law. From this perspective the circumvention of the preliminary ruling procedure has a considerable different importance than in the *Eco Swiss-Decision*. Indeed, the uniform application of EU law may be heavily endangered through arbitral proceedings.

4. Further safeguards to ensure the uniform application of EU law (criterion n° 5)

One could argue that the uniform application can still be enforced through other means such as the infringement mechanisms provided for in Art. 258 to 260 TFEU or the claim for damages under the extra-contractual liability of either the EU or the member states in case of failure to (correctly) apply EU law.[1045] The importance attributed to such a mechanism as a complement to ensure the respect of EU law by national courts and their member states as well to prevent a circumvention of Art. 267 TFEU was stressed in the *PC-Opinion.*[1046]

When member states or courts fail to apply EU law or courts (erroneously) deny to activate the preliminary ruling procedure, the persons concerned could seek for damages under the extra-contractual liability. The Commission or other member states might (additionally or alternatively) engage infringement proceedings for a violation of EU law under Art. 259, 260 TFEU.[1047]

In the *PC-Opinion* these mechanisms could not apply, because the Court was supposed to have a distinct legal personality. Consequently, its

---

lic aspects (such as competition law) need to be evaluated under a certain minimum standard of control regarding their compliance with EU law and cannot be left entirely to private arbitrations outside any control mechanism. However, public law espects are the very essence of mixed arbitrations.

1045 This is advanced by the *Electrabel-Tribunal* as being a suffienct safeguard, cf.: *Electrabel vs. Hungary*, 30.11.2012 – ICSID Case No. ARB/07/19: Decision on Jurisdiction, Applicable Law and Liability, para 4.159 ff.

1046 *CJEU*, 08.03.2011 – Opinion 1/09 - Patents Court = ECLI:EU:C:2011:123, para 86 f; cf. also: *Hindelang*, AVR Vol. 53 (2015), 68, 77 in footnote 39; *Eilmansberger*, CMLR Vol. 46 (2009), 383, 405 f also stresses out these possibilities as sufficient to „*rescue*“ mixed arbitration provisons in IIAs.

1047 *Electrabel vs. Hungary*, 30.11.2012 – ICSID Case No. ARB/07/19: Decision on Jurisdiction, Applicable Law and Liability, para 4.159 ff.

acts could not be attributed to the member states or the EU.[1048] Arbitral tribunals do not have a distinct legal personality which would lead to the same setting as in the PC-Opinion. Hence *a priori* the setting is different. However, it is rather doubtful whether acts of arbitral tribunals could be attributed to the member states.[1049] Under Art. 258, 259 TFEU only acts of the member states' organs are potential causes of action.[1050] Acts by private individuals will only be attributed to a member state, if the latter can sufficiently determine and influence their action.[1051] Arbitral tribunals are, by their very nature, neither state organs, nor does a member state have considerable influence on their action. Thus, to attribute the potential violations of EU law through the arbitral tribunal, one would need to base such a claim on the prior conclusion of the IIA (as through the conclusion of the IIA the host state enabled the access to arbitration).[1052] A similar approach has also been adopted regarding unclear legislative acts by member states, which might lead national courts to ignore or misapply EU law. Given that courts as judicial bodies are considered to be generally independent from the state's influence, this misapplication of laws by courts may only constitute a violation of EU law, if it occurs in a considerable amount of cases.[1053] If only few courts ignore EU law, the attribution of its violation via the legislative act remains impossible.[1054] Arbitral tribunals are ad-hoc tribunals which might respect precedents but are in no way bound by any case law. Furthermore, the majority of decisions is not published. Hence, it is impossible to determine, whether EU law is misapplied in a considerable amount of cases (and if this misapplication is due to the IIA not sufficiently ensuring the compliance of arbitral tribunals with EU

1048 Cf. also: *Hindelang*, LIEI Vol. 39, Iss. 2 (2012), 179, 204.

1049 For the opposite: *Hindelang*, AVR Vol. 53 (2015), 68, 77 who seems to consider that such an attribution is possible.

1050 *Calliess/Ruffert*, in: *Calliess/Ruffert EUV/AEUV.*, Art. 258, para 27 f.

1051 *Calliess/Ruffert*, in: *Calliess/Ruffert EUV/AEUV.*, Art. 258, para 27 f.

1052 *Ehricke* in: Streinz EUV/AEUV, Art. 258 TFEU, para 9; this also seems to be the Commission's standpoint in the *Micula vs Romania* Case: *European Commission*, Commission Decision (EU) 2015/1470 - notified under C(2015) 2112: Decision on State aid SA.38517 (2014/C) (ex 2014/NN) implemented by Romania-Arbitral award Micula v Romania of 11 December 2013 (30/03/2015), para 102; cf. also: *Parish*, EJIL Vol. 23, No. 1, 141, 152.

1053 *CJEU*, 09.12.2003 – C-129/00 - Commission vs. Italy = ECLI:EU:C:2003:656, para 32 f.

1054 *CJEU*, 09.12.2003 – C-129/00 - Commission vs. Italy = ECLI:EU:C:2003:656, para 32 f.

law). Thus, the possibility of other sanctions or control mechanisms to ensure the uniform application of EU law is more than doubtful as well.[1055]

5. Contravention of the principle of mutual trust (criterion n° 6)

Arbitration clauses in IIAs potentially also conflict with the principle of mutual trust among EU member states, undermining the autonomy of the EU's legal order.

The CJEU held that:

> „the regulation [is] based on the principle of mutual trust between Member States in the fact that their respective national legal systems are capable of providing an equivalent and effective protection of fundamental rights, recognised at European Union level, in particular, in the Charter of Fundamental Rights.“[1056]

The importance of this principle to guarantee the observance of the principle of autonomy in the EU has once again be strengthened by the Court in the *Opinion 2/13*:

> "That principle requires, particularly with regard to the area of freedom, security and justice, each of those States, save in exceptional circumstances, *to consider all the other Member States to be complying with EU law* and particularly with the fundamental rights recognised by EU law
>
> (…), save in exceptional cases, they may not check whether that other Member State has actually, in a specific case, observed the fundamental rights guaranteed by the EU."[1057]

The arbitration mechanism established by an arbitration clause might enable such a control to be exercised by the arbitral tribunal. It needs to be admitted that the arbitral tribunal will not directly question the compatibility of another member state's actions with EU law. It will predominantly evaluate the conformity of the host state's actions with the IIA. However, whenever a conflict with provisions of EU law occurs this also includes or at least might include the analysis by the arbitral tribunal whether the host state observed provisions of EU law. Thus, the arbitral tribunal would (also) exercise a control of another member state's observance of EU law.

1055 Cf. also: *Parish*, EJIL Vol. 23, No. 1, 141, 143.

1056 *CJEU*, 22.12.2010 – C-491/10 PPU - Aguirre Zarraga = ECLI:EU:C:2010:828, para 70 [emphasis added].

1057 *CJEU*, 18.12.2014 – Opinion 2/13 - ECHR = ECLI:EU:C:2014:2454, para 192 [emphasis added]; cf. also: *Schill*, JWIT Vol. 16, No. 3 (2015), 379, 381.

This control might include fundamental rights but is not necessarily limited to those rights. It might as well be a control of observance of internal market provisions or secondary legislation.

However, the type of provision the control is exercised upon is irrelevant. The principle of mutual trust is not limited to the observance of fundamental rights. It has a multitude of manifestations differing widely in the type of EU law or national member states laws concerned.[1058] The underlying idea, and thus the guideline to observe if the principle is set aside, is the risk for the autonomy of the EU's legal order.[1059] The control of a member state's compliance with EU law should in general only be exercised by the CJEU, as any other method of control would (at least potentially) disrupt the uniform interpretation and application of EU law. At the same time the uniformity of its application and interpretation are substantial provisions for the functioning of the entire legal framework in the EU.[1060]

1058 Regarding the fundamental freedoms the principle has been developed by the CJEU since *CJEU*, 20.02.1979 – C-120/78 - Cassis de Dijon = ECLI:EU:C:1979:42 stating that the member states need – except exceptional reasons – to recognise the (potentially) diverging standards of production and distribution, cf. *Oppermann/Classen et al.*, 5. Edn. (2011), §22, para 31; the same has *inter alia* been admitted for services legally provided in one member state, which needs to be recognised by all member states (*CJEU*, 25.07.1991 – C-76/90 - Saeger vs. Dennemeyer = ECLI:EU:C:1991:331), cf. : *Oppermann/Classen et al.*, 5. Edn. (2011) § 25, para 14. In matters of procedural law the CJEU further developed the principle of mutual trust, including the general principle that – except particular circumstances such as a violation of a member states public order – judgements from other member states need to be reciprocally recognised: Regulation EU/1215/2012 - Brussels Regulation, Official Journal of the European Union L 351 (12/12/2012), 1, cf. also: *Oppermann/Classen et al.*, 5. Edn. (2011) § 36, para 32 ff. Even in the – traditionally protectionist – subject matter of judicial cooperation in criminal matters, the principle of mutual trust has been at the origin of the European arrest warrant and surrender procedures between Member States (Council Framework Decision 2002/584/JHA of 13 June 2002), cf. also: *Oppermann/Classen et al.*, 5. Edn. (2011), § 37, para 9.

1059 The Court states that clearly in *CJEU*, 18.12.2014 – Opinion 2/13 - ECHR = ECLI:EU:C:2014:2454, para 194: "*even though EU law imposes an obligation of mutual trust between those Member States, [the ECHR-accession] is liable to upset the underlying balance of the EU and undermine the autonomy of EU law (...)*"; also given the variety of cases in which the principle applied and the broad terms of the CJEU, it cannot be limited to any specific area of EU law.

1060 Cf. also: *Kleinheisterkamp*, JIEL Vol. 15, No. 1 (2012), 85, 102 f. This is challenged by *Söderlund*, JOIA Vol. 24, Iss. 5 (2007), 455, 465 who considers the

The dispute settlement mechanism in IIAs is deliberately based on the idea to internationalise the conflict between investor and host state. This approach was based on the underlying idea that national remedies do not provide an adequate protection for the investor, either because these courts might be biased, proceedings might take too long or because basic principles of legal and judicial protection are most likely not observed.[1061] Hence, it is the very essence of the international investment arbitration system to mistrust national courts as objective judges *vis-à-vis* the investor. However, this fundamentally clashes with the principle of mutual trust, at least in *inter se* relations.[1062]

It was also objected to this idea that – consequently – any national arbitration law adopted by EU member states would violate the principle of mutual trust as the state would express distrust *vis-à-vis* its own national courts.[1063] This objection is unconvincing. First, in private arbitrations the arbitral tribunal would not evaluate the acts of a member state. It will apply the law designated by the parties to acts of private parties. Thus, there is no control of sovereign acts of a host state, which largely differs the situation from investor-state arbitrations. Second, EU law does not prohibit a

---

mutual trust principle to be soft law only; a position which can hardly be followed given the recent decisions by the CJEU.

1061 Cf.: *Sattorova*, LIEI Vol. 39, No. 2 (2012), 223, 226 f; *Engel*, SchiedsVZ, 2015, 218, 219; *Sornarajah*, 3. Edn. (2010), p. 217; *Herdegen*, 10. Edn. (2014), p. 353; cf. also: *Kleinheisterkamp*, JIEL Vol. 15, No. 1 (2012), 85, 101 f; *Dimopoulos*, CMLR Vol. 48, No. 1 (2011), 63, 92; *Ghouri*, Int. A.L.R. Vol. 14, No. 6, 189, 190. This argument is also advanced by the European Commission: as to the Commission, which is correct in the authors view, the principle of mutual trust would require all member states to consider all other member states not to influence their courts and that any national courts are judging the case absolutely unbiased. Hence, by applying the *mutual trust* principle, the justification for an internationalisation of the conflict, eludes and – on the contrary – "*reveals mistrust in courts of the courts of EU member states*", cf.: *European Commission*, Amicus Curia Brief filed in Achmea (former Eureko BV) vs. Slovak Republic (PCA Case n°2008-13) - arbitration proceedings, 07/07/2010, para 34; also cf. paras 49 ff.

1062 Clearly supporting this view: *Dimopoulos*, CMLR Vol. 48, No. 1 (2011), 63, 92; this was also supported by the Czech Republic and the European Commission, cf.: *Eastern Sugar vs. Czech Republic*, 27.03.2007 – SCC No. 088/2004 - Partial award, para 107 and 110 with a main focus on the breach of the principle of mutual trust, which would form part of the inherent principles of the judicial framework in the EU.

1063 Cf. also: *Higher Regional Court Frankfurt*, SchiedsVZ (2013), 119, 10.05.2012 – 26 SchH 11/10, 125.

state to consider its *own* courts to be untrustworthy. The principle of mutual trust perfectly allows EU member states to adopt different regulations regarding their appeal procedures. However, the principle prohibits a member state to consider the courts of *other* member states to be untrustworthy.

6. Overall assessment of the criteria n° 1 to n° 6

Given the diverse effects by which the arbitration clause contained in IIAs endangers the uniform application of EU law and its autonomy, the arbitration clause violates the specific characteristics of the EU's legal order and judicial framework.[1064] There are only few safeguards, which are even uncertain, to prevent arbitral tribunals from large impediments on these specific characteristics. Even more, the mechanism, such as it is currently shaped, is rather designed to expressly circumvent EU law wherever possible. The former resistance expressed by arbitral tribunals and even several national courts to adopt an unbiased view on the conflict demonstrates these risks. Given that, as to the CJEU, in the overall assessment a considerable risk to impede on the autonomy of EU law is sufficient, mixed arbitration clauses in IIAs are incompatible with EU law.

IV. Interim conclusions on the arbitration clause's incompatibility with the autonomy of the EU's legal order and its specific characteristics

It was demonstrated that the arbitration clause is incompatible with EU law as it impedes severely on the autonomy of the EU's legal order and its specific characteristics. Hence, EU law and the IIAs arbitration clause conflict. Given that EU law is considered as international law applicable to the arbitration dispute and the relevant conflict rule is the principle of primacy, the latter will deny effect to the arbitration clause. As an immediate consequence, the arbitral tribunal lacks jurisdiction. After a brief outlook on the consequences and particularities of mixed agreements (cf. *infra* V.), further potential incompatibilities of the arbitration clause with EU law will be analysed (cf.: "*B. Incompatibility of the arbitration clause*

1064 For the opposite: *Lang*, Der EuGH und die Investor-Staat-Streitbeilegung in TTIP und CETA (Beit. zum Transnat. Wirt.-R, Vol. 138, 2015), p. 16 f.

with EU law due to the violation of competencies" and "*C. Incompatibility of the arbitration clause with the principle of non-discrimination* ").

V. Excursus for mixed agreements

Whenever mixed agreements (such as e.g. the Energy Charter Treaty, "*ECT*") are concerned the arguments mentioned above – regarding intra-EU relations – apply as well. However, it is worth mentioning that in those cases, two further difficulties occur.

Especially in the case of the ECT, the *Electrabel-Tribunal* underlined that the EU itself is party to the investment agreement. As to the tribunal, through signing the treaty, the EU admitted that they accept the jurisdiction of an arbitral tribunal with regard to investment disputes.[1065] However, signing a treaty does not mean that the treaty itself and the provisions contained therein are lawful with regard to EU law.[1066]

One might take the example of a bill passing the parliament, which may as well be considered unconstitutional by the courts. Admitting that the executive and legislative powers are capable of committing acts contrary to the constitution, is one of the most predominant features of the modern understanding of the rule of law.[1067] This also applies in the EU context. An international treaty signed by the EU, can as well be contrary to EU primary law.[1068] However, this will not affect the external validity of the treaty, as long as the competences were respected.[1069] The mere fact that the EU signed a treaty like the ECT thus cannot be considered as a decisive argument for the compatibility of the arbitration clause with EU law.

Mixed agreements however reveal another difficult issue questioning the compatibility of EU law and arbitration clauses under a different an-

---

1065 *Söderlund*, JOIA Vol. 24, Iss. 5 (2007), 455, 462 f.

1066 *Dimopoulos*, LIEI Vol. 39, No. 4 (2012), 447, 450; *Dimopoulos*, CMLR Vol. 48, No. 1 (2011), 63, 70.

1067 *Grzeszick* in: Maunz/Dürig GG, Art. 20 GG, para 37 in German Constitutional Law referred to as "*materieller Rechtsstaatsbegriff*", *Maurer*, Grundlagen, Verfassungsorgane, Staatsfunktionen, 5. Edn. (2007), p. 204; cf. also for the European context: *Streinz*, 10. Edn. (2016), para 530 with reference to *CJEU*, 27.11.2012 – C-370/12 - Pringle vs. Ireland (ESM) = ECLI:EU:C:2012:756 which will be analysed *infra* (II.).

1068 *Dimopoulos*, LIEI Vol. 39, No. 4 (2012), 447, 450.

1069 *Dimopoulos*, LIEI Vol. 39, No. 4 (2012), 447, 450; *Dimopoulos*, CMLR Vol. 48, No. 1 (2011), 63, 70.

gle. As both, the EU and its member states are party to mixed agreements, they may – theoretically – both be sought in arbitration proceedings for having violated the substantive guarantees under an IIA.[1070] After an investor filed its claim, the arbitral tribunal – or a different mechanism provided to do so, as it is conceived in the CETA-Draft-Agreement – would need to determine the question whether the EU or its member states are the correct respondents.[1071] Determining this question would potentially imply the necessity to resolve the question of competencies within the EU.[1072] However, the CJEU considers this task to be one of the cornerstones of the autonomy of the legal order, which was expressly (re-) affirmed in the *Opinion 2/13*.[1073] Hence, to assure the compatibility of any arbitration clause contained in a mixed agreement, it would be necessary (besides eliminating the other existing difficulties) to create a mechanism of allocation of the respondent which safeguard's the CJEU's hostility to this particular subject.[1074]

B. Incompatibility of the arbitration clause with EU law due to the violation of competencies exclusively attributed to the EU?

Besides the incompatibility with the autonomy of the EU's legal order, the arbitration clause needs to be evaluated with regard to the member states' *competencies* to agree upon a separate dispute settlement mechanism outside the framework of the European Treaties. This is a question which is

1070 *Hindelang*, AVR Vol. 53 (2015), 68, 80 ff.

1071 Cf. *Hindelang*, AVR Vol. 53 (2015), 68, 81 ff for the general description of the problem and the mechanism provided in the CETA-Draft agreement; cf. also: *Schill*, JWIT Vol. 16, No. 3 (2015), 379, 384.

1072 *Hindelang*, AVR Vol. 53 (2015), 68, 81; *Lang*, Der EuGH und die Investor-Staat-Streitbeilegung in TTIP und CETA (Beit. zum Transnat. Wirt.-R, Vol. 138, 2015), p. 12 and 14.

1073 *CJEU*, 18.12.2014 – Opinion 2/13 - ECHR = ECLI:EU:C:2014:2454, para 224; cf. also: *Hindelang*, AVR Vol. 53 (2015), 68, 82 f; the statement was already the cornerstone of the *Mox-Plant* decision, cf.: *Lang*, Der EuGH und die Investor-Staat-Streitbeilegung in TTIP und CETA (Beit. zum Transnat. Wirt.-R, Vol. 138, 2015), p. 13.

1074 *Hindelang*, AVR Vol. 53 (2015), 68, 83, cf. Part IV. for further implications.

predominantly treated within the question of extra-EU IIAs.[1075] However, the question also needs to be addressed in the context of intra-EU IIAs.

Various awards stressed out that private arbitration, based on national arbitration laws, was judged admissible by the CJEU *inter alia* in the *Eco Swiss-Case*. Therefore, mixed arbitration, such as investor-state arbitration, based on IIAs should be perfectly admissible as well.[1076] This argument lacks a sufficient examination of the allocation of competencies between the EU and its member states. It should therefore be analysed whether the member states still had the competence to agree – by virtue of an international agreement – upon a dispute settlement mechanism which is likely to upset essential provisions of EU law, especially state aid provisions, fundamental-freedoms and EU competition law.

It should be kept in mind that in the context of the EU the member states agreed upon a certain distribution of competences between the EU and themselves. This distribution has two consequences. First, the EU is only entitled to act upon conferral of competences by the member states through the European Treaties (Art. 5 (1), (2) TFEU).[1077] Second, the member states limit their sovereignty in the areas, which have been transferred (Art. 2, 3 TFEU).[1078] If the Treaties provide for an exclusive competency of the EU, the member states are precluded from any interaction in this field (Art. 2 (1), Art. 3 TFEU).[1079] In matters of divided competences between the EU and the member states, the later may still act if the EU did not yet use or no longer uses its competences (Art. 2 (2), Art. 3 TFEU).[1080] Hence, if an international agreement among member states containing an arbitration clause falls into the scope of an exclusive competence or in the matters of divided competences where the EU decid-

---

1075 Cf. inter alia: *Burgstaller* in: *Bungenberg/Griebel/Hindelang* (Eds.), International investment law and EU law, 2011, p. 62 ff; *Bungenberg* in: *Bungenberg/Griebel/Hindelang* (Eds.), International investment law and EU law, 2011, p. 29 ff; *Chaisse*, JIEL Vol. 15, No. 1 (2012), 51, 57 ff; *Eilmansberger*, CMLR Vol. 46 (2009), 383, 394 ff; cf. for a comprehensive analysis: *Schmitt*, 2013.

1076 Cf. inter alia: *Euram vs. Slovak Republic*, 22.10.2012 – PCA Case no. 2010-17: First Award on Jurisdiction, para 256; *Achmea vs. Slovak Republic*, 26.10.2012 – PCA Case No. 2008-13 - Award on Jurisdiction, Arbitrability and Suspension, para 274.

1077 *Hobe*, 8. Edn. (2014), para 71.

1078 *Hobe*, 8. Edn. (2014), para 71.

1079 *Schwarze* in: Schwarze EU-Kommentar, Art. 2 TFEU, para 9.

1080 *Hobe*, 8. Edn. (2014), para 71.

ed to exercise its competences, the member states would be precluded to undertake an agreement containing such an arbitration clause.

Member states would especially lack the external competence to conclude an international agreement, if the conditions set forth in Art. 3 (2) TFEU are fulfilled, i.e. if entering into an international agreement may (sufficiently) affect common rules or alter their scope (Art. 3 (2) TFEU). In this case there would be an exclusive competence attributed to the EU.[1081] Regarding international agreement *with non-member states*, this has been developed under the *ERTA-Case* and the following precedents, reshaping at diverse occasions the prerequisites for the admission of an (implicit) exclusive competence of the EU.[1082] The conditions were finally codified in Art. 3 (2) and 216 TFEU with the Lisbon Treaty in 2009.[1083]

Although the *ERTA-Doctrine* (and thus its codification in Art. 3 and 216 TFEU) has been mainly applied to question of external relations of the EU or its member states with non-member states[1084], the principle in Art. 3 (2) TFEU also applies to *inter se* relations.[1085]

This enhancement of the *ERTA-Doctrine* after the revision through the Lisbon Treaty has been clearly underlined by the CJEU in the *Pringle vs.*

1081 *CJEU*, 31.03.1971 – C-22/70 - ERTA = ECLI:EU:C:1971:32, para 15 ff; settled case law since then, reiterated *inter alia* in: *CJEU*, 15.11.1994 – Opinion 1/94 = ECLI:EU:C:1994:384; *CJEU*, 07.02.2006 – Opinion 1/03 - Lugano Agreement = ECLI:EU:C:2006:81; cf. also: *Obwexer* in: v. d. Groeben/Schwarze AEUV/EUV, Art. 3 TFEU, para 40 ff; *Nettesheim* in: Grabitz/Hilf/Nettesheim EUV/AEUV, Art. 3 TFEU, para 40.

1082 *Hobe*, 8. Edn. (2014), para 150 ff.

1083 *Hobe*, 8. Edn. (2014), para 150; *Schroeder*, Grundkurs Europarecht, 4. Edn. (2015), p. 114 f; *Vedder* in: von Heinegg/Vedder EUV/AEUV, Art. 3 TFEU, para 5 ff.

1084 The *ERTA-Case* concerned five of six member states of the former European Economic Area and several non-member states, the Opinion 1/94 concerned the conclusion of the GATT-Treaty, the Opinion 1/2003 dealt with the conlcusion of the Lugano Agreement between the EU member states and the states of the European Free Trade Assocition (except Liechtenstein); the Open-Skies agreements related to several bilateral agreements of EU member states with the United States of America (Joined Cases C-466 to 469; 471 to 472; 475 to 476/98).

1085 *CJEU*, 27.11.2012 – C-370/12 - Pringle vs. Ireland (ESM) = ECLI:EU:C:2012:756, para 100 ff; cf. also: *Rossi* in: Calliess/Ruffert EUV/AEUV, Art. 352 TFEU, para 53.

Ireland Case on the compatibility of the European Stability Mechanism (ESM) with the European Treaties.[1086] The CJEU states:

> "In that regard, it must be recalled that, under Article 3(2) TFEU, the Union is to have 'exclusive competence for the conclusion of an international agreement when its conclusion … may affect common rules or alter their scope'.
>
> It follows also from that provision that Member States are prohibited from concluding an agreement *between themselves* which *might affect common rules or alter their scope.*"[1087]

Compared to the *ERTA-Case* and the following decisions, the decision adds a different angle to the doctrine. The *ERTA-Case* and the following decisions focused on the competence of either the EU or the member states (jointly) to conclude an agreement with member *and* non-member states.[1088] The *Pringle-Case* clearly admits that the principles developed in *ERTA* and laid down in Art. 3 (2) TFEU also apply *to purely intra-EU relationships*.[1089]

Thus, it needs to be evaluated if an arbitration clause in an intra EU agreement might affect common rules or alter their effects (cf. Art. 3 (2) TFEU). If this was the case, the member states would no longer have the power to agree upon such a mechanism in an IIA. It would then be an exclusive competence for the EU to create (or not to create) such a mechanism. The arbitration clause contained in an IIA concluded between member states would therefore be contrary to EU law, especially Art. 3 (2) TFEU.

The terms "*might affect common rules or alter their effect*" is derived from the *ERTA-Case*.[1090] The *Opinion 1/03* tried to reshape the terms to a more general approach, indicating the criterion to decide whether or not an

---

1086 *CJEU*, 27.11.2012 – C-370/12 - Pringle vs. Ireland (ESM) = ECLI:EU:C:2012 :756.

1087 *CJEU*, 27.11.2012 – C-370/12 - Pringle vs. Ireland (ESM) = ECLI:EU:C:2012 :756, para 100 f [emphasis added].

1088 *CJEU*, 07.02.2006 – Opinion 1/03 - Lugano Agreement = ECLI:EU:C:2006 :81, para 114 ff.

1089 *CJEU*, 27.11.2012 – C-370/12 - Pringle vs. Ireland (ESM) = ECLI:EU:C:2012: 756, para 101; *Dahlquist/Lenk et al.*, European Policy Analysis, 2016:4, 1, 6; questioned by *Nettesheim*, NJW, 2013, 14, 15 who considers that the underlying idea was the effet utile of the European Treaties.

1090 *CJEU*, 31.03.1971 – C-22/70 - ERTA = ECLI:EU:C:1971:32, para 22; *Pelka* in: Schwarze EU-Kommentar, Art. 3 AEUV, para 17; *Ahner*, Investor-Staat-Schiedsverfahren nach Europäischem Unionsrecht, 2015, p. 163.

agreement might affect common rules or alter its effects.[1091] As to the CJEU the relevant provisions of the agreement and in EU law need to be compared by taking into consideration their nature, their content and their scope of application.[1092] The final criterion should be the risk of the agreement to alter the "*uniform and consistent application of the Community rules*" as well as the "*proper functioning of the system which [the Community rules] establish in order to preserve the full effectiveness of Community law*".[1093] The infringement needs to be of sufficient severity.[1094]

The question whether IIAs affect such rules needs to be addressed under two different angles. First, it needs to be analysed *which type of provisions need to be affected* to trigger the denial of the member states competences (I.). Second, the compatibility could either be challenged with regard to the jurisdictional rules of the EU or with regard to the substantive provisions regulating the internal market (II.).

I. The type of provisions to be affected to trigger the application of the ERTA-jurisprudence

The first issue to be addressed is the scope of provisions meant by "*common rules*" in the *ERTA*- and *Pringle-Decision*. One could argue that common rules only refer to either those fields of EU law which are fully harmonised or at least harmonised to such a considerable extent (or planned to be harmonised) that further rules would potentially affect those measures.[1095] From the rather extensive formula given by the CJEU, one

1091 *Vedder* in: von Heinegg/Vedder EUV/AEUV, Art. 3 TFEU, para 7.

1092 *CJEU*, 07.02.2006 – Opinion 1/03 - Lugano Agreement = ECLI:EU:C:2006:81, para 122-124.

1093 *CJEU*, 07.02.2006 – Opinion 1/03 - Lugano Agreement = ECLI:EU:C:2006:81, para 128; cf. also: *Vedder* in: von Heinegg/Vedder EUV/AEUV, Art. 3 TFEU, para 7; *Terhechte* in: Schwarze EU-Kommentar, Art. 216 TFEU, para 9.

1094 *Terhechte* in: Schwarze EU-Kommentar, Art. 216 TFEU, para 9.

1095 Similar: *Tietje*, Intra-EU BITs als Herausforderung im Mehrebenensystem des Rechts (Beit. zum Transnat. Wirt.-R, Vol. 104, 2011), p. 11 and *Ahner*, Investor-Staat-Schiedsverfahren nach Europäischem Unionsrecht, 2015, p. 165 who however refers to rules setting a minimum standard of harmonization, which is expressly denied by the CJEU, *CJEU*, 07.02.2006 – Opinion 1/03 - Lugano Agreement = ECLI:EU:C:2006:81, para 123.

could also argue that all kind of community regulations are to be analysed to assess whether an agreement may affect their uniform application within the member states. The CJEU refers to the

> "conclusion of an agreement by the Member States being incompatible with the unity of the common market and the uniform application of Community law"[1096]

A teleological analysis would also support this wider approach. The *ERTA-Doctrine* is often regarded as a safeguard to guarantee the *effet utile* of the European Treaties and prevent member states to engage or compromise the uniform application of EU law by concluding divergent international agreements, which might raise conflicts as to the relation of the principle of primacy in EU law and the *pacta sunt servanda* principle toward non-member states.[1097] Others argue that extending Art. 3 (2) TFEU too extensively, would violate the principle of conferral of competencies to the EU.[1098]

Interpreting the *ERTA-Doctrine* in the *inter se* context set by the *Pringle-Case* however reveals the necessity to limit the terms "*common rules*". The *ERTA-Doctrine* was conceived in the particular circumstances of external competencies attributed to the EU. The above-mentioned reasoning of the conflicting principles of supremacy and *pacta sunt servanda*, do not rise at the same level in *inter se* agreements. For those agreements, as aforementioned, the principle of primacy takes pre-eminence. Hence, the *effet utile* of the treaties is not endangered. Furthermore, it follows from the *Pringle-Case* that the CJEU seems to apply a rather restrictive approach considering the rules to be taken into account. It can hardly be argued that the inauguration of the ESM would not affect any rules such as the free movement of capital or any other provision related to the internal market. However, the CJEU seems to restrain its examination to those regulations which particularly target the same subject (i.e. the stability of the Euro market through banking regulations).[1099] The same can be ob-

1096 *CJEU*, 07.02.2006 – Opinion 1/03 - Lugano Agreement = ECLI:EU:C:2006:81, para 122.

1097 *Pitschas*, EuZW, 2003, 82, 93; *Streinz/Mögele* in: Streinz EUV/AEUV, Art. 3 TFEU, para 16; *Obwexer* in: v. d. Groeben/Schwarze AEUV/EUV, Art. 3 TFEU, para 40 ff.

1098 *Ahner*, Investor-Staat-Schiedsverfahren nach Europäischem Unionsrecht, 2015, p. 167.

1099 *CJEU*, 27.11.2012 – C-370/12 - Pringle vs. Ireland (ESM) = ECLI:EU:C:2012:756, para 101 ff, referring to Directive 407/2010/EU and Art. 119 ff TFEU only.

served in the *Opinion 1/03* regarding the Lugano Agreement, where the CJEU extensively argues, why the Brussels Convention and Lugano Agreement contain overlapping rules and subjects of regulation.[1100]

II. Scope of comparison under the ERTA-Doctrine / Pringle-Case

Given this rather restrictive interpretation of the term "*common rules*" in the *inter-se* context, it should be assessed which "*rules*" of EU law could be particularly affected by an *inter se* IIA and which contain a (sufficiently) dense community regulation in order to trigger an incompatibility with Art. 3 (2) TFEU.

The jurisdictional regulations by the EU in the Art. 19 TEU, Art. 251 ff TFEU could in no way be sufficient to enact an exclusive competence attributed to the EU. The level of regulation is extremely low in this regard.[1101] They rather contain general principles which cannot be deemed sufficient in this context. Furthermore, if those general principles were deemed to be sufficient to attribute an exclusive competency to the EU, private arbitration would be impossible as well (as it is not foreseen in these provisions). However, private arbitration has been endorsed by the CJEU in the *Eco-Swiss-Case* (cf. *supra*).

Other contradicting common rules might be the Minimum Platform on Investment adopted in 2006.[1102] However, this negotiation proposal only regulates questions of market access, national treatment and a most favoured nations standard and thus relates to (particular) *substantive* protection standards.[1103]

1100 *CJEU*, 07.02.2006 – Opinion 1/03 - Lugano Agreement = ECLI:EU:C:2006:81, para 134 ff.

1101 Similar: *Tietje*, Intra-EU BITs als Herausforderung im Mehrebenensystem des Rechts (Beit. zum Transnat. Wirt.-R, Vol. 104, 2011), p. 11.

1102 *European Commission - DG Competition*, Minimum platform on investment for EU FTAs – Provisions on establishment in template for a Title on "Establishment, trade in services and e-commerce", 28/07/2006; cf. also: *Burgstaller*, JOIA Vol. 26, No. 2 (2009), 181, 202 ff; *Eilmansberger*, CMLR Vol. 46 (2009), 383, 393 f.

1103 *European Commission - DG Competition*, Minimum platform on investment for EU FTAs – Provisions on establishment in template for a Title on "Establishment, trade in services and e-commerce", 28/07/2006; cf. also: *Burgstaller*, JOIA Vol. 26, No. 2 (2009), 181, 202 ff; *Eilmansberger*, CMLR Vol. 46 (2009), 383, 393 f.

Lastly, one might argue that the *substantive* provisions of the internal market, which indeed contain particularly dense regulations, could be understood as such "*common rules*". Regarding both, the provisions of the internal market and the Minimum Platform on Investment, the question is whether the limits to the member state competencies in the *Pringle-Decision* need to be examined by a subject related analysis ("*common rules*" on jurisdiction vs. jurisdictional rules in the IIA) or if there could be cross-subject interferences ("*common rules*" on the internal market vs. jurisdictional rules in the IIA).

With regard to this subject, on the one hand, the CJEU states that the legal basis for the common rule is irrelevant, as this basis is determined by its "*principal component, whereas the rule which may possibly be affected may be merely an ancillary component of that legislation.*"[1104] This would argue in favour of a potential cross-subject analysis. However, the CJEU also stated that "*a chance that bilateral agreements would lead to distortions in the flow of services in the internal market*"[1105] cannot trigger an exclusive competence of the EU. The regulations do not need to be "*precisely the same*". However, at least they need to have a particular link.[1106] Indeed, such *de facto* impediments may exist on various occasions and hence would lead to an exhaustive set of competences for the EU. Consequently, provisions affecting the full effect of EU law may, by virtue of the principle of primacy, be set aside, but will not automatically lead to the missing competence of member states to act in the respective field.[1107] This would also create an unbearable uncertainty as to the competencies of the member states and the EU. Once again, also in the *Pringle-Decision*, the CJEU did not seem to apply such a large approach in its comparison,

---

1104 *CJEU*, 07.02.2006 – Opinion 1/03 - Lugano Agreement = ECLI:EU:C:2006:81, para 131; cf. also: *Obwexer* in: v. d. Groeben/Schwarze AEUV/EUV, Art. 3 TFEU, para 43.

1105 *CJEU*, 15.11.1994 – Opinion 1/94 = ECLI:EU:C:1994:384, para 78 f and reiterated in *CJEU*, 07.02.2006 – Opinion 1/03 - Lugano Agreement = ECLI:EU:C:2006:81, para 123; *CJEU*, 05.11.2002 – C-467/98 - Open Skies = ECLI:EU:C:2002:625, para 85 f; against the taking into account of de facto impediments: *Pitschas*, EuZW, 2003, 82, 93.

1106 Terms supported by AG Kokott in *Opinion of Advocate General Kokott*, 27.06.2013 – C-137/12 = ECLI:EU:C:2013:441, para 116; also supporting a restrictive interpretation: *Nettesheim* in: Grabitz/Hilf/Nettesheim EUV/AEUV, Art. 3 TFEU, para 24.

1107 However this approach seems to be supported by: *Dahlquist/Lenk et al.*, European Policy Analysis, 2016:4, 1, 6 f.

as it does not even mention any substantive rules relating to the internal market to be potentially affected by the creation of the ESM. Lastly, it should be noted that in the *Opinion 1/94* the CJEU expressly restricted the competencies attributed under the former CCP, which should have strong indications regarding the allocation of competences with regard to IIAs.[1108]

Hence from the lens of a potential limitation of the member state's competencies (i.e. Art. 3 (2) TFEU), one cannot determine any incompatibility of the arbitration clauses contained in IIAs with EU law. As a conflict on the competence level is denied, the question whether shifting competences after the conclusion of IIAs has affected their validity, which is raised in the extra-EU context, is obsolete.[1109]

III. Interim conclusion on the arbitration clause's incompatibility due to violation of the EU's exclusive competences

It was found that the conclusion of IIAs did not violate EU law from the competence perspective. Hence, this objection will not lead to any incompatibility of EU law and the arbitration clauses contained in IIAs.

C. Incompatibility of the arbitration clause with the principle of non-discrimination

It should now be analysed whether the arbitration clause contained in intra-EU IIAs is incompatible with the principle of non-discrimination in Art. 18 TFEU or the fundamental freedoms.[1110]

1108 Cf. for a comprehensive analysis: *Burgstaller* in: *Bungenberg/Griebel /Hindelang* (Eds.), International investment law and EU law, 2011; cf. also: *Johannsen*, Die Kompetenz der EU für ausländische Direktinvestitionen nach Lissabon (Beit. zum Transnat. Wirt.-R, Vol. 90, 2009), p. 6-8.

1109 For a comprehensive analysis of the subject matter: *Burgstaller* in: *Bungenberg/Griebel/Hindelang* (Eds.), Internationaler Investitionsschutz und Europarecht, 2010, p. 62 ff.

1110 For the reasoning of several arbitral tribunals to deny an incompatibility cf.: *infra* footnote 1112; the principle of non-discrimination constitutes one of the cornerstones of the fundamental freedoms. The reasoning can thus apply irrespective of whether one relies on Art. 18 TFEU or on one of the fundamental

The compatibility of arbitration clauses contained in IIAs has been raised by several respondents in arbitration proceedings involving intra-EU IIAs.[1111]

This objection has generally not been further assessed by the tribunals. The arbitral tribunals mainly reduced the question to the statement that even though the clause might be discriminatory, this discrimination would need to be resolved by extending its benefits to any other investor from another EU member state.[1112] The *EURAM-Tribunal* additionally noted that even though the clause might be discriminatory, this could not affect the investor's rights. The only consequence could be that the EU member state would be exposed to infringement proceedings.[1113]

However, this analysis is somehow short-sighted. It should first be analysed whether the arbitration clause actually violates Art. 18 TFEU, before addressing the legal consequences of such violation.

---

freedoms, cf. also: *Dahlquist/Lenk et al.*, European Policy Analysis, 2016:4, 1, 4.

1111 Cf. inter alia: *Achmea vs. Slovak Republic*, 26.10.2012 – PCA Case No. 2008-13 - Award on Jurisdiction, Arbitrability and Suspension, para 112 and 117 ff; *Euram vs. Slovak Republic*, 22.10.2012 – PCA Case no. 2010-17: First Award on Jurisdiction, para 101.

1112 *Inter alia: Eastern Sugar vs. Czech Republic*, 27.03.2007 – SCC No. 088/2004 - Partial award, para 170; ; *Euram vs. Slovak Republic*, 22.10.2012 – PCA Case no. 2010-17: First Award on Jurisdiction, para 270 f and 274, basing its considerations on the non-existence of a discrimination and the fact that – if there is discriminiation – the effect would be to extend rights rather than to restrict them; *Achmea vs. Slovak Republic*, 26.10.2012 – PCA Case No. 2008-13 - Award on Jurisdiction, Arbitrability and Suspension, para 274; cf. also *Reinisch*, LIEI Vol. 39, No. 2 (2012), 157, 176; *Eilmansberger*, CMLR Vol. 46 (2009), 383, 407; *Dimopoulos*, CMLR Vol. 48, No. 1 (2011), 63, 84; the position of *Dahlquist/Lenk et al.*, European Policy Analysis, 2016:4, 1, 5 is not entirely clear: rights should be extended but if this was not possible, the (extra-EU) BITs would need to be terminated; cf. also: *Söderlund*, JOIA Vol. 24, Iss. 5 (2007), 455, 462 and *Wehland*, ICLQ Vol. 58, Iss. 2 (2009), 297, 310 ff who both seem to consider that there is no discrimination; an extension is also suggested by *Kottmann*, EuZW, 2016, 512, 520.

1113 As to the tribunal, a violation of Art. 18 TFEU could be qualified as a violation of the European Treaties by the host state, but could not deprive the investor from ist right to rely on the arbitration clause, cf.: *Euram vs. Slovak Republic*, 22.10.2012 – PCA Case no. 2010-17: First Award on Jurisdiction, para 270.

I. Violation of the principle of non-discrimination by the arbitration clause

To address the first question, *Wehland* correctly points out that two perspectives should be distinguished: the perspective of other EU member states (and their investors) towards the home state (outbound perspective) and the perspective of other EU member states (and their investors) towards the host state (inbound perspective).[1114]

1. Inbound perspective (host state discriminating non-IIA protected investors)

The inbound perspective focuses on the "*benefits*" in terms of an additional or – allegedly – more efficient legal remedy granted by the host state to investors from some member states but denied to others. As to Art. 18 TFEU:

> "Within the scope of application of the Treaties, and without prejudice to any special provisions contained therein, any discrimination on grounds of nationality shall be prohibited."

It is common ground that the provision applies to both the EU as well as EU member states.[1115] Intra-EU investment protection disputes will touch fundamental questions of the internal market, the fundamental freedoms and several other provisions of the European Treaties, including *inter alia* Art. 267, 344 TFEU (cf. *supra*). Arbitration clauses will hence, at least indirectly, fall within the material scope of application of the European Treaties, which is sufficient to apply Art. 18 TFEU.[1116]

However, it is questionable whether the conclusion of an IIA including an arbitration clause constitutes a discrimination. A "*discrimination*" requires a less favourable treatment of two comparable circumstances or sit-

---

1114 For this distinction: *Wehland*, ICLQ Vol. 58, Iss. 2 (2009), 297, 310 ff referring to an 'export' perspective and an 'import' perspective; also: *Dimopoulos*, CMLR Vol. 48, No. 1 (2011), 63, 80 and 82.

1115 *Rust* in: v. d. Groeben/Schwarze AEUV/EUV, Art. 18, para 38 f; cf. *CJEU*, 09.09.2004 – C-304/01 = ECLI:EU:C:2004:495, para 30 f, 46.

1116 *CJEU*, 20.03.1997 – C-323/95 - Hayes = ECLI:EU:C:1997:169, para 17: *"an effect, even though indirect" is sufficient; Holoubek* in: Schwarze EU-Kommentar, Art. 18 TFEU, para 26 f; *Epiney* in: Calliess/Ruffert EUV/AEUV, Art. 18 TFEU, para 18 f.

uations. If such a discrimination exists, the subsequent question would be, if the discrimination can be justified ("*three-step approach*").[1117]

(1) Difference in treatment between investors from different nationalities

There can be no doubt that access to arbitration constitutes a more favourable treatment attributed to those investors being nationals of a home state which signed an IIA with an EU member state.

The arbitration clause grants access to arbitration only to investors being nationals of the host-state. Thus, the treaty clearly differentiates on the basis of nationality between different investors of different nationalities. One could however argue whether the one or the other mechanism is more favourable. The tribunal in *Binder vs. Czech Republic* e.g. stated:

> "(…) when there is no BIT between two Member States, the remedy available to an investor (…) is legal action before the national courts of the [host] state. The fact that, when there is a BIT, such national remedy is replaced or supplemented by an international arbitration mechanism does not (…) involve any discrimination."[1118]

Hence, the tribunal apparently recognises a legal action before national courts and an (international) arbitral tribunal to be sort of equivalent, at least to the degree that it does not constitute a discrimination.[1119] Other tribunals opposed to this and considered that arbitral proceedings are more favourable than national proceedings in the host state.[1120] However, in that regard it is irrelevant if the access to arbitration is more favourable than the access to national courts or if both are equivalent.[1121] As the German

1117 *Streinz* in: Streinz EUV/AEUV, Art. 18 TFEU, para 45; cf. also: *Bogdandy* in: Grabitz/Hilf/Nettesheim EUV/AEUV, Art. 18 TFEU, para 8; *Holoubek* in: Schwarze EU-Kommentar, Art. 18 TFEU, para 21-24.

1118 *Binder vs. Czech Republic*, 06.06.2007 – UNCITRAL - Award on Jurisdiction, para 65.

1119 *Binder vs. Czech Republic*, 06.06.2007 – UNCITRAL - Award on Jurisdiction, para 65.

1120 Cf. the conclusions in: *Eastern Sugar vs. Czech Republic*, 27.03.2007 – SCC No. 088/2004 - Partial award, para 164-166; *Achmea vs. Slovak Republic*, 26.10.2012 – PCA Case No. 2008-13 - Award on Jurisdiction, Arbitrability and Suspension, para 264.

1121 For the idea of equivalence: cf. *Binder vs. Czech Republic*, 06.06.2007 – UNCITRAL - Award on Jurisdiction, para 65; *Söderlund*, JOIA Vol. 24, Iss. 5

Supreme Court correctly pointed out, at least the fact that an investor can chose from several means of dispute resolution is a more favourable treatment than being restricted on either the one or the other mechanism.[1122] As arbitration clauses contained in IIAs typically enable this choice, the host states through the conclusion of the IIA attribute a more favourable treatment to one investor than to another.[1123].

(2) Comparable circumstances between such investors

Given that there is a more favourable treatment, the question is whether investors from one EU member state (having signed an IIA with the host state) and investors from other EU member states (not having signed an IIA) are in comparable circumstances. This leads to the question whether Art. 18 TFEU (or the fundamental freedoms) imposes the general obligation to all member states to extend benefits granted in bilateral agreements to all other member state, which would result in an intra-EU most-

(2007), 455, 462 seems to consider that a procedural guarantee cannot constitute a discrimination at all.

1122 *German Federal Supreme Court*, 03.03.2016 – I ZB 2/15, para 702; cf. also: *Eilmansberger*, CMLR Vol. 46 (2009), 383, 402; *Wehland*, ICLQ Vol. 58, Iss. 2 (2009), 297, 310 f; *Clodfelter*, Santa Clara Jour. of Int. Law Vol. 12, Iss. 1 (2013), 159, 181 who points out that the mere possibility of better treatment is sufficient to constitute a discrimination under EU law.

1123 *Lenk*, EJLS Vol. 8, No. 2 (2015), 6, 11 f and 17; *Johannsen*, Die Kompetenz der EU für ausländische Direktinvestitionen nach Lissabon (Beit. zum Transnat. Wirt.-R, Vol. 90, 2009), 22; *Dimopoulos*, CMLR Vol. 48, No. 1 (2011), 63, 80 f; *Dahlquist/Lenk et al.*, European Policy Analysis, 2016:4, 1, 4 f and 11; for the opposite: *Söderlund*, JOIA Vol. 24, Iss. 5 (2007), 455, 462. Nevertheless, it also argued that not the arbitration clause itself contains the discrimination, but the denial of the host state to grant any investor from another member state its benefits in terms of the access to arbitration, cf.: *Eilmansberger*, CMLR Vol. 46 (2009), 383, 407. This view should be rejected. From the jurisprudence of the CJEU it clearly appears that a discrimination may result from the simple existence of a provision granting a benefit to a national from one state and denying it to nationals from other states. The mere existence of the provision may constitute a discrimination: cf. *CJEU*, 05.11.2002 – C-471/98 - Commission vs. Belgium (Open Skies) = ECLI:EU:C:2002:628, para 141: "*[the] source of discrimination is not the possible conduct [of a third party] but the Article [contained in the agreement]*", cf. also: *Clodfelter*, Santa Clara Jour. of Int. Law Vol. 12, Iss. 1 (2013), 159, 181.

favoured nations treatment by all member states.[1124] On the other hand, if such an obligation does not exist (at least under certain conditions) the arbitration clause contained in an IIA could not constitute a violation of Art. 18 TFEU either, as the differentiation would be irrelevant from the EU law perspective. The question of whether the investors are in comparable circumstances, should be analysed by reference to case law of the CJEU in tax matters, which deals with similar difficulties and questions.

(a) The perception of an obligation of intra-EU MFN treatment in tax matters

The question of the existence of an intra-EU most favoured nations (MFN) obligation has intensively been discussed in matters related to bilateral tax treaties. Indeed, such treaties represent several similarities to the situation of intra-EU IIAs. The matters of tax law are currently not subject to particular (exhaustive) regulations under EU law.[1125] Hence, the member states concluded several bilateral international treaties which regulate double-taxation issues by either granting particular tax exemptions, tax rates or particular tax treatment to nationals, residents or incorporations of the other contracting party. The result is a scattered system of tax treatment within the EU, depending on the nationality, residence or seat of incorporation. Consequently, the question of comparability between similar entities from different nationalities (horizontal comparability) arises.[1126] As an example, a double taxation agreement between Germany and Belgium may grant a particular benefit to nationals of both states having its residence in the other member state. A German tax payer, resident in Belgium would thus be granted a particular benefit. A Dutch taxpayer, being resident in Belgium however might be denied the same benefit, given that the Netherlands and Belgium would not have concluded a similar agreement. A MFN treatment might enable the Dutch tax payer to claim identi-

---

1124 *Wehland*, ICLQ Vol. 58, Iss. 2 (2009), 297, 315; cf. also: *Dahlquist/Lenk et al.*, European Policy Analysis, 2016:4, 1, 4 f.

1125 *Kofler*, European Taxation Vol. 45, No. 12 (2005), 530, 531. Under the EC-Treaty, Art. 293 provided for the possibility to conclude a multilateral treaty to avoid double-taxations. However, the member states did not make use of it and the article was abolished under the Treaty of Lisbon; cf. also: *Dahlquist/Lenk et al.*, European Policy Analysis, 2016:4, 1, 5.

1126 *Kofler*, European Taxation Vol. 45, No. 12 (2005), 530, 537.

cal benefits as the German tax payer, based on the non-discrimination principle in EU law. The situation is very similar to intra-EU IIAs which contain arbitration clauses. Dutch investors may likewise argue that the denial of access to arbitration constitutes a horizontal discrimination towards them compared to German investors.

In two particular cases ("*D*" and "*Test Claimants ACT*") the CJEU addressed the question with regard to such double-taxation issues.[1127] In both cases the CJEU rejected the application of a MFN approach to bilateral preferences. It stated:

> "The fact that those reciprocal rights and obligations apply only to persons resident in one of the two Contracting Member States [of a bilateral agreement] is an inherent consequence of bilateral double taxation conventions. It follows that a taxable person resident in [the other Member State being contracting party of the agreement] is not in the same situation as a taxable person resident outside [this Member State] (…)."[1128]

For some scholars these decisions mark the abandon of any idea of intra-EU MFN treatment.[1129] Having a particular look on the reasoning of the

1127 *CJEU*, 05.07.2005 – C-376/03 - D. vs. Inspecteur van de Belastingdienst = ECLI:EU:C:2005:424 which was based on the following facts: Belgium and the Netherlands concluded a bilateral double-taxation agreement and reciprocally agreed that residents in one of the two states are granted the same personal allowances, concessions and reductions in the other state than in their state of residence. Mr. D, a German national, claims that these benefits need to be extended to all other EU member state nationals in the Netherlands, irrespective of any double-taxation-agreement being concluded between the Netherlands and the other EU member states. Any denial of this benefits, would constitute a discrimination towards nationals of other EU member states equally being non-residents in either Belgium or the Netherlands; *CJEU*, 12.12.2006 – C-374/04 - Test Claimants in Class IV of ACT Group Litigation = ECLI:EU:C:2006:773 relates to tax credit which leads to taxes paid on dividendes in the UK only being paid once by corporates and shareholders. The UK concluded several double-taxation agreements with member states, some of them applying the benefits of the tax credit also to nationals from this country, others not.

1128 *CJEU*, 05.07.2005 – C-376/03 - D. vs. Inspecteur van de Belastingdienst = ECLI:EU:C:2005:424, para 61.

1129 Cf. *inter alia*: *Kofler*, European Taxation Vol. 45, No. 12 (2005), 530, 538; *Kampermann*, Policy Papers on Transnational Economic Law, October 2005 p 3 ff; *Tietje*, Intra-EU BITs als Herausforderung im Mehrebenensystem des Rechts (Beit. zum Transnat. Wirt.-R, Vol. 104, 2011), p. 16 f; possibly arguing for an unconditioned legality of such agreements: *Ress/Ukrow* in: Grabitz/Hilf/Nettesheim EUV/AEUV, Art. 63 TFEU, para 201 ff; also: *Kofler*, European Taxation Vol. 45, No. 12 (2005), 530, 538.

decisions, the CJEU reveals several preconditions for its denial to extend the benefits of the double-taxation agreements to all other member state nationals.

The CJEU first observes that the granting of benefits in the double-taxation agreement creates reciprocal rights for the member states.[1130] Second, the CJEU states that the differentiation is an inherent consequence of the bilateral nature of the agreement and its provisions. Third, it holds that

> "[the provisions granting the reciprocal benefits] *cannot be* regarded as a benefit *separable* from the remainder of the Convention, *but is an integral part thereof and contributes to its overall balance*."[1131]

Indeed, this limitation to the admittance of differential treatments is crucial to the decisions. The only justification for both decisions and their 'departure' from the internal market's inherent principles that nationals from one member states should not be discriminated against nationals from other member states is that the different nationals are not in comparable circumstances, as the differentiation is an "*inherent consequence*" of the bilateral treaty.[1132] Hence, the differentiation is not *per se* admitted, simply because both member states concluded a bilateral agreement. It is only admitted because the persons claiming the extension of the benefits are not in comparable situations, which is a prerequisite to constitute a discrimination.[1133] In the *Test-Claimants-Case* this finding becomes more obvious:

> "In order to determine whether such a *difference in treatment is discriminatory*, it is necessary to consider whether, as regards the measures at issue, the non-resident companies concerned are in an objectively comparable situation. […]

1130 *CJEU*, 05.07.2005 – C-376/03 - D. vs. Inspecteur van de Belastingdienst = ECLI:EU:C:2005:424, para 60.

1131 *CJEU*, 05.07.2005 – C-376/03 - D. vs. Inspecteur van de Belastingdienst = ECLI:EU:C:2005:424, para 62 [emphasis added].

1132 Cf. also: *Lehner* in: *Dürrschmidt/Lehner/Vogel* (Eds.), Doppelbesteuerungsabkommen der Bundesrepublik Deutschland auf dem Gebiet der Steuern vom Einkommen und Vermögen, 2015, para 271 ff.

1133 Cf. also: *Sedlaczek/Züger* in: Streinz EUV/AEUV, Art. 65 TFEU, para 16; *Groot*, Intertax Vol. 42, Iss. 6&7 (2014), 405, 412 f; *Lehner* in: *Dürrschmidt/Lehner/Vogel* (Eds.), Doppelbesteuerungsabkommen der Bundesrepublik Deutschland auf dem Gebiet der Steuern vom Einkommen und Vermögen, 2015, para 271 ff; *Weggenmann*, RIW, 2005, 717, 718 ff.

> Thus, the grant of a tax credit [...] cannot be regarded as a benefit separable from the remainder of those DTCs, but is an integral part of them and contributes to their overall balance [...]
>
> It follows that the Treaty provisions on freedom of establishment do not preclude [such treatment] [as] such a situation does not discriminate against [other EU-nationals]."[1134]

It follows that horizontal differences in treatment, even based on *inter se* agreements (given the competencies to conclude such agreements remain with the member states (cf. *supra* under B.)) are not *per se* compatible with the principle of non-discrimination. On the other hand, the CJEU also points out, a differentiated treatment is not *per se* illegal under EU law.[1135] It will only become a (prohibited) discrimination if it is applied to nationals in comparable circumstances and when no justification is provided for the different treatment. Comparable circumstances might be denied if the advantage is granted in a *bilateral agreement* and constitutes an *inherent consequence* deriving from this agreement, as the advantage is *inseparable* from the integrity of the agreement.[1136] If the benefit is the result of a unilateral act of one state and thus not the consequence of the negotiation of the agreement and its inherent balancing, there is no reason to exclude this behaviour by a member state from being discriminatory.[1137]

(b) Consequences from the "D" and "Test Claimant" cases for arbitration clauses contained in IIAs

Hence, the essential question to resolve this issue is whether the investors of different nationalities are considered to be in "*comparable circumstances*" and whether the differentiation can be justified. It is highly ques-

1134 *CJEU*, 12.12.2006 – C-374/04 - Test Claimants in Class IV of ACT Group Litigation = ECLI:EU:C:2006:773, para 83, 88, 92 and 93 [footnotes omitted; changes as indicated to facilitate the reading, emphasis added].

1135 *Groot*, Intertax Vol. 42, Iss. 6&7 (2014), 405, 412 and 413.

1136 Cf. also: *Sedlaczek/Züger* in: Streinz EUV/AEUV, Art. 65 TFEU, para 16; *Groot*, Intertax Vol. 42, Iss. 6&7 (2014), 405, 412 f; *Lehner* in: *Dürrschmidt/Lehner/Vogel* (Eds.), Doppelbesteuerungsabkommen der Bundesrepublik Deutschland auf dem Gebiet der Steuern vom Einkommen und Vermögen, 2015, para 271 ff.

1137 Cf. also: *Groot*, Intertax Vol. 42, Iss. 6&7 (2014), 405, 413; *Kofler*, European Taxation Vol. 45, No. 12 (2005), 530, 538; *CJEU*, 20.05.2008 – C-94/06 - OESF = ECLI:EU:C:2008:289, para 54.

tionable if the jurisprudence in tax matters could be extended to an arbitration clause contained in IIAs.[1138]

First, benefits from double-taxation agreements are the only and inherent sense of such agreements. There would be merely no useful provision in such a treaty, if the tax benefit is carved out from the treaty. Indeed, considering this particularity, the benefit is an inherent consequence of the double-taxation agreement. Assuming the same for a dispute settlement clause contained in an IIA, seems doubtful.[1139] Nothing in the structure of an IIA would require an arbitration clause to be inserted in such agreement. Given the substantive guarantees, the IIA would even have an impact without any dispute resolution clause at all.

Second, supporting the same idea, an arbitration clause is not such an "*integral part*" of the IIA that it could not be separated from the agreement.[1140] Several arbitral tribunals pointed out the particular importance of a neutral forum to guarantee the efficiency of the IIA.[1141] However, even without any neutral forum at all, the IIA cannot be considered useless. It may be less effective but by far not deprived of any sense.[1142]

However, arbitration clauses contained in IIAs, are of substantial importance for the equilibrium of an IIA. To some extent, states limit their consent to arbitration to particular guarantees contained in the IIA or to further conditions. A wide consent to arbitration may thus be a reason why states limit certain substantive guarantees. In terms of the CJEU's juris-

---

1138 The *EURAM-Tribunal* argued that the jurisprudence of the CJEU should be transposed to IIAs. As to the tribunal, it results from the CJEU's judgements in tax matters that the member states would be free to agree on reciprocal rights and obligations as long as there is no specific treaty prohibiting such behaviour and the European measures of harmonization did not extend to a degree to prohibit such inter-se agreements. IIAs should be treated accordingly as there would neither be a treaty prohibiting IIAs between member states, nor any European regulation would be sufficiently dense to prohibit further action by the member states, cf.: *Euram vs. Slovak Republic*, 22.10.2012 – PCA Case no. 2010-17: First Award on Jurisdiction, para 274 ff. This argument confuses the question of competence with the question of a (potentially justified) discrimination and violation of EU law.

1139 For the opposite: *Wehland*, ICLQ Vol. 58, Iss. 2 (2009), 297, 316 f.

1140 Cf. also: *German Federal Supreme Court*, 03.03.2016 – I ZB 2/15, para 74.

1141 Cf. *inter alia* the conclusions in: *Eastern Sugar vs. Czech Republic*, 27.03.2007 – SCC No. 088/2004 - Partial award, para 164-166; *Achmea vs. Slovak Republic*, 26.10.2012 – PCA Case No. 2008-13 - Award on Jurisdiction, Arbitrability and Suspension, para 264.

1142 *German Federal Supreme Court*, 03.03.2016 – I ZB 2/15, para 74.

prudence in the *D-* and *Test Claimants-Case*, the arbitration clause may thus be some sort of result of the bargaining processes. However, this same argument shows that arbitration clauses and substantive guarantees can be separated. If an arbitration clause was an inherent consequence of an IIA, there could be no difference between substantive guarantees and procedural protection. However, treaty practice shows various examples, where either the consent given to arbitration is less extensive than the substantive guarantees or the consent to arbitration extends even beyond the substantive guarantees provided for in an IIA (e.g. to claims arising from state contracts as well, etc.).[1143]

Also with regard to the reciprocity from the host state's perspective, IIAs are not comparable to double-taxation agreements.[1144] Whereas under the latter, reciprocity will be one of the major considerations, most of the IIAs, have for a long time been concluded in perfect knowledge of *de facto* attributing rights in one direction only. The situation regarding IIAs might nearly be compared to a unilateral attribution of claimable rights by the host state. The guarantees are not literally conceived as an exchange for guarantees by the other state, but rather for the promotion of investments flowing from the home state to the host state.[1145] Lastly, it should be noted that Art. 65 (1) TFEU expressly refers to the ability to differentiate between taxpayers "*who are not in the same situation with regard to their place of residence*".[1146] Such a provision is inexistent for IIAs.

Given these considerations, investors from different member states need to be considered as being in comparable circumstances as those being granted access to arbitration through an intra-EU IIA's arbitration clause.[1147]

1143 For an example of a more restrictive arbtiration clause: Art. 7 of the Cyprus - Hungarian Bilateral Investment Treaty (entry into force: 25/05/1990): "*Any dispute [...] concerning exppropritation of an investment (...)*". For the coppo-site, extending a clause beyond treaty claims: *SGS vs. Paraguay*, 12.02.2010 – ICSID Case No. ARB/07/29 - Decision on Jurisdiction, para 129; for a range of further examples although in a different context: *Schreuer*, McGill Jour of Disp. Res. Vol. 1, No. 1 (2014), 1, 6 ff.

1144 For the opposite: *Dimopoulos*, CMLR Vol. 48, No. 1 (2011), 63, 81.

1145 *Dahlquist/Lenk et al.*, European Policy Analysis, 2016:4, 1, 10.

1146 Cf. also: *Dahlquist/Lenk et al.*, European Policy Analysis, 2016:4, 1, 5.

1147 Obviously supporting this view: *Lenk*, EJLS Vol. 8, No. 2 (2015), 6, 11 f and 17.

(3) Justification for the differential treatment in comparable circumstances

It is hard to perceive how this difference in treatment should be justified as it is the result of purely discretionary decision of the respective member state. A justification for this differentiation based on ownership, nationality or any sort of indirect control is *per se* impermissible under EU law. Hence, the arbitration clause itself constitutes a discrimination in terms of Art. 18 TFEU from the inbound-perspective.[1148]

2. Outbound perspective (home state favoring its national investors towards non-national investors)

In the outbound perspective, the alleged discrimination becomes an issue of national-treatment under EU law. *De facto*, from the home state's perspective, own nationals are treated differently than nationals from other member states (non-nationals) because national investors are granted benefits under an IIA, which are not granted to non-nationals.[1149]

Analysing the jurisprudence of the CJEU on this matter reveals that one needs to distinguish two set of situations.[1150] The benefit granted to nationals in a bilateral agreement can be the result of an advantage granted by the home state or by the other signatory state (i.e. the host state). In the first situation, there is strictly no difference to situations in which the home state would attribute particular benefits to its nationals by virtue of domestic laws.[1151] Hence, the mere fact that those benefits are attributed

1148 Obviously supporting this view: *Lenk*, EJLS Vol. 8, No. 2 (2015), 6, 11 f and 17; *Dahlquist/Lenk et al.*, European Policy Analysis, 2016:4, 1, 5 who also refer to: *CJEU*, 25.07.1991 – C-221/89 - Factortame = ECLI:EU:C:1991:320, para 29 ff: *"[provisions] which stipulates that where a vessel is owned or chartered by natural persons they must be of a particular nationality and where it is owned or chartered by a company the shareholders and directors must be of that nationality is contrary to Article 52 of the Treaty (...)"*; inisofar also: *Dimopoulos, CMLR Vol. 48, No. 1 (2011), 63, 84.*

1149 *Dimopoulos*, CMLR Vol. 48, No. 1 (2011), 63, 82 f; *Wehland*, ICLQ Vol. 58, Iss. 2 (2009), 297, 320; *Tietje*, Intra-EU BITs als Herausforderung im Mehrebenensystem des Rechts (Beit. zum Transnat. Wirt.-R, Vol. 104, 2011), p. 15 f; *Dahlquist/Lenk et al.*, European Policy Analysis, 2016:4, 1, 5 but with reference to the differences in substantive protection.

1150 Cf. also: *Wehland*, ICLQ Vol. 58, Iss. 2 (2009), 297, 312 ff.

1151 *Wehland*, ICLQ Vol. 58, Iss. 2 (2009), 297, 314.

through a bilateral agreement, instead of national laws, does not provide any justification for such differences, as extending those benefits would in no way impede on any rights of the other contracting party or on the equilibrium and reciprocity of the treaty.[1152] This was clearly admitted by the CJEU.[1153]

The second situation reveals to be more complex. In this situation, the benefit is granted by the other contracting party (i.e. the host-state) and a unilateral extension of rights beyond the home state's nationals would have considerable impact on the host state as other contracting party. This reasoning already appeared in the abovementioned *Saint Gobain-* and *Gottardo-Cases*.[1154] However, in the *Open Skies* decision the CJEU clearly disapproved justifications based on the considerations that the benefits would be granted by the other contracting party. As to the CJEU the discrimination is the consequence of the fact that the discriminating included a clause in the agreement which now enables the other country to grant particular benefits to nationals of the home state.[1155] Hence, the state should have abstained from concluding an agreement including such a provision. It is argued that the CJEU comes to this conclusion as otherwise the agreement would enable to circumvent fundamental norms of the internal market. As to some authors, these considerations cannot be trans-

1152 *CJEU*, 21.09.1999 – C-307/97 - Saint Gobain = ECLI:EU:C:1999:438, para 59; *CJEU*, 15.01.2002 – C-55/00 - Gottardo = ECLI:EU:C:2002:16, para 34, 36 and 37, especially 37: *"the unilateral extension by the Italian Republic, to workers who are nationals of other Member States, of the benefit of having insurance periods which they completed in Switzerland taken into account for the purpose of acquiring entitlement to Italian old-age benefits would in no way compromise the rights which the Swiss Confederation derives from the Italo-Swiss Convention and would not impose any new obligations on that country (...)*"; *Wehland*, ICLQ Vol. 58, Iss. 2 (2009), 297, 314; *Dimopoulos*, CMLR Vol. 48, No. 1 (2011), 63, 83 f.

1153 *CJEU*, 21.09.1999 – C-307/97 - Saint Gobain = ECLI:EU:C:1999:438, para 59; *CJEU*, 15.01.2002 – C-55/00 - Gottardo = ECLI:EU:C:2002:16, para 37; *Wehland*, ICLQ Vol. 58, Iss. 2 (2009), 297, 314; *Dimopoulos*, CMLR Vol. 48, No. 1 (2011), 63, 83 f.

1154 *CJEU*, 21.09.1999 – C-307/97 - Saint Gobain = ECLI:EU:C:1999:438, para 59; *CJEU*, 15.01.2002 – C-55/00 - Gottardo = ECLI:EU:C:2002:16, para 37; cf. also: *Dahlquist/Lenk et al.*, European Policy Analysis, 2016:4, 1, 5.

1155 *CJEU*, 05.11.2002 – C-471/98 - Commission vs. Belgium (Open Skies) = ECLI:EU:C:2002:628, para 141; *Dahlquist/Lenk et al.*, European Policy Analysis, 2016:4, 1, 5; for a different reading of the judgment: *Wehland*, ICLQ Vol. 58, Iss. 2 (2009), 297, 313.

posed to IIAs, as the extension of rights from an arbitration clause would not affect the internal market and the competitor's positions.[1156] Admitting for the sake of the argument that the consideration by the CJEU in *Open Skies* was indeed based on potential implications for the internal market, the same would apply for IIAs. The access to arbitration to challenge state measures for e.g. changes in the legal framework which affect the business model of an investor (such as *inter alia* in the *Micula-Case*) constitute a major impediment on competitors by the simple chance that damages are granted for violation of any standard.[1157] Hence the internal market is affected in the same way as in the *Open Skies-Decision*. However, a better understanding of the jurisprudence of the CJEU in the *Open Skies*-Case would rather be to refer to the question whether the equivalence or reciprocity of an IIA would be disturbed by extending the benefits of an arbitration clause to all non-nationals by the *home state*. The home state would hence decide who can sue the host state in front of an arbitral tribunal. As already pointed out, IIAs can be conceived as the overlap of two unilateral attributions of rights by each host state to investors from the home state.[1158] Hence, it cannot be upon the home state to extend those rights unilaterally, as the rights are granted by the host state.[1159] Under the outbound perspective, the discrimination hence needs to be considered justified by applying the criteria set forth in *Saint-Gobain* and *Gottardo*.[1160]

1156 *Wehland*, ICLQ Vol. 58, Iss. 2 (2009), 297, 314 f.

1157 Cf. also: *Kerkemeyer*, EuZW, 2016, 10, 15.

1158 Hence, whereas in the inbound perspective (cf. *supra*), the reciprocity cannot justify the discrimination as the host state does not grant those rights in an exchange but it can be perceived as an unilateral attribution of rights to the investor, following this idea it needs to be admitted that in the outbound perspective the fact that its upon the host state to grant such benefits, indeed justifies the same discrimination as the home state would impede on those rights by unilaterally extending the rights.

1159 Similar: *Tietje*, Intra-EU BITs als Herausforderung im Mehrebenensystem des Rechts (Beit. zum Transnat. Wirt.-R, Vol. 104, 2011), p. 15; for the opposite: *Dimopoulos*, CMLR Vol. 48, No. 1 (2011), 63, 84 f; cf. also: *Dahlquist/Lenk et al.*, European Policy Analysis, 2016:4, 1, 5 who consider that both member states would need to extend it unilaterally by national legislations, which would, consequently applied for all intra-EU IIAs deprive the IIA of any sense.

1160 For the opposite: *Wehland*, ICLQ Vol. 58, Iss. 2 (2009), 297, 314 f; once again it should be clarified that the argument stating that the EU commisison did not base infringement proceedings based on this argument, is a non-argument. The Commission enjoys considerable discretion whether to instaure such proceedings. Furthermore, the infringement proceedings in 2015 reveal to be based on

Hence, arbitration clauses are discriminatory under the inbound perspective but justified under the outbound perspective.

II. Legal consequences of the violation of the principle of non-discrimination

As in the inbound-scenario, arbitration clauses reveal to be discriminatory, the legal consequences of this discrimination need to be assessed. Until now, these legal consequences were merely the only question arbitral tribunals, being confronted with the argument of a potential discrimination, dealt with. It was nearly unequivocally held that any discrimination should be resolved by extending the benefits to all investors from all EU member states. [1161] This indeed seems to be the perspective of the CJEU relating to outbound-discriminations in tax matters.[1162] Regarding inbound-discrimination, the CJEU did not pronounce any clear solution yet,[1163] but

the violation of the principle of non-discrimination as well, cf.: *Dahlquist/Lenk et al.*, European Policy Analysis, 2016:4, 1, 4.

1161 *Inter alia: Eastern Sugar vs. Czech Republic*, 27.03.2007 – SCC No. 088/2004 - Partial award, para 170; ; *Euram vs. Slovak Republic*, 22.10.2012 – PCA Case no. 2010-17: First Award on Jurisdiction, para 270 f and 274, basing its considerations on the non-existence of a discrimination and the fact that – if there is discriminiation – the effect would be to extend rights rather than to restrict them; *Achmea vs. Slovak Republic*, 26.10.2012 – PCA Case No. 2008-13 - Award on Jurisdiction, Arbitrability and Suspension, para 274; cf.also *Reinisch*, LIEI Vol. 39, No. 2 (2012), 157, 176; *Eilmansberger*, CMLR Vol. 46 (2009), 383, 407; *Dimopoulos*, CMLR Vol. 48, No. 1 (2011), 63, 84; the position of *Dahlquist/Lenk et al.*, European Policy Analysis, 2016:4, 1, 5 is not entirely clear: rights should be extended but if this was not possible, the (extra-EU) BITs would need to be terminated; cf. also: *Söderlund*, JOIA Vol. 24, Iss. 5 (2007), 455, 462 and *Wehland*, ICLQ Vol. 58, Iss. 2 (2009), 297, 310 ff who both seem to consider that there is no discrimination.

1162 *CJEU*, 21.09.1999 – C-307/97 - Saint Gobain = ECLI:EU:C:1999:438, para 58; cf. also: *Dahlquist/Lenk et al.*, European Policy Analysis, 2016:4, 1, 5.

1163 The questions until now were resolved on the previous stage of denying a discrimination, cf.: *Weggenmann*, RIW, 2005, 717, 718 ff; However, regarding the effects, of applying a MFN approach, was and is subject to considerable debate: cf.*inter alia* for the debate before the rulings in "D" and "Test Claimants": *Kemmeren*, EC Tax Review Iss. 6, No° 3 (1997), 146 and after the decision: *Kofler*, European Taxation Vol. 45, No. 12 (2005), 530, 539 with further references.

it is indeed arguable that if the CJEU admits a discrimination, this could in principle be resolved by extending the benefit.[1164]

However, two considerations do not support this conclusion in the particular case of an inbound discrimination relating to arbitration clauses in IIAs.

First, a nearly identical problem as regarding the application of a MFN clause to dispute settlement clauses in IIAs would occur on the European level. The consent given by a host state to submit itself to arbitration is a (wilful) limitation of its sovereignty. Allowing EU law to overcome this, would be questionable regarding the allocation of competences.[1165] Furthermore, it is doubtful how such an extension should be conceived. Would this also extend to investors from those states, with whom the EU member state did not conclude any IIA at all and on which substantive provision should those investors base their claim on? Lastly, there might be major difficulties how to determine which arbitration clause might be the most favourable.[1166] One might occur the impossibility to compare a procedure under the ICSID-Convention but requiring a waiting-period of six months with procedures under the UNCITRAL rules with a four months waiting period. Another question would be, whether the annulment procedure is considered more favourable than the national setting-aside proceedings or *vice-versa*.[1167] All this reveals the impossibility of an

---

1164 *CJEU*, 07.02.1991 – C-184/89 - Nimz = ECLI:EU:C:1991:50, para 21: "*(...) where there is indirect discrimination [...], the national court is required to set aside that provision, without requesting or awaiting its prior removal by collective bargaining or any other procedure, and to apply to members of the group disadvantaged by that discrimination the same arrangements as are applied to other employees (...)" [emphasis added]*; cf. *Oppermann/Classen et al.*, 5. Edn. (2011) § 17, para 78; this seems to be denied by: *Lemke* in: v. d. Groeben/Schwarze AEUV/EUV, Art. 20 of the Charter, para 19; cf. also.: *Dahlquist/Lenk et al.*, European Policy Analysis, 2016:4, 1, 5; favouring such approach *inter alia*: *Kottmann*, EuZW, 2016, 512, 519 and *Bücheler/Vasiljevic*, SchiedsVZ, 2016, 328, 338.

1165 Simliar: *Wehland*, ICLQ Vol. 58, Iss. 2 (2009), 297, 314 who however seems to consider this difficulties to be a justification for a discrimination, which is doubtful.

1166 Supporting this view: *Clodfelter*, Santa Clara Jour. of Int. Law Vol. 12, Iss. 1 (2013), 159, 181 f.

1167 The German expression is „*keine Gleichheit im Unrecht*“. This subject has predominantly also been discussed in the context of the scope of MFN-clauses in IIAs, *Griebel*, (2008), p. 80 ff; cf. in this direction also: *Daimler Financial*

approach to extended the dispute settlement mechanism to all other EU nationals.

Second, an extension to all EU member state nationals is unconceivable if the mixed arbitration mechanism contained in IIAs itself is contrary to EU law for other reasons. EU law cannot extend illegal benefits based on a discrimination argument.[1168] As it has just been demonstrated, arbitration clauses contained in IIAs are incompatible with EU law not only because they are discriminatory, but also due to their disrespect of the general principals of the EU's legal order and judicial framework (cf. *supra* under A.). Hence, the legal consequence of a discrimination cannot be to extend the effects of arbitration clauses but to deny effect to those clauses.

D. Interim conclusions on conflicts between EU law and arbitration clauses contained in IIAs

The foregoing analysis revealed that arbitration clauses contained in IIAs are compatible with several provisions of EU law but that there are incompatibilities with others. Summarizing the findings in this Chapter it can be stated that:

- Arbitration clauses offering access to mixed arbitration impede on the principle of autonomy of the EU's legal order and its specific characteristics (cf. *supra* under A.);
- Arbitration clauses offering access to mixed arbitration do not violate the division of competences between the EU and its member states

Services AG vs. Argentina, 22.08.2012 – ICSID Case No. ARB/05/1 - Award, para 260.

1168 *European Commission*, Amicus Curia Brief filed in U.S. Steel Golbal Holdings I B.V. vs. Slovak Republic (PCA Case n°2013-6) - arbitration proceedings, 15/05/2014, p. 11; *European Commission*, Amicus Curia Brief filed in Achmea (former Eureko BV) vs. Slovak Republic (PCA Case n°2008-13) - arbitration proceedings, 07/07/2010, para 32-34; *Kleinheisterkamp*, JIEL Vol. 15, No. 1 (2012), 85, 100 f; *Clodfelter*, Santa Clara Jour. of Int. Law Vol. 12, Iss. 1 (2013), 159, 181 f; for the general application of this principle in EU law: *Lemke* in: v. d. Groeben/Schwarze AEUV/EUV, Art. 20 of the Charter, para 18; *Jarass*, 2. Edn. (2013), para 10; according to *Kottmann*, EuZW, 2016, 512, 520 the illegality under EU law does not need to be taken into account as EU law would only constitute domestic law of the hosts state. The opposite was demonstrated *supra* (Chapter 7).

although the CJEU extended its control in this subject matter through the *Pringle-Decision* (cf. *supra* under B.);

- Arbitration clauses offering access to mixed arbitration also violate the principle of non-discrimination. The discrimination cannot be resolved by extending the benefits of an arbitration clause to all investors from other EU member states (cf. *supra* under C.).

As aforementioned, by virtue of the principle of primacy being the relevant conflict rule, these incompatibilities imperatively lead to the non-application of the arbitration clause. The arbitral tribunals hence lack jurisdiction regarding intra-EU investment arbitration proceedings.

Chapter 10: Primacy of EU law on the merits

According to the results regarding the jurisdiction of the tribunals in the previous chapter, the question of how to address potential conflicts of EU law and IIAs at the *merits' stage* becomes a purely auxiliary question. It should however be addressed briefly.

It was previously demonstrated that EU law also forms part of the applicable law to the merits. Furthermore, the considerations regarding the principle of primacy being the relevant conflict rule in *inter se* relations remain identical (cf. *supra*).

A. Inconsistency with substantive guarantees provided in the IIA

The main conflict on the merits stage may arise from incompatible obligations under EU law and the IIA. Hence, if indeed EU law requires a behaviour by the host state which would be deemed to violate the protection standards under the IIA, EU law needs to take primacy. Any obligation under the IIA cannot set aside the effective application of EU law (principle of supremacy, cf. *supra*).[1169]

The existence of such conflicts was demonstrated *supra*. As an example, one might once again refer to the *Micula-Case*. The order to pay compensation for the revocation of benefits qualified as state aid by the European Commission, would *de facto* lead to a result which is equivalent to

1169 *Eilmansberger*, CMLR Vol. 46 (2009), 383, 422.

not revoking the benefit.[1170] Hence, the compensation granted through the award disabled the application of Art. 107 TFEU. Under the principle of primacy, this is unconceivable. The full and effective application of Art. 107 ff TFEU is circumvented.

However, it should be clarified that the principle of primacy will only apply if EU law mandates the EU member state to act in a certain way. If EU law allows a margin of discretion and if any of the eligible actions would be compatible with the IIA, the principle of supremacy does not apply.[1171] This was e.g. the case regarding the attribution of stranded-costs in the *Electrabel-Case*. As Hungary can pay those costs under EU law, IIA and EU law would not conflict. The tribunal then has the discretion to evaluate whether the choice made by the EU member state when exercising this discretion complies with the IIA.[1172]

B. How to implement EU law's primacy on the merits

The remaining major problem is the correct application of EU law through the arbitral tribunal itself. If e.g. the tribunal concludes that a particular provision of EU law is not applicable to the case (although it would be, given the correct interpretation of this provision), this would *de facto* set aside the primacy of EU law. Hence, the predominant issue becomes how to correctly implement the primacy of EU law on the merits.[1173]

The first and most obvious possibility would be to allow private arbitral tribunals to refer questions to the CJEU by virtue of the preliminary ruling procedure.[1174] However, in the light of the current jurisprudence of the

1170 *Eilmansberger*, CMLR Vol. 46 (2009), 383, 424-426.

1171 Similar also: *Eilmansberger*, CMLR Vol. 46 (2009), 383, 423 f.

1172 *Electrabel vs. Hungary*, 25.11.2015 – ICSID Case No. ARB/07/19 - Award, para 177 ff. It should be noted that the tribunal did not found Hunagry in breach of the IIA, as it exercised its discretion in compliance with the obligations under the IIA.

1173 Also referring to this risk of incorrect application: *Eilmansberger*, CMLR Vol. 46 (2009), 383, 406.

1174 This is supported by *Hindelang*, LIEI Vol. 39, Iss. 2 (2012), 179, 201-205 and *Hindelang*, AVR Vol. 53 (2015), 68, 84 f who also considers that the CJEU should consider mixed-arbitral tribunals being courts of the member states as they are supposed to substnatially differ from arbitral tribunals resolving private disputes. However, he also admits that recent decisions of the CJEU point

CJEU, this solution would require an amendment of the European Treaties, which seems unlikely.[1175]

Some authors argue that an approach similar to the *Bosphorus-Case* of the ECtHR should be adopted.[1176] In this decision the ECtHR stated that acts, which are mandatorily required by EU law, are *prima facie* considered to comply with the obligations from the ECHR as well, except for the demonstration of a manifest deficiency of EU law with regard to human rights protection in the concrete case. Although the author favours this approach to be adopted regarding extra-EU IIAs, it cannot be transposed to the merits of an intra-EU dispute. This is due to the fact that the underlying idea in the *Bosphorus-Decision* and the conflict in intra-EU IIAs cannot be compared. In the *Bosphorus-Case* the ECtHR expressly considers that EU member states keep being obliged under the ECHR, even if they are implementing mandatory provisions of EU law. Hence, EU law does not take primacy. This would be contrary to the finding that in the conflicts relating to intra-EU IIAs, EU law takes precedence.[1177] However, it needs to be acknowledged that adopting such an approach on the merits, would already considerably reduce potential frictions.

---

in the opposite direction (especially the *Opinion 1/09*); cf.: *Hindelang*, LIEI Vol. 39, Iss. 2 (2012), 179, 203 f.

1175 Cf. similar: *Burgstaller*, LIEI Vol. 39, No. 2 (2012), 207, 220 f.

1176 *Tietje*, Intra-EU BITs als Herausforderung im Mehrebenensystem des Rechts (Beit. zum Transnat. Wirt.-R, Vol. 104, 2011), p. 18 f; *Tietje/Wackernagel*, JWIT Vol. 16, Iss. 2 (2015), 205, 242 f similiar, speacking of "*mutual recognition*" in connection with a provision for exhausting local remedies: *Lang*, Der EuGH und die Investor-Staat-Streitbeilegung in TTIP und CETA (Beit. zum Transnat. Wirt.-R, Vol. 138, 2015), p. 20-22 who both seeks to implement a *Bosphorus* approach by requiring the arbitral tribunals to adopt a certain, more restrictive interpretation. If those limits were observed, the CJEU (and national courts) should not challenge the awards; cf. also: *Dimopoulos*, LIEI Vol. 39, No. 4 (2012), 447, 467; not really following the Bosphorus approach but resolving the conflict on the level of treaty interpretation: *Electrabel vs. Hungary*, 30.11.2012 – ICSID Case No. ARB/07/19: Decision on Jurisdiction, Applicable Law and Liability, para 4.142 and 4.168; cf.also in so far: *Kulick*, SchiedsVZ, 2013, 81, 84 f; considering such an approach but finally rejecing it: *Eilmansberger*, CMLR Vol. 46 (2009), 383, 422.

1177 Adopting *Tietje's* approach that EU law cannot be regarded as international law and hence the IIA takes primacy, the *Bosphorus* approach is perfectly in line with this solution, cf.: *Tietje*, Intra-EU BITs als Herausforderung im Mehrebenensystem des Rechts (Beit. zum Transnat. Wirt.-R, Vol. 104, 2011), p. 18 f.

One could also think about requiring investors to exhaust local (EU and national) remedies before being able to bring a claim under the IIA.[1178] This would lead to various national tribunals and – if the investor engages the respective proceedings – European courts having pronounced their view on the compatibility of the measure with EU law.[1179] However, as long as the arbitral tribunal is sought, it is obliged to decide the dispute. It cannot, without further provision in the IIA enabling the tribunal to do so, restrain from judging the case, even though this might include difficult questions with regard to EU law. If the tribunal – contrary to the authors point of view – accepts its jurisdiction in the intra-EU context, it needs to render a decision.

The potentially most promising solution would be the strengthening of the *amicus curiae* position of the European Commission. Arbitral tribunals, if the host state argues that a certain action was mandatory under EU law, may seek the opinion of the Commission on this precise point and ask the Commission to demonstrate their view on the correct interpretation, including e.g. if compensation ordered for this particular measure would endanger the efficient and unanimous application of particular provisions of EU law. Depending on the opinion delivered by the Commission, the tribunal could either proceed or reject the claim. However, this solution would require the willingness of the Commission to participate in such an approach and the willingness of the arbitral tribunals to accept the interpretation given in such statements. The previous *amicus curia* briefs seem to demonstrate that the Commission is willing to advance its considerations on the effects of a particular judgments on the merits with regard to particular provisions of EU law.[1180] However at least some of the arbitral tribunals seemed to demonstrate a large hostility to accept the opinions rendered by the Commission.

1178 Cf.: *Schill*, JWIT Vol. 16, No. 3 (2015), 379, 386 f; cf. in a different context: *Hindelang*, AVR Vol. 53 (2015), 68, 86 who considers this to be a solution to the incompatibility of arbitration clauses with the autonomy of EU law.

1179 *Dimopoulos*, CMLR Vol. 48, No. 1 (2011), 63, 92 f supporting either a suspension or the necessity for the arbitral tribunals to deny jurisdiction; cf. also: *Dimopoulos*, LIEI Vol. 39, No. 4 (2012), 447, 447, 467.

1180 *Inter alia*: *European Commission*, Amicus Curia Brief filed in Electrabel vs. Hungary (ICSID Case n° ARB/07/19) - arbitration proceedings, 12/06/2009, p. 5 ff.

Chapter 11: Challenges to the results due to the particular interests and rights in question

The key findings of the two previous chapters should now be challenged against two further considerations. The key findings of the previous chapters were the following:

Arbitration clauses are incompatible with EU law and needs to remain unapplied by virtue of the principle of primacy; hence an arbitral tribunal which is sought based on such arbitration clause lacks jurisdiction;

If any substantive guarantee under an IIA requires the state to act in a manner which is inconsistent with its obligations under EU law, such guarantee cannot prevail; in application of the principle of primacy, such guarantee needs to remain unapplied by any dispute resolution body being sought with such clause.

However, several IIAs include so called sunset-clauses which might affect the aforementioned results as they extend the application of an IIA even beyond the point in time when it became inapplicable ("*A. Impact of sunset clauses on the results*"). Second the results should be challenged *vis-à-vis* to the general interests of the parties involved, which have been previously outlined ("*B. Conformity of the solution with the interests in question*").

A. Impact of sunset clauses on the results

The overall results as aforementioned could be questioned by the implications of so-called sunset clauses in IIAs. As an example of such a clause, Art. 13 (3) of the German Model BIT states:

> "In respect of investments made prior to the date of termination of this Treaty, the provisions of the above Articles shall continue to be effective for a further period of twenty years from the date of termination of this Treaty"[1181]

It might be argued that even if EU law leads to the inapplicability of the IIA or particular provisions contained therein, this could not impede on the investor's rights, as the sunset clause grandfathers the IIA and its provisions for a certain timeframe.[1182]

1181 Art. 13 (3) German Model BIT (2008).

1182 Discussed by *Dahlquist/Lenk et al.*, European Policy Analysis, 2016:4, 1, 8 ff; *Leeks*, U. Toronto Fac. L. Rev. Vol. 65, No. 2 (2007), 1, 35 and 39.

The *Eastern Sugar-Tribunal* expressly dismissed any objection to the IIAs validity by referring to a sunset clause contained in the IIA which would in any event uphold the investor's rights.[1183]

The argument needs to be rejected for several reasons:

First, it is doubtful whether sunset clauses would apply in such cases. Under a literal ("*termination*") and systematic interpretation of such sunset clauses, one could argue that they are restricted to situations in which one contracting party unilaterally revokes the treaty.[1184] In the German Model BIT, Art. 13 (3) follows Art. 13 (2), which relates to the minimum application period of the treaty and the possibilities to unilaterally terminate the treaty. No reference is made to any (mutual) modification of the treaty by the contracting parties, neither to an inapplicability of any treaty provisions relating to a conflict rule or Art. 30 (3) VCLT being applied.[1185]

Second, admitting such effects to a sunset clause would be equivalent to limit the parties' possibilities to modify the IIA at any time. Any modification, notwithstanding if contained in the IIA or in any other instrument of international law, could only be applied after the period in the sunset clause expired. This seems a too far reaching consequence. Furthermore, theoretically the parties also need to have the possibility to set aside the sunset clause itself, if it e.g. contradicts with a specific rule of conflict they agreed upon in a different treaty. This mechanism of mutual termination, which immediately sets an end to the performance of the treaty, is even accepted by Art. 54 (b) of the VCLT.[1186]

1183 *Eastern Sugar vs. Czech Republic*, 27.03.2007 – SCC No. 088/2004 - Partial award, para 174 f expressly referred to the sunset clause to set aside any objection based on the arbitration clause being void. The German Federal Supreme Court however – implicitly – seems to admit that a sunset-clause contained in the IIA might not grandfather the arbitration clause in the IIA, cf.: *German Federal Supreme Court*, 03.03.2016 – I ZB 2/15, para 77 f. The subject is touched in *Binder vs. Czech Republic*, 06.06.2007 – UNCITRAL - Award on Jurisdiction, para 62 without that the tribunal provides a clear answer.

1184 *Dahlquist/Lenk et al.*, European Policy Analysis, 2016:4, 1, 8 f.

1185 *Dahlquist/Lenk et al.*, European Policy Analysis, 2016:4, 1, 8 who however gives an example of a sunset clause which under a literal interpretation may also take effect upon mutual termination of the IIA; similarly *Voon/Mitchell et al.*, ICSID Rev. Vol. 29, No. 2 (2014), 451, 465 f; *Braun*, Ausprägungen der Globalisierung: Der Investor als partielles Subjekt im Internationalen Investitionsrecht, 2012, p. 169 f supports that under a teleological interpretation the sunset clause would need to cover the mutual termination as well.

1186 *Dahlquist/Lenk et al.*, European Policy Analysis, 2016:4, 1, 9 who also correctly refers to Art. 70 of the VCLT as a limit but points out that the limitation

Third, and most striking, granting this effect to a sunset clause would contradict the principle of primacy. Applying this principle would set aside the sunset clause as well.[1187] Admitting a clause which preserves a situation incompatible with EU law, would deny full effect and application to EU law.[1188]

---

contained therein, does not apply to third parties; cf. similar: *Wackernagel*, EU Judicial Proceedings, Consenual Termination of Intra-EU BITs (Beit. zum Transnat. Wirt.-R, Vol. 140, 2016), 5, 12 f; also p. 265: *International Law Commission*, Yearbook of the International Law Commission (Volume II / 1966), 1967, p. 265: "*[Art. 70] (b) relates only to the right, obligation or legal situation of the States parties to the treaties created through the execution, and is not in any way concerned with the question of the "vested interests"of individuals*" for the opposite: *Söderlund*, JOIA Vol. 24, Iss. 5 (2007), 455, 460 who seems to consider that the accession of an EU member state is a unilateral act, which ignores the mutual character of the accession treaty; for the position of the CJEU: *CJEU*, 10.07.1991 – T-70/89 - BBC vs. Commission = ECLI:EU:T:1991:40, para 77.

1187 This seems to be implicitly admitted by *German Federal Supreme Court*, 03.03.2016 – I ZB 2/15 as well, which leave the arguments reagrding the sunset clause completely aside.

1188 The *Achmea-Tribunal* advanced an interesting argument which somehow differs from raising the effects of a sunset clause. According to the tribunal, independently from any conflict rule which may result in setting aside the IIA or any obligation thereunder, the IIA has not been terminated, as the invalidity or termination must be invoked according to Art. 65 VCLT. According to the tribunal, the Slovak Republic never duly invoked the termination vis à vis the Netherlands as the investor's home state and the objections raised in the mixed proceedings itself would not be sufficient, cf.: *Achmea vs. Slovak Republic*, 26.10.2012 – PCA Case No. 2008-13 - Award on Jurisdiction, Arbitrability and Suspension, para 234 ff. This is somehow surprising as Art. 65 (4) VCLT states that "*Without prejudice to article 45, the fact that a State has not previously made the notification prescribed in paragraph 1 shall not prevent it from making such notification in answer to another party claiming performance of the treaty or alleging its violation (...)*". According to the Achmea-Tribunal, the claimant is not "*another party claiming performance of the treaty*" in terms of Art. 65 (5) VCLT. Parties to the arbitration dispute are the investor and the Slovak Republic as respondent and host state. However, the IIA has been concluded between the Netherlands and the Slovak Republic. Thus, "*other party*" in terms of Art. 65 VCLT could only be the Netherlands themselves cf.: *Achmea vs. Slovak Republic*, 26.10.2012 – PCA Case No. 2008-13 - Award on Jurisdiction, Arbitrability and Suspension, para 237 f. This seems incorrect as Art. 65 (4) VCLT expressly includes the possibility to raise the objection in the proceedings itself. If those proceedings take place between an investor and the host state, the host state must be entitled to raise the objections towards the counterparty in the current proceedings.

If a substantive provision contained in an international treaty which contradicts EU law cannot be applied under EU law, a provision safeguarding this incompatible provision can *a forteriori* not be applied as well.[1189] This is challenged by few authors having dealt with this subject before, by reference to the investor's perspective. Such an effect would jeopardise the investor's rights (which would be personally attributed to such investor) and its legitimate expectations in the continuous application of the IIA.[1190]

However, it is doubtful if such legitimate expectations and irrevocably attributed rights exist under an IIA and whether the application of the principle of primacy would indeed jeopardise these rights and expectations.[1191] Art. 34, 37 of the VCLT address the question but these provisions are limited to irrevocable rights attributed to third-party states.[1192] One could indeed argue that the article can apply by analogy, but this – once again – presupposes that the rights attributed to the investor are *irrevocable*.[1193]

1189 Cf. also: *Eilmansberger*, CMLR Vol. 46 (2009), 383, 422.

1190 Expressed by *Eastern Sugar vs. Czech Republic*, 27.03.2007 – SCC No. 088/2004 - Partial award, para 174; *Söderlund*, JOIA Vol. 24, Iss. 5 (2007), 455, 460; Similar: *Happ*, Int. A.L.R. Iss. 3 (2007), 74, 76; cf. also: *Dahlquist/Lenk et al.*, European Policy Analysis, 2016:4, 1, 9 ff; *Wackernagel*, EU Judicial Proceedings, Consenual Termination of Intra-EU BITs (Beit. zum Transnat. Wirt.-R, Vol. 140, 2016), 5, 16, both with reference to Art. 37 VCLT; *Leeks*, U. Toronto Fac. L. Rev. Vol. 65, No. 2 (2007), 1, 38 f who refers to the "*fairness*" of letting investor's bear the consequences of such changes; *Braun*, Ausprägungen der Globalisierung: Der Investor als partielles Subjekt im Internationalen Investitionsrecht, 2012, p. 174 clearly refers to the investor's legitimate expectations as crucial determinant.

1191 Cf. also: *Dahlquist/Lenk et al.*, European Policy Analysis, 2016:4, 1, 9 ff; *Voon/Mitchell et al.*, ICSID Rev. Vol. 29, No. 2 (2014), 451,468-472 deying any effect when the parties mutually termiante the agreement.

1192 *Dahlquist/Lenk et al.*, European Policy Analysis, 2016:4, 1, 10 f; *Wackernagel*, EU Judicial Proceedings, Consenual Termination of Intra-EU BITs (Beit. zum Transnat. Wirt.-R, Vol. 140, 2016), 5, 16.

1193 *Dahlquist/Lenk et al.*, European Policy Analysis, 2016:4, 1, 10 f; *Wackernagel*, EU Judicial Proceedings, Consenual Termination of Intra-EU BITs (Beit. zum Transnat. Wirt.-R, Vol. 140, 2016), 5, 16; this issue is adressed by *Klabbers*, Treaty conflict and the European Union, 2009 p 126 ff with regard to Art. 351 TFEU and the principle of primacy as well; although being generally reluctant *Klabbers* seems to admit that from the perspective of the CJEU, individual rights do not set an obstacle.

However, the investor's rights are derived from the IIA and thus mediated by its home state.[1194] One needs to distinguish between the capability of an investor being (partial) subject of international law (which is merely undisputed) and the question, whether the rights conferred to the investor are directly possessed by the investor (and hence may no longer be abrogated by the home or host states without its approval).[1195] Whereas it is true that IIAs grant claimable rights to investors, those rights are not attributed to the investors for their personal benefit. Indeed, states agree upon mechanisms of mutual promotion of investment to reciprocally promote the investment in the respective territories.[1196] Hence, nationals are protected as a mean to achieve an overall goal. Some even consider that the dispute of the investor under mixed arbitration proceedings is ultimately still a dispute between the home state and the host state.[1197] This is based on the consideration that the investor's rights are an auxiliary to the rights granted to the contracting parties through conclusion of the IIA.[1198]

1194 *Hindelang*, LIEI Vol. 39, Iss. 2 (2012), 179, 200; for the opposite: *Happ*, Int. A.L.R. Iss. 3 (2007), 74, 76; this concept is contested by *Braun*, Ausprägungen der Globalisierung: Der Investor als partielles Subjekt im Internationalen Investitionsrecht, 2012, p. 98 ff who however does not suggest that the substantive rights cannot be amended or terminated by the contracting states, cf. p. 167, 174 f.

1195 *Voon/Mitchell et al.*, ICSID Rev. Vol. 29, No. 2 (2014), 451, 454; cf. also: *Ipsen*, Völkerrecht, 6. Edn. (2014), p. 311-314; *Braun*, Ausprägungen der Globalisierung: Der Investor als partielles Subjekt im Internationalen Investitionsrecht, 2012, p. 98 ff and 103 ff considers that the investors are attributed own substantive rights which might be abrogated if there are no legitimate expectations hindering such abrogation, cf. p. 164, 174 f.

1196 *Sornarajah*, 3. Edn. (2010), p. 186 and 217 who also refers to the right of the home state to pay out the investor and take over its claim as a considerable feature of the inter-state nature of the disputes; *Vandevelde*, U.C. Davis Jour. of Int. Law & Policy Vol. 12, No. 1 (2005), 157, 171; cf. also: *Dahlquist/Lenk et al.*, European Policy Analysis, 2016:4, 1, 10 f; similarly: *Wackernagel*, EU Judicial Proceedings, Consenual Termination of Intra-EU BITs (Beit. zum Transnat. Wirt.-R, Vol. 140, 2016), 5, 25 -27 who however doubts that IIAs do not also attribute personal rights; also supporting the opposite: *Happ*, Int. A.L.R. Iss. 3 (2007), 74, 76.

1197 *Hindelang*, LIEI Vol. 39, Iss. 2 (2012), 179, 200; *Sornarajah*, 3. Edn. (2010), p. 217.

1198 *Dahlquist/Lenk et al.*, European Policy Analysis, 2016:4, 1, 10 f; *Sornarajah*, 3. Edn. (2010), p. 217; *Voon/Mitchell et al.*, ICSID Rev. Vol. 29, No. 2 (2014), 451, 458 correctly point out that this feature distinguishes investors' rights from human rights protection, as the latter are based on an idea of universality; hwoever doubting this approach: *Wackernagel*, EU Judicial Proceedings,

The fact that IIAs regularly also contain dispute settlement clauses which admit inter-state arbitration is a great indicator that IIA's are still primarily conceived as an inter-state instrument. Even in the fields of human rights protection, the second great domain in which the attribution of individual rights through international treaties appeared, the attribution of irrevocable rights seems being matter of debate. *A forteriori* in IIAs, which are of less universal character, investors' rights should not be perceived as being separated from the states' consent.[1199] Lastly, the fact that the parties deem it necessary to include a sunset clause in case of termination, reveals *a contrario* that such rights are not protected without such conventional agreements.[1200]

Regarding legitimate expectations of the investor, it is doubtful if such legitimate expectations exist. First, the investor is not "*protected*" against interpretative notes by the member states as well, which might heavily affect its alleged rights under the treaty. This has been perfectly demonstrated relating to the FET standard under the NAFTA.[1201] Second, in the context of a state's accession to a regional international organisation such as the EU, through a lasting accession process of several years, it is highly doubtful if any legitimate expectation that the regime of IIAs would remain completely unaffected, although the effects and the perception of EU law are well known, really exists. Lastly, but this will be demonstrated *infra* in Chapter 15, legitimate expectations are not effectively jeopardised, as EU law provides for equivalent protection as such under IIAs.

Consenual Termination of Intra-EU BITs (Beit. zum Transnat. Wirt.-R, Vol. 140, 2016), 5, 21 ff.

1199 *Ascensio* in: Corten/Klein VCLT - II, Art. 70 VCLT, para 24; cf. also: *Dahlquist/Lenk et al.*, European Policy Analysis, 2016:4, 1, 10 f.

1200 *Ascensio* in: Corten/Klein VCLT - II, Art. 70 VCLT, para 22; considering that even regarding human rights, those rights depend on the parties' agreements: *Ipsen*, Völkerrecht, 6. Edn. (2014), p. 314; supporting this view regarding IIAs: *Voon/Mitchell et al.*, ICSID Rev. Vol. 29, No. 2 (2014), 451, 458 f.

1201 As a countermovement to the far reaching interpretation of the FET standard by some tribunals, NAFTA the Free Trade Commission issued an interpretative note stating that the protection granted under the FET standard should not go beyond what is agreed under the international minimum standard, cf: *NAFTA Free Trade Commission*, Notes of Interpretation of Certain Chapter 11 Provisions, issued on 31/07/2001.

B. Conformity of the solution with the interests in question

The solution developed for the conflict in the intra-EU context meets the benchmark criteria previously developed and hence complies with the diverging interests in question (cf. *supra*: *Chapter 5 D. II. „Enjeux en question" – Guiding principles which should be respected by any solution to this conflict of laws)*.

The first angle refers to the general principles of the legal frameworks involved. Regarding EU law, the inherent principles, such as the principle of primacy and its mandatory character, are respected to the most possible extent. The legal framework of EU law prevails. Investors and states need to comply with this framework but may also claim all rights granted by this legal framework.

With regard to international investment law, the specific characteristics are preserved as well. IIAs are international agreements concluded by two or more states. Those states are deliberately free to change those treaties or alter their effects, e.g. by concluding other agreements or agreeing upon conflict clauses with regard to IIAs. However, unless changed or amended by mutual agreement, no unilateral act of a contracting party may change the guarantees provided for in an IIA. Through the accession to the EU, both member states mutually altered the effects of the IIA. The agreement on the primacy of EU law as relevant rule of conflict does not constitute a unilateral act of any of the states which violates its obligations undertaken in the IIA. All contracting parties of the IIA are also contracting parties of the European Treaties, which means that they are deliberately free to decide to amend the rights and obligations undertaken in the treaty.[1202] Although the accession to the EU may have taken place at subsequent dates, the situation does not differ from an amendment to an existing treaty between two or more parties which is extended in time.

The second angle refers to the interests of the parties involved. From the perspective of the EU member states, the solution conforms with their interest in not being exposed to diverging, incompatible obligations and their general duty to comply with the mandatory character of EU law. Regarding the investors' perspective, the situation is less obvious. As aforementioned, one might argue that investors are deprived of their rights. However, two considerations should refute this objection. First, the inves-

---

1202 Similar *inter alia*: *Eilmansberger*, CMLR Vol. 46 (2009), 383, 425 f and generally *supra* (Chapter 8).

tor's rights are conceived and mediated through the parties' intention, expressed in the IIA. Consequently, its rights can be enlarged whenever the contracting parties decide to leverage the protection standard or diminished whenever the contracting parties decide to shorten the protection guaranteed. Second, given the considerable level of protection under EU law, the investors' objectively legitimate expectations regarding its protection against major risks affecting its investment, are preserved. It should be kept in mind that forum shopping and cherry-picking is inadmissible and the investor's business risks should not be passed on to the member states.[1203]

The last angle requires to take into consideration the practical issues and consequences of the solution. As the arbitral tribunals do not admit their jurisdiction and leave the decisions to either national courts or European Courts, the solution does not create any specific disruption on later stages of the proceedings.[1204]

1203 For a more detailed analysis of the equivalence, cf. *infra* (Chapter 15); similar with regard to the interests in question: *Eilmansberger*, CMLR Vol. 46 (2009), 383, 405.

1204 If tribunals admit jurisdiction, the principle of primacy at least needs to be respected on the merits stage, which would disable possible "*public interest*" objections regarding EU law on the level of setting aside proceedings or enforcement proceedings. However, the challenge of the tribunal's jurisdiction would still contain major uncertainties for the investors.

Part III: Conflicts between IIAs and EU Law in the extra-EU setting

Extra-EU conflicts are characterised by involving non-member states (and their investors) and an EU-member state as a host state. Hence, the analysed setting should be a (potential) legal remedy against an EU member state based on an IIA which was concluded between the member state and a non-member state as the investor's home state.

Therefore, the findings in Part II regarding intra-EU IIAs cannot simply be transposed. The fundamental difference is that there is only one state (the host state) which is bound by two legal orders, i.e. the IIA and EU law. The home state is only bound by the IIA but not by the European Treaties.

The extra-EU context currently attracts significantly less attention than intra-EU conflicts. The reasons might be manifold. First, the Commission – contrary to the intra-EU context – endorsed the existence of extra-EU IIAs and tries to renegotiate diverse mixed agreements with non-member states to unify the investment protection regime and hence abrogate the existing treaties.[1205] The success of those negotiations and especially the question whether investment related provision will, after all, be included in such agreements, looks increasingly doubtful.[1206] However, in 2014, 16 ICSID cases involving EU member states as respondents in extra-EU proceedings were pending.[1207] Hence, the question of how to consider the ex-

---

1205 *European Commission*, Communication COM(2010)343 final: Communication from the Commission to the Council, the European Parliament, the European Economic and Social Committee and the Committee of the Regions - Towards a comprehensive European international investment policy, 07/07/2010 and the various publications available in the meantime at: http://ec.europa.eu/trade/policy/accessing-markets/investment [last accessed on 11.02.2017]; cf. also for the challenges in this context: *Chaisse*, JIEL Vol. 15, No. 1 (2012), 51.

1206 Cf. also: *Lentner*, JOLAS No. 2 (2014), 156, 161. Given the recent developments under the Trump administration, this reveals to be even more uncertain at least regarding TTIP.

1207 *International Centre for Settlement of Investment Disputes*, The ICSID caseload: statistics - special focus European Union, disclosure: 12/01/2015, p. 13; some recent examples are: *Ping An vs. Belgium*, 30.04.2015 – ICSID Case No.

isting extra-EU IIAs in potential proceedings, is of particular importance. This question becomes even more important, when one takes into account that disputes and proceedings resulting from such IIAs could lead to similar difficulties as in the intra-EU context.[1208] Furthermore, if the mixed agreements enter into force, the difficulties may also appear in this context.

Three findings are crucial for the analysis of the extra-EU conflict and for the further developments in this thesis:

First, the findings in Chapter 5, 9 and 10 regarding potentially incompatible provisions in IIAs and EU law[1209] persist also in the extra-EU context. Arbitration clauses contained in IIAs remain being incompatible with the specific characteristics of the EU's legal order and its autonomy.[1210] Also, substantive guarantees contained in IIAs may reveal to be incompatible with e.g. the state-aid provisions.[1211] The fundamental difference between the intra-EU and extra-EU context is the question how this incompatibility needs to be resolved. As aforementioned, the mere fact that two legal systems provide for different regulations and are applied to the same facts, even though they might be contradictory, does not as such imply any further consequences. It depends on the respective legal frameworks to determine how to resolve such incompatibility.[1212]

ARB/12/29 - Award which was dismissed due to jurisdictional objections but involved a decision of revocation of state aid (cf. para 100); cf. also: *Poštová vs. Greece*, 09.04.2015 – ICSID Case No. ARB/13/8 - Award which was also dismissed on the jurisdictional stage but included objections as to measures adopted during the Greek financial crisis, cf. para 44 ff.

1208 Cf. also: *Dimopoulos/Sattorova*, LIEI Vol. 39, Iss. 2 (2012), 153, 155; This is also addressed by *Lang*, Der EuGH und die Investor-Staat-Streitbeilegung in TTIP und CETA (Beit. zum Transnat. Wirt.-R, Vol. 138, 2015), p. 23, who considers that the ongoing negotiations in the TTIP and CETA context reveal a chance to find solutions for the ongoing difficulties with the existing BITs.

1209 It has been demonstrated that arbitration clauses contained in IIAs are incompatible with the specific characteristics of the EU's legal order and its autonomy, cf. Chapter 9. It has also been demonstrated that substantive guarantees in IIAs might be incompatible with certain provisions of EU primary and secondary law, cf. Chapter 10. This shall not be repeated here.

1210 This has been demonstrated at length in Chapter 9.

1211 This has been demonstrated *supra* Chapter 5 and 10.

1212 *Vitzthum/Bothe*, Völkerrecht, 5. Edn. (2010), para 46 ff; cf. also the remarks by *Nettesheim*, EuR, 2006, 737, 738 ff; for an empiric analysis of the various national constitutions: *Peters*, Vienna Online Journal on International Constitutional Law, 2009, 170, 187 ff.

Second, the conflict does no longer appear on the same level and among the same parties. Whereas in the intra-EU context two sources of international law, applicable to both parties (i.e. the home state and the host state) compete on the same level, the perspective is different in the extra-EU context. Although EU law and IIAs might still be sources of international law, EU law is applicable to the host state only. Hence, the host state is the only party to which both frameworks, the IIA and EU law apply and which may hence need to deal with the resulting (potential) incompatibilities, as it might be exposed to contradicting legal obligations under both frameworks.

Third, one might argue that the aforementioned conflicts are a non-issue and does not reveal any further difficulties as each legal framework needs to determine its own rules on how to deal with conflicting legal frameworks. As long as EU law or the internal law of the host state would grant (unconditional) primacy to the IIA, the investors should not be concerned about any conflict the host state might be exposed to. Even if EU law does not acknowledge such primacy, the investor should, from its personal perspective, not be concerned by any conflict the host state might be exposed to, as long as such conflict does not have any influence on its own rights and the security offered through the IIA.

However, the question reveals to be more difficult in the context of potential conflicts between extra-EU IIAs and EU law. It will be demonstrated that regarding extra-EU IIAs one needs to distinguish between an external perspective (of investors and non-member states) and an internal perspective of the EU member state (including its obligations *vis-à-vis* the other member states). This later view will be referred to as the "*unionist*" view.[1213] Whereas from the external perspective (which refers to the perspective of public international law) IIAs remain in force and need to take primacy over conflicting provisions under EU law, EU law as such, analysed from a *unionist* perspective, does not, or at least not unconditionally, accept the primacy of IIAs over EU law. This should be demonstrated in Chapter 12 by analysing the status of extra-EU IIAs under international law and EU law which reveals these different perspectives.

It follows from the foregoing that the two frameworks claim primacy at the same time. Again, it could be argued that investors should not be concerned about the *unionist view* if their rights are not affected by the diverg-

1213 The term „*unionist*“ refers to a denomination used by *Tietje/Wackernagel*, JWIT Vol. 16, Iss. 2 (2015), 205.

ing classifications. However, Chapter 12 and 13 will demonstrate that the diverging perspectives may interfere with the investors' rights at various occasions throughout the arbitral proceedings based on an extra-EU IIA. These interferences result from the fact that although the *unionist* view may not alter the validity of the extra-EU IIAs under public international law, it has particular importance for the member states and their national courts but also for arbitral tribunals which might all interfere with investors' rights.[1214]

After having found that there might be a disruptive potential for both, EU member states as well as investors ignoring EU law in those proceedings, a more comprehensive approach between EU law and international investment law will be developed and suggested in Chapter 14 and 15. This approach will favour transposing the *Bosphorus-Doctrine* of the ECtHR to the present conflict. It should then be outlined how such approach should be implemented in practice, in particular its practical consequences, and in how far the solution complies with the parties' interests (Chapter 16).

Chapter 12: The current status of extra-EU IIAs under public international law and EU law

Adopting, as mentioned above, both a third-party as well as a *unionist* lens, it will be first demonstrated that extra-EU IIAs remain fully in force from the perspective of public international law. This result cannot be altered by EU law (A.). However, under EU law and hence also from the perspective of an EU member state as a potential respondent in arbitration proceedings, further legal consequences may derive from EU law, which may also be the basis for potential interferences with the investor (B.).

A. External perspective: continuous validity of extra-EU IIAs under public international law

Under the angle of international law, extra-EU IIAs are generally submitted to the principle of *pacta sunt servanda.*

1214 *Tietje/Wackernagel*, JWIT Vol. 16, Iss. 2 (2015), 205, 207 ff., especially, p. 209.

Other than in the *inter se* context, this principle has not been set aside by other principles and conflict rules (I.). Hence, these IIAs remain fully in force from the public international law perspective. Potentially the only remedy to end the application of those treaties, besides the mutual agreement to terminate the IIA or by means of unilateral use of a clause providing for termination contained in the IIA, would be to invoke the principle of *rebus sic stanibus*, which, however, seems to be of questionable promise (II.).

I. Principle of pacta sunt servanda

Generally, the extra-EU IIAs were concluded, entered into force and hence are subject to the general principle of *pacta sunt servanda* under international law. One could however argue, similar to the intra-EU context, that this principle might have been set aside upon accession of the EU member state or by conclusion of further amendments to the European Treaties.

Following the same considerations as in the intra-EU context, potential conflict rules concluded by the parties would need to be respected first. IIAs, as already demonstrated, usually do not contain such conflict rules. EU law contains an inherent conflict rule (the principle of primacy) but the European Treaties are not applicable to the non-member state. Hence, different from the *inter se* relations, the parties to the IIA have not agreed on a particular conflict rule to govern their relations.

In the absence of conflict rules contained in the IIA, one could only refer to Art. 59 or 30 VCLT. Even though the European Treaties may, regarding several IIAs, be regarded as *lex posterior*, both articles only apply between the same parties.

Whereas in Art. 59 VCLT this is demonstrated by the wording "*A treaty shall be considered as terminated if all the parties to it conclude a later treaty*", Art. 30 (4) lit b VCLT is even clearer regarding the present situation. It states:

> "When the parties to the later treaty *do not include all the parties* to the earlier one:
>
> […] as between a State party to both treaties and a State party to only one of the treaties, the *treaty to which both States are parties* governs their mutual rights and obligations."

Consequently, Art. 59 and 30 VCLT cannot be applied either. In the absence of any further conflict rule, the extra-EU IIAs remain fully in force from a public international law perspective.[1215]

II. No fundamental change of circumstances upon accession to the EU (Art. 62 VCLT)

Some scholars refer to Art. 62 VCLT and the *clausula rebus sic stanibus* as a possibility to challenge the validity of extra-EU IIAs (which would *a priori* set aside any conflict between IIAs and EU law).[1216]

The accession of a state to the EU or the later implementation of primary or secondary law by the EU should constitute a fundamental change in the circumstances under which the extra-EU IIA was concluded. This would, in accordance with the principles laid down in Art. 62 VCLT result in the possibility for the member states to dishonour their obligations under an IIA.

It is however highly doubtful if such arguments can succeed. Generally, Art. 62 VCLT requires an unforeseeable, objective change in the circumstances compared to the conclusion of the treaty and this change in circumstances needs to be qualified as fundamental.[1217] As Art. 62 VCLT endangers the fundamental principle of *pacta sunt servanda*, it should be interpreted restrictively.[1218]

In the authors view the foundation of the EU, the accession of any state thereto and the implementation of any act through the European institutions does not fulfil the criteria set forth in Art. 62 VCLT.

1215 *Hahn* in: Calliess/Ruffert EUV/AEUV, Art. 351 TFEU, para 83; *Eilmansberger*, CMLR Vol. 46 (2009), 383, 412 f; *Khan* in: GKK EUV/AEUV, Art. 351 TFEU, para 3; *Keller/Schmitt* in: KHN - EU Außenwirtschaftsrecht, XII. Investitionsschutzpolitik, Erwägungsgründe, para 22; *Lavranos*, TDM Vol. 10, Iss. 2 (2013), 1, 3; *Terhechte* in: Schwarze EU-Kommentar, Art. 351 TFEU, para 16; *Schmitt*, 2013, p. 289.

1216 Cf. *inter alia*: *Schmalenbach* in: Calliess/Ruffert EUV/AEUV, Art. 351 TFEU, para 17; *Hummer* in: von Heinegg/Vedder EUV/AEUV, Art. 351 TFEU, para 19.

1217 *Shaw*, International law, 6. Edn. (2008), p. 855 and *Shaw/Fournet* in: Corten/Klein VCLT - II, Article 62 VCLT, para 24 ff.

1218 *Shaw/Fournet* in: Corten/Klein VCLT - II, Article 62 VCLT, para 1 and 40; *Vitzthum/Bothe*, Völkerrecht, 5. Edn. (2010), p. 60.

None of these events constitute an objective and fundamental change compared to the moment when the extra-EU IIA was concluded.[1219]

For a change to qualify as '*objective*' under any given circumstances, it must be independent from a "*mere subjective change of attitude of the party invoking the principle*".[1220] Similarly, motives of concluding a treaty or the wish to no longer perform obligations derived from a treaty are no objective circumstances. The *res sic stanibus - doctrine* should protect those situations, in which one could (objectively) assume the parties' intention of not having the treaty concluded or at least not pursuing it, if they had known of the newly arisen circumstances.[1221] Nothing would lead to such conclusions due to the mere adherence of some contracting parties to a regional organisation such as the EU and the fact that following decisions of this organisation could be contrary to other obligations. The non-member state could even have a larger interest in protecting its investments and investors.

Second, the criteria of a fundamentality seem not to be fulfilled either. Changes should be qualified as fundamental if they "*radically transform the extent of the obligations still to be performed*".[1222] This would mean that the change is fundamental because EU member states now need to fulfil potentially contradicting obligations from two sets of legal frameworks. Although the member state's burden to fulfil contradicting obligations cannot be ignored by international law, it cannot *per se* alter the validity of an international treaty either.[1223] This would indeed open a *Pandora's box* for states to escape from existing conventional obligations under international law. From such teleological point of view, none of the acts as referred above, can be qualified as fulfilling the criteria set forth in Art. 62 VCLT.

1219 Similar: *Eilmansberger*, CMLR Vol. 46 (2009), 383, 411; for the opposite: *Johannsen*, Die Kompetenz der EU für ausländische Direktinvestitionen nach Lissabon (Beit. zum Transnat. Wirt.-R, Vol. 90, 2009), p. 27.

1220 *Shaw/Fournet* in: Corten/Klein VCLT - II, Article 62 VCLT, para 24.

1221 *Shaw/Fournet* in: Corten/Klein VCLT - II, Article 62 VCLT, para 25.

1222 *ICJ*, I.C.J. Reports (1973), 49, 02.02.1973 – ICJ Fisheries Case, 63: cf. also: *Brownlie*, Principles of public international law, 7. Edn. (2008), p. 652 and *Shaw*, International law, 6. Edn. (2008), p. 856. *Shaw/Fournet* in: Corten/Klein VCLT - II, Article 62 VCLT, para 31 even state that – with regard to the unforseable character of the change – any act by the contracting parties favouring the change, cannot be invoked under Art. 62 VCLT.

1223 Similarly: *Eilmansberger*, CMLR Vol. 46 (2009), 383, 411.

Hence, the principle of *rebus sic stanibus* cannot be invoked to set aside extra-EU IIAs.[1224]

III. Consequences for obligations arising from IIAs under public international law

Hence, from the perspective of public international law the IIA remains fully valid including the obligations contained therein. As there is no particular conflict rule regarding potentially conflicting provisions contained in IIAs, *ab initio* the host state will be forced to comply the obligations arising from the IIA.

1224 Some member states referred to the instruments of international law in infringement proceedings before the CJEU which were initiated for a failure to comply with Art. 351 (2) TFEU, cf. *infra*. The member states argued that they might rely on instruments, such as the principle of *rebus sic stanibus* when measures being contrary to an IIA would need to be implemented based on mandatory EU Law, which would then set aside the obligations under the IIA, cf.: *CJEU*, 03.03.2009 – C-249/06 - Commission vs Sweden = ECLI:EU:C:2009:119, para 23; *CJEU*, 19.11.2009 – C-118/07 - Commission vs. Finland = ECLI:EU:C:2009:715, para 17; However, the line of argumentation was not endorsed by the Court, cf.: *CJEU*, 03.03.2009 – C-249/06 - Commission vs Sweden = ECLI:EU:C:2009:119, para 23 and 41; cf. also: *Opinion of Advocate General Maduro*, 10.07.2008 – C-205/06 and C-249/06 = ECLI:EU:C:2008:391, para 55-57. In *CJEU*, 03.03.2009 – C-249/06 - Commission vs Sweden = ECLI:EU:C:2009:119, para 41 the member states also especially referred to the "*within the authorised law*" clause contained in the IIA, which should be a contractual instrument to avoid conflicts between IIAs and EU law. The CJEU firmly rejected this approach. Any mechanism of international law would be too unsecure and time consuming to grant full effectiveness to the Art. 64 (3), 66 and 75 TFEU. All these provisions in the European Treaties would be set up for situations of emergency, where long lasting negotiations or discussions about how to implement restrictive measures and to comply with other obligations under international law, would render them less effective. Furthermore, whether the requirements especially of the *rebus sic stanibus* principle would be fulfilled, is considered to be highly doubtful by the Court, cf.: *CJEU*, 03.03.2009 – C-249/06 - Commission vs Sweden = ECLI:EU:C:2009:119, para 40 and 41; *CJEU*, 03.03.2009 – C-205/06 - Commission vs. Austria = ECLI:EU:C:2009:118, para 39 and 40.

B. Unionist perspective: primacy of EU law despite contradicting obligations under public international law

After having assessed the perspective of public international law on extra-EU IIAs, the *unionist view* should be analysed. In this context, the international law perspective and the *unionist* perspective need to be clearly distinguished.[1225]

Under international law, the EU member states are deliberately free to agree upon any regulation in their *inter se relations*. They might even completely deny effect to any international agreement with third parties *within their respective relations* or agree upon sanctions if other obligations are honoured.[1226] This is an integral part of their sovereignty. However, this may not have any effect on a non-member state as a third party (cf. Art. 34 VCLT).[1227] From the perspective of those third-party states, the general rules of international law would apply and determine the legal consequences of any behaviour by the EU member state conceived therein (i.e. claim for specific performance, damages, etc.).[1228]

It will be demonstrated that *a priori* EU law recognises, under certain conditions, the validity of such conventions and admits that the member states will need to fulfil the obligations contained therein. This is the general legal consequence as set forth in Art. 351 (1) TFEU. As long as Art. 351 (1) TFEU applies, the conflict between incompatible provisions in IIAs and EU law is resolved as follows: as the IIA claims full primacy and EU law recognises, in application of Art. 351 (1) TFEU that the mem-

1225 Cf. also: *Tietje/Wackernagel*, JWIT Vol. 16, Iss. 2 (2015), 205, 207-209.

1226 *Streinz*, 10. Edn. (2016), p. 48; *Eilmansberger*, CMLR Vol. 46 (2009), 383, 398.

1227 *Lavranos* in: v. d. Groeben/Schwarze AEUV/EUV, Art. 351 TFEU, para 5; *Hummer* in: von Heinegg/Vedder EUV/AEUV, Art. 351 TFEU, para 3; *CJEU*, 14.10.1980 – C-812/79 -Burgoa = ECLI:EU:C:1980:231, para 10.

1228 *Hummer* in: von Heinegg/Vedder EUV/AEUV, Art. 351 TFEU, para 3 with reference to the fact that Art. 351 TFEU prevents the member states from breaching either their prior obligations or the obligations under EU law, as both are fully in force. Same was reiterated by the CJEU on various occasions, also *inter alia* in the particular cases regarding pre-accession BITs: *CJEU*, 03.03.2009 – C-205/06 - Commission vs. Austria = ECLI:EU:C:2009:118; *CJEU*, 03.03.2009 – C-249/06 - Commission vs Sweden = ECLI:EU:C:2009:119; *CJEU*, 19.11.2009 – C-118/07 - Commission vs. Finland = ECLI:EU:C:2009:715, where the CJEU however stated that the member states violated their duties under Art. 351 (2) TFEU.

ber states are entitled to fulfil such obligations arising from the IIA, the "conflict" is resolved by granting primacy to the IIA. This general situation will be treated first (I.).

However, Art. 351 TFEU imposes several restrictive conditions to be fulfilled in order to admit that EU member states are, from the *unionist* perspective, entitled to fulfil an incompatible obligation arising from the international conventions they concluded (including IIAs). This considerably limits the legal effects of Art. 351 (1) TFEU and hence leads to the situation where the host state under public international law will be forced to comply with the IIA but under EU law (i.e. in its *inter se* relation with the other EU member states) might be prohibited to do so (II.). Hence, the *unionist* perspective and the international law perspective "*clash*" leaving the host state with the situation of not being able to honour both obligations. In how far this might affect an investor will be treated *infra* (cf. Chapter 13).

I. The effects of Art. 351 TFEU: grandfathering of conflicting obligations

The previously mentioned Art. 351 TFEU expressly deals with the relationship of obligations under EU law and obligations EU member states might have undertaken in agreements with non-member states.

Art. 351 (1) TFEU generally admits that treaties which were concluded before the 1st of January 1958 or alternatively the member state's accession to the EU (*prior treaties*) remain fully in force from the *unionist* view and hence expressly endorses the principle of *pacta sunt servanda.*[1229] Hence, Art. 351 (1) TFEU allows the EU member states to honour obligations arising from *prior treaties* even though those obligations might conflict with EU law. Fulfilment of those obligations is not considered to be a breach of the obligations under the European Treaties or EU law in general. The member state may not be exposed to infringement proceedings

1229 *Schmalenbach* in: Calliess/Ruffert EUV/AEUV, Art. 351 TFEU, para 1; *Kokott* in: Streinz EUV/AEUV, Art. 351 TFEU, para 1; *Lavranos* in: v. d. Groeben/Schwarze AEUV/EUV, Art. 351 TFEU, para 1; *Keller/Schmitt* in: KHN - EU Außenwirtschaftsrecht, XII. Investitionsschutzpolitik, Erwägungsgründe, para 24, 28; *Schmitt*, 2013, p. 293 f.

or otherwise held liable when the (compelling) fulfilment[1230] of the obligation from a *prior* treaty leads to a violation of EU law.[1231]

Hence, at least for the IIAs concluded before the transferal of competencies for foreign direct investment to the EU (cf. Art. 207 TFEU), the member states remained competent to conclude IIAs with non-member states. EU law generally does not challenge their validity from the *unionist* perspective as well.

The shift of competences to the EU cannot alter this effect either.[1232] Without wanting to enter into the extensive debates regarding this subject matter, it seems that this shift cannot question the agreement's validity. Remaining doubts have been at least clarified by the grandfathering rule in Regulation 1219/2012/EU.[1233] Consequently: as long as a EU member state concluded an extra-EU IIA before its accession to the EU, Art. 351 (1) TFEU generally applies. In such cases, Art. 351 (1) TFEU states that EU law acknowledges that the EU member state may fulfil its obligations under the IIA, even though the obligations contained therein might be contradictory to EU law.

1230 As to the CJEU, the exemption of Art. 351 (1) TFEU applies only, if the act which simultaneously leads to a breach of EU law is compelling under the *prior* treaty. If the *prior* treaty grants discretion to the member state and any eligible action under the scope of action is compatible with EU law, the latter requires the member state to exercise this discretion in a way that renders both treaties compatible. Hence, Art. 351 (1) TFEU only targets true conflicts of treaties, cf.: *CJEU*, 14.01.1997 – C-124/95 - Centro-Com = ECLI:EU:C:1997:8, para 57 and 60: „*It should, [...], be remembered that, when an international agreement allows, but does not require, a Member State to adopt a measure which appears to be contrary to Community law, the Member State must refrain from adopting such a measure*"; cf. also: *Hummer* in: von Heinegg/Vedder EUV/AEUV, Art. 351 TFEU, para 14; *Kokott* in: Streinz EUV/AEUV, Art. 351 TFEU, para 8; *Schmitt*, 2013, p. 294 f.

1231 Inter alia: *Eilmansberger*, CMLR Vol. 46 (2009), 383, 398.

1232 *Keller/Schmitt* in: KHN - EU Außenwirtschaftsrecht, XII. Investitionsschutzpolitik, Erwägungsgründe, para 25; *Eilmansberger*, CMLR Vol. 46 (2009), 383, 397 f pointing out that an invalidity could only occur from the treaty being "*ultra vires*" at the time of conclusion, which is not the case; *Schmitt*, 2013, p. 290. For a comprehensive analysis of the situation after the Treaty of Lisbon: cf. *Schmitt*, 2013, p. 289 ff.

1233 *Keller/Schmitt* in: KHN - EU Außenwirtschaftsrecht, XII. Investitionsschutzpolitik, Erwägungsgründe, para 28-30; *Engel*, SchiedsVZ, 2015, 218, 222; It should be noted that the regulation does not necessarily state that all extra-EU BITs are in compliance with EU law. The only effect of this regulation, if there is any besides a declaratory effect, is to maintain them in force.

II. Limits to Art. 351 (1) TFEU and its consequences for the unionist perspective on extra-EU IIAs

However, Art. 351 TFEU contains several limitations which limit its scope of application and may hence result in EU law challenging (from a purely *inter-se* perspective) the primacy of extra-EU IIAs with regard to EU Law.[1234]

The first limit results from the (allegedly clear) wording of Art. 351 (1) TFEU. The article, at first glance, explicitly excludes treaties being concluded after respectively the 1st of January 1958 or the member state's accession to the EU (*posterior treaties*). Such treaties are, other than *prior treaties*, in principle not covered by Art. 351 (1) TFEU. The limitations as to the point in time when extra-EU IIAs were concluded will be treated *infra* under (2.).[1235] But even regarding *prior* treaties, which are clearly covered by Art. 351 (1) several limitations apply. Art. 351 (2) TFEU imposes strict obligations even regarding such treaties and may reduce the grandfathering effect of Art. 351 (1) TFEU. In addition and regarding both, *prior* and *posterior* treaties, the CJEU developed particular restrictions as to the particular principles or provisions of EU law which are set aside by application of Art. 351 (1) TFEU.[1236] In all these cases Art. 351 (1) TFEU will not apply. Consequently, from a *unionist* view, and hence stressing the internal perspective among EU member states, EU law contains limitations to the authorisation granted to the other member states to fulfil international obligations which are incompatible with EU law without being in violation of EU law itself. Given the considerable scope of these exceptions to Art. 351 (1) TFEU, the conflict between IIAs and EU law, which

1234 It should once again be clarified that this *unionist* perspective is a priori a purely internal consequence for the EU member states among each other. It cannot challenge the IIAs validity under international law. From the international law perspective, it would even be irrelevant if Art. 351 (1) only recognises this principle regarding *prior* treaties. The same will apply for extra-EU IIAs concluded after this date or any immanent restriction applied by the CJEU, cf.: *Hummer* in: von Heinegg/Vedder EUV/AEUV, Art. 351 TFEU, para 7; *Eilmansberger*, CMLR Vol. 46 (2009), 383, 397 f; *Tietje/Wackernagel*, JWIT Vol. 16, Iss. 2 (2015), 205, 208 f.

1235 Cf. also: *Lavranos* in: v. d. Groeben/Schwarze AEUV/EUV, Art. 351 TFEU, para 6, however with the reference to the possibility to apply Art. 351 TFEU to posterior treaties by analogy in case of a transfer of competencies to the EU; *Hummer* in: von Heinegg/Vedder EUV/AEUV, Art. 351 TFEU, para 2 and 7.

1236 *Hummer* in: von Heinegg/Vedder EUV/AEUV, Art. 351 TFEU, para 14.

seemed being resolved by Art. 351 (1) TFEU, reappears in a multitude of cases. Hence, EU law and IIAs will conflict in various situations depending on whether an actor (such as e.g. the arbitral tribunal or national courts) adopt the *unionist* perspective or the international law perspective.

1. Limits to Art. 351 (1) TFEU regarding *prior treaties*

Even regarding prior treaties, which are clearly covered by the wording of Art. 351 (1) TFEU, two limitations apply.

The first one is derived from inherent limits to the application of Art. 351 (1) TFEU which have been developed by the CJEU.

The CJEU limited Art. 351 (1) TFEU in particular circumstances. In the *Kadi-Cases* it held:

> "Article 307 EC may in no circumstances permit any challenge to the principles that form part of the *very foundations of the Community legal order*, one of which is the protection of fundamental rights, including the review by the Community judicature of the lawfulness of Community measures as regard their consistency with those fundamental rights."[1237]

This means that even though Art. 351 TFEU generally enables member states to honour obligations from *prior* treaties, this obligation may – from a *unionist* view – be limited if fulfilling the respective obligation impedes on the very foundations of the EU's legal order. [1238] The scope of the very foundations of the Community legal order is hence of crucial importance to the effects of Art. 351 TFEU. The broader it is, the less effective Art. 351 TFEU becomes.

The term "*very foundations of the Community legal order*" has not yet been assessed in detail regarding investment protection.

Tietje/Wackernagel argue that the term cannot be equivalent to "*public policy*" (which may potentially hinder the enforcement of an award issued from private arbitration, cf. *supra*). They tend to limit it to the context of human rights protection, in which it was used and to political principles in the EU.[1239] Such interpretation seems to narrow.

1237 *CJEU*, 03.09.2008 – Joined Cases C-402/05 P and C-415/05 P - Kadi = ECLI:EU:C:2008:461, para 304 [emphasis added].

1238 *Tietje/Wackernagel*, JWIT Vol. 16, Iss. 2 (2015), 205, 211 f; *Schmitt*, 2013, p. 295.

1239 *Tietje/Wackernagel*, JWIT Vol. 16, Iss. 2 (2015), 205, 211 f.

First, a literal interpretation of the term "*foundations of the Community legal order*" does not contain such limitations. Foundations of the Community legal order may as well be a feature of EU law which is not related to the protection of human rights but rather to more generalist principals or even economical principals.[1240] The wording itself hence does not provide for a particular restriction of the terms.

Second, the CJEU presented particular severity in defending several economic principles and especially the principle of the autonomy of the EU's legal order, which it considers to be cornerstones of the EU's legal order.[1241] The principle of autonomy is even expressly considered to form part of the "*foundations of the Community legal order*".[1242] Hence, the term is broader than only a guarantee of fundamental human rights. One could argue that such fundamental norms also include the uniform application of fundamental and basic rules of the internal market, such as e.g. state aid provisions.[1243]

Consequently, EU law would, from its internal perspective, not accept that a member state fulfils its obligations under an extra-EU IIA, even though the IIA might have been concluded prior to the member state's accession to the EU or the foundation of the EU, if fulfilling such obligations contravene the above-mentioned provision.

The second limitation concerns the legal effects of Art. 351 (1) TFEU. Although in application of Art. 351 (1) TFEU the member states may be released from fulfilling an incompatible obligation arising from EU law, Art. 351 (1) TFEU does not set aside the duty of EU member states to implement necessary changes, whenever an IIA is in conflict with EU law,

---

1240 Cf. also: *Lavranos* in: v. d. Groeben/Schwarze AEUV/EUV, Art. 351 TFEU, para 24 ff who seems to consider that the underlying idea is more general and extends to a general primacy for several fundamental provisions of the EU legal order (both economic and political).

1241 Cf. the provisions on EU competition law in *CJEU*, 23.03.1982 – C-102/81 - Nordsee = ECLI:EU:C:1982:107.

1242 *CJEU*, 03.09.2008 – Joined Cases C-402/05 P and C-415/05 P - Kadi = ECLI:EU:C:2008:461.

1243 Similar: *Schmitt*, 2013, p. 295 who seems to consider that the provision could also extend to questions of extra-EU BITs; for the opposite: *Tietje/Wackernagel*, JWIT Vol. 16, Iss. 2 (2015), 205, 212; for a restrictive interpretation which however does not seem limited to human rights only: *Lavranos* in: v. d. Groeben/Schwarze AEUV/EUV, Art. 351 TFEU, para 25; cf. similar: *Kokott* in: Streinz EUV/AEUV, Art. 351 TFEU, para 5.

Art. 351 (2) TFEU.[1244] Hence, EU member states have a duty, deriving from their general duty of loyalty *vis-à-vis* other member states and the EU itself, to align their obligations from those treaties with their obligations under EU law. Not fulfilling this duty may expose the member state to infringement proceedings as the obligation under Art. 351 (2) TFEU is a self-standing obligation for the member state.[1245]

Art. 351 (2) TFEU gained particular importance in a couple of judgements by the CJEU regarding extra-EU IIAs, which demonstrates the severity of the CJEU towards potential incompatibilities of investment protection standards with EU law.[1246]

In those proceedings, the Commission sought the member states in front of the CJEU for failure of their obligations under Art. 351 (2) TFEU by not taking the appropriate steps to eliminate incompatibilities between free transfer clauses in *prior* extra-EU IIAs and the (current) Art. 64 (3), 66 and 75 TFEU. The Commission argued that if any measure is undertaken by the EU based on these articles, the member states would be unable to grant full effect to those measures, as they would conflict with contradicting provisions in the extra-EU IIAs.[1247] As the member states did not take any appropriate steps to eliminate those incompatibilities, they would have infringed Art. 351 (2) TFEU.[1248]

1244 Also demonstrated by the infringement proceedings regarding extra-EU BITs: *CJEU*, 03.03.2009 – C-249/06 - Commission vs Sweden = ECLI:EU:C:2009:119; *Kleinheisterkamp*, JIEL Vol. 15, No. 1 (2012), 85, 88; *Lorenzmeier* in: Grabitz/Hilf/Nettesheim EUV/AEUV, Art. 351 TFEU, para 30; *Lavranos* in: v. d. Groeben/Schwarze AEUV/EUV, Art. 351 TFEU, para 8.

1245 *Khan* in: GKK EUV/AEUV, Art. 351 TFEU, para 6.

1246 *CJEU*, 03.03.2009 – C-249/06 - Commission vs Sweden = ECLI:EU:C:2009:119; *CJEU*, 03.03.2009 – C-205/06 - Commission vs. Austria = ECLI:EU:C:2009:118; *CJEU*, 19.11.2009 – C-118/07 - Commission vs. Finland = ECLI:EU:C:2009:715.

1247 *CJEU*, 03.03.2009 – C-249/06 - Commission vs Sweden = ECLI:EU:C:2009:119, para 16; *CJEU*, 03.03.2009 – C-205/06 - Commission vs. Austria = ECLI:EU:C:2009:118, para 17.

1248 *CJEU*, 03.03.2009 – C-249/06 - Commission vs Sweden = ECLI:EU:C:2009:119, para 15; *CJEU*, 03.03.2009 – C-205/06 - Commission vs. Austria = ECLI:EU:C:2009:118, para 16. The Commission might have had concerns regarding three sets of situations: first, the existence of such obligations could indirectly bias the member states' decisions in e.g. the European Council, when deciding about such measures to be implemented. Second, after such measures had been decided, the member state may be unwilling to actually implement them. Third, imagining the freezing of funds for a particular person to be ordered by EU law, compensation granted by an arbitral tribunal for

The member states argued that the conflict would be purely hypothetical as there has not been any concrete situation yet in which the member states did not fulfil their obligations under EU law by referring to an IIA. In their view, a conflict of EU law and any *prior* treaty under Art. 351 TFEU needs to be an actual conflict.[1249] Sweden even argued that regarding two countries (Cote d'Ivoire and the former Socialist Republic of Yugoslavia), existing IIAs would not have prevented Sweden from (effectively) implementing such measures.[1250] Hence, the member states referred to the objection that an obligation under international law will only lead to the member state's responsibility, but may not *de jure* influence its sovereignty and hence the decision to adopt restrictive measures notwithstanding the existence of contradicting obligations on the international level.[1251] The CJEU firmly rejected the objection and declared that the member states failed to comply with Art. 351 (2) TFEU. A hypothetical, *de jure*, incompatibility of EU law and provisions of an IIA was judged sufficient for Art. 351 (1), (2) TFEU. Hence, a conflict in the sense of Art. 351 (1), (2) TFEU would not require an actual (imminent) situation of incompatibility but two legally contradicting obligations were sufficient. Consequently, under Art. 351 (2) TFEU, member states were also obliged

---

such measures may indeed undermine the effectiveness of such a decision. This duty to minimise any potential friction is also pointed out by *Opinion of Advocate General Maduro*, 10.07.2008 – C-205/06 and C-249/06 = ECLI:EU:C:2008:391, para 43 ff; cf. also: *Burgstaller*, JOIA Vol. 26, No. 2 (2009), 181, 196-199.

1249 *CJEU*, 03.03.2009 – C-249/06 - Commission vs Sweden = ECLI:EU:C:2009:119, para 18 f; *CJEU*, 03.03.2009 – C-205/06 - Commission vs. Austria = ECLI:EU:C:2009:118, para 20 f.

1250 *CJEU*, 03.03.2009 – C-249/06 - Commission vs Sweden = ECLI:EU:C:2009:119, para 21.

1251 Similarly: *Eilmansberger*, CMLR Vol. 46 (2009), 383, 410; acknowledging this point: *Opinion of Advocate General Maduro*, 10.07.2008 – C-205/06 and C-249/06 = ECLI:EU:C:2008:391, para 24; cf. also: *Burgstaller*, JOIA Vol. 26, No. 2 (2009), 181, 196-199. The member states also rised a discrimination objection, as the Commission did not target other IIAs of other member states having the same structure and hence the judgement could disadvantage particular investors in the concerned member states vis à vis other member states, cf.: *CJEU*, 19.11.2009 – C-118/07 - Commission vs. Finland = ECLI:EU:C:2009:715, para 44. The CJEU also rejects the discrimination-objection. No member state could rely on the non-performance of the obligations under EU law by another member state to justify its own failure to comply with EU law, cf.: *CJEU*, 19.11.2009 – C-118/07 - Commission vs. Finland = ECLI:EU:C:2009:715, para 48 f.

to eliminate potential incompatibilities, although they might not have occurred yet.[1252] This demonstrates the particular severity of EU law when enforcing "*its own*" primacy, although this may interfere with external obligations of the member states. In case of conflict, the CJEU requires the member states to admit absolute primacy to EU law.[1253]

Following this severe interpretation, the effects of the member states not complying with their obligation under Art. 351 (2) TFEU and its implications on Art. 351 (1) TFEU are not entirely clear. Whereas some scholars argue that the only legal consequence of not complying with Art. 351 (2) TFEU is that EU member states might be sanctioned by the EU (or potentially by individuals in an extra-contractual claim for violating EU law such as the aforementioned infringement proceedings)[1254], others argue that the principle of Art. 351 (1) TFEU is limited in time by the fulfilment of the member states' obligations under Art. 351 (2) TFEU.[1255] In other words, EU law would only accept the fulfilment of obligations from *prior* treaties as long as the EU member states complies with its obligations under Art. 351 (2) TFEU. As *Terhechte* puts it:

> "(…) the most effective way to eliminate an incompatibility [in terms of Art. 351 (2)] is the non-application of the respective agreement".[1256]

1252 *CJEU*, 03.03.2009 – C-249/06 - Commission vs Sweden = ECLI:EU:C:2009:119, para 37 and 38; *CJEU*, 03.03.2009 – C-205/06 - Commission vs. Austria = ECLI:EU:C:2009:118, para 37.

1253 In a very recent decision regarding the Slovak Republic, the CJEU admitted a slightly different approach, which may however be due to the particular facts of the case. It stated that the Slovak Republic did not violate its obligations to transpose a directive, as the implementation of the directive would set aside rights guaranteed under a *prior* IIA (cf. *CJEU*, 15.09.2011 – C-264/09 = ECLI:EU:C:2011:580, para 44 ff) However, the case did not concern the obligation under Art. 351 (2) TFEU. Furthermore, the Slovak Republic did undertake necessary steps and was *de facto*, by the particular terms of the investment contract (which should be denounced to comply with the directive), despite these efforts, unable to comply with its obligations under EU law. This setting cannot be generalised (cf. para 14 f for the terms of the contract).

1254 *Schmalenbach* in: Calliess/Ruffert EUV/AEUV, Art. 351 TFEU, para 13; *Hummer* in: von Heinegg/Vedder EUV/AEUV, Art. 351 TFEU, para 21; *Kokott* in: Streinz EUV/AEUV, Art. 351 TFEU, para 13; *Khan* in: GKK EUV/AEUV, Art. 351 TFEU, para 3, 5 f.

1255 *Terhechte* in: Schwarze EU-Kommentar, Art. 351 TFEU, para 9; similar: *Schmid*, NJW 1998, 190, 193 f.

1256 *Terhechte* in: Schwarze EU-Kommentar, Art. 351 TFEU, para 9.

Following this idea, from the perspective of the member states, in case of conflict, EU law could take absolute primacy, as the right in Art. 351 (1) TFEU would cease to have effect if the member states did not comply with their obligation resulting from Art. 351 (2) TFEU (i.e. to amend international agreements which are incompatible with EU law). This interpretation of the possible legal effects would be in line with the severe attitude the CJEU demonstrated especially towards incompatible obligations arising from extra-EU IIAs. Hence, national courts of the member states, when sought with a decision, such as an arbitral award, which would lead to a conflict of EU law with the obligations under an IIA (given that the EU member state did not take appropriate steps for eliminating such conflicting obligation), would need to grant EU law primacy, although under international law the IIA remains fully in force.

2. Non-application of Art. 351 (1) TFEU to substantial conflicts in posterior treaties

Regarding *posterior* treaties, EU law in principle does not accept their unhindered application within the EU. The wording of Art. 351 (1) TFEU is particularly clear on this subject matter. At first glance all extra-EU IIAs having been concluded after the respective state acceded the EU, would not be covered by Art. 351 (1) TFEU. Consequently, EU law would claim primacy in case of a conflicting obligation between EU law and the IIA.

However, some authors argue that Art. 351 (1) TFEU should apply by analogy to *posterior* treaties, which cover a subject matter that is now part of the EU competencies, as long as the member states could not have foreseen the shift of competences.[1257] As the EU's competencies for foreign direct investments were transferred to the EU through the Lisbon Treaty in 2009, such an analogous application could affect (and "*safeguard*") a considerable number of IIAs.

1257 *Terhechte* in: Schwarze EU-Kommentar, Art. 351 TFEU, para 16; *Lavranos* in: v. d. Groeben/Schwarze AEUV/EUV, Art. 351 TFEU, para 6; *Pache/Bielitz*, EuR, 2006, 316, 326 f; *Eilmansberger*, CMLR Vol. 46 (2009), 383, 397 f; *Johannsen*, Die Kompetenz der EU für ausländische Direktinvestitionen nach Lissabon (Beit. zum Transnat. Wirt.-R, Vol. 90, 2009), p. 24 f; *Schmitt*, 2013, p. 298-300 who however considers that with the signature of the Treaty of Lisbon on 13.07.2007 the member states could forsee the change relating to their competences.

The CJEU did not express a clear position on the possibility to apply Art. 351 (1) TFEU by analogy so far.[1258] It however stated that the member states have the duty *not* to enter into any international commitment, which would *de facto* prevent the EU from exercising its powers in the future.[1259]

Generally, it is doubtful if Art. 351 (1) TFEU can really be applied by analogy (1) and if such analogy is accepted, what would be the correct consequences (2).

(1) Arguments against the application of Art. 351 (1) TFEU by analogy

Those scholars favouring the application of Art. 351 (1) TFEU to certain *posterior* treaties generally advance two arguments: first, as long as regarding a certain subject matter, the EU does not hold competencies, the member states must be free to conclude international conventions. Otherwise, there would be an imminent danger that at a later point in time, the agreement may be contrary to EU law.[1260] Second, this danger may affect EU member states' willingness to deepen the European integration, as this might be contrary to their existing international obligations.[1261]

Considering the wording of Art. 351 (1) TFEU and the *effet utile* of EU law, such an analogy seems doubtful. First, as an exception to the principle of primacy it should *per se* be applied restrictively. Second, applying Art. 351 (1) TFEU by analogy may heavily alter the uniform application of EU law, even regarding substantial elements of e.g. the internal market.[1262] Third, the underlying idea of Art. 351 TFEU is to reduce the fric-

1258 *Lavranos* in: v. d. Groeben/Schwarze AEUV/EUV, Art. 351 TFEU, para 6; *Schmitt*, 2013, p. 298.

1259 *CJEU*, 14.07.1976 – Joined cases 3, 4 and 6-76 - Kramer = ECLI:EU:C:1976:114, para 44 f; cf. also: *Schmitt*, 2013, p. 299 and *Lavranos* in: v. d. Groeben/Schwarze AEUV/EUV, Art. 351 TFEU, para 6.

1260 *Schmitt*, 2013, p. 299; *Pache/Bielitz*, EuR, 2006, 316, 327. *Lorenzmeier* in: Grabitz/Hilf/Nettesheim EUV/AEUV, Art. 351 TFEU, para 24; *Johannsen*, Die Kompetenz der EU für ausländische Direktinvestitionen nach Lissabon (Beit. zum Transnat. Wirt.-R, Vol. 90, 2009), p. 24-26.

1261 *Pache/Bielitz*, EuR, 2006, 316, 327 and references above.

1262 Cf. regarding the underlying idea of Art. 351 TFEU also: *Terhechte* in: *Bungenberg/Griebel/Hindelang* (Eds.), International investment law and EU law, 2011, p. 81 and 90, who also seems to see considerable substantive conflicts when transposing Art. 351 TFEU to those IIAs as well.

tions due to contradicting obligations, which could not have been evaded due to the conclusion *prior* to the European Treaties. Upon entering the EU, the member states are under a duty of loyalty under Art. 4 (3) TEU. They might be competent to conclude agreements but they still need to ensure that by concluding such agreements, they do not alter full effect to their commitments under EU law.[1263] Furthermore, EU member states could still enter into agreements. They however need to ensure that they may terminate the obligations thereof in case of future conflicts.[1264]

(2) Limitations to the grandfathering effect of Art. 351 (1) TFEU if applied by analogy

If Art. 351 (1) TFEU is applied by analogy, its effects are limited. It could only apply regarding primary or secondary law which entered into force after the agreement was concluded. For primary and secondary law issued before the agreement was concluded, the member states were already subject to these provisions and cannot circumvent their application by virtue of an international agreement concluded on a subject matter which is not yet (entirely) transferred to the EU.[1265] Otherwise, Art. 351 (1) TFEU would widely affect the principle of primacy and the uniform application of EU law. This was recently clearly admitted by the CJEU:

> "[Art. 351 TFEU cannot apply to a posterior treaty] when, because of a development in European Union law, a legislative measure adopted by a Member State in accordance with the power offered by an earlier international agreement appears contrary to European Union law. In such a situation, *the Member State concerned cannot rely on that agreement in order to exempt itself from the obligations that have arisen subsequently from European Union law.*"[1266]

Hence, regarding IIAs, if they provide for standards being potentially in conflict with EU primary or secondary law which was already in force when the agreements were concluded, Art. 351 (1) cannot apply by analogy. Regarding conflicts of provisions in IIAs and EU law, this will be the

1263 For this duty cf. also: *Eilmansberger*, CMLR Vol. 46 (2009), 383, 411.

1264 *Manzini*, EJIL Vol. 12, No. 4 (2001), 781, 786.

1265 *Schmalenbach* in: Calliess/Ruffert EUV/AEUV, Art. 351 TFEU, para 8; *Lorenzmeier* in: Grabitz/Hilf/Nettesheim EUV/AEUV, Art. 351 TFEU, para 27 f.

1266 *CJEU*, 09.02.2010 – C-277/10 - Luksan = ECLI:EU:C:2012:65, para 63 referring to a national law which relied on Article 14*bis* of the Berne Convention but was contrary to EU directives in the respective subject matter.

case for the overwhelming number of IIAs, as the state aid provisions, fundamental freedoms, etc. were already included in the European Treaties for decades.[1267] However, regarding several provisions of secondary law, this particular limitation may not apply as they were adopted after the conclusion of several *posterior* IIAs.

In addition, two further limitations should apply regarding those rules: First, if one were to admit the possibility to apply Art. 351 (1) TFEU by analogy to posterior treaties, this needs to be compensated by a stricter application of Art. 351 (2) TFEU. [1268]To safeguard the *effet utile* of EU law, which may be substantially affected by the analogy, the legal effects of Art. 351 (1) TFEU should be limited in time and cease to have effect upon non-compliance with the duty to align the obligations under Art.351 (2) TFEU. Hence, given a failure to adopt the obligations in case of incompatibility, the member states would need to accept the primacy of EU law, despite the international obligation in the *posterior* treaty. From the perspective of a national court of an EU member state, obligations from an extra-EU IIA would need to be unapplied in such cases of conflict with EU law.

Second, *posterior* treaties, which were concluded when the shift of competences was foreseeable (which must at least by the time of conclusion of the Lisbon Treaty on 13th of December 2007, if not earlier given the debate about the Treaty establishing an European Constitution), Art. 351 (1) TFEU cannot apply by analogy either.[1269] In total this affects

1267 *Wallenberg/Schütte* in: Grabitz/Hilf/Nettesheim EUV/AEUV, Art. 107 TFEU, para 1 f; cf. also: *Schmalenbach* in: Calliess/Ruffert EUV/AEUV, Art. 351 TFEU, para 8; for the potential implications of the CJEU's decisions on IIAs: *Lorenzmeier* in: Grabitz/Hilf/Nettesheim EUV/AEUV, Art. 351 TFEU, para 28.

1268 Also supporting an application of Art. 351 (2) TFEU in this case but without clearly stating which kind of consequences should be derived therefrom: *Eilmansberger*, CMLR Vol. 46 (2009), 383, 398; *Schmitt*, 2013, p. 300-302.

1269 These IIAs would need to fully comply with EU law, as *Bungenberg* in: *Bungenberg/Griebel/Hindelang* (Eds.), International investment law and EU law, 2011, p. 38 points out, even the Commission's "*consent*" would not change this, as it could only cover the signature, not the entry into force. Furthermore, a breach of EU law is not evaded by the mere conclusion of an agreement. All international agreements, even those of concluded by the EU, need to comply with (at least) primary EU law, cf.: *Nettesheim*, EuR, 2006, 737, 761; *Streinz/Ohler et al.*, Der Vertrag von Lissabon zur Reform der EU, 3. Edn. (2010), p. 99.

an extensive number of extra-EU IIAs for which EU law would take absolute primacy in case of conflict.[1270]

III. Summary regarding the unionist perspective and the status of extra-EU IIAs

To summarise, the *unionist* view puts considerable doubt upon the continuous applicability of IIA's in the respective relationship of the EU member states under EU law:

- Regarding *prior* IIAs, the extent to which Art. 351 (2) TFEU requires the member states to act and to e.g. suspend the obligations from IIAs remains doubtful, even more given the severe jurisprudence of the CJEU;
- Regarding *posterior* IIAs, the question if Art. 351 (1) TFEU can be applied by analogy for treaties concluded before the shift of competences in Art. 207 (1) TFEU was foreseeable is still unsolved. If one accepts to apply Art. 351 (1) by analogy to posterior treaties, it should be limited in time by fulfilling the obligations under Art. 351 (2) TFEU; in any case, for provisions of EU law which were already in place before the conclusion of the respective IIA, Art. 351 (1) TFEU cannot apply by analogy.
- For *posterior* IIAs concluded after the signature of the Lisbon Treaty, which made the shift of competencies become apparent, if not earlier, Art. 351 (1) TFEU cannot apply by analogy either as the general duty of loyalty (Art. 4 (3) TEU) requires the member states to abstain from concluding any international agreement which could alter the effects of this transferal;
- Generally, regarding *prior* and *posterior* IIAs, the scope of the inherent limits of Art. 351 (1) TFEU, as expressed by the CJEU in the *Kadi-Cases*, may also apply to extra-EU IIAs, given considerable interferences of provisions in IIAs with substantial provisions of EU law.

Hence, from the *unionist* view, there are multitudes of situations in which EU law will take primacy on the obligations derived from an IIA or in which it remains at least highly doubtful if extra-EU IIAs could fully be

1270 Supporting this view regarding the foreseeability upon time of conclusion for the Treaty of Lisbon: *Schmitt*, 2013, p. 300.

applied. The potential effects of this *unionist* view and Art. 351 TFEU for the investors will be analysed in the following Chapter.

C. Excursus for mixed agreements and future comprehensive trade agreements

Before assessing the consequences for investors, several consequences regarding future mixed investment agreements (and the Energy Charter Treaty) should be stressed out. In such scenarios, the above mentioned "*clash*" between the *unionist* and the international law perspective could even be of greater importance. Irrespective of their substantive compatibility with EU law, those treaties, if signed by the EU, will become binding upon the member states and the EU (Art. 216 (2) TFEU). Hence, in this context, Art. 351 TFEU will not apply at all and the member states will be fully exposed to all obligations under the IIA and EU law.[1271] If the "*carve-out*" clauses or reshaped protection standards considered so far could eliminate these difficulties, is rather doubtful.[1272] First, they seem to have only a limited scope of application.[1273] Second, the interpretation given to these clauses by arbitral tribunals remains doubtful as well.[1274]

1271 Cf. *inter alia*: *Schmalenbach* in: Calliess/Ruffert EUV/AEUV, Art. 216 TFEU, para 25-27.

1272 Cf.: *Hoffmeister/Alexandru*, JWIT Vol. 15 (2014), 379, 398 regarding exceptions for financial regulations, cf. also: *Clodfelter*, Santa Clara Jour. of Int. Law Vol. 12, Iss. 1 (2013), 159, 163-165; cf. also regarding CETA: *Peterson/Dahlquist*, IA Reporter Vol. 9, No. 6 (2016), 2, 5 f.

1273 De facto such a carve out clause was dealt with in the proceedings against Finland: *CJEU*, 19.11.2009 – C-118/07 - Commission vs. Finland = ECLI:EU:C:2009:715. The CJEU expressly rejected the possibility to eliminate a potential incompatibility of EU law and the IIA by reference to such a clause, cf. footnote 1224.

1274 This concern was expressed by the CJEU regarding a similar clause in several of the Finish BITs, stating that investments are protected "*under all circumstances, within the limits authorised by its own laws*", cf.: *CJEU*, 19.11.2009 – C-118/07 - Commission vs. Finland = ECLI:EU:C:2009:715, para 41.

Chapter 13: *Current perception of EU law in extra-EU arbitration proceedings*

Having assessed the international and *unionist* view on extra-EU IIAs, it will now be analysed how these diverging concepts could interfere with the investors' rights in arbitration proceedings.

EU law might intervene in the arbitration proceedings by various means in the extra-EU context. However, the interference is fundamentally different from the intra-EU context. As aforementioned, EU law cannot set aside the validity of the IIA in general. Hence, it should be analysed how EU law might intervene in the arbitration proceedings despite not being international law *applicable to both parties*.

The underlying idea of this chapter is the following:

EU law is not only international law applicable to the host state but also, through the reception of such international law in each member state, part of the domestic legal framework of each EU member state. As such, EU law may interfere with investment arbitration proceedings at various occasions and may also affect the investors' rights. Generally, one might refer to Art. 27 VCLT which states that the host state's domestic law may not set aside the host state's obligations under international law. If Art. 27 VCLT would be generally applied in extra-EU investment proceedings, the investors' rights under the IIA would not be affected. However, and this should be further demonstrated, such analysis reveals to be too short-sighted.

EU law may interfere with the investor's rights despite being only qualified as domestic law of the host state, whenever the tribunal judging the case will grant primacy to the domestic law rather than to the IIA. This will occur, if the tribunal will be forced to adopt, or adopts, the *unionist view* as developed *supra* in Chapter 12. The very essence of the *unionist view* is to grant primacy to EU law rather than to the IIA, whenever there is a conflict with EU law and Art. 351 (1) TFEU does not grandfather the conflicting obligation under the IIA. Hence, the *unionist view* somehow rejects the traditional public international law perspective which would refer to Art. 27 VCLT. Consequently, whenever this *unionist view* is adopted by a tribunal ruling the investment proceedings, EU law may largely interfere with the investor's rights.[1275] Such situations will be demonstrated *infra* (B. II. and C.).

1275 Cf. also: *Tietje/Wackernagel*, JWIT Vol. 16, Iss. 2 (2015), 205, 207 ff.

However, it should not be neglected that the investor's rights may also be affected if the IIA itself contains references to the host state's domestic legal framework and hence limits the protection offered to the investor by requiring the latter to observe certain provisions of the host state's domestic law. Such situations will be demonstrated *infra* (B. I.).

In order to structure the aforementioned ideas, the dual nature of EU law will be demonstrated first (A.) as this is a prerequisite for EU law interfering with the main stage of the investment proceedings before an arbitral tribunal.

After having found that EU law can also be qualified as domestic law of the host states, the potential negative implications EU law might have for an investor at the main stage of the arbitration proceedings will be analysed (B.). In a further step, the role of EU law in potential subsequent proceedings (and the potential interferences with the investor's rights at this stage) will be further developed (C.). These demonstrations will show a large potential for frictions, both for the investor and the EU member states when ignoring EU law in the investment claim (D.).

A. The dual nature of EU law in extra-EU arbitration proceedings: international law but also domestic law of the member state

It will be demonstrated that EU law has a dual nature which besides its nature as international law, also should be qualified as domestic law of each member state. This qualification potentially triggers its influences on the arbitration proceedings which will be further developed in the following sub-section.

It was demonstrated *supra* (Chapter 7) that EU law remains international law, although it has several diverging characteristics. However, EU law also needs to be considered as part of the host state's domestic law. This characteristic is often described as the "*dual nature*"[1276] of EU law and is the final consequence of the reception of primary and secondary law within the EU member states.[1277] It is nearly undisputed, even among those

1276 Cf. e.g.: *Achmea vs. Slovak Republic*, 26.10.2012 – PCA Case No. 2008-13 - Award on Jurisdiction, Arbitrability and Suspension, para 69.

1277 *Opinion of Advoacte General Maduro*, 16.01.2008 – C-402/05 P = ECLI:EU:C:2008:11, para 22: *"In other words, the Treaty has created a municipal legal order of trans-national dimensions"*; *Komninos*, CMLR Iss. 37 (2000), 459, 473 who considers EU law to be *„an integral part of each nation-*

who consider EU law to be a legal framework *sui generis* that this framework is (directly or by means of the prior consent of the member states) integrated in the legal framework of all member states.[1278] *Inter alia*, in Germany this reception is based on the consent given by the national legislator to the government to ratify the European Treaties or its amendments.[1279] Consequently, it forms part of the domestic legal framework as well. The underlying idea is that international law, and hence EU law, irrespective of the means by which its reception in the national legal order takes place, will *in fine* form part of this legal order.[1280] By virtue of the principle of territoriality and sovereignty, the national states remain free to decide upon the application of a norm on its territory, notwithstanding particular consequences of this behaviour, especially regarding its responsibility on the international level.[1281] This approach is largely supported by arbitral tribunals as well.[1282]

---

al law"; cf. also: *Electrabel vs. Hungary*, 30.11.2012 – ICSID Case No. ARB/07/19: Decision on Jurisdiction, Applicable Law and Liability, para 4.118; *Hahn* in: *Bungenberg/Griebel/Hobe et al.* (Eds.), International Investment Law, 2015, p. 674; *Dörr* in: Grabitz/Hilf/Nettesheim EUV/AEUV, Art. 47 TEU, para 79.

1278 Cf. *inter alia*: *Wackernagel*, EU Judicial Proceedings, Consenual Termination of Intra-EU BITs (Beit. zum Transnat. Wirt.-R, Vol. 140, 2016), 5, 10 f who however stresses the fact that in his opinion, EU law cannot be both and should only be treated "*like* domestic law" (p. 10 [emphasis in original]).

1279 *German Constitutional Court*, BVerfGE 123, 267, 30.06.2009 – 2 BvE 2/08, 397 f.

1280 Cf.also: *Oppermann/Classen et al.*, 5. Edn. (2011) § 10, para 9; para 13 for a reference to various member states and the national perception of how to integrate EU law in the national legal orders; cf. also from the more traditional international law perspective: *Stein/Buttlar*, Völkerrecht, 13. Edn. (2012), para 174, 180 ff which concludes that either from the monist or dualist approach, both would finally lead to apply international law as part of the domestic legal order; similar: *Herdegen*, Völkerrecht, 15. Edn. (2016), p. 171 ff; *Dörr* in: Grabitz/Hilf/Nettesheim EUV/AEUV, Art. 47 TEU, para 79; *Heintschel von Heinegg, Wolff* in: Beck-OK GG, Art. 25 GG, para 13 ff; cf. also: *Electrabel vs. Hungary*, 30.11.2012 – ICSID Case No. ARB/07/19: Decision on Jurisdiction, Applicable Law and Liability, para 4.125.

1281 *Stein/Buttlar*, Völkerrecht, 13. Edn. (2012), para 181; *Brownlie*, Principles of public international law, 7. Edn. (2008), p. 33; cf. also: *Ipsen*, Völkerrecht, 6. Edn. (2014), p. 11; *Herdegen*, Völkerrecht, 15. Edn. (2016), p. 8-11.

1282 *Oostergetel & Laurentius vs. Slovak Republic*, 30.04.2010 – UNICTRAL - Award on Jurisdiction, para 99 f; *AES Summit vs. Hungary*, 23.09.2010 – ICSID Case No. ARB/07/22 - Award, para 7.6.6: *Electrabel vs. Hungary*, 30.11.2012 – ICSID Case No. ARB/07/19: Decision on Jurisdiction, Applica-

Hence, whereas in the intra-EU context EU law will predominantly be considered in the arbitration proceedings by its role as *international law applicable to the parties of the intra-EU IIA*, in the extra-EU context it may only be taken into consideration as part of *EU member states' domestic law*. Thus, a distinction needs to be drawn between the extent to which the host state's domestic law could interfere with the jurisdiction of the tribunal and the merits of the proceedings. This will depend on the applicable law at each of these stages and the way conflicts between different applicable laws should be resolved.

It should be recalled (cf. *supra*) that the applicable law to the merits and the jurisdiction is not necessarily the same.[1283] Whereas the jurisdictional stage is predominantly governed by the law applicable to the instrument the consent to arbitration derives from (e.g. the IIA), the applicable law to the merits is determined by the choice of the parties or by reference to the procedural framework the arbitration takes place in (ICSID, ICC, etc.).[1284] This distinction is crucial for the developments in the following subsections.

B. Potential interferences of EU law with extra-EU investment proceedings

Given this qualification of EU law as being also part of the host state's domestic legal framework, two sorts of interferences by EU law with extra-EU investment proceedings shall be treated which are the result of the aforementioned qualification. First, interferences which result from the IIA itself (I.). The particularity of these interferences is that they result

ble Law and Liability, para 4.118; *Achmea vs. Slovak Republic*, 26.10.2012 – PCA Case No. 2008-13 - Award on Jurisdiction, Arbitrability and Suspension, para 242; it should be pointed out that the European Commission also defends this viewpoint, cf.: *European Commission*, Amicus Curia Brief filed in U.S. Steel Golbal Holdings I B.V. vs. Slovak Republic (PCA Case n°2013-6) - arbitration proceedings, 15/05/2014, para 64.

1283 *Schreuer*, McGill Jour of Disp. Res. Vol. 1, No. 1 (2014), 1, 2 f; cf. more generally: *Fouchard/Gaillard et al.*, Fouchard, Gaillard, Goldman on international commercial arbitration, 1999, p. 632 f.

1284 For the law applicable to the jurisdiction: among others: *Schreuer*, McGill Jour of Disp. Res. Vol. 1, No. 1 (2014), 1, 3 f; for the law applicable to the merits, cf. *inter alia*: *Banifatemi* in: *Yannaca-Small* (Ed.), Arbitration under international investment agreements, 2010 and cf. *supra* (Chapter 4).

from the IIA as the (international) instrument on which the investor bases its claim. Other than the interferences which will be dealt with under (II.), they are hence independent from any tribunal adopting a *unionist* or an internationalist view on the potential conflict between EU law and IIAs. Consequently, there is no question of hierarchy of laws between EU law and IIA as the restraints are contained in the same instrument (i.e. the IIA) and hence occur on the same legal level.

Second, potential interferences which result from the application of EU law as law applicable to the dispute besides the IIA shall be treated (II.). These interferences may only occur if a tribunal grants primacy to EU law rather than to the IIA, despite of EU law being qualified as domestic law only. This will mainly be the case if the tribunal adopts or is forced to adopt the *unionist view* which has been developed *supra*. In this scenario, there will be a true conflict of laws between EU law and extra-EU IIAs which may negatively affect the investor as EU law might set aside the protection (allegedly) granted under the IIA.

I. Interferences of EU law with extra-EU investment proceedings through the IIA itself

The first possibility for EU law to interfere with extra-EU arbitration proceedings despite not being international law applicable to both parties but only domestic law of the host state is by means of the IIA itself. IIAs contain mainly two possibilities which force the arbitral tribunal to take into consideration requirements as set forth by the host state's domestic law. The first interference results from the so-called legality requirement which is linked to the qualification of any economic undertaking as "*investment*" under the IIA. If the investor does not comply with particular provisions of the host state's legal framework, its economic operation may be disqualified from being an investment. This is equivalent to deny any protection to the investor as the substantive guarantees under an IIA only provide protection for economic operations being qualified as "*investments*" under the IIA (1.).

The second potential interference results from the interpretation of certain protection standards, predominantly the FET standard, which required arbitral tribunals to take into consideration several limits as set forth by the host state's domestic legal framework when determining the investors' legitimate expectations (2.).

1. The legality requirement: investments made in accordance with the law of the host state

The first aspect which leads to a certain interference of EU law even in the case of extra-EU IIAs is linked to legality of the investment under domestic law at the time of the establishment, which is (generally) considered to be a further requirement to admit the investor's claim under an IIA. This has considerable consequences for the scope of protection offered for investments under IIAs. Before assessing the consequences for a potential conflict of a host state measure with EU law (2), the current state of arbitral jurisprudence regarding legality requirements for investors will be summarised (1).

(1) The prerequisite of the investment's legality under the law of the host state

In several cases the protection offered by an IIA is limited to investments which are "*made in accordance with the law of the host states*".[1285] Several IIAs indeed contain provisions which expressly lay down this requirement. The Czech-Israel BIT e.g. provides:

> "The Term 'investment' shall compromise any asset [etc.] in connection with economic activity by an investor of one contracting party in the territory of another contracting party, *in accordance with the laws and regulations of the latter.*"[1286]

But even in cases where the IIA omits to state the explicit requirement of an investment being made in accordance with the law of the host states, several tribunals consider this prerequisite to be an implicit condition contained in *all* IIAs.[1287] The tribunal in *Phoenix Action* held:

> "In the Tribunal's view, States cannot be deemed to offer access to the ICSID dispute settlement mechanism to investments made in violation of their laws. (….)

1285 *Tietje* in: *Ehlers/Schoch* (Eds.), Rechtsschutz im Öffentlichen Recht, 2009, p. 68; *Herdegen*, 10. Edn. (2014), p. 339.

1286 Art. 1 of the Czech Republic - Israel Bilateral Investment Treaty (entry into force: 16/03/1999) [emphasis added].

1287 *Phoenix Action vs. Czech Republic*, 15.04.2009 – ICSID Case No. ARB/06/5 - Award, para 101 ff; *Plama vs. Bulgaria*, 27.08.2008 – ICSID Case No. ARB/03/24 - Award, para 138 and 139 with reference to the Energy Charter Treaty; cf. also *Diel-Gligor/Hennecke* in: *Bungenberg/Griebel/Hobe et al.* (Eds.), International Investment Law, 2015, p. 566 f.

> These are illegal investments according to the national law of the host State and cannot be protected through an ICSID arbitral process. And it is the Tribunal's view that this condition – the conformity of the establishment of the investment with the national laws – is implicit even when not expressly stated in the relevant BIT."[1288]

This requirement would apply regardless of international law to be the applicable law with regard to jurisdiction, as it directly flows from the notion of investment under the IIA. The limitation is hence conceived within the IIA itself.[1289] Only if the economic operation the investor undertakes is qualified as an investment under the IIA, the protection standards as conceived therein will apply. IIAs only protect such economic operations which qualify as investments. If the definition of investment includes as a further precondition the legality requirement, failure to comply with such requirement will lead to the absence of protection under the IIA.

The meaning and scope of such legality requirements is matter of intensive debate. [1290]

1288 *Phoenix Action vs. Czech Republic*, 15.04.2009 – ICSID Case No. ARB/06/5 - Award, para 101 ff.

1289 *Diel-Gligor/Hennecke* in: *Bungenberg/Griebel/Hobe et al.* (Eds.), International Investment Law, 2015, p. 566; cf. also: *Schreuer*, McGill Jour of Disp. Res. Vol. 1, No. 1 (2014), 1, 4 f.

1290 Besides the question of the scope of this requirement, several tribunals and scholars extensively argue whether the compliance with the host state's national law is a question of jurisdiction or the merits. This later question should be left aside for the purpose of this thesis, as it will hardly influence the overall outcome, cf. for the discussion *inter alia*: *Tietje*, Int. Investitionsschutzrecht im Spannungsverhältnis (Beit. zum Transnat. Wirt.-R, Vol. 93, 2010), 5, 16 f; *Diel-Gligor/Hennecke* in: *Bungenberg/Griebel/Hobe et al.* (Eds.), International Investment Law, 2015, p. 570 f. Without wanting to deepen the discussion, the author considers that the question is well known from other types of proceedings. Predominantly it is refered to the following differentiation: obvious infringements should be dealt with at the stage of jurisdiction, more difficult assessments, which are necessarily interlinked with deeper factual inquiries, should be treated at the merits state, cf. e.g. for claims alleging violations of the German Constitution before the German Constitutional Court, *Scherzberg* in: *Ehlers/Schoch* (Eds.), Rechtsschutz im Öffentlichen Recht, 2009, p. 293 f. However, in arbitration proceedings jurisdicitonal questions often also require a deeper assessment of the factual matrix, e.g. to determine the notion of investment. In this situation, there is no real need or advantage from transposing the question to the merits. Furthermore, the assessment of the term investment which usually states the requirement of complaince with the host state's legislation is a question of jurisdiction. It would be artificial to carve out one particular aspect of this question and defer it to the merits stage; supporting this

It is common sense that the requirement of compliance with the host state's national laws and regulations cannot extend to all potentially applicable laws and regulation in the host state. Such an extensive interpretation would deprive IIAs of any sense.[1291]

In order to determine the scope of provisions to be respected, some tribunals have followed a very narrow approach, wanting to limit the requirement to the observance of the host state's most "*fundamental legal principles*".[1292] Such fundamental principles would e.g. consist of the prohibition of fraud, obfuscating true ownership, corruption or similar behaviour.[1293] Other tribunals opposed this approach and included a broader scope of legislations, in no way limited to the most fundamental principles.[1294]

---

view: *Carlevaris*, JWIT Vol. 9 (2008), 35, 49; However *Diel-Gligor/Hennecke* in: *Bungenberg/Griebel/Hobe et al.* (Eds.), International Investment Law, 2015, p. 570 argue that on the merits, the tribunal may take a weighted approach and consider different approaches how to take into accout the "*illegality*" of the investment, e.g. by reducing compensation.

1291 *Tietje* in: *Ehlers/Schoch* (Eds.), Rechtsschutz im Öffentlichen Recht, 2009, p. 68; cf. also: *Tokios Tokelés vs. Ukraine*, 29.04.2004 – ICSID Case No. ARB/02/18 - Decision on Jurisdiction, para 68: "*Even if we were able to confirm the Respondent's allegations, which would require a searching examination of minute details of administrative procedures in Ukrainian law, to exclude an investment on the basis of such minor errors would be inconsistent with the object and purpose of the Treaty.*"; *Herdegen*, 10. Edn. (2014), p. 340; *Schreuer* in: *Wolfrum* (Ed.), Max Planck Encyclopedia of Public International Law, 2008, para 46.

1292 *Rumeli vs. Kazakhstan*, 29.07.2008 – ICSID Case No. ARB/05/16 - Award, para 319; *LESI vs. Algeria*, 10.01.2005 – ICSID Case No. ARB/03/08 - Award, p. 28. *Desert Line vs. Yemen*, 06.02.2008 – ICSID Case No. ARB/05/17 - Award, para 104.

1293 *Desert Line vs. Yemen*, 06.02.2008 – ICSID Case No. ARB/05/17 - Award, para 104.

1294 *Quiborax vs. Bolivia*, 27.09.2012 – ICSID Case No. ARB/06/2 - Decision on Jurisdiction, para 263 ff; *Saluka vs. Czech Republic*, 17.03.2006 – UNCITRAL - Partial Award, para 204 ff; *Teinver vs. Argentina*, 21.12.2012 – ICSID Case No. ARB/09/1 - Decision on Jurisdiction, para 327 f although none of these awards de facto found a breach of the national law, they did not limit their examination to any fundamental principles; the tribunal in *Quiborax vs. Bolivia*, 27.09.2012 – ICSID Case No. ARB/06/2 - Decision on Jurisdiction even expresly rejected such an approach, cf. para 263 f; cf. also for no limitations: *Schreuer* in: *Wolfrum* (Ed.), Max Planck Encyclopedia of Public International Law, 2008, para 46 ff.

Second, some tribunals tried to limit the requirements for investors not by referring to fundamental principles but by excluding such provisions which are "*unrelated to the very nature of investment regulation*".[1295] Interestingly the *Saba Fakes Tribunal,* which applied such an approach, then excludes regulations regarding the telecommunications sector and competition law (given that the investment was in the telecommunications sector) from such rules to be observed by the investor to claim protection.[1296] This has been challenged by several other tribunals in the following, which denied such restrictions on the subject matter of the regulations.[1297]

In order to obtain a reasonable interpretation of investments made in "*accordance with the laws and regulations of the host state*", one needs to address the wording, the intent as well as the context of the provisions in the IIAs (cf. Art. 31 ff VCLT).

First, regarding the wording, the terms *"in accordance with the laws and regulations of the host state"* do not imply any specific reference to the gravity of a violation. All the more, there is no reference to any fundamental principle of the host state's legal order. On the contrary, given the pure wording, one could consider that *"laws and regulations of the host state"* includes all sorts of provisions which apply to the investment.

Hence, from a literal understanding, the restrictive approach in the aforementioned cases cannot be supported. However, certain limitations seem to be necessary when considering the consequences of the terms and the intention of an IIA in general. Extending the investor's duty to comply with the national legislation to a wide range of provision will, at the same time, considerably reduce the scope of protection offered by the IIA.[1298] It may also be a possibility to circumvent the general rule of Art. 27 VCLT, which states that no national provision may justify a breach of international law. Although the question of the investment's legality does not directly

1295 *Saba Fakes vs. Turkey*, 14.07.2010 – ICSID Case No. ARB/07/20 - Award, para 119.

1296 *Saba Fakes vs. Turkey*, 14.07.2010 – ICSID Case No. ARB/07/20 - Award, para 119 ff.

1297 Cf. *inter alia*: *Anderson vs. Costa Rica*, 19.05.2010 – ICSID Case No. ARB(AF)/07/3 - Award, para 57 f; *Hamester vs. Ghana*, 18.06.2010 – ICSID Case No. ARB/07/24 - Award, para 123 f.; for further references: *Carlevaris*, JWIT Vol. 9 (2008), 35, 37 ff.

1298 This is a consequence of treating the legality on the jurisdictional stage: *Diel-Gligor/Hennecke* in: *Bungenberg/Griebel/Hobe et al.* (Eds.), International Investment Law, 2015, p. 568; *Carlevaris*, JWIT Vol. 9 (2008), 35, 40 and 49; *Borris/Hennecke*, SchiedsVZ, 2008, 49, 58.

relate to the justification of a breach of the IIA, if the protection is denied to the investment in general, the tribunal will not be able to evaluate any breach of substantive provision either. The admittance of protection accorded to the investment in general is a precondition to any protection guaranteed under specific protection standards.[1299] However, when concluding an IIA the parties expressly intended to grant this protection.[1300]

On the other hand, the substantial interest of the host state – expressed in such limitations – to force the investor to comply with the host state's national framework, should be taken into account as well.[1301] Although foreign investors should be granted protection, especially against measures by the host state which discriminate the investor or destroy the level playing field for economic operators, this protection should not lead to discharging the investor from the entire national regulations. The idea of a level playing field for national and foreign investors also implies a certain respect for the national legislation by foreign investors. When taking this into consideration, the tribunal in *Quiborax vs. Bolivia*[1302] found a pertinent approach to address the threshold of the legality requirement:

> "The subject-matter scope of the legality requirement is limited to [alternatively] (i) non-trivial violations of the host State's legal order [...] [or] (ii) violations of the host State's foreign investment regime [...] and (iii) fraud – for instance, to secure the investment (...)"[1303]

Addressing these alternative conditions, each of them seems appropriate.

Investments built on fraud should be excluded from any protection, because the principles of *dolo agit* and *ex turpi causa non oritur actio* is a commonly accepted principle, including in international law.[1304]

1299 *Carlevaris*, JWIT Vol. 9 (2008), 35, 49 and cf. references above.

1300 *Carlevaris*, JWIT Vol. 9 (2008), 35, 44 correctly points out that the host state cannot be presumed to consent to an arbitration regarding an obviously illegal investment which disregards substantial elements of its national legal framework.

1301 Similar: *Diel-Gligor/Hennecke* in: *Bungenberg/Griebel/Hobe et al.* (Eds.), International Investment Law, 2015, p. 571-574.

1302 *Quiborax vs. Bolivia*, 27.09.2012 – ICSID Case No. ARB/06/2 - Decision on Jurisdiction.

1303 *Quiborax vs. Bolivia*, 27.09.2012 – ICSID Case No. ARB/06/2 - Decision on Jurisdiction, para 266.

1304 This was admitted by all tribunals, even though the threshold determined by these tribunals regarindg the investment's illegality was considerably high: *Rumeli vs. Kazakhstan*, 29.07.2008 – ICSID Case No. ARB/05/16 - Award, para 319; *LESI vs. Algeria*, 10.01.2005 – ICSID Case No. ARB/03/08 - Award,

Similarly, the host state's foreign investment regime is somehow the most crucial precondition for the state to accept the presence of foreign investors on its territory. If there are specific rules related to the admittance of investments, the observance of these rules is a precondition to any protection.

Third, non-trivial violations of the host state's legal order should be included in the legality requirement. This refers to all rules which constitute the fundamental cornerstones for the competitive and economic landscape in the host state and thus ensure the level playing field for all economic operators. Dispensing investors from those rules would considerably disadvantage other operators. The host state will presumably not have such an intention. In general, those obligations do not set up an unreasonable burden for the investor. On the contrary, they provide a reasonable balance of the investor's good faith and "*clean-hands*"-requirement with its interest in enjoying investment protection under the IIA.[1305]

The requirement of legality is an absolute duty and not subject to the observance of due-diligence by the investor. Any failure of the investor related to any kind of the provisions mentioned above, should deprive the investor of being granted protection under IIA.[1306] However, the requirement only extends to the legal basis which was already set up at the time of establishment. Further changes in national legislation may not affect the protection enjoyed under the IIA.[1307]

---

p. 28. *Desert Line vs. Yemen*, 06.02.2008 – ICSID Case No. ARB/05/17 - Award, para 104 but also *Fraport vs. Philippines*, 16.08.2007 – ICSID Case No. ARB/03/25 - Award, para 402.

1305 *Khachaturian/Moloo*, Fordham International Law Journal Vol. 34, Iss. 6 (2011), 1473, 1485, cf. also: *Anderson vs. Costa Rica*, 19.05.2010 – ICSID Case No. ARB(AF)/07/3 - Award, para 58; cf. similar: *Diel-Gligor/Hennecke* in: *Bungenberg/Griebel/Hobe et al.* (Eds.), International Investment Law, 2015, p. 573 and *Carlevaris*, JWIT Vol. 9 (2008), 35, 48 f; *Hammerstein/Roegele*, SchiedsVZ, 2015, 275, 278-280.

1306 *Herdegen*, 10. Edn. (2014), p. 339; *Salacuse*, The law of investment treaties, 2. Edn. (2015) 7.6 Limitations on Defitions of Investment (a) Legal Requirements; for the opposite: *Fraport vs. Philippines*, 16.08.2007 – ICSID Case No. ARB/03/25 - Award, para 396.

1307 Cf. *inter alia*: *Diel-Gligor/Hennecke* in: *Bungenberg/Griebel/Hobe et al.* (Eds.), International Investment Law, 2015, p. 575.

(2) Consequences for interferences of investments with EU law

It will be analysed to what extent the legality requirement as perceived in (1) may interfere with the investment protection under an IIA if the investor violates provisions of EU law. In situations where the investor is denied protection under the IIA due to non-compliance with provisions of EU law, such interference occurs. At the same time, the "*conflict*" between EU law and IIAs would be eliminated in favour of EU law. In such cases the investor may not rely on the protection under the IIA if the economic operation conducted by such investor violates EU law.

Indeed, the respect of several provisions of EU law are part of the non-trivial violations conceived as part of the legality requirement imposed upon investors.

This includes most of the fundamental provisions of EU competition and procurement law as well as the state aid rules.

Regarding state aid rules, the Art. 107 ff TFEU and the general procedure to comply with when seeking to be granted any financial or non-financial benefit which might mitigate the charges usually to be borne by the investor, are core elements of the EU legal framework. The overall goal of these provisions is to ensure an unhindered competition within the internal market and a level playing field for all economic operators.[1308] The general prohibition of state aid is one of the most important provisions to achieve this goal. The EU member states should not be able to interfere with the economic success of any particular entity or a sector by any means.[1309] If any aid, by whatever means, is granted to an economic operator, it should be granted by an independent authority (the Commission) and following procedural and substantive criteria, which take into consideration the effects and the necessity for such interference with an unhindered competition.[1310] The observance of these general principles

---

1308 Art. 3 lit. g of the EC – Treaty expressly declared this as an overall goal of the Treaty. Although the Lisbon Treaty abandonned this declaration, it still remains valid, cf. *Hobe*, 8. Edn. (2014), para 1064; *Wallenberg/Schütte* in: Grabitz/Hilf/Nettesheim EUV/AEUV, Art. 107 TFEU, para 10; *Kühling* in: Streinz EUV/AEUV, Art. 107 TFEU, para 1 f; *Haratsch*, 2016, p. 609 f.

1309 *Oppermann/Classen et al.*, 5. Edn. (2011) § 21, para 1 ff; cf. also references above.

1310 *Oppermann/Classen et al.*, 5. Edn. (2011) § 21, para 2; *Rusche* in: Immenga/Mestmäcker AEUV, D. Art. 107 (3) TFEU, para 43-53; *Kühling* in: Streinz EUV/AEUV, Art. 107 TFEU, para 109.

laid down in Art. 107 and 108 TFEU and implemented through the directives, are crucial for the entire functioning of the EU's internal market. The Commission and the member states in general also openly address all economic operators when publishing guidelines, communications or other publications to build a reliable and transparent procedure as to the conditions to obtain the approval for a certain state measure which could be qualified as state aid.[1311] The CJEU even refers to those guidelines as setting up a certain legitimate expectation for other competitors.[1312]

For foreign investors this legal framework should be among the most basic understandings when entering the internal market. Any economic undertaking operating within the EU should be aware of these principles which feature among the most prominent achievements of EU competition law. Consequently, no economic operator should be entitled to build its business in violation of the legal requirements under Art. 107 ff TFEU. Indeed, compliance with state aid rules is of such importance within the EU that an investment construed in violence of these rules should be excluded from the scope of protected investments. Given that the requirement of specific procedures to obtain such aid is commonly known in the public sphere, one could even perceive that an investor ignoring any necessity of prior approval of a state aid measure tries to condone the circumvention of those rules. Approving such behaviour is nearly equal to intentionally trying to set aside an existing legislation.

A similar reasoning should apply for the general rules regarding competition in Art. 101 ff TFEU and the public procurement procedures. All of these contain substantial elements to establish a free and unhindered internal market within the EU. They contribute to set up the previously cited level playing field among economic operators and thus determine the boundaries to be respected by businesses and economic operators in general. The prohibition of abuse of a dominant market position is a fundamental idea in the conception of the internal market.[1313] The same applies,

1311 Cf. also: *Oppermann/Classen et al.*, 5. Edn. (2011) § 21, para 19; *Bär-Bouyssière* in: Schwarze EU-Kommentar, Art. 107 TFEU, para 5; *CJEU*, 24.03.1993 – C-313/90 - CIRFS = ECLI:EU:C:1993:111, para 41 ff.

1312 *CJEU*, 24.03.1993 – C-313/90 - CIRFS = ECLI:EU:C:1993:111, para 41 ff.

1313 *Hobe*, 8. Edn. (2014), para 996; *Eilmansberger* in: Streinz EUV/AEUV, Art. 101 TFEU, para 1-3; *Schröter* in: v. d. Groeben/Schwarze AEUV/EUV, Art. 101 TFEU, para 18-20.

at least since the last directives on public procurement, for the procedures to follow in the attribution of orders in the public procurement.[1314]

Thus, establishing an investment by circumventing these rules or even directly disregarding these rules certainly also directly disregards basic provisions in the EU member states to establish the general circumstances of exercising economic freedoms. Those investments should therefore equally be considered as not being construed in accordance with the laws and regulations of the host state.

However, this exception for granting protection to investments should not apply if further developments after the establishment of the investment lead to a (potentially) abusive market position by the investor and thus to measures in terms of Art. 101 ff TFEU. Such later changes of the legal framework cannot set aside the investment's legality and its protection.

Similar considerations should apply for secondary law applying to a certain field of investments, especially particular sectors such as the energy or banking sector. Those provisions, although being of interventionist character, set up the general rules of the game. *Inter alia*, the previously mentioned third energy package implements certain basic and common rules to observe in the energy market through the directives 2009/72/EC and 2009/73/EC. The same would be true regarding the SSM-directive in the banking sector. Any particular promises which circumvents those rules cannot be accepted as being an investment made in accordance with the host state's laws. All operators, irrespective of their origin, will need to comply with these measures when entering this market. However, once again, energy suppliers being established in 2008, before adoption of the directives in 2009, would only need to comply with the former rules, e.g. in the energy sector established in the 2003 directives.[1315] The legality requirement cannot extend to changes to the legal framework which happen after the establishment of the investor (cf. *supra*).

1314 *Tiedje* in: v. d. Groeben/Schwarze AEUV/EUV, Art. 53 TFEU, para 129-132; *Höfler*, NZBau, 2010, 73, 74 f.

1315 Directive 2003/55/EC - Common rules for the internal market in natural gas, Official Journal of the European Communities L 176 (26.06.2003 (repealed)), 57 and Directive 2003/54/EC - Common rules for the internal market in electricity, Official Journal of the European Communities L 176 (26.06.2003 (repealed)), 37.

2. Interpretation of the Fair and Equitable Treatment standard

Another limitation derived from EU law on the merits could be drawn regarding the FET standard. FET is generally admitted to be one of the most commonly used standards by investors when referring to the type of measures subject to this thesis. Especially regulatory changes or the revocation of preferential promises to the investor are predominantly challenged in arbitration proceedings involving EU member states.[1316]

It was already demonstrated that the cornerstone of admitting the violation of the FET standard is the definition of "*legitimate*" expectations. Determining the threshold of these expectations considerably influences the margin of action attributed to the host state when changing its legislations. When addressing the question of potential conflicts of mandatory provisions of EU law with extra-EU IIAs, one could argue that several of the requirements mandated by EU law need to be taken into account when considering the legitimacy of the investor's expectations. This would indeed considerably reduce the potential conflicts.

Jacob/Schill underline that legitimate expectations are:

> "limited to [protect] what an investor, based on objective government conduct and based on the *circumstances prevailing in the host state* can legitimately expect at the time of investing abroad. It is not a purely subjective test. (…) The issue becomes one of *how regulatory charges are ushered* in, rather than whether."[1317]

These circumstances also include the lawfulness of an act under domestic law. When assessing the investor's (alleged) expectations the *Electrabel-Tribunal*[1318] stated:

> "Electrabel cannot point to EU law for its expectations, given that Hungary was *seeking at all times, necessarily, to comply with EU law, as Electrabel and Dunamenti both knew* (…); Electrabel cannot found its case on Hungary's regulated or deregulated pricing, given that it was common knowledge that long-term PPAs could not cohabit, unchanged, with deregulation. (…) Electrabel knew (as did Dunamenti) that Dunamenti bore the commercial risks of its operations in Hungary under the PPA in a difficult *transitional period towards market liberalisation and*

1316 Cf. *inter alia*: *Eastern Sugar vs. Czech Republic*, 27.03.2007 – SCC No. 088/2004 - Partial award, para 199 f; *Electrabel vs. Hungary*, 30.11.2012 – ICSID Case No. ARB/07/19: Decision on Jurisdiction, Applicable Law and Liability, para 6.14 f; *AES Summit vs. Hungary*, 23.09.2010 – ICSID Case No. ARB/07/22 - Award, para 9.1.1.

1317 *Jacob/Schill* in: *Bungenberg/Griebel/Hobe et al.* (Eds.), International Investment Law, 2015, p. 747 [emphasis added].

1318 *Electrabel vs. Hungary*, 25.11.2015 – ICSID Case No. ARB/07/19 - Award.

> *membership of the European Union, including the application of EU law and the role of the Commission.*"[1319]

In other words: an investor cannot expect that a host state would breach fundamental norms in its favour, including those of EU law. This was indeed concluded by various tribunals dealing with the FET standard.[1320] The *Electrabel-Tribunal* refers to two considerations, when addressing the scope of the expectations the investor could reasonably have. First, an investor cannot rely on the non-compliance of the host state with EU law.[1321] Second, the investor's expectations need to be backed up against the political, judicial and social background of the host state's accession to the EU and hence includes a certain anticipation. A similar approach – although outside the context of EU law – was also followed in the *Duke Energy vs. Ecuador*[1322] award when the tribunal expressly held that the

> "assessment of the reasonableness or legitimacy must take into account all circumstances, including not only the facts surrounding the investment, but also the political, socioeconomic, cultural and historical conditions prevailing in the host State."[1323]

The tribunal in *Saluka vs. Czech Republic* also held that:

> "[the investor] had no basis for expecting that there would be no future change in the Government's policy towards the banking sector's bad loan problem or in the Government's willingness to adhere during the pre-accession period to the rules on State aid in the Europe Agreement."[1324]

This approach seems correct. Similarly, as concerning the legality of the investment, the claim for damages under the FET standard requires a cer-

---

1319 *Electrabel vs. Hungary*, 25.11.2015 – ICSID Case No. ARB/07/19 - Award, para 156 [emphasis added].

1320 *LG&E vs. Argentina*, 03.10.2006 – ICSID Case No. ARB/02/1 - Decision on Liability, para 130; *Duke Energy vs. Ecuador*, 18.08.2008 – ICSID Case No. ARB/04/19 - Award, para 347; *Continental vs. Argentina*, 05.09.2008 – ICSID Case No. ARB/03/9 - Award, para 261; *Parkerings vs. Lithuania*, 11.09.2007 – ICSID Case No. ARB/05/8 - Award, para 331.

Ioan Micula, Viorel Micula & others vs. Romania, 11.12.2013 – ICSID Case No. ARB/05/20 - Final Award, para 529.

1321 Endorsing this approach: *Kniebaum*, ELTE Law Journal, 27,34; cf. also: *Schreuer*, JWIT Vol. 6, No. 3 (2005), 357, 369.

1322 *Duke Energy vs. Ecuador*, 18.08.2008 – ICSID Case No. ARB/04/19 - Award.

1323 *Duke Energy vs. Ecuador*, 18.08.2008 – ICSID Case No. ARB/04/19 - Award, para 340.

1324 *Saluka vs. Czech Republic*, 17.03.2006 – UNCITRAL - Partial Award, para 351: cf. also: *Burgstaller*, JOIA Vol. 26, No. 2 (2009), 181, 193 f.

tain due diligence by the investor. The burden of an undisturbed relationship of economic operators within the territory of the host state cannot be exclusively borne by the host-states. This due diligence, which refers to assessing the general legal framework but also potential circumstances which might (fundamentally) alter this legal framework, should be borne by the investor. Hence the assessment of this due diligence should be part of the expectations the investor reasonably *was entitled to have (its legitimate expectations)*.[1325] The investor cannot reasonably believe that the host state would not observe fundamental legal provisions, including those issued by a supra-national institution, which would expose the host state to further sanctions by this organisation such as *inter alia* infringement proceedings by the European Commission.[1326]

Relating to EU law, such due diligence of course requires the investor to be informed about fundamental provisions and their *mise en oeuvre*, such as the state aid provisions in Art. 107 ff TFEU and the competition law regulations under Art. 101 ff TFEU. [1327]

However, the scope is not limited to those provisions. Other than for the legality of the investment at the time of establishment, the due diligence regarding its legitimate expectations includes a certain kind of anticipation of further changes which might occur due to the host state being an EU member state and which are reasonably foreseeable.[1328]

This is not limited – as in the specific factual circumstances of the *Electrabel-Decision* – to the changes occurring in the context of the host state's accession to the EU. Indeed, these circumstances which were the result of a long-lasting process of integration, starting with the signing of the association agreements, were so obvious that none of the investors

---

1325 Cf. also: *Hammerstein/Roegele*, SchiedsVZ, 2015, 275, 278-280; *Kniebaum*, ELTE Law Journal, 27, 34; *Burgstaller*, JOIA Vol. 26, No. 2 (2009), 181, 193f; *Eilmansberger*, CMLR Vol. 46 (2009), 383, 417.

1326 Cf. also: *Kniebaum*, ELTE Law Journal, 27,34; *Eilmansberger*, CMLR Vol. 46 (2009), 383, 417 who considers that there "*can be no protection for illegal [..] measures [even] under the Europe Agreement*"; *Burgstaller*, JOIA Vol. 26, No. 2 (2009), 181, 195.

1327 Cf.also: *Kniebaum*, ELTE Law Journal, 27,34; regarding the fundamental character of these provisions cf. *supra* Chapter 5 and 13.

1328 For the opposite however: *Eilmansberger*, CMLR Vol. 46 (2009), 383, 417 who considers that potential further evolutions cannot be part of the investor's due dilligence regarding the legailty of its investment; also: *Burgstaller*, JOIA Vol. 26, No. 2 (2009), 181, 195.

could reasonably disregard the changes which might affect the entire business upon accession.

Such a due diligence and duty to anticipate should also relate to sectors which are already subject to a certain regulation by the EU based on the further deepening of the internal market and which have a considerably high probability of further regulations by the EU. The third energy package is a pertinent example of such regulations.

The regulation in the energy market dates back to the first directives being issued in 1996.[1329] Since then, the EU has regularly intervened in the market and has extended its regulations to obtain a more competitive energy and gas market, which is less dominated by national interferences and large monopolies or oligopolies. In this context, the third energy package was issued to counter the inefficiencies perceived after the 2003 directives and the second legislative package. Even though no fourth edition of these regulation has been issued yet, the Commission's communication on the adoption of the third package, dated 15th of November 2012,[1330] clearly indicates that further regulations in this field, aiming to foster competition and to further reduce particular advantages of large suppliers, transmission companies or national member states, will be adopted soon. An investor investing in this context cannot reasonably expect that the legislative framework in a particular member state, which probably contravenes these requirements, will persist over the coming years. This is reminiscent of the accession context, where the Europe Agreements already contained specific provisions which made clear that particular advantages may not persist. The same applies here.[1331] If the in-

1329 *Roggenkamp/Redgwell/Rønne u. a.* (Eds.), Energy law in Europe, 3. Edn. (2016), para 4.197 f; cf. also: *Theobald/Gey-Kern*, EuZW, 2011, 896, 896 with further references regarding the implications in a Germany as a member state when implementing the directive.

1330 *European Commission*, Communication COM(2012) 663 final: Communication from the Commission to the European Parliament, the Council, the European Economic and Social Committee and the Committee of the Regions - Making the internal energy market work, 15/11/2012.

1331 Cf. inter alia: Art. 64 of the Europe Agreements: "*The following are incompatible with the proper functioning of the Agreement in so far as they may affect trade beween the Community and [the member state]: [...] (iii) any public aid which distorts or threatens to distort competition by favouring certain undertakings or the production of goods (...)*"; also advanced by the Commission in its amicus curiae brief in the U.S. Steel vs Slovak Republic proceedings to demonstrate that no legitimate expectations could exist or persist (although this

vestor decides to bear the risk of particular changes to affect its business, it is a pure business risk which may pay in the form of high margins or lead to large losses but which should not be borne by EU member states on the basis of an IIA.

II. Interferences of EU law with extra-EU investment proceedings through domestic law being applicable law to the arbitration proceedings

The second type of interference may result from EU law being applicable law to the investment proceedings as domestic law of the host state. However, in this situation, EU law may only interfere with the investor's rights if the tribunal grants primacy to EU law rather than to the IIA which will be predominantly the case if it adopts or is forced to adopt the *unionist view* on the relationship between EU law and IIAs. If the tribunal relies on the public international law perspective, extra-EU IIAs remain fully in force and cannot be set aside by EU law, cf. Art. 27 VCLT. Only if and to the extent the tribunal favours the unionist view, EU law may endanger the unrestricted application of the IIA.

The potential application of EU law to the dispute will be subdivided to the situations and implication of EU law being applicable law to the jurisdictional stage and to the merits state.

1. EU law being the applicable law to the jurisdictional stage as *lex loci arbitri*.

Generally, the law applicable to determine the arbitral tribunal's jurisdiction is derived from the instrument the arbitration clause is contained in.[1332] Hence, regarding treaty claims (i.e. claims based on an IIA), this will usually be the IIA. Domestic law, even though it might be applicable

---

view is focused on the judgements of the CJEU), cf.: *European Commission*, Amicus Curia Brief filed in U.S. Steel Golbal Holdings I B.V. vs. Slovak Republic (PCA Case n°2013-6) - arbitration proceedings, 15/05/2014, para 14 and 66.

1332 *Banifatemi* in: *Yannaca-Small* (Ed.), Arbitration under international investment agreements, 2010, p. 191 f; *Schreuer*, McGill Jour of Disp. Res. Vol. 1, No. 1 (2014), 1, 3 f; *Azurix Corp. vs. Argentina*, 08.12.2003 – ICSID Case No. ARB/01/12 - Decision on Jurisdiction, para 48.

to the merits stage by e.g. a choice of law clause, should not affect the tribunals jurisdiction as it will generally not question the validity of an agreement under international law.[1333] However, the validity of the arbitration clause could be questioned, if EU law is applicable as *lex loci arbitri*, which will be the case if the arbitral tribunal has its seat in an EU member state.

The *lex loci arbitri* usually refers to the domestic law at the seat of the tribunal and will determine the validity of the arbitration clause as well as set the mandatory limits for the procedure to be applied.[1334] It is usually not applicable to the merits. Being applicable to the jurisdiction phase, it needs to be taken into account when evaluating the validity of the arbitration agreement contained in the IIA, irrespective of whether it is international law applicable to both parties.[1335] It is applied as the domestic law of the host state where the arbitral tribunal has its seat.[1336]

This having said, EU law might set aside the tribunals jurisdiction by rendering the arbitration clause invalid. Such clauses are incompatible with the specific characteristics of EU law, especially its autonomy. This has been demonstrated in Chapter 9. As the submission of mixed disputes regarding an EU member state to arbitration is considered to impede on the autonomy of the EU's legal order and its specific characteristics, the

---

1333 *Schreuer*, McGill Jour of Disp. Res. Vol. 1, No. 1 (2014), 1, 3 f; *Azurix Corp. vs. Argentina*, 08.12.2003 – ICSID Case No. ARB/01/12 - Decision on Jurisdiction, para 48; *CMS vs. Argentina*, 17.07.2003 – ICSID Case No. ARB/01/8 - Decision of the Tribunal on Objections to Jurisdiction, para 42 and 88; Similar: *Daimler Financial Services AG vs. Argentina*, 22.08.2012 – ICSID Case No. ARB/05/1 - Award, para 50.

1334 *Böckstiegel*, Arbitration International Vol. 28, Iss. 4 (2012), 577, 579 f; *Trittmann*, SchiedsVZ, 2016, 7, 10; *Park*, The International and Comparative Law Quarterly Vol. 32, No. 1 (1983), 21, 22 f; *Horn*, SchiedsVZ, 2008, 209, 211 f; The concept of lex loci arbitry gets challenged by several scholars and some arbitral tribunals which suggest to grant larger autonomy to the arbtiration clause and its proceedings (cf. e.g: *Fouchard/Gaillard et al.*, Fouchard, Gaillard, Goldman on international commercial arbitration, 1999, p. 213 ff). However, at least regarding EU member states, the above-mentioned principles would apply regarding the effects of EU law.

1335 *Park*, The International and Comparative Law Quarterly Vol. 32, No. 1 (1983), 21, 23; cf. also: *Higher Regional Court Frankfurt*, SchiedsVZ (2013), 119, 10.05.2012 – 26 SchH 11/10, 122.

1336 *Böckstiegel*, Arbitration International Vol. 28, Iss. 4 (2012), 577, 579 f; *Trittmann*, SchiedsVZ, 2016, 7, 10; *Park*, The International and Comparative Law Quarterly Vol. 32, No. 1 (1983), 21, 22 f; *Horn*, SchiedsVZ, 2008, 209, 211 f.

lex loci arbitri through the application of EU law would render the arbitration clause invalid. This applies irrespective of whether both parties are EU member states or just the host state. From its internal perspective, EU law will still consider arbitration clauses such as contained in IIAs to be incompatible with EU law. The question whether this incompatibility has any effects on the arbitration proceedings is a matter of the applicable conflict clause. The *lex loci arbitri* can be considered as such conflict clause as it grants primacy to the law of the arbitral tribunal's seat in order to determine the validity of the arbitration clause. If the *lex loci arbitri* includes EU law, which will be the case in all EU member states, it will render the arbitration clause invalid for violation of the specific characteristics of the EU's legal order and the principle of autonomy. This general principle cannot be set aside by any EU member state, irrespective if by virtue of an intra-EU or extra EU agreement.[1337] The grandfathering provisions in Art. 351 (1) TFEU cannot safeguard the arbitration clause in this context. If they would apply, the conflict between EU law (stating that the arbitration clause is invalid as it is incompatible with the principle of autonomy of EU law) and the IIA (containing the arbitration clausc) would be resolved in favour of the IIA. However, this safeguard does not apply in this scenario for multiple reasons.

First, regarding *posterior* IIAs, in the authors view, Art. 351 (1) TFEU may not apply and hence EU law would require the arbitration clause to be set aside. The grandfathering rule in Art. 351 (1) cannot authorise member states to violate substantive principles such as the autonomy of EU law (which forms part of EU law since its beginning) through *posterior* IIAs.

The same issue may arise for *prior* IIAs (or if one wants to apply Art. 351 (1) TFEU by analogy to several *posterior* treaties as well), if one adopts the opinion that non-compliance with the obligation under Art. 351 (2) TFEU will terminate the grandfathering effects of Art. 351 (1) TFEU.

1337 Clearly supporting this thesis: *Lenk*, EJLS Vol. 8, No. 2 (2015), 6, 18; Cf. for future IIAs: *Burgstaller*, LIEI Vol. 39, No. 2 (2012), 207, 216 ff; regarding the negotiations for mixed agreements such as TTIP and CETA: *Lang*, Der EuGH und die Investor-Staat-Streitbeilegung in TTIP und CETA (Beit. zum Transnat. Wirt.-R, Vol. 138, 2015), p. 8 ff; *Schill*, JWIT Vol. 16, No. 3 (2015), 379; the perspective by those commentators is slighlty different as they focus on the unionist view and the possibilities of the EU to conclude future agreements without infringing EU law. However, the idea can be transposed to the setting of applying EU law by the *lex loci arbitri* as again, this would lead to the *unionist* view to take primacy.

Furthermore, the CJEU expressly considered the autonomy of the EU's legal order to be part of its fundamental principles which Art. 351 (1) TFEU may not impede on in any way, irrespective the time of conclusion of the treaties.

However, two considerations limit the implication of this scenario: First, regarding ICSID-Proceedings, the *lex loci arbitri* remains unapplied. Second, in non-ICSID-Proceedings, EU law would only be part of the *lex loci arbitri* if the seat of the tribunal is in an EU member state.[1338]

2. EU law at the merits stage

Besides its role as *lex loci arbitri*, EU law may apply as domestic law to the merits of the arbitration dispute. This will however depend on the applicable law to the dispute and the internal hierarchy of laws between domestic law and international law.

It has been shown that the applicable law to the merits is primarily determined by the parties' choice. In absence of any choice, arbitral tribunals will usually refer to the procedural framework governing the arbitration.[1339] Under Art. 42 (1) of the ICSID-Convention[1340], domestic law will then apply conjointly with international law, whereas under other (relevant) frameworks, the arbitral tribunal will need to determine the most appropriate laws to be applied.[1341]

Hence, following this hierarchy, the parties either in the IIA or in a disjoint instrument, may expressly agree to apply domestic law (and thus EU

1338 This has been the case in *Achmea vs. Slovak Republic*, 26.10.2012 – PCA Case No. 2008-13 - Award on Jurisdiction, Arbitrability and Suspension, para 242: "*This second stage operates both under international law and, here, also under German law as the lex loci arbitri applying to UNCITRAL arbitration proceedings where the agreed place of arbitration is Frankfurt in the Federal Republic of Germany [...] Germany is a founding member of the EU; and German law includes, of course, EU law*".

1339 *Fouchard/Gaillard et al.*, Fouchard, Gaillard, Goldman on international commercial arbitration, 1999, p. 865 ff; *Böckstiegel*, Arbitration International Vol. 28, Iss. 4 (2012), 577, 580.

1340 Art. 42 (1) of the ICSID Convention: "*In the absence of such agreement, the Tribunal shall apply the law of the Contracting State party to the dispute (including its rules on the conflict of laws) and such rules of international law as may be applicable (...)*".

1341 Cf. *supra* Chapter 4 for the entire demonstration.

law) to the merits. However, this possibility is of minor importance. Most of the IIAs in force, if they contain a choice of law, refer – at least concerning treaty claims – to the provisions of the agreement as well as the relevant or applicable rules of international law.[1342]

In absence of an express agreement, EU law may theoretically apply by choice or determination of the tribunal when addressing either Art. 42 of the ICSID-Convention or the similar provisions in the private forums' procedural frameworks.[1343] However, it was demonstrated that arbitral tribunals tend to admit an implicit choice of law when sought with a treaty claim. This implicit choice will refer to the provisions of the IIA in conjunction with international law.[1344] The most prominent reasoning is to refer to the basis of the claim. In a treaty claim, this will be an international agreement, which *a priori* seems to demonstrate the parties' intention of wanting this instrument to be governed by the rules it derives from.[1345] Admitting such an implicit choice would once again disqualify EU law from having any *legal* implications on potential violations of the IIA's protection standards. It may then be assessed primarily as a fact (except for two particular cases demonstrated *supra*).

In those cases, where domestic law and international law, especially the provisions of the IIA, will be applied simultaneously, arbitral tribunals tend to grant primacy to the IIA by following two considerations. First, regarding the obligations under the IIA, Art. 27 VCLT generally requires that an obligation undertaken on the international level cannot be set aside by virtue of domestic law.[1346] Hence, EU law does not take primacy in the

---

1342 *Spiermann* in: *Muchlinski/Ortino/Schreuer* (Eds.), The Oxford handbook of international investment law, 2008, p. 107; however also admitting the growing importance of domestic law in the choice of law clauses: *Schreuer*, McGill Jour of Disp. Res. Vol. 1, No. 1 (2014), 1, 12; *Böckstiegel*, Arbitration International Vol. 28, Iss. 4 (2012), 577, 580 f.

1343 Art. 22 of the SCC Arbitration Rules (2010); Art. 21 (1) of the ICC Arbitration Rules (2012); Arrt. 35 of the UNCITRAL Arbitration Rules (2013); cf. also: *Schreuer*, McGill Jour of Disp. Res. Vol. 1, No. 1 (2014), 1, 11 ff; cf. also: *Böckstiegel*, Arbitration International Vol. 28, Iss. 4 (2012), 577, 580.

1344 *Banifatemi* in: *Yannaca-Small* (Ed.), Arbitration under international investment agreements, 2010, p. 204-206 and cf. *supra*.

1345 *Kjos*, Applicable law in investor-state arbitration, 2013, p. 223, 224 ff and particularly p. 229 f with further references; *Spiermann* in: *Muchlinski/Ortino/Schreuer* (Eds.), The Oxford handbook of international investment law, 2008, p. 107-109.

1346 *Kjos*, Applicable law in investor-state arbitration, 2013, p. 239 f.

extra-EU context, although the obligations impounded on the host state by EU law and the IIA might be contradictory and conflicting. Second, even in matters which are not primarily governed by a substantive provision of an IIA and which will therefore be primarily governed by domestic law (e.g. the validity of contracts, etc.), arbitral tribunals tend to grant international law a "*corrective*" function.[1347] This corrective function should especially become relevant, if the application of national law conflicts with fundamental norms of international law, such as e.g. when determining the amount of compensation or when maintaining the binding force of (contractual or conventional) obligations.[1348]

The following scenario should illustrate the situation: even though the investor's claim is based on the IIA and hence international law, arbitral tribunals regularly admit that particular questions may be exclusively determined by reference to the host state's national law as it is the appropriate legal framework to resolve this – mainly preliminary – question.[1349] An example of such a question might be the validity of a particular promise given to the investor, which could influence its legitimate expectations under the FET standard, or the existence of a contractual obligation which is claimed as a treaty claim under an umbrella clause.[1350] Domestic law will be applied to determine this question. However, international law

1347 *Kjos*, Applicable law in investor-state arbitration, 2013, p. 195 f and 207 f with further examples; also: *Spiermann* in: *Muchlinski/Ortino/Schreuer* (Eds.), The Oxford handbook of international investment law, 2008, p. 114 f; *Leeks*, U. Toronto Fac. L. Rev. Vol. 65, No. 2 (2007), 1, 18 f; *Gaillard/Banifatemi*, ICSID Rev. Vol. 18, Iss. 2 (2003), 375, 387 strongly contest this interpretation.

1348 *CME vs. Czech Republic*, 14.03.2003 – UNCITRAL - Final award, para 504; *LG&E vs. Argentina*, 03.10.2006 – ICSID Case No. ARB/02/1 - Decision on Liability, para 94 f; somehow also: *Annullment Committee in Wena Hotels vs. Egypt*, 05.02.2002 – ICSID Case No. ARB/98/4 - Decision on Annulment, para 50 – 53; cf. also: *Kjos*, Applicable law in investor-state arbitration, 2013, p. 207 f; *Leeks*, U. Toronto Fac. L. Rev. Vol. 65, No. 2 (2007), 1, 18.

1349 *Spiermann* in: *Muchlinski/Ortino/Schreuer* (Eds.), The Oxford handbook of international investment law, 2008, p. 110-112; *Kjos*, Applicable law in investor-state arbitration, 2013, p. 241; cf. also: *Schreuer*, McGill Jour of Disp. Res. Vol. 1, No. 1 (2014), 1,17-20.

1350 *Kjos*, Applicable law in investor-state arbitration, 2013, p. 241 ff who also refers to expropriation claims whenever the BIT in question refers to preexisting property rights under the national laws of the host state; cf. also: *Spiermann* in: *Muchlinski/Ortino/Schreuer* (Eds.), The Oxford handbook of international investment law, 2008, p. 110-112; *Schreuer*, McGill Jour of Disp. Res. Vol. 1, No. 1 (2014), 1, 18 f.

keeps a corrective function if the results under domestic law seem unacceptable from an international perspective. This grants particular discretion to the tribunals on the question of how far the influences of domestic law might extend in the proceedings. One could conclude that domestic law is somehow disregarded from the merits, irrespective of whether it is considered as applicable law to the dispute or not.

However, and this was expressly stressed by the ad-hoc Committee in the *MTD vs. Chile-Case*:

> "However, it will often be necessary for BIT tribunals to apply the law of the host State, and this necessity is reinforced for ICSID tribunals by Article 42(1) of the ICSID Convention. Whether the applicable law here derived from the first or second sentence of Article 42(1) does not matter: *the Tribunal should have applied [domestic] law to those questions which were necessary for its determination and of which Chilean law was the governing law.* At the same time, the implications of some issue of Chilean law for a claim under the BIT were for international law to determine. In short, both laws were relevant."[1351]

Hence, if domestic law (and hence EU law) is applicable to the merits, arbitral tribunals generally are required to take its effects into consideration. If they wish to set aside its particular legal consequences, at least they carry a particular burden of proof.[1352]

C. The role of EU law in the subsequent proceedings

Once an award has been rendered by an arbitral tribunal based on an extra-EU IIAs, the award may be exposed to subsequent proceedings. Subsequent proceedings refer to annulment, setting-aside or enforcement proceedings (I.) – if any of those are necessary – but also to actions by e.g. the European Commission regarding an award rendered based on an extra-EU IIA (II.). Assuming that the award did not take into account EU law (properly), both may widely interfere with this award.

1351 *Annulment Committee in MTD vs. Chile*, 21.03.2007 – ICSID Case No. ARB/01/7 - Decision on Annulment, para 72 [emphasis added].

1352 The extensive use of the "*corrective*" function of international law or the blunt disregard of domestic law without further justification raises constant critisism: cf. *inter alia*: *Sattorova*, LIEI Vol. 39, No. 2 (2012), 223, 241 f; *Gaillard/Banifatemi*, ICSID Rev. Vol. 18, Iss. 2 (2003), 375; *Leeks*, U. Toronto Fac. L. Rev. Vol. 65, No. 2 (2007), 1, 18 f.

I. Setting-aside or enforcement proceedings

Setting-aside proceedings or enforcement proceedings in an EU member state may present a major risk for the investor. National courts in an EU member state will need to primarily evaluate the validity of the arbitration clause and the compliance of the award with the *ordre public* with regard to their national law. This includes EU law. When applying EU law, those courts will need to focus on the rights and obligations under EU law, which generally takes primacy over conflicting obligations from public international law. These tribunals, being national tribunals of a member state, will most probably apply the *unionist view* assuming that they want to avoid exposing the member state to a violation under EU law with the respective potential consequences (i.e. infringement proceedings, etc.). Hence, even though an IIA might be valid under international law, based on either the incompatibility of the arbitration clause with EU law or if the award disregards fundamental provisions of EU law, national courts will even be under the duty to set aside the award or deny its enforcement as it conflicts with EU law.[1353] This could only be eliminated by virtue of Art. 351 (1) TFEU. However, the limits to this article have already been developed (cf. Chapter 12). Hence, as soon as the award comes into contact with an EU member state, its validity or enforceability will be questioned. Given the ongoing debate on the relationship of Art. 53, 54 of the ICSID-Convention and EU law, this question might even appear when dealing with an ICSID-Award.[1354] After all, the ICSID-Convention also constitutes an international convention which has been concluded by the member states. From a *unionist* perspective, as soon as Art. 351 (1) TFEU does not apply, a member state cannot honour its obligations deriving from the ICSID-Convention if those contradict EU law. From this perspective, national tribunals of the member states could be forced to deny enforcement to an arbitral award which disrespects EU law even though such an award was rendered under the ICSID-Framework.[1355]

1353 *Kleinheisterkamp*, JIEL Vol. 15, No. 1 (2012), 85, 92 f; *Tietje/Wackernagel*, JWIT Vol. 16, Iss. 2 (2015), 205, 235 for the context of enforcement of an ICSID-Award. However, the general idea is applicable in all situations described above.

1354 *Tietje/Wackernagel*, JWIT Vol. 16, Iss. 2 (2015), 205, 235.

1355 *Tietje/Wackernagel*, JWIT Vol. 16, Iss. 2 (2015), 205, 224 ff.

II. Potential decisions by the European Commission

Another obstacle for the investor after having obtained an award in its favour was revealed in the *Micula* proceedings and might be used in a couple of further cases. The facts should be recalled briefly: an investor accepted to provide particular services in disfavoured regions in Romania. Romania granted particular benefits to the investor for rendering the respective services.[1356] These incentives and subsidies have not been in line with the state aid provisions and were hence cancelled by Romania.[1357] The tribunal considered the revocation to be a breach of the FET standard an ordered Romania to pay damages to the investor.[1358] After having rendered the award, the Commission issued a decision upon which it considered the enforcement of the award (ordering compensation for the revoked state aid) to be itself qualified as state aid and hence prohibited under Art. 107 TFEU.[1359] Consequently, a member state court will be prevented from enforcing this award as such enforcement would be a breach of EU law.

As this decision refers to a more general principle which could be applied in further cases, it should be assessed briefly.

Generally, the CJEU held at various occasions that the payment of damages or the enforcement of judgements will not constitute illegal state aid and will not be contrary to EU law in general, as it is qualified as an involuntary act of the member state and based on the general legal framework issued for (extra-contractual or contractual) liability of the member states.[1360] Hence, not every decision of a dispute settlement body which

---

1356 Cf.: *Ioan Micula, Viorel Micula & others vs. Romania*, 23.09.2008 – ICSID Case No. ARB/05/20 - Decision on Jurisdiction and Admissibility, para 28.

1357 *Ioan Micula, Viorel Micula & others vs. Romania*, 23.09.2008 – ICSID Case No. ARB/05/20 - Decision on Jurisdiction and Admissibility, para 40 ff.

1358 *Ioan Micula, Viorel Micula & others vs. Romania*, 11.12.2013 – ICSID Case No. ARB/05/20 - Final Award, para 872 for the tribunal's conclusion after an extensive analysis of the parties' arguments.

1359 *European Commission*, Commission Decision (EU) 2015/1470 - notified under C(2015) 2112: Decision on State aid SA.38517 (2014/C) (ex 2014/NN) implemented by Romania-Arbitral award Micula v Romania of 11 December 2013 (30/03/2015); cf. also the comment by *Peterson*, IA Reporter Vol. 9, No. 6 (2016), 14, 16 f.

1360 *CJEU*, 27.09.1988 – Joined cases 106 to 120/87 - Asteris = ECLI:EU:C:1988:457, para 23: "*It follows that State aid, that is to say measures of the public authorities favouring certain undertakings or certain*

orders that a state is obliged to pay damages would be affected. However, the CJEU has equally set up boundaries regarding this jurisprudence. If the decision itself is not issued based on a general system of liability, applicable to all economic operators, and if the decision by any dispute settlement body is used to circumvent the provisions under EU law, especially the state aid provisions, the prohibition of Art. 107 TFEU also extends to the enforcement of the award (*criterion of selectivity*).[1361]

It is argued that the prohibition only concerns these cases and cannot extend further.[1362] However, arbitral awards based on an IIA perfectly fit with the exception as set forth by the CJEU. The award is not based on a general system of liability but rather on a particular mechanism which has been voluntarily put in place by the EU member state, the extra-EU IIA. This system of liability also only favours particular persons (investors from a particular country) and hence targets a selective group of person. These considerations are reinforced if one takes into account the underlying idea of the reasoning in the *Micula-Case*. The underlying idea is to grant *effet utile* to the provisions under EU law and the fact that through

---

products, is fundamentally different in its legal nature from damages which the competent national authorities may be ordered to pay to individuals in compensation for the damage they have caused to those individuals"; cf. also: European Commission, Commission Decision (2008/408/EC) - notified under C(2007) 5400: on the State aid C 36/A/06 (ex NN 38/06) implemented by Italy in favour of ThyssenKrupp, Cementir and Nuova Terni Industrie Chimiche (20/11/2007), para 70-75; *CJEU*, 27.03.1980 – C-61/79 - Denkavit = ECLI:EU:C:1980:100, para 31; *Tietje/Wackernagel*, JWIT Vol. 16, Iss. 2 (2015), 205, 220 f; *European Commission*, Amicus Curia Brief filed in U.S. Steel Golbal Holdings I B.V. vs. Slovak Republic (PCA Case n°2013-6) - arbitration proceedings, 15/05/2014, para 82 ff.

1361 *CJEU*, 18.07.2007 – C-119/05 - Lucchini = ECLI:EU:C:2007:434; para 59 – 63: even the principle of res judicata cannot prevent a judgement to be set aside if it is contrary to EU Law; cf. also: *Tietje/Wackernagel*, JWIT Vol. 16, Iss. 2 (2015), 205, p. 222 f who refer to the *Opinion of Advocate General Ruiz-Jarabo Colomer*, 28.04.2005 – Joined Cases C-346/03 and C-529/03 - Atzeni et al = ECLI:EU:C:2005:256, para 194 ff and especially para 198; cf. also: *European Commission*, Amicus Curia Brief filed in U.S. Steel Golbal Holdings I B.V. vs. Slovak Republic (PCA Case n°2013-6) - arbitration proceedings, 15/05/2014, para 82 f; *European Commission*, Commission Decision (EU) 2015/1470 - notified under C(2015) 2112: Decision on State aid SA.38517 (2014/C) (ex 2014/NN) implemented by Romania-Arbitral award Micula v Romania of 11 December 2013 (30/03/2015), para 109-115.

1362 *Tietje/Wackernagel*, JWIT Vol. 16, Iss. 2 (2015), 205, 223.

an IIA particular persons are granted the possibility to disable this *effet*.[1363] If an explicit prohibition under EU law is circumvented by whatever mean, EU law should prohibit accepting this circumvention, irrespective of whether this turns out to be done by virtue of an award issued by a separate dispute settlement mechanism. Reconsidering member states' obligations under Art. 351 (2) TFEU regarding *prior* extra-EU IIAs, one might argue that by not renegotiating or terminating the extra-EU IIAs, although they conflict with EU law, the member states keep in force a mechanism which, through the arbitral proceedings, serves to circumvent EU law.[1364] Under their duty of loyalty (Art. 4 (3) TEU) and by respect to the principle of primacy, member states will then need to deny enforcement to an award or the Commission might initiate proceedings based on Art. 258 TFEU for breach of EU law, which could have considerable effects on EU member state and their tribunals.

A short example should illustrate this idea: A public procurement procedure was not in conformity with the principles laid down in the directives 2014/24/EU and 2014/25/EU. It directly attributed a contract to an investor without prior public call for tenders. Upon a claim by a competitor, EU law would force the member state to revoke the contract with the investor. The investor, having lost considerable amounts in profits, files a claim based on an extra-EU IIA subject to the grandfathering rule in Art. 351 (1) TFEU. The tribunal attributes damages in the amount of the investor's lost profits upon cancellation of the contract. *De facto* the investor received what was initially due. The competitive landscape, transparency and good use of public resources, which are the underlying ideas of public procurement law[1365], are circumvented at its best.

Numerous other cases might be construed which have the same underlying idea. From the perspective of EU law this is not acceptable. There-

1363 *European Commission*, Commission Decision (EU) 2015/1470 - notified under C(2015) 2112: Decision on State aid SA.38517 (2014/C) (ex 2014/NN) implemented by Romania-Arbitral award Micula v Romania of 11 December 2013 (30/03/2015), para 109-115, cf. also: *European Commission*, Amicus Curia Brief filed in U.S. Steel Golbal Holdings I B.V. vs. Slovak Republic (PCA Case n°2013-6) - arbitration proceedings, 15/05/2014, para 83.

1364 Although *Tietje/Wackernagel* seem to limit their analysis to the state-aid provisions, they expressly accept the underlying idea of preventing circumvention and hence providing full effect to EU law in the *Micula- Decision*, cf.: *Tietje/Wackernagel*, JWIT Vol. 16, Iss. 2 (2015), 205, 223.

1365 Cf. for the underlying ideas of public procurement law: *Kilian*, Europäisches Wirtschaftsrecht, 5. Edn. (2016), para 484, 488.

fore, the reasoning of the *Micula Case* might be applied to awards based on extra-EU IIAs as well. However, such an approach will considerably hinder and weaken the judicial force of an award disregarding EU law.

D. Interim conclusion on the disruptive potential of ignoring EU law in extra-EU investment proceedings

Hence, ignoring EU law at the stage of the arbitration proceedings may have considerable disruptive potential for the EU member state as well as the investor. For the investor, discharging EU law may at first glance provide numerous advantages, as it may potentially hinder the success of its claim.[1366] On the other hand, the investor needs to bear the risk that its award is set aside in the subsequent proceedings and that enforcement will probably not be granted, at least in EU member states.[1367] This could considerably weaken the success of the dispute mechanism in total. The investor then would need to seek a forum outside the EU and enforce the award outside the EU as well.

Second, the interferences which might occur on various stages of the proceedings, including by means of interpretation of the IIA (cf. legality requirement and interpretation of the FET standard) generate a considerable risk of highly diverging decisions by the multitude of dispute settlement bodies which decide in particular matters. As an example, the arbitral tribunals will regularly need to decide on matters of EU law without having the possibility to consult the CJEU on the interpretation of such particular question. This does not only leverage the risk of diverging decisions by different dispute settlement bodies, but also creates uncertainty for the investor and the host state. This is a highly unsatisfactory outcome for both, investor and the home state, which seek to strengthen the legal certainty and stability through the conclusion of the IIA.

Third, from the EU member state's perspective, the disruptive potential becomes even greater. It has several sets of potentially conflicting obligations. Not complying with its obligations under EU law may expose the

1366 Cf. more generally for domestic vs. international law: *Leeks*, U. Toronto Fac. L. Rev. Vol. 65, No. 2 (2007), 1, 16 f; cf. also: *Gaillard/Banifatemi*, ICSID Rev. Vol. 18, Iss. 2 (2003), 375, 380.

1367 Cf. similarly: *Kleinheisterkamp*, JIEL Vol. 15, No. 1 (2012), 85, 92 f.

member state to sanctions. Not complying with an award rendered based on an IIA, is a breach of its obligations under international law.[1368]

The state therefore is left with only two further options: Rethinking its membership of the EU or rethinking the upholding of IIAs with non-member states in their current format.

Both decisions would have considerable impact, including for investors. In the medium to long term, a well perceived protection mechanism may be revoked due to the impossibility for member states to comply with their obligations if both frameworks keep trying to be self-contained regimes which ignore each other.[1369]

Chapter 14: Cooperative approach: transposing Solange and Bosphorus to extra-EU investment proceedings

The following chapter will try to offer a different solution which takes into consideration the aforementioned difficulties and risks.

The conflict between EU law and IIAs is not the first conflict in the multi-nexus of converging or diverging treaties, rights and obligations under international (and national) law.[1370] Indeed, there have been numerous examples of courts, tribunals and other institutions dealing with a nexus of legal frameworks and providing a solution for the respective conflict.

Two of the most noted approaches were the *Solange-Jurisprudence* by the German Constitutional Court and the *Bosphorus-Decision*[1371] by the European Court of Human Rights (ECtHR).

Both approaches, including their underlying ideas, will be analysed first (A.) in order to establish that the approach taken in these decisions can be transposed to the extra-EU IIA context (B.).

1368 Cf. similar: *Tietje/Wackernagel*, JWIT Vol. 16, Iss. 2 (2015), 205, 230.

1369 Similar: *Tietje/Wackernagel*, JWIT Vol. 16, Iss. 2 (2015), 205, 241 ff.

1370 *Klabbers*, Treaty conflict and the European Union, 2009, p. 8; *Tietje*, Intra-EU BITs als Herausforderung im Mehrebenensystem des Rechts (Beit. zum Transnat. Wirt.-R, Vol. 104, 2011).

1371 *European Court of Human Rights*, 30.06.2005 – Application n° 45036/98 - Bosphorus.

A. The reception of "similar conflicts" by other courts: Solange and Bosphorus

From the several other tribunals having dealt with the question, two decisions should be highlighted here, as they point out a similar and well recognised approach for how to resolve potential overlapping legal frameworks in the context of EU law. First, the German Constitutional Court, through its *Solange-Decision,* found a particular solution to address the overlap between national law and EU law, based on a self-constraint in its control (I.). The ECtHR endorsed this approach and transposed it to the situation of conflicting obligations between several international treaties, in particular EU law and the ECHR (II.).

I. German Constitutional Court: Solange II

The German Constitutional Court rendered several judgments on the interference of national law with EU law, finally leading to its *Solange-II-Decision* which is now widely accepted and frequently reiterated.[1372]

The task of the German Constitutional Court is to observe the compliance of the German legislative and executive powers with the German Constitution. Germany is a member state of the EU but the German Constitutional Court is not part of the European courts. Thus, in principle it does not examine the validity of any act issued by the European Institutions and their conformity with EU (primary or secondary) law. However, it was doubtful whether the court would consider itself competent to challenge the validity of an act of (primary or secondary) EU law by examining the conformity of this act with the German constitution.[1373] The *Solange-II-Decision*[1374] clearly denied such a control:

> „As long as the European Communities, especially the jurisprudence by the CJEU, generally guarantee an effective protection of fundamental rights with regard to

1372 Cf. inter alia: *German Constitutional Court*, BVerfGE 102, 147, 07.06.2000 – 2 BvL 1/97 - Bananenmarkt, 162 ff; cf. also: *German Constitutional Court*, BVerfGE 123, 267, 30.06.2009 – 2 BvE 2/08.

1373 This was the former position of the German Constitutional Court, cf: *German Constitutional Court*, BVerfGE 37, 271, 29.05.1974 – 2 BvL 52/71 - Solange I, 280.

1374 *German Constitutional Court*, BVerfGE 73, 339, 22.10.1986 – 2 BvR 197/83 - Solange II.

> the public authorities of the Community, which is considered equivalent to the protection required inalienably under the German Constitution, [...] the German Constitutional Court will not exercise its control whether the act of secondary law upon which the national authorities based their act, is compatible with the requirements of the fundamental rights guaranteed under the German Constitution."[1375]

Consequently, the court denies its jurisdiction and restrains from interfering with acts issued by the European legal order as long as (*"solange"*) it considers the protection under this order to be generally equivalent.[1376]

The underlying idea of *Solange-II* is to admit a certain primacy of EU law[1377] but also to minimise the conflicts within two separate legal frameworks as long as this does not lead to a – manifest – decrease of the level of protection granted to the individuals protected by both legal frameworks.[1378] This later idea could also be transposed to the extra-EU IIA setting. As the interference of both legal frameworks might create frictions and results which are inadequate due to a double standard applied to the same act, one legal framework accepts to reduce the margin of control as long as the level of protection is not undermined by this approach. This approach found a certain support in matters of conflicting obligations under international law by the ECtHR in the *Bosphorus-Decision.*

II. ECtHR: Bosphorus vs. Ireland

The *Bosphorus-Decision* by the ECtHR has often been qualified as an equivalent to the *Solange-Decision* by the German Constitutional Court.[1379] This approach is correct, considering the underlying idea to ex-

---

1375 *German Constitutional Court*, BVerfGE 73, 339, 22.10.1986 – 2 BvR 197/83 - Solange II, 387 [translated].

1376 *Hobe*, 8. Edn. (2014), para 454 ff.

1377 *Hobe*, 8. Edn. (2014), para 462.

1378 For a comprehensive summary of the different implications within the German Constitutional order and jurisprudence: *Schwerdtfeger*, EuR, 2015, 290; cf. also regarding this idea: *Lang*, Der EuGH und die Investor-Staat-Streitbeilegung in TTIP und CETA (Beit. zum Transnat. Wirt.-R, Vol. 138, 2015), p. 20 f who also stresses the incentivising idea for the other legal framework to observe a certain level of protection to enable the *Solange*-approach to apply; also stressed by *Schwerdtfeger*, EuR, 2015, 290, 306 f. This idea will be treated *infra* (Chapter 16).

1379 *Grabenwarter/Pabel*, Europäische Menschenrechtskonvention, 6. Edn. (2016) § 18, para 23; *Haratsch*, ZaöVR 66 (2006), 927.

ercise limited control on certain acts.[1380] However, both decisions differ as to their setting and their reasoning. Whereas the *Solange-Decision* dealt with conflicts of national law and EU law, the *Bosphorus-Decision* clearly addresses the conflict of international obligations. Furthermore, the conclusions how to deal with the conflict differ widely.

In *Bosphorus vs. Ireland* the Turkish based airline (Bosphorus Airlines) tried to oppose the seizure of two of its airplanes by the Irish government. The seizure was based on a Regulation (990/93)[1381] by the (former) European Community which implemented the Resolution 820 (1993) by the Security Council of the United Nations.[1382] Based on the resolution all states should

> "impound all vessels, freight vehicles, rolling stock and aircraft in their territories in which a majority or controlling interest is held by a person or undertaking in or operating from the Federal Republic of Yugoslavia (Serbia and Montenegro)"[1383]

The Regulation 990/93 implemented Resolution 820 (1993) within the former European Community member states.[1384] Based on Art. 8 of the regulation, the Irish Government seized two aircraft belonging to a Yugoslavian airline and leased by Bosphorus Airways during a stay in Ireland. Bosphorus Airlines initiated judicial review proceedings in Ireland, leading to a preliminary ruling reference of the Irish Supreme Court to the CJEU. The CJEU declared the seizure to be in perfect compliance with EU law.[1385] The Irish Court, following the CJEU judgment, dismissed Bosphorus Airline's objections, which led the latter to address the ECtHR for violation of its right to property protected by Art. 1 of Protocol No.1 to the ECHR.[1386]

Thus, the situation to be evaluated by the ECtHR was the following:

The Court needed to examine the compliance of an act by the Irish Government with the obligations undertaken by the latter towards the

1380 *Haratsch*, ZaöVR 66 (2006), 927, 928; *Meyer* in: Karpenstein/Mayer EMRK, Einl, para 138.

1381 Council Regulation (EEC) No 990/93 - Sanctions on Former Yugoslavia, Official Journal of the European Communities L102 (26.04.1993), 14.

1382 *European Court of Human Rights*, 30.06.2005 – Application n° 45036/98 - Bosphorus, para 14 ff; *Haratsch*, ZaöVR 66 (2006), 927, 928; *Janik*, ZaöVR, 2010, 127, 137 f.

1383 Resolution S/RES/820 (1993) (17.04.1993), para 24.

1384 *European Court of Human Rights*, 30.06.2005 – Application n° 45036/98 - Bosphorus, para 14 ff; *Haratsch*, ZaöVR 66 (2006), 927, 928.

1385 *CJEU*, 30.07.1996 – C-84/95 - Bosphorus = ECLI:EU:C:1996:312.

1386 *Haratsch*, ZaöVR 66 (2006), 927, 928 f; *Janik*, ZaöVR, 2010, 127, 137 f.

Turkish Republic in the ECHR. However, the act potentially violating Ireland's obligations under the ECHR was based on the European Regulation 990/93, which ordered the Irish Government to act the way it did.

By not doing so, it would indeed have violated its obligations undertaken towards the other EU member states in the European Treaties.

The different conventional obligations of Ireland as an EU member state in the *Bosphorus-Case* are displayed by the following illustration:

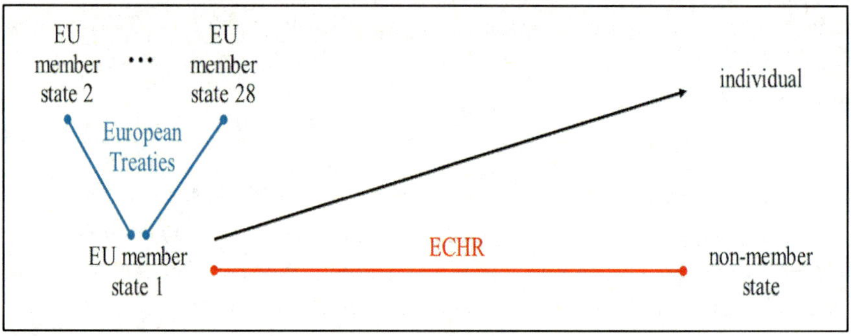

Illustration 4

This situation is very comparable, if not identical, to a host state's obligations under an IIA (with a non-member state) when the act challenged under the IIA is based on mandatory EU law.

The solution adopted by the ECtHR strongly differs from the solution by arbitral tribunals in matters of international investment law, as it limits its own capacity and duty to verify the lawfulness of acts under EU law with the ECHR under certain conditions.

The ECtHR firstly holds that the right to property could be limited only for the purpose of a legitimate general interest-objective and that the compliance of an EU member state with its obligations under the European Treaties constitutes such a legitimate interest.[1387]

1387 *European Court of Human Rights*, 30.06.2005 – Application n° 45036/98 - Bosphorus, para 149 ff.

Second, the Court observes that although the compliance constitutes a legitimate general interest:

> "absolving Contracting States completely from their Convention responsibilities in the areas covered by such a transfer would be incompatible with the purpose and object of the Convention."[1388]

Third, an absolute control of those acts is judged to be inadequate as well. The Court therefore holds,

> "In the court's view, state action taken in compliance with such legal obligations is justified as long as the relevant organization is considered to protect fundamental rights, as regard both the substantive guarantees offered and the mechanisms controlling their observance, in a manner which can be considered at least equivalent to that for which the Convention provides."[1389]

Thus, the ECtHR claims a presumption of legality of the act of an EU member state as long as three conditions are met:

- The state's act was determined by EU law;[1390] *and*
- The level of protection offered by the EU law in the field protected by the ECHR is equivalent on substantive guarantees;[1391] *and*
- The level of protection offered by the EU law in the field protected by the ECHR is equivalent on procedural guarantees to enforce substantive rights.[1392]

This presumption can be rebutted if the claimant demonstrates that either:

- The level of protection in the EU is no longer equivalent, either on substantive but also on procedural guarantees (*continual overall control*);[1393] *or*
- The protection is manifestly deficient for the specific case (*particular control*).[1394]

1388 *European Court of Human Rights*, 30.06.2005 – Application n° 45036/98 - Bosphorus, para 154.

1389 *European Court of Human Rights*, 30.06.2005 – Application n° 45036/98 - Bosphorus, para 155.

1390 *European Court of Human Rights*, 30.06.2005 – Application n° 45036/98 - Bosphorus, para 155-157.

1391 *European Court of Human Rights*, 30.06.2005 – Application n° 45036/98 - Bosphorus, para 155 and 159 f.

1392 *European Court of Human Rights*, 30.06.2005 – Application n° 45036/98 - Bosphorus, para 155 and 160 ff.

1393 *European Court of Human Rights*, 30.06.2005 – Application n° 45036/98 - Bosphorus, para 155.

The ECtHR derives this approach from an interpretation of the ECHR and its Art. 1 and the interpretation given to the scope of its obligations. It reiterates the general duty of the contracting states to comply with the obligations undertaken under the convention.[1395] It holds that the ECHR does not prohibit the contracting parties to access an international or supranational organisation and to transfer powers to this organisation, even though this might affect fields covered by the convention.[1396] The court also recognises the interest of states to enter into such organisations and the "*consequent need to secure [the organisations'] proper functioning*".[1397]

Given these considerations, in accordance with Art. 31 (3) lit. c VCLT, the obligations under the ECHR should be interpreted:

> "(…) in the light of any relevant rules and principles of international law applicable in relations between the Contracting parties (…)"[1398]

On the one hand, this includes the principle of *pacta sunt servanda*. On the other hand, "*any relevant rules of international law*" should also include the European Treaties, as the acting state is bound by those rules.[1399] The ECHR and its obligations could not be considered on a stand-alone ba-

1394 *European Court of Human Rights*, 30.06.2005 – Application n° 45036/98 - Bosphorus, para 156; cf. for a summary of the argumentation also: *Haratsch*, ZaöVR 66 (2006), 927, 929 and *Winkler*, EuGRZ Vol. 34 (2007), 641, 643 ff.

1395 Article 1 of European Convention on Human Rights (entry into force: 03/09/1950): „*The High Contracting Parties shall secure to everyone within their jurisdiction the rights and freedoms defined in Section I of this Convention*".

1396 *European Court of Human Rights*, 30.06.2005 – Application n° 45036/98 - Bosphorus, para 152; *Meyer* in: Karpenstein/Mayer EMRK, Einl, para 126.

1397 *European Court of Human Rights*, 30.06.2005 – Application n° 45036/98 - Bosphorus, para 150; *Meyer* in: Karpenstein/Mayer EMRK, Einl, para 126-128; this has been reapplied at multiple occasions, among others recently in *European Court of Human Rights*, 23.05.2016 – Application No. 17502/07 (Avotiņš vs. Lettland); the presumption hence remains constantly applied by the ECtHR. This is questioned by *Ress*, EuZW, 2016, 800 who refers to the fact that the Bosphorus-Decision was adopted unanimously but the recent decision in *Avotins vs. Lettland* was rendered including a dissenting opinion; this seems to be a doubtful argument.

1398 *European Court of Human Rights*, 30.06.2005 – Application n° 45036/98 - Bosphorus, para 150.

1399 *European Court of Human Rights*, 30.06.2005 – Application n° 45036/98 - Bosphorus, para 150; *Haratsch*, ZaöVR 66 (2006), 927, 933; cf. also: *Dörr*, JuS, 2006, 442, 444.

sis.[1400] Relevant rules of international law in terms of Art. 31 VCLT should, as to the ECtHR, also include those rules of international law which are only applicable to one or certain parties to the convention.[1401] Following the logic of the ECtHR Art. 31 (3) lit. c VCLT should thus be read by "*any relevant rules of international law applicable in the relations between the parties to the convention*" but not "*applicable in the relations between the parties to the dispute*".[1402] As Turkey is not a member state to the EU, the membership in the EU could not (completely) exempt the member states from their obligations under the ECHR. However, Ireland's membership in the EU enables the ECtHR to differentiate on its own authority to challenge the lawfulness of acts committed upon duties under the respective organisation as long as an equivalent level of protection is guaranteed.[1403]

B. Transposing Solange and Bosphorus to extra-EU IIA investment arbitration

The "*conflict*" which occurred for Ireland in the *Bosphorus* case, although it concerned the respect of fundamental rights, is comparable to the conflict for host states under an extra-EU IIA. The compliance with one conventional obligation could possibly lead to the disrespect of another conventional obligation with another state. It should therefore be analysed whether the *Bosphorus* doctrine could also be applied to international investment arbitration proceedings based on extra-EU IIAs.[1404] To be able to

1400 *Haratsch*, ZaöVR 66 (2006), 927, 933; cf. also on a more general level regarding Art. 31 VCLT: *Broekhuijsen*, Bulletin for International Taxation Vol. 67, No. 9 (2013), 1.

1401 *Tams/Tzanakopoulos et al.*, Research handbook on the law of treaties, 2014, p. 34; cf. for this analysis: *Broekhuijsen*, Bulletin for International Taxation Vol. 67, No. 9 (2013), 1,4 citing various other cases decided by the ECtHR with references to non-binding rules of international law, notwithstanding the parties concerned.

1402 Cf. also: *Tams/Tzanakopoulos et al.*, Research handbook on the law of treaties, 2014, p. 34.

1403 *Haratsch*, ZaöVR 66 (2006), 927, 933, *Dörr*, JuS, 2006, 442, 444 f; *Herr-Reißmann*, NJW 2006, 192, 193 f.

1404 The general idea of using this approach for multi-level conflicts including those in IIAs is generally supported by a couple of scholars, which however widely diverge in their propositions and who did not analyse the concrete mechanism and its requirements, cf.*inter alia*: *Lang*, Der EuGH und die Inves-

transpose the solution, the EU law needs to, first of all, be applicable to (at least the interpretation of) the obligations under the IIA which is at the origin of the investment dispute. This is the fundamental idea on which the EctHR bases its approach. It will hence be demonstrated first, that this fundamental idea can also be applied in investment disputes (cf. this section (B.).

The second prerequisite is that the *Bosphorus* doctrine could only apply, if investment protection under the IIA and under EU law are considered to be at least equivalent regarding substantive and procedural guarantees. This is the final and most important argument, why the ECtHR accepts to reduce its control on acts by EU member states which are based on mandatory provisions of EU law. This however, will be treated with in a second step in the next chapter (cf. *Chapter 15*).

I. EU law as a mean of interpretation for obligations under an IIA

The setting in international investment arbitrations differs from the *Bosphorus-Case.* However, some particularities of investment proceedings may render the reasoning why EU law shall be taken into consideration when interpreting the IIA in extra-EU disputes even easier. Other than for the ECtHR, arbitral tribunals may even be bound by the parties to apply not only the IIA but also the domestic law of the host state (1.). This includes, as demonstrated, EU law. In any other situation, i.e. where EU law is not as such part of the applicable law in the investment dispute, arbitral tribunals may follow the approach of the *Bosphorus-Case* and render EU law at least applicable to the interpretation of the IIA's obligations by virtue of Art. 31 (3) lit c VCLT (2.).

---

tor-Staat-Streitbeilegung in TTIP und CETA (Beit. zum Transnat. Wirt.-R, Vol. 138, 2015), p. 20-22; *Eilmansberger*, CMLR Vol. 46 (2009), 383, 418; *Tietje*, Intra-EU BITs als Herausforderung im Mehrebenensystem des Rechts (Beit. zum Transnat. Wirt.-R, Vol. 104, 2011), p. 18 f; *Tietje/Wackernagel*, JWIT Vol. 16, Iss. 2 (2015), 205, 242 f however all with a different focus and mechanism; cf. also: *European Commission*, Amicus Curia Brief filed in Electrabel vs. Hungary (ICSID Case n° ARB/07/19) - arbitration proceedings, 12/06/2009, para 74 and 77; considering such an approach but finally rejecing it in the intra-EU context: *Eilmansberger*, CMLR Vol. 46 (2009), 383, 422.

1. EU law as domestic law being applicable law to the investment dispute

It was demonstrated *supra* that in several situations arbitral tribunals will apply both EU law as domestic law and the IIA to the dispute. As mentioned above, the most common situations will be those featuring an explicit choice of the parties which refers to domestic law as applicable law as well or – in the absence of an explicit choice – the application by virtue of the arbitral tribunal's choice under the procedural framework. Given the considerable amount of ICSID-Proceedings and the general reference to domestic law (and hence EU law) in Art. 42 (1) of the ICSID-Convention, there are several cases in which EU law might be deemed applicable in the dispute. However, it should be kept in mind that arbitral tribunals so far express frequent hostility as to the application of domestic law and tend to circumvent its application by several means (cf. *supra*). Nonetheless, the priority granted to international law does not exclude taking into consideration EU law when interpreting obligations under the IIA. Furthermore, in the *Bosphorus-Case* the ECHR has *in fine* primacy but the solution was found by means of interpretation.

Hence in these situations, EU law may be part of the rules which the arbitral tribunal will need to take into consideration when interpreting the IIA. For the ECtHR this has been the first prerequisite to be able to apply the *Bosphorus-Approach*, as the entire approach is based on an interpretation of the state's obligation under the ECHR (i.e. the IIA in the investment setting).

2. Considering EU law by virtue of Art. 31 (3) lit. c VCLT

If domestic law is not applicable to the dispute, the remaining situations (*per se)* lead to the *Bosphorus*-Scenario: the arbitral tribunal is called to examine the host state's compliance with the IIA towards the investor. At the same time, for the host state EU law also applies and may force the state to undertake a certain measure, which is consequently challenged by the investor under the IIA. This is precisely the situation in which the ECtHR in the *Bosphorus-Case* decided to apply Art. 31 (3) lit. c VCLT to the interpretation of the "*host state's*" obligations under the convention. However, when evaluating whether this can also be applied in investment proceedings, a distinction needs to be drawn between mixed investment protection agreements (such as the Energy Charter Treaty) and extra-EU IIAs.

(1) Mixed agreements (e.g. Energy Charter Treaty)

Regarding mixed agreements, the situation is precisely the same as in *Bosphorus*. Several of the contracting parties to the IIA (the European member states) are also contracting parties to the European Treaties. When interpreting the scope of the host state's obligations under the IIA, the arbitral tribunals will therefore need to recourse to Art. 31-33 VCLT, including Art. 31 (3) lit. c VCLT. When e.g. seeking the true meaning of "*the Contracting Party['s]*" obligation to "*encourage and create stable, equitable, favourable and transparent conditions for Investors of other Contracting Parties to make Investments*"[1405], the arbitral tribunals may take into consideration (all) other rules of international law "*applicable in the relation between the parties [to the Energy Charter Treaty]*". Those rules will, at least following the ECtHR's considerations, also include the European Treaties, as there is at least a partial overlap of the contracting parties to both treaties.[1406] Although the obligations under the IIA could not be set aside by the European Treaties, the situation deriving from the transfer of powers to the EU could and should not be completely set aside when interpreting the host state's obligations under the IIA.

(a) Challenges to the role attributed to Art. 31 (3) lit. c VCLT

However, this role attributed to Art. 31 VCLT did not remain unchallenged in public international law. Several aspects of Art. 31 (3) lit. c VCLT are matter of debate. The article reads as follows:

> "(3) There shall be taken into account, together with the context: [...] (c) any relevant rules of international law applicable in the relations between the parties."

Whether Art. 31 (3) lit. c VCLT is limited to general principles of international law or whether it refers to all sources of international law (potentially even non-binding sources[1407]) is a questioned asked by scholars and tri-

1405 Art. 10 (1) 1 Enery Charter Treaty which is generally referred to as the fair and equtiable treatment clause in the Treaty.

1406 *European Court of Human Rights*, 30.06.2005 – Application n° 45036/98 - Bosphorus, para 150.

1407 For the interpretation of treties in the light of non-binding sources, especially regarding tax-issues: *Broekhuijsen*, Bulletin for International Taxation Vol. 67, No. 9 (2013), 1.

bunals.[1408] If one arrives at the conclusion that also other treaties should be included in the scope of Art. 31 (3) lit. c VCLT, the second doubt refers to the question which treaties (especially concluded between which parties) could be used as a point of reference for interpreting the treaty in question.[1409]

Regarding the type of rules to take into account when interpreting a treaty, several tribunals tried to limit the additional sources to take into consideration by virtue of Art. 31 (3) lit. c VCLT to general principles of international law only.[1410] Thus Art. 31 (3) lit. c VCLT would state that for the interpretation of any treaty (i.e. the IIA), the tribunals should take into account any general principles of international law.

However, such an interpretation would be far too narrow. First, the term "*general*" does not appear in Art. 31 (3) lit. c VCLT.[1411] Second, it has been expressly rejected when considering the text of the article.[1412] Third, as the ILC states, if the article was limited to general principles of international law only, it would be of no further use.[1413] Those principles should be part of any interpretation and execution of a treaty, due to their nature as general principles of international law.[1414] What has indeed been considered by the ILC when adopting Art. 31 (3) lit. c VCLT was to include

1408 *International Law Commission*, ILC Report on Fragmentation of International Law, 13/04/2006, para 421 f with reference to various case law examples: e.g. *Ireland vs. United Kingdom*, 02.07.2003 – PCA Case (MOX Plant/OSPAR) - Final Award, para 105 and 143 or *WTO Appellate Body, United States - Certain Shrimp and Shrimp Products*, 12.10.1998 – WT/DS58/AB/R, para 126-134.

1409 *International Law Commission*, ILC Report on Fragmentation of International Law, 13/04/2006.

1410 *Netherlands vs. France*, 12.03.2004 – UNRIAA - Affaire concernant l'apurement des comptes, para 103.

1411 Cf. also: *International Law Commission*, ILC Report on Fragmentation of International Law, 13/04/2006, para 422.

1412 *International Law Commission*, ILC Report on Fragmentation of International Law, 13/04/2006, para 422 and 430.

1413 *International Law Commission*, ILC Report on Fragmentation of International Law, 13/04/2006, para 422.

1414 *International Law Commission*, ILC Report on Fragmentation of International Law, 13/04/2006, para 468: "*These general rules and principles are applicable as a function of their mere "generality" and their validity is based on nothing grander than their having passed what Thomas Franck calls the 'but of course test'*".

in the sources of interpretation of one treaty such further treaties which are relevant for the relations of the parties.[1415]

As to the question of the parties involved in the treaties to be considered in the interpretative task, the scope differs widely between answers from different international tribunals. Some consider that only those treaties which are signed by all contracting parties of the treaty which is to be interpreted should be taken into account.[1416] This would lead to (at least) two unsolicited effects. First, the wider the application of a treaty is – which goes along with a wide recognition of its content – the more it will stay isolated from any other rules of international law. To carry it to the extreme, 159 contracting states would be impossible to agree upon – even *inter se* – an interpretation of a certain obligation in a treaty to which 160 states are contracting states.[1417] Furthermore, it would also block any possibility to take into consideration regional particularities which may have been laid down by states in an interpretative treaty.[1418] Hence, this narrow approach should be rejected.

Besides this strict interpretation, others seem to require the parties of the dispute to be parties in the treaty to take into consideration.[1419] Still others do not seem to limit it to the parties in the dispute but one party in the dispute and include non-binding frameworks as well. Especially the ECtHR seems to adopt the latter approach.[1420] The reasoning why this lat-

1415 *International Law Commission*, ILC Report on Fragmentation of International Law, 13/04/2006, para 422.

1416 *WTO Pannel, EC - Measures Affecting the Approval and Marketing of Biotech Products*, 07.02.2006 – WT/DS291-293/INTERIM, para 7.68.

1417 *International Law Commission*, ILC Report on Fragmentation of International Law, 13/04/2006, para 470 f.

1418 *International Law Commission*, ILC Report on Fragmentation of International Law, 13/04/2006, para 471.

1419 This seems to be the opinion of the ILC in its 2006 Report: *International Law Commission*, ILC Report on Fragmentation of International Law, 13/04/2006, para 470 f.

1420 *European Court of Human Rights*, 26.11.2013 – Application no. 5809/08 - Al Dulimi, para 116 which does not even contain a reference to both parties; similarly in *European Court of Human Rights*, 30.06.2005 – Application n° 45036/98 - Bosphorus the case did not include two parties (Ireland and Turkey) which were parties to the European Treaties; for references made to non-binding rules or frameworks and for a summary of the ideas regarding non-binding sources: *Broekhuijsen*, Bulletin for International Taxation Vol. 67, No. 9 (2013), 1; cf. also *Winkler*, EuGRZ Vol. 34 (2007), 641, 648.

ter approach should be followed will be treated in the following subsection.

(b) Reasons to support the ECtHR's way of treaty interpretation

The way of interpretation applied by the ECtHR is correct and should even be extended. Hence, when interpreting the scope of the state's obligation resulting from one treaty's, the tribunals should take into account all international treaties which are applicable to such state which is deemed having violated its conventional obligations.

There are four main reasons to support this view:

First, no treaty is a stand-alone provision that should be interpreted in a "*vacuum*"[1421]. The ILC in its report on the fragmentation of international law puts it clearly when stating:

> "[The principle of systematic integration, displayed in Art. 31 (3) lit. c VCLT] points to a need to take into account the normative environment more widely."[1422].

The ILC concludes on these thoughts by stating:

> "More generally, if it is indeed the point of international law to coordinate the relations between States, then it follows that specific norms must be read against other norms bearing upon those same facts as the treaty under interpretation."[1423]

It is indeed correct that a treaty should be interpreted and applied in "*good faith*" and referring to its "*ordinary meaning*", as Art. 31 (1) VCLT states.

1421 The notion was employed by the ECtHR in *European Court of Human Rights*, 21.11.2001 – Application no. 35763/97 - Al-Adsani, para 55: "*The Convention, including Article 6, cannot be interpreted in a vacuum. The Court must be mindful of the Convention's special character as a human rights treaty, and it must also take the relevant rules of international law into account ...The Convention should so far as possible be interpreted in harmony with other rules of international law of which it forms part, including to those relating to the grant of State immunity.*"; reiterated at various occasions, inter alia.: *European Court of Human Rights*, 26.11.2013 – Application no. 5809/08 - Al Dulimi, para 112; several authors support this view, cf. among others: *Broekhuijsen*, Bulletin for International Taxation Vol. 67, No. 9 (2013), 1,2 ff; *Leeks*, U. Toronto Fac. L. Rev. Vol. 65, No. 2 (2007), 1, 33 f and 36; *Tietje/Wackernagel*, JWIT Vol. 16, Iss. 2 (2015), 205, 241.

1422 *International Law Commission*, ILC Report on Fragmentation of International Law, 13/04/2006, para 415.

1423 *International Law Commission*, ILC Report on Fragmentation of International Law, 13/04/2006, para 416.

An interpretation in good faith will necessarily include the external context of the treaty, the legal framework it was based on or which interferes with the treaty, as well as the perception and evolution of the international relationships the contracting parties are subject to.[1424] This framework may be a crucial factor to understand the true meaning of the convention the tribunal is obliged to interpret.[1425] And it may be the only possibility to understand what both parties intended or – legitimately – are entitled to expect and understand from the obligations undertaken in the treaty.

Second, the ECtHR stresses the principle of systematic integration and the need for contracting states of a particular treaty to be able to access regional, supranational or international organisations and confer or transfer parts of their sovereignty to those organisations in the objective to strengthen the "*cooperation in certain fields of activity*".[1426] The importance of such organisations and integration for states should not be neglected. It is crucial for any state, as part of its sovereignty, to be able to push forward such cooperation and (constantly) (re-)shape its external relations with other states. Denying the importance of such cooperation would lead to the paradoxical situation that it could indeed be impossible for a state to enter such cooperation except for very limited fields of activities, as to avoid any potential conflict or breach of its various obligations undertaken in international treaties. It is important to stress that the principle of *pacta sunt servanda* cannot be set aside by the simple accession to such an organisation. However, an existing treaty cannot be read as the prohibition to enter in such organisations as well. By means of inter-

1424 *Tietje/Wackernagel*, JWIT Vol. 16, Iss. 2 (2015), 205, 241; also implicitly pointed out by the tribunals in: *WTO Appellate Body, United States - Certain Shrimp and Shrimp Products*, 12.10.1998 – WT/DS58/AB/R, para 129 f; *Ireland vs. United Kingdom*, 02.07.2003 – PCA Case (MOX Plant/OSPAR) - Final Award, para 105; this is also stressed out by *Lavranos* who however seems to deduct this approach by the principle of comity as forming part of the general principles of international law, which should force the tribunals to interpret treaty obligations in a way to avoid a further fragmentation of international law, cf.: *Lavranos*, ZaöVR, 2008, 575, 613 ff,, especially p. 615.

1425 *Belgium vs. France*, UN Reports of International Arbitration III, 1701, 01.03.1937 – Différend concernant l'Accord Tardieu-Jaspar, 1713; cf.: *International Law Commission*, ILC Report on Fragmentation of International Law, 13/04/2006, para 414-416.

1426 *European Court of Human Rights*, 26.11.2013 – Application no. 5809/08 - Al Dulimi, para 114 ff; *European Court of Human Rights*, 30.06.2005 – Application n° 45036/98 - Bosphorus, para 150 ff; *Meyer* in: Karpenstein/Mayer EMRK, Einl, para 126.

pretation, tribunals will need to ensure a counter-balancing between the obligations undertaken in the convention (and hence the protection contained therein) and the importance of supra- or international organisations and their proper functioning for the international level.[1427]

Third, interpreting a convention underlying a dispute also requires taking into consideration the evolution of the parties and the necessity for international law to consider such evolutions. Leaving aside especially those treaties which have been concluded by the contracting parties since the IIA was concluded would lead to a steady-locked interpretation of a treaty, which cannot be a "*good faith*"-interpretation of the state's obligations undertaken in the treaty. It should be kept in mind that the aim is not to terminate the treaty or to exonerate the state of any obligation, but to give reasonable scope and interpretation to its obligations by (also) taking into consideration the consequent evolution of circumstances and the legal framework the obligations are performed in.[1428]

Fourth, the question is whether the contracting parties of the conflicting agreement should be a limiting criterion. What the ECtHR truly refers to is a more general – underlying – principle of *systematic integration,* which is used to determine a state's obligations under the convention. Such a principle would operate outside the context of specific conventional obligations and its contracting parties. One could even consider – given its wide reiteration by various tribunals and courts – whether it is evolving into a sort of general principle of treaty interpretation in international law, which courts will need to take into account.[1429] This method of interpretation re-

---

1427 *Peters/Altwicker*, Europäische Menschenrechtskonvention, 2. Edn. (2012), p. 18; *Grabenwarter*, European Convention for the Protection of Human Rights and Fundamental Freedoms, (2014) Art. 1, para 8 f; cf. also: *Winkler*, EuGRZ Vol. 34 (2007), 641, 647.

1428 *Shaw/Fournet* in: Corten/Klein VCLT - II, Article 62 VCLT Article 62, para 44 insist on the fact that the state – in principle – cannot rely on changes of circumstances to terminate the performance of its obligations under a certain treaty except for those grounds provided by international law; however, it should be pointed out that it is not a question of non-performance of the obligations under the treaty but to take into consideration the changing context to define the scope of a – still valid – treaty; similar to this approach: *Lavranos*, ZaöVR, 2008, 575, 614 f ; cf. also: *Winkler*, EuGRZ Vol. 34 (2007), 641, 648.

1429 *European Court of Human Rights*, 30.06.2005 – Application n° 45036/98 - Bosphorus; *European Court of Human Rights*, 26.11.2013 – Application no. 5809/08 - Al Dulimi; *WTO Appellate Body, United States - Certain Shrimp and Shrimp Products*, 12.10.1998 – WT/DS58/AB/R; *Netherlands vs. France*, 12.03.2004 – UNRIAA - Affaire concernant l'apurement des comptes; *Ireland*

fers to respecting the state's various – potentially diverging – obligations and trying to reconcile them to the maximum extent. As the ECtHR puts it in *Al-Dulimi and Montana vs. Switzerland*:

> "It thus takes the view that the presumption of equivalent protection is intended, in particular, to ensure that a State Party is not faced with a dilemma when it is obliged to rely on the legal obligations incumbent on it as a result of its membership of any international organisation which is not party to the Convention"[1430]

The underlying idea of this principle is to differentiate between internal actions omitted by a host state and those acts which are external to the immediate influence of the host state. For internal actions, the host state needs to be fully reliable as it can control them at any time. By no means can such actions justify a breach of international obligations undertaken by the state (cf. Art. 27 VCLT). However, for external acts, which are not fully controlled by the host state, one cannot apply the same logic. Especially for acts decided in international organisations which are binding on its members, the idea of full control to avoid conflicts and a breach of obligations fails.[1431] The only way to prevent such conflicts would be to either abstain completely from participating in such organisations or to implement a veto-mechanism for every single participating state, which deprives any organisation of the potential for operational success.[1432] Admit-

---

vs. United Kingdom, 02.07.2003 – PCA Case (MOX Plant/OSPAR) - Final Award; As to *International Law Commission*, ILC Report on Fragmentation of International Law, 13/04/2006, para 430, the principle has not even been challenged during the discussion of the VCLT, but was taken as "*granted*"; cf.also: *Meyer* in: Karpenstein/Mayer EMRK, Einl, para 126-128. Not going that far but also supporting this view: *Tietje/Wackernagel*, JWIT Vol. 16, Iss. 2 (2015), 205, 229 f and 234. *Lavranos* refers to the principle of comity which however seems to be of similar extend, cf.: *Lavranos*, ZaöVR, 2008, 575, 614 f.

1430 *European Court of Human Rights*, 26.11.2013 – Application no. 5809/08 - Al Dulimi, para 116.

1431 Similar: *Tietje/Wackernagel*, JWIT Vol. 16, Iss. 2 (2015), 205, 229 f and 234; *Grabenwarter/Pabel*, Europäische Menschenrechtskonvention, 6. Edn. (2016), p. 152. It should not be further developped, which has often been discussed in the context of the Bosphorus-Decision, whether the act quesitioned still constitutes an act which is attributable to the "*host*" state although it was determined by an international organisation, cf.: *Janik*, ZaöVR, 2010, 127, 137 ff for a further analysis in the context of human rights. The reasons are that in the context of IIAs, host states will very likely have at least a minimum of discretion when implementing mandatory measures or provisions under EU law.

1432 These difficulties seem to be admitted by *Tietje/Wackernagel*, JWIT Vol. 16, Iss. 2 (2015), 205, 229 f as well, although the considerations raised in the article are on a different topic.

ting the importance of such structures thus imperatively requires to admit the conflict potential resulting from the restriction for the state's margin of operation in those structures or organisations.

(2) Transposing the underlying idea of the Bosphorus-Approach to extra-EU-IIAs

Transposing these considerations to extra-EU IIAs reveals that the obligations under an IIA should be interpreted in the light of the EU member states' obligations under EU law. Regarding IIA's, one could argue that there are not two overlapping multi-national treaties but solely a bilateral treaty (the IIA) and one multi-national treaty (i.e. the Lisbon Treaty as the latest of the European Treaties, establishing the TFEU and TEU) but that none of the other EU member states is a contracting party to the IIA. It could thus be difficult to conceive how the European Treaties should be any other rule of international law "*applicable in the relations between the parties*".[1433] However, given the argument of a more general, underlying principle of *systematic integration* behind the ECtHR's interpretation, this literal approach may not succeed. As already explained, the logic of a reduced margin of action in international organisations applies beyond the limits of contractual obligations undertaken by one or another party. The decisive factor is the accession of one party to an international or supranational organisation. Even in a bilateral treaty the host state loses its margin of action regarding matters imperatively decided by EU law. Recognizing the possibility to enter in supra- or international organisations and to transfer powers to these organisations leads to the necessity to take into account the accession's effects when interpreting any treaty undertaken by the host state.[1434] Again, this could be referred to as the only possible interpretation which complies with the obligation to interpret treaties in good faith according to Art. 31 (1) VCLT as it would minimise potential harm to either the one or the other framework.[1435]

1433 Art. 31 (3) lit. c VCLT [emphasis added].

1434 For an integrative approach also: *Tietje*, Intra-EU BITs als Herausforderung im Mehrebenensystem des Rechts (Beit. zum Transnat. Wirt.-R, Vol. 104, 2011), p. 18 f; *Tietje/Wackernagel*, JWIT Vol. 16, Iss. 2 (2015), 205, 229 ff.

1435 *Tietje/Wackernagel*, JWIT Vol. 16, Iss. 2 (2015), 205, 241.

Especially the underlying idea of IIAs and international investment protection does not fully apply for acts issued within a supra- or international framework as well. This idea was to create a legal framework protecting the investors' rights, which is governed by international law and operates outside the national legislative context, as this national legislation is subject to full discretion of the host state. Regarding a legal environment which derives from a supra- or international organisation, the host state has (at least partially) lost its discretion and influence on the framework.[1436] Intentionally depriving the investor of its rights through an act issued by this organisation would therefore require a conjoint approach of all members of the organisation.[1437] Theoretically this is still possible. However, given that IIA should generally not prevent host states from adapting their (general) regulations to new situations, a targeted action against one particular investor or a range of investors definitely becomes less probable. Second, following the *Bosphorus-Approach*, such supranational framework needs to provide certain (equivalent) guarantees, which the host state may not set aside unilaterally either. This idea justifies to take into consideration the specific situation of a host state having transferred powers to the EU when interpreting an extra-EU IIA as well.

II. Interim results on the possibility to transpose the Bosphorus Approach to IIAs

It has hence been demonstrated that arbitral tribunals should take EU law into account when interpreting the obligations resulting from an IIA in extra-EU investment proceedings.

First, for some of these extra-EU disputes, EU law will be applicable as domestic law to the dispute. As such, arbitral tribunal cannot simply disregard EU law when determining whether the EU member state, as host-state, violated its obligations under the IIA.

Second, even if the IIA solely refers to international law as applicable law to the investment dispute EU law should be taken into account by means of Art. 31 (c) VCLT.

1436 Also admitted by *Tietje/Wackernagel*, JWIT Vol. 16, Iss. 2 (2015), 205, 229 f; *Tietje*, Intra-EU BITs als Herausforderung im Mehrebenensystem des Rechts (Beit. zum Transnat. Wirt.-R, Vol. 104, 2011), p. 18 f.

1437 *Tietje*, Intra-EU BITs als Herausforderung im Mehrebenensystem des Rechts (Beit. zum Transnat. Wirt.-R, Vol. 104, 2011), p. 18 f.

As a result, the preliminary prerequisite to transpose the *Bosphorus-Approach* to extra-EU proceedings is met: the arbitral tribunals are entitled to take EU law into account when interpreting the EU member states' obligations under the IIA.

Hower, in the *Bosphorus-Decision* the ECtHR stated that the margin of control, which is exercised by the court or tribunal, can only be reduced, if the two legal frameworks in question offer an *equivalent level of (substantive and procedural) protection*. This second, most important, prerequisite will be analysed in the following Chapter 15.

Chapter 15: Conditions to reduce the margin of control according to the Bosphorus-Approach

Having demonstrated that the reasoning of the ECtHR in the *Bosphorus-Decision* regarding which provisions to take into account when interpreting a treaty can be transposed to the interpretation of extra-EU IIAs, the further conditions set forth by the ECtHR to apply the *Bosphorus-Presumption* should be assessed.

The ECtHR requires one fundamental condition to be met to reduce the margin of control regarding mandatory acts of EU law, which is the equivalence of substantive and procedural protection within the EU regarding human rights. Being able to transpose the *Bosphorus-Presumption* to investment protection within the EU would thus require the substantive and procedural protection for investments under EU law being at least equivalent to the protection offered by IIAs.[1438]

Two important remarks must be stressed before examining this further:

First, the ECtHR did not require both legal frameworks to be identical in their level of protection. Both indeed simply need to be equivalent. Thus, the threshold is substantially lower.[1439]

Second, the presumption will only apply for "*mandatory*" acts of EU law, meaning those acts which require a certain action or a limited scope

---

1438 *Grabenwarter*, European Convention for the Protection of Human Rights and Fundamental Freedoms, (2014) Art. 1, para 8 f; *Meyer* in: Karpenstein/Mayer EMRK, Einl, para 145.

1439 Cf. also: *Tietje/Wackernagel*, JWIT Vol. 16, Iss. 2 (2015), 205, 234; *Peters/Altwicker*, Europäische Menschenrechtskonvention, 2. Edn. (2012), p. 18 f; *Grabenwarter/Pabel*, Europäische Menschenrechtskonvention, 6. Edn. (2016), p. 151; *Janik*, ZaöVR, 2010, 127, 163.

of actions by the EU member state. Consequently, the level of protection will only need to be equivalent for this sort of action. This has, as it will be demonstrated, a considerable impact on the question of applicability of the Charter of Fundamental Rights of the EU and the potential procedural remedies.[1440]

The equivalence of substantive protection standards in IIAs and under EU law will be demonstrated first. The second sub-section will address the equivalence of procedural protection offered by both frameworks.

A. Equivalence of substantive protection under EU law

The equivalence of protection offered by EU law with regard to protection standards will be demonstrated by referring to the most common protection guarantees contained in IIAs and the interpretation given to these standards by arbitral tribunals. Differences linked to particular wordings or particular scope of the guarantees of specific IIAs might potentially set aside the *Bosphorus-Presumption* and will be treated *infra* (Chapter 16).

I. Protection against (direct and indirect) expropriations

The first standard to be analysed should be the prohibition of expropriation contained in several IIAs.

The protection against expropriation in EU law is generally guaranteed by the national constitutions or the national legal framework. This would – obviously – not be sufficient to establish an equivalence of protection. However, regarding (all) acts of the EU institutions or the EU member states which *implement* EU law, the protection of the right to property is guaranteed by Art. 17 of the Charter of Fundamental Rights of the EU.[1441]

1440 *Peters/Altwicker*, Europäische Menschenrechtskonvention, 2. Edn. (2012), p. 18; This is why several arguments claiming an obvious non-equivalence of EU law and IIAs (mostly in the context of the notion of sameness under Art. 59, 30 VCLT) cannot sustain, as those comparisions do generally compare EU law to IIAs, without distinction to the type of act in question and its determination by EU law, cf. e.g.: *Reinisch*, LIEI Vol. 39, No. 2 (2012), 157, 170 f.

1441 Similarly: *Dimopoulos*, CMLR Vol. 48, No. 1 (2011), 63 65; this seems to be ignored by *Tietje*, Intra-EU BITs als Herausforderung im Mehrebenensystem des Rechts (Beit. zum Transnat. Wirt.-R, Vol. 104, 2011), p. 14.

Such supra-national protection as conceived by the Charter may be an equivalent mean of protection. The applicability of the Charter however depends on the interpretation given to the notion of "*implementing*" EU law. The notion was already discussed previously.

It was demonstrated that the CJEU considers the EU member states to "*implement*" EU law in the sense of Art. 51 (1) of the Charter whenever:

- The state measure is mandatory under EU law[1442] *or*
- The state measure limits fundamental freedoms, as such limitations can only be justified if they also comply with the rights and guarantees of the Charter[1443] *or*
- In all other cases where the state measure is somehow related to EU law by its objective, by the intention to implement EU law or even if it only indirectly affects provisions of EU law as long as the specific characteristics of EU law such as the principle of supremacy, the direct effect or the autonomy are questioned.[1444]

Hence, when transposing this approach to the questions arising under the *Bosphorus-Presumption,* all acts for which arbitral tribunals could make use of the presumption, i.e. acts which are to a certain extent mandated by EU law, would be acts which implement EU law as to the above-mentioned definition. The first situation where the presumption is invoked might concern mandatory acts of the EU. In such cases the Charter will obviously be applicable. Other cases might concern regulations such as the energy unbundling regulations, which leave a certain discretion to EU member states but the eligible scope of action is outside the remaining scope of action under an IIA. For those actions the Charter will apply as well. If the EU issues secondary regulation which expressly regulates a certain subject matter and thus forces the EU member states to undertake a certain range of measures, this will obviously be a measure which is somehow related to the EU either by its objective or by the intention to implement EU law. Such measures by the host state will hence necessarily

1442 *Terhechte* in: v. d. Groeben/Schwarze AEUV/EUV, Art. 51 of the Charter, para 10.

1443 *Terhechte* in: v. d. Groeben/Schwarze AEUV/EUV, Art. 51 of the Charter, para 10.

1444 *Terhechte* in: v. d. Groeben/Schwarze AEUV/EUV, Art. 51 of the Charter, para 11; *CJEU*, 10.07.2014 – C-198/13 - Hernández = ECLI:EU:C:2014:2055, para 37.

"*implement*" EU law according to the interpretation given to the term by the CJEU. [1445]

Even though a state measure might "*implement*" EU law, some authors argued that the protection guaranteed under Art. 17 of the Charter would be considerably weakened by the interference of the Art. 17 of the Charter with Art. 345 TFEU. [1446] Art. 345 TFEU reads as follows:

> "The Treaties shall in no way prejudice the rules in Member States governing the system of property ownership."

However, one cannot deduct from Art. 345 TFEU that the member states should not be bound by the Charter when property rights are concerned.[1447] Art. 345 TFEU does not limit the right to property. A fundamental distinction needs to be drawn between the terms "*right to property*" and the terms "*system of property ownership*".[1448] The system of property ownership rather refers to a concept, whereas the right to property to the individual right of each natural person or legal entity. Hence, Art. 345 TFEU does not refer to the individual right itself but to the concept of property.[1449]

Second, one needs to bear in mind that Art. 345 TFEU is part of the chapter "*final provisions*" in the TFEU and should thus have a general use within the application of the TFEU, whereas Art. 17 of the Charter figures among the rights which are attributed to individuals in the Charter. Given these differences, Art. 345 TFEU should only be read as a demarcation of competencies between the EU and its member states regarding the regulation of the system of property ownership, without impeding or having any

1445 Compared e.g. to the *Fransson Case (CJEU*, 26.12.2013 – C-617/10 - Hans Åkerberg Fransson = ECLI:EU:C:2013:105), in which the CJEU also admitted the measure to "*implement*" EU law, the relationship between the national measure and the provision of EU law to be implemented will be much closer.

1446 Cf. for an overview of the differencies: *Calliess* in: Becker/Ehlers Europäische Grundfreiheiten (2014), § 20, para 4 ff and *Hatje* in: Schwarze EU-Kommentar, Art. 345 TFEU, para 2 ff.

1447 Cf. inter alia: *Jarass*, 2. Edn. (2013), Art. 17, para 5.

1448 In German, the terms refer to "Eigentums*recht*" and "Eigentums*ordnung*" which seems to give a clearer indication on the scope of each of both articles as it indicates the difference more precisely.

1449 *Jarass*, 2. Edn. (2013) Art. 17, para 5; *Bernsdorff* in: Meyer (Ed.) Charta der Grundrechte der EU, Art. 17 of the Charter, para 4; *Hatje* in: Schwarze EU-Kommentar, Art. 345 TFEU, para 9; *Calliess* in: Becker/Ehlers Europäische Grundfreiheiten (2014), § 20, para 10 f.

impact on the right to property guaranteed in Art. 17 of the Charter.[1450] Art. 345 TFEU guarantees that no provision in the European Treaties would prevent the member states to deliberately decide on their allocation of private or state-owned property, depending on their idea on economic politics.[1451] Thus, the member states are free to decide to either nationalise or to privatise property without being hindered from doing so by the European Treaties.[1452] The EU recognises this choice and omits to interfere with it.[1453] However, this does not mean that any decision by the member states in execution of this choice, cannot violate other provisions of the Treaties.[1454] Especially such measures will need to comply with Art. 17 of the Charter as well as the principle of non-discrimination.[1455] Art. 345 TFEU does neither prohibit nationalising measures by the EU (cf. also: Art. 17 (1) 2 of the Charter which would otherwise be useless), nor would it affect or reduce the scope of protection guaranteed by Art. 17 of the Charter or the competency of the CJEU to determine the scope of this article.[1456]

Hence, the equivalence of protection under the IIA provisions and Art. 17 of the Charter need to be compared. To address the equivalence, three distinct features of the standard will be compared:

First, the conditions required to exceptionally enable expropriations without infringing the general prohibition of expropriation need to be addressed (*equivalence of conditions for a lawful expropriation*).

1450 *Jarass*, 2. Edn. (2013) Art. 17, para 5; *Bernsdorff* in: Meyer (Ed.) Charta der Grundrechte der EU, Art. 17 of the Charter, para 4; *Hatje* in: Schwarze EU-Kommentar, Art. 345 TFEU, para 9; *Calliess* in: Becker/Ehlers Europäische Grundfreiheiten (2014), § 20, para 10 f.

1451 *Jarass*, 2. Edn. (2013) Art. 17, para 5; *Bernsdorff* in: Meyer (Ed.) Charta der Grundrechte der EU, Art. 17 of the Charter, para 4.

1452 *Hatje* in: Schwarze EU-Kommentar, Art. 345 TFEU, para 2 ff.

1453 *Hatje* in: Schwarze EU-Kommentar, Art. 345 TFEU, para 8 f.

1454 *Hatje* in: Schwarze EU-Kommentar, Art. 345 TFEU, para 4 ff.

1455 *Hatje* in: Schwarze EU-Kommentar, Art. 345 TFEU, para 9 f; *CJEU*, 06.11.1984 – C-182/83 - Fearon = ECLI:EU:C:1984:335, para 7: „*Consequently, although Article [345 TFEU] does not call in question the member states' right to establish a system of compulsory acqusition by public bodies, such a system remains subject to the fundamental rule of non-discrimination (...)*".

1456 *Jarass*, 2. Edn. (2013) Art. 17, para 5; *Calliess* in: Becker/Ehlers Europäische Grundfreiheiten (2014), § 20, para 1; denying any right of the European Union to nationalise but agreeing considering the remaining aspects: *Streinz*, 10. Edn. (2016), para 793.

Second, the state measures covered by the general prohibition of expropriation should be evaluated (*equivalence of measures being qualified as expropriation*).

Third, the scope of protection offered by the standards with regard to the protected assets should be analysed (*equivalence of protected assets*).

1. Equivalence of measures being qualified as expropriations

The different measures being qualified as expropriations should be addressed first, as this will determine if any justification for an impediment on the right of property is necessary and which conditions will need to be fulfilled. IIAs generally protect the investor against *direct* (*de jure* or *formal*) and *indirect* (*de facto*) expropriations.

As demonstrated, a formal expropriation in investment law is characterised by a formal transfer of the title as well as depriving the investor of further enjoyment of their previous rights.[1457]

Art. 17 of the Charter states a nearly identical definition. A formal expropriation consists of a transfer of ownership by a "*measure completely and errantly depriving the owner of her/his ownership*"[1458].[1459]

IIAs generally also prohibit indirect expropriations.[1460] Despite differences in how to determine the existence of an indirect expropriation, the common elements of such measures remain identical. Indirect expropriations leave the formal right with the owner but deprive him of any substantial use of this right. This might *inter alia* appear through the "*effective*

1457 *Kniebaum* in: *Bungenberg/Griebel/Hobe et al.* (Eds.), International Investment Law, 2015, p. 970 f.

1458 *Wollenschläger* in: Peers, Hervey et al. - European Union Charter of Fundamental Rights, Art. 17 (1) of the Charter, para 17(1).32.

1459 *Jarass*, 2. Edn. (2013) Art. 17, para 18; the requirement of a transfer was expressly stressed out by the CJEU: *CJEU*, 10.07.2003 – Joined Cases C-20/00 and C-64/00 - Booker et al. = ECLI:EU:C:2003:397, especially paras 80, 81.

1460 It is doubtful if the difference in terminology between indirect, de facto or creepeing expropriations should realy translate by a difference in substance. Kniebaum argues that creeping expropriation involve a long lasting changement, whereas de facto expropriation should be instant. As the general definition of an indirect expropriation remains the same, the notion of indirect expropriation will be used as a superset for creeping and de facto expropriations, cf. for further details: *Kniebaum* in: *Bungenberg/Griebel/Hobe et al.* (Eds.), International Investment Law, 2015, p. 971 ff.

loss of management, use or control, or a significant depreciation in value, of the assets".[1461] Generally the same definition applies regarding indirect expropriations in the context of Art. 17 of the Charter.[1462]

Regarding the concrete interpretation (i.e. the application) of these definitions under the IIA and EU law, it should be demonstrated that the application of the terms covers mainly the same state measures.

Regarding IIAs, the criteria to determine the threshold between a regulation of the right of property and an (indirect) expropriation are the duration and the degree of interference with the potential economic use of the investment. The interference needs to be of such substance that *de facto* the investor's ability to reasonably use its investment is either completely destroyed or diminished to a negligible extent.[1463] To determine the intensity, the state measures cannot be evaluated in isolation, but the overall effects need to be determined.[1464] However, there is considerable debate, whether the impact of the measure should be sufficient to qualify a measure as indirect expropriation. Some tribunals consider the effect of the state measure as the only element which should be taken into account (*sole effect doctrine*), regardless of the state's intention or any public policy necessities to act the way the state did.[1465] Others want to exclude specific acts from being qualified as indirect expropriations, even though they might have considerable economic effects. Mainly two criteria have been used in recent arbitral practice to limit the consequences of the *sole effect doctrine*. Some tribunals exercised an additional test of proportionality, which means that the expropriation will be balanced against the public interest requiring the measure. Only if the public interest could not over-

1461 *UNCTAD*, United Nations Conference on the Law of Treaties: Series on issues in international investment agreements: Taking of Property, 2000, p. 4.

1462 *Jarass*, 2. Edn. (2013) Art. 17, para 18 f; *European Court of Human Rights*, 24.06.1993 – Application no. 14556/89 - Papamichalopoulos, para 43 ff.

1463 *Kniebaum* in: *Bungenberg/Griebel/Hobe et al.* (Eds.), International Investment Law, 2015, p. 983; *CME vs. Czech Republic*, 13.09.2001 – UNCITRAL - Partial Award, para 604: "*effectively neutralize the benefit of the property*"; *Pope & Talbot vs. Canada*, 10.04.2001 – UNCITRAL - Awards on the Merits of Phase 2, para 102: "*[measure needs to be] sufficiently restrictive to support a conclusion that the property has been 'taken' [...]*".

1464 *Kniebaum* in: *Bungenberg/Griebel/Hobe et al.* (Eds.), International Investment Law, 2015 p.979; *Siemens A.G. vs. Argentina*, 17.01.2007 – ICSID Case No. ARB/02/8 - Award.

1465 *Kniebaum* in: *Bungenberg/Griebel/Hobe et al.* (Eds.), International Investment Law, 2015, p. 982.

weight the private interest in the property, the act is deemed to be considered as indirect expropriation.[1466] Others focus on the objectives of the measure and deny an indirect expropriation, regardless the harm the action may cause, if the objective were public power measures or legitimate public regulations.[1467]

The comparison of measures having been qualified as indirect expropriations under IIAs and EU law will be, regarding IIAs, based on the *sole effect* doctrine for two reasons: first, it seems as if a significant number of arbitral tribunals continue to apply this approach. Second, the other criteria advanced by several tribunals only leverage the threshold for a measure to be qualified as indirect expropriation. Hence those are additional criteria which are taken into consideration to *exclude* a measure from being qualified as expropriation. Those criteria will be dealt with when evaluating the requirements to justify an expropriation (as EU law mainly takes these criteria into consideration under this angle as well).

The CJEU as well as the ECtHR have dealt with several cases regarding indirect expropriations. Measures such as the construction of a canal system on private property, the restrictions as to the use of an immovable property which leaves the owner without substantial use (*Köktepe-Case*) or the destruction of any assets were conceived as indirect expropriation.[1468] The CJEU further seems to consider that administrative restrictions as to the sale of a product might constitute indirect expropriations.[1469] Adopting the same perspective, the CJEU admits that the right to property also includes the guarantee for the owner to at least have the possibility to reach the commercial break-even point.[1470] However, in the *Ka-*

1466 *Tecmed vs. Mexico*, 29.05.2003 – ICSID Case No. ARB (AF)/00/2 - Award, para 122; *LG&E vs. Argentina*, 03.10.2006 – ICSID Case No. ARB/02/1 - Decision on Liability, para 189 ff; cf. also: *Kniebaum* in: *Bungenberg/Griebel/Hobe et al.* (Eds.), International Investment Law, 2015, p. 1003 ff; *Nikièma*, Best Practices: Indirect Expropriation, 03/2012, p. 15 f.

1467 *Methanex vs. USA*, 03.08.2005 – UNCITRAL- Final Award of the Tribunal on Jurisdiction and Merits Part. IV Chapter D, para 15; cf. also: *Nikièma*, Best Practices: Indirect Expropriation, 03/2012, p. 17 ff.

1468 *European Court of Human Rights*, 22.07.2008 – Application no 35785/03 - Köktepe, para 84 ff; *Jarass*, 2. Edn. (2013) Art. 17, para 19.

1469 *Wollenschläger* in: v. d. Groeben/Schwarze AEUV/EUV, Art. 17 of the Charter, para 27; *Calliess* in: Calliess/Ruffert EUV/AEUV, Art. 17 of the Charter, para 19.

1470 *CJEU*, 16.10.2003 – C-363/01 - Flughaften Hannover-Langenhagen = ECLI:EU:C:2003:548, para 55 and 56: "*As to the right to property, the fact*

di cases the CJEU denied considering the freezing of funds to be an indirect expropriation and qualified those measures as regulations of the use of property.[1471]

Compared to the jurisprudence of arbitral tribunals, the applications seem to overlap broadly. *Inter alia*, in the *Metalclad-Case* refusing a construction permit for an immovable property, especially designated to a certain business purpose, was judged to be an indirect expropriation. The case seemingly reflects the *Köktepe-Case*, where the authorities deprived the owner of any use of the property by qualifying it as national forest.[1472] Similarly, the revocation of a license to operate the business, which was qualified as an indirect expropriation in *Tecmed,* might find its counterpart in the jurisprudence of the CJEU (although it has not yet been formally decided).[1473]

---

that the managing body of an airport is not authorised to collect an access fee does not mean, contrary to the Flughafen's assertions, that that body is deprived of the possibility of profiting from the economic services that it provides on the groundhandling market to which it must grant access. Article 16(3) of the Directive requires that the fee which may be collected in return for access to airport installations must be determined according to relevant, objective, transparent and non-discriminatory criteria. Therefore, that provision does not prevent the fee from being determined in such a way that the mananging body of the airport is able not only to cover the costs associated with the provision and maintenance of airport installations, but also to make a profit." However, a contrario, if the legislation had put the airport in the position of not being able to at least cover its costs, the CJEU seems having addmitted an interference with the right to property, cf. also: *Calliess* in: Calliess/Ruffert EUV/AEUV, Art. 17 of the Charter, para 19.

1471 *CJEU*, 03.09.2008 – Joined Cases C-402/05 P and C-415/05 P - Kadi = ECLI:EU:C:2008:461, para 368 ff and *CJEU*, 30.09.2010 – T-85/09 - Kadi = ECLI:EU:T:2010:418, para 192 ff.

1472 *European Court of Human Rights*, 22.07.2008 – Application no 35785/03 - Köktepe, para 84 f.

1473 *CJEU*, 12.05.2005 – C-347/03 - ERSA = ECLI:EU:C:2005:285 which concerned the necessity to use a specific description for selling its wine – which might to some degree be compared to a revocation or non-attribution of a license to operate a business model. In para 121 and 122 the Court held: *"It is therefore necessary to examine whether the prohibition of the use of the word 'Tocai' for the description and presentation of certain Italian quality wines psr from 1 April 2007, resulting from the exchange of letters on Tocai, constitutes disproportionate and intolerable interference, impairing the very substance of the fundamental right to property of the economic operators concerned. That prohibition, in so far as it does not exclude any reasonable method of marketing the Italian wines concerned, does not constitute a deprivation of posses-*

Regarding the limits of measures being qualified as indirect expropriation, one can find similar approaches as well: *Inter alia*, the tribunal's decision in *LG&E* denied the existence of a *de facto* expropriation as the investor was still enabled to control its investment even though the market position of the investment was heavily affected by Argentina's monetary policy measures.[1474] Hence, even though arbitral tribunals are more focused on the economic effects of a state measure, the threshold to admit an indirect expropriation remains relatively high.

Even the *Kadi-Case* finds some equivalence in the tribunals' jurisprudence. The *S. D. Myers-Tribunal* equally disqualified an export ban to be qualified as an indirect expropriation, as the measure, which took 18 months, was only temporary.[1475]

In addition to the fact that the delimiting criteria broadly overlap, the concrete delimitation under EU law between measures above and below the threshold to qualify a measure as indirect expropriation is less important. Under an IIA, if a measure does not qualify as an indirect expropriation, the expropriation standard will not apply and does not provide any further protection. Other than under the investment protection mechanism, any measure not being qualified as indirect expropriation would still be either qualified as regulations of the use of property or other limitations on the right of property, which both are subject to further justification under Art. 17 of the Charter.[1476]

It will be demonstrated that the conditions which need to be met by a member state under EU law in case of expropriations but also in case of (severe) regulations of the right to property are equivalent to the expropriation standard guaranteed in IIAs.[1477]

---

sions as referred to in the first paragraph of Article 1 of Protocol No 1 to the ECHR (...)".

1474 *LG&E vs. Argentina*, 03.10.2006 – ICSID Case No. ARB/02/1 - Decision on Liability, para 198 ff.

1475 *S. D. Myers vs Canada*, 13.11.2000 – UNCITRAL - Partial Award, para 287.

1476 *Wollenschläger* in: v. d. Groeben/Schwarze AEUV/EUV, Art. 17 of the Charter, para 28.

1477 Cf. also regarding the question of compensation being a general criteria within the test of proportionality and thus considering the qualification as *de facto* expropriation being of no further use: *Wollenschläger* in: v. d. Groeben/Schwarze AEUV/EUV, Art. 17 of the Charter, para 28; the equivalence of both standards (EU Law and IIA) seems to be admitted by *Dimopoulos*, LIEI Vol. 39, No. 4 (2012), 447, 464 f, who however expresses doubts as to the equivalence of requirements regarding the amount due for compensation.

2. Equivalence of conditions for a lawful expropriation

As demonstrated, IIAs generally require four conditions to be fulfilled in order to qualify the expropriation as lawful. Those are[1478]:

- the expropriation needs to serve a public purpose;
- it needs to be non-discriminatory;
- the host state needs to expropriate with respect to the due process of law (with the availability of a judicial review of the expropriating measure);
- fair compensation needs to be paid for the expropriated good.

Art. 17 of the Charter sets slightly different conditions as to the lawfulness of an *expropriation*:

- the expropriation needs to be in the public interest;
- it needs to be based on a precise legal basis which sets forth the major modalities of the expropriation;[1479]
- it needs to comply with the test of proportionality (Art. 52 (1) of the Charter): the deprivation needs to be suitable to pursue the public interest, necessary to obtain it and appropriate compared to the interest pursued;[1480]
- due compensation needs to be paid in return to the expropriation.

Regarding the *regulations of the use of property*, Art. 17 of the Charter generally requires:

- the measures need to have a legal basis;
- the measure needs to serve the public interest;
- it needs to pass the test of proportionality;
- compensation may need to be paid in cases of severe restrictions.

Indeed, irrespective of whether a measure is still qualified as direct or indirect expropriation or if it is 'only' considered to be a regulation of the right to use its property (with a considerable impact on the investor), the criteria to justify such limitations on the right of property are equivalent to

---

1478 Cf. *supra* Chapter 4; cf. also: *Kniebaum* in: *Bungenberg/Griebel/Hobe et al.* (Eds.), International Investment Law, 2015, p. 1017 with extensive jurisprudence of the arbitral tribunal regarding each of the conditions on, p. 1018 ff.

1479 *Wollenschläger* in: Peers, Hervey et al. - European Union Charter of Fundamental Rights, Art. 17 (1) of the Charter, para 17(1).39.

1480 *Jarass*, 2. Edn. (2013) Art. 17, para 28; cf. also: *Wollenschläger* in: Peers, Hervey et al. - European Union Charter of Fundamental Rights, Art. 17 (1) of the Charter, para 17(1).40; *Wollenschläger* in: v. d. Groeben/Schwarze AEUV/EUV, Art. 17 of the Charter, para 33.

the conditions in investment protection law if the state measure is sufficiently severe. This should be demonstrated by assessing the aforementioned criteria.

(1) Public purpose / public interest

The first condition for an expropriation to be qualified as lawful is that the expropriation needs to serve a public purpose (IIA) or public interest (EU law). The conditions requiring a public purpose / public interest under both frameworks are not only equivalent but nearly identical. Neither EU law nor IIAs positively list potential interests which might justify an expropriation.[1481] Under both frameworks, the requirement generally excludes expropriations for the purpose of private benefit only (hence it does not at least additionally serve a valid public interest).[1482] Generally both frameworks grant considerable discretion to the authorities to determine the public interest but would deny the existence of a public interest / public purpose if the latter only serves as a pretext to an expropriation for the purely private benefit of a particular person.[1483]

The same applies for measures which will be qualified as regulations of the use of property under EU law. According to Art. 52 (1) of the Charter, each limitation of the right to property needs to serve a legitimate public purpose.[1484] Especially considering that arbitral tribunals also grant host states a considerable margin of appreciation to determine the public interest, the differences regarding the requirement should be negligible.

(2) Due process of law

The second condition for an expropriation to be qualified as lawful under an IIA is the observance of a due process of law when expropriating the owner. Despite some differences in the details, the requirement of a due

1481 *Kniebaum* in: *Bungenberg/Griebel/Hobe et al.* (Eds.), International Investment Law, 2015, p. 1018; *Jarass*, 2. Edn. (2013) Art. 17, para 27.

1482 *Jarass*, 2. Edn. (2013) Art. 17, para 27; *Kniebaum* in: *Bungenberg/Griebel/Hobe et al.* (Eds.), International Investment Law, 2015, p. 1018 f.

1483 *Jarass*, 2. Edn. (2013) Art. 17, para 27; *Kniebaum* in: *Bungenberg/Griebel/Hobe et al.* (Eds.), International Investment Law, 2015, p. 1018 f.

1484 *Jarass*, 2. Edn. (2013), para 30 ff.

process of law in IIAs usually includes several aspects reflecting a prior involvement of the owner and the future possibility to challenge the expropriating act.[1485] The prior involvement requires a notice of expropriation, the involvement of the investor / owner prior to the expropriating measure and the possibility to advance its case and arguments to the authorities.[1486]

These requirements are also well established under the test of proportionality in EU law and especially regarding the right to property guaranteed under Art. 17 of the Charter.[1487] First, the general requirement of the expropriation being based on a sufficiently precise legal basis reduces the possibility of arbitrary and unadvised expropriations. Second, limitations, including expropriation as one of the most fundamental restrictions to the right of property, need to follow a due process of law. This was expressly recognised in the *Kadi* judgements[1488], which were interpreted as regulations of the use of property but, due to their far-reaching impact, would have required a due process including the ability for Mr. Kadi to present the case to the relevant authorities before the measure was taken to meet the test of proportionality.[1489] If this requirement is even imposed for the – less severe – regulation of the right to property, it is *a forteriori* imposed regarding the more far reaching deprivation of the right to property.

(3) Prohibition of discrimination

IIAs further guarantee that any expropriating measures need to be non-discriminatory. With reference to the principle of national treatment, a measure being discriminatory is generally defined as a difference in treatment taking place in comparable circumstances without adequate reasons

---

1485 *Kniebaum* in: *Bungenberg/Griebel/Hobe et al.* (Eds.), International Investment Law, 2015, p. 1028 f.

1486 *Kniebaum* in: *Bungenberg/Griebel/Hobe et al.* (Eds.), International Investment Law, 2015, p. 1029.

1487 Cf. for the general requirement: *Jarass*, 2. Edn. (2013) Art. 52, para 44a.

1488 *CJEU*, 03.09.2008 – Joined Cases C-402/05 P and C-415/05 P - Kadi = ECLI:EU:C:2008:461, *CJEU*, 30.09.2010 – T-85/09 - Kadi = ECLI:EU:T:2010:418.

1489 *CJEU*, 03.09.2008 – Joined Cases C-402/05 P and C-415/05 P - Kadi = ECLI:EU:C:2008:461, para 368 ff and *CJEU*, 30.09.2010 – T-85/09 - Kadi = ECLI:EU:T:2010:418, para 192 ff; cf. also: *Jarass*, 2. Edn. (2013) Art. 17, para 38.

for this difference.[1490] In EU law the exact same right is generally admitted under Art. 20 of the Charter (and regarding EU nationals in Art. 18 TFEU), which requires all EU institutions and the member states to act in a non-discriminatory manner. This obviously also applies to restrictions to the right to property, irrespective of whether they constitute an expropriation or only a regulation of the use of property. The standards can be considered as identical to this regard, which will be explained in detail concerning the principle of national treatment and non-discrimination (cf. *infra "II. National treatment and non-discrimination clauses"*).

(4) Due compensation

The last condition for an expropriation to be qualified as lawful is the due compensation for the loss of the right to property. The requirement of due compensation in case of an expropriation is well established under both EU law and the expropriation standards in IIAs. As to the determination of the amount to be paid and its modalities, both frameworks tend to refer to the *Hull-Formula*, which requires the compensation to be "*prompt, adequate and effective*".[1491] Referring to the same standard of international law when determining the compensation should serve as considerable proof of the equivalence of both systems. Judging whether the concrete determination of an *adequate* compensation is sufficient or not is mostly a matter of fact which cannot be reasonably compared. However, what can be compared are the criteria which are used by both frameworks to determine the value. These criteria are mostly the same:

Arbitral tribunals generally refer to a comparative approach which estimates the value of an asset by reference to the price achieved upon sale of equivalent asset or other market data. Others refer to cash flow discounted methods, which try to project future revenues.[1492] Similar approaches are conducted by courts within the EU. They generally take the market value, including subsequent deductions from the amount paid (e.g.

1490 *Kniebaum* in: *Bungenberg/Griebel/Hobe et al.* (Eds.), International Investment Law, 2015, p. 1025.

1491 *Bernsdorff* in: Meyer (Ed.) Charta der Grundrechte der EU, Art. 17 of the Charter, para 20; *Jarass*, 2. Edn. (2013) Art. 17, para 29.

1492 Cf. for a detailed analysis: *Marboe* in: *Bungenberg/Griebel/Hobe et al.* (Eds.), International Investment Law, 2015, p. 1073-1083.

taxes), into consideration when determining whether or not the compensation was adequate.[1493] Inflexible determinations of the market value by member states are denied any effect to lower the amount to be paid.[1494]

In particular circumstances, EU law may admit that the amount to be paid is considerably lower than the market value.[1495] This is in particular admitted when such a reduction is linked to substantial considerations of public policy, such as the restructuring of entire governance systems or far reaching social or political reforms.[1496]

Regarding measures which are not qualified as indirect expropriations (e.g. because the impediment on the right to property is not sufficiently severe), compensation is usually not required by Art. 17 (1) 2 of the Charter. However, especially for measures of a certain severity which are close to the effects of an indirect expropriation, compensation is usually required under the test of proportionality to render the measure proportional.[1497] This further demonstrates the equivalence of both frameworks. Additionally, compensation for such measure can be obtained by referring to the host state's or the EU's failure to meet "*legitimate expectations*" under the extra-contractual liability of the EU or the member states.[1498] Such claims are the consequence of EU law requiring the member states to observe certain standards and conditions even if the member states' measure does not qualify as an expropriation but 'only' constitutes a regulation of the use of the right to property. If the member states fail to observe the se-

---

1493 *European Court of Human Rights*, 29.03.2006 – Application no. 36813/97 - Scordino, para 101 ff.

1494 Cf. *Jarass*, 2. Edn. (2013), Art. 17, para 29 f for further references.

1495 *Wollenschläger* in: v. d. Groeben/Schwarze AEUV/EUV, Art. 17 of the Charter, para 34.

1496 *Wollenschläger* in: v. d. Groeben/Schwarze AEUV/EUV, Art. 17 of the Charter, para 34; *Dimopoulos*, LIEI Vol. 39, No. 4 (2012), 447, 465 considers this to be problematic regarding the equivalence of both provisions.

1497 *Wollenschläger* in: v. d. Groeben/Schwarze AEUV/EUV, Art. 17 of the Charter, para 28; *Jarass*, 2. Edn. (2013) Art. 17, para 43; *Bernsdorff* in: Meyer (Ed.) Charta der Grundrechte der EU, Art. 17 of the Charter, para 21.

1498 Cf. for the rules governing the liability of the European Union and the member states: *infra* (Chapter 15) regarding the equivalence of procedural protection; *CJEU*, 14.05.1975 – C-74/74 - CNTA = ECLI:EU:C:1975:59, para 44: "(…) *the Commission has violated a superior rule of law, thus rendering the [EU] liable by failing to include in [the regulati*on] *transitional measures for the protection of the confidence which a trader might legitimiatly have had in the community rules."; cf. also: CJEU, 19.05.1992 – C-104/89 and C-37/90 - Mulder et al. = ECLI:EU:C:1992:217, para 12 ff.*

vere conditions outlined above (i.e. the regulation serves a public interest, due process, non-discrimination, overall proportionality of the measure) the regulation constitutes a violation of the right contained in Art. 17 of the Charter and hence may engage the member states' liability.[1499]

3. Equivalence of protected assets and holders of these rights

It has been demonstrated that EU law and IIAs refer to equivalent criteria as to which measures constitute an expropriation and require equivalent conditions to be fulfilled in order to qualify a measure as a lawful expropriation. However, equivalence of the standard also requires the protected assets under both frameworks to be equivalent.

At first glance there is a sharp difference between Art. 17 of the Charter and the expropriation standards of IIAs regarding the protected assets under each of the frameworks. IIAs refer to investments, whereas Art. 17 of the Charter refers to the right to property. Expropriating investments does not necessarily mean expropriating property (1). Furthermore, protection granted to investments regularly also extends to indirect ownership, which might lead to further difficulties compared to the scope of protection offered to property under the Charter (2).

(1) Protected assets and difficulties arising thereof

Although capturing the integrity of cases which will potentially be qualified as "*investments*" under an IIA seems fairly impossible, the most common features should be benchmarked against the right to property and further protected rights under the Charter. This comparison reveals that most cases are either covered directly by Art. 17 of the Charter or that protection may be achieved under Art. 16 of the Charter.

The existence of an investment is generally approached by a broad definition in the respective IIA. As however investment protection considerably depends on the access to arbitration, the definition of investment should, for the purpose of this comparison, refer to the *Salini-Test* adopted

1499 *Calliess* in: Calliess/Ruffert EUV/AEUV, Art. 17 of the Charter, para 25; *Bernsdorff* in: Meyer (Ed.) Charta der Grundrechte der EU, Art. 17 of the Charter, para 20.

with regard to Art. 25 ICSID-Convention (and which might be adopted in other frameworks as well in order to define the access to arbitration). Under this approach, an investment is defined by a certain financial contribution, over a certain duration, including a certain risk this contribution is exposed to as well as a contribution to the development of the host state.[1500] This definition usually leads to various types of assets and rights being protected. This obviously includes any kind of "*movable and immovable property as well as any other rights in rem*"[1501] and intellectual property rights, such as "*copyrights and related rights, patents, utility-model patents, industrial designs, trademarks, plant variety rights [,] trade-names, trade and business secrets, technical processes*".[1502]

Regarding these assets, no real difference between the scope of assets falling under the term of investments and the scope of the term property can be assessed. Property under Art. 17 of the Charter, which is defined as pecuniary rights exclusively assigned to the individual for their private use and interest,[1503] generally refers *inter alia* to all moveable and immoveable property rights as well as several immaterial rights.[1504] Immaterial property is protected explicitly under Art. 17 (2) of the Charter.[1505]

1500 Although the test is not undisputed, it should be the reference for this thesis. The discussions are mainly based on the necessity of further, more restrictive criteria, or the irrelevance of the contribution to the host state's development (cf.: *Bischoff/Happ* in: *Bungenberg/Griebel/Hobe et al.* (Eds.), International Investment Law, 2015, p. 512 ff). Both will not fundamentally impede on the results of this thesis, as the last criteria has been adressed with great flexibility by arbitral tribunals and further restrictive criteria will only strengthen the result of the findings in this chapter. For a more comprehensive approach regarding the discussion about the scope of the term investment, cf.: *Bischoff/Happ* in: *Bungenberg/Griebel/Hobe et al.* (Eds.), International Investment Law, 2015, p. 510 ff; *Johannsen*, Der Investitionsbegriff nach Art. 25 Abs. 1 der ICSID-Konvention (Beit. zum Transnat. Wirt.-R, ol. 87, 2009), 5.

1501 German Model BIT 2009 Art. 1 (1) lit. a.

1502 German Model BIT 2009 Art. 1 (1) lit. d and e.

1503 *Wollenschläger* in: Peers, Hervey et al. - European Union Charter of Fundamental Rights, Art. 17 (1) of the Charter, para 17(1).16; *Jarass*, 2. Edn. (2013), para 6.

1504 *Wollenschläger* in: Peers, Hervey et al. - European Union Charter of Fundamental Rights, Art. 17 (1) of the Charter, para 17(1).16; *Wollenschläger* in: v. d. Groeben/Schwarze AEUV/EUV, Art. 17 of the Charter, para 10 f; *Jarass*, 2. Edn. (2013) Art. 17, para 8.

1505 *Jarass*, 2. Edn. (2013) Art. 17, para 9.

The holding of shares in a company is also qualified as an investment.[1506] Likewise, shares also fall under the scope of property rights to be protected by Art. 17 of the Charter.[1507]

More difficult questions arise from two specific categories of investments. First, loans, debts and other contractual claims and concessions, to which economic value is attributed, are usually also referred to as investments.[1508] Second, the investment is often defined through a holistic approach of the overall economic activity, which might lead to the fact that the state measure does not properly interfere with a particular asset (such as the factory) but with the business entity as such.[1509] This also includes the fact that shareholders are generally not only protected against interference with their rights as shareholders but against impediment on the business entity as well.[1510]

The first aforementioned difficulty relates to the scope of (private and public) rights protected under both frameworks. The term investment is usually understood to refer to a range of contractual claims. Some opponents want to limit this definition by requiring a slightly higher standard and demanding a certain gravity or duration of such claims or a particular impact. However, in light of the Charter this would not make any difference, as under Art. 17 of the Charter the protection of privately owned contractual claims, as long as one can attribute an economic value to those claims, is recognised.[1511] The same has been expressly admitted by the CJEU for contractual claims derived from a public procurement process which the investor owns.[1512] Regarding public concessions or similar public rights, Art. 17 of the Charter will cover those rights granted under public law schemes either if those rights were granted in return for any (monetary or non-monetary) contribution or alternatively protected by legitimate

1506 *Herdegen*, 10. Edn. (2014), p. 338.

1507 *Wollenschläger* in: Peers, Hervey et al. - European Union Charter of Fundamental Rights, Art. 17 (1) of the Charter, para 17(1).16; *Jarass*, 2. Edn. (2013), para 6.

1508 *Herdegen*, 10. Edn. (2014), p. 338; cf. also: German Model BIT 2009 Art. 1 (1) lit. c and f.

1509 *Bischoff/Happ* in: *Bungenberg/Griebel/Hobe et al.* (Eds.), International Investment Law, 2015, p. 516, 518 and 519 ff.

1510 *Herdegen*, 10. Edn. (2014), p. 338.

1511 *Wollenschläger* in: v. d. Groeben/Schwarze AEUV/EUV, Art. 17 of the Charter, para 10; *Jarass*, 2. Edn. (2013) Art. 17, para 8.

1512 *CJEU*, 18.07.2007 – C-503/04 - Commission vs. Germany = ECLI:EU:C:2007:432, para 36.

expectations of the owner (protection of *acquired rights* or *droit acquis*).[1513] From this perspective, one cannot identify a major difference between the scope of protection under IIAs and Art. 17 of the Charter.

The second difficulty points to the question of protection for the enterprise, economic activity, market position and the good-will as such under Art. 17 of the Charter. The question is matter of intense debates.[1514] Leaving aside *acquired rights*, general interferences with the market position, general and unspecified business opportunities as well as chances or economic interests do not constitute property in the sense of Art. 17 of the Charter.[1515] This also excludes market shares.[1516] Hence, the economic enterprise or the estate as such are not protected under Art. 17 of the Charter. Recently, frequent reference has been made to the *Sky Österreich-Case*, in which the CJEU indeed denied the protection under Art. 17 of the Charter relating to a measure under Austrian law affecting Sky's remuneration paid to grant other broadcasting providers access to its exclusively purchased broadcasting rights related to sport events.[1517] As the expectation to obtain remuneration for granting access to those broadcasting rights was not qualified as *droit acquis*, the claim based on Art. 17 of the Charter failed as the interference was only related to Sky's general market posi-

1513 *Bernsdorff* in: Meyer (Ed.) Charta der Grundrechte der EU, Art. 17 of the Charter, para 15; *Jarass*, 2. Edn. (2013) Art. 17, para 10 f; and 14 *CJEU*, 23.02.1995 – Joined Cases C-358/93 and C-416/93 - Bordessa and others = ECLI:EU:C:1995:54, para 50: *"transfer for consideration would confer on undertakings purchasing quotas ownership over them"; European Court of Human Rights*, 29.11.1991 – Application no. 12742/87 - Pine Valley.

1514 *Bernsdorff* in: Meyer (Ed.) Charta der Grundrechte der EU, Art. 17 of the Charter, para 14 ff; *Wollenschläger* in: Peers, Hervey et al. - European Union Charter of Fundamental Rights, Art. 17 (1) of the Charter, para 17(1).20 ff; *Jarass*, 2. Edn. (2013) Art. 17, para 10 ff.

1515 *Wollenschläger* in: Peers, Hervey et al. - European Union Charter of Fundamental Rights, Art. 17 (1) of the Charter, para 17(1).20: *Jarass*, 2. Edn. (2013) Art. 17, para 11 and 14; *Wollenschläger* in: v. d. Groeben/Schwarze AEUV/EUV, Art. 17 of the Charter, para 14 ff; cf. *inter alia*: *CJEU*, 18.03.1980 – Joined cases 154/78, 205/78 et al - SpA Ferriera Valsabbia = ECLI:EU:C:1980:81, para 89: "*the guarantee afforded to the ownership of property cannot be extended to protect commercial interests, the uncertainties of which are part of the very essence of economic activity (...)*".

1516 *Wollenschläger* in: v. d. Groeben/Schwarze AEUV/EUV, Art. 17 of the Charter, para 14.

1517 *CJEU*, 22.01.2013 – C-283/11 - Sky Österreich = ECLI:EU:C:2013:28; cf. also: *Wollenschläger* in: v. d. Groeben/Schwarze AEUV/EUV, Art. 17 of the Charter, para 17.

tion.[1518] This is a major difference to IIAs, which do protect such entities, as they can easily be qualified as investment following the *Salini-Criteria.*[1519] Hence, an entity can be (especially indirectly) expropriated by measures affecting the business model.

The difference is however reduced considerably by two considerations. First, if the impediment on the business entity translates to an impediment on its substance or assets, e.g. through reallocation or revoking of particular production quotas or the revocation of a concession, Art. 17 of the Charter grants protection.[1520] Second, it can be deduced from the CJEU's jurisprudence that if the interference with the business entity as such reaches the degree required to constitute an indirect expropriation, Art. 17 of the Charter would apply despite the general statement that protection is not granted to the economic entity as such.[1521] Identically, the IIA only grants protection via the expropriation clause in these particular circumstances. Under an IIA the right to property is not protected as such but only against expropriations as one particular interference. Hence, both frameworks merge in the case of an indirect or direct expropriation. Additionally, in cases where the CJEU would not allow Art. 17 to intervene, investors may still rely on Art. 16 of the Charter. The conditions to restrict the general freedom to conduct business would clearly encompass the economic activity as such.[1522] However, the conditions of legality vary.

1518 *CJEU*, 22.01.2013 – C-283/11 - Sky Österreich = ECLI:EU:C:2013:28, para 35-40.

1519 For an example of this approach: *Waste Management vs. Mexico*, 30.04.2004 – ICSID Case No. ARB(AF)/00/3 - Award, para 81-83.

1520 *Wollenschläger* in: Peers, Hervey et al. - European Union Charter of Fundamental Rights, Art. 17 (1) of the Charter, para 17(1).20: *Jarass*, 2. Edn. (2013) Art. 17, para 12; *Wollenschläger* in: v. d. Groeben/Schwarze AEUV/EUV, Art. 17 of the Charter, para 16; *Calliess* in: Becker/Ehlers Europäische Grundfreiheiten (2014), § 20, para 21.

1521 *A contrario* from *CJEU*, 18.03.1980 – Joined cases 154/78, 205/78 et al - SpA Ferriera Valsabbia = ECLI:EU:C:1980:81, para 89: „*(...) Moreover, it should be noted that no close of an undertaking as a result of the application of [the regulation] has been recorded.*"; *Vosgerau* in: Stern/Sachs EU GrCH, Art. 17 of the Charter, para 35; *Wollenschläger* in: Peers, Hervey et al. - European Union Charter of Fundamental Rights, Art. 17 (1) of the Charter, para 17(1).20: *Jarass*, 2. Edn. (2013) Art. 17, para 12; *Wollenschläger* in: v. d. Groeben/Schwarze AEUV/EUV, Art. 17 of the Charter, para 16.

1522 *Jarass*, 2. Edn. (2013) Art. 16, para 9; *Everson/Goncalves* in: Peers, Hervey et al. - European Union Charter of Fundamental Rights, Art. 16 of the Charter, para 16.34.

Whereas Art. 16 also requires the test of proportionality to be fulfilled, it does not refer to the necessity of being compensated. This may however be achieved through the action for extra-contractual liability of either the EU or the member states (cf. above for this idea; this will be explained in more detail *infra*). Furthermore, one could consider that obtaining primary relief is even better than being referred to secondary relief through compensation only (cf. *infra* for this idea regarding the equivalence of procedural protection). Finally, it should be called to mind that the frameworks only need to provide equivalent protection. Particular circumstances could be addressed by virtue of proofing a manifest deficiency of protection in the case at hand (cf. *infra* Chapter 16 for the practical mise en oeuvre of the *Bosphorus-Presumption*).

(2) Implications of the chain of control: indirectly owned investments

Two issues, linked to the notion of investor and hence the personal scope of application under an IIA but also to the term of investment, should be briefly addressed here. To offer equivalent protection, the personal scope of protected persons needs to be equivalent as well. Generally, IIAs admit protection for loosely or indirectly controlled assets as well. To what degree such indirect control is protected, is a matter of considerable debate.[1523] The predominant criteria to determine the personal scope of protection is the exercise of either ownership or (at least *de facto*) control over the invested asset.[1524] It should be assumed that at least the so-called one-layer structure should be subject to protection under IIAs as well.[1525] However, arbitral tribunals have also granted the right to claim violation of an IIA to more elaborated structures.[1526] Furthermore, shareholders, in-

1523 The debate is mostly related to the question of control in multi-layer relations and the avoidance of treaty shopping.

1524 *Herdegen*, 10. Edn. (2014), p. 335 f; *Bischoff/Happ* in: *Bungenberg/Griebel/Hobe et al.* (Eds.), International Investment Law, 2015, p. 526 f, 530 ff.

1525 *Herdegen*, 10. Edn. (2014), p. 334 f.

1526 Example of more sophisticated structures by the awards in *Plama vs. Bulgaria*, 08.02.2005 – ICSID Case No. ARB/03/24 - Decision on Jurisdiction, para 170; *International Thunderbird Gaming Corporation vs. Mexico*, 26.01.2006 – UNCITRAL - Arbitral Award, para 107 f; or the example provided by *Herdegen*, 10. Edn. (2014), p. 335 f with reference to *Aguas del Tunaris vs. Bolivia*,

cluding minority shareholders, are also protected against measures which do not necessarily directly touch upon their rights as shareholders but also against interferences with the business entity.[1527] From the perspective of the equivalence of protection under the IIA and EU law, the question reveals itself as simple.

Regarding shareholders and their rights which might be affected by impediments on economic activity, the equivalence has already been duly demonstrated. Whenever the shareholders are *de facto* expropriated by a measure affecting the economic entity, protection will be offered through application of Art. 17 of the Charter (cf. *supra*).

Regarding multi-layer structures, it should be stressed that the right under Art. 17 of the Charter is attributed to the formal owner of the property (except in the case just mentioned). Hence, it will be the responsibility of the formal owner to claim its rights under the Charter. However, from the perspective of an equivalent protection, it should not be deemed unreasonable to ask an investor exercising at least *de facto* control over the entity that's rights were violated, to claim its rights through this, controlled, entity.[1528]

In case there is a lack of protection in particular minority shareholding situations and the investor is able to demonstrate such lack, this could be addressed by rebutting the *Bosphorus-Presumption*.

II. National treatment and non-discrimination clauses

It should now be demonstrated that EU law also provides an equivalent level of protection compared to the protection offered by IIAs through the national treatment standard and non-discrimination clauses. The standard of national treatment and general non-discrimination clauses will be treated in parallel. According to the first standard, unjustified less favourable treatment of national and foreign investors in comparable or like circum-

21.10.2005 – ICSID Case No. ARB/02/3 - Decision on Respondent's Objections to Jurisdiction, para 264.

1527 *Herdegen*, 10. Edn. (2014), p. 338.

1528 *Inter alia*: *International Thunderbird Gaming Corporation vs. Mexico*, 26.01.2006 – UNCITRAL - Arbitral Award, para 108, which holds that the investor, despite of not having ownership or legal control, still is enabled to "*decide and implement the key decisions*" which should hence also enable to claim the violation of rights.

stances is prohibited.[1529] The latter standard refers to a general prohibition of treating investors in comparable or like circumstances differently whenever such differential treatment is not justified, irrespective of whether the treatment is based on the investor's nationality or on other grounds.[1530]

Both standards are usually evaluated based on three steps[1531]:

- the finding of a less favourable treatment of one entity compared to another entity;
- both entities need to be in comparable/similar/like circumstances;
- the question whether difference in treatment can be justified.

Under EU Law, one can refer to two provisions that cover these aspects: the free movement of capital and the general prohibition of discrimination under Art. 20 of the Charter. Art. 18 TFEU cannot be raised here as it addresses only discrimination among nationals of EU member states (i.e. intra-EU scenarios).[1532]

1. Equivalence of prohibition of national treatment under the free movement of capital

The guarantee of free movement of capital under Art. 63 TFEU is commonly referred to as the most far reaching guarantee for non-member state nationals. Generally, as already explained, it prohibits any measure by the EU or a member state which hinders, or renders less attractive (i.e. restricts: "*beschränken*") the free movement of capital to or from other

1529 *Reinisch* in: *Tietje* (Ed.), Internationales Wirtschaftsrecht, 2015, p. 411.

1530 Cf. e.g.: *Griebel*, (2008) p.73; *Schreuer* in: *Rogers/Alford* (Eds.), The future of investment arbitration, 2009, p. 183, 193; *Kniebaum* in: *Bungenberg/Griebel/Hobe et al.* (Eds.), International Investment Law, 2015, p. 802.

1531 For the *three-step-test* under the national treatment standard: *Methanex vs. USA*, 03.08.2005 – UNCITRAL- Final Award of the Tribunal on Jurisdiction and Merits, para 13; cf. also: *Reinisch* in: *Bungenberg/Griebel/Hobe et al.* (Eds.), International Investment Law, 2015, p. 855; for the standard under the general non-discrimination clause: *Kniebaum* in: *Bungenberg/Griebel/Hobe et al.* (Eds.), International Investment Law, 2015, p. 802.

1532 This is generally accepted, cf. *inter alia*: *Epiney* in: Calliess/Ruffert EUV/AEUV, Art. 18 TFEU, para 41.

member states or non-member states (*erga omnes* protection).[1533] This general prohibition of restriction (*Beschränkungsverbot*) includes but is not limited to the prohibition of (direct or indirect) discriminatory measures. Even indistinctly applied measures, i.e. non-discriminatory measures, which impede on the free movement are – in general – prohibited and subject to justification.[1534]

Hence, compared to the national treatment standard and the general prohibition of discrimination, the guarantee under the free movement of capital seems even wider at first glance. It does not necessarily require a less favourable treatment and both entities do not need to be in similar circumstances. The EU's and the member state's margin of action is generally restricted within the scope of application of the free movement of capital.

Hence, to evaluate the equivalence, the scope of application of both guarantees needs to be assessed. This includes the protected behaviour under each of the standards (1). Second, both frameworks provide means of justification which should be compared to derive that no major difference can be established (2). Third, a particular problem reducing the protection for non-member state investors under EU law will be addressed (3), which relates to a partial overlap of the free movement of capital and other fundamental freedoms, given that those freedoms do not provide for an *erga omnes* protection.

(1) Protected assets: "investment" and "free movement of capital"

When addressing the scope of application of the free movement of capital compared to the protection provided by IIAs, the type of assets and the type of action needs to be compared.

The national treatment and non-discrimination clauses provide protection for "*investments*" under the IIA. The free movement of capital refers to the "*movement of capital*". Both terms however reveal to be nearly identical.

1533 *Hobe*, 8. Edn. (2014), para 862; *Wojcik* in: v. d. Groeben/Schwarze AEUV/EUV, Art. 63 TFEU, para 14; *Glaesner* in: Schwarze EU-Kommentar, Art. 63 TFEU, para 16.

1534 *Wojcik* in: v. d. Groeben/Schwarze AEUV/EUV, Art. 63 TFEU, para 14; *Glaesner* in: Schwarze EU-Kommentar, Art. 63 TFEU, para 16.

As aforementioned, investments under an IIA refer to moveable or immovable as well as immaterial property, loans or debts, good-will as well as commercial claims or publicly granted rights such as concessions.

The free movement of capital covers a range of direct investments and portfolio investments, including long term loans, etc. The CJEU usually refers to the extremely broad *"definition"* provided by the nomenclature in the capital directive to assess the scope of the fundamental freedom, which overlaps broadly with the investment definition. The freedom applies to all sorts of transfer or flow (and hence use) of these assets from member states to other member states or from non-member states to member states. The terms mentioned in the capital lead to the conclusion that the movement of capital includes all sort of creation, establishment, transmission and somehow even use of pecuniary rights.[1535] The directive e.g. refers to direct investments such as the *"[e]stablishment and extension of branches or new undertakings belonging solely to the person providing the capital, and the acquisition in full of existing undertakings*", participations within "*new or existing undertaking with a view to establishing or maintaining lasting economic links*", reinvestment of profits, long term loans, investments in real estate, dealing with or holding of shares, bonds or other financial instruments, insurances or even guarantees or securities provided.[1536] As soon as these assets by any mean "*cross*" the border between EU member states or between third-states and EU member states, the protection under the free movement of capital applies.[1537] Hence, the type of protected assets or behaviours is nearly identical with those of an investment under the IIA, except for purely commercial claims and granted public rights. These will need to be evaluated under the general prohibition of discrimination by Art. 20 of the Charter (cf. *infra*: "*2. Compensation of protection through application of Art. 20 of the* Charter").

Second, the type of actions to be covered should be assessed. The national treatment standard refers to all sorts of actions by the host state. However, the types of actions for which the national treatment standard will usually apply are those which refer to the setting of a level playing

1535 *Wilmowsky* in: Becker/Ehlers Europäische Grundfreiheiten (2014), § 12, para 2; *Hobe*, 8. Edn. (2014), para 856.

1536 Annex I of the Council Directive 88/361/EEC - Capital Directive, Official Journal of the European Communities L 178 (24.06.1988), 5.

1537 *Wilmowsky* in: Becker/Ehlers Europäische Grundfreiheiten (2014), § 12, para 3; *Glaesner* in: Schwarze EU-Kommentar, Art. 63 TFEU, para 17 f.

field to operate in the host state. If the state will impede on *particular rights* (such as e.g. the investor's property) through behaviour which is revealed to be *also* discriminatory, such as through an expropriating measure, the guarantee provided in this case (prohibition of expropriation, FET) will also protect against (unjustified) discriminatory measures. Hence, the remaining scope of application for the national treatment standard will usually be limited to more general restrictions applied to foreign investors, e.g. relating to the corporate structure, shareholder rights, particular requirements to register or run a company, etc..[1538] This type of state measures are also widely covered by the protection under the free movement of capital. Especially all national tax measures or provisions by which a state tries to keep particular forms of influence on certain companies or formerly privatised undertakings are prohibited under Art. 63 TFEU.[1539] The free movement of capital relates especially to those measures but more generally to all measures which might affect the allocation of capital in a member state.[1540] Competition should be enabled within the internal market without reference to the economic operator's nationality. This is equivalent to a level playing field for national and non-national operators.[1541] Regarding actions which may not be covered under the free movement of capital, Art. 20 of the Charter (cf. *infra 2.*) will provide further protection.

(2) Exceptions and justifications to guarantees under the IIA and under EU law

Neither Art. 63 TFEU nor the national treatment / non-discrimination standard apply unconditionally. Art. 63 TFEU is restricted by Art. 64, 65, 66 and 75 TFEU as well as the *rule of reason* (being recognised as a gen-

1538 *Hobe*, 8. Edn. (2014), para 857 f; *Glaesner* in: Schwarze EU-Kommentar, Art. 63 TFEU, para 21.

1539 *Wilmowsky* in: Becker/Ehlers Europäische Grundfreiheiten (2014), § 12, para 20 and 24.

1540 *Wojcik* in: v. d. Groeben/Schwarze AEUV/EUV, Art. 63 TFEU, para 10; *Glaesner* in: Schwarze EU-Kommentar, Art. 63 TFEU, para 18 f; *Hobe*, 8. Edn. (2014), para 856.

1541 *Wojcik* in: v. d. Groeben/Schwarze AEUV/EUV, Art. 63 TFEU, para 10 „*that capital – irrespective of ist orgin – may be used freely withhin the Union*"; *Glaesner* in: Schwarze EU-Kommentar, Art. 63 TFEU, para 18 f.

eral limitation to the fundamental freedoms). Under the IIA standards, less favourable treatment can be justified if either it is not applied to undertakings in like circumstances, if the IIA allows certain exceptions, or if it is generally justified by legitimate reasons of public policy.[1542]

When comparing these exceptions, the exceptions to Art. 63 TFEU through the *rule of reason* do not need to be taken into account to demonstrate the equivalence. The *rule of reason* only applies to indistinctly applied measures.[1543] Indistinctly applied restrictions exclude *qua definitionem* measures which are discriminatory. However, under an IIA, an *indistinctly* applied measure would not even be prohibited by the substantive protection standard of national treatment or prohibition of discrimination as both protection standards only relate to *discriminatory* measures.[1544]

Hence, only the expressly named exceptions under Art. 64-66 and Art. 75 TFEU should be benchmarked against the limitations in the substantive standards in IIAs.

Art. 64 and Art. 65 TFEU contain particular provisions to enable restrictions on the free movement of capital. Whereas Art. 64 (1) TFEU mainly contains a grandfathering rule for existing limitations, Art. 64 (2) and (3) TFEU enable restrictions on the free movement of capital with third countries if those are adopted following the ordinary legislative procedure (para 2) or in a specific procedure (para 3). Those restrictions are

---

1542 The approach of introducing justification in the assessment of whether two entities are in like circumstances was adopted by the tribunals in *Pope & Talbot vs. Canada*, 10.04.2001 – UNCITRAL - Awards on the Merits of Phase 2, para 78 and *S. D. Myers vs Canada*, 13.11.2000 – UNCITRAL - Partial Award, para 250; other tribunals admitted the justification as a separate ground for denying a breach of the national treatment standard: *Contact Champion Trading et al vs. Egypt*, 27.08.2006 – ICSID Case No. ARB/02/9 - Award, para 134 and *Parkerings vs. Lithuania*, 11.09.2007 – ICSID Case No. ARB/05/8 - Award, para 368; cf. also: *Reinisch* in: *Tietje* (Ed.), Internationales Wirtschaftsrecht, 2015, p. 863 f and *Ortino* in: *Dupuy/Francioni/Petersmann* (Eds.), Human rights in international investment law and arbitration, 2009, p. 360.

1543 *Glaesner* in: Schwarze EU-Kommentar, Art. 63 TFEU, para 24; *Khan/Eisenhut* in: von Heinegg/Vedder EUV/AEUV, Art. 63 TFEU, para 19: "*conditio sine qua non for any immanent restriction is to be non-discriminatory*".

1544 This is the consequence of the less favorable treatment in like circumstances: cf. *Reinisch* in: *Bungenberg/Griebel/Hobe et al.* (Eds.), International Investment Law, 2015, p. 856 and 860; if a measure applies to both, national and non-national competitors, it will not be discriminatory under the IIA.

only possible regarding direct investment, establishments, the provision of financial services or the admission of securities to capital markets. Additionally, as an exception it must be interpreted strictly. Furthermore, the general limits to such restrictions apply, *inter alia* the test of proportionality regarding the restricting measure.[1545]

Art. 65 TFEU enables national measures in the domain of tax law or for the reasons of protecting public policy or public security. Additionally, Art. 66 TFEU generally admits restrictions to counter serious difficulties for the EU or the Eurozone. Neither Art. 66, nor Art. 64 (2), (3) TFEU have ever been used so far. [1546] Art. 75 TFEU enables the European Parliament and the European Council to restrict the free movement of capital if such a restriction is necessary to prevent or fight terrorism. The provision is mostly used to execute sanctions issued by the UN Security Council.[1547]

Art. 64 TFEU will be treated with later. Especially the fact that so far neither Art. 64 (2) nor Art. 64 (3) TFEU have been used and represent mostly a restriction introduced for further negotiations with non-member states on the political level justifies to primarily focus on Art. 65, 66 and 75 TFEU.[1548]

Art. 65 TFEU enables restrictions relating to

> "*tax provisions* for taxpayers not being in the same situations; [*or* all kind of] requisite measures to *prevent infringements of national law* and regulations, in particular in the field of taxation and the prudential supervision of financial institutions, [*or* …] procedural requirements for the *purposes of* administrative or *statistical information* [or] measures which are *justified on grounds of public policy or public security*."[1549]

1545 *Wojcik* in: v. d. Groeben/Schwarze AEUV/EUV, Art. 64 TFEU, para 21; *CJEU*, 13.05.2003 – C-463/00 - Commission vs. Spain = ECLI:EU: C:2003: 272, para 72 and 73, „*However, the Court has also held that the requirements of public security, as a derogation from the fundamental principle of free movement of capital, must be interpreted strictly [...] and [that the restrictions] do not go beyond what is necessary for that purpose (...)*".

1546 *Bröhmer* in: Calliess/Ruffert EUV/AEUV, Art. 66 TFEU, para 1.

1547 *Bröhmer* in: Calliess/Ruffert EUV/AEUV, Art. 75 TFEU, para 1; cf. also: *CJEU*, 03.03.2009 – C-249/06 - Commission vs Sweden = ECLI:EU:C:2009: 119, para 32.

1548 Cf. for the use and the underlying idea of this provision being more a political power in negotiations with third countries: *Wojcik* in: v. d. Groeben/Schwarze AEUV/EUV, Art. 64 TFEU, para 15.

1549 Art. 65 (1) TFEU [emphasis added and lit. a) and lit. b.) omitted].

Upon first perception, these exceptions seem to be deliberately wide. However, the CJEU considerably restricted these exceptions in its jurisprudence. One could argue that the provisions could *per se* not be identical with those under an IIA, given that the CJEU (in the infringement proceedings mentioned in Chapter 12 and 13) considered the free flow of capital standards in IIAs to be incompatible with EU law, especially due to their unconditional scope of application compared to the restrictions in Art. 66 and Art. 75 TFEU.[1550] However, it should be noted that this incompatibility was based on a strictly hypothetical evaluation of both guarantees (and hence not on actual incompatibilities) and that the CJEU declared those provisions to be incompatible based on the consideration that the existing limitations under an IIA are too vague. The member states, to comply with their duty in Art. 351 (2) TFEU, should have obtained a mechanism which *guarantees* that the diverging obligations could not conflict. However, the perspective adopted in this analysis is different as it aims to demonstrate a general equivalence of protection and it takes into account arbitral tribunal's interpretation of the textual standard (which seems to have been carved out by the CJEU).

Generally, exceptions based on Art. 65 (1) TFEU may not be justified if they constitute an arbitrary discrimination or a disguised restriction of the freedom (cf. Art. 65 (3) TFEU). Art. 65 (3) TFEU requires any difference to be founded on an objective reason demonstrating a particular public interest (which excludes any economic considerations by the EU member state) and satisfying the test of proportionality. As already described, this refers to the measure being suitable to obtain the public interest, necessary to obtain it and being ultimately proportional after balancing the reasons of public policy with the importance of the fundamental freedom.[1551] The CJEU often puts considerable weight on the necessity of a measure, requiring it to be the least harmful measure possible to obtain the public interest invoked, which leads to less weight on the last criteria of overall proportionality.[1552] However, the results obtained constitute a severe re-

---

1550 Cf. infringement proceedings in *CJEU*, 03.03.2009 – C-249/06 - Commission vs Sweden = ECLI:EU:C:2009:119; *CJEU*, 03.03.2009 – C-205/06 - Commission vs. Austria = ECLI:EU:C:2009:118; *CJEU*, 19.11.2009 – C-118/07 - Commission vs. Finland = ECLI:EU:C:2009:715 which were referred to *supra* footnote 1224.

1551 *Khan/Eisenhut* in: von Heinegg/Vedder EUV/AEUV, Art. 65 TFEU, para 17; *Glaesner* in: von Heinegg/Vedder EUV/AEUV, Art. 65 TFEU, para 9 and 12.

1552 Similar: *Oppermann/Classen et al.*, 5. Edn. (2011) § 22, para 12.

striction of the state measure by requiring strict conditions to be fulfilled.[1553] The CJEU e.g. limited the interests of public policy and public security to grounds which provide for a "*genuine and sufficiently serious threat to a fundamental interest of society*".[1554] *Inter alia*, prior admission requirements by public authorities regarding any measures of direct investment or exercise of shareholder rights are generally considered not necessary in terms of the test of proportionality, as a notification mechanism would be sufficient to prevent abuse and criminal behaviour.[1555] Hence, if the member states try to restrict the free movement of capital based on Art. 65 TFEU, these restrictions are subject to a high level of control by the CJEU and will only be admitted in after due observance of their overall proportionality.

Similar approaches have been used by the arbitral tribunals in order to justify a difference in treatment under the national treatment standard or the general non-discrimination clause. *Inter alia* the *Pope & Talbot-Tribunal* admitted "*rational government polices*"[1556] to justify the difference in treatment. In the case at hand the tribunal even admitted the avoidance of trade disputes with the US as a valid public interest[1557], which would be doubtful under EU law as it constitutes an economics-related reason.[1558] Additionally, generally, arbitral tribunals put considerable weight on the comparability of circumstances between different investors.[1559] Most IIAs restrain the application of national treatment standards to a

1553 Cf. also: *Wojcik* in: v. d. Groeben/Schwarze AEUV/EUV, Art. 65 TFEU, para 32.

1554 *CJEU*, 14.03.2000 – C-54/99 - Association Église de Scientologie de Paris = ECLI:EU:C:2000:124, para 17.

1555 *CJEU*, 14.12.1995 – C-165/94 - Sanz de Lera et al. = ECLI:EU:C:1995:451, para 23 ff; C-367/98, para 13 f (regarding the maximum of 55% of all shares being held by foreign sharehodlers under national law); cf. also: *Bröhmer* in: Calliess/Ruffert EUV/AEUV, Art. 65 TFEU, para 14 ff with further illustrations.

1556 *Pope & Talbot vs. Canada*, 10.04.2001 – UNCITRAL - Awards on the Merits of Phase 2, para 78; similar: *Parkerings vs. Lithuania*, 11.09.2007 – ICSID Case No. ARB/05/8 - Award, para 368.

1557 *Pope & Talbot vs. Canada*, 10.04.2001 – UNCITRAL - Awards on the Merits of Phase 2, para 86 and 87.

1558 C-367/98, para 52; cf. also: *Glaesner* in: von Heinegg/Vedder EUV/AEUV, Art. 65 TFEU, para 1.

1559 *Griebel*, (2008), p. 82.

treatment in "*similar circumstances*" or "*like circumstances*".[1560] Although some tribunals applied an extensive approach which even extends the benchmarks for comparison beyond economic sectors (i.e. the *Occidental vs. Ecuador Case* where the tribunal considered an oil producing foreign investor to be in similar circumstances than flower exporting national companies regarding tax refunds[1561]), the more reasonable and predominant interpretation of the similarity at least requires a certain amount of similarity between the national and foreign companies to compare as otherwise the host state's margin of action would be completely eluded. It is impossible to ensure – especially in tax matters – a cross-industry equal treatment regarding all matters.[1562] In this regard the interpretation given by the *Pope & Talbot Case* and other cases seems more appropriate which requires the compared entities to be at least addressing the "*same business or economic sector*".[1563] This excludes comparison between economic

---

1560 Article 1102 (1) of the NAFTA: "*Each Party shall accord to investors of another Party treatment no less favorable than that it accords, in like circumstances, to its own investors (...)*"; Similar Art. 3 of the US-Model BIT (2012), Art. III. 3. of the Wolrd Bank Guidelines on the Treatment of Foreign Investment: "be as favorable as that accorded by the State to national investors in *similar circumstance*" [emphasis added].

1561 *Occidental Exploration vs. Ecuador*, 01.07.2004 – LCIA Case No. UN3467 - Final Awardpara 168: the Tribunal holds that Claimant was right to argue a breach of the national treatment provision as other companies *"involved in the export of other goods, particularly flowers, mining and seafood products are entitled to receive VAT refund and continuously enjoy this benefit*" whereas Claimant did not.

1562 *Griebel*, (2008), p. 82; cf. also: *Herdegen*, 10. Edn. (2014), p. 348.

1563 *Pope & Talbot vs. Canada*, 10.04.2001 – UNCITRAL - Awards on the Merits of Phase 2, para 75 f; cf. also: *Griebel*, (2008), p. 82; approach also adopted by the Tribunal in *S. D. Myers vs Canada*, 13.11.2000 – UNCITRAL - Partial Award, para 250 ff. When addressing the question whether the sector should be considered to be the same, the approach developed by the WTO Appellate Body seems to be an appropriate benchmark, although the WTO-jurisprudence refers to "*like products*" instead of "*like circumstances*". The tribunal in *Methanex vs. USA*, 03.08.2005 – UNCITRAL- Final Award of the Tribunal on Jurisdiction and Merits, para 35 held that the differences in the respective wording would rather indicate a difference. Similar reasonings can be found by the tribunal in *Occidental Exploration vs. Ecuador*, 01.07.2004 – LCIA Case No. UN3467 - Final Award, para 175 ff. Although the wording is different, the underlying criteria can serve as well established benchmarks. Both, the WTO-Regulations as well as the national treatment standard in international investment law, try to create a level playing field for national and foreign competitors, cf.: *Dolzer/Stevens*, Bilateral Investment Treaties, 1995, p. 65. This under-

sectors, which exercise their business under fundamentally different conditions. Requiring the host state to extend the equal treatment across all industries considerable restraints its margin of action. In any case, if one wants to enable a cross-sector comparison, the threshold to justify a differential treatment needs to be considerably lowered to guarantee a certain (and fair) right to regulate to the host state.[1564] In this context, public policy reasons have also been used to justify that two or more undertakings are not in comparable circumstances.[1565] Arbitral tribunals regularly consider the host state's possibility to justify a differential treatment.[1566] Such justifications may either be considered separately or introduced in the test of like circumstances, denying the similarity of two situations if there are sufficient reasons of "*public policy*" for a differentiation.[1567] If two entities

---

lying idea should at least justify to take into account the criteria derived in the WTO-jurisprudence. The Appellate Body regularly refers – besides physical properties of the product, which does not seem appropriate in the investment context – to the "*same, or similar, functions (end-uses)*" (substitutable produces) or "*the extent to which consumers are willing to use the products to perform these functions*" (consumer's preferences), cf: *WTO Appellate Body, EC-Asbestos*, 12.03.2001 – WT/DS135/AB/R, para 117; *Schöbener/Herbst et al.*, 2010, p. 160 for the overall approach of the WTO-Dispute Settlement Bodies. Both indicators, transposed to services and all sorts of products, goods or any other economic use made in the host state, provide two indicators, which can serve as first benchmarks to determine the sameness of the economic sector, cf.: *Corn Products vs. Mexico*, 15.01.2208 – ICSID Case No. ARB (AF)/04/1 - Decision on Responsibility, para 122; cf. also for this approach: *Reinisch* in: *Tietje* (Ed.), Internationales Wirtschaftsrecht, 2015, p. 867 and 869.

1564 *National Grid vs. Argentina*, 03.11.2008 – UNCITRAL - Award, para 200; *Enron vs. Argentina*, 22.05.2007 – ICSID Case No. ARB/01/3 - Award, para 282.

1565 For this approach, e.g *National Grid vs. Argentina*, 03.11.2008 – UNCITRAL - Award, para 200.

1566 *Reinisch* in: *Tietje* (Ed.), Internationales Wirtschaftsrecht, 2015, p. 863; *Griebel*, (2008), p. 82 f.

1567 The approach to analyse whether a different treatment may be justified in the determination of whether two entities are in "*like circumstances*" was adopted by the tribunals in *Pope & Talbot vs. Canada*, 10.04.2001 – UNCITRAL - Awards on the Merits of Phase 2, para 78 and *S. D. Myers vs Canada*, 13.11.2000 – UNCITRAL - Partial Award, para 250; other tribunals admitted the justification as a separate ground for denying a breach of the national treatment standard: *Contact Champion Trading et al vs. Egypt*, 27.08.2006 – ICSID Case No. ARB/02/9 - Award, para 134 and *Parkerings vs. Lithuania*, 11.09.2007 – ICSID Case No. ARB/05/8 - Award, para 368; cf. also: *Reinisch* in: *Tietje* (Ed.), Internationales Wirtschaftsrecht, 2015, p. 863 f and *Ortino* in:

being compared are found not to be in like circumstances the entire standard is dismissed.

Hence, one can indeed observe the wide overlap of restrictions between EU law or IIAs. Additionally, EU law enumerates the potential public interest, which leads to a restriction as to the type of interest being able to justify exceptions to Art. 63 TFEU. Under IIAs the scope of interests is *ab initio* unlimited, meaning it will then be balanced against the interest in question in the particular case. From this perspective, the exceptions under EU law are at least seem to be clearer, if not more restrictive.

Assuming that the balancing of particular interests would lead to different results under the different frameworks does not, however, question the overall general equivalence of the protection offered under both frameworks. This is the particular and inherent risk of different dispute settlement bodies to rule the same case.

Regarding the potential restrictions based on Art. 66 ("*serious difficulties for the operation of economic and monetary union*") or Art. 75 TFEU ("*combating terrorism and related activities*"), the same considerations apply. They enumerate further, limited, ground of public interest, which may serve as a justification for a restriction of the free movement of capital. Any measure implementing such restrictions would be subject to a (strict) test of proportionality, which is also reflected by the wording of the clauses (cf. "*strictly necessary*" in Art. 66, "*necessary*" in Art. 75).[1568] The same should apply for Art. 64 (2) and (3) TFEU.[1569] By contrast, the protection through the free movement of capital is set aside if a national measure falling under Art. 64 (1) TFEU enables the discrimination regarding pre-existing national legislation. However, Art. 64 (1) TFEU should not be taken into account as a conflict between mandatory EU law and

---

Dupuy/Francioni/Petersmann (Eds.), Human rights in international investment law and arbitration, 2009, p. 360.

1568 *Wojcik* in: v. d. Groeben/Schwarze AEUV/EUV, Art. 66 TFEU, para 8; furthermore, measures under Art. 66 TFEU are limited to maximum 6 months of application; *Bröhmer* in: Calliess/Ruffert EUV/AEUV, Art. 75 TFEU, para 5; the CJEU in the Kadi-Cases exercised a particularily strict control regarding the measures, even though they were taken in order to implement measures by Security Council of the United Nations, cf: *CJEU*, 03.09.2008 – Joined Cases C-402/05 P and C-415/05 P - Kadi = ECLI:EU:C:2008:461, p. 333 ff.

1569 *Khan/Eisenhut* in: von Heinegg/Vedder EUV/AEUV, Art. 64 TFEU, para 8 with reference to the wording "*without prejudice to the other Chapters of the Treaties*"; for the opposite however: *Wilmowsky* in: Becker/Ehlers Europäische Grundfreiheiten (2014), § 12, para 45.

IIAs cannot occur based on this provision. It only enables member states to uphold existing provisions but does not require a certain act. Hence, under the consideration of this comparison Art. 64 (1) TFEU cannot set aside the general equivalence of both regimes. A measure based on Art. 64 (1) TFEU would always result in a situation where investors are entitled to claim non-respect of the IIA as EU law will not mandate any measure and hence there is no conflict between the IIA and EU law.

(3) Scope of application of the free movement of capital: *erga omnes* protection?

Although there is a general far reaching equivalence between the discrimination related protection standards under an IIA and the free movement of capital under EU law, this protection is weakened by a certain overlap between the freedom of establishment and the free movement of capital.[1570] The freedom of establishment may be a powerful guarantee once an investor has established itself in the EU and then tries to expand its business in multiple EU member states. However, this guarantee does not apply to undertakings or nationals from non-member states. Hence, whereas the same state measure would need to be justified towards other undertakings or nationals from EU member states, such justification is not necessary towards undertakings or nationals from non-member states.[1571]

Thus, the relation between both fundamental freedoms becomes crucial regarding the protection of foreign investors from non-member states.[1572] The jurisprudence of the CJEU is far from being well established in this particular question. The CJEU tends to apply both freedoms to a particular measure, and – under certain criteria – considers that one of the freedoms

1570 Cf. also: *Hahn* in: *Bungenberg/Griebel/Hobe et al.* (Eds.), International Investment Law, 2015, p. 679 f and *Hindelang/Maydell* in: *Bungenberg/Griebel/Hindelang* (Eds.), International investment law and EU law, 2011, p. 3.

1571 *Wojcik* in: v. d. Groeben/Schwarze AEUV/EUV, Art. 63 TFEU, para 61; *Hahn* in: *Bungenberg/Griebel/Hobe et al.* (Eds.), International Investment Law, 2015, p. 679 f; *Hindelang/Maydell* in: *Bungenberg/Griebel/Hindelang* (Eds.), International investment law and EU law, 2011, p. 2 f.

1572 *Hahn* in: *Bungenberg/Griebel/Hobe et al.* (Eds.), International Investment Law, 2015, p. 680.

should be *lex specialis*.[1573] Difficulties arise with regard to the purchase of immobile property or direct investments.[1574] Portfolio investments are exclusively covered by the free movement of capital.[1575]

With regard to questions of acquisition or the use of immobile property, the CJEU so far tends to apply the free movement of capital only.[1576] However, regarding direct investments, the focus seems to shift towards determining the scope of application of the concurring freedoms by referring to the principle "*aim*" of the state measure in question.[1577] If the measure aims particularly to regulate investments capable of exercising a definite influence on the undertaking, the freedom of establishment will be considered *lex specialis*. If, however, the regulation indistinctly applies to all sorts of investments, without predominantly targeting investors exercising definite influence on the undertaking, either both freedoms apply or the free movement of capital will be *lex specialis*.[1578]

This has particular influence on protected investments. A considerable number of provisions, especially with regard to taxation matters, will still be controlled *vis-à-vis* the free movement of capital as general taxes will rarely specifically target investors exercising sufficient control on the un-

1573 *Wojcik* in: v. d. Groeben/Schwarze AEUV/EUV, Art. 63 TFEU, para 63 and 64; *Glaesner* in: Schwarze EU-Kommentar, Art. 63 TFEU, para 11.

1574 *Glaesner* in: Schwarze EU-Kommentar, Art. 63 TFEU, para 11; *Wojcik* in: v. d. Groeben/Schwarze AEUV/EUV, Art. 63 TFEU, para 62; *Khan/Eisenhut* in: von Heinegg/Vedder EUV/AEUV, Art. 63 TFEU, para 15.

1575 *Glaesner* in: Schwarze EU-Kommentar, Art. 63 TFEU, para 12; *Khan/Eisenhut* in: von Heinegg/Vedder EUV/AEUV, Art. 63 TFEU, para 15.

1576 *CJEU*, 01.06.1999 – C-302/97 - Kone = ECLI:EU:C:1999:271,para 55; *CJEU*, 25.01.2007 – C-370/05 - Fetersen = ECLI:EU:C:2007:59, para 47; *Wojcik* in: v. d. Groeben/Schwarze AEUV/EUV, Art. 63 TFEU, para 63.

1577 *CJEU*, 19.07.2012 – C-31/11 - Scheunemann = ECLI:EU:C:2012:481, para 20: „*In order to determine whether national legislation falls within the scope of one or other of the freedoms of movement, it is clear from now well established case-law that the aim of the legislation concerned must be taken into consideration*"; *Hindelang/Maydell* in: *Bungenberg/Griebel/Hindelang* (Eds.), International investment law and EU law, 2011, p. 5 referring to the "centre of gravity".

1578 *CJEU*, 19.07.2012 – C-31/11 - Scheunemann = ECLI:EU:C:2012:481, para 22; *CJEU*, 24.05.2007 – C-157/05 - Holböck = ECLI:EU:C:2007:297, para 24; *CJEU*, 03.10.2006 – C-452/04 - Fidium Finanz = ECLI:EU:C:2006:631, para 34 and 38; ff; *Bröhmer* in: Calliess/Ruffert EUV/AEUV, Art. 63 TFEU; *Wojcik* in: v. d. Groeben/Schwarze AEUV/EUV, Art. 63 TFEU, para 65; *Hindelang/Maydell* in: *Bungenberg/Griebel/Hindelang* (Eds.), International investment law and EU law, 2011, p. 4 f.

dertaking.[1579] Furthermore, with regard to shareholder rights and the interference with these rights by national measures, the CJEU has so far still relied on the free movement of capital.[1580] Regarding the requirement to obtain a license for exercising its business in Germany, in *Fidium Finanz* the CJEU, however, concluded the opposite.[1581] Generally, only for taxation matters the primacy of the freedom of establishment was established on a constant basis, depriving the free movement of capital of being applied to such cases. In all other situations, at least the free movement of capital was applied additionally and would hence offer protection for extra-EU investors.[1582]

Assuming that the distinction will be applied to future cases as well, several cases of investors under EU law may only be evaluated *vis-à-vis* the freedom of establishment. This freedom, however, does not apply to non-member state nationals or undertakings. At first glance, this seems to lead to a considerable lack of protection. However, the lack in protection, also regarding potential types of actions or assets not covered under the free movement of capital, is reduced by three elements:

- First, investment protection generally requires a certain degree of control on the investment. If however, the investor is able to exercise such control, he might exercise its control on the legal entity established in the EU and claim its rights through this entity and hence through the freedom of establishment.[1583]
- Furthermore, a certain further compensation may be achieved by the general rule of non-discrimination based on Art. 20 of the Charter.
- If even through Art. 20 of the Charter, protection is obviously denied in the concrete case, the *Bosphorus-Presumption* should be rebutted in this particular case (cf. *infra* Chapter 16).

1579 Regarding earnings and dividendes *inter alia*: *CJEU*, 24.05.2007 – C-157/05 - Holböck = ECLI:EU:C:2007:297.

1580 *CJEU*, 13.05.2003 – C-98/01 - Commission vs. UK and Northern Ireland = ECLI:EU:C:2003:273, para 52; cf. also: *Glaesner* in: Schwarze EU-Kommentar, Art. 63 TFEU, para 11.

1581 *CJEU*, 03.10.2006 – C-452/04 - Fidium Finanz = ECLI:EU:C:2006:631, para 48.

1582 *Tietje* in: Becker/Ehlers Europäische Grundfreiheiten (2014), § 10, para 396.

1583 The CJEU ruled on various occasions that the mere ownership or control of foreign nationals in an entity based in the EU may not justify a restriction of the fundamental freedoms, cf.: *CJEU*, 19.06.1990 – C-213/89 - Queen vs. Secretary of State for Transport = ECLI:EU:C:1990:257.

2. Compensation of protection through application of Art. 20 of the Charter

The general principle of non-discrimination laid down in Art. 20 of the Charter applies indistinctly to all EU nationals and non-nationals and to any measures by the EU or its member states which fall under the scope of application of the Charter (cf. *supra*).[1584] Hence, for the purpose of the acts to be considered in this section it fully applies to all potential measures to be challenged. As several scholars state, Art. 20 of the Charter can be referred to as the underlying general principle in EU law of prohibiting discrimination.[1585] It may especially provide protection, where the free movement of capital does not apply.

As for the CJEU, the principle of equality laid down in Art. 20 of the Charter requires:

> "that comparable situations must not be treated differently and that different situations must not be treated in the same way unless such treatment is objectively justified."[1586]

One can immediately observe the nearly identical criteria of this requirement compared to the national treatment or the prohibition of discrimination under an IIA. It should be noted that the difference in nationality as such will never be a sufficient differentiator, neither to deny comparable circumstances nor to justify a treatment without a further public purpose underlying this differentiation.[1587] Hence, regarding the wording of the cri-

---

1584 *Bell* in: Peers, Hervey et al. - European Union Charter of Fundamental Rights, Art. 20 of the Charter, para 20.17; *Jarass*, 2. Edn. (2013) Art. 20, para 6.

1585 *Bell* in: Peers, Hervey et al. - European Union Charter of Fundamental Rights, Art. 20 of the Charter, para 20.01 and 20.13 f; *Jarass*, 2. Edn. (2013), para 1; *Lemke* in: v. d. Groeben/Schwarze AEUV/EUV, Art. 20 of the Charter, para 2. All three stress the reference to the explanations attached to the Charter stating that the principle is well settled case law and a general principle of EU law as deducted by the CJEU; cf. e.g.: *CJEU*, 13.11.1984 – C-283/83 - Racke II = ECLI:EU:C:1984:344.

1586 *CJEU*, 03.05.2007 – C-303/05 - Advocaten voor de Wereld = ECLI:EU:C: 2007:261, para 56.

1587 Whereas *CJEU*, 12.09.2006 – C-479/04 - Østre Landsret vs. Denmark = ECLI:EU:C:2006:549, para 69 seems to deny this statement, it should be kept in mind that the purpose of this thesis is to deal with investments operating in the European Union, which has not been the case in the above-mentioned decision. For two undertakings operating under EU law, it should be hard to demonstrate that the difference in treatment can be soley based on the difference of nationality if both operate their business in the European Union; also

teria, Art. 20 of the Charter should indeed cover merely the same guarantees as the substantive provisions of the IIAs. Furthermore, analysing the application and interpretation given to the criteria also demonstrates the equivalence of protection to be obtained under both forums.

First, the interpretation of comparable circumstance turns out to be fairly similar. The CJEU applies a wide interpretation of what can be considered as comparable circumstances. It held in the *Arcelor-Case*:

> "The elements which characterise different situations, and hence their comparability, must in particular be determined and assessed in the light of the subject-matter and purpose of the Community act which makes the distinction in question (…)."[1588]

It is sufficient, if both situations are "*fairly comparable*" with regard to the subject matter they deal with.[1589] Especially regarding undertakings belonging to different economic sectors or producing different goods, the CJEU has adopted a very broad approach, which is consistent with what has been developed by the majority of arbitral tribunals regarding investment protection.[1590] Undertakings are considered to be in comparable circumstances, if their products are either substitutes or compete against each other, or even if they are in cross-sectors which do not enter into competition, if the state measure in question refers to criteria (e.g. greenhouse emissions) which puts the two sectors into fairly comparable circumstanc-

Hindelang/Maydell in: *Bungenberg/Griebel/Hindelang* (Eds.), International investment law and EU law, 2011, p. 7 consider this to "*remain in dark*". Second, a guarantee applying to member state nationals only, would deprive Art. 20 of the Charter, especially its application to nationals and non-nationals of any sense; cf. also: *CJEU*, 22.01.1976 – C-55/75 - Balkan-Import Export GmbH = ECLI:EU:C:1975:177, para 15 which clearly reveals that the CJEU refers to a justification of the differntial treatment; cf. also: *Sachs* in: Stern/Sachs EU GrCH, Art. 20 of the Charter, para 11 and 23.

1588 *CJEU*, 16.12.2008 – C-127/07 - Arcelor = ECLI:EU:C:2008:728, para 26.

1589 *Jarass*, 2. Edn. (2013), Art. 20, para 7; cf. also: *Lemke* in: v. d. Groeben/Schwarze AEUV/EUV, Art. 20 of the Charter, para 15.

1590 For the approach by arbitral tribunals: refusing a cross sector approach: *CMS vs. Argentina*, 12.05.2005 – ICSID Case No. ARB/01/8 - Award, para 287-293; admitting such an approach: *Occidental Exploration vs. Ecuador*, 01.07.2004 – LCIA Case No. UN3467 - Final Award, para 167-179; for EU law: *CJEU*, 16.12.2008 – C-127/07 - Arcelor = ECLI:EU:C:2008:728, para 26. Except for the extreme approach in the *Occidental-Case*, there does not seem to be a major difference, cf. also: *Kniebaum* in: *Bungenberg/Griebel/Hobe et al.* (Eds.), International Investment Law, 2015, para 803 f.

es.[1591] Hence, the definition of comparable circumstances does not reveal a major difference in both frameworks.

Regarding the second criterion, a difference in treatment may be any kind of factual or legal treatment which is less favourable. Neither the text of Art. 20 of the Charter nor the jurisprudence provide any further limitation to this criterion.[1592] Especially a minor degree of disadvantage will not *per se* justify the differential treatment.[1593]

With regard to a possible justification, the general test of proportionality under Art. 52 (1) of the Charter applies. Similar as regarding the free movement of capital, any differentiation needs to be the consequence of a legitimate public interest, strictly necessary and overall proportional with regard to the limitation of the principle of equal treatment.[1594] It has been duly demonstrated that with regard to these criteria the requirements by arbitral tribunals in arbitration proceedings and under EU law converge.

Hence, the cases being uncovered by the free movement of capital could be supplemented by the guarantee provided under Art. 20 of the Charter, which demonstrates an equivalence with regard to the national treatment and prohibition of discrimination as well.

III. Fair and equitable treatment

Assessing the equivalence of the FET standard with protection offered by EU law requires a different approach than regarding the previously analysed standards. This is due to the particular nature of the FET standard, which unifies different aspects of the rule of law in one protection stand-

1591 *CJEU*, 16.12.2008 – C-127/07 - Arcelor = ECLI:EU:C:2008:728, para 36.

1592 *Jarass*, 2. Edn. (2013), para 11; similar: *Sachs* in: Stern/Sachs EU GrCH, Art. 20 of the Charter, para 19-21 who points out that the CJEU, similar as several arbitral tribunals, lacks claritiy on whether differences in the different situations are consideres as a justification for a different treatment in comparable circumstances or if they already lead to non-comparable circumstances.

1593 *CJEU*, 22.05.2003 – C-462/99 - Connected Austria = ECLI:EU:C:2003:297, para 115; *Jarass*, 2. Edn. (2013), para 11; *Lemke* in: v. d. Groeben/Schwarze AEUV/EUV, Art. 20 of the Charter, para 16.

1594 *Lemke* in: v. d. Groeben/Schwarze AEUV/EUV, Art. 20 of the Charter, para 16; *Sachs* in: Stern/Sachs EU GrCH, Art. 20 of the Charter, para 22; *Graser* in: Schwarze EU-Kommentar, Art. 20 of the Charter, para 6.

ard.[1595] Other legal systems, including EU law, although they imply the rule of law in their respective legal framework, usually do not provide for one overarching standard which includes all sub-aspects. Instead, the different requirements will be part of different principles the public authorities are subject to. Hence, to address the equivalence the different aspects included in the FET standard will need to be separated and analysed one-by-one.

As aforementioned, the FET standard includes several key elements of protection:[1596]:

- Guarantee of due process by the host state;[1597]
- Absence of obviously arbitrary and discriminatory measures, including duress or action intentionally causing (financial or physical) harm;[1598]
- Obligation of stability, consistency and transparency, which offers the investor the possibility to react and plan its investment and to comply with such regulations;[1599]

1595 *Jacob/Schill* in: *Bungenberg/Griebel/Hobe et al.* (Eds.), International Investment Law, 2015, p. 716 f; *Schreuer* in: *Hoffmann* (Ed.), Protection of foreign investments through modern treaty arbitration: diversity and harmonisation, 2010, p. 125, 126.

1596 For further explanations regarding the FET standard cf. *supra* (Chapter 4) and also, among others: *Hammerstein/Roegele*, SchiedsVZ, 2015, 275; *Wehland* in: *Balthasar* (Ed.), International Commercial Arbitration, 2016, p. 177 ff.

1597 *Rumeli vs. Kazakhstan*, 29.07.2008 – ICSID Case No. ARB/05/16 - Award, para 617; cf. also: *Jacob/Schill* in: *Bungenberg/Griebel/Hobe et al.* (Eds.), International Investment Law, 2015, p. 48 ff; *Schreuer*, JWIT Vol. 6, No. 3 (2005), 357, 373; *Schreuer* in: *Hoffmann* (Ed.), Protection of foreign investments through modern treaty arbitration: diversity and harmonisation, 2010, p. 125, 128; *Reinisch* in: *Tietje* (Ed.), Internationales Wirtschaftsrecht, 2015, p. 416.

1598 *Waste Management vs. Mexico*, 30.04.2004 – ICSID Case No. ARB(AF)/00/3 - Award, para 98; *Rumeli vs. Kazakhstan*, 29.07.2008 – ICSID Case No. ARB/05/16 - Award, para 609; cf. also: *Jacob/Schill* in: *Bungenberg/Griebel/Hobe et al.* (Eds.), International Investment Law, 2015, p. 731 ff; cf. also: *Schreuer* in: *Hoffmann* (Ed.), Protection of foreign investments through modern treaty arbitration: diversity and harmonisation, 2010, p. 125, 126 f; *Schreuer*, JWIT Vol. 6, No. 3 (2005), 357, 374; *Reinisch* in: *Tietje* (Ed.), Internationales Wirtschaftsrecht, 2015, p. 416.

1599 *Metalclad vs. Mexico*, 30.08.2000 – ICSID Case No. ARB(AF)/97/1 - Award, para 99; *Maffezini vs. Spain*, 25.01.2000 – ICSID Case No. ARB/97/7 - Decision on Jurisdiction, para 83; *Rumeli vs. Kazakhstan*, 29.07.2008 – ICSID Case No. ARB/05/16 - Award, para 617; *Tecmed vs. Mexico*, 29.05.2003 – ICSID Case No. ARB (AF)/00/2 - Award, para 154; *Jacob/Schill* in: *Bungenberg/Griebel/Hobe et al.* (Eds.), International Investment Law, 2015, p. 728 ff

- Honouring legitimate expectations and acting in a foreseeable manner, based on what an objective, reasonable and informed investor could expect in the concrete circumstances;[1600]
- Absence of disproportional interferences with the investor's rights when comparing the degree of interference with the host state's objectives and the public interest in question.[1601]

1. Administrative and judicial due process (element no°1)

The FET standard requires the host state to guarantee due process in its administrative and judicial proceedings.[1602] This is equivalently guaranteed under EU law.

(1) Due process in judicial proceedings

Regarding judicial proceedings, this requires the host state to guarantee not only access to justice but also a fair and unbiased trial.[1603] This may

---

and 733 ff; cf. also: *Schreuer* in: *Hoffmann* (Ed.), Protection of foreign investments through modern treaty arbitration: diversity and harmonisation, 2010, p. 125, 126 f.

1600 *Jacob/Schill* in: *Bungenberg/Griebel/Hobe et al.* (Eds.), International Investment Law, 2015, p. 723-728; *Schreuer* in: *Hoffmann* (Ed.), Protection of foreign investments through modern treaty arbitration: diversity and harmonisation, 2010, p. 125, 126 f; *Schreuer*, JWIT Vol. 6, No. 3 (2005), 357, 373 f.

1601 *Jacob/Schill* in: *Bungenberg/Griebel/Hobe et al.* (Eds.), International Investment Law, 2015, p. 735 ff; *Saluka vs. Czech Republic*, 17.03.2006 – UNCITRAL - Partial Award, para 306 f.

1602 *Jacob/Schill* in: *Bungenberg/Griebel/Hobe et al.* (Eds.), International Investment Law, 2015, p. 721 f; *Herdegen*, 10. Edn. (2014), p. 346 f; *Schreuer* in: *Hoffmann* (Ed.), Protection of foreign investments through modern treaty arbitration: diversity and harmonisation, 2010, p. 125, 128; regarding administrative due process: *International Thunderbird Gaming Corporation vs. Mexico*, 26.01.2006 – UNCITRAL - Arbitral Award, para 200: "*As acknowledged by [the investor], the [administrative] proceedings should be tested against the standards of due process and procedural fairness applicable to administrative officials*"; regarding judicial due process: *Loewen et al. vs. USA*, 26.06.2003 – ICSID Case No. ARB(AF)/98/3 - Award, para 123; *Mondev vs. USA*, 11.10.2002 – ICSID Case No. ARB(AF)/99/2 - Award, para 127.

1603 *Jacob/Schill* in: *Bungenberg/Griebel/Hobe et al.* (Eds.), International Investment Law, 2015, p. 722 f; *Herdegen*, 10. Edn. (2014), p. 346 f.

include the right of being heard, the unbiased decision-making and conduct of a case in general, the rendering of a decision within reasonable delays as well as the protection against arbitrary misapplication of the laws applicable to the case.[1604]

The same principles are also well established under EU law. Especially Art. 47 of the Charter guarantees the right to a fair trial in a nearly identical way when compared to the requirements set up by arbitral tribunals. Art. 47 (1) and (2) of the Charter read as follows:

> „(1) Everyone whose rights and freedoms guaranteed by the law of the Union are violated has the right to an effective remedy before a tribunal in compliance with the conditions laid down in this Article.
>
> (2) Everyone is entitled to a fair and public hearing within a reasonable time by an independent and impartial tribunal previously established by law. Everyone shall have the possibility of being advised, defended and represented."

The guarantee in Art. 47 of the Charter codifies a well settled case law of the CJEU which previously admitted the right to a fair trial and the access to justice as being part of the general principles of EU law.[1605] Through the Charter, this right, however, is granted the status of a subjective right.[1606] Through this right, individuals and legal entities[1607], irrespective of their nationality, are granted access to a court that is independent (free from instructions by other public authorities) and impartial (free from any appearance of being bigoted or biased) and which was previously established by law (which requires the objective and previous determination of which court will hear the case and hence excludes influences by the host

1604 *Jacob/Schill* in: *Bungenberg/Griebel/Hobe et al.* (Eds.), International Investment Law, 2015, p. 723; *Herdegen*, 10. Edn. (2014), p. 346 f. cf. e.g.: *Loewen et al. vs. USA*, 26.06.2003 – ICSID Case No. ARB(AF)/98/3 - Award, para 123 which essentially dealt with the host state's courts failure to prevent the investor from being insulted by racist and other defamatory comments in court proceedings.

1605 *Jarass*, 2. Edn. (2013) Art. 47, para 1.

1606 Art. 47 requires the (alleged) violation of "*rights and freedoms guaranteed by the law of the Union*". This requirement will not limit the protection for investors, as it extends to all rights and freedoms guaranteed by EU law, irrespective of being contained in the Charter, primary law or secondary law. It is sufficient if the claimant demonstrates an legitimate interest in its claim to overcome this hurdle, which is deliebratly wide, cf. *Jarass*, 2. Edn. (2013) Art. 47, para 7 f. Especially it cannot be compared to the German "*Schutznormtheorie*", which is more demanding. Whenever any right of an investor is *de facto* affected, Art. 47 will also apply: *Jarass*, 2. Edn. (2013) Art. 47, para 8.

1607 *Jarass*, 2. Edn. (2013) Art. 47, para 12.

states or the EU such as the building of *ad hoc* courts).[1608] Impartiality requires the state to abstain from e.g. legislative interventions in a pending case by issuing a specific law to influence the outcome of a case.[1609] Violations were conceived by *inter alia* the participation of members of the executive powers in judicial bodies (even if only in a consolatory function) or the accumulation of functions by judges.[1610] The right to a fair process includes the right to be duly informed by the tribunal, the right to be able to make submissions and the right to be heard (which includes the tribunal's duty to take into consideration the submitted arguments and to deal with those in the proceedings).[1611] These rights need to be ensured on an equal basis, granting a level playing field for all parties to the proceedings.[1612]

Given these principles, the requirements under both frameworks seem identical. In the *Loewe* Case the arbitral tribunal found a violation of the FET standard by virtue of the national court's endorsements of discriminatory and racist behaviour by the other party.[1613] This would also violate the tribunal's impartiality and hence disregards Art. 47 of the Charter. The same can be concluded regarding the most demanding aspect of the denial of due process under the FET standard, which is the prohibition of significant misapplication of law. Arbitral tribunals concluded that courts which reveal to be arbitrary due to manifest disregard for the applicable law, are

1608 *Jarass*, 2. Edn. (2013) Art. 47, para 18, 20 f and 22 f.

1609 *European Court of Human Rights*, 09.12.1994 – Application no. 13427/87 - Stran Greek Refineries, para 49 and 50: *"The principle of the rule of law and the notion of fair trial enshrined in Article 6 (art. 6) preclude any interference by the legislature with the administration of justice designed to influence the judicial determination of the dispute. [...] In conclusion, the State infringed the applicants' rights under Article 6 para. 1 (art. 6-1) by intervening in a manner which was decisive to ensure that the - imminent - outcome of proceedings in which it was a party was favourable to it (...)".*

1610 *Jarass*, 2. Edn. (2013) Art. 47, para 20 f.

1611 *Jarass*, 2. Edn. (2013) Art. 47, para 32-35.

1612 *Jarass*, 2. Edn. (2013) Art. 47, para 37 f.

1613 *Loewen et al. vs. USA*, 26.06.2003 – ICSID Case No. ARB(AF)/98/3 - Award, para 123, 136 f; which is unperceiveable under EU law as even the appearance of partiality is sufficient to deny the court's impartiality, which will in any case be questioned if the judges endorse a discriminatory behaviour, cf. also: *Alber* in: Stern/Sachs EU GrCH, Art. 47 of the Charter, para 103 ff.

considered to deny justice to the claimant.[1614] Such arbitrary disregards of the applicable law will equally be a violation of the principle of fair trial under Art. 47 of the Charter.[1615] Although under both framework, the requirement should not inaugurate a judicial review of the decision itself, it provides protection against measures which *de facto* deprive the parties of their judicial review, given that the "*court*" does not judge the case in accordance with the law but somehow in bad faith or *ex aequo et bono*.[1616] This is well established under EU law as well. Under EU law a court might even have the duty to provide additional and extensive reasons when changing its jurisprudence on a certain matter. This imposes a more demanding duty, as it requires the court to comply with an additional burden of proof that its decision is unbiased and non-arbitrary.[1617]

Hence, regarding the requirement of due process in judicial proceedings, EU law at least offers equivalent guarantees to those granted in IIAs.

(2) Due process in administrative proceedings

The FET standard also requires the host state to observe the requirements of due process in administrative processes. The threshold is considerably lower than regarding judicial due process, as the administrative authorities cannot be required to act impartially or independently in the same way as judicial authorities.[1618] The elements to be observed by the host state are the involvement of the investor in administrative proceedings which might affects its substantive rights, the chance of being heard and its arguments to be considered. Furthermore, the decisions need to have a legal basis and the authorities need to exercise their (potential) discretion by respecting the legal limits and the purpose of the provisions they are implement-

---

1614 *Jacob/Schill* in: *Bungenberg/Griebel/Hobe et al.* (Eds.), International Investment Law, 2015, p. 723; *Oostergetel & Laurentius vs. Slovak Republic*, 30.04.2010 – UNICTRAL - Award on Jurisdiction, para 291 f.

1615 *van Vormizeele* in: Schwarze EU-Kommentar, Art. 47 of the Charter, para 13; *Jarass*, 2. Edn. (2013) Art. 47, para 38.

1616 *Jacob/Schill* in: *Bungenberg/Griebel/Hobe et al.* (Eds.), International Investment Law, 2015, p. 723, for the FET standard; for the absence of arbitrary decisions under the fair trial standard: *Jarass*, 2. Edn. (2013) Art. 47, para 38.

1617 *European Court of Human Rights*, 14.01.2010 – Application no. 36815/03 - Atansovski, para 38; *Jarass*, 2. Edn. (2013) Art. 47, para 38.

1618 *International Thunderbird Gaming Corporation vs. Mexico*, 26.01.2006 – UNCITRAL - Arbitral Award, para 200.

ing.[1619] None of these elements is considered as a stand-alone requirement but rather part of an overall approach to determine whether the requirements of due process were fulfilled.

Under EU law nearly identical if not more extensive guarantees are provided by either Art. 41 of the Charter (regarding administrative decisions by the EU) or by the general principles of EU law acknowledged by the CJEU (regarding the acts of the member states when implementing EU law).[1620] Violation of these guarantees will either render the measure void or enable secondary relief by claims for compensation by virtue of the extra-contractual liability. The guarantees expressly refer to the principle of legality, which requires a (precise) legal basis for any administrative act to be issued (*Vorbehalt des Gesetzes*) and the observance of the boundaries and limitations set up by the entire legal framework the host state or the EU operates in (*Vorrang des Gesetzes*).[1621] The principles also require the prior involvement of the addressee of the measure, the communication of the decision's reasoning and the respect of fundamental principles of good administration.[1622] Any discretion attributed to the public authorities, either of the EU or the member states, needs to be exercised in accordance with its legal basis, its purpose and following the principle of proportionality.[1623] Same as regarding the FET standard, some of these requirements

1619 *International Thunderbird Gaming Corporation vs. Mexico*, 26.01.2006 – UNCITRAL - Arbitral Award, para 200; *Alex Genin et al vs. Estonia*, 25.06.2001 – ICSID Case No. ARB/99/2 - Award, para 364; *FPS vs. Czech Republic*, 12.11.2010 – UNCITRAL - Final award, para 292; cf. also: *Jacob/Schill* in: *Bungenberg/Griebel/Hobe et al.* (Eds.), International Investment Law, 2015, p. 722.

1620 *Jarass*, 2. Edn. (2013) Art. 41, para 9 f; *Danwitz*, Europäisches Verwaltungsrecht, 2008, p. 341; *Gundel* in: Becker/Ehlers Europäische Grundfreiheiten (2014), § 27, para 6 ff.

1621 *Danwitz*, Europäisches Verwaltungsrecht, 2008, p. 346; *Lasok/Millett et al.*, 2004, p. 317.

1622 *CJEU*, 03.09.2008 – Joined Cases C-402/05 P and C-415/05 P - Kadi = ECLI:EU:C:2008:461, para 335 f which clearly aligns with the requirements set forth in *Alex Genin et al vs. Estonia*, 25.06.2001 – ICSID Case No. ARB/99/2 - Award, para 364; cf. also: *Danwitz*, Europäisches Verwaltungsrecht, 2008, p. 356; *Jarass*, 2. Edn. (2013), para 21, 24, 28; *Lasok/Millett et al.*, 2004, p. 323 f.

1623 *CJEU*, 19.09.2000 – Joined Cases C-177/99 and C-181/99 = ECLI:EU:C:2000:470, para 42: "*It should be pointed out at the outset that since the principle of proportionality has been consistently recognised by the Court as forming part of the general principles of Community law* [...], *the validity of acts of the Community institutions may be reviewed on the basis of that general principle*

may be set aside in exceptional circumstances for specific reasons.[1624] However in an overall assessment the procedure needs to follow the same standards.[1625]

2. Prohibition of arbitrary and discriminatory measures and measures causing intentional harm (element no°2)

The general prohibition of arbitrary and discriminatory measures is guaranteed under the FET standard, although it overlaps with the national treatment standard and the general prohibition of discrimination. It does not seem that the guarantee under the FET standard would go any further than the obligations established under those standards. In this context, it was duly demonstrated that EU law offers equivalent protection for investors (cf. *supra* II.).

As regards arbitrary measures which intend to cause financial or physical duress[1626], they might either be contained in the aforementioned discriminatory measures (as *Jacob/Schill* point out, the general rule of equality *a forteriori* also prohibits "*targeted harassment*"[1627]) or purely arbitrary – but non-discriminatory – measures (which are difficult to perceive), which are prohibited under the general principle of legality and the boundaries set up for the exercise of discretionary powers under EU law.[1628]

---

of law" [references ommitted]; *Danwitz*, Europäisches Verwaltungsrecht, 2008, p. 368-370; *Lasok/Millett et al.*, 2004, p. 335-338.

1624 E.g. in the *Kadi-Decision*, the CJEU stated that the very nature of the measures to be implemented, they could not involve a prior hearing of the adresses. However, this lack of involvement in the prior proceedings will need to be compensated by the posterior possibility to challenge the decision and through the providing of reasonings in short delays which enable an efficient judicial challenge of the measure, cf. *CJEU*, 03.09.2008 – Joined Cases C-402/05 P and C-415/05 P - Kadi = ECLI:EU:C:2008:461, para 335 ff; cf. also: *Gundel* in: Becker/Ehlers Europäische Grundfreiheiten (2014), § 27, para 11 ff.

1625 Similar: *Jacob/Schill* in: *Bungenberg/Griebel/Hobe et al.* (Eds.), International Investment Law, 2015, p. 721.

1626 Referring to this nomenclature: *Herdegen*, 10. Edn. (2014) p 344 and *Desert Line vs. Yemen*, 06.02.2008 – ICSID Case No. ARB/05/17 - Award, para 186.

1627 *Jacob/Schill* in: *Bungenberg/Griebel/Hobe et al.* (Eds.), International Investment Law, 2015, p. 731.

1628 It should be pointed out that EU law does not require a subjective harmful intention to be proven, but already admits a "misuse of powers [...] if it appears, on the basis of objective, relevant and consistent evidence [that the measure

3. Obligation to provide legality, stability and transparency in exercising legislative or regulatory powers (element no°3)

FET further requires to enable investors to run their investment in a stable legal environment.[1629] Without '*freezing*' the host state's ability to change its legislation, the FET standard requires to enable changes in the legislative framework by admittance to the *rule of law*, in a *transparent* manner and by providing a certain *predictability* and *stability*.[1630]

The *stability* of a legal framework often refers to changes occurring in a legal framework and the ability of an investor to plan its business and especially the compliance of the latter with the legislative framework of the host state. When setting up a normative environment A on day one, the host state may not turn to an opposite environment B on day two.[1631]

The requirements of *predictability and transparency* cannot be strictly separated.[1632] They both refer to the way an investor may react to changes in the legislative framework and its possibility to assess and evade potential interferences with its business planning. The *Metalclad-Tribunal*, stated:

---

was] taken with the exclusive or main purpose of achieving an end other than that stated or evading a procedure specifically prescribed by [EU law]", cf.: CJEU, 14.11.2002 – Joined cases T-332/00 and T-350/00 - Rica Foods = ECLI:EU:T:2002:274, para 200; cf. also: Danwitz, Europäisches Verwaltungsrecht, 2008, p. 368-370 with further references from the case law of the CJEU.

1629 *Jacob/Schill* in: *Bungenberg/Griebel/Hobe et al.* (Eds.), International Investment Law, 2015, p. 728 and 733.

1630 *Jacob/Schill* in: *Bungenberg/Griebel/Hobe et al.* (Eds.), International Investment Law, 2015, p. 728; *Schreuer*, JWIT Vol. 6, No. 3 (2005), 357, 374 f.

1631 *Jacob/Schill* in: *Bungenberg/Griebel/Hobe et al.* (Eds.), International Investment Law, 2015, p. 729 with refrence to the decision in: *PSEG Global vs. Turkey*, 19.01.2007 – ICSID Case No. ARB/02/5 - Award, para 250 which perfectly summarises how not to comply with the stability requirement: *"what has been described above as 'roller-coaster' effect of the continous legislative changes. This is particularly the case of the requirements, in law or practice, to the continous change in the conditions governing the corporate status of the Project, and the constant alterations between private law status and administrative concessions."*; in *AES Summit vs. Hungary*, 23.09.2010 – ICSID Case No. ARB/07/22 - Award, para 9.3.29 it was pointed out that stability cannot refer to denying the host state's right to regulate.

1632 *Schreuer* in: *Hoffmann* (Ed.), Protection of foreign investments through modern treaty arbitration: diversity and harmonisation, 2010, p. 125, 126.

> "[the host state] failed to ensure a transparent and predictable framework for Metalclad's business planning and investment. The totality of these circumstances demonstrates a lack of orderly process and timely disposition in relation to an investor."[1633]

In the same light, but with a slightly different focus, the *Tecmed-Tribunal* found (in a criticised decision which possibly constitutes the maximum of what can be expected under the FET[1634]) that:

> "[it is required that the investor] may know beforehand any and all rules and regulations that will govern its investments, as well as the goals of the relevant policies and administrative practices or directives, to be able to plan its investment and comply with such regulations."[1635]

In other words: the legal framework governing the investment and hence determining the administrative decisions and potential interferences with the investment needs to be accessible for the investor; any legal requirement needs to be transparent to enable the actual compliance with the framework by the investor. Failure to do so, by provisions being excessively vague, meaningless or unclear, the host state will violate the FET standard.[1636] This also includes the steady and uniform application of the legal framework by administrative authorities.[1637]

The *legality* requirement (i.e. existence of a legal basis for the state measure) may somehow be assessed as an auxiliary to the obligation of

---

1633 *Metalclad vs. Mexico*, 30.08.2000 – ICSID Case No. ARB(AF)/97/1 - Award, para 99; cf. for the criticisms: *Jacob/Schill* in: *Bungenberg/Griebel/Hobe et al.* (Eds.), International Investment Law, 2015, p. 734; also *AES Summit* as cited *supra* footnote (1631).

1634 *Potestà*, ICSID Rev. Vol. 28 (2013), 88, 98 ff and *Dolzer*, Santa Clara Jour. of Int. Law Vol. 12 (2013), 7, 20 ff stressing the more distinct approach of current tribunals regarding different situations and the degree of comittment demanded by the host state.

1635 *Tecmed vs. Mexico*, 29.05.2003 – ICSID Case No. ARB (AF)/00/2 - Award, para 154, cf. also: *Jacob/Schill* in: *Bungenberg/Griebel/Hobe et al.* (Eds.), International Investment Law, 2015, p. 730.

1636 *Jacob/Schill* in: *Bungenberg/Griebel/Hobe et al.* (Eds.), International Investment Law, 2015, p. 730, referring to *Occidental Exploration vs. Ecuador*, 01.07.2004 – LCIA Case No. UN3467 - Final Award, para 184; *Schreuer* in: *Hoffmann* (Ed.), Protection of foreign investments through modern treaty arbitration: diversity and harmonisation, 2010, p. 125, 126.

1637 *Schreuer* in: *Hoffmann* (Ed.), Protection of foreign investments through modern treaty arbitration: diversity and harmonisation, 2010, p. 125, 127; cf. *inter alia*: *MTD vs. Chile*, 25.05.2004 – ICSID Case No. ARB/01/7 - Award, para 165; *Ronald S. Lauder vs. Czech Republic*, 03.09.2001 – UNCITRAL- Final Award, para 292 ff.

stability, transparency and predictability. A measure which impedes on subjective rights of an investor will require a legal basis to avoid being qualified as non-transparent or unpredictable, simply because if such legal basis is missing the investor may not have foreseen the requirements its investment needs to comply with.[1638]

EU law generally acknowledges the aforementioned requirements in member states' and the EU's regulations by referring to the principle of legal certainty (*Rechtssicherheit*).[1639] It forms part of the general principles of EU law and hence needs to be respected by both the EU as well as member states whenever implementing EU law.[1640] As these principles form part of EU primary law, all acts by member states as well as secondary legislation can be declared void if they do not meet these requirements.[1641]

Based on the principle of legal certainty, the CJEU developed different requirements which widely overlap with the requirements under the FET standard.

First, regarding the obligation of *transparency and predictability*, the CJEU ruled:

> "In particular, the principle of legal certainly requires that Community rules enable those concerned to *know precisely the extent of the obligations which are imposed on them*. Individuals must be able to ascertain unequivocally what their rights and obligations are and take steps accordingly (…)."[1642]

The similarities with the above cited decision by the *Tecmed-Tribunal* are remarkable. This requirement under the principle of legal certainty has been stressed on various occasions by the CJEU, constantly referring to the overall goal to enable individuals to ascertain the legal framework under which it operates.[1643] This necessarily includes the elemental require-

---

1638 *Jacob/Schill* in: *Bungenberg/Griebel/Hobe et al.* (Eds.), International Investment Law, 2015, p. 728 ff.

1639 *Jacob/Schill* in: *Bungenberg/Griebel/Hobe et al.* (Eds.), International Investment Law, 2015, p. 729; *Tridimas*, The general principles of EU law, 2. Edn. (2007), p. 242 and 244-251.

1640 *CJEU*, 10.03.2009 – C-345/06 - Gottfried Heinrich = ECLI:EU:C:2009:140, para 45 with further references; *Tridimas*, The general principles of EU law, 2. Edn. (2007), p. 244; cf. also: *Jarass*, 2. Edn. (2013) Einl., para 36.

1641 *Jarass*, 2. Edn. (2013) Einl., para 36.

1642 *CJEU*, 10.03.2009 – C-345/06 - Gottfried Heinrich = ECLI:EU:C:2009:140, para 44 [footnotes omitted; emphasis added].

1643 Also admitted in *CJEU*, 15.02.1996 – C-63/93 = ECLI:EU:C:1996:51, para 20; *CJEU*, 20.01.1989 – C-234/87 - Casio Computer = ECLI:EU:C:1989:27, pa-

ments of transparency, which apply both in legislative and administrative proceedings.[1644] The principle of legal certainty may also require member states to concretise any general, unspecific legislation when implementing EU law if the particular rights and obligations provided for by e.g. secondary legislation are not clearly identifiable.[1645]

Second, the principle of legal certainty also requires the coherent and uniform application of the rules issued in the EU legal order. This is also derived from the principle of primacy and the principle of effectiveness of EU law (cf. *supra*), which should ensure that no national provisions deprive EU law of taking full effect in all member states.[1646] Conjointly with the general requirements of due administrative process and the principle of non-discrimination imposing on the national authorities in application of EU law (cf. *supra*), this guarantees that any provision of EU law should be consistently applied in all member states.[1647]

Third, the EU legal order requires all institutions and the member states to obey to the principle of legality (*Vorrang und Vorbehalt des Gesetzes*). This ensures a predictable administrative and legislative framework, as any obligation or right imposed needs to have a legal basis, which in turn needs to be sufficiently transparent and unequivocal. Hence, the principle of legal certainty and legality cover wide varieties of the obligations under the IIA regarding the predictability, transparency and legality of the legal framework in the EU.

---

ra 11-13; cf. also: *Tridimas*, The general principles of EU law, 2. Edn. (2007), p. 244-246; *Lasok/Millett et al.*, 2004, p. 341-343 with multiple references.

1644 Regarding the administrative proceedings cf. *supra* and the reference to Art. 41 of the Charter (e.g. including the duty to provide reasons, prior hearing and involvement, etc.); the duty to provide transparency in the legislative proceedings is clearly adressed in *CJEU*, 10.03.2009 – C-345/06 - Gottfried Heinrich = ECLI:EU:C:2009:140, para 46 ff but also through the general provisions under EU law, e.g. the duty to publish legislative acts (Art. 297 TFEU), cf.: *Jacob/Schill* in: *Bungenberg/Griebel/Hobe et al.* (Eds.), International Investment Law, 2015, p. 733.

1645 *CJEU*, 19.09.1996 – C-326/95 = ECLI:EU:C:1996:341 regarding a Greek regulation of review for public procurement conracts which did not mention the possibility of judicial review sufficiently clear, also: *CJEU*, 29.03.2011 – Joined Cases C-201/09 P and C-216/09 P - Arcelor = ECLI:EU:C:2011:190, para 68; cf: *Tridimas*, The general principles of EU law, 2. Edn. (2007), p. 246 f.

1646 Similar: *Tridimas*, The general principles of EU law, 2. Edn. (2007), p. 248.

1647 Cf.: *CJEU*, 20.01.1989 – C-234/87 - Casio Computer = ECLI:EU:C:1989:27, para 11-12; *Lasok/Millett et al.*, 2004, p. 343.

The *stability* requirement should be assessed conjointly with the legitimate expectations and the requirement for consistency in the following sub-paragraph.

4. Honouring of legitimate expectations and stability of legislation (element no°4)

The principles of stability, consistency and the honouring of legitimate expectations under an IIA are another essential element of the FET standard. The host state is required to take into consideration the investor's objectively determined expectations regarding the investment and the essential conditions of its operation.[1648] In other words: if the investor was entitled to rely upon a particular setting, commitment or framework regarding its investment, the host state cannot frustrate these expectations by abruptly changing the framework or essential circumstances.[1649]

The scope of protection under the FET standard is limited by two ideas. First, the expectations in question are not determined from the *individual* investor's perspective. It is meaningless if the investor relied on a certain legal framework or certain circumstances as long as these expectations would not have been shared by an objective, reasonable and informed third party.[1650] The crucial element which determines if an expectation is legitimate is thus not the individual perspective of the concrete investor in question but an objectivised level of expectations attributed to an investor in the concrete circumstances.

1648 *Schreuer* in: *Hoffmann* (Ed.), Protection of foreign investments through modern treaty arbitration: diversity and harmonisation, 2010, p. 125, 126 f; *Schreuer*, JWIT Vol. 6, No. 3 (2005), 357, 374 f; *Herdegen*, 10. Edn. (2014), p. 344-346; *Jacob/Schill* in: *Bungenberg/Griebel/Hobe et al.* (Eds.), International Investment Law, 2015p. 723-731.

1649 *Jacob/Schill* in: *Bungenberg/Griebel/Hobe et al.* (Eds.), International Investment Law, 2015, p. 725 f; *Herdegen*, 10. Edn. (2014), p. 344 f; *Reinisch* in: *Tietje* (Ed.), Internationales Wirtschaftsrecht, 2015, p. 415.

1650 *International Thunderbird Gaming Corporation vs. Mexico*, 26.01.2006 – UNCITRAL - Arbitral Award, para 147: *"'legitimate expectations' relates to a situation where a Contracting Party's conduct creates reasonable and justifiable expectations on the part of an investor"*; *Griebel*, (2008) p.72; *Dolzer*, Santa Clara Jour. of Int. Law Vol. 12 (2014), 7, 18-20.

Second the host state is not forced to keep the "*circumstances prevailing at the time the investment is made [...] totally unchanged*"[1651], as this cannot be the legitimate expectation of an objective, reasonable and informed third party. But any changes of the host state's legal frameworks need to be foreseeable and offer the investor the *possibility to react and plan its investment and to comply with such regulations*.[1652] The question if the FET standard is violated can only be determined by a consideration of all (legitimate) interests, the purpose of the state measure as well as a balancing of the state's interest, the circumstances the measure was taken in and the way in which the measure was implemented.[1653]

Hence, the mere existence of a regulatory framework cannot entail such expectations. Objectively, reasonable expectations require a certain link with an action of the host state, such as a particular, granted advantage, an administrative decision or even a particular setting of a legislative framework (e.g. under the consistency requirement, which would prohibit frequent changes regarding the same subject matter).[1654]

EU law addresses these guarantees through the angle of the principle of legal security, which includes the protection of legitimate interests (*Vertrauensschutz*) and the prohibition of retroactive regulations (*Rückwirkungsverbot*).[1655] Conjointly applied, both principles will provide nearly an identical scope of protection to that under the FET standard.

1651 *Saluka vs. Czech Republic*, 17.03.2006 – UNCITRAL - Partial Award, para 305.

1652 *Schreuer* in: *Hoffmann* (Ed.), Protection of foreign investments through modern treaty arbitration: diversity and harmonisation, 2010, p. 125, 126 f; *Jacob/Schill* in: *Bungenberg/Griebel/Hobe et al.* (Eds.), International Investment Law, 2015, p. 730.

1653 *Saluka vs. Czech Republic*, 17.03.2006 – UNCITRAL - Partial Award, para 305; *Schreuer* in: *Hoffmann* (Ed.), Protection of foreign investments through modern treaty arbitration: diversity and harmonisation, 2010, p. 125, 126 f; *Dolzer*, Santa Clara Jour. of Int. Law Vol. 12 (2014), 7, 21; *Jacob/Schill* in: *Bungenberg/Griebel/Hobe et al.* (Eds.), International Investment Law, 2015, p. 728-730 and 733 ff.

1654 *Jacob/Schill* in: *Bungenberg/Griebel/Hobe et al.* (Eds.), International Investment Law, 2015, p. 726 f; . *Herdegen*, 10. Edn. (2014), p. 345; *Reinisch* in: *Tietje* (Ed.), Internationales Wirtschaftsrecht, 2015, p. 415.

1655 Cf. also: *Jacob/Schill* in: *Bungenberg/Griebel/Hobe et al.* (Eds.), International Investment Law, 2015, p. 724 stating that this protection would be well established under EU law.

Regarding the protection of legitimate expectations, the CJEU stated in the *Hauer-Case*:

> "[...] that any economic operator to whom an institution has given justified hopes may rely on the principle of the protection of legitimate expectations."[1656]

Such "*justified hopes*" may, similarly as under the FET standard, e.g. be based on particular commitments provided by the institutions of the EU.[1657] Revoking administrative decisions which grant particular advantages to the addressee are subject to strict conditions: they may only be revoked in a particular timeframe and meeting the principle of proportionality, which also requires to balance the interest of revoking the act against the expectations of the addressee that the act will sustain.[1658] However, EU law reveals to be particularly strict when it comes to building legitimate expectations on non-specific commitments and regarding commitments which are in breach of EU law:

First, the mere existence of a legislative framework or a market setting may not raise legitimate expectations. The CJEU constantly states that:

> "[...] traders are not justified in having a legitimate expectation that an existing situation *which is capable of being altered* by the Community institutions in the exercise of their discretionary power will be maintained, particularly in an area such as that of the common organisation of the markets, the objective of which involves constant adjustment to reflect changes in economic circumstances."[1659]

Hence, mere changes of the conditions the economic activity is exercised in will usually not be sufficient to raise legitimate expectations. The same would apply for non-specific measures such as monetary payments over a certain timeframe or other general measures.[1660] However, e.g. internal provisions and administrative rules of practice may build legitimate expectations, if they are published and it is implied that these measures will apply to future case.[1661]

1656 *CJEU*, 14.07.1998 – T-119/95 - Hauer = ECLI:EU:T:1998:161, para 54; cf.also *CJEU*, 14.06.2012 – C-606/10 - ANAFE = ECLI:EU:C:2012:348, para 78; *Jarass*, 2. Edn. (2013) Einl, para 37.

1657 *Jarass*, 2. Edn. (2013) Einl, para 37; *Tridimas*, The general principles of EU law, 2. Edn. (2007), p. 280 f; *Lasok/Millett et al.*, 2004, p. 353.

1658 *Jarass*, 2. Edn. (2013) Einl, para 37; *Lasok/Millett et al.*, 2004, p. 354 f.

1659 *CJEU*, 15.07.2004 – Joined Cases C-37/02 and C-38/02 - Adriano et al = ECLI:EU:C:2004:443, para 70. [emphasis added].

1660 *Jarass*, 2. Edn. (2013) Einl, para 38; *Lasok/Millett et al.*, 2004, p. 356.

1661 *CJEU*, 28.06.2005 – Joined cases C-189/02 P, C-202/02 P, C-205/02 P to C-208/02 P and C-213/02 P = ECLI:EU:C:2005:408, para 211, which also – once

Second, the CJEU emphatically denies any legitimate expectations where the commitment which gives rise to the expectations is unlawful. Under EU law, legitimate expectations may only arise when the economic operator conducted a due diligence to assess the legal requirements and fully complied with those requirements.[1662] Only if the investor is acting in good faith and could not have reasonably foreseen that the measure is illegal under EU law (e.g. due to a retroactive measure), which is strictly controlled, legitimate expectations can be granted.[1663]

This seems to differ from the protection offered by – at least several – arbitral tribunals, which admitted less explicit behaviours to raise legitimate expectations or some did not put such considerable weight on the legality of the state measure rising the expectations.[1664] However, the gap is reduced by the following considerations:

- As explained *supra* when analysing the "*legality requirement*" (Chapter 13), such objective, reasonable expectations cannot be based on actions or commitments which would constitute a violation of the substantial and important provisions of the host state's legal framework, including EU law. Excluding non-compliance with substantial provisions from raising legitimate expectations will have the effect that even under an IIA only promises based on minor illegalities may raise legitimate expectations. In such cases, it could be argued that the investor was probably acting in good faith regarding the commitment's legality under EU law;

again – underlines the need to act consistently and predictable in administrative decisions.

1662 *Tridimas*, The general principles of EU law, 2. Edn. (2007), p. 281.

1663 *CJEU*, 17.04.1997 – C-90/95 - de Compte vs. Parliament = ECLI:EU:C:1997 :198; *Tridimas*, The general principles of EU law, 2. Edn. (2007), p. 284 f.

1664 *Lemire vs. Ukraine*, 28.03.2011 – ICSID Case No. ARB/06/18 - Award, para 70; however this is opposed by various tribunals, which require a more specific commitment of the state: *Plama vs. Bulgaria*, 27.08.2008 – ICSID Case No. ARB/03/24 - Award, para 218; *Glamis Gold vs. United States*, 08.06.2009 – UNCITRAL - Award, para 766; the Argentina Cases are doubtful, as the stability was abrubtly changed with tremendous economic effects, which probably at least require a transition period under EU law, cf.: for the tribunal's reasonings: *LG&E vs. Argentina*, 03.10.2006 – ICSID Case No. ARB/02/1 - Decision on Liability, para 133.

- EU law does not generally prevent legitimate expectations from being based on particular rights granted under a legislative provision.[1665] The provision, however, needs to lead to a result which *de facto* is equivalent to a particular advantage granted by an authority of the EU;[1666]
- The prohibition of retroactive application (*Rückwirkungsverbot*) will generally prohibit laws from taking retroactive effect, even regarding laws which only set a new regulatory framework. Depending on the severity of the changes, a transition period may be necessary to render the measure compatible with the principle of legal security.[1667] As measures which especially target investors will in general be provisions having a larger impact, the difference is further reduced;[1668]
- Additionally, Art. 16 and 17 of the Charter set a further general requirement for EU law, the principle of proportionality. Although a certain behaviour may not give rise to legitimate expectations, the impediment on particular rights, especially under Art. 16 of the Charter, will need to comply with the principle of proportionality. With regard to this principle, the CJEU regularly requires a certain uniformity, consistency and a fair balancing of interests. In this balancing, the prior actions and (non-specific) commitments given to an individual or legal entity will also need to be taken into account.[1669]

Given all these considerations, the difference is further and considerably diminished to an extent that reveals that both criteria are at least equivalently protected under EU law and IIAs.

1665 *CJEU*, 14.05.1975 – C-74/74 - CNTA = ECLI:EU:C:1975:59, para 41-43; *CJEU*, 26.06.1990 – C-152/88 - Sofrimport = ECLI:EU:C:1990:259, para 26; *Tridimas*, The general principles of EU law, 2. Edn. (2007), p. 252.

1666 Cf.also: *CJEU*, 28.06.2005 – Joined cases C-189/02 P, C-202/02 P, C-205/02 P to C-208/02 P and C-213/02 P = ECLI:EU:C:2005:408, para 209-211; similar: *Tridimas*, The general principles of EU law, 2. Edn. (2007), p. 252.

1667 Similar: *CJEU*, 14.05.1975 – C-74/74 - CNTA = ECLI:EU:C:1975:59, para 41-43; *CJEU*, 26.06.1990 – C-152/88 - Sofrimport = ECLI:EU:C:1990:259, para 26.

1668 *Jarass*, 2. Edn. (2013) Einl, para 39; *CJEU*, 17.07.1997 – C-183/95 - Affish BV vs. Rijksdienst = ECLI:EU:C:1997:373, para 56.

1669 *CJEU*, 06.11.2003 – C-243/01 - Gambelli = ECLI:EU:C:2003:597, para 67: *„[regulations] must serve to limit betting activities in a consistent and systematic manner"*, cf. also: *Oppermann/Classen et al.*, 5. Edn. (2011) § 22, para 12.

5. Principle of proportionality (element no°5)

The last criterion to be assessed is the overall compliance of the host state with the principle of proportionality. Several tribunals introduced this criterion in their assessment of the FET standard and tried to balance the overall impediment on the investor's rights with the overall goal and public interest in question. This principle, is identically and strictly applied by the CJEU to any measure impeding e.g. the right to conduct business (Art. 16 of the Charter), the right to property (Art. 17 of the Charter) or any limitation to a fundamental freedom or further right guaranteed by EU law (cf. *supra*). Hence, regarding this element of the FET standard one cannot reasonably conduct any difference in protection between EU law and the substantive protection offered by IIAs.

6. Overall comparative assessment regarding the FET standard

The overall assessment of the FET standard and the protection under EU law reveals that the inherent principles and the protection derived thereof broadly overlap. Differences may arise especially regarding the balancing of particular interests and the necessary commitment to raise legitimate expectations. These differences may result in either action being declared in violation of an IIA but not violating the principles under EU law and *vice versa*. However, criticism of the wide and far-reaching application of the FET standard and its interference with the right to regulate attributed to a host state has led to a certain decline and reservations of arbitral tribunals in making extensive use of the provision.[1670] EU law generally attributes a fair protection under the FET standard. In a comprehensive approach, this should not question the overall equivalence of those standards. Where investors are seriously threatened by a measure and subject to considerable losses, both EU law as well as the FET standard under an IIA will provide at least equivalent protection.

1670 Cf. already in 2010: *Tietje*, Int. Investitionsschutzrecht im Spannungsverhältnis (Beit. zum Transnat. Wirt.-R, Vol. 93, 2010), 5, 12 f with reference to *Duke Energy vs. Ecuador*, 18.08.2008 – ICSID Case No. ARB/04/19 - Award, para 339 ff; *Saluka vs. Czech Republic*, 17.03.2006 – UNCITRAL - Partial Award, para 305. The trend became even more obvious in the meantime, cf.: *Dolzer*, Santa Clara Jour. of Int. Law Vol. 12 (2013), 7, 20 ff and *Potestà*, ICSID Rev. Vol. 28 (2013), 88, 98 ff with further references to recent decisions.

IV. Further principles: Prohibition of arbitrary measures and umbrella clauses

Finally, two further clauses of minor importance in IIAs should be addressed at this stage. They relate to protection against arbitrary measures in general (1.) and the protection offered by an umbrella clause (2.).

1. Protection against arbitrary measures

As already explained in the context of the legal framework under IIAs, the protection against arbitrary measures is largely covered by the FET and FPS standard. It was demonstrated that under both frameworks, EU law as well as IIAs, the protection offered to investors is merely equivalent. *A forteriori*, this will also apply to separate clauses in IIA, which refer to the prohibition of arbitrary measures. Generally speaking, the EU law principle of proportionality should as such be sufficient to guarantee that member states refrain from such measures.

2. Umbrella clauses

EU law surely does not provide for a guarantee which is completely equivalent to an umbrella clause.

It shall be recalled, that through an umbrella clause, the violation of e.g. contractual obligations *vis-à-vis* the investor should not only constitute a violation of this contractual agreement but also of the IIA. Hence, the clause leverages a so-called *contract claim* (for fulfilment of a contract, which might also be submitted to the national law of the host state) to a *treaty claim* (for breach of the IIA).[1671] The same may apply for other obligations undertaken towards the investor which do not root in contractual commitments.[1672]

The scope of protection offered by these clauses remains highly controversial, which is especially related to the question of what kind of viola-

1671 *Reinisch* in: *Tietje* (Ed.), Internationales Wirtschaftsrecht, 2015, p. 429; This commonly recognised terminology was also used by the tribunal in: *SGS vs. Pakistan*, 06.08.2003 – ICSID Case No. ARB/01/13 - Decision of the Tribunal on Objections to Jurisdiction, para 146.

1672 *Griebel*, (2008), p. 85.

tion of which obligation may be challenged under the IIA through the umbrella clause.[1673] Some consider this term to cover all obligations undertaken by the host state towards the investor, irrespective of their nature.[1674] Others restrict the clause to cover contractual obligations only.[1675] However, the concrete scope of the obligation and the umbrella clause does not really impact this analysis of equivalence. In the absence of an umbrella clause under EU law, contractual obligations or other obligations undertaken by the host state will need to be enforced by means of national law addressing national tribunals. The umbrella clause itself only *leverages an existing claim on the international level.* [1676] The existence of the obligation will still be dependent on the national law of the host state. Even if one were to admit that several interferences of the host state with such obligations such as retroactive abrogation or impediment may be set aside by a corrective function of international law, similar if not identical principles (prohibition of retroactivity, protection of legitimate interests) exist under EU law as has just been demonstrated in the context of the FET standard (cf. *supra*).

Hence, the true question arising in the context of an umbrella clause is one of the equivalence of procedural protection. If those systems are equivalent, the clause leveraging the contract claim to a treaty claim is of no further use to enhance the investor's protection.

1673 *Herdegen*, 10. Edn. (2014), p. 340; *Griebel*, (2008), p. 85.

1674 *SGS vs. Philippines*, 29.01.2004 – ICSID Case No. ARB/02/6 - Decision of the Tribunal on Objections to Jurisdiction, para 115 f and 127 f, which although dealing with a treaty claim does not seem to limit the scope of the umbrella clause in the BIT to those contractual obligations only; same applies for: *Noble Ventures vs. Romania*, 12.10.2005 – ICSID Case No. ARB/01/11 - Award, para 61.

1675 *Reinisch* in: *Tietje* (Ed.), Internationales Wirtschaftsrecht, 2015, p. 429; *Eureko vs. Poland*, 19.08.2005 – Ad Hoc Arbitration - Partial Award, para 244 and 250 f although it is not expressly stated by the tribunal.

1676 *Reinisch* in: *Tietje* (Ed.), Internationales Wirtschaftsrecht, 2015, p. 429; This commonly recognised terminology was also used by the tribunal in: *SGS vs. Pakistan*, 06.08.2003 – ICSID Case No. ARB/01/13 - Decision of the Tribunal on Objections to Jurisdiction, para 146.

V. Additional protection for investors established within the EU and operating in other EU member states

Assuming an investor would be established in the EU and operates in another member state, which essentially leads to an intra-EU setting, the equivalence would *a forteriori* be guaranteed. In this scenario, additionally the fundamental freedoms such as the freedom of establishment or the freedom to provide services would apply, which also set up a prohibition of restrictions. Additionally, Art. 18 TFEU would provide for a broader prohibition of discrimination, which requires more restrictive reasons to justify a difference in treatment.

VI. Overall assessment of substantive protection under EU law and IIAs

The comparison of the substantive guarantees under both legal frameworks reveals an overall equivalence of both protection systems, with regard to member states' measures being mandated by EU law. Differences may arise as to the concrete balancing of interests, where both legal frameworks assign different priorities to different regulatory interests. Some stress the fact that the degree to which EU law and arbitral tribunals admit policy exceptions diverge substantially.[1677] However, even though EU law may in particular circumstances be more attentive to regulatory interferences, it guarantees the overall proportionality of the measures by various means (e.g. the test of proportionality or the general prohibition of restrictions).[1678] Furthermore, the overall objective of investment protection, which is the stability of the host state's legal framework and the predictability of changes for the investor – is at least equivalently guaranteed under EU law. IIAs generally contain very broad protection standards, which always leave considerable room for interpretation und uncertainty. The more precise standards under EU law, and the general adherence to the rule of law, reduce this uncertainty and hence may even result in a more predictable framework: e.g. the reasons of public policy, which may be invoked to justify a certain measure, are enumerated in the respective articles of the TFEU and the jurisprudence of the CJEU adds further cer-

1677 *Dahlquist/Lenk et al.*, European Policy Analysis, 2016:4, 1, 6.

1678 Similarly but with a focus on intra-EU IIAs: *Dimopoulos*, CMLR Vol. 48, No. 1 (2011), 63, 66.

tainty as to their scope of application. This even enforces the investors' protection.

The most considerable differences between both frameworks, the (alleged) scope of legitimate expectations as well as the protection of indirectly affected investors, cannot compromise the overall equivalence. Regarding legitimate expectations, it has been demonstrated that both frameworks protect those expectations. However, EU law is particularly demanding regarding the actions leading to such expectations. Illegal measures may, in general, not rise legitimate expectations at all. Broad, unspecific commitments, may not be relied on either. With regard to IIAs, the interpretation given to the FET standard by arbitral tribunals differs widely and may be of a broader scope, at least regarding particular decisions (e.g. *Tecmed vs. Mexico)*. However, as to the legality requirement to raise legitimate expectations, it was demonstrated that arbitral tribunals tend to put more weight on the "clean-hands" requirement for investors. These differences are hence reduced to a considerable degree. Furthermore, the remaining differences cannot be considered to be of such degree to compromise an equivalence. It should be reminded that both frameworks do not need to offer identical protection. Regarding one particular aspect, protection may be more narrow. However, this is compensated by other standards where IIAs might offer less protection than EU law. Additionally, arbitral tribunals are increasingly recognising the state's need to regulate and to balance diverging interests. EU law provides for established mechanisms which guarantee this precise feature.

Regarding investors being indirectly affected by state measures, EU law will require the harmed subsidiary or owner to seek for judicial protection. Hence, the only real difference between both frameworks is the way to implement judicial protection. Furthermore, the reason for e.g. shareholders to claim damages for a measure affecting a subsidiary, is to be attributed any protection at all under an IIA. IIAs generally require the investor and the host state to be of different nationality. However, subsidiaries are often established under the law of the host state and hence do not fulfil this criterion. As an investment under an IIA generally requires considerable control over the investment, the investor should be able to address its claims through the originally harmed object. If, regarding the particular facts of the case, such claims are impossible, the presumption could still be rebutted based on a manifest deficiency of protection in the specific case.

B. Equivalence of procedural guarantees under EU law

After having established an equivalence of substantive guarantees, the following sub-section should address the equivalence of procedural protection offered by EU law and IIAs. Such an equivalence is denied by several authors as well as several arbitral tribunals having addressed the question in the intra-EU context.[1679] When analysing their statements, one has to doubt, whether the question has been correctly addressed so far. Discussion tends to focus on the (undisputable) fact that EU law does not provide for a separate internationalised dispute settlement mechanism by means of arbitration open to investors as a vehicle for damage claims against host states. The *Eastern Sugar-Tribunal* e.g. stated:

> "The BIT also provides for a special procedural protection in the form of arbitration between the investor state and the host state and, especially arbitration of a 'mixed' or 'diagonal' type been the investor and the host state, as in the present case [...]"[1680]

Without further analysis, it concludes that:

> "EU law does not provide such a guarantee."[1681]

Hence, the analysis seems to be based on the search for a provision or an institution under EU law which would provide a similar form of access to a mixed internationalised dispute mechanism. This analysis is based on circular reasoning, as it presupposes a mechanism to be provided by EU law because IIAs chose this particular mechanism. To avoid this reasoning (and in order to be able to appropriately address the question of equivalence), the underlying idea of the mixed arbitration mechanism will be developed to enable evaluating the equivalence (I.). Based on the characteristics provided by investment protection law to ensure this underlying idea (II.), the characteristics and mechanisms of EU law will be analysed (III.). The chapter will finish with an overall assessment of the equivalence

1679 *Tietje*, Intra-EU BITs als Herausforderung im Mehrebenensystem des Rechts (Beit. zum Transnat. Wirt.-R, Vol. 104, 2011), p. 14 mainly relying on the fact that domestic and international dispute settlement mechanisms cannot be equivalent; *Tietje/Wackernagel*, JWIT Vol. 16, Iss. 2 (2015), 205, 243; *Eastern Sugar vs. Czech Republic*, 27.03.2007 – SCC No. 088/2004 - Partial award, para 164-166.

1680 *Eastern Sugar vs. Czech Republic*, 27.03.2007 – SCC No. 088/2004 - Partial award, para 164.

1681 *Eastern Sugar vs. Czech Republic*, 27.03.2007 – SCC No. 088/2004 - Partial award, para 165.

(IV.), which demonstrates that the procedural guarantees under IIAs and EU law are equivalent.

I. How to address the equivalence of procedural protection

To be able to assess the equivalence of procedural protection under an IIA and EU law, the criteria how to address this question need to be developed. As mentioned above, it is obvious that EU law does not provide for a mixed arbitration mechanism which might cover the integrity of cases currently pending under investment arbitration rules. Furthermore, the investment arbitration mechanism is focused on granting immediate compensation to investors which pledge the violation of their rights under an IIA. One might doubt whether EU law provides such immediate access to compensation (cf. *infra* for the role of secondary relief in EU law).

However, this is not necessary either. The question of equivalence of procedural protection cannot be addressed in the same way as the equivalence of substantial guarantees by comparing two sorts of rules and demonstrating that they largely cover the same situations and provide for largely the same level of protection. Procedural protection has the sole task to ensure the effective application of substantive guarantees. Procedural guarantees are no self-contained system which exists for its own sake. They are designed to support substantive guarantees.[1682] In other words, as the ECtHR puts it:

> "[...] the effectiveness of such substantive guarantees of fundamental rights depends on the mechanisms of control in place *to ensure their observance.*"[1683]

Hence, the equivalence of procedural guarantees under IIAs and EU law should be addressed by comparing how far the procedural systems enables achieving the overarching goal, which is to efficiently ensure the proper

---

1682 Cf. for the different mechanisms in national and international law how enforcement of the substantive guarantees is ensured by dispute settlement mechanisms and other mechanisms: *Wiegandt*, ZaöVR, 2011, 31, 60 ff; cf. also *Walter*, ZaöVR, 2016, 363, 375 and 379 f; for a more theoretical approach integrating various other means, cf.: *Benedek*, ZaöVR, 2016, 345 and p. 347 regarding the judicial supervision as a mean to enforce obligations deriving from public international law.

1683 *European Court of Human Rights*, 30.06.2005 – Application n° 45036/98 - Bosphorus, para 160 [emphasis added].

application of the substantive guarantees and hence their effectiveness. This should be addressed by reference to three considerations:

- Multiple claims by individual do not necessarily mean that the system is effective overall: the best substantive protection is guaranteed if it ensures that *no violation occurs*;
- If substantive guarantees are violated, the system will need to ensure the *effective compliance of the host state with these guarantees for the future*;
- Any individual suffering *definite, irrevocable harm*, should be able to *obtain compensation* through the system.

II. The implementation of procedural investment protection by mixed arbitration

IIAs generally address procedural protection by referring to mixed arbitration. The (theoretical) possibility of inter-state remedies is also available under IIAs; however, the occasional use of this instrument justifies to leave them aside for this comparison. The mixed arbitration mechanism tries to guarantee the effectiveness of substantive protection by mainly three elements:

- *Procedural protection through a non-national court system*: The reference to a non-national dispute settlement body, which allows to exclude interferences or biased judgements which might occur when host state's national tribunals are required to hear cases which concern compensation to be paid by their "*own*" state[1684];
- *Enforcement of substantive guarantees through deterrence*: A deterrent effect[1685], which results from the granting of compensation to an investor whenever the host state violates the substantive guarantees;
- *Guarantee of compensation for irreparable harm*: The individual compensation for the investor, which might at least obtain monetary compensation if definite harm occurs.

These characteristics should now be benchmarked against the procedural protection under EU law to determine to what extent the overarching goal

---

1684 *Sornarajah*, 3. Edn. (2010), p. 217; *Ghouri*, Int. A.L.R. Vol. 14, No. 6, 189, 190; *Sattorova*, LIEI Vol. 39, No. 2 (2012), 223, 227 and further references in footnote 24.

1685 In German: "*Abschreckungseffekt*".

of rendering the substantive guarantees effective is equivalently protected under EU law.

III. Equivalence of procedural investment protection under EU law compared to IIAs

The characteristics of the mixed arbitration system under IIAs should be used as starting points to demonstrate to what extent EU law provides similar characteristics and – if not – to what extent the mechanisms provided by EU law will equivalently ensure the effective application and enforcement of the investors' substantive guarantees under EU law. This requires an analysis of the distribution of judicial protection between EU courts and national courts ("*1. Procedural protection through a non-national court system*") as well as the evaluation of possibilities to obtain primary or secondary relief ("*2. Specific performance instead of deterrence: how to ensure observance of substantive guarantees*"). Furthermore, the influence of additional mechanisms under EU law which might cover potential *lacunas* will be analysed ("*3. Complementary means offered by EU law to enforce compliance with substantive guarantees*").

It should be recalled that the equivalence of protection refers to those acts for which the *Bosphorus-Presumption* may apply in investment proceedings. Hence, the comparison will focus on those acts which are (at least partially) mandated by EU law and hence reduce the host state's margin of action to such a point that any further action will be considered as a breach of the IIA. This might e.g. be a decision directly issued by the Commission or the Council, which is binding on member states, a regulation which leads to a particular change in the legislative framework, or a directive which will then be transposed by member states into national legislation. However, it may also refer to acts of the member states, which execute such decisions or which amend legislation to comply with imperative requirements of EU law (such as procurement law, competition law or unjustified limitations of the fundamental freedoms). Regarding all other acts (i.e. these which are not effectively determined by EU law), there is no potential for a conflict between EU law and the IIA as the host state may fulfil the requirements of both legal frameworks. Hence the presumption has no need to be applied.

1. Procedural protection through a non-national court system

Mixed arbitration essentially relies on a non-national dispute settlement body which excludes any necessity to seek protection of the investor's rights before national courts. Hence it will be analysed to what extent EU law provides a similar non-national dispute resolution system.

Proceedings in front of the CJEU can generally be considered equivalent to a non-national dispute settlement body. The CJEU is a permanent supra-national court. Its composition excludes any substantial interference of the member states with its judgements. Hence, for acts which might be directly challenged before the CJEU, no major difference can be found to the mixed arbitration mechanism (1). Regarding acts which require an involvement of national courts (2), other mechanisms of EU law will guarantee the unbiased judgement of those courts, including the protection offered through Art. 19 TEU, Art. 47 of the Charter and the extra-contractual liability of the member states (3).

(1) Direct actions before the CJEU

EU law enables direct actions to the CJEU essentially by virtue of Art. 263, 264 TFEU (action for annulment). The action for annulment in Art. 263, 264 TFEU enables to directly challenge acts of the European institutions producing legal effects *vis-à-vis* third parties.[1686] As to Art. 263 (1) TFEU two sorts of acts of the institutions can be challenged:

First, all *legislative acts* (cf. Art. 289 (3) TFEU) of the Council, the Commission or the European Central Bank, except for recommendations and opinions (which lack a legally binding effect (Art. 288 (5) TFEU)). This includes directives and regulations. Second, *all acts* of the European Parliament or the European Council or other bodies, offices or agencies of the EU which are *intended to produce legal effects towards third parties*. The type of act itself is not limited, as long such act is intended to produce legal effects towards third parties.[1687]

1686 *Oppermann/Classen et al.*, 5. Edn. (2011) § 13, para 5; *Wegener* in: Calliess/Ruffert EUV/AEUV, Art. 19 TEU, para 44 f.

1687 *Pache* in: von Heinegg/Vedder EUV/AEUV, Art. 263 TFEU, para 16; *Hobe*, 8. Edn. (2014), para 506; *Oppermann/Classen et al.*, 5. Edn. (2011) § 13, para 44.

It should be recalled what has already been said at the beginning of this sub-chapter. The acts for which a procedural equivalence should be demonstrated are acts which are (at least partially) mandated by EU law and hence reduce the host state's margin of action to such a point that any further action will be considered as a breach of the IIA. This might include the following:

- a decision directly issued by the Commission or the Council, which is binding on member states;
- a regulation which leads to a particular change in the legislative framework; or
- a directive which will then be transposed by member states into national legislation; or
- any act of the member states which implements such decisions or which amends legislation to comply with imperative requirements of EU law (such as secondary law, public procurement law, competition law, etc.).

Regarding the aforementioned acts to be evaluated, the action for annulment potentially covers all acts which are issued by the EU itself, especially decisions, regulations and directives as they are intended to produce legal effects towards third parties.

Implementation or transposition measures by the member states, and member state laws which are issued to achieve general compliance (e.g. with EU primary law), will not be challengeable under Art. 263 TFEU. However, the legal basis of these acts (such as e.g. the directive) may be challenged under the annulment procedure. Hence, Art. 263 TFEU generally seems to cover a wide procedural guarantee against acts issued by the EU.

However, Art. 263 TFEU differentiates as to the claimant and restricts the *locus standi* for individuals and legal entities in Art. 263 (4) TFEU. [1688] The claimants enumerated in Art. 263 (2) TFEU are considered to be privileged plaintiffs. Their action for annulment is admissible without proving a further legal interest in the action. Individuals and legal entities can only bring an action for annulment if they fulfil the criteria set forth in Art. 263

1688 *Schwarze* in: Schwarze EU-Kommentar, Art. 263 TFEU, para 38; *Gaitanides* in: v. d. Groeben/Schwarze AEUV/EUV, Art. 263 TFEU, para 49; cf. also: *Hobe*, 8. Edn. (2014), para 512; *Oppermann/Classen et al.*, 5. Edn. (2011) § 13, para 42 and 56 ff.

(4) TFEU.[1689] Investors as natural persons or legal entities are not part of the privileged claimants and hence subject to the restrictions set forth in Art. 263 (4) TFEU. The effects of this provision will hence influence the access for investors to direct claims at the CJEU. The interpretation given to these criteria remains rather restrictive, despite of an enlargement pursued in the Lisbon Treaty.[1690] Art. 263 (4) reads as follows:

> "Any natural or legal person may (…) institute proceedings against an act addressed to that person or which is of direct and individual concern to them, and against a regulatory act which is of direct concern to them and does not entail implementing measures."

The *locus standi* is hence granted in three different situations:

- The challenged act is addressed to that person;
- The challenged act is of direct and individual concern to the applicant;
- The challenged act is a regulatory act which is of direct concern to the individual / legal entity and does not entail implementing measures.

(a) Act addressed to that person

The first group (addressee of the act) includes nearly all decisions which are directly addressed to the investor, e.g. by the Commission or the Council. Any individual or legal entity, regardless of its nationality, is entitled to institute proceedings under Art. 263 TFEU if the act in question is addressed to the person (i.e. the addresses as to Art. 288 (4) TFEU). This may essentially concern e.g. decisions based on Art. 101 ff TFEU and decisions ordering the revocation of state aid based on Art. 107 ff TFEU. [1691] It should be noted that even in multi-layer structures (which may be of

1689 *Schwarze* in: Schwarze EU-Kommentar, Art. 263 TFEU, para 38; *Gaitanides* in: v. d. Groeben/Schwarze AEUV/EUV, Art. 263 TFEU, para 49; cf. also: *Hobe*, 8. Edn. (2014), para 512; *Oppermann/Classen et al.*, 5. Edn. (2011) § 13, para 42 and 56 ff.

1690 *Hobe*, 8. Edn. (2014), para 513.

1691 *Gaitanides* in: v. d. Groeben/Schwarze AEUV/EUV, Art. 263 TFEU, para 50; *Oppermann/Classen et al.*, 5. Edn. (2011) § 13, para 56; the CJEU seems to admit the individual / legal entity to be adressed even though the revocation is formally adressed to the member state, cf. *CJEU*, 17.09.1980 – C-730/79 - Philip Morris = ECLI:EU:C:1980:209, para 5; as *Dörr* in: Grabitz/Hilf/Nettesheim EUV/AEUV, Art. 263 TFEU, para 100 and footnote 6 argues that the CJEU universally accepts the *locus standi* in these constellations without further evaluating the (correct) alternative in Art. 263 (4) TFEU on which it is based.

particular relevance for investment disputes) the parent company may be granted *locus standi* if the act in question is addressed to the subsidiary.[1692] Actions brought by competitors should be better assessed by the second alternative of Art. 263 (4).[1693]

(b) Act of direct and individual concern to the applicant

The second group covers acts of direct and individual concern to the applicant. For any acts other than demonstrated under (a), *locus standi* is only granted if the applicant demonstrates that the act is of direct *and* individual concern to him. Both criteria set a major hurdle for seeking the annulment of legislative acts, although the Lisbon Treaty eliminated several hurdles as to this type of acts.

The terms "*acts*" now potentially addresses all kind of acts, including legislative acts, which eliminates any doubts arising from diverging formulations in the previous treaties. However, these acts need to be of direct and individual concern to the applicant.[1694]

Thc term "*direct concern*" is related to the discretion left to the member states when implementing the act. If there is no reasonable discretion left in the application of the act, the act is of direct concern for the applicant. The underlying idea is that, the applicant is *de facto* already concerned by the act of the EU itself, although there is technically an implementing measure which follows the act.[1695]

Regarding the *individual concern*, the CJEU still adopts the restrictive *Plaumann-Formula*[1696] to determine the admissible applications under

---

1692 The CJEU accepted the *locus standi* for a fully owned subsidiary in *CJEU*, ECR 1983, 00911, 17.03.1983 – C-294/81 - Control Data = ECLI:EU:C:1993:285, para 10. Any other decision would constitue an "*excess of formalism*".

1693 Cf. inter alia: *Dörr* in: Grabitz/Hilf/Nettesheim EUV/AEUV, Art. 263 TFEU, para 93 and 99 ff regarding competiton law and state-aid provisions.

1694 *Hobe*, 8. Edn. (2014), para 513 f; *Oppermann/Classen et al.*, 5. Edn. (2011) § 13, para 44; *Gaitanides* in: v. d. Groeben/Schwarze AEUV/EUV, Art. 263 TFEU, para 53-58; *Schwarze* in: Schwarze EU-Kommentar, Art. 263 TFEU, para 41-43.

1695 *Gaitanides* in: v. d. Groeben/Schwarze AEUV/EUV, Art. 263 TFEU, para 62; *Schwarze* in: Schwarze EU-Kommentar, Art. 263 TFEU, para 45; *Oppermann/Classen et al.*, 5. Edn. (2011) § 13, para 58.

1696 *CJEU*, 15.07.1963 – C-25/62 - Plaumann = ECLI:EU:C:1963:17.

Art. 263 TFEU. As to this Formula applicants are only individually concerned if

> "that decision affects them by reason of certain attributes which are peculiar to them or by reason of circumstances in which they are differentiated from all other persons and by virtue of these factors distinguishes them individually just as in the case of the person addressed."[1697]

This excludes an action for annulment if the applicant is subject to a regulation which does not affect him in particular compared to other participants in the market. An individual concern has been admitted in several categories:

- The first relates to those (legislative) acts where the affected individuals / legal entities of the provisions are fixed, although they are not formally addressees of the provisions (e.g. by being mentioned by name or through a particular description) and the addressed audience will not be further extended.[1698] These cases are usually referred to as *collective decisions*.[1699]
- The second category relates to those individuals / legal entities which are attributed particular formal or procedural rights through the (legislative) act, *inter alia* through *prior* hearings, inclusion in the administrative proceedings, etc. The CJEU extended this category to cases in which the entity seeking annulment was not attributed procedural rights by law but in the concrete factual circumstances. The fact of being included in the proceedings related to a regulation generates a *distinctive token*.[1700]

1697 *CJEU*, 15.07.1963 – C-25/62 - Plaumann = ECLI:EU:C:1963:17.

1698 *Schwarze* in: Schwarze EU-Kommentar, Art. 263 TFEU, para 47; *Gaitanides*, in: Groeben/Schwarze AEUV/EUV, Art. 263 TFEU, para 66; *CJEU*, 29.03.1979 – C-113/77 - NTN Toyo Bearing = ECR 1979, 01185; *Gaitanides* in: v. d. Groeben/Schwarze AEUV/EUV, Art. 263 TFEU; *Oppermann/Classen et al.*, 5. Edn. (2011) § 13, para 58.

1699 *CJEU*, 29.03.1979 – C-113/77 - NTN Toyo Bearing = ECR 1979, 01185: "*a natural or legal person is individually concerned by a provision (...) where that provision in fact constitutes a collective decision relating to named addressees*"; *Schwarze* in: Schwarze EU-Kommentar, Art. 263 TFEU, para 47; *Gaitanides*, in: Groeben/Schwarze AEUV/EUV, Art. 263 TFEU, para 66.

1700 *Schwarze* in: Schwarze EU-Kommentar, Art. 263 TFEU, para 48; *Gaitanides* in: v. d. Groeben/Schwarze AEUV/EUV, Art. 263 TFEU, para 69; *CJEU*, 04.10.1983 – C-191/82 - Fediol vs. Commission = ECLI:EU:C:1983:259, para 30.

- Third, the individual concern may be demonstrated if the act constitutes an impediment on particular or specific rights granted to the individual or legal entity. These specific rights might be licenses attributed to a company or economic circumstances which *single out the applicant's interest* in seeking the annulment of the act.[1701]

Regarding the acts of the EU to be analysed here, it will generally not be possible to challenge directives, as they require further implementation and hence are not of direct concern to the applicant (except collective measures).

Regulations, which generally do not entail implementing measures (and hence are of direct concern), may be subject to Art. 263 TFEU if they fulfil the *Plaumann-Criteria*.[1702] The same applies for decisions of EU authorities which do not leave reasonable discretion to the member states.

In these later cases, the particular nature of investment claims will lead to several situations being covered by the *Plaumann-Criteria.* Hence, numerous acts of the EU related to investment protection are directly challengeable under Art. 263 (4) TFEU.

This relates to the fact that the possibility to raise substantive claims is often linked to the attribution of particular rights to investors (such as those which might lead to an expropriation, grant legitimate expectations or are subject to public rights, e.g. concessions, etc.). In those cases, the third category of cases under the *Plaumann-Criteria* (impediment on particular rights) will apply.

Other substantive claims will be linked to inconsistent administrative behaviour or other forms of previous involvement, which will also lead to the admission of the claim under Art. 263 (4) TFEU. These cases may also include the challenge of decisions on matters of competition law or state aid provision by competitors or general measures of the EU (such as e.g.

1701 *CJEU*, 23.11.1995 – C-10/95 P - Asocarne = ECLI:EU:C:1996:159, para 43: *Court held that a normative provision may, in certain circumstances, be of individual concern to certain interested economic agents. However, as the Court of First Instance rightly observed, that case-law cannot be relied on in the present case since, unlike the regulation contested in that case, the directive contested at first instance has not adversely affected specific rights of the appellant or of its members"; CJEU*, 24.04.1996 – C-87/95 P - CNPAAP = ECLI:EU:C:1996:159, para 36; *Schwarze* in: Schwarze EU-Kommentar, Art. 263 TFEU, para 49; *Oppermann/Classen et al.*, 5. Edn. (2011) § 13, para 61.

1702 *Schwarze* in: Schwarze EU-Kommentar, Art. 263 TFEU, para 45.

the block exemptions) if the investor is denied the attribution of a certain benefit by an EU member state based on these general measures.[1703]

Additionally, the category of collective measures should have considerable impact on investors. It generally refers to directives which, by virtue of its scope of application, only apply to particular persons and excludes the possibility that the category of persons is further extended in the future. Such measures will also be directly challengeable under Art. 263 (4) TFEU.[1704] Although the cases were usually developed regarding anti-dumping-provisions, investors in particular might rely on this provision regarding specific and targeted measures. *Inter alia* the energy unbundling directives, at least regarding the unbundling requirement itself, also target a very particular, specified group of providers, which will not extend further (as future bundling of supply and transmission functions is inconceivable) and hence may be challenged under Art. 263 (4) TFEU.

(c) Regulatory act which is of direct concern to them and does not entail implementing measures

The possibilities demonstrated so far are supplemented by the third group of acts in Art. 263 (4), which relates to *regulatory acts* that do not entail implementation measures and are of direct concern. Art. 263 (3) 3. Var. TFEU directly concerns regulatory acts. The CJEU did not extend this alternative to all directives, which has been supported by several scholars in literature.[1705]

As to the CJEU, *regulatory acts* in Art. 263 (4) should be opposed to *legislative acts* in Art. 289 (3) TFEU. Hence, the CJEU excludes the ability to challenge all legislative acts and thus all type of (usual) regulations

1703 *CJEU*, 22.11.2007 – C-260/05 P - Sniace = ECLI:EU:C:2007:700, para 57 ff; *Dörr* in: Grabitz/Hilf/Nettesheim EUV/AEUV, Art. 263 TFEU, para 99 and 100.

1704 *CJEU*, 29.03.1979 – C-113/77 - NTN Toyo Bearing = ECR 1979, 01185, para 11; *Schwarze* in: Schwarze EU-Kommentar, Art. 263 TFEU, para 49.

1705 *Gaitanides* in: v. d. Groeben/Schwarze AEUV/EUV, Art. 263 TFEU, para 74 for an overview; for an extension also to legislative acts: *Pache* in: von Heinegg/Vedder EUV/AEUV, Art. 263 TFEU, para 44 *Schwarze* in: Schwarze EU-Kommentar, Art. 263 TFEU, para 51; for the opposite: *Ehricke* in: Streinz EUV/AEUV, Art. 263 TFEU, para 53-55.

and directives under Art. 263 (4) TFEU.[1706] Those legislative acts are only challengeable if they are of direct and individual concern under Art. 263 (4) 2. Var. TFEU. However, the third category under Art. 263 (4) TFEU provides protection against measures under Art. 290 and 291 TFEU issued by the Commission or the Council if they do not entail further implementation measures.

As those measures (e.g. the dumping-regulations and other acts implemented in the former comitology procedure) may have considerable impact on the economic operators, including investors, the *locus standi* granted against these measures without necessity to refer to an *individual concern* further strengthens the procedural protection under Art. 263 TFEU.

As a consequence and general summary of the analysis in this subsection, there is a considerable number of investment related disputes for which investors may directly seek court action before the CJEU by way of the annulment proceedings. This applies regardless of the fact that the annulment procedure still remains subject to particular preconditions to be fulfilled to enable direct access to the CJEU, as most cases of investment disputes will potentially raise in situations where those preconditions are fulfilled.

(2) Supplementary function of national courts under EU law

Regarding all other types of acts, EU law general does not provide a particular direct action to the CJEU. This basically refers to directives which cannot be qualified as collective decisions, general regulations which do not impede on particular rights or implementing measures of the member states as well as acts which tend to generally comply with EU law. In these cases, investors will need to rely on the procedural protection provided by national courts. Whereas one could generally argue that a recourse to national courts is insufficient as mixed arbitrations especially tried to internationalise the conflict, EU law presents several particularities

1706 It should be noted that directives would in any case fall outside the scope of Art. 263 (4) 3. Alt. as they need further implementation measures in the member state. The discussion is therefore focused on the general admissibility of claims against regulations which constitute legislative acts under Art. 288 (3) TFEU, cf. also: *Gaitanides* in: v. d. Groeben/Schwarze AEUV/EUV, Art. 263 TFEU, para 74 ff.

which will diminish numerous threats commonly associated with judicial relief before national courts.

(a) Enforcement through the preliminary ruling procedure

The most obvious particularity is the interaction of national courts with the CJEU by virtue of the preliminary ruling procedure (Art. 267 TFEU).[1707] Through this procedure, the determining aspects of the dispute, if they are related to the interpretation of a national provision in the light of EU law, are referred to the CJEU as a supra-national dispute settlement body, which will ultimately judge on the correct interpretation of EU law and its application within the national legal framework. This applies to all national measures, no matter if they are directly based on EU law or by virtue of a transposing provision in national law. The procedure may also be engaged for questions of validity of either a national norm (allegedly) conflicting with EU law or a provision of EU law which conflicts with supreme EU law. Other than in a purely national court system, the ultimate and binding interpretation regarding substantive guarantees of EU law will hence be rendered by a supra-national court, instead of the court of last resort in the domestic legal system.

Reference is frequently made to non-mandatory character of Art. 267 TFEU, which would considerably weaken the mechanism.[1708] Three considerations should set aside this criticism:

First, courts of last resort are under the duty to refer the question to the CJEU if they cannot establish an *acte clair* or *éclairé*. Practice has shown that there has not been much reluctance on part of national courts to refer

1707 This was also recognised by the ECtHR in *European Court of Human Rights*, 30.06.2005 – Application n° 45036/98 - Bosphorus, para 164.

1708 *Euram vs. Slovak Republic*, 22.10.2012 – PCA Case no. 2010-17: First Award on Jurisdiction, para 250 and 252. As to the tribunal, even national courts of last resort do not necessarily refer the question to the CJEU. By applying the *acte clair* doctrine, they might apply and interpret EU law as long as they consider that there is no reasonable doubt about the interpretation and application. Whether courts admit to have reasonable doubts or not, would be subject to a wide range of discretionary power; the same has been argued by the tribunal in *Achmea vs. Slovak Republic*, 26.10.2012 – PCA Case No. 2008-13 - Award on Jurisdiction, Arbitrability and Suspension, para 278 ff and *Electrabel vs. Hungary*, 30.11.2012 – ICSID Case No. ARB/07/19: Decision on Jurisdiction, Applicable Law and Liability, para 4.148.

questions to the CJEU. The increase in preliminary ruling references serves as strong proof of this.[1709]

Second, regarding the validity of any act of the EU, the reference is mandatory.[1710]

Third, even for inferior courts, the denial to make use of the preliminary ruling procedure is a violation of the member state's obligations under EU law, which may lead to infringement proceedings and engage the member state's responsibility in case the interpretation reveals to be wrong (cf. *infra* for the assistance-function of secondary relief).[1711]

Hence, the mechanisms in implementing Art. 267 TFEU substantially guarantee the final and uniform application of EU law in all member states and also disable national particularities and influences on the effective application of any guarantees contained therein.[1712] By the means of indirect control, Art. 267 TFEU fills the gap in individual protection by a non-national court, which is left due to the limited *locus standi* in Art. 263 (4) TFEU.[1713]

(b) Principle of supremacy and direct effect

Furthermore, EU law limits the possibilities for EU member states to interfere with judicial proceedings by supra-national and overarching standards all national procedural frameworks need to comply with. The national procedural framework is limited by the boundaries of EU law, especially through the principle of supremacy. If any provision, even of procedural law, reveals to be contrary to a guarantee provided in EU law, this provision of national law must not be applied. National courts are bound by this principle. An impediment on this principle constitutes a violation of EU law and may engage infringement proceedings or the member state's lia-

---

1709 *Oppermann/Classen et al.*, 5. Edn. (2011) § 13, para 69.

1710 *CJEU*, 21.02.1981 – Joined Cases C-143/88 and C-92/89 - Zuckerfabrik Süderdithmarschen = ECLI:EU:C:1991:65, para 14 f; *Oppermann/Classen et al.*, 5. Edn. (2011), para 79; *Gaitanides* in: v. d. Groeben/Schwarze AEUV/EUV, Art. 267 TFEU, para 65.

1711 *Pache* in: von Heinegg/Vedder EUV/AEUV, Art. 267 TFEU, para 35; *Wegener*, EuR, 2002, 785, 789; *Augsberg* in: v. d. Groeben/Schwarze AEUV/EUV, Art. 340 TFEU, para 100.

1712 *Pache* in: von Heinegg/Vedder EUV/AEUV, Art. 267 TFEU, para 1.

1713 *Pache* in: von Heinegg/Vedder EUV/AEUV, Art. 267 TFEU, para 10 ; similarly: *Oppermann/Classen et al.*, 5. Edn. (2011) § 13, para 70.

bility. Hence, other than "*traditional*" procedural frameworks, EU member states are not deliberately free to change or adapt provisions of their procedural law and hence interfere with substantial rights, as they will need to respect the outer limits set up by EU law. The principle of supremacy may even require to grant particular procedural protection if this is necessary to grant EU law (and hence also the investor's substantial protections thereunder) full effect (cf. *infra*).[1714]

Furthermore, the principle of direct effect, which renders certain rights and obligations under EU law directly applicable to individuals in the EU member states and may set aside contradicting national measures or provisions, also provides further guarantees for the investor's substantial protection. If e.g. EU law requires member states, by means of a directive, to provide a particular legal remedy, upon omission or deficient transposal of the member states' individuals (and hence the investor) may directly rely on the directive and base its claim on the provision setting up the obligation to provide the legal remedy.[1715]

(c) Principle of effectiveness (*Effektivitätsgrundsatz*) and Art. 19 (1) TEU, Art. 47 of the Charter

Lastly, a major deficiency of the traditional recourse to national remedies is the possibility for the host state to reduce these remedies or exclude particular acts from being submitted to judicial control. EU law insures against such a denial of justice by two means, once again reducing the disadvantages for investors of being partially subject to national remedies.

First, the principle of effectiveness requires national courts to give full effect to EU law, including by means of interpreting or setting-aside na-

1714 *CJEU*, 19.06.1990 – C-213/89 - Queen vs. Secretary of State for Transport = ECLI:EU:C:1990:257, para 20; *CJEU*, 13.03.2007 – C-432/05 - Unibet = E-CLI:EU:C:2007:163, para 43; further references in: *Gundel* in: Becker/Ehlers Europäische Grundfreiheiten (2014), § 27, para 49 f.

1715 Cf. e.g. relating to the "*enforcement-directive*" in intellectual property law, *CJEU*, 05.06.2008 – C-395/07 - Commission vs. Germany = ECLI:EU:C:2008:325, for the direct application: *Jaeger*, System einer Europäischen Gerichtsbarkeit für Immaterialgüterrechte, 2013, p. 400 f; for the opposite: *Eisenkolb*, GRUR, 2007, 387.

tional remedies, if this is necessary to guarantee the supremacy of EU law.[1716] The CJEU states in settled case law:

> "In that regard, the detailed procedural rules governing actions for safeguarding an individual's rights under Community law must be no less favourable than those governing similar domestic actions (principle of equivalence) and must not render practically impossible or excessively difficult the exercise of rights conferred by Community law (principle of effectiveness) [...].
>
> Moreover, it is for the national courts to interpret the procedural rules governing actions brought before them, such as the requirement for there to be a specific legal relationship between the applicant and the State, in such a way as to enable those rules, wherever possible, to be implemented in such a manner as to contribute to the attainment of the objective [...] of ensuring effective judicial protection of an individual's rights under Community law."[1717]

Second, Art. 19 (1) TEU and Art. 47 of the Charter guarantee the right of access to justice. Hence, judicial recourse needs to be available regarding every act of the EU or any act of the member states when implementing EU law. This may require national courts to even grant previously unaccepted or unknown forms of judicial control under national procedural law and the national legislator to implement the necessary procedural remedies.[1718] As especially Art. 49 of the Charter is conceived as a fundamental right, the individual has a claimable right to ensure this provision and may engage EU member state's extra-contractual liability besides potential infringement proceedings initiated by the Commission (cf. *infra*).

(3) The assisting function of secondary relief: compensation for violation of EU law

Additionally, the secondary relief by engaging the EU's or the member states' responsibility under the extra-contractual liability for violation of

---

1716 *CJEU*, 19.06.1990 – C-213/89 - Queen vs. Secretary of State for Transport = ECLI:EU:C:1990:257, para 20 relating to a provision of national law which precluded from granting interim relief relating to a measure potentially conflicting with EU law.

1717 *CJEU*, 13.03.2007 – C-432/05 - Unibet = ECLI:EU:C:2007:163, para 43 f.

1718 *CJEU*, 25.07.2002 – C-50/00 - Unión de Pequeños = ECLI:EU:C:2002:462, para 38 f and 41; *CJEU*, 13.03.2007 – C-432/05 - Unibet = ECLI:EU:C:2007:163, para 43 f with further references in para 43; cf. also: *Jarass*, 2. Edn. (2013) Art. 47, para 25a; *Schwarze* in: Schwarze EU-Kommentar, Art. 19 TEU, para 14.

EU law may compensate for individual and definite harm which results from the infringement of EU law. It may also have an incentivising function to guarantee observance of EU law, similar to the deterring effect in the mixed arbitration context.

Although the extra-contractual liability requires a sufficiently serious breach of EU law, the criteria developed by the CJEU to assess this restriction are particularly favourable for investors in claiming compensation for major impediments on their rights. The criteria are the following:

- the discretion left to the authorities upon deciding or issuing a normative provision;
- the gravity of the damage;
- the limited number of persons concerned compared to the overall addressees of the provision (which might, according to the CJEU in the *Mulder-Case*, include up to thousands of aggrieved parties, if those are still far less than the overall addresses of the provision); and
- the type of provision violated.

Impediments on fundamental provisions, such as provisions under the Charter or the fundamental freedoms will more likely lead to the attribution of damages. In investment disputes which relate to particularly targeted measures, the number of aggrieved parties will be low whereas the potential damage will be typically high.[1719] Also the type of provision violated will potentially concern more fundamental norms of EU law, as those provisions are among the essential features of substantial protection for investments under EU law. Hence, especially in the context of investment disputes, the extra-contractual liability may become particularly relevant as the aforementioned criteria are likely to be fulfilled.

Second, the denial to make use of the preliminary ruling procedure by national courts will also reduce the threshold to engage the extra-contractual liability. If the measure is found to be contrary to EU law, the denial is a strong indicator to engage the liability.[1720] Second, the non-referral to the CJEU may itself be a breach of EU law and hence engage the responsibility of the member state if the denial is arbitrary or wil-

1719 *Augsberg* in: v. d. Groeben/Schwarze AEUV/EUV, Art. 340 TFEU para 49 ff; *Berg* in: Schwarze EU-Kommentar, Art. 340 TFEU, para 43 ff.

1720 *Augsberg* in: v. d. Groeben/Schwarze AEUV/EUV, Art. 340 TFEU, para 100; cf. also: *Wegener*, EuR, 2002, 785, 789.

ful.[1721] Hence, by this mechanism, the extra-contractual liability also contributes to the effective application and engagement of the procedure in Art. 267 TFEU.

It should also be noted that the extra-contractual liability of the EU is not suspect to having previously engaged primary relief.[1722] The liability of the member states may be suspect of such an exhausting-legal remedies requirement. However, compensation may be granted for damages occurred during those proceedings.[1723]

2. Specific performance instead of deterrence: how to ensure observance of substantive guarantees

After having assessed the access to a non-national court system enforcing the rights of investors, the second criterion, relating to the type of decision rendered by the dispute settlement mechanisms, will be evaluated.

Mixed arbitration tribunals generally issue decisions granting compensation (secondary relief). Primary relief is not commonly accepted, although several tribunals try to pave the way to implementing such measures.[1724] EU law generally grants primary protection by *restitution in*

1721 *Gaitanides* in: v. d. Groeben/Schwarze AEUV/EUV, Art. 263 TFEU, para 71; cf.also but more general: *CJEU*, 13.06.2006 – C-173/03 = ECLI:EU:C: 2006:391, para 32 and 35.

1722 *Berg* in: Schwarze EU-Kommentar, Art. 340 TFEU, para 19; *Augsberg* in: v. d. Groeben/Schwarze AEUV/EUV, Art. 340 TFEU, para 26.

1723 *Berg* in: Schwarze EU-Kommentar, Art. 340 TFEU, para 69; similar: *Augsberg* in: v. d. Groeben/Schwarze AEUV/EUV, Art. 340 TFEU, para 78.

1724 For a recent example of a tribunal which seems to be willing to order restitution of a legal framework instead of compensation: *Ioan Micula, Viorel Micula & others vs. Romania*, 23.09.2008 – ICSID Case No. ARB/05/20 - Decision on Jurisdiction and Admissibility, para 166 – 168; some consider restitution to be in practice impossible (e.g. *CME vs. Czech Republic*, 13.09.2001 – UNCITRAL - Partial Award, para 618; cf. also for the general challenge of restitution in kind to be the appropriate measure to be ordered by an arbitral tribunal: *inter alia*: *Hindelang*, AVR Vol. 53 (2015), 68, 78; others point out the fact that BITs generally (with several exceptions) do not limited to secondary relief but given e.g. Art. 53, 54, which only relate to the enforcement of awards attributing compensation, restitution may not be the best choice for the investors, cf.: *Dugan*, Investor-state arbitration, 2008, p. 569 f; Under public international law however restitution should be the first option to be addressed: cf.: *ICJ*, Case concerning the factory at Chrozow, p. 47.

kind (or the declaration of how to interpret several norms, which will have comparable effects after being applied by national courts), whereas secondary relief mainly has a supporting function (cf. *supra*).

Considering that the overarching goal of procedural protection should be to enforce substantive guarantees, granting (only) compensation even seems less effective than primary relief. Indeed, the preference by arbitral tribunals to grant compensation is due to the fact that *restitution in kind* would be far more difficult to enforce in the host state. From the investor's perspective, keeping its investment and e.g. rendering a particular provision, which used to harm this investment, void, should be perceived as being even more desirable than only being granted compensation.[1725] R*estitution in kind* enables the investor to pursue the investment and generate further profits, whereas compensation refers to compensating the economic harm, which can never be a full equivalent to the first possibility. EU law especially provides this possibility of *restitution in kind* and – if further damages subsist – to grant compensation for these damages. This possibility, which does not need to rely on a deterrent effect[1726] for the host state to refrain from further interferences, should be considered even more effective to guarantee the substantive protection offered by EU law.

3. Complementary means offered by EU law to enforce compliance with substantive guarantees

Finally, reference will be made to the infringement proceedings as an additional guarantee provided by EU law, which further strengthens the effective application of substantive guarantees. As previously described, Art. 258 TFEU enables the Commission to initiate proceedings against a member state if it considers that any of the member state's acts violates EU law.[1727]

1725 Based on several IIAs, tribunals consider that they do not have jurisdiction to order restitution in kind (cf. *supra* footnote above). However, several tribunals expressed their (general) willigness and favour of granting restitutio in kind: *Ioan Micula, Viorel Micula & others vs. Romania*, 23.09.2008 – ICSID Case No. ARB/05/20 - Decision on Jurisdiction and Admissibility, para 166-168.

1726 The German expression is "*Abschreckungseffekt*".

1727 *Oppermann/Classen et al.*, 5. Edn. (2011), para 33; *Pache* in: von Heinegg/Vedder EUV/AEUV, Art. 258 TFEU, para 21.

This instrument enables an external objective control of legality for the member states and their judicial framework.[1728] Taken individually, these proceedings cannot guarantee an equivalent protection for investors. However, the additional mechanism further distinguishes procedural protection under EU law from traditional procedural protection under domestic law. The Commission as an independent institution, which considers itself to be the "*guardian of the [European] Treaties*"[1729], seeks to observe member states and their compliance with EU law. Hence, investors may also address to the Commission, if they consider any act of a member state to be in violation of EU law. After having evaluated the act, the Commission may then engage proceedings.

The mechanism is particularly interesting because it represents similarities with the inter-state and diplomatic protection mechanism under previous investment protection mechanisms (such as the FCNs). One could argue that mixed arbitration was especially designed to counter such dispute resolution mechanisms. Infringement proceedings, however, substantially differ from the aforementioned mechanisms and especially their shortcomings. One major inefficiency of inter-state remedies and diplomatic protection was their dependency on the claimant's home state to claim rights.[1730] The home state, however, may have several reasons not to engage itself in such claims, especially considering the possible lack of a genuine incentive to do so and potential diplomatic repercussions acting as a further disincentive.[1731] The situation regarding the Commission is different. Diplomatic influences may be reduced, as the Commission itself is recognised as a superior authority under the European Treaties. The Commission also has a genuine interest in detecting and eliminating infringements of member state's obligations under EU law. The uniform and effective applica-

1728 *Pache* in: von Heinegg/Vedder EUV/AEUV, Art. 258 TFEU, para 3; *Hobe*, 8. Edn. (2014), para 499 and 501. Stressing the importance of such meachanism: *Walter*, ZaöVR, 2016, 363, 375 ff.

1729 Cf. *inter alia*: *European Commission*, Amicus Curia Brief filed in Micula vs. Romania to the U.S. Court of Appeals, 04/02/2016, p. 6.

1730 *Herdegen*, 10. Edn. (2014), p. 330; *Ghouri*, Int. A.L.R. Vol. 14, No. 6, 189, 191; *Vandevelde*, U.C. Davis Jour. of Int. Law & Policy Vol. 12, No. 1 (2005), 157, 160; *Lang*, Der EuGH und die Investor-Staat-Streitbeilegung in TTIP und CETA (Beit. zum Transnat. Wirt.-R, Vol. 138, 2015), p. 5.

1731 *Ghouri*, Int. A.L.R. Vol. 14, No. 6, 189, 191; *Vandevelde*, U.C. Davis Jour. of Int. Law & Policy Vol. 12, No. 1 (2005), 157, 160; *Lang*, Der EuGH und die Investor-Staat-Streitbeilegung in TTIP und CETA (Beit. zum Transnat. Wirt.-R, Vol. 138, 2015), p. 5; cf. *supra* (Chapter 2 and 3).

tion of EU law is one of the fundamental tasks attributed to the Commission (Art. 17 (1) TEU).[1732] Hence, this sort of external control further contributes to the equivalence of the judicial systems under EU law and IIAs.

IV. Overall assessment of the equivalence of procedural protection under IIAs and EU law

Comparing the procedural protection under EU law and IIAs reveals that both systems equally enforce the substantive protection standards of the respective legal framework and ensure that the enforcement of substantive provisions is guaranteed by a supranational mechanism and independent from the host states. Art. 263 (4) TFEU reveals to offer protection in numerous situations which might particularly affect investors, even though the *locus standi* of individuals and legal entities is restricted. As this mechanism enables a direct claim in front of the CJEU, there is no major difference to a claim brought to an international arbitral tribunal. In those cases, where investors would need to rely on domestic tribunals to enforce their rights, EU law offers several particularities which distinguish the overall judicial framework considerably from other purely domestic frameworks. These particularities ensure an equivalent enforcement of substantive protection (and hence the overall protection for investors). Especially the preliminary ruling procedure enables to leverage the interpretation regarding substantive guarantees to the supranational level and hence disable domestic courts to interfere with investors' rights. Furthermore, the rights of fair trial and due process guaranteed by the Charter of Fundamental Rights of the EU provides essential guarantees of due process within the member states. Upon non-compliance with those features, investors may claim damages. Additionally, the Commission has a supervisory function regarding EU member states' compliance with substantive provisions of EU law. All these features are of supranational character and may not be altered by EU member states, which differentiates the overall system from "*usual*" local remedies. EU law hence provides a framework which *in general* enables to guarantee the procedural enforcement of substantive protection standards. Hence, *in general,* it offers an equivalent protection mechanism. The investor may still be *de facto* hindered to en-

1732 *Oppermann/Classen et al.*, 5. Edn. (2011) § 5, para 119 and 130; *Epping* in: von Heinegg/Vedder EUV/AEUV, Art. 5 TEU, para 5.

force its rights through a denial of justice (e.g. the national courts may deny to engage the preliminary ruling procedure, although they are under the duty to do so). Hence, the question of actual enforcement of the investors' rights turns out to be a question of whether or not the procedural framework (including its various guarantees) is actually observed. However, failure to do so would constitute a denial of justice. The fact that a denial occurred should be one of the most prominent cases to rebut the *Bosphorus-Presumption* in arbitration proceedings (cf. *infra*). However, the fact that such denial of justice may theoretically occur, cannot compromise the overall equivalence of the procedural system.

Chapter 16: Implementing the Bosphorus-Approach in extra-EU investment arbitration proceedings

The following section evaluates how arbitral tribunals could implement the *Bosphorus-Doctrine* in investment proceedings. This includes a proposal how arbitral tribunals should deal with and establish thc presumption of lawfulness (A.) and its conditions. Subsequently it should be analysed how investors should be enabled to rebut the presumption and which exceptions should apply to the presumption (B.). Once the *Bosphorus-Presumption* would be applied by arbitral tribunals, the courts in the EU and arbitral tribunals would need to enter into a dialogue which respects the limits the *Bosphorus-Presumption* tries to establish to the level of control in each judicial framework (C.). Implementing the Bosphorus-Presumption in such a way would satisfy the involved parties' interests and could hence constitute a lasting solution to the conflict of EU law with extra-EU IIAs (D.).

A. The presumption of lawfulness: how to determine if an act is 'mandatory' under EU law

The presumption of lawfulness should be a mechanism to resolve conflicts between the IIA and EU law which result from the host state's obligation to obey to both legal orders, even though they might require different sets of actions. As demonstrated this conflict may only occur where the EU member state is subject to mandatory requirements under EU law. This crucial element should be analysed first (I.). This question is inextricable from the repartition of the burden of proof, which should be addressed subsequently (II.).

I. Mandatory actions by the host states under EU law

The qualification of an act as mandatory under EU law will be the crucial determinant to engage the presumption. It would be excessive to require an act to be strictly mandatory in the sense of EU law, leaving only one option to the EU member state (simple execution such as in the revocation of state aid). Besides those acts which require one particular action by member states, the presumption should also include measures where EU law leaves a certain discretion to the host state, but all remaining actions may fall outside the scope of eligible actions under the IIA. This will include e.g. provisions which leave several options to the member states how to implement a certain goal, but definitely require a certain result to be obtained.[1733] However, achieving this result would be a potential violation of the IIA (cf. for the concrete implementation regarding the burden of proof: *infra* under II.). The presumption could hence apply e.g. regarding decisions by the Commission or regulatory acts by the Commission which require the member state to execute these decisions in a particular manner (such as state aid approvals or disapprovals) and regulations by EU law which require administrative implementation (such as e.g. Regulation 1031/2010/EU[1734] for the attribution of greenhouse-gas certificates). It may also extend to directives such as the aforementioned SSM-directive or the third energy package which intend to achieve a certain goal (e.g. separation of transit and energy suppliers) by leaving a certain (limited) discretionary scope of action to the member states how to achieve that goal.

However, the flexibility of the approach should *per se* not render the investor's rights and claims useless. On the other hand, the host state

---

1733 This also seems to be the standard which is (now) applied by the ECtHR after the *Biret-Decision*: *European Court of Human Rights*, 09.12.2008 – Application no. 13427/87 - Biret, para 2; The court expressly applies the *Bosphorus-Presumption* to a state measure which left a certain discretion to the state adopting such measure but which was based on a compulsory act by an international organisation, cf.: *Janik*, ZaöVR, 2010, 127, 169.

1734 Regulation (EU) No 1031/2010 - Greenhouse Gas Emission Scheme, Official Journal of the European Union L 302 (12/11/2010), 1.

needs to have a fair chance to rely on the presumption. Therefore, the burden of proof regarding the mandatory character should be carefully redistributed between investor and host state.

II. The burden of proof relating to an act being "mandatory"

To fairly redistribute the burden of proof and make the presumption applicable in practice, the following mechanism should be established whenever EU law could have considerable influence on the host state's actions which are challenged under an extra-EU IIA.

- The investor will challenge several state measures in its claim and describe to what extent these measures may have infringed its rights under an IIA;
- The host state may invoke the *Bosphorus-Presumption* by demonstrating that the measures were the consequence of mandatory provisions of EU law. The host state will be required to demonstrate that the measure was the direct consequence of provisions of EU law and to what extent this provision of EU law determined the remaining scope of action. This should be referred to as the *prima facie* evidence of the mandatory character;
- The investor may now reply to this *prima facie* establishment by demonstrating that under the relevant provisions of EU law the host state was able to undertake alternative measures which would have been less harmful by naming such measures in a concrete way;
- The host state may then reply by demonstrating that either such measures would have equally violated the IIA and hence all eligible actions lead to a conflicting situation *or* the measure being less harmful would violate other, at least equal rights of third parties (such as other investors, etc.).

This distribution of the burden of proof translates the flexibility of the approach to determine a mandatory act into a balanced repartition of risks and difficulties. Whereas the state, which raises the presumption as a defence, generally needs to first prove the mandatory character, it would be unreasonable to require the host state to demonstrate from the very beginning of the proceedings that all potential acts would equally violate the IIA. For the investor, demonstrating other, less harmful measures should be reasonable as well. This requires the investor to determine concrete measures which it would have expected and hence translate its "*legitimate expectations*". If this succeeds, again, the host state will need to reply and justify why those measures do not constitute a feasible alternative to the measure which was undertaken and which is challenged under the IIA.

B. Rebutting the presumption: when to consider the protection to be manifestly deficient

Upon having demonstrated the mandatory character of the measure, the presumption of lawfulness will apply to the act. In other words: the act is presumed not having violated the IIA either, given the principal equivalence of EU law and the IIA. At this stage, the consequences of prior proceedings under EU law will need to be taken into account (I.). Second, the investor may rebut the presumption upon demonstrating that there has been a general downgrade in the level of protection (II.) or that in the case at hand EU law proves to be manifestly deficient (III.). Finally, the consequences of a denial of justice on the *Bosphorus-Presumption* need to be evaluated (IV.).

I. Consequence of prior proceedings

A presumption of legality, which is based on the fact that an act is considered lawful under EU law, necessarily requires that the act was challenged under EU law. Hence, the investor may be forced to engage judicial review against the act by procedural means under EU law first.

At this stage, the tribunal may be required to stay the proceedings if lawfulness has not yet been definitively established under EU law and the "*EU proceedings*" are still pending.

The investor may deliberately refrain from undertaking proceedings under EU law. This will, however, need to be sanctioned by the arbitral tribunal. One can reasonably ask the investor to engage judicial proceedings which offer an equivalent scope of protection (cf. *supra*). The sanction could e.g. be introduced by deeming an act lawful under EU law until it has been challenged by an investor. In this case, the investor loses the possibility to demonstrate that the act was unlawful under EU law. Hence, the only possibility for the investor to succeed with its claim would be to rebut the presumption, which, as will be demonstrated *infra*, may be particularly difficult when not seeking judicial protection under EU law.

II. Downgrade in the level of protection

The first exception where the *Bosphorus-Presumption* shall not apply any longer is the general downgrade in the level of protection under EU law (*continuous overall control of the equivalence*). However, this seems to be more of a theoretical issue. This scenario would e.g. apply if either the CJEU considerably restricts its application of e.g. the Charter of Fundamental Rights on the member states or if EU law is amended to such a degree that equivalence would no longer be justifiable. However, continuous overall control is necessary to ensure that the principle of *pacta sunt servanda,* which renders the IIA fully applicable in the relations between member states and non-member states is not set aside. Only as long as the EU provides for an overall equivalent protection the presumption may apply. This shall not mean that any arbitral tribunal needs to reconsider the equivalence. If an investor wants to rebut the presumption based on the argument of a general downgrade in the level of protection, it should be forced to denominate the (grave) changes in EU law which would lead to such general downgrade compared to the *status quo*.

III. Considerable lack of protection in the particular case depriving the investor of any protection

The second exception where the *Bosphorus-Presumption* shall not apply is of more practical importance and an essential feature of the overall suggestion. The investor should be enabled to demonstrate that *in the case at hand*, EU law does not provide any sufficient protection. The burden of proof to demonstrate this lack of protection, should be entirely attributed to the investor.

The overall approach should be flexible enough to enable the arbitral tribunal to take into consideration changing circumstances and facts. However, three guidelines and general remarks will be pointed out regarding the implementation of this approach:

First, the lack of protection regarding particular facts, e.g. because EU law will not grant legitimate protection under *these particular circumstances or a particular case* will *not* be considered as an indirect expropriation, should not *per se* lead to rebutting the presumption. The term *equivalence* itself demonstrates that there could be differences in the assessment of a particular level of protection regarding the facts of the case at hand. Hence, a considerable lack of protection in the concrete circumstances will require demonstration that the protection offered by EU law regarding a particular measure is either completely missing or manifestly deficient. *Inter alia*, a difference in the balancing of particular interests may never justify rebutting the presumption.

Second, from the assessment of the current level of protection, one might only perceive four options under which such an assessment may eventually succeed, given that there is no settled case law yet on that particular regard.

- First, if the CJEU – in a particular case – will accept compensation for expropriation which is far below the real market value. The threshold should *inter alia* be fixed below 50%.
- Second, if EU law will substantially limit the protection under the non-discrimination principle, e.g. accepting that a non-member state national can *per se* not be compared to a member state national, this would render the non-discrimination argument useless under EU law.
- Third, if relating to particular guarantees provided for in the IIA (e.g. due to a specific wording which is considerably broader than the typical scope of protection which was analysed in this thesis), EU law does not enable any protection mechanism which reveals to be at least equivalent.
- Finally, in situations in which due to an indirectly controlled investment, judicial protection cannot be obtained under EU law (as a result of the potential divergence between the notion of investment under an IIA and the protection offered under EU law), the investor should be able to refer to the full protection under the IIA. However, it has been demonstrated that such situations are more of theoretical nature.

The last exception where the *Bosphorus-Presumption* shall not apply is to a manifest deficiency of protection shall be the case of a denial of justice having occurred in the national proceedings where the investor claimed the violation of EU law. This procedural side of protection should be addressed in the following section, given the particular court system in the EU.

IV. Denial of justice: forcing the EU member states to grant sufficient procedural protection

Applying the *Bosphorus-Presumption* to matters of investment law enables shifting the attention for investment protection to the procedural guarantees under EU law. The predominant criticism regarding the court system under EU law is related to its partial reliance on the national courts of member states, therefore not constituting a genuine supra-national court system. It has already been demonstrated that EU law provides for particular additional mechanisms to compensate these structural difficulties.

However, when applying the *Bosphorus-Presumption* in investment proceedings, a further safeguard should be implemented. This could even strengthen the guarantees for the investor. The *Bosphorus-Presumption* shall be rebutted if the investor demonstrates a denial of justice, which either translates via the non-availability of judicial relief against the measure, the obviously missing prospect of success or the wilful disregard of fundamental procedural guarantees, such as guaranteed by Art. 47 of the Charter. This may also include cases in which, contrary to Art. 19 (1) TEU and Art. 47 of the Charter, a legal remedy is not implemented by the member states.[1735]

It is evident that this objection will only be applicable to those investors which have previously sought judicial protection under EU law. However, if, after exhausting potential remedies, including the (potentially denied) references to the CJEU, the investor was deprived of its rights due to a denial of justice of the national courts (which has not been compensated by superior courts), the presumption of lawfulness will be rebutted due to the *violation of the procedural safeguards in the concrete case*. It should be noted that denial of justice does not necessarily require to exhaust all

1735 This idea, which is mainly based on the fact that under an equivalent protection protection is more reduced to procedural aspects, may also be observed in the drafting of the FET standard in the CETA agreement. The draft artice enumerates several measures to be considered as a breach of the FET, which (nearly) exclusively relate to denial of either administrative of judicial due process or purely arbitrary measures, cf.: *Lentner*, JOLAS No. 2 (2014), 156, 159; cf. for the underlying idea of the waiving of local remedies with reference to "*developped states*": *Sattorova*, LIEI Vol. 39, No. 2 (2012), 223, 231 ff underlining the importance of due process. However, in recent investment arbitration proceedings, the acknowledgement of a denial of justice remains rather rare, as the tribunals often focus on other potential breaches of the IIA (cf.: *IA Reporter Team*, IA Reporter Vol. 8, No. 26 (2015), 17, 20. Recently in an intra-EU case, the ICSID-Tribunal however held that such denial occurred: *Dan Cake S.A. vs. Hungary*, 24.08.2015 – ICSID Case No. ARB/12/9 - Decision on jurisdiction and Liability, para 146 ff. This also seems to be applied by the ECtHR when evaluating the manifest deficiency, cf.: *Janik*, ZaöVR, 2010, 127, 167.

available remedies, where those remedies are inefficient or obviously without prospect of success.[1736]

The approach presents two particular advantages:

First, the criteria leading to a denial of justice are commonly agreed in various systems of (national and international) law, including EU law, investment law and the ECHR. By reference to the various cases decided under these frameworks, both, investors and host states may have clear guidelines of conduct for national tribunals. Upon violation of these guidelines, the investor may claim full damages.

Second, this approach would incentivise national court systems to effectively implement EU law and the substantive guarantees contained therein, as this would lead to the presumption of lawfulness under concurring legal frameworks.[1737] In order to avoid conflicting situations, EU member states would have a further reason to ensure the proper application of EU law within their domestic judicial frameworks.

C. The required dialogue of the judges

The application of the *Bosphorus-Presumption* in investment arbitration proceedings would also require the cooperation of European courts when confronted with an award being rendered based on the presumption. The *Bosphorus-Presumption* – if correctly applied by the arbitral tribunals – would ensure that questions of EU law and especially the compliance of EU member states with mandatory provisions of EU law, would in principle be respected by arbitral tribunals. Only those cases which translate by grave disregards of the investor's rights, or situations in which the member state's acts *de facto* have not been the result of mandatory require-

1736 This is a rule which is even agreed upon under customary international law regarding the epousal and diplomatic protection system, cf.: *Sattorova*, LIEI Vol. 39, No. 2 (2012), 223, 235-237; the general rule was also established by the CJEU, cf.: *CJEU*, 08.03.2001 – Joined cases C-397/98 and C-410/98 - Metallgesellschaft = ECLI:EU:C:2001:134, para 102-106; *CJEU*, 24.03.2009 – C-445/06 - Danske = ECLI:EU:C:2009:178, para 62 f.

1737 Although in another setting, the idea of incentivising the other legal framework to guarantee certain standards by the applicaiton of the Bosphorus / Solange approach is also discussed by *Lang*, Der EuGH und die Investor-Staat-Streitbeilegung in TTIP und CETA (Beit. zum Transnat. Wirt.-R, Vol. 138, 2015), p. 20-22; similarily a coordinated approach of the CJEU and arbitral tribunals is favored by: *Schill*, JWIT Vol. 16, No. 3 (2015), 379, 386.

ments of EU law, will lead to awards attributing compensation to the investors. When faced with such cases, e.g. in setting-aside or enforcement proceedings, the European courts should also refrain from full control over awards and limit themselves to control whether:

- the presumption was applied;
- the tribunal did not commit manifest errors in applying this presumption.

In all other cases, the courts should refrain from any interference. There would also be no necessity to do so. As tribunals will regularly not apply and interpret provisions of EU law (except to determine the mandatory character, which can be easily controlled), the spillover effects on EU law would be considerably reduced, which could also deprive the jurisdictional objection based on the "*invalidity of the arbitration clause*" as one of the set-aside grounds of its force. Second, the presumption should in principle guarantee that no fundamental provisions of EU law should be misapplied by the tribunal and hence also render less effective the objection based on the violation of *ordre public*.

D. Conformity of the solution with the interests in question

The solution matches with the several interests in question which have been developed as benchmarks *supra* (Chapter 5, D, II.). First, through the application of the *Bosphorus-Presumption*, the principles of the diverging legal instruments are preserved to its most possible extent. As to EU law, regarding mandatory acts which are considered lawful under EU law, arbitral tribunal would in principle not challenge these acts. Only in particular circumstances, such as a denial of justice, which would also be contrary to EU law guarantees, the IIAs would fully apply. The impediment on the principle of supremacy which results from the full application of the IIA in situations where EU law does not offer any protection at all in the particular case, are of minor importance and need to be accepted to reduce the overall frictions. From the perspective of international investment law, the inherent principles remain protected as well. First, the IIA remains fully in force and *per se* applicable. Only for those acts where EU member states are mandated to undertake a certain measure, the presumption applies. Given that both frameworks reveal to offer equivalent protection, the *de facto* difference for the investor should be minimal. If the measure is illegal under EU law, protection will be obtained by EU law. If it is lawful, the presumption can still be rebutted if the level of protection is insufficient or in the case of a denial of justice.

Furthermore, the solution complies with the parties' interests. First, EU member states entered into conventional obligations under an IIA. Hence, in principal they need to accept being submitted to the restrictions which are derived thereof. In the particular case where they cannot fulfil both obligations, they will in principle be exempted as long as they comply with EU law, including in the domestic court proceedings (i.e. also provide sufficient procedural protection in the concrete case). However, also the EU member states' particular interest in entering into a regional cooperation within the EU will be honoured by the solution. Regarding investors, the level of protection obtained is considerably high. As demonstrated, the presumption will only apply as long as EU law guarantees an equivalent overall protection and as long as this protection was also offered in the case at hand. Applying the presumption will only eliminate those claims which are *de facto* based on forum shopping by certain investors, as they seek to enforce a level of protection on the detriment of the host states' legitimate interests.

Lastly, the solution is sustainable in the long term, as soon as it is consequently applied. It will reduce the risk of setting-aside arbitral awards due to potential conflicts with EU law. On the other hand, member states could keep their system of IIAs, until a coherent external policy was agreed upon by the EU and its member states.

Part IV: Outlook regarding the EU's future investment policy

The previously demonstrated conflicts and their solutions regarding intra-EU and extra-EU IIAs can only be a starting point for a more in-depth discussion regarding the future of investment protection within the EU. While this thesis deliberately focused on the existing IIAs, the solutions reveal to be of major importance for the EU's future investment policy, especially through the conclusion of comprehensive trade agreements such as TTIP, CETA or the EUSFTA.

These agreements reveal similar difficulties and raise identical issues as those regarding intra-EU and extra-EU IIAs treated *supra*, both regarding the member states' *inter se* relations as well as the external relations. At first glance, such mixed agreements could be understood as a combination of various intra-EU and extra-EU IIAs in one comprehensive agreement. Hence, given the aforementioned findings, this would rise the following issues to consider:

If such agreements should generally include references to mixed arbitration mechanisms, they need to be rendered compatible with the principle of autonomy of the EU's legal order and its specific characteristics. Otherwise, a judgement of the CJEU, rejecting to endorse the mixed arbitration mechanism, may, similar as in the context of the EU's accession to the ECHR (economically and politically) ruin long lasting negotiations with important trading partners.[1738] The recent communication of several member states regarding a (major) reform of the dispute settlement mechanism, e.g. through establishing a permanent court for investment arbitration in La Hague, is a first step to start a debate about these difficulties.[1739] Hopefully, the CJEU's judgment in the preliminary questions regarding the *Achmea-Case* will provide further clarifications. If (which should also be debated) mixed arbitration should be a distinctive feature of these fu-

1738 *Lenk*, EJLS Vol. 8, No. 2 (2015), 6, 14 f; *Lang*, Der EuGH und die Investor-Staat-Streitbeilegung in TTIP und CETA (Beit. zum Transnat. Wirt.-R, Vol. 138, 2015), p. 16 ff.

1739 Cf. Non-paper from Austria, Finland, France, Germany and the Netherlands, presented to the European Council on 01.10.2015 [not publicly available – obtainable through acess to documents service of the European Commission].

ture agreements, further research is necessary to develop adequate mechanisms which consider the CJEU's concerns in this regard.[1740]

Those agreements also lead to a more general question which addresses the structure of mixed agreements and their applicability in the inter se relations, a question which is already matter of debate in the context of the ECT. It can indeed be questioned if the member states, by concluding mixed agreements (such as the ECT and the future agreements), agreed to set up an additional protection mechanism for investors besides the European Treaties.[1741] Some argue that those agreements contain an implicit disconnection clause, others firmly reject this approach.[1742] If the latter approach is favoured, the question of conflicting obligations regarding the member states *inter se* reoccurs.

However, also in the external context, there are remaining concerns how to reconcile the member states' obligations under EU law and the obligations from such future agreements. For agreements concluded by the EU, Art. 351 TFEU may not be invoked. Such agreements are binding upon the EU and its member states. However, as duly demonstrated, this may lead to a dead-lock situation for the member states. It seems as if the negotiators in the CETA and TTIP agreement wish to address this issue by reshaping protection standards.[1743] However, it is highly doubtful if one can address the multitude of potentially conflicting obligations in such clauses without rendering the entire scope of protection useless. Hence, the recognition of the difficulties in this context can only be the first step to resolve them.

1740 The idea to completely reshape the investment dispute settlement mechanism is e.g. advanced by: *Hindelang*, AVR Vol. 53 (2015), 68; cf. also: *Schill*, JWIT Vol. 16, No. 3 (2015), 379; cf. also: *Peterson/Dahlquist*, IA Reporter Vol. 9, No. 6 (2016), 2, 3 ff.

1741 *Kulick*, SchiedsVZ, 2013, 81, 86 ff argues in favour of an implicit disconnection clause in the ECT; similar, or at least arguing that this should be the path to follow: *Kleinheisterkamp*, JIEL Vol. 15, No. 1 (2012), 85 104 f.

1742 Against this approach and considering that mixed agreements apply fully in the inter se relations: *Tietje*, Applicability of the ECT in ICSID Arbitration (Beit. zum Transnat. Wirt.-R, Vol. 78, 2008), 5, 10 ff; recently: *Tietje/Wackernagel*, JWIT Vol. 16, Iss. 2 (2015), 205, 227 f.

1743 Cf. for a comprehensive overview: *Clodfelter*, Santa Clara Jour. of Int. Law Vol. 12, Iss. 1 (2013), 159, 163-165; cf. also: *Hoffmeister/Alexandru*, JWIT Vol. 15 (2014), 379 for the content of the currently negotiated agreements; cf. also: *Peterson/Dahlquist*, IA Reporter Vol. 9, No. 6 (2016), 2, 3 ff.

Despite these questions, the negotiations in the TTIP and CETA context predominantly seem to address the criticisms provided by the civil society, including the transparency of the proceedings and the establishment of an appeal mechanism to unify the application and interpretation of protection standards.[1744] However, the aforementioned difficulties question the overall approach and should be at least at an equivalent level with the other concerns relating to the procedural implementation of investor state arbitration.

1744 Similarly: *Lenk*, EJLS Vol. 8, No. 2 (2015), 6, 13 f.

Conclusion

In the following, the different theses which were developed in the previous chapters will be briefly summarised:

Thesis no.1 (Part I): EU law and international investment law are competing and conflicting legal frameworks

International investment protection in the EU is characterised by an overlapping framework of IIAs and EU law, which both intend to protect investors against harmful state measures. Both systems grew in parallel but have not been set up in a coordinate approach.

1. Sub-Thesis (Chapter 1 and 2): Investment protection through IIAs was conceived as a counter-movement to several shortcomings in previously established investment protection mechanisms (such as the international minimum standard or FCN treaties). IIAs provide for a specialised mechanism of investment protection through offering wide ranging substantive guarantees and procedural enforcement through an immediate access to international arbitration proceedings for the investor (e.g. under the ICSID-Convention or private arbitration forums (ICC, SCC, etc.)).

2. Sub-Thesis (Chapter 3 and 4): The rise of the EU since 1958 has established an additional framework for investors within the EU member states through the ongoing integration and the construction of the internal market. EU law seeks to protect economic activity and unhindered competition within the internal market. Especially the freedom of establishment and the free movement of capital protect economic operators from harmful interventions of EU member states on their business activities. Since the Charter of Fundamental Rights of the EU became binding in 2009, the right to property and the freedom to conduct business provide further guarantees for economic operators (and hence investors). Procedural protection is guaranteed by a coordinated system of legal protection, partially relying on EU member states' national courts but *in fine* implementing an interpretative authority and final recourse to the CJEU regarding matters of application validity and interpretation of EU law.

Both frameworks however have not been built up in a coordinate approach. Their potential interferences have never been expressly addressed so far.

3. Sub-Thesis (Chapter 5 – 1st and 2nd sub-chapter): The separate legal frameworks of EU law and international investment law may conflict, regarding both, procedural provisions and substantive guarantees.

Although both, EU law and IIAs, primarily seek to protect investors, they might enter into conflict. Conflicts arise when an EU member state cannot fulfil its obligations under EU law and the IIA simultaneously. This occurs, whenever EU law mandates member states to undertake a certain (scope of) action(s) which necessarily lead(s) to violate the IIA or whenever a provision or guarantee expressly granted under one framework is prohibited in the second framework. Conflicts may be observed regarding the procedural protection (the investor's access to arbitration through the arbitration clause) or the substantive guarantees (the protection standards) of an IIA. The conflict of EU law with the investor's access to arbitration is of general concern as the access to mixed arbitration itself may violate EU law, whereas conflicts regarding substantive guarantees largely depend on the particular facts of the case. The latter may especially occur due to particular provisions of EU law, which are of more interventionist character and seek to establish a balance between economic activities and other (public) interest (*inter alia* revoking a benefit previously attributed to the investor as the benefit is qualified as state aid may violate the FET standard or constitute an indirect expropriation).

4. Sub-Thesis (Chapter 5 – 3rd sub-chapter): These conflicts may interfere with investment arbitration proceedings or subsequent proceedings by various means and cast doubt on the successful enforcement of an award ignoring these conflicts.

Ignoring the conflict of EU law and IIAs in the arbitration proceedings is unconceivable as EU law may interfere with the proceedings by numerous means: Beside the consequences on the jurisdictional and merits stage of the main investment proceedings before an arbitral tribunal, objections such as the incompatibility of the arbitration clause or substantive guarantees with EU law may also occur within the subsequent proceedings. With regard to ICSID-Awards, the manifest lack of powers is a ground for annulment in the annulment proceedings, which enable to reintroduce objections related to the tribunal's jurisdiction or the applicable law. The uncertainties as to the relationship of Art. 53, 54 of the ICSID-Convention (which generally grant unhindered enforcement of an award) and the principle of supremacy in EU law, cast further doubts on the enforceability of an award contrary to EU law at least within EU member states. Arbitration in private forums (ICC, SCC, etc.) is subject to setting-aside proceedings in the state of the tribunal's seat and enforcement proceedings in all states the award should be enforced in. In these national proceedings, the same objections may be raised, referring to either the invalidity of the arbitration clause or the violation of public interest in the respective state (which as to the CJEU, includes the respect of mandatory provisions of EU law). An award rendered in violation of EU law may hence at least potentially be set aside or denied enforcement.

5. Sub-Thesis (Chapter 5 – 4th sub-chapter): Correctly addressing conflicts between EU law and international investment law requires to distinguish between the intra-EU and extra-EU context

Whereas in an intra-EU context all relevant actors are EU member states (which are bound by the European Treaties and an IIA), the extra-EU context includes an EU member state and a non-member state (which is not bound by the European Treaties). This difference in the involved actors justifies to separately address the conflicts, as different set of rules will apply in each context. However, the general interests in question remain the same. Any solution to the aforementioned conflict should observe the fundamental principles of both legal frameworks (e.g. *pacta sunt servanda* but also the principle of primacy), the parties' interests (a fair level of investment protection and the host state's interest to comply with its obligations under both frameworks) as well as the sustainability of the solution in practice.

Thesis no. 2 (Part II): In intra-EU arbitration proceedings, arbitral tribunals lack jurisdiction due to the IIA's arbitration clause being incompatible with EU law; in any case arbitral tribunals will need to respect the principle of supremacy of EU law when dealing with the merits of an investment claim

1. Sub-thesis (Chapter 6): EU law could interfere with the arbitral tribunal's jurisdiction or the merits of the proceedings by rendering the arbitration clause (and hence the host state's consent to arbitration) or substantive guarantees invalid; this however requires that EU law is qualified as international law applicable to the dispute.

Investment arbitration disputes are based on IIAs as international conventions between states. They contain the host state's consent to arbitration (which might then be accepted by the investor, e.g. through filing the claim) and substantive protection standards (which may engage the host state's liability). Generally domestic law may not set aside an international convention (cf. Art. 27 VCLT). However, if EU law can be qualified as international law, any arbitral tribunal would need to take into account the consequences EU law might have for the IIA. If EU law renders the entire IIA void or inapplicable, the host state's consent to arbitration as well as any substantive guarantee would be evaded. If EU law renders particular provisions of the IIA void or inapplicable, the tribunal may either lack jurisdiction (if the arbitration clause is void or inapplicable) or substantive protection standards may not be applied (if these standards are void or inapplicable).

2. Sub-Thesis (Chapter 7): EU law, despite its particularities, must still be qualified as international law which is applicable to the investment dispute (at the jurisdictional and at the merits stage).

EU law has several distinctive characters compared to traditional international law, such as the principles of autonomy, supremacy and direct effect. Also, the ability of European institutions to issue secondary law on various subject matters (which is then binding on member states) grants formerly unknown powers to the EU. However, EU law, despite these characteristics, remains rooted in international law and still needs to be qualified as such. The entire legal framework of EU law and its institutions operates within the boundaries set by the European Treaties, which are subject to (unanimous) amendments by EU member states. Each member state remains free to implement EU law or to quit the EU. The particular *inter se* principles of direct effect, supremacy and autonomy constitute principles intending to enforce the unanimous application of EU law within member states. However, the state's choice of a particular mechanism which ensures the observance of their *inter se* relations, cannot disqualify the entire framework of being international law.

3. Sub-Thesis (Chapter 8): The conflict between two competing frameworks of international law (EU law and IIAs) in an intra-EU context needs to be resolved by referring to the principle of supremacy as an inherent conflict rule agreed upon by EU member states

Conflicts of different legal frameworks on the international level need to be resolved by referring to conflict rules. States may mutually agree on conflict rules, which determine the priority of several provisions on others. If such rules are missing, Art. 30 and 59 VCLT constitute default rules. In the intra-EU context, a conjoint reading of Art. 351 and 350 TFEU as well as the jurisprudence of the CJEU reveal the underlying principle of supremacy to be the applicable (inherent) conflict rule between EU member states. In their respective relations, EU member states agreed upon the fundamental principle that any rule which hinders EU law to take full effect, may not be applied. This applies both to member states' national laws or to intra-EU international agreements (such as IIAs). The principle of primacy only requires a conflicting provision to remain unapplied. Hence, it does not render IIAs void. However, conflicting provisions of the IIA cannot be applied between EU member states.

4. Sub-Thesis (Chapter 9): By agreeing on a mixed dispute settlement mechanism in IIAs, EU member states violate EU law. Three potential violations need to be assessed. First, the potential violation of EU law by infringing on an exclusive competence attributed to the EU. Second, the compatibility of the IIA's arbitration clause with the autonomy of the EU's legal order and its specific characteristics. Third the potential violation of the principle of non-discrimination. The IIA's arbitration clause violates the principle of non-discrimination and the specific autonomy of EU law. Given the principle of supremacy as relevant conflict rule, the IIA's arbitration clause needs to be set aside and the arbitral tribunal lacks jurisdiction.

Analysing potential incompatibilities of EU law and arbitration clauses contained in IIAs, reveals that by agreeing upon such clauses, member states did not violate an exclusive competence of the EU. Although the CJEU ruled in the *Pringle-Case*, that such infringements on the EU's competence may render an *inter se* agreement incompatible with EU law, the EU did not hold an exclusive competence with regard to dispute settlement clauses contained in intra-EU IIAs.

However, arbitration clauses contained in IIAs conflict with the principle of autonomy of the EU's legal order and its specific characteristics. Although not every dispute settlement mechanism outside the European Treaties is incompatible with EU law, mixed arbitration's impediment on the autonomy of EU law and its specific characteristics is of such severity, that it reveals to be contrary to EU law. These impediments are *inter alia* characterised by the degree to which the preliminary ruling procedure is circumvented. Furthermore, mixed arbitration may lead to *de facto* contradicting interpretations of EU law between the arbitral tribunals and the CJEU, which may considerably alter the uniform application of EU law. Lastly, mixed arbitration also reveals to be contrary to the principle of mutual trust.

Arbitration clauses contained in IIAs also violate the principle of non-discrimination. The choice offered to an investor between national and arbitral proceedings is a benefit, which is granted to several investors only (that are part of a member state having concluded an IIA). This difference in treatment cannot be justified. The discrimination cannot be resolved by extending the benefit to all investors. This extension would further support the aforementioned impediment on the autonomy of the EU's legal order. Hence, the discrimination can only be resolved by denying effect to the arbitration clause.

Consequently, EU law renders the arbitration clause invalid. An arbitral tribunal, sought with an intra-EU investment dispute, hence lacks jurisdiction.

5. Sub-Thesis (Chapter 10): Supposed for the sake of the argument, that an arbitral tribunal would not deny its jurisdiction, any conflict between EU member states' obligations under an IIA and EU law needs to be resolved in favour of the latter (given the principle of primacy as inherent conflict rule).

If the arbitral tribunal does not decline its jurisdiction, given the principle of primacy as the relevant conflict rule in intra-EU proceedings, EU member states cannot be held liable for breaches of the IIA, if the breach results from an implementation of mandatory provisions of EU law. This also includes the hypothesis that the EU member state may (under EU law) exercise discretion (e.g. when implementing EU law) but all eligible actions violate the IIA.

6. Sub-Thesis (Chapter 11): This result cannot be altered by reference to the investors' personal rights or sunset / survival clauses contained in an IIA.

Although the investor is a (partial) subject of international law, its rights remain mediated through the IIA and may be revoked by mutual consent of the contracting parties to an IIA. This is underlined by the character of IIAs as reciprocal agreements on the protection of investments as means to foster the economic development in the respective host state. Contrary to human rights, the investor's rights are entirely based on the IIA (and hence a conventional agreement) and not conceived as universal, underlying rights. Hence, they can be revoked by the contracting parties. This includes the right to revoke a previously stipulated survival clause. Through the accession to the EU the member states agreed to revoke such rights.

Thesis no. 3 (Part III): In extra-EU arbitration proceedings EU law may not alter the validity of an IIA; however, given the numerous interferences EU law may have upon an investment claim, the Bosphorus approach of the ECtHR should be transposed to extra-EU arbitration proceedings as long as EU member states execute mandatory provisions of EU law

1. Sub-Thesis (Chapter 12): Extra-EU IIAs remain fully valid from a public international law perspective; however, from an internal, EU member states' perspective, IIAs cannot claim full primacy on EU law.

In the extra-EU context, a dual perspective needs to be adopted. From the perspective of public international law, extra-EU IIAs remain fully valid as the European Treaties are not applicable to both contracting parties. Nevertheless, from an internal (EU law) perspective, IIAs cannot claim full primacy. Art. 351 (1) TFEU generally acknowledges the primacy of obligations from extra-EU IIAs, which have been concluded before the 1st of January 1958 (or accession of member states to the EU (*prior* IIAs)). However, regarding extra-EU IIAs being concluded after the 1st of January 1958 or a member state's accession (*posterior* IIAs), Art. 351 TFEU cannot be applied, at least regarding provisions of EU law already being in force at the time of the conclusion of the *posterior* IIA. With regard to these IIAs, EU law claims primacy.

Furthermore, in the *Kadi-Case* the CJEU concluded that Art. 351 (1) TFEU, irrespective of the time the treaty was concluded, cannot allow any obligation to touch upon the foundations of the EU's legal order (including its autonomy). Hence, whenever a tribunal needs to take into account the internal (EU law) perspective, the conflicts between EU law and IIAs may reappear.

2. Sub-Thesis (Chapter 13 – 1st to 3rd sub-chapter): EU law cannot be applicable to extra-EU IIA arbitration proceedings as international law (as it is not applicable to both parties in the conflict); however, due to its dual nature, it may still apply as domestic law of the host state. As such EU law needs to be taken into account at various occasions even in extra-EU investment dispute proceedings.

EU law cannot be regarded as international law applicable to the dispute in extra-EU investment proceedings, as it is not applicable to both parties. However, it may apply as part of the host state's domestic law. This may be relevant whenever the parties chose to apply international law and domestic law to the dispute or whenever the arbitral tribunal has its seat within EU member states. In this later hypothesis, EU law is applied as *lex loci arbitri* and may render the arbitration clause invalid. However, this later scenario does not apply to ICSID-Proceedings, as they are delocalised and do not contain any reference to the *lex loci arbitri*.

Besides these general considerations, EU law may also interfere with the arbitration proceedings in two distinct manners. First, to obtain protection under an IIA, investments need to be made *"in accordance with the law of the host states"*. Manifestly illegal investments are refused protection. Several substantial provisions of EU law, such as the state aid rules and general competition law constitute such fundamental rules with regard to investments, as they set up the general level playing field for all (domestic or foreign) investors within the internal market. Violation of these rules upon establishment, results in denying protection under an IIA to this particular investment.

Additionally, the FET standard requires to take into account the conformity with substantive rules of the host state and even certain future changes of the legal framework, when correctly determining the scope of legitimate expectations under the protection standard. An investor cannot legitimately expect the host state to violate substantial provisions of EU law, such as the state aid, public procurement or competition law rules but also the relevant rules establishing a certain environment for business sectors (such as e.g. the energy market directives).

3. Sub-Thesis (Chapter 13 – 4th sub-chapter): Even only being considered as domestic law of the host state, EU law may widely interfere with the protection offered by an IIA, if it is completely ignored in the proceedings.

Ignoring the internal, *unionist* perspective in arbitration proceedings may result in setting-aside the award or denying its enforcement when national courts of EU member states are sought with such proceedings. Also, the recent decision by the European Commission in the *Micula-Case* demonstrates a further obstacle, as the Commission considered the member state's compliance with an award disrespecting the Art. 107 ff TFEU to constitute itself prohibited state aid and hence prevented the member state to comply with the award. In the long term, EU member states are dead-locked. They cannot comply with both obligations. Hence, they will be either forced to reconsider their membership within the EU or their system of investment protection through IIAs.

4. Sub-Thesis (Chapter 14): The specific character of the EU as a supranational organisation and the host state's reduced margin of action *vis-à-vis* to acts under EU law, justifies to transpose the approach adopted in the *Bosphorus-Decision* by the ECtHR to extra-EU conflicts.

Analysing the reasons of this dead-locked situation, one can observe that the situation of EU member states is different from the traditional setting under international law. Generally national acts may not justify the violation of obligations on the international level (cf. Art. 27 VCLT). This idea is based on the premise, that the state can fully determine all of its actions. Regarding supra-national organisations, this premise fails. Upon accession and transferal of competences, EU member states lost their discretion regarding particular fields of action, which leads to the aforementioned conflicts. The ECtHR based its decision in the *Bosphorus-Case* on the principle of *systematic integration,* which seeks to take the reciprocally overlapping obligations into account and acknowledges that international conventions cannot be interpreted as being self-contained regimes. This approach should also be applied to the conflict of EU law and extra-EU-IIAs.

Transposing the *Bosphorus* approach leads to acknowledging the primacy of an IIA, but to reduce the margin of control exercised by arbitral tribunals if several conditions are fulfilled, i.e. an equivalent level of substantive and procedural protection under both frameworks.

The *Bosphorus* approach accepts that the IIA remains fully in force. However, as long as EU law would guarantee an equivalent level of substantial and procedural protection, an act being mandatory (and lawful) under EU law is presumed being in conformity with the obligations under the IIA as well. This presumption can be rebutted if either the level of protection under EU law (in future) reveals to be insufficient or if the protection is manifestly deficient in the particular case.

5. Sub-Thesis (Chapter 15): EU law and IIAs offer equivalent substantive and procedural protection regarding acts being determined by EU law.

Comparing the level of protection regarding acts being mandatory under EU law, reveals that the substantive protection is at least equivalent under both frameworks. Especially the protection offered under Art. 16 (freedom to conduct business) and Art. 17 (right to property) of the Charter, as well as the free movement of capital, the principle of non-discrimination (Art 20 of the Charter) and the general principles of fair trial, due process and legal security offer an equivalent level of protection under EU law when compared to substantive protection guarantees contained in IIAs.

The procedural protection offered by EU law and IIAs reveals to be equivalent as well. Equivalence of procedural guarantees cannot require to offer a mixed arbitration mechanism under EU law. Equivalence needs to be understood as requiring a mechanism which guarantees the effective enforcement of the investor's substantive protection standards. From this perspective, EU law and IIAs offer an equivalent procedural protection as well. Procedural enforcement of substantive standards under EU law is either guaranteed by a direct action to the CJEU (Art. 263 TFEU) or by virtue of the interaction of national courts with the CJEU through the preliminary ruling procedure. The correct and uniform application of guarantees provided by EU law is further supplemented by the right to a fair trial, the infringement proceedings and the possibility to engage the extra-contractual liability of member states violating EU law which set up a supra-national framework of procedural rules the member state needs to observe.

6. Sub-Thesis (Chapter 16): Implementing the *Bosphorus* approach in extra-EU arbitration proceedings requires a balanced distribution of the burden of proof and a dialogue of the different courts involved which strengthens the importance of due process in implementing investment protection under EU law.

When implementing this approach, the tribunal will need to balance the burden of proof regarding the mandatory character of an act under EU law (which should in principle be borne by EU member states) and the manifest deficiency (borne by the investor). Denial of justice will take a predominant place within this context. It guarantees that investors may enforce their rights under the IIA when national courts of a member states, despite their obligations under EU law, did not respect guarantees under EU law or their duty to interact with the CJEU. On the other side, European courts should respect the choice by arbitral tribunals when the presumption is applied and reduce their control on arbitral awards as well. Only manifest disregards of EU law when applying the presumption should enable to question the validity of the award.

Arbitral Awards

Asian Agricultural Products Ltd. (United Kingdom) vs. Republic of Sri Lanka, referred to as: *AAP vs. Sri Lanka*, 27.06.1990 – ICSID Case No. ARB/87/3 - Final Award

Achmea B.V. (formerly Eureko B.V.) (The Netherlands) vs. The Slovak Republic, UNCITRAL, referred to as: *Achmea vs. Slovak Republic*, 26.10.2012 – PCA Case No. 2008-13 - Award on Jurisdiction, Arbitrability and Suspension

Achmea B.V. (formerly Eureko B.V.) (The Netherlands) vs. The Slovak Republic, UNCITRAL, referred to as: *Achmea vs. Slovak Republic*, 07.12.2012 – PCA Case No. 2008-13 - Award

ADC Affiliate Limited and ADC & ADMC Management Limited (Republic of Cyprus) vs. The Republic of Hungary, referred to as: *ADC vs. Hungary*, 02.10.2006 – ICSID Case No. ARB/03/16 - Award

AES Summit Generation Limited (United Kingdom) and AES-Tisza Erömü Kft vs. The Republic of Hungary, referred to as: *AES Summit vs. Hungary*, 23.09.2010 – ICSID Case No. ARB/07/22 - Award

Aguas del Tunari, S.A. (The Netherlands) vs. Republic of Bolivia,, referred to as: *Aguas del Tunaris vs. Bolivia*, 21.10.2005 – ICSID Case No. ARB/02/3 - Decision on Respondent's Objections to Jurisdiction

Alex Genin, Eastern Credit Limited, Inc. and A.S. Baltoil (United States of America) vs. The Republic of Estonia, referred to as: *Alex Genin et al vs. Estonia*, 25.06.2001 – ICSID Case No. ARB/99/2 - Award

Alasdair Ross Anderson et al (Canada) vs. Republic of Costa Rica, referred to as: *Anderson vs. Costa Rica*, 19.05.2010 – ICSID Case No. ARB(AF)/07/3 – Award

Austrian Airlines (Austria) vs. The Slovak Republic, UNCITRAL, referred to as: *Austrian Airlinces vs. Slovak Republic*, 09.10.2009 – UNCITRAL - Final Award

Archer Daniels Midland Company and Tate & Lyle Ingredients Americas, Inc. (United States of America) vs. The United Mexican States, referred to as: *ADM and Tate & Lyle vs. Mexico*, 21.11.2007 – ICSID Case No. ARB (AF)/04/5 - Award

Azurix Corp. (United States of America) vs. The Argentine Republic, referred to as: *Azurix Corp. vs. Argentina*, 08.12.2003 – ICSID Case No. ARB/01/12 - Decision on Jurisdiction

Azurix Corp. (United States of America) vs. The Argentine Republic, referred to as: *Azurix Corp. vs. Argentina*, 14.07.2006 – ICSID Case No. ARB/01/12 – Award

Mr. Binder (The Federal Republic of Germany) vs. The Czech Republic, referred to as: *Binder vs. Czech Republic*, 06.06.2007 – UNCITRAL - Award on Jurisdiction

Biwater Gauff (Tanzania) Ltd. (United Kingdom) vs. United Republic of Tanzania, referred to as: *Biwater Gauff vs. Tanzania*, 24.07.2008 – ICSID Case No. ARB/05/22 – Award

Cargill, Inc. (Unied States of America) vs. Republic of Poland, referred to as: *Cargill vs. Poland*, 01.03.2008 – UNCITRAL - Award

CME Czech Republic B.V. (The Netherlands) vs. The Czech Republic, referred to as: *CME vs. Czech Republic*, 13.09.2001 – UNCITRAL - Partial Award

CME Czech Republic B.V. (The Netherlands) vs. The Czech Republic, referred to as: *CME vs. Czech Republic*, 14.03.2003 – UNCITRAL - Final award

CMS Gas Transmission Company (United States of America) vs. The Republic of Argentina, referred to as: *CMS vs. Argentina*, 17.07.2003 – ICSID Case No. ARB/01/8 - Decision of the Tribunal on Objections to Jurisdiction

CMS Gas Transmission Company (United States of America) vs. The Republic of Argentina, referred to as: *CMS vs. Argentina*, 12.05.2005 – ICSID Case No. ARB/01/8 – Award

CMS Gas Transmission Company (United States of America) vs. The Republic of Argentina - Annullment Proceedings, referred to as: *Annullment Committee in CMS vs. Argentina*, 25.09.2007 – ICSID Case No. ARB/01/8 - Decision on Annulment

Compañiá dc Aguas del Aconquija S.A. and Vivendi Universal S.A. (formerly Compañía de Aguas del Aconquija, S.A. and Compagnie Générale des Eaux) (France) vs. Argentine Republic - Annullment Proceedings, referred to as: *Annulment Committee in Vivendi vs. Argentina*, 03.07.2002 – ICSID Case No. ARB/97/3 - Decision on Annulment

Consortium Groupement L.E.S.I.- DIPENTA (Italy) vs. République algérienne démocratique et populaire, referred to as: *LESI vs. Algeria*, 10.01.2005 – ICSID Case No. ARB/03/08 - Award

Contact Champion Trading Company, Ameritrade International, Inc. (formerly Champion Trading Company, Ameritrade International, Inc., James T. Wahba, John B. Wahba, Timothy T. Wahba) (United States of America) vs. Arab Republic of Egypt, referred to as: *Contact Champion Trading et al vs. Egypt*, 27.08.2006 – ICSID Case No. ARB/02/9 - Award

Continental Casualty Company (United States of America) vs. The Argentine Republic, referred to as: *Continental vs. Argentina*, 05.09.2008 – ICSID Case No. ARB/03/9 - Award

Corn Products International, Inc. (United States of America) vs. United Mexican States, referred to as: *Corn Products vs. Mexico*, 15.01.2208 – ICSID Case No. ARB (AF)/04/1 - Decision on Responsibility

Daimler Financial Services AG (The Federal Republic of Germany) vs. The Argentine Republic, referred to as: *Daimler Financial Services AG vs. Argentina*, 22.08.2012 – ICSID Case No. ARB/05/1 - Award

Dan Cake S.A. (Portugal) vs. The Republic of Hungary, referred to as: *Dan Cake S.A. vs. Hungary*, 24.08.2015 – ICSID Case No. ARB/12/9 - Decision on jurisdiction and Liability

Desert Line Projects LLC (Oman) vs. The Republic of Yemen, referred to as: *Desert Line vs. Yemen*, 06.02.2008 – ICSID Case No. ARB/05/17 – Award

Différend concernant l'Accord Tardieu-Jaspar, referred to as: *Belgium vs. France*, 01.03.1937 – Différend concernant l'Accord Tardieu-Jaspar, UN Reports of International Arbitration III, 1701

Duke Energy Electroquil Partners & Electroquil S.A. (United States of America) vs. Republic of Ecuador, referred to as: *Duke Energy vs. Ecuador*, 18.08.2008 – ICSID Case No. ARB/04/19 – Award

Eastern Sugar B.V. (The Netherlands) vs. The Czech Republic, referred to as: *Eastern Sugar vs. Czech Republic*, 27.03.2007 – SCC No. 088/2004 - Partial award

Edenred S.A. (France) vs. Republic of Hungary, referred to as: *Edenred S.A. vs. Hungary*, 13.12.2016 – ICSID Case No. ARB/13/21 - Award

EDF International S.A. (France) vs. Republic of Hungary, referred to as: *EDF vs. Hungary*, 04.12.2014 – UNCITRAL - Award

EDF (Services) Limited (United Kingdom) vs. Romania, referred to as: *EDF vs. Romania*, 08.10.2009 – ICSID Case No. ARB/05/13 - Award

El Paso Energy International Company (United States of America) vs. The Argentine Republic, referred to as: *El Paso vs. Argentina*, 31.11.2011 – ICSID Case No. ARB/03/15 - Award

El Paso Energy International Company (United States of America) vs. The Argentine Republic, referred to as: *El Paso vs. Argentina*, 27.04.2006 – ICSID Case No. ARB/03/15 - Decision on Jurisdiction

Electrabel S.A. (Kingdom of Belgium) vs. Republic of Hungary, referred to as: *Electrabel vs. Hungary*, 30.11.2012 – ICSID Case No. ARB/07/19: Decision on Jurisdiction, Applicable Law and Liability

Electrabel S.A. (Kingdom of Belgium) vs. Republic of Hungary, referred to as: *Electrabel vs. Hungary*, 25.11.2015 – ICSID Case No. ARB/07/19 – Award

Emilio Agustín Maffezini (The Argentine Republic) vs. The Kingdom of Spain, referred to as: *Maffezini vs. Spain*, 25.01.2000 – ICSID Case No. ARB/97/7 - Decision on Jurisdiction

Enron Corporation and Ponderosa Assets, L.P. (also known as: Enron Creditors Recovery Corp. and Ponderosa Assets, L.P.) (United States of America) vs. The Argentine Republic, referred to as: *Enron vs. Argentina*, 22.05.2007 – ICSID Case No. ARB/01/3 - Award

European American Investment Bank AG (Austria) vs. The Slovak Republic, referred to as: *Euram vs. Slovak Republic*, 22.10.2012 – PCA Case no. 2010-17: First Award on Jurisdiction

Eureko B.V. (The Netherlands) vs. Republic of Poland, referred to as: *Eureko vs. Poland*, 19.08.2005 – Ad Hoc Arbitration - Partial Award

Frontier Petroleum Services Ltd. (Canada) vs. The Czech Republic, referred to as: *FPS vs. Czech Republic*, 12.11.2010 – UNCITRAL - Final award

Fraport AG Frankfurt Airport Services Worldwide (The Federal Republic of Germany) vs. The Republic of the Philippines, referred to as: *Fraport vs. Philippines*, 16.08.2007 – ICSID Case No. ARB/03/25 – Award

Georg Nepolsky (The Federal Republic of Germany) vs. The Czech Republic, referred to as: *Nepolsky vs. Czech Republic*, 01.10.2010 – UNCITRAL - Award

Glamis Gold Ltd. (Canada) vs. The United States of America, referred to as: *Glamis Gold vs. United States*, 08.06.2009 – UNCITRAL - Award

Gustav F W Hamester GmbH & Co KG (The Federal Republic of Germany) vs. Republic of Ghana, referred to as: *Hamester vs. Ghana*, 18.06.2010 – ICSID Case No. ARB/07/24 – Award

Impregilo S.p.A. (Italy) vs. The Argentine Republic, referred to as: *Impregilo vs. Argentina*, 21.6.2011 – ICSID Case No. ARB/07/17 - Award

International Thunderbird Gaming Corporation (United States of America) vs. The United Mexican States, referred to as: *International Thunderbird Gaming Corporation vs. Mexico*, 26.01.2006 – UNCITRAL - Arbitral Award

Ioan Micula, Viorel Micula, S.C. European Food S.A, S.C. Starmill S.R.L. and S.C. Multipack S.R.L. (Sweden) vs. Romania, referred to as: *Ioan Micula, Viorel Micula & others vs. Romania*, 23.09.2008 – ICSID Case No. ARB/05/20 - Decision on Jurisdiction and Admissibility

Ioan Micula, Viorel Micula, S.C. European Food S.A, S.C. Starmill S.R.L. and S.C. Multipack S.R.L. (Sweden) vs. Romania, referred to as: *Ioan Micula, Viorel Micula & others vs. Romania*, 11.12.2013 – ICSID Case No. ARB/05/20 - Final Award

Ioan Micula, Viorel Micula, S.C. European Food S.A, S.C. Starmill S.R.L. and S.C. Multipack S.R.L. (Sweden) vs. Romania - Annulment Proceedings, referred to as: *Annulment Committee in Micula vs. Romania*, 26.02.2016 – ICSID Case No. ARB/05/20 - Decision on Annulment

Ioannis Kardassopoulos (Hellenic Republic) vs. The Republic of Georgia, referred to as: *Ioannis Kardassopoulos vs. Georgia,*, 03.03.2010 – ICSID Case No. ARB/05/18 – Award

Jan Oostergetel and Theodora Laurentius (The Netherlands) vs. The Slovak Republic, referred to as: *Oostergetel & Laurentius vs. Slovak Republic*, 30.04.2010 – UNICTRAL - Award on Jurisdiction

Joseph Charles Lemire (United States of America) vs. Ukraine, referred to as: *Lemire vs. Ukraine*, 28.03.2011 – ICSID Case No. ARB/06/18 – Award

LG&E Energy Corp., LG&E Capital Corp., and LG&E International, Inc. (United States of America) vs. The Argentine Republic, referred to as: *LG&E vs. Argentina*, 03.10.2006 – ICSID Case No. ARB/02/1 - Decision on Liability

Loewen Group, Inc. and Raymond L. Loewen (Canda) vs. United States of America, referred to as: *Loewen et al. vs. USA*, 26.06.2003 – ICSID Case No. ARB(AF)/98/3 – Award

Metalclad Corporation (United States of America) vs. The United Mexican States, referred to as: *Metalclad vs. Mexico*, 30.08.2000 – ICSID Case No. ARB(AF)/97/1 - Award

Methanex Corporation (Canada) vs. United States of America, referred to as: *Methanex vs. USA*, 03.08.2005 – UNCITRAL- Final Award of the Tribunal on Jurisdiction and Merits

Mondev International Ltd. (Canada) vs. United States of America, referred to as: *Mondev vs. USA*, 11.10.2002 – ICSID Case No. ARB(AF)/99/2 - Award

MTD Equity Sdn. Bhd. and MTD Chile S.A. (Malaysia) vs. Republic of Chile, referred to as: *MTD vs. Chile*, 25.05.2004 – ICSID Case No. ARB/01/7 – Award

MTD Equity Sdn. Bhd. and MTD Chile S.A. (Malaysia) v. Republic of Chile - Annulment Proceedings, referred to as: *Annulment Committee in MTD vs. Chile*, 21.03.2007 – ICSID Case No. ARB/01/7 - Decision on Annulment

National Grid plc (United Kingdom) vs. The Argentine Republic, referred to as: *National Grid vs. Argentina*, 03.11.2008 – UNCITRAL - Award

Noble Ventures, Inc. (United States of America) vs. Romania, referred to as: *Noble Ventures vs. Romania*, 12.10.2005 – ICSID Case No. ARB/01/11 – Award

OAO Gazprom (Russian Federation) vs. The Republic of Lithuania, referred to as: *Gazprom vs. Lithuania*, PCA Case No. 2011-16 (ongoing)

Occidental Exploration and Production Company (United States of America) vs. The Republic of Ecuador, referred to as: *Occidental Exploration vs. Ecuador*, 01.07.2004 – LCIA Case No. UN3467 - Final Award

Parkerings-Compagniet AS (Norway) vs. Republic of Lithuania, referred to as: *Parkerings vs. Lithuania*, 11.09.2007 – ICSID Case No. ARB/05/8 - Award

Phoenix Action, Ltd. (Israel) vs. The Czech Republic, referred to as: *Phoenix Action vs. Czech Republic*, 15.04.2009 – ICSID Case No. ARB/06/5 - Award

Ping An Life Insurance Company, Limited and Ping An Insurance (Group) Company, Limited (China) vs. The Government of Belgium, referred to as: *Ping An vs. Belgium*, 30.04.2015 – ICSID Case No. ARB/12/29 - Award

Plama Consortium Limited (Cyprus) vs. Republic of Bulgaria, referred to as: *Plama vs. Bulgaria*, 08.02.2005 – ICSID Case No. ARB/03/24 - Decision on Jurisdiction

Plama Consortium Limited (Cyprus) vs. Republic of Bulgaria, referred to as: *Plama vs. Bulgaria*, 27.08.2008 – ICSID Case No. ARB/03/24 - Award

Pope & Talbot, Inc. (United States of America) vs. The Government of Canada, referred to as: *Pope & Talbot vs. Canada*, 10.04.2001 – UNCITRAL - Awards on the Merits of Phase 2

Poštová banka, a.s. and ISTROKAPITAL SE (Cyprus) vs. Hellenic Republic, referred to as: *Poštová vs. Greece*, 09.04.2015 – ICSID Case No. ARB/13/8 - Award

PSEG Global, Inc., The North American Coal Corporation, and Konya Ingin Electrik Üretim ve Ticaret Limited Sirketi (United States of America) vs. Republic of Turkey, referred to as: *PSEG Global vs. Turkey*, 19.01.2007 – ICSID Case No. ARB/02/5 – Award

Quiborax S.A., Non Metallic Minerals S.A. and Allan Fosk Kaplún (Chile) vs. Plurinational State of Bolivia, referred to as: *Quiborax vs. Bolivia*, 27.09.2012 – ICSID Case No. ARB/06/2 - Decision on Jurisdiction

Ronald S. Lauder (United States of America) vs. The Czech Republic, referred to as: *Ronald S. Lauder vs. Czech Republic*, 03.09.2001 – UNCITRAL- Final Award

Rumeli Telekom A.S. and Telsim Mobil Telekomunikasyon Hizmetleri A.S. (Republic of Turkey) vs. Republic of Kazakhstan, referred to as: *Rumeli vs. Kazakhstan*, 29.07.2008 – ICSID Case No. ARB/05/16 – Award

Saba Fakes (The Netherlands) vs. Republic of Turkey, referred to as: *Saba Fakes vs. Turkey*, 14.07.2010 – ICSID Case No. ARB/07/20 - Award

Salini Costruttori S.p.A. and Italstrade S.p.A. (Italy) vs. The Hashemite Kingdom of Jordan, referred to as: *Salini vs. Jordan*, 09.11.2004 – ICSID Case No. ARB/02/13 - Award

Salini Costruttori S.p.A. and Italstrade S.p.A. (Italy) vs. Kingdom of Morocco, referred to as: *Salini vs. Morocco*, 31.07.2001 – ICSID Case No. ARB/00/4 - Decision on Jurisdiction

Saluka Investments B.V. (The Netherlands) vs. The Czech Republic, referred to as: *Saluka vs. Czech Republic*, 17.03.2006 – UNCITRAL - Partial Award

SAUR International SA (France) vs. The Argentine Republic, referred to as: *SAUR vs. Argentina*, 06.06.2012 – ICSID Case No. ARB/04/4 - Decision on Jurisdiction and Liability

S.D. Myers, Inc. (United States of America) vs. Government of Canada, referred to as: *S. D. Myers vs Canada*, 13.11.2000 – UNCITRAL - Partial Award

SGS Société Générale de Surveillance S.A. (Switzerland) vs. Islamic Republic of Pakistan, referred to as: *SGS vs. Pakistan*, 06.08.2003 – ICSID Case No. ARB/01/13 - Decision of the Tribunal on Objections to Jurisdiction

SGS Société Générale de Surveillance S.A. (Switzerland) vs. The Republic of Paraguay, referred to as: *SGS vs. Paraguay*, 12.02.2010 – ICSID Case No. ARB/07/29 - Decision on Jurisdiction

SGS Société Générale de Surveillance S.A. (Switzerland) vs. Republic of the Philippines, referred to as: *SGS vs. Philippines*, 29.01.2004 – ICSID Case No. ARB/02/6 - Decision of the Tribunal on Objections to Jurisdiction

Siemens A.G. (The Federal Republic of Germany) vs. The Argentine Republic, referred to as: *Siemens A.G. vs. Argentina*, 17.01.2007 – ICSID Case No. ARB/02/8 - Award

Suez, Sociedad General de Aguas de Barcelona, S.A. (Spain) and Vivendi Universal, S.A. (France) (formerly Aguas Argentinas, S.A., Suez, Sociedad General de Aguas de Barcelona, S.A.and Vivendi Universal, S.A.) vs. The Argentine Republic, referred to as: *Suez vs. Argentina*, 30.07.2010 – ICSID Case No. ARB/03/19 - Decision on Liability

Técnicas Medioambientales Tecmed, S.A. (Spain) vs. The United Mexican States, referred to as: *Tecmed vs. Mexico*, 29.05.2003 – ICSID Case No. ARB (AF)/00/2 - Award

Teinver S.A., Transportes de Cercanías S.A. and Autobuses Urbanos del Sur S.A. (Spain) vs. The Argentine Republic, referred to as: *Teinver vs. Argentina*, 21.12.2012 – ICSID Case No. ARB/09/1 - Decision on Jurisdiction

Telenor Mobile Communications A.S. (Norway) v. The Republic of Hungary, referred to as: *Telenor vs. Hungary*, 13.09.2006 – ICSID Case No. ARB/04/15 - Award

Tokios Tokelés (Lithunia) vs. Ukraine, referred to as: *Tokios Tokelés vs. Ukraine*, 29.04.2004 – ICSID Case No. ARB/02/18 - Decision on Jurisdiction

U.S. Steel Global Holdings I B.V. (The Netherlands) vs. The Slovak Republic, referred to as: *U.S. Steel vs. Slovak Republic*, PCA Case No. 2013-6 (ongoing)

Vattenfall AB, Vattenfall Europe AG, Vattenfall Europe Generation AG (formerly Vattenfall AB, Vattenfall Europe AG, Vattenfall Europe Generation AG & Co. KG) (Sweden) vs. The Federal Republic of Germany, referred to as: *Vattenfall vs. Germany I*, 11.03.2011 – ICSID Case No. ARB/09/6 – Award

Waguih Elie George Siag and Clorinda Vecchi (Italy) vs. The Arab Republic of Egypt, referred to as: *Siag and Vecchi vs. Egypt*, 01.06.2009 – ICSID Case No. ARB/05/15 - Award

Waste Management, Inc. (United States of America) vs. United Mexican States ("Number 2"), referred to as: *Waste Management vs. Mexico*, 30.04.2004 – ICSID Case No. ARB(AF)/00/3 - Award

Wena Hotels Ltd. (United Kingdom) vs. Arab Republic of Egypt, referred to as: *Wena vs. Egypt*, 08.12.2000 – ICSID Case No. ARB/98/4 – Award

Wena Hotels Ltd. vs. Arab Republic of Egypt - Annullment Proceedings, referred to as: *Annullment Committee in Wena Hotels vs. Egypt*, 05.02.2002 – ICSID Case No. ARB/98/4 - Decision on Annulment

Wintershall Aktiengesellschaft (The Federal Republic of Germany) vs. The Argentine Republic, referred to as: *Wintershall vs. Argentina*, 08.12.2008 – ICSID Case No. ARB/04/14

Literature

Abedian, Hossein: Judicial Review of Arbitral Awards in International Arbitration – A Case for an Efficient System of Judicial Review, Journal of International Arbitration Vol. 28, Iss. 6 (2011), p. 553–590 (cited as: *Abedian*, JOIA, Vol. 28, Iss. 6 (2011))

Ahner, Juliane: Investor-Staat-Schiedsverfahren nach Europäischem Unionsrecht, Zulässigkeit und Ausgestaltung in Investitionsabkommen der Europäischen Union, Tübingen - Germany, 2015

Alschner, Wolfgang: Americanization of the BIT Universe: The Influence of Friendship, Commerce and Navigation (FCN) Treaties on Modern Investment Treaty Law, Goettingen Journal of International Law Vol. 5, No. 2 (2013), p. 455–486 (cited as: *Alschner*, Goettingen Journal of International Law, Vol. 5, No. 2 (2013))

Balthasar, Stephan (Ed.): International Commercial Arbitration, Best Practice Guide, 1st Ed., Munich (München) - Germany, 2016 (cited as: *Author,* in *Balthasar* (Ed.), International Commercial Arbitration)

Bartosch, Andreas: EU-Beihilfenrecht, Art. 106 - 109 AEUV, De-minimis-Verordnung, DAWI-Paket, Allgemeine Gruppenfreistellungsverordnung sowie Verfahrensverordnung : Kommentar, 2nd Ed., Munich (München) - Germany, 2016

Beljin, Saša/Schulze, Reiner/Zuleeg, Manfred: Europarecht, Handbuch für die deutsche Rechtspraxis, 2nd Ed., Baden-Baden - Germany, 2010

Benedek, Wolfgang: Grundlagen und Rahmenbedingungen der Steuerungskraft des Völkerrechts, Zeitschrift für ausländisches und öffentliches Recht und Völkerrecht (2016), p. 345–362 (cited as: *Benedek*, ZaöVR, (2016))

Bernsdorff, Norbert/Meyer, Jürgen (Eds.): Charta der Grundrechte der Europäischen Union, 4th Ed., Baden-Baden - Germany, 2014 (cited as: *Author*, in: *Meyer (Ed.) Charta der Grundrechte der EU*).

Bieber, Roland/Epiney, Astrid/Haag, Marcel: Die Europäische Union, Europarecht und Politik, 11th Ed., Baden-Baden - Germany, 2015

Blanke, Hermann-Josef/Mangiameli, Stelio: The Treaty on European Union (TEU), A commentary, Berlin - Germany, 2013

Böckstiegel, Karl Heinz: Commercial and Investment Arbitration: How Different are they Today?, Arbitration International Vol. 28, Iss. 4 (2012), p. 577–590 (cited as: *Böckstiegel*, Arbitration International, Vol. 28, Iss. 4 (2012))

Borris, Christian/Hennecke, Rudolf: Das Kriterium der Einhaltung von Vorschriften nationalen Rechts in ICSID-Schiedsverfahren – Anmerkungen zum Schiedsspruch in der Sache Fraport v. Philippines, Zeitschrift für Schiedsverfahren (2008), p. 49–58 (cited as: *Borris/Hennecke*, SchiedsVZ, (2008))

Braun, Tillmann Rudolf: Ausprägungen der Globalisierung: Der Investor als partielles Subjekt im Internationalen Investitionsrecht, Qualität und Grenzen dieser Wirkungseinheit, Baden-Baden - Germany, 2012

Bräuninger, Laura: Investitionsschiedsgerichtsbarkeit und Diskriminierungsverbote, Die Vereinbarkeit von Schiedsklauseln in Extra-EU BITs mit den Diskriminierungsverboten des AEUV, Berlin - Germany, 2015

Broekhuijsen, Dirk M.: A Modern Understanding of Article 31(3)(c) of the Vienna Convention (1969): A New Haunt for the Commentaries to the OECD Model?, , 2013 (Volume 67), No. 9, Bulletin for International Taxation Vol. 67, No. 9 (2013), p. 1–8 (cited as: *Broekhuijsen*, Bulletin for International Taxation, Vol. 67, No. 9 (2013))

Brownlie, Ian: Principles of public international law, 7th Ed., Oxford - United Kingdom, New York - United States of America, 2008

Bücheler, Gebhard/Vasiljevic, Igor: EUGH Vorlage zur Wirksamkeit von Schiedsvereinbarungen in unionsinternen BIT, Case Comment: German Federal Supreme Court: Achmea Set Aside Proceedings, Order 03.03.2016 - I ZB 2/15, Zeitschrift für Schiedsverfahren (2016), p. 328–339 (cited as: *Bücheler/Vasiljevic*, SchiedsVZ, (2016))

Bungenberg, Marc/Griebel, Jörn/Hindelang, Steffen (Eds.): International investment law and EU law, Heidelberg - Germany, New York - United States of America, 2011 (cited as: *Author,* in *Bungenberg/Griebel/Hindelang* (Eds.), International investment law and EU law)

Bungenberg, Marc/Griebel, Jörn/Hobe, Stephan/Reinisch, August (Eds.): International Investment Law, A Handbook, First Ed., Munich (München) - Germany, Oxford - United Kingdom, Baden-Baden - Germany, 2015 (cited as: *Author,* in *Bungenberg/Griebel/Hobe/Reinisch* (Eds.), International Investment Law)

Burgstaller, Markus: European Law and Investment Treaties, Journal of International Arbitration Vol. 26, No. 2 (2009), p. 181–216 (cited as: *Burgstaller*, JOIA, Vol. 26, No. 2 (2009))

Ibid.: Investor-State Arbitration in EU International Investment Agreements with Third States, Legal Issues of Economic Integration Vol. 39, No. 2 (2012), p. 207–222 (cited as: *Burgstaller*, LIEI, Vol. 39, No. 2 (2012))

Cairns, David J. A.: The Spanish Application of the UNCITRAL Model Law on International Commercial Arbitration, Arbitration International Vol. 22, No. 4 (2006), p. 573–596 (cited as: *Cairns*, Arbitration International, Vol. 22, No. 4 (2006))

Calliess, Christian/Ruffert, Matthias (Eds.): EUV, Das Verfassungsrecht der Europäischen Union mit Europäischer Grundrechtecharta, 5th Ed., Munich (München) - Germany, 2016 (cited as: *Author*, in: *Calliess/Ruffert EUV/AEUV*).

Carlevaris, Andrea: Conformity of Investments with the Law of the Host State and the Jurisdiction of International Tribunals, The Journal of World Investment & Trade Vol. 9 (2008), p. 35–49 (cited as: *Carlevaris*, JWIT, Vol. 9 (2008))

Chaisse, Julien: Promises and Pitfalls of the European Union Policy on Foreign Investment—How will the New EU Competence on FDI affect the Emerging Global Regime?, Journal of International Economic Law Vol. 15, No. 1 (2012), p. 51–84 (cited as: *Chaisse*, JIEL, Vol. 15, No. 1 (2012))

Clodfelter, Mark A.: The Future Direction of Investment Agreements in the European Union, Santa Clara Journal of International Law Vol. 12, Iss. 1 (2013), p. 159–182 (cited as: *Clodfelter*, Santa Clara Jour. of Int. Law, Vol. 12, Iss. 1 (2013))

Commission, Jeffery P.: Precedent in Investment Treaty Arbitration - A Citation Analysis of a Developing Jurisprudence, Journal of International Arbitration Vol. 24, Iss. 2 (2007), p. 129–158 (cited as: *Commission*, JOIA, Vol. 24, Iss. 2 (2007))

Corten, Olivier/Klein, Pierre (Eds.): The Vienna Conventions on the Law of Treaties: Volume I, A commentary, Oxford - United Kingdom, New York - United States of America, 2011 (cited as: *Author*, in: *Corten/Klein VCLT - I*).

Ibid.: The Vienna Conventions on the Law of Treaties: Volume II, A commentary, Oxford - United Kingdom, New York - United States of America, 2011 (cited as: *Author*, in: *Corten/Klein VCLT - II*).

Coyle, John F.: The Treaty of Friendship, Commerce and Navigation in the Modern Era, Columbia Journal of Transnational Law Vol. 51 (2013), p. 302–359 (cited as: *Coyle*, Columbia Journal of Transnational Law, Vol. 51 (2013))

Cremer, Wolfram: Der programmierte Verfassungskonflikt: Zur Bindung der Mitgliedstaaten an die Charta der Grundrechte der Europäischen Union nach dem Konventsentwurf für eine Europäische Verfassung, Neue Zeitschrift für Verwaltungsrecht (2003), p. 1452–1457 (cited as: *Cremer*, NVwZ, (2003))

Dahlquist, Joel: Investigation: EU member-states table differing responses in face of Commission's infringement proceedings related to intra-EU BITs, Investment Arbitration Reporter Vol. 9, No. 4 (2016), p. 46–49 (cited as: *Dahlquist*, IA Reporter, Vol. 9, No. 4 (2016))

Dahlquist, Joel/Lenk, Hannes/Rönnelid, Love: The infringement proceedings over intra-EU investment treaties – an analysis of the case against Sweden, European Policy Analysis (2016:4), p. 1–12 (cited as: *Dahlquist/Lenk/Rönnelid*, European Policy Analysis, (2016:4))

Dimopoulos, Angelos: The Validity and Applicability of International Investment Agreements between EU Member States under EU and International Law, Common Market Law Review Vol. 48, No. 1 (2011), p. 63–93 (cited as: *Dimopoulos*, CMLR, Vol. 48, No. 1 (2011))

Ibid.: The Compatibility of Future EU Investment Agreements with EU Law, Legal Issues of Economic Integration Vol. 39, No. 4 (2012), p. 447–472 (cited as: *Dimopoulos*, LIEI, Vol. 39, No. 4 (2012))

Dimopoulos, Angelos/Sattorova, Mavluda: The Present and Future of EU International Investment Treaties, Legal Issues of Economic Integration Vol. 39, Iss. 2 (2012), p. 153–155 (cited as: *Dimopoulos/Sattorova*, LIEI, Vol. 39, Iss. 2 (2012))

Dolzer, Rudolf: Fair and Equitable Treatment: Today's Contours, Santa Clara Journal of International Law Vol. 12 (2014), p. 7–33 (cited as: *Dolzer*, Santa Clara Jour. of Int. Law, Vol. 12 (2014))

Dolzer, Rudolf/Stevens, Margrete: Bilateral Investment Treaties, The Hague -The Netherlands, Boston - United States of America, London - United Kingdom, 1995

Dörr, Dieter: Case Comment to ECtHR - Bosphorus, Decision dated 30.06.2005 – Application No. 45036/98, Juristische Schulungen (2006), p. 442–445 (cited as: *Dörr*, JuS, (2006))

Dörr, Oliver/Schmalenbach, Kirsten (Eds.): Vienna Convention on the Law of Treaties, A commentary, Heidelberg - Germany [et. al.], 2012 (cited as: *Author*, in: *Dörr/Schmalenbach VCLT*).

Dralle, Tilman Michael: Der Fair and Equitable Treatment-Standard im. Investitionsschutzrecht am Beispiel des. Schiedsspruchs Glamis Gold v. United States, Beiträge zum Transnationalen Wirtschaftsrecht Vol. 115 (2011), p. 5–33 (cited as: *Dralle*, Der FET Standard im Investitionsschutzrecht (Beit. zum Transnat. Wirt.-R, Vol. 115, 2011))

Dugan, Christopher F.: Investor-state arbitration, New York - United States of America, 2008

Dupuy, Pierre-Marie/Francioni, Francesco/Petersmann, Ernst-Ulrich (Eds.): Human rights in international investment law and arbitration, New York - United States of America, 2009 (cited as: *Author,* in *Dupuy/Francioni/Petersmann* (Eds.), Human rights in international investment law and arbitration)

Dürrschmidt, Daniel/Lehner, Moris/Vogel, Klaus (Eds.): Doppelbesteuerungsabkommen der Bundesrepublik Deutschland auf dem Gebiet der Steuern vom Einkommen und Vermögen, Kommentar auf der Grundlage der Musterabkommen, 6th Ed, Munich (München) - Germany, 2015 (cited as: *Author,* in *Dürrschmidt/Lehner/Vogel* (Eds.), Doppelbesteuerungsabkommen der Bundesrepublik Deutschland auf dem Gebiet der Steuern vom Einkommen und Vermögen)

Echandi, Roberto/Sauvé, Pierre: Prospects in international investment law and policy, World Trade Forum, Cambridge - United Kingdom, 2013

Ehlers, Dirk/Schoch, Friedrich (Eds.): Rechtsschutz im Öffentlichen Recht, Berlin - Germany, 2009 (cited as: *Author,* in *Ehlers/Schoch* (Eds.), Rechtsschutz im Öffentlichen Recht)

Eilmansberger, Thomas, Bilateral Investment Treaties and EU law, Common Market Law Review Vol. 46 (2009), p. 383–429 (cited as: *Eilmansberger*, CMLR, Vol. 46 (2009))

Heintschel von Heinegg, Wolff/Vedder, Christoph (Eds.): Europäisches Unionsrecht, EUV, AEUV, Grundrechte-Charta ; Handkommentar ; mit den vollständigen Texten der Protokolle und Erklärungen und des EAGV, First Ed., Baden-Baden - Germany [et. al.], 2012 (cited as: *Author*, in: *von Heinegg/Vedder EUV/AEUV*).

Eisenkolb, Julia: Eisenkolb: Die Enforcement-Richtlinie und ihre Wirkung - Ist die Enforcement-Richtlinie mit Ablauf der Umsetzungsfrist unmittelbar wirksam?, Gewerblicher Rechtsschutz und Urheberrecht (2007), p. 387–393 (cited as: *Eisenkolb*, GRUR, (2007))

Elscher, Alfred/Sliskovic, Violeta: Aktuelle Entwicklungen des Investitionsschutzrechts, Recht der internationalen Wirtschaft (2016), p. 190–201 (cited as: *Elscher/Sliskovic*, RIW, (2016))

Engel, Daniel: Investitionsschutzstreitigkeiten in der Europäischen Union, Zeitschrift für Schiedsverfahren (2015), p. 218–225 (cited as: *Engel*, SchiedsVZ, (2015))

Epping, Volker/Hillgruber, Christian (Eds.): Beck'scher Online-Kommentar Grundgesetz, 31st Ed., Munich (München) - Germany, 2016 (as of 01.01.2016) (cited as: *Author*, in: *Beck-OK GG*).

Evans, Malcolm D.: International law, Second Ed., Oxford - United Kingdom, New York - United States of America, 2006

Ferrari, Franco/Kieninger, Eva Maria/Mankowski, Peter/Otte, Karsten/Sänger, Ingo/Schulze, Götz/Staudinger, Ansgar (Eds.): Internationales Vertragsrecht, Rom I-VO, CISG, CMR, FactÜ, 2nd Ed., Munich (München) - Germany, 2012 (cited as: *Author*, in: *Ferrari/Kieninger/Mankoswki Internat. Vertragsrecht*).

Fietta, Stephen: Most Favoured Nation Treatment and Dispute Resolution under Bilateral Investment Treaties: A turning point? , International Arbitration Law Review Iss. 4 (2005), p. 131–138 (cited as: *Fietta*, Int. A.L.R., Iss. 4 (2005))

Fouchard, Philippe/Gaillard, Emmanuel/Goldman, Berthold/Savage, John: Fouchard, Gaillard, Goldman on international commercial arbitration, The Hague -The Netherlands, Boston - United States of America, 1999

Franzius, Claudio: Zwischen Selbstbehauptung und Selbstbeschränkung der Rechtsordnungen und ihrer Gerichte, Zeitschrift für ausländisches und öffentliches Recht und Völkerrecht (2015), p. 383–412 (cited as: *Franzius*, ZaöVR, (2015))

Frenz, Walter: Europarecht, Heidelberg - Germany [et. al.], 2011

Füracker, Matthias: Relevance and Structure of Bilateral Investment Treaties, Zeitschrift für Schiedsverfahren (2006), p. 236–245 (cited as: *Füracker*, SchiedsVZ, (2006))

Gaillard, Emmanuel/Banifatemi, Yas: The Meaning of "and" in Article 42(1), Second Sentence, of the Washington Convention: The Role of International Law in the ICSID Choice of Law Process, ICSID Review - Foreign Investment Law Journal Vol. 18, Iss. 2 (2003), p. 375–411 (cited as: *Gaillard/Banifatemi*, ICSID Rev., Vol. 18, Iss. 2 (2003))

Gáspár-Szilágyi, Szilárd: EU Member State Enforcement of 'Mixed' Agreements and Access to Justice: Rethinking Direct Effect, Legal Issues of Economic Integration Vol. 40, No. 2 (2013), p. 163–190 (cited as: *Gáspár-Szilágyi*, LIEI, Vol. 40, No. 2 (2013))

Geiger, Rudolf/Kotzur, Markus/Khan, Daniel-Erasmus (Eds.): EUV, AEUV, Vertrag über die Europäische Union und Vertrag über die Arbeitsweise der Europäischen Union ; Kommentar, 5th Ed., Munich (München) - Germany, 2010 (cited as: *Author*, in: *GKK EUV/AEUV*).

Ghouri, Ahmad Ali: The Evolution of Bilateral Investment Treaties, Investment Treaty Arbitration and International Investment Law, International Arbitration Law Review Vol. 14, No. 6, p. 189–204 (cited as: *Ghouri*, Int. A.L.R., Vol. 14, No. 6)

Ibid.: Resolving Incompatibilities of Bilateral Investment Treaties of the EU Member States with the EC Treaty: Individual and Collective Options, European Law Journal Vol. 16, No. 5 (2010), p. 806–830 (cited as: *Ghouri*, ELJ, Vol. 16, No. 5 (2010))

Grabenwarter, Christoph: European Convention for the Protection of Human Rights and Fundamental Freedoms, Frist Ed., Munich (München) - Germany, 2014

Ibid.: Rechtliche Rahmenbedingungen des Verhältnisses zwischen EU und Europarat aus der Perspektive des Europarates und die Rolle der Mitgliedstaaten, Zeitschrift für ausländisches und öffentliches Recht und Völkerrecht (2014), p. 419–444 (cited as: *Grabenwarter*, ZaöVR, (2014))

Grabenwarter, Christoph/Pabel, Katharina: Europäische Menschenrechtskonvention, Ein Studienbuch, 6th Ed., Munich (München) - Germany, Basel - Switzerland, Vienna (Wien) - Austria, 2016

Grabitz, Eberhard/Nettesheim, Martin/Bandilla, Rüdiger/Hilf, Meinhard (Eds.): Das Recht der Europäischen Union, [Kommentar zu den Verträgen], 41st supplement (Ergänzungslieferung), Munich (München) - Germany, 2010 (continiously updated) – Volume I (cited as: *Author*, in: *Grabitz/Hilf/Nettesheim EUV/AEUV*).

Ibid.: Das Recht der Europäischen Union, [Kommentar zu den Verträgen], 41st supplement (Ergänzungslieferung), Munich (München) - Germany, 2010 (continiously updated) – Volume II (cited as: *Author*, in: *Grabitz/Hilf/Nettesheim EUV/AEUV*).

Ibid.: Das Recht der Europäischen Union, [Kommentar zu den Verträgen], 41st supplement (Ergänzungslieferung), Munich (München) - Germany, 2010 (continiously updated) – Volume III (cited as: *Author*, in: *Grabitz/Hilf/Nettesheim EUV/AEUV*).

Gramlich, Ludwig/Conen, Claudia: Streitbeilegung bei Auslandsinvestitionen - "Guter" Rechtsschutz für (private) Investoren, Zeitschrift für Schiedsverfahren (2015), p. 225–235 (cited as: *Gramlich/Conen*, SchiedsVZ, (2015))

Griebel, Jörn: Internationales Investitionsrecht, Lehrbuch für Studium und Praxis, First Ed., Munich (München) - Germany, 2008, (2008), (cited as: Griebel, (2008))

Hammerstein, Christian v./Roegele, Peter: Der Fair and Equitable Treatment-Standard im Investitionsschutzrecht, Zeitschrift für Schiedsverfahren (2015), p. 275–280 (cited as: *Hammerstein/Roegele*, SchiedsVZ, (2015))

Happ, Richard: The legal status of the Investor vis-à-vis the European Communities: some salient thoughts, International Arbitration Law Review Iss. 3 (2007), p. 74–81 (cited as: *Happ*, Int. A.L.R., Iss. 3 (2007))

Haratsch, Andreas: Die Solange -Rechtsprechung des Europäischen Gerichtshofs für Menschenrechte, Zeitschrift für ausländisches und öffentliches Recht und Völkerrecht 66 (2006), p. 927–947 (cited as: *Haratsch*, ZaöVR, 66 (2006))

Ibid.: Europarecht, Tübingen - Germany, 2016, (2016), (cited as: Haratsch, (2016))

Hepburn, Jarrod: In upholding intra-EU Energy Charter award, Swiss court considers EU state aid issue, as well as umbrella clause reservation and tribunal's damages methodology, Investment Arbitration Reporter Vol. 8, No. 25 (2015), p. 16–19 (cited as: *Hepburn*, IA Reporter, Vol. 8, No. 25 (2015))

Herdegen, Matthias: Internationales Wirtschaftsrecht, 10th Ed., Munich (München) - Germany, 2014, 10. Edn. (2014), (cited as: Herdegen, 10. Edn. (2014))

Ibid.: Europarecht, 17th Ed., Munich (München) - Germany, 2015

Ibid.: Völkerrecht, 15th Ed., Munich (München) - Germany, 2016

Herr-Reißmann, Christine: Straßburg oder Luxemburg? - Der EGMR zum Grundrechtsschutz bei Verordnungen der EG in der Rechtssache Bosphorus, Neue Juristische Wochenschrift 2006, p. 192–194 (cited as: *Herr-Reißmann*, NJW, 2006)

Heselhaus, F. Sebastian M./Nowak, Carsten (Eds.): Handbuch der Europäischen Grundrechte, Munich (München) - Germany, 2006 (cited as: *Author,* in *Hesselhaus/Nowak* (Eds.), Handbuch der Europäischen Grundrechte)

Heuer, Jan: Art. 51 Abs. 1 Satz 1 GRC: Die Bindung der Mitgliedstaaten an die Unionsgrundrechte, Munich (München) - Germany, 2014

Hindelang, Steffen: Circumventing Primacy of EU Law and the CJEU's Judicial Monopoly by Resorting to Dispute Resolution Mechanisms Provided for in Inter-se Treaties? The Case of Intra-EU Investment Arbitration, Legal Issues of Economic Integration Vol. 39, Iss. 2 (2012), p. 179–206 (cited as: *Hindelang*, LIEI, Vol. 39, Iss. 2 (2012))

Ibid.: Repellent Forces: The CJEU and Investor-State Dispute Settlement, On how the CJEU's Concept of Autonomy of EU Law Could Fundamentally Alter Investor-State Arbitration's Current DNA, or what the ECtHR, the European Patent Court, and Investment Tribunals in the EU-Canada Comprehensive Economic Trade Agreement (CETA) Might Have in Common, Archiv des Völkerrechts Vol. 53 (2015), p. 68–89 (cited as: *Hindelang*, AVR, Vol. 53 (2015))

Hobe, Stephan: Europarecht, 8th Ed., Munich (München) - Germany, 2014, 8. Edn. (2014),
(cited as: Hobe, 8. Edn. (2014))

Ibid.: Einführung in das Völkerrecht, 10th Ed., Tübingen - Germany, 2014

Hoffmann, Anne K. (Ed.): Protection of foreign investments through modern treaty arbitration: diversity and harmonisation, ASA Special Series - No. 34, Zurich - Switzerland, 2010 (cited as: *Author,* in *Hoffmann* (Ed.), Protection of foreign investments through modern treaty arbitration: diversity and harmonisation)

Hoffmeister, Frank/Alexandru, Gabriela: A First Glimpse of Light on the Emerging Invisible EU Model BIT, The Journal of World Investment & Trade Vol. 15 (2014), p. 379–401 (cited as: *Hoffmeister/Alexandru*, JWIT, Vol. 15 (2014))

Höfler, Heiko: Transparenz bei der Vergabe öffentlicher Aufträge, Neue Zeitschrift für Baurecht und Vergaberecht (2010), p. 73–78 (cited as: *Höfler*, NZBau, (2010))

Horn, Norbert: Zwingendes Recht in der internationalen Schiedsgerichtsbarkeit, Zeitschrift für Schiedsverfahren (2008), p. 209–222 (cited as: *Horn*, SchiedsVZ, (2008))

Hwang, Shu-Perng: Anwendungsvorrang statt Geltungsvorrang? Normlogische und institutionelle Überlegungen zum Vorrang des Unionsrechts, Zeitschrift Europarecht (2016), p. 355–373 (cited as: *Hwang*, EuR, (2016))

IA Reporter Team Dan Cake vs. Hungary Liability Ruling: Tribunal finds Hungarian court's handling of bankruptcy proceedings to be flawed, leading to finding of a denial of justice under intra-EU BIT, Investment Arbitration Reporter Vol. 8, No. 26 (2015), p. 17–21 (cited as: *IA Reporter Team*, IA Reporter, Vol. 8, No. 26 (2015))

Immenga, Ulrich/Mestmäcker, Ernst-Joachim (Eds.): Wettbewerbsrecht, 5th Ed., Munich (München) - Germany, 2016 (cited as: *Author*, in: *Immenga/Mestmäcker AEUV*).

Ipsen, Knut: Völkerrecht, 6th Ed., Munich (München) - Germany, 2014

Jaeger, Thomas: System einer Europäischen Gerichtsbarkeit für Immaterialgüterrechte, Grundlagen - Struktur - Verfahren, Berlin - Germany, Heidelberg - Germany, 2013

Janik, Cornelia: Die EMRK und internationale Organisationen - Ausdehnungen und Restriktionen der equivalent protection-Formel in der neuen Rechtsprechung des EGMR, Zeitschrift für ausländisches und öffentliches Recht und Völkerrecht (2010), p. 127–179 (cited as: *Janik*, ZaöVR, (2010))

Jarass, Hans D.: EU-Grundrechte, Ein Studien- und Handbuch, Munich (München) - Germany, 2005

Ibid.: Charta der Grundrechte der Europäischen Union, Unter Einbeziehung der vom EuGH entwickelten Grundrechte, der Grundrechtsregelungen der Verträge und der EMRK; Kommentar, Munich (München) - Germany, 2. Edn. (2013), (cited as: Jarass, 2. Edn. (2013))

Jarass, Hans D./Beljin, Saša: Die Bedeutung von Vorrang und Durchführung des EG-Rechts für die nationale Rechtsetzung und Rechtsanwendung, Neue Zeitschrift für Verwaltungsrecht (2004), p. 1–11 (cited as: *Jarass/Beljin*, NVwZ, (2004))

Jensen, J. Ole: Die Auslegung von Investitionsschutzabkommen am Beispiel der "umbrella clause", Rechtssicherheit durch höhere Präzision, Recht der internationalen Wirtschaft (2016), p. 277–286 (cited as: *Jensen*, RIW, (2016))

Johannsen, Sven Leif Erik: Der Investitionsbegriff nach Art. 25 Abs. 1 der ICSID-Konvention, Beiträge zum Transnationalen Wirtschaftsrecht Vol. 87 (2009), p. 5–

36 (cited as: *Johannsen*, Der Investitionsbegriff nach Art. 25 Abs. 1 der ICSID-Konvention (Beit. zum Transnat. Wirt.-R, ol. 87, 2009))

Ibid.: Die Kompetenz der Europäischen Union für ausländische Direktinvestitionen nach dem Vertrag von Lissabon, Beiträge zum Transnationalen Wirtschaftsrecht Vol. 90 (2009) (cited as: *Johannsen*, Die Kompetenz der EU für ausländische Direktinvestitionen nach Lissabon (Beit. zum Transnat. Wirt.-R, Vol. 90, 2009))

Jörn, Nils: With money and bloode, Der Londoner Stahlhof im Spannungsfeld der englisch-hansischen Beziehungen im 15. und 16. Jahrhundert, Cologne (Köln) - Germany, 2000

Jung, Peter: Anwendung der Gründungstheorie auf Gesellschaften schweizerischen Rechts?, Zugleich eine Anmerkung zu den beim BGH anhängigen Revisionsverfahren II ZR 158/06 und II ZR 290/07, Neue Zeitschrift für Gesellschaftsrecht (2008), p. 681–685 (cited as: *Jung*, NZG, (2008))

Kampermann, Karoline: Keine Meistbegünstigung im Steuerrecht – Das Urteil des EuGH in der Rs. C-376/03 vom 5. Juli 2005, Policy Papers on Transnational Economic Law (October 2005) (cited as: *Kampermann*, Policy Papers on Transnational Economic Law, (October 2005))

Karpenstein, Ulrich/Mayer, Franz C. (Eds.): EMRK, Konvention zum Schutz der Menschenrechte und Grundfreiheiten, 2nd Ed., Munich (München) - Germany, 2015 (cited as: *Author*, in: *Karpenstein/Mayer EMRK*).

Kemmeren, Eric: The termination of the 'most favoured nation clause' dispute in tax trea law and the necessity of a Euro Model Tax Convention, EC Tax Review Iss. 6, No° 3 (1997), p. 146–152 (cited as: *Kemmeren*, EC Tax Review, Iss. 6, No° 3 (1997))

Kempen, Bernhard/Hillgruber, Christian: Völkerrecht, 2nd Ed., Munich (München) - Germany, 2012

Kerkemeyer, Andreas: Unionsrecht und Internationales Investitionsschutzrecht auf Kollisionskurs, Europäische Zeitschrift für Wirtschaftsrecht (2016), p. 10–16 (cited as: *Kerkemeyer*, EuZW, (2016))

Khachaturian, Alex/Moloo, Rahim: The Compliance with the Law Requirement in International Investment Law, Fordham International Law Journal Vol. 34, Iss. 6 (2011), p. 1473–1501 (cited as: *Khachaturian/Moloo*, Fordham International Law Journal, Vol. 34, Iss. 6 (2011))

Kilian, Wolfgang: Europäisches Wirtschaftsrecht, 5th Ed., Baden-Baden - Germany, 2016

Kjos, Hege Elisabeth: Applicable law in investor-state arbitration, The interplay between national and international law, Oxford - United Kingdom, 2013

Klabbers, Jan: Treaty conflict and the European Union, Cambridge - United Kingdom, New York - United States of America, 2009

Kleinheisterkamp, Jan: Investment Protection and EU law: The Intra- and Extra-EU Dimension of The Energy Charter Treaty, Journal of International Economic

Law Vol. 15, No. 1 (2012), p. 85–109 (cited as: *Kleinheisterkamp*, JIEL, Vol. 15, No. 1 (2012))

Knahr, Christina (Ed.): Investment and commercial arbitration, Similarities and divergences Vol. 3, Utrecht - The Netherlands, Portland - United States of America, 2010 (cited as: *Author,* in *Knahr* (Ed.), Investment and commercial arbitration)

Kniebaum, Ursula: The Fate of Intra-EU BITs from an Investment Law and Public International Law Perspective, ELTE Law Journal, p. 27–35 (cited as: *Kniebaum*, ELTE Law Journal,)

Kofler, Georg W.: "Dancing with Mr D": The ECJ's Denial of Most-Favoured-Nation Treatment in the "D" case, European Taxation Vol. 45, No. 12 (2005), p. 530–540 (cited as: *Kofler*, European Taxation, Vol. 45, No. 12 (2005))

Komninos, Assimakis P.: Case C-126/97 Eco Swiss China Time Ltd. v. Benetton International NV, Judgement of 1 June 1999, Full Court - Case Law, Common Market Law Review Iss. 37 (2000), p. 459–478 (cited as: *Komninos*, CMLR, Iss. 37 (2000))

Kottmann, Matthias: Case Comment: German Federal Supreme Court: Achmea Set Aside Proceedings, Order 03.03.2016 - I ZB 2/15, Europäische Zeitschrift für Wirtschaftsrecht (2016), p. 512–520 (cited as: *Kottmann*, EuZW, (2016))

Krajewski, Markus: Wirtschaftsvölkerrecht, 2nd Ed., Heidelberg - Germany [et. al.], 2009

Krenzler, Horst-Günther/Herrmann, Christoph/Niestedt, Marian/Baule, Sylvia (Eds.): EU-Aussenwirtschafts- und Zollrecht, 6th supplement (Ergänzungslieferung), Munich (München) - Germany, 2015 (cited as: *Author*, in: *KHN - EU Außenwirtschaftsrecht*).

Kropholler, Jan/Neuhaus, Paul Heinrich: Internationales Privatrecht, Einschließlich der Grundbegriffe des internationalen Zivilverfahrensrechts, 6th Ed., Tübingen - Germany, 2006

Kühn, Wolfgang/Wiegel, Ulrike: The Application of International Law and Treaty Provisions by Arbitrators, Journal of World Investment Vol. 4, No. 3, p. 451–472 (cited as: *Kühn/Wiegel*, Journal of World Investment, Vol. 4, No. 3)

Kulick, Andreas: Electrabel locuta, causa finita? - Intra-EU-Investitionsstreitigkeiten unter dem Energiecharta-Vertrag, Zeitschrift für Schiedsverfahren (2013), p. 81–87 (cited as: *Kulick*, SchiedsVZ, (2013))

Lachmann, Jens-Peter: Handbuch für die Schiedsgerichtspraxis, 3rd Ed., Cologne (Köln) - Germany, 2008

Lang, Andrej: Der Europäische Gerichtshof und die Investor-Staat-Streitbeilegung in TTIP und CETA: Zwischen Konfrontation, Konstitutionalisierung und Zurückhaltung, Beiträge zum Transnationalen Wirtschaftsrecht Vol. 138 (2015) (cited as: *Lang*, Der EuGH und die Investor-Staat-Streitbeilegung in TTIP und CETA (Beit. zum Transnat. Wirt.-R, Vol. 138, 2015))

Lasok, K. Paul. E./Millett, Timothy/Howard, Anneli: Judicial control in the EU, Procedures and principles, Richmond - United States of America, 2004, (2004), (cited as: Lasok; Millett; Howard, (2004))

Lavranos, Nikos: Regulating competing jurisdictions among international courts and tribunals, Zeitschrift für ausländisches und öffentliches Recht und Völkerrecht (2008), p. 575–621 (cited as: *Lavranos*, ZaöVR, (2008))

Ibid.: In Defence of Member States' BITs Gold Standard: The Regulation 1219/2012 Establishing a Transitional Regime for Existing Extra-EU BITs, A Member State's Perspective, Transnational Dispute Management Vol. 10, Iss. 2 (2013), p. 1–14 (cited as: *Lavranos*, TDM, Vol. 10, Iss. 2 (2013))

Leeks, Annie: The Relationship between Bilateral Investment Treaty Arbitration and the Wider Corpus of International Law; the ICSID-Approach, University of Toronto Faculty of Law Review Vol. 65, No. 2 (2007), p. 1–40 (cited as: *Leeks*, U. Toronto Fac. L. Rev., Vol. 65, No. 2 (2007))

Lenk, Hannes: Challenging the Notion of Coherence in EU Foreign Investment Policy, European Journal of Legal Studies Vol. 8, No. 2 (2015), p. 6–20 (cited as: *Lenk*, EJLS, Vol. 8, No. 2 (2015))

Lentner, Gabriel M.: A Uniform European Investment Policy?: The unwritten EU Model BIT, Journal of Law and Administrative Sciences No. 2 (2014), p. 156–165 (cited as: *Lentner*, JOLAS, No. 2 (2014))

Ličková, Magdalena: European Exceptionalism in International Law, European Journal of International Law Vol. 19, No. 3 (2008), p. 463–490 (cited as: *Ličková*, EJIL, Vol. 19, No. 3 (2008))

Manzini, Pietro: The Priority of Pre-Existing Treaties of EC Member States within the Framework of International Law, European Journal of International Law Vol. 12, No. 4 (2001), p. 781–792 (cited as: *Manzini*, EJIL, Vol. 12, No. 4 (2001))

Maunz, Theodor/Dürig, Günter (Eds.): Grundgesetz, Kommentar, 76th supplement (Ergänzungslieferung), Munich (München) - Germany, 2015 (cited as: *Author*, in: *Maunz/Dürig GG*).

Maurer, Hartmut: Grundlagen, Verfassungsorgane, Staatsfunktionen, 5th Ed., Munich (München) - Germany, 2007

Muchlinski, Peter/Ortino, Frederico/Schreuer, Christoph (Eds.): The Oxford handbook of international investment law, Oxford - United Kingdom, New York - United States of America, 2008 (cited as: *Author,* in *Muchlinski/Ortino/Schreuer* (Eds.), The Oxford handbook of international investment law)

Mus, Jan B.: Conflicts between Treaties in International Law, Netherlands International Law Review (1998), p. 208–232 (cited as: *Mus*, Netherlands International Law Review, (1998))

Nettesheim, Martin: Normenhierarchien im EU-Recht, Zeitschrift Europarecht (2006), p. 737–772 (cited as: *Nettesheim*, EuR, (2006))

Ibid.: Europarechtskonformität des Europäischen Stabilitätsmechanismus, Neue Juristische Wochenschrift (2013), p. 14–16 (cited as: *Nettesheim*, NJW, (2013))

Neun, Andreas/Otting, Olaf: Die EU-Vergaberechtsreform 2014, Europäische Zeitschrift für Wirtschaftsrecht (2014), p. 446–452 (cited as: *Neun/Otting*, EuZW, (2014))

Newcombe, A./Paradell, L.: Law and Practice of Investment Treaties: Standards of Treatment, New York - United States of America [et. al.], 2009

Notter, Markus Peter: Völkerrechtlicher Investitionsschutz, Unter besonderer Berücksichtigung der bilateralen Investitionsschutzverträge der Schweiz, Rechts- und staatswissenschaftlichen Fakultät der Universität Zürich, Zürich - Switzerland, 1989

Nowak, Carsten: Europarecht nach Lissabon, Baden-Baden - Germany, 2011

Oppermann, Thomas/Classen, Claus Dieter/Nettesheim, Martin: Europarecht, 5th Ed., Munich (München) - Germany, 2011, 5. Edn. (2011), (cited as: Oppermann; Classen; Nettesheim, 5. Edn. (2011))

Pache, Eckhard/Bielitz, Joachim: Das Verhältnis der EG zu den völkerrechtlichen Verträgen ihrer Mitgliedstaaten, Zeitschrift Europarecht (2006), p. 316–339 (cited as: *Pache/Bielitz*, EuR, (2006))

Parish, Matthew: International Courts and the European Legal Order, European Journal of International Law Vol. 23, No. 1, p. 141–153 (cited as: *Parish*, EJIL, Vol. 23, No. 1)

Park, William W.: The Lex Loci Arbitri and International Commercial Arbitration, The International and Comparative Law Quarterly Vol. 32, No. 1 (1983), p. 21–5 (cited as: *Park*, The International and Comparative Law Quarterly, Vol. 32, No. 1 (1983))

Peers, Steve/Hervey, Tamara K./Kenner, Jeff/Ward, Angela (Eds.): The EU Charter of Fundamental Rights, A commentary, Hart Publishing, Oxford - United Kingdom, Portland - United States of America, Oregon - United States of America, 2014 (cited as: *Author*, in: *Peers, Hervey et al. - European Union Charter of Fundamental Rights*).

Peters, Anne: Supremacy Lost: International Law Meets Domestic Constitutional Law, Vienna Online Journal on International Constitutional Law (2009), p. 170–198 (cited as: *Peters*, Vienna Online Journal on International Constitutional Law, (2009))

Peters, Anne/Altwicker, Tilmann: Europäische Menschenrechtskonvention, 2nd Ed., Munich (München) - Germany, 2012

Peterson, Luke Erik: Edenred S.A. vs. Hungary: French investor wins 23 million EUR under France-Hungary BIT, Investment Arbitration Reporter 2016 (Vol.9, No. 29), p. 8–9 (cited as: *Peterson*, IA Reporter, 2016 (Vol.9, No. 29))

Idem.: Water extraction claim dries up in absence of funds; claimant ordered to cover half of state's expenses in UNCITRAL arbitration, Investment Arbitration Reporter

Vol. 3, No. 9 (2010), p. 10–12 (cited as: *Peterson*, IA Reporter, Vol. 3, No. 9 (2010))

Idem.: Electrabel v. Hungary Decision on Liability: Tribunal in Electrabel case finds that Hungary did not breach Energy Charter Treaty, but one claim reserved for future determination, Investment Arbitration Reporter Vol. 5, No. 23 (2012), p. 3–5 (cited as: *Peterson*, IA Reporter, Vol. 5, No. 23 (2012))

Idem.: Intra-EU treaty claims controversy: new decisions and developments in claims brought by EU investors vs. Spain and Hungary, Investment Arbitration Reporter Vol. 9, No. 13 (2014), p. 4–5 (cited as: *Peterson*, IA Reporter, Vol. 9, No. 13 (2014))

Idem.: Intra-EU-BITs: European Court of Justice is (finally) invited to weigh in on compatibility of intra-EU bilateral investment treaties and EU law, Investment Arbitration Reporter Vol. 9, No. 11 (2016), p. 2–3 (cited as: *Peterson*, IA Reporter, Vol. 9, No. 11 (2016))

Idem.: Micula vs. Romania annulment ruling: European Commission's arguments before Micula annulment committee are dismissed, but E.C. says that its non-enforceability arguments are gaining purchase in member-state courts, Investment Arbitration Reporter Vol. 9, No. 6 (2016), p. 14–17 (cited as: *Peterson*, IA Reporter, Vol. 9, No. 6 (2016))

Idem.: Micula vs. Romania annulment ruling: exploring the reasons why an ICSID annulment committee has declined Romania's bid to annul Micula award, Investment Arbitration Reporter Vol. 9, No. 6 (2016), p. 7–14 (cited as: *Peterson*, IA Reporter, Vol. 9, No. 6 (2016))

Peterson, Luke Erik/Dahlquist, Joel: Canada-EU Free Trade Agreement: Canada-EU treaty sees radical changes to investment dispute settlement, as Canada falls in line behind EU demands for reforms, Investment Arbitration Reporter Vol. 9, No. 6 (2016), p. 2–7 (cited as: *Peterson/Dahlquist*, IA Reporter, Vol. 9, No. 6 (2016))

Idem.: Frustration of investor's intra-EU water export scheme leads to notice of investment treaty breach Vol. 9, No. 16 (2016), p. 2 (cited as: *Peterson/Dahlquist*, , Vol. 9, No. 16 (2016))

Idem: Investigation: Denmark proposes mutual termination of its nine BITs with fellow EU member-states, against spectre of infringement cases, Investment Arbitration Reporter Vol. 9, No. 11 (2016), p. 1–4 (cited as: *Peterson/Dahlquist*, IA Reporter, Vol. 9, No. 11 (2016))

Pitschas, Christan: EuGH: Open-Skies-Abkommen mit USA, Europäische Zeitschrift für Wirtschaftsrecht (2003), p. 82–94 (cited as: *Pitschas*, EuZW, (2003))

Polter, Dirk-Meints: Auslandsenteignungen und Investitionsschutz, Berlin - Germany, 1975

Posner, Richard A.: The Rise and Fall of Judical Self-Restraint, California Law Review Vol. 100, No. 3 (2012), p. 519–556 (cited as: *Posner*, California Law Review, Vol. 100, No. 3 (2012))

Potestà, Michele: Legitimate expectations in investment treaty law: Understanding the roots and the limits of a controversial concept, ICSID Review - Foreign Investment Law Journal Vol. 28 (2013), p. 88–122 (cited as: *Potestà*, ICSID Rev., Vol. 28 (2013))

Idem.: Legitimate Expectations in Investment Treaty Law: Understanding the Roots and the Limits of a Controversial Concept, ICSID Review - Foreign Investment Law Journal (2013), p. 88–122 (cited as: *Potestà*, ICSID Rev., (2013))

Poudret, Jean-François/Basson, Sebastian: Comparative law of international arbitration, 2nd Ed., London - United Kingdom, 2007

Reinisch, August: The Role of Precedent in ICSID Arbitration, Austrian Arbitration Yearbook (2008), p. 495–510 (cited as: *Reinisch*, Austrian Arbitration Yearbook, (2008))

Idem: Articles 30 and 59 of the Vienna Convention on the Law of Treaties in Action: the Decisions on Jurisdiction in the Eastern Sugar and Eureko Investment Arbitrations, Legal Issues of Economic Integration Vol. 39, No. 2 (2012), p. 157–178 (cited as: *Reinisch*, LIEI, Vol. 39, No. 2 (2012))

Rengeling, Hans-Werner/Middeke, Andreas/Gellermann, Martin (Eds.): Handbuch des Rechtsschutzes in der Europäischen Union, 3rd Ed., Munich (München) - Germany, 2014 (cited as: *Author,* in *Rengeling/Middeke/Gellermann* (Eds.), Handbuch des Rechtsschutzes in der Europäischen Union)

Repasi, René: Völkervertragliche Freiräume für EU-Mitgliedstaaten, Zeitschrift Europarecht (2013), p. 45–75 (cited as: *Repasi*, EuR, (2013))

Ress, Georg: EMRK: Bosphorus-Vermutung - Grundsatz des gleichwertigen Schutzes und der Kontrolle auf Vorliegen einer "manifest deficiency", Europäische Zeitschrift für Wirtschaftsrecht (2016), p. 800 (cited as: *Ress*, EuZW, (2016))

Rogers, Catherine A./Alford, Roger P. (Eds.): The future of investment arbitration, Oxford - United Kingdom, New York - United States of America, 2009 (cited as: *Author,* in *Rogers/Alford* (Eds.), The future of investment arbitration)

Roggenkamp, Martha M./Redgwell, Catherine/Rønne, Anita/Guayo, Iñigo del (Eds.): Energy law in Europe, National, EU and international regulation, 3rd Ed., Oxford - United Kingdom, 2016 (cited as: *Author,* in *Roggenkamp/Redgwell/Rønne/Guayo* (Eds.), Energy law in Europe)

Sachs, Wayne: The New U.S. Bilateral Investment Treaties, Berkeley Journal of International Law Vol. 2, Iss. 1 (1984) (cited as: *Sachs*, Berkeley Journal of International Law, Vol. 2, Iss. 1 (1984))

Saenger, Ingo (Ed.): Zivilprozessordnung, Familienverfahren, Gerichtsverfassung, Europäisches Verfahrensrecht ; Handkommentar, 6th Ed., Baden-Baden - Germany, 2015 (cited as: *Author*, in: *Sänger/ZPO*).

Salacuse, Jeswald W.: The law of investment treaties, 2nd Ed., Oxford - United Kingdom, 2015

Sattorova, Mavluda: Return to the Local Remedies Rule in European BITs? Power (Inequalities), Dispute Settlement and Change in Investment Treaty Law, Legal Issues of Economic Integration Vol. 39, No. 2 (2012), p. 223–248 (cited as: *Sattorova*, LIEI, Vol. 39, No. 2 (2012))

Schill, Stephan W.: Opinion 2/13 – The End for Dispute Settlement in EU Trade and Investment Agreements?, The Journal of World Investment & Trade Vol. 16, No. 3 (2015), p. 379–388 (cited as: *Schill*, JWIT, Vol. 16, No. 3 (2015))

Schmid, Christoph: Immer wieder Bananen: Der Status des GATT/WTO-Systems im Gemeinschaftsrecht, Zur Lage nach dem Beschluß des WTO-Streitbeilegungsgremiums über die EG-Bananenmarktordnung vom 25. 9. 1997, Neue Juristische Wochenschrift 1998, p. 190–197 (cited as: *Schmid*, NJW, 1998)

Schmitt, Ramona: Die Kompetenzen der Europäischen Union für ausländische Investitionen in und aus Drittstaaten, Munich (München) - Germany, 2013, (2013), (cited as: Schmitt, (2013))

Schöbener, Burkhard/Herbst, Jochen/Perkams, Markus: Internationales Wirtschaftsrecht, Heidelberg - Germany, Munich (München) - Germany [et. al.], 2010, (2010), (cited as: Schöbener; Herbst; Perkams, (2010))

Schreuer, Christoph: Travelling the BIT Route. Of Waiting Periods, Umbrella Clauses and Forks in the Road, The Journal of World Investment & Trade Vol. 5, No. 2 (2004), p. 231–256 (cited as: *Schreuer*, JWIT, Vol. 5, No. 2 (2004))

Ibid.: Fair and Equitable Treatment in Arbitral Practice, The Journal of World Investment & Trade Vol. 6, No. 3 (2005), p. 357–368 (cited as: *Schreuer*, JWIT, Vol. 6, No. 3 (2005))

Ibid.: The ICSID Convention, A commentary, 2nd Ed., Cambridge - United Kingdom, 2009

Ibid.: Full Protection and Security, Journal of International Dispute Settlement Vol. 1, No. 2 (2010), p. 353–369 (Stand: 07.02.2014) (cited as: *Schreuer*, Journal of International Dispute Settlement, Vol. 1, No. 2 (2010))

Ibid.: Jurisdiction and Applicable Law in Investment Treaty Arbitration, McGill Journal of Dispute Resolution Vol. 1, No. 1 (2014), p. 1–25 (cited as: *Schreuer*, McGill Jour of Disp. Res., Vol. 1, No. 1 (2014))

Schroeder, Werner: Grundkurs Europarecht, 4th Ed., Munich (München) - Germany, 2015

Schwab, Karl Heinz/Walter, Gerhard/Baumbach, Adolf: Schiedsgerichtsbarkeit, Systematischer Kommentar zu den Vorschriften der Zivilprozessordnung, des Arbeitsgerichtsgesetzes, der Staatsverträge und der Kostengesetze über das privatrechtliche Schiedsgerichtsverfahren, 6th Ed. (initiated by Adolf Baumbach), Munich (München) - Germany, 2000

Schwarze, Jürgen (Ed.): EU-Kommentar, 3rd Ed., Baden-Baden - Germany, 2012 (cited as: *Author*, in: *Schwarze EU-Kommentar*).

Schweisfurth, Theodor: Völkerrecht, Tübingen - Germany, 2006

Schwerdtfeger, Angela: Europäisches Unionsrecht in der Rechtsprechung des Bundesverfassungsgerichts – Grundrechts-, ultra-vires- und Identitätskontrolle im gewaltenteiligen Mehrebenensystem, Zeitschrift Europarecht (2015), p. 290–310 (cited as: *Schwerdtfeger*, EuR, (2015))

Shaw, Malcolm N.: International law, 6th Ed., Cambridge - United Kingdom, New York - United States of America, 2008

Söderlund, Christer: Intra-EU BIT Investment Protection and the EC Treaty, Journal of International Arbitration Vol. 24, Iss. 5 (2007), p. 455–468 (cited as: *Söderlund*, JOIA, Vol. 24, Iss. 5 (2007))

Sornarajah, M.: The International law on foreign investment, 3rd Ed., Cambridge - United Kingdom [et al.], 2010, 3. Edn. (2010), (cited as: Sornarajah, 3. Edn. (2010))

Stein, Torsten/ von Buttlar, Christian: Völkerrecht, 13th Ed., Munich (München) - Germany, 2012

Steindl, Barbara Helene: ICSID annulment vs. set aside by state courts - compared to ICSID ad hoc annulment Committees, is it the state courts that are now more hesitant to set aside awards?, Yearbook on International Arbitration Vol. 4 (2015), p. 181–206 (cited as: *Steindl*, Yearbook on International Arbitration, Vol. 4 (2015))

Steiner, Josephine/Woods, Lorna/Twigg-Flesner, Christian: EU law, 9th Ed., Oxford - United Kingdom, New York - United States of America, 2006

Stern, Klaus/Sachs, Michael (Eds.): Europäische Grundrechte-Charta, GRCh ; Kommentar, Munich (München) - Germany, 2016 (cited as: *Author*, in: *Stern/Sachs EU GrCH*).

Stevenson, Angus: Oxford dictionary of English, 3rd Ed., New York - United States of America, 2010

Stier, Anna: The jurisdiction of the arbitral tribunal in intra-EU investment treaty disputes after the decision in Electrabel v Hungary, Arbitration International Vol. 31 (2015), p. 163–170 (cited as: *Stier*, Arbitration International, Vol. 31 (2015))

Streinz, Rudolf (Ed.): EUV/AEUV, Vertrag über die Europäische Union und Vertrag über die Arbeitsweise der Europäischen Union, 2nd Ed. Vol. 57, Munich (München) - Germany, 2012 (cited as: *Author*, in: *Streinz EUV/AEUV*).

Streinz, Rudolf: Europarecht, 10th Ed., Heidelberg - Germany, 2016, 10. Edn. (2016), (cited as: Streinz, 10. Edn. (2016))

Streinz, Rudolf/Ohler, Christoph/Herrmann, Christoph: Der Vertrag von Lissabon zur Reform der EU, 3rd Ed., Munich (München) - Germany, 2010

Tams, Christian J./Tzanakopoulos, Antonios/Zimmermann, Andreas/Richford, Athene E.: Research handbook on the law of treaties, Cheltenham - United Kingdom, Northampton - United States of America, 2014

Terhechte, Jörg Philipp (Ed.): Verwaltungsrecht der Europäischen Union, Zur Ausdifferenzierung und Globalisierung der europäischen Verwaltungsrechtsordnung, Baden-Baden - Germany, 2011 (cited as: *Author,* in *Terhechte* (Ed.), Verwaltungsrecht der Europäischen Union)

Tettinger, Peter J. (Ed.): Kölner Gemeinschaftskommentar zur Europäischen Grundrechte-Charta, Munich (München) - Germany, 2006 (cited as: *Author*, in: *Tettinger/Stern Europäische Grundrechte-Charta*).

Theobald, Christian/Gey-Kern, Tanja: Das dritte Energiebinnenmarktpaket der EU und die Reform des deutschen Energiewirtschaftsrechts 2011, Europäische Zeitschrift für Wirtschaftsrecht (2011), p. 896–901 (cited as: *Theobald/Gey-Kern*, EuZW, (2011))

Thiele, Alexander: Der Austritt aus der EU - Hintergründe und rechtliche Rahmenbedingungen eines "Brexit", Zeitschrift Europarecht (2016), p. 281–304 (cited as: *Thiele*, EuR, (2016))

Tietje, Christian: The Applicability of the Energy Charter Treaty in ICSID Arbitration of EU Nationals vs. EU Member States, Beiträge zum Transnationalen Wirtschaftsrecht Vol. 78 (2008), p. 5–17 (cited as: *Tietje*, Applicability of the ECT in ICSID Arbitration (Beit. zum Transnat. Wirt.-R, Vol. 78, 2008))

Ibid.: Die Außenwirtschaftsverfassung der EU nach dem Vertrag von Lissabon, Beiträge zum Transnationalen Wirtschaftsrecht Vol. 83 (2009) (cited as: *Tietje*, Die Außenwirtschaftsverfassung der EU nach dem Vertrag von Lissabon (Beit. zum Transnat. Wirt.-R, Vol. 83, 2009))

Ibid.: Internationales Investitionsschutzrecht im Spannungsverhältnis von staatlicher Regelungsfreiheit und Schutz wirtschaftlicher Individualinteressen, Beiträge zum Transnationalen Wirtschaftsrecht Vol. 93 (2010), p. 5–22 (cited as: *Tietje*, Int. Investitionsschutzrecht im Spannungsverhältnis (Beit. zum Transnat. Wirt.-R, Vol. 93, 2010))

Ibid.: Bilaterale Investitionsschutzverträge zwischen EU-Mitgliedstaaten (Intra-EU-BITs) als Herausforderung im Mehrebenensystem des Rechts, Beiträge zum Transnationalen Wirtschaftsrecht Vol. 104 (2011) (Stand: 19.03.2014) (cited as: *Tietje*, Intra-EU BITs als Herausforderung im Mehrebenensystem des Rechts (Beit. zum Transnat. Wirt.-R, Vol. 104, 2011))

Tietje, Christian (Ed.): Internationales Wirtschaftsrecht, 2nd Ed., Berlin - Germany, 2015 (cited as: *Author,* in *Tietje* (Ed.), Internationales Wirtschaftsrecht)

Tietje, Christian/Wackernagel, Clemens: Enforcement of Intra-EU ICSID Awards, Multilevel Governance, Investment Tribunals and the Lost Opportunity of the Micula Arbitration, The Journal of World Investment & Trade Vol. 16, Iss. 2 (2015), p. 205–247 (cited as: *Tietje/Wackernagel*, JWIT, Vol. 16, Iss. 2 (2015))

Tridimas, Takis: The general principles of EU law, 2nd Ed., Oxford - United Kingdom, 2007

Trittmann, Rolf: The interplay between procedural and substantive law in international arbitration, Zeitschrift für Schiedsverfahren (2016), p. 7–15 (cited as: *Trittmann*, SchiedsVZ, (2016))

Vandevelde, Kenneth J.: The Bilateral Investment Treaty Program of the United States, Cornell International Law Journal Vol. 21, Iss. 2 (1988), p. 201–276 (cited as: *Vandevelde*, Cornell Int. Law. J., Vol. 21, Iss. 2 (1988))

Ibid.: A Brief History of International Investment Agreements, U.C. Davis Journal of International Law & Policy Vol. 12, No. 1 (2005), p. 157–194 (cited as: *Vandevelde*, U.C. Davis Jour. of Int. Law & Policy, Vol. 12, No. 1 (2005))

Verosta, Stephan/Fischer, Peter/Köck, Heribert Franz/Verdross, Alfred (Eds.): Völkerrecht und Rechtsphilosophie, Internationale Festschrift für Stephan Verosta zum 70. Geburtstag, Berlin - Germany, 1980 (cited as: *Author,* in *Verosta/Fischer/Köck/Verdross* (Eds.), Völkerrecht und Rechtsphilosophie)

Vierdag, E. W.: The Time of the 'Conclusion' of a Multilateral Treaty: Article 30 of the Vienna Convention on the Law of Treaties and Related Provisions, British Yearbook of International Law Vol. 58, Iss. 1 (1988), p. 75–111 (cited as: *Vierdag*, British Yearbook of International Law, Vol. 58, Iss. 1 (1988))

Villiger, Mark Eugen (Ed.): Commentary on the 1969 Vienna Convention on the Law of Treaties, Leiden - The Netherlands, Boston - United States of America, 2009 (cited as: *Author*, in: *Villiger VCLT*).

Vitzthum, Wolfgang/Bothe, Michael: Völkerrecht, 5th Ed., Berlin - Germany, New York - United States of America, 2010

Vogel, Walther: Kurze Geschichte der Deutschen Hanse, Munich (München) - Germany, Leipzig - Germany, 1915

von Danwitz, Thomas: Europäisches Verwaltungsrecht, Berlin - Germany [et. al.], 2008

von der Groeben, Hans / Schwarze, Jürgen/Hatje, Armin (Eds.): Europäisches Unionsrecht, Vertrag über die Europäische Union, Vertrag über die Arbeitsweise der Europäischen Union, Charta der Grundrechte der Europäischen Union, 7th Ed. Volume I (Art. 1 - 55 TEU, Art. 1 - 66 TFEU, Art. 1 - 64 of the Charter), Baden-Baden - Germany, 2015 (cited as: *Author*, in: *v. d. Groeben/Schwarze AEUV/EUV*).

Ibid.: Europäisches Unionsrecht, Vertrag über die Europäische Union, Vertrag über die Arbeitsweise der Europäischen Union, Charta der Grundrechte der Europäischen Union, 7th Ed. Volume II (Art. 67 - 105 TFEU), Baden-Baden - Germany, 2015 (cited as: *Author*, in: *v. d. Groeben/Schwarze AEUV/EUV*).

Ibid.: Europäisches Unionsrecht, Vertrag über die Europäische Union, Vertrag über die Arbeitsweise der Europäischen Union, Charta der Grundrechte der Europäischen Union, 7th Ed. Volume III (Art. 106 - 173 TFEU), Baden-Baden - Germany, 2015 (cited as: *Author*, in: *v. d. Groeben/Schwarze AEUV/EUV*).

Ibid.: Europäisches Unionsrecht, Vertrag über die Europäische Union, Vertrag über die Arbeitsweise der Europäischen Union, Charta der Grundrechte der Europäischen Union, 7th Ed. Volume IV (Art. 174 - 358 TFEU), Baden-Baden - Germany, 2015 (cited as: *Author*, in: *v. d. Groeben/Schwarze AEUV/EUV*).

Voon, Tania/Mitchell, Andrew/Munro, James: Parting Ways: The Impact of Mutual Termination of Investment Treaties on Investor Rights, ICSID Review - Foreign

Investment Law Journal Vol. 29, No. 2 (2014), p. 451–473 (cited as: *Voon/Mitchell/Munro*, ICSID Rev., Vol. 29, No. 2 (2014))

Wackernagel, Clemens: The Twilight of the BITs? EU Judicial Proceedings, the Consensual Termination of Intra-EU BITs and Why that Matters for International Law, Beiträge zum Transnationalen Wirtschaftsrecht (2016), p. 5–42 (cited as: *Wackernagel,* EU Judicial Proceedings, Consenual Termination of Intra-EU BITs (Beit. zum Transnat. Wirt.-R, Vol. 140, 2016))

Walter, Christian: Grundlagen und Rahmenbedingungen für die Steuerungskraft des Völkerrechts, Zeitschrift für ausländisches und öffentliches Recht und Völkerrecht (2016), p. 363–389 (cited as: *Walter*, ZaöVR, (2016))

Wegener, Bernhard W.: Staatshaftung für die Verletzung von Gemeinschaftsrecht durch nationale Gerichte?, Zeitschrift Europarecht (2002), p. 785–800 (cited as: *Wegener*, EuR, (2002))

Weggenmann, R. Hans: Keine Meistbegünstigung aus Doppelbesteuerungsabkommen, Recht der internationalen Wirtschaft (2005), p. 717–720 (cited as: *Weggenmann*, RIW, (2005))

Wegner, Kilian: Die "Fransson"-Entscheidung des EuGH - Eine Erschütterung im System der europäischen Grundrechte, HRR-Strafrecht.de - Online-Zeitschrift und Rechtsprechungsdatenbank (2013), p. 126–131 (cited as: *Wegner*, HRRS, (2013))

Wehland, Hanno: Intra-EU Investment Agreements and Arbitration: Is European Community Law an Obstacle?, International and Comparative Law Quaterly Vol. 58, Iss. 2 (2009), p. 297–320 (cited as: *Wehland*, ICLQ, Vol. 58, Iss. 2 (2009))

Wetzel, Ralf Günter/Rauschning, Dietrich: The Vienna Convention on the Law of Treaties, Travaux préparatoires = Die Wiener Vertragsrechtskonvention : Materialien zur Entstehung der einzelnen Vorschriften, Frankfurt am Main - Germany, 1978

Wiegandt, Jan: Internationale Rechtsordnung oder Machtordnung? - Eine Anmerkung zum Verhältnis von Macht und Recht im Völkerrecht, Zeitschrift für ausländisches und öffentliches Recht und Völkerrecht (2011), p. 31–76 (cited as: *Wiegandt*, ZaöVR, (2011))

Winkler, Sebastian: Die Vermutung des "äquivalenten" Grundrechtsschutzes im Gemeinschaftsrecht nach dem Bosphorus-Urteil des EGMR, Europäische Grundrechte Zeitschrift Vol. 34 (2007), p. 641–654 (cited as: *Winkler*, EuGRZ, Vol. 34 (2007))

Wolff, Reinmar/Borris, Christian (Eds.): The New York Convention, Convention on the Recognition and Enforcement of Foreign Arbitral Awards of 10 June 1958 : commentary, Munich (München) - Germany, Baden-Baden - Germany, Oxford - United Kingdom, 2012 (cited as: *Author*, in: *Wolff New York Convention*).

Wolfrum, Rüdiger (Ed.): Max Planck Encyclopedia of Public International Law, Oxford - United Kingdom, 2008 (cited as: *Author,* in *Wolfrum* (Ed.), Max Planck Encyclopedia of Public International Law)

Wong, Jarrod: Umbrella Clauses in Bilateral Investment Treaties, George Mason Law Review Vol. 14, Iss. 1, p. 135–221 (Stand: 04.02.2014) (cited as: *Wong*, George Mason Law Review, Vol. 14, Iss. 1)

Yannaca-Small, Katia (Ed.): Arbitration under international investment agreements, A guide to the key issues, New York - United States of America, 2010 (cited as: *Author,* in *Yannaca-Small* (Ed.), Arbitration under international investment agreements)

Further Sources

Decisions by the Court of Justice of the European Union as well as national courts are intentionally omitted, a reference can be found in the respective footnote.

Amicus Curia Briefs filed by the European Commission

European Commission: Amicus Curia Brief filed in Electrabel vs. Hungary (ICSID Case n° ARB/07/19) - arbitration proceedings, 12/06/2009, available at: http://ec.europa.eu/dgs/legal_service/submissions/arbitrage/icsid_arb_2007_19_obs_en.pdf [last checked on 28.02.2017].

European Commission: Amicus Curia Brief filed in Achmea (former Eureko BV) vs. Slovak Republic (PCA Case n°2008-13) - arbitration proceedings, 07/07/2010, available at: http://ec.europa.eu/dgs/legal_service/submissions/pca/2008_13_obs_en.pdf [last checked on 28.02.2017].

European Commission: Amicus Curia Brief filed in EURAM vs. Slovak Republic (PCA Case n°2010-17) - arbitration proceedings, 13/10/2011, available at: http://ec.europa.eu/dgs/legal_service/submissions/pca/2010_17_obs_en.pdf [last checked on 28.02.2017].

European Commission: Amicus Curia Brief filed in EDF vs. Hungary (PCA Case n°2009-13) - arbitration proceedings, 14/05/2013, available at: http://ec.europa.eu/dgs/legal_service/submissions/arbitrage/pca_2009_13_obs_en_red.pdf [last checked on 28.02.2017].

European Commission: Amicus Curia Brief filed in U.S. Steel Golbal Holdings I B.V. vs. Slovak Republic (PCA Case n°2013-6) - arbitration proceedings, 15/05/2014, available at: http://ec.europa.eu/dgs/legal_service/submissions/pca/2013_6_amicus_en.pdf [last checked on 28.02.2017].

European Commission: Amicus Curia Brief filed in Micula vs. Romania to the U.S. Court of Appeals, 04/02/2016, available at: http://www.italaw.com/sites/default/files/case-documents/italaw7096.pdf [last checked on 28.02.2017].

Miscellaneous Documents

European Commission: referred to as: Commission Communication on State aid elements in sales of land and buildings by public authorities (97/C209/03), Official Journal of the European Communities C 209 - Vol. 40 (1997), p. 3–5.

European Commission: Commission letter SG (2001) D/290869 of 06/08/2001: Commission Communication relating to the methodology for analysing State aid linked to stranded costs, adopted by the Commission on 26/07/2001, available at: http://ec.europa.eu/competition/state_aid/legislation/stranded_costs_en.pdf [last checked on 28.02.2017].

European Commission: Commission Decision (2008/408/EC) - notified under C(2007) 5400: on the State aid C 36/A/06 (ex NN 38/06) implemented by Italy in favour of ThyssenKrupp, Cementir and Nuova Terni Industrie Chimiche, 20/11/2007

European Commission: Press Release: Commission opens German gas market to competition by accepting commitments from RWE to divest transmission network, Brussels - Belgium, 18/03/2009, [available at: http://europa.eu/rapid/press-release_IP-09-410_en.htm].

European Commission: Communication COM(2010)343 final: Communication from the Commission to the Council, the European Parliament, the European Economic and Social Committee and the Committee of the Regions - Towards a comprehensive European international investment policy, Brussels - Belgium, 07/07/2010, available at: http://trade.ec.europa.eu/doclib/docs/2010/july/ tradoc_146307.pdf [last checked on 28.02.2017].

European Commission: Communication COM(2012) 663 final: Communication from the Commission to the European Parliament, the Council, the European Economic and Social Committee and the Committee of the Regions - Making the internal energy market work, Brussels - Belgium, 15/11/2012, available at: http://www. europarl.europa.eu/RegData/docs_autres_institutions/commission_europeenne/com/2012/0663/COM_COM(2012)0663_EN.pdf [last checked on 28.02.2017].

European Commission: Commission Staff Working Document SWD(2013) 177 final: Ownership Unbundling, The Commission's Practice in Assessing the Presence of a Conflict of Interest Including in Case of Financial Investors, Brussels - Belgium, 08.05.2013, available at: https://ec.europa.eu/energy/sites/ener/files/documents/ swd_2013_0177_en.pdf [last checked on 28.02.2017].

European Commission: Press Release: Commission fines Microsoft for non-compliance with browser choice commitments, Brussels - Belgium, 06/03/2013, [available at: http://europa.eu/rapid/press-release_IP-13-196_en.htm].

European Commission: Commission Decision (EU) 2015/1470 - notified under C(2015) 2112: Decision on State aid SA.38517 (2014/C) (ex 2014/NN) implemented by Romania-Arbitral award Micula v Romania of 11 December 2013, 30/03/2015

European Commission: Press Release: European Commission to request a Court of Justice opinion on the trade deal with Singapore, Brussels - Belgium, 04/03/2015, [available at: http://trade.ec.europa.eu/doclib/press/index.cfm?id=1269].

European Commission: Press Release: Commission asks Member States to terminate their intra-EU bilateral investment treaties, Brussels - Belgium, 18/06/2015, [available at: http://europa.eu/rapid/press-release_IP-15-5198_en.htm].

European Commission: Commission Staff Working Document - Interpretative note on Directive 2009/72/EC concerning common rules for the internal market in electricity and Directive 2009/73/EC concerning common rules for the internal market in natural gas, Brussels - Belgium, 22/10/2010, available at: https://ec.europa.eu /energy/sites/ener/files/documents/2010_01_21_the_unbundling_regime.pdf [last checked on 28.02.2017].

European Commission - DG Competition: Minimum platform on investment for EU FTAs – Provisions on establishment in template for a Title on "Establishment, trade in services and e-commerce", 28/07/2006, available at: http://www.iisd.org/ pdf/2006/itn_ecom.pdf [last checked on 28.02.2017].

European Financial Committee: Report ECFIN/CEFCPE(2006)REP/56882 final: Annual EFC Report to the Commission and the Council on the Movement of Capital and the Freedom of Payments, Brussels - Belgium, 15/11/2006, available at: http://register.consilium.europa.eu/doc/srv?l=EN&f=ST%205044%202007%20INI T [last checked on 28.02.2017].

Governments of Austria, Finland, France, Germany and the Netherlands: Intra-EU Investment Treaties: Non-paper from Austria, Finland, France, Germany and the Netherlands, 2015, available at: https://www.rijksoverheid.nl/documenten/ publicaties/2016/05/18/non-paper-investeringsbescherming-tussen-eu-lidstaten [last checked on 28.02.2017].

Hindelang, Steffen/Reuling, Martin/Kuijper, Pieter Jan/Pernice, Ingolf/Scharz, Michael: Investor State Dispute Settlement Provisions in the EU's International Investment Agreements, Study conducted for the European Parliament, Brussels - Belgium, 04/09/2014, available at: http://www.jura.fu-berlin.de/fachbereich/ einrichtungen/oeffentliches-recht/lehrende/hindelangs/Studie-fuer-Europaeisches-Parlament/Volume-2-Studies.pdf [last checked on 28.02.2017].

International Centre for Settlement of Investment Disputes: The ICSID caseload: statistics - special focus European Union, Washington D.C. - United States of America, disclosure: 12/01/2015, available at: https://icsid.worldbank.org/apps/ICSI DWEB/resources/Documents/Stats%20EU%20Special%20Issue%20-%20Eng.pdf [last checked on 28.02.2017].

International Law Commission: Yearbook of the International Law Commission (Volume II / 1966), Documents of the second part of the seventeenth session and of the eighteenth session including the reports of the Commission to the General Assembly, New York, 1967, available at: http://legal.un.org/ilc/publications/yearbooks /english/ilc_1966_v2.pdf [last checked on 28.02.2017].

International Law Commission: ILC Report on Fragmentation of International Law, Difficulties arising from the diversification and expansion of international law - Report of the Study Group of the International Law Commission, 13/04/2006, available at: http://legal.un.org/ilc/documentation/english/a_cn4_l682.pdf [last checked on 28.02.2017].

NAFTA Free Trade Commission: Notes of Interpretation of Certain Chapter 11 Provisions, issued on 31/07/2001, available at: http://www.sice.oas.org/tpd/nafta/ Commission/CH11understanding_e.asp [last checked on 28.02.2017].

Nikièma, Suzy H.: Best Practices: Indirect Expropriation, Report published by the International Institute for Sustainable Development (IISD), 03/2012, available at: http://www.iisd.org/pdf/2012/best_practice_indirect_expropriation.pdf [last checked on 28.02.2017].

OECD: "Indirect Expropriation" and the "Right to Regulate" in International Investment Law, Working Papers on International Investment Law, 2004, available at: https://www.oecd.org/daf/inv/investment-policy/WP-2004_4.pdf [last checked on 28.02.2017].

UNCTAD: United Nations Conference on the Law of Treaties: Series on issues in international investment agreements: Taking of Property, 2000, available at: http://unctad.org/en/docs/psiteiitd15.en.pdf [last checked on 28.02.2017].

UNCTAD: Bilateral Investment Treaties: 1995–2006, Trends in Investment Rulemaking, New York - United States of America, Geneva - Switzerland, 2007, available at: http://unctad.org/en/docs/iteiia20065_en.pdf [last checked on 28.02.2017].

UNCTAD: World Investment Report, United Nations, Geneva - Switzerland, 2016, available at: http://unctad.org/en/PublicationsLibrary/wir2016_en.pdf [last checked on 28.02.2017].

United Nations Conference on the Law of Treaties: Summary records of the plenary meetings and of the meetings of the Committee of the Whole Second session, Official Records, Vienna (Wien) - Austria, 09/04.1969 to 22/05/1969, available at: http://legal.un.org/diplomaticconferences/lawoftreaties-1969/vol/english/2nd_sess .pdf [last checked on 28.02.2017].

International Treaties and further Legislative Acts

The International Energy Charter - Consolidated Energy Charter Treaty with Related Documents, referred to as: Energy Charter Treaty (1994), available at: http://www.energycharter.org/fileadmin/DocumentsMedia/Legal/ECTC-en.pdf [last checked on 28.02.2017].

Model Document for Bilateral Investment Treaties by Italy in 2003, referred to as: Italian Model BIT (2003), available at: http://www.italaw.com/sites/default/ files/archive/ITALY%202003%20Model%20BIT%20.pdf [last checked on 28.02.2017].

Model Document for Bilateral Investment Treaties by Canada in 2004, referred to as: Canadian Model BIT (2004), available at: -http://www.italaw.com/documents/Canadian2004-FIPA-model-en.pdf [last checked on 28.02.2017].

Model Document for Bilateral Investment Treaties by the United States of America in 2004, referred to as: U.S. Model BIT (2004), available at: http://www.state.gov/documents/organization/117601.pdf [last checked on 28.02.2017].

Model Document for Bilateral Investment Treaties by the Germany in 2008, referred to as: German Model BIT (2008), available at: http://investmentpolicyhub.unctad.org/Download/TreatyFile/2865[last checked on 28.02.2017].

Model Document for Bilateral Investment Treaties by Germany in 2009, referred to as: German Model BIT (2009), available at: https://tu-dresden.de/gsw/jura/ifve/jfoeffl9/ressourcen/dateien/lehrveranstaltungen/lehrveranstaltungen_material/sose2011/german_model_treaty2009?lang=de [last checked on 28.02.2017].

Model Document for Bilateral Investment Treaties by the United States of America in 2012, referred to as: U.S. Model BIT (2012), available at: http://www.state.gov/documents/organization/188371.pdf [last checked on 28.02.2017].

Albania; The Netherlands. Agreement on Encouragement and Reciprocal Protection of Investments between the Kingdom of the Netherlands and the Republic of Albania, signed 15.04.1994, entry into force: 01.09.1995, referred to as: Albania - Netherlands Bilateral Investment Treaty (entry into force: 01.09.1995)

Conference on International Commercial Arbitration: Convention on the Recognition and Enforcement of Foreign Arbitral Awards (New York Convention), referred to as: New York Convention on the Recognition and Enforcement of Foreign Arbitral Awards (1958)

Council of Europe: Convention for the Protection of Human Rights and Fundamental Freedoms (signed: 04/11/1950), referred to as: European Convention on Human Rights (entry into force: 03/09/1950), available at: http://www.echr.coe.int/Documents/Convention_ENG.pdf [last checked on 28.02.2017].

Cyprus; Hungary: Agreement between the Government of the Republic of Cyprus and the Government of the Hungarian Peoples Republic on Mutual Promotion and Protection of Investments (signed: 24/05/1989), referred to as: Cyprus - Hungarian Bilateral Investment Treaty (entry into force: 25/05/1990), available at: http://investment policyhub.unctad.org/IIA/country/94/treaty/1161 [last checked on 28.02.2017].

Czech Republic; Israel: Agreement between the Government of the Czech Republic and the Government of the State of Israel for the Reciprocal Promotion and Protection of Investments (signed: 23/09/1997), referred to as: Czech Republic - Israel Bilateral Investment Treaty (entry into force: 16/03/1999), available at: http://www.italaw.com/sites/default/files/laws/italaw6079.pdf [last checked on 28.02.2017].

European Commission: Commission Regulation (EU) No 1031/2010 of 12 November 2010 on the timing, administration and other aspects of auctioning of greenhouse gas emission allowances pursuant to Directive 2003/87/EC of the European Parliament and of the Council establishing a scheme for greenhouse gas emission allowances trading within the Community - Text with EEA relevance, referred to as: Regulation (EU) No 1031/2010 - Greenhouse Gas Emission Scheme, Official Journal of the European Union L 302 (12/11/2010), p. 1–41.

European Commission: Commission Regulation (EU) No 1407/2013 on the application of Articles 107 and 108 of the Treaty on the Functioning of the European Union to de minimis aid, referred to as: Regulation (EU) No 1407/2013 - De Minimis State Aid, Official Journal of the European Union L 352/1 (24/12/2013), p. 1–8.

European Commission: Commission Regulation (EU) No 651/2014 declaring certain categories of aid compatible with the internal market in application of Articles 107 and 108 of the Treaty - Text with EEA relevance, referred to as: Regulation (EU) No 651/2014 - General Block Exemption Regulation, Official Journal of the European Union L 187/1 (17/06/2014), p. 1–78.

European Council: Council Directive 88/361/EEC for the implementation of Article 67 of the Treaty, referred to as: Council Directive 88/361/EEC - Capital Directive, Official Journal of the European Communities L 178 (24.06.1988), p. 5–18.

European Council: Regulation (EC) No 1/2003 of on the implementation of the rules on competition laid down in Articles 81 and 82 of the Treaty - Text with EEA relevance, referred to as: Council Regulation (EC) No 1/2003 - Implementation of Antitrust Regulations, Official Journal of the European Communities L 1/1 (16/12/2002), p. 1–25.

European Council: Council Regulation (EU) No 1024/2013 of 15 October 2013 conferring specific tasks on the European Central Bank concerning policies relating to the prudential supervision of credit institutions, referred to as: Council Regulation (EU) No 1024/2013 - SSM Regulation, Official Journal of the European Union L 287 (15.10.2013)

European Union: Council Regulation (EEC) No 990/93 of 26 April 1993 concerning trade between the European Economic Community and the Federal Republic of Yugoslavia (Serbia and Montenegro), referred to as: Council Regulation (EEC) No 990/93 - Sanctions on Former Yugoslavia, Official Journal of the European Communities L102 (26.04.1993), p. 14–16.

European Union: Directive 2000/12/EC of the European Parliament and of the Council of 20 March 2000 relating to the taking up and pursuit of the business of credit institutions, referred to as: Directive 2000/12/EC - Capital Markets, Official Journal of the European Communities L 126 (20.03.2000 (repealed)), p. 1–59.

European Union: Directive 2003/54/EC of the European Parliament and of the Council of 26 June 2003 concerning common rules for the internal market in electricity and repealing Directive 96/92/EC - Statements made with regard to decommissioning and waste management activities, referred to as: Directive 2003/54/EC - Common rules for the internal market in electricity, Official Journal of the European Communities L 176 (26.06.2003 (repealed)), p. 37–56.

European Union: Directive 2003/55/EC of the European Parliament and of the Council of 26 June 2003 concerning common rules for the internal market in natural gas and repealing Directive 98/30/EC., referred to as: Directive 2003/55/EC - Common rules for the internal market in natural gas, Official Journal of the European Communities L 176 (26.06.2003 (repealed)), p. 57–78.

European Union: Directive 2006/48/EC of the European Parliament and of the Council of 14 June 2006 relating to the taking up and pursuit of the business of credit institutions (recast) - Text with EEA relevance, referred to as: Directive 2006/48/EC - Capital Markets Directive, Official Journal of the European Communities L 177 (14.06.2006), p. 1–200.

European Union: Directive 2009/72/EC of the European Parliament and of the Council of 13 July 2009 concerning common rules for the internal market in electricity and repealing Directive 2003/54/EC - Text with EEA relevance, referred to as: 2009/72/EC - Common Rules for the Internal Market in Electricity Directive, Official Journal of the European Communities L 211 (13/07/2009), p. 55–93.

European Union: Directive 2009/73/EC of the European Parliament and of the Council of 13 July 2009 concerning common rules for the internal market in natural gas and repealing Directive 2003/55/EC - Text with EEA relevance, referred to as: 2009/73/EC - Common Rules for the Internal Market in Natural Gas Directive, Official Journal of the European Communities L 211 (13/07/2009), p. 94–136.

European Union: Regulation (EU) No 1219/2012 of the European Parliament and of the Council establishing transitional arrangements for bilateral investment agreements between Member States and third countries, referred to as: Regulation (EU) 1219/2012 on bilateral investment agreements between member states and third countries, Official Journal of the European Union L 351 (12/12/2012), p. 40–46.

European Union: Regulation (EU) No. 1215/2012 of the European Parliament and of the Council on jurisdiction and the recognition and enforcement of judgments in civil and commercial matters, referred to as: Regulation EU/1215/2012 - Brussels Regulation, Official Journal of the European Union L 351 (12/12/2012), p. 1–32.

European Union Member States: Single European Act amending the Treaties establishing the European Economic Community, signed on 17/02/1986 (nine member states) and 28/02/1986 (Denmark, Italy and Greece), entered into force on 01/07/1987, referred to as: Single European Act, Official Journal of the European Communities L 169 (1987)

ICSID Administrative Council: Additional Facility Rules adopted by the Administrative Council of the International Centre of Settlement of Investment Disputes, referred to as: ICSID Additional Facility Rules (April 2006), available at: https://icsid.worldbank.org/apps/ICSIDWEB/icsiddocs/Documents/AFR_English-final.pdf [last checked on 28.02.2017].

UNCITRAL: UNCITRAL Model Law on International Commercial Arbitration 1985 with amendments as adopted in 2006, referred to as: UNCITRAL Model Law (as amended in 2006), available at: https://www.uncitral.org/pdf/english/texts/arbitration/ml-arb/07-86998_Ebook.pdf [last checked on 28.02.2017].

United Kingdom; Argentina: Agreement between the Government of the United Kingdom of Great Britain and Northern Ireland and the Government of the Republic of Argentina for the Promotion and Protection of Investments, referred to as: United Kingdom - Argentina Bilateral Investment Treaty (entered into force: 19/02/1993), available at: http://investmentpolicyhub.unctad.org/ Download/TreatyFile/126 [last checked on 28.02.2017].

United Nations: Resolution S/RES/820 by the Security Council of the United Nations, referred to as: Resolution S/RES/820 (1993) (17.04.1993)

United States of America; Mexico; Canada: North American Free Trade Agreement between the United States of America, The United Mexican States and Canada, referred to as: North American Free Trade Agreement (1994)